IN THE
IMAGE OF GOD

IN THE IMAGE OF GOD

A Feminist Commentary on the Torah

Judith S. Antonelli

JASON ARONSON INC.

Northvale, New Jersey

London

First Jason Aronson Inc. softcover edition—1997

This book was set in 10 pt. Times by Alpha Graphics in Pittsfield, New Hampshire.

For Acknowledgments, see page 521.

Library of Congress Cataloging-in-Publication Data

Antonelli, Judith S., 1952–
   In the image of God : a feminist commentary on the Torah / Judith
S. Antonelli.
     p. cm.
   Includes bibliographical references and index.
   ISBN 1-56821-438-3 (hardcover)
   ISBN 0-7657-9952-9 (softcover)
   1. Bible. O.T. Pentateuch—Commentaries. 2. Bible. O.T.
Pentatuech—Feminist criticism. 3. Feminism—Religious aspects—
Judaism. I. Title.
BS1225.3.A58 1995
222'.106—dc20
                                                  95-15872

Manufactured in the United States of America. Jason Aronson Inc. offers books and cassettes. For information and catalog write to Jason Aronson Inc., 230 Livingston Street, Northvale, New Jersey 07647.

And Elokim created humanity in God's image,
In the image of God Elokim created it;
Male and female God created them.

Genesis 1:27

Contents

✾✾✾ ✾✾✾

Figures and Tables

FIGURES

TABLES

✿✿✿ ✿✿✿

Introduction

This book is a unique blend of traditional Judaism and radical feminism. "Isn't that an oxymoron?" more than one person asked upon hearing of my topic. It was precisely to correct such an unfortunate misunderstanding that I wrote *In the Image of God: A Feminist Commentary on the Torah.*

My basic thesis is that the Torah, which was revealed by God to Moses on Mount Sinai over 3,300 years ago, is not the root of misogyny, sexism, or male supremacy (I use these three terms interchangeably). Instead of projecting our own twentieth-century consciousness back in time, we must look at the Torah in the context in which it was given—the pagan world of the ancient Near East. By doing so, it becomes very clear that, far from *oppressing* women, the Torah actually *improved* the status of women as it existed in the surrounding societies. If this was the Torah's mandate in ancient times, how much more so should it continue to be in modern times!

The notion that male supremacy is rooted in the Bible, beginning with the story of Adam and Eve, is a basic tenet of Western civilization. This universal tendency to attribute the origins of male domination to the "Old Testament" is primarily due to the spread of Christianity as the major religion of the West. However, whether they are Christians, Jews, or self-proclaimed "pagans," both the proponents *and* the opponents of women's subordination have united as strange bedfellows in pointing to the Torah as the source.

Using traditional Jewish sources as well as supplementary material from history, anthropology, sociology, psychology, ancient religion, and feminist theory, I have examined in detail every woman and every issue pertaining to women in the Torah, *parshah* by *parshah.* The Torah is divided into fifty-four portions; each portion, or *parshah,* is read in the synagogue on the Sabbath (combining a few to make a yearly cycle of readings). This book is modeled on that structure; hence, there are fifty chapters, each of which corresponds (again, with a few combinations) to a *parshah.*

One may, therefore, read this book from beginning to end, or use it sporadically as a study guide for the *parshah* of the week. I recommend that the reader have a Hebrew–English copy of the Torah itself available for reference; personally, I have found Rabbi Aryeh Kaplan's *The Living Torah* to be the clearest, most readable modern English translation. I have purposely separated traditional Jewish sources from other scholarly sources in my citations; the former are noted, usually in abbreviated form, in parentheses in the text (and explained following this introduction), while the latter are footnoted in standard academic style.

As a radical feminist and a religious Jew, my purpose in writing this book has been twofold: (1) to refute the common feminist stereotype that Judaism is a "patriarchal religion," and (2) to refute the sexism in Judaism by exposing it as sociology rather than "divine law."

To accomplish the first of these goals, I need to demonstrate the male supremacist nature of paganism. In order to do so, I must describe many pagan deities and rituals in detail. Religious Jews are taught not to inquire into such matters and may therefore take issue with the extent to which I delve into them. Thus, I quote the following words of a 1960 ruling by the late Rabbi Moshe Feinstein.

A Jew may teach pagan religion and mythology if it is presented

> in a way that the students understand that it is meaningless nonsense, that any rational person has nothing but contempt for the foolishness these people believed in. There may even be some benefit to this. The students will begin to understand that even today there are ideologies that many people believe in that in reality are absurd, yet people follow them blindly, just as in the ancient past many generations erred by believing in paganism and millions of people adhered to it. . . . [Thus], teaching about the irrational beliefs of the people of antiquity is a good thing and will have beneficial results.[1]

Since I am both a committed feminist and an observant Jew, my criticism of where feminism and Judaism have each "gone wrong" should surely not be interpreted as either anti-feminist or anti-Semitic; neither should it be used as ammunition by members of one group to try to discredit the other.

FEMINIST ANTI-JUDAISM

In 1898, in the first wave of American feminism, which culminated in the women's suffrage movement, Elizabeth Cady Stanton and a group of Christian feminists published *The Woman's Bible,* purporting to "revise . . . those texts and chapters directly referring to women, and those also in which women are made prominent by exclusion."[2]

Although the feminist impulse at the heart of their work—to dispel the myth that a biblical divine authority demands sexism—is one with which I fully concur, the result seldom moved beyond nineteenth-century Christian anti-Semitism. Jewish

---

1. Quoted in Avraham Yaakov Finkel, "Teaching Mythology," in *The Responsa Anthology* (Northvale, NJ: Jason Aronson, 1990), p. 171.

2. Stanton, Elizabeth Cady, and the Revising Committee, *The Woman's Bible* (New York: European Publishing Co., 1898), p. 5. This began to be reprinted in 1974 by the Coalition Task Force on Women and Religion in Seattle.

sources do not figure in their discussion of Jewish scriptures at all. Unfortunately, their conclusion rejects divine authority rather than sexism! (My own perspective on the divine origin of Torah will be discussed shortly.)

Thus, it is asserted that a particular passage "was manipulated by some Jew";[3] that "the Jews evidently believed the males the superior sex";[4] that Jews have "contempt" for women and that "the Mosaic code and customs so plainly degrade the female sex";[5] and that "the Hebrew laws regulating the relations of men and women are never complimentary to the latter."[6]

Finally, we are told, toward the end of the section on the Five Books of Moses, that "surely such records are enough to make the most obstinate believer doubt the divine origin of Jewish history and the claim of that people to have been under the special guidance of Jehovah [sic]. Their claim to have had conversations with God daily and to have acted under His commands in all their tergiversations of word and action is simply blasphemous." Rather, it is concluded, the Torah is a product of "the most obscene minds of a barbarous age."[7]

The second wave of American feminism, which began in the late 1960s, led to the emergence of the "feminist spirituality movement" in the early to mid-1970s. This time, spiritual feminists have gone way beyond simply rebelling within Christianity; they have reclaimed paganism, witchcraft, and goddess worship as components of an ancient "women's religion."

For the past twenty years, feminist spirituality has promoted a revisionist history of the ancient world—that paganism was a prowoman religion whose sexual rites "honored" women and nature, until the time when a band of warlike Hebrew men with a stern and vengeful male god came along and wiped it out. While the Jewish insistence on premarital virginity and marital monogamy for women are viewed as repressive, pagan phallus worship, male castration, and human—even child—sacrifice are not. (Some authors completely deny these latter phenomena, dismissing them as "male bias," while others seem to take a certain satisfaction in the idea of ritual male castration.)

Unfortunately, just like their foremothers, contemporary "neopagan" feminists have blamed Judaism for the sexism in Christianity. This ignores the fact that *Christian misogyny is its own phenomenon,* stemming mostly from the New Testament, the Church Fathers, and Greco-Roman paganism. (The impact of male celibacy—a totally foreign concept in Judaism—should also not be underestimated.) Moreover, even in cases where Christian sexism does stem from the Church's *appropriation and reinterpretation of* Jewish scriptures, by attempting to understand the "Old Testament" without any rabbinic commentaries, this should certainly not be confused with Judaism itself.

---

3. Ibid., p. 18.
4. Ibid., p. 35.
5. Ibid., pp. 73, 76.
6. Ibid., p. 80.
7. Ibid., pp. 119–120, 126.

Four major examples, spanning fifteen years (1972–1987), will suffice to give a clear picture of the anti-Judaic bias in feminist spirituality. While this is certainly a result of ignorance and *not* a conscious, malicious attitude toward Jews, it nevertheless draws upon some inaccurate and historically dangerous beliefs.

Elizabeth Gould Davis, a U.S. naval intelligence officer who was given a full military burial upon her death,[8] hardly fits the standard image of a spiritual feminist heroine. However, her book about matriarchy, *The First Sex,* caught on tremendously with spiritual feminists because it gives the reader a glimpse of a different reality, a world predating male supremacy.

The inspirational power of her book is highly dangerous, however, because embedded within it is the Nazi occult myth of Aryan supremacy.[9] Davis hypothesizes a "long-lost superrace" of blue-eyed, golden-haired people.[10] All early civilizations, she says, belonged to the Indo-European race, while "the Semites never achieved a civilization of their own."[11] She calls the Amazons, the warrior women who lived in what are now Libya and Turkey, a "blue-eyed race of women,"[12] while the subjugation of women is labeled "Judaic 'morality.'"[13]

Davis asserted, "It is significant that only the Jews strove to deny the feminine creation."[14] "The Semitic myth of male supremacy" is attributed to men whose "Semitic souls were outraged at the freedom and authority granted to Western women. . . . We must not forget that the leaders of the early church were Jews, bred in the Hebraic tradition that women were of no account and existed solely to serve men."[15]

She believes that captivity and slavery were good for Jews, as they "imbibed a modicum of culture from their long sojourn in civilized Egypt," while "the Babylonian captivity was another civilizing episode in the life of the Hebrews." Jews were "later shrewd enough to adopt the civilization of Canaan, but to this already established culture they contributed nothing."[16]

Merlin Stone, an archaeologist, continued this "Aryan" line of thinking in her book, *When God Was a Woman,* in which she asserted, "at the risk of overwhelming religious, emotional, and academic reactions," that both Avraham and the Levites were probably not Semitic, but Indo-European, similar to "the Aryan priestly caste of In-

---

8. See Rhoda Lerman, "In Memoriam: Elizabeth Gould Davis," *Ms.* (Dec. 1974): 74–75, 95.

9. That the Nazis were involved in the occult and used "Aryan" prehistory to promote their mystical-racial ideology of Jew-hatred has been explored in several works. See, for instance, Nicholas Goodrick-Clarke, *The Occult Roots of Nazism* (Wellingborough, Great Britain: Aquarian Press, 1985); Dusty Sklar, *The Nazis and the Occult* (New York: Dorset Press, 1977); Nigel Pennick, *Hitler's Secret Sciences* (Suffolk, England: Neville Spearman, 1981); and Wilhelm Wulff, *Zodiac and Swastika* (New York: Coward, McCann and Geoghegan, 1973).

10. Elizabeth Gould Davis, *The First Sex* (Baltimore: Penguin, 1972), pp. 25–26.

11. Ibid., pp. 140–141.

12. Ibid., p. 49.

13. Ibid., p. 287.

14. Ibid., p. 144.

15. Ibid., p. 230.

16. Ibid., p. 141.

dia, the Brahmins."[17] Her primary evidence is the fact that Indo-European male deities (such as Zeus) were often worshiped as thunder, lightning, and on volcanic mountains (like Sinai), and she posits a linguistic connection between the words *Levite* and *lava*.[18] This, too, is a compelling analysis if one lacks enough knowledge to refute it.

Stone, like other spiritual feminists, refers to "the warlike aspect of the Hebrews" and "the Hebrew suppression of the worship of the Goddess,"[19] which was accomplished through "massacres perpetuated by the Hebrews on the original inhabitants of Canaan."[20] (This language, implying genocide against a native people, creates a very insidious image, which is certainly bound to color feminist perceptions of modern Israel and its soldiers.) Moreover, she asserts that the Hebrews were "an isolated patriarchal society which worshiped the male deity alone."[21]

Stone condemns Judaism's disgust with the pagan prostitution of women, calling it "anti-sexual," and views the emphasis on knowledge of paternity *only* in terms of men claiming the ownership of women's bodies.[22] While I certainly do not dispute that effect, it is important to *also* recognize that *knowledge of paternity is a necessary prerequisite for the demand that men take responsibility for the consequences of sex.*

The pagan temple was the original brothel. Such a naive view of the pagan exploitation of female sexuality as "sacred" leads me to believe that someday, extraterrestrials could land on the earth, dig up a *Playboy* magazine, and conclude that the inhabitants of this planet must have "worshiped" women!

Z. Budapest was a "guru" among feminist witches—Hungarian-born, she was *raised* as a witch by her mother and is not a renegade Christian or Jew, like most spiritual feminists. She asserted in her writing that Jews had destroyed their goddess, Lilith. "The Jews, however, carried a deep burden of guilt about what they had done to Lilith, the Great Goddess. . . . Lilith cursed them as a result, and in effect told them that nothing would go right for Jews again until her worship was reinstated. Could this be the final solution of the Middle East crisis?"[23]

Budapest later issued a statement of regret "that passages in my book . . . have been understood as anti-semetic [*sic*]," as well as for using the term "final solution," which was the Nazis' euphemism for their plan of Jewish extermination. She did *not* admit that the passages *were indeed* anti-Semitic, nor did she include in this retraction her statement, in the same book, that "Judaism has an inherent backlash to femi-

---

17. Merlin Stone, *When God Was a Woman* (New York: Harcourt Brace Jovanovich, 1976), pp. 103–104.

18. Ibid., pp. 114–122.

19. Ibid., p. 126.

20. Ibid., p. xix.

21. Ibid., p. 54.

22. Ibid., pp. 153–162.

23. Zsuzsanna Emese Budapest, *The Holy Book of Women's Mysteries*, part 2 (Los Angeles: author, 1980), pp. 196–197. The frontispiece of this book is her Certificate of Appreciation from then-Los Angeles Mayor Tom Bradley lauding Budapest's "outstanding efforts and accomplishments which have been of great benefit to your community and particularly to the city of Los Angeles. Your community spirit and interest have helped make our City a better place in which to live."

nist spirituality built into it. Christianity simply helped itself, through Judaism, to write its own sexist war story."[24]

Monica Sjöö and Barbara Mor, authors of *The Great Cosmic Mother*, pit women against Judaism in their statement that the "constant fight against matriarchal religion and custom is the primary theme of the Old Testament."[25] The Levites were "punitive and misogynistic" men who "seem consumed with hatred of the Goddess and of women, especially the Canaanite and other neighboring matriarchal women who in sensual joy and freedom practiced their ancient moon rites."[26]

The Hebrews are characterized as "showing the restlessness of mind and ego characteristic of the Bronze Age," being "greedy, violent, plundering, and corrupt," and bearing a "psychological hostility to the entire living earth." The God of Israel is nothing more than a "newly militant, self-aggrandizing, and righteous male ego."[27]

Judaism is blamed for being "violently anti-sexual"; "eliminating the female sex entirely from the creation or purpose of the world"; distorting the ancient concept of taboo in "a psychological fetish for cleanliness," having an "abhorrence of the body" and a "revulsion against the sick, the elderly, and the disabled"; and developing the doctrine of "racial purity."[28]

The Canaanites, on the other hand, are portrayed as a peaceful, agricultural, "matriarchal" culture where women had "sensuality, vivacity, and autonomy under the Goddess." By asserting that "Hebrew women of biblical times were the first to undergo" the oppression of a "patriarchal misogynist worldview,"[29] the authors *appear* to be allies of modern "Jewish" women against ancient "Hebrew" men. This divide-and-conquer approach only serves to emphasize even further the anti-Semitic nature of their analysis.

Such revisionism has, unfortunately, spread even to segments of the women's movement that are unrelated to spirituality. An otherwise excellent book on battered women, for example, makes the assertion that "prior to the creation of the Bible, women were not treated this way; rather, women were worshiped as the Goddesses of Life."[30] In other words, this author is telling her readers—whether she realizes it or not—that *the Jews* started the custom of wife beating!

This kind of "feminism" can drive a Jewish woman crazy. If she wants to fight sexism without getting slapped in the face as a Jew, where does she go? Dare she discuss her problems with Jewish men in such an environment? The twin evils of feminist anti-Semitism and Jewish men's sexism thus led to the emergence of an independent Jewish-feminist movement by 1980.

---

24. Ibid., p. 215. The retraction was an "Author's Insert" enclosed in subsequent copies of the book.

25. Monica Sjöö and Barbara Mor, *The Great Cosmic Mother* (San Francisco: Harper and Row, 1987), pp. 264–265. Norwegian and German translations of at least parts of this book have also been published.

26. Ibid., p. 267.

27. Ibid., pp. 268–269.

28. Ibid., pp. 270–272.

29. Ibid., p. 273.

30. Lenore E. Walker, *The Battered Woman* (New York: HarperPerennial, 1979), p. 11.

However, even many Jewish women have accepted various aspects of feminist spirituality's anti-Judaic theology. "When Jewish women take a central place in their religion, they will no longer be practicing Judaism," wrote Naomi Goldenberg.[31] Starhawk (Miriam Simos), a feminist pagan priestess of Jewish origin, equated Judaism and Christianity in seeing "spirit and matter as separate" and identifying "matter with evil and corruption."[32] Margot Adler, another feminist pagan priestess of Jewish origin, concluded that Judaism's view of idolatry is nothing more than a "patronizing superiority" for "dull natives debasing themselves before a stone idol."[33]

Even *Lilith,* "the independent Jewish women's magazine," has fallen prey to this trend, to some degree. In its early days, this refreshing Jewish feminist voice published a ground-breaking critique of feminist theological anti-Semitism,[34] and to this day, it continues to monitor "secular" feminist anti-Semitism, as well as publishing many positive articles. However, in the 1990s, neopagan revisionism began to appear in its pages.

Paganism was portrayed as a "feminine" Judaism squelched by traditional Judaism (defined as "male") in a 1991 article:

> Like other peoples long ago, Jews lived close to nature and had an appropriate awe and reverence for her. We knew her by her various names: Ashtoreth, Ashera, Ishtar, Adama[,] . . . the Great Mother, the Great Goddess. In their zeal to smash idol worship, our forefathers crushed the reverencing of Ashera, and with her destruction, the respect of nature began to disappear. Religion went to our heads, became encased in bound volumes, was endlessly debated by bearded male scholars in dark, dusty rooms."[35]

In 1992, an article on the Shekhinah by a Christian woman defined the term as "the name for the Feast of the Full Moon, which once celebrated the menstruation of the Great Goddess."[36] In 1993, an article exploring how Jewish women can blend a Jewish identity with pagan goddess worship appeared—complete with a picture of an Egyptian goddess and a sidebar listing the eight annual Nordic pagan "Sabbats," or festivals.[37] That the Egyptians were the quintessential slavemasters of the Jews and that Nordic paganism formed the mystical backbone of Nazi ideology should be of great concern to Jewish women who feel like worshiping those goddesses and celebrating those holidays.

---

31. Naomi R. Goldenberg, *Changing of the Gods* (Boston: Beacon Press, 1979), pp. 7–8.
32. Starhawk, *The Spiral Dance* (New York: Harper and Row, 1979), p. 110.
33. Margot Adler, *Drawing Down the Moon* (Boston: Beacon Press, 1979), p. 27.
34. Judith Plaskow, "Blaming Jews for Inventing Patriarchy," and Annette Daum, "Blaming Jews for the Death of the Goddess," both in *Lilith,* no. 7 (1980/5741): 11–12, 12–13.
35. Mary Gendler, "Cornstalks, Conch Shells and My Jewish Problem," *Lilith,* 16:4 (Fall 1991): 32. While I fully agree with her association of Jewish holidays with the cycles of nature, I take issue with her assertion that (a) this is embodied by pagan goddesses, whom she calls "Jewish," and (b) that *traditional Judaism* is antinature just because her own Jewish upbringing and education failed to communicate this aspect of it to her.
36. Carolyn McVickar Edwards, "Shekhina: The Door to the Soul," *Lilith* 17:4 (Fall 1992): 5.
37. Rahel Musleah, "When the Goddess Calls, Jewish Women Answer," *Lilith* 18:4 (Fall 1993): 8–13.

That Jewish feminists have become susceptible to neopaganism is a result of ignorance, but *this is not the fault of feminism*. The main culprit here, unfortunately, is the sexism that has invaded and pervaded Jewish culture.

JEWISH SEXISM

Judaism should not be confused with Jewish *men*. Some modern Jews assert that Judaism is simply "whatever Jews do," but this is inaccurate. If most Jews ate pork, eating pork would still not be "Jewish." If most Jews decided to observe the Sabbath on Sunday, Sunday would still never become the *Jewish* Sabbath.

Similarly, misogyny and male supremacy are not inherently "Jewish"; that is, not endemic to *Judaism*. This does not deny, however, that misogyny and male supremacy have entered Jewish *culture* as a sociological phenomenon. Just as this book refutes feminist anti-Judaism, so too does it seek to separate Torah (divine law) from men's sexism, which is an unfortunate and all-too-widespread part of Jewish sociology.

In the right-wing ("black-hat" or "ultra") Orthodox Jewish world, the claim is frequently made that feminism is a "gentile custom" (which the Torah forbids Jews to emulate). "Imitating the non-Jews includes incorporating the secular philosophy of feminism into Judaism," asserted one right-wing Orthodox woman.[38] (If the insights of a gentile mind are prohibited, should Jews be using telephones and toilets?)

Indeed, this woman's argument proves exactly the *reverse* of her claim! She states that there is no need for feminism in Judaism because there are no injustices against women to rectify. If there are no injustices against women in Judaism, that means there is no male supremacy in Judaism, and if there is no male supremacy in Judaism, it must be a gentile custom!

Therefore, *male supremacy is the gentile custom that Jews should not emulate.* That Jews *have* emulated it means we are obligated to work to get rid of it. Although male supremacy is not inherently Jewish, Jews have nevertheless adopted some of the worst practices of the cultures in which they live. Feminism, as a struggle for freedom, human dignity, and equal opportunity, is a *very strong Jewish value.*

Feminism is a term that has taken a lot of battering over the years. Accusations of "male bashing" have led many women to say, "I'm no feminist, but . . ." and then express a very feminist opinion. This dynamic should be familiar to Jews. *Zionism*, too, has become a dirty word in some circles. Those who feel threatened by Jewish strength and independence have attempted to distort and twist the meaning of the term (calling it "Arab bashing") in order to discredit its adherents and weaken public support for the cause.

---

38. Lisa Aiken, *To Be a Jewish Woman* (Northvale, NJ: Jason Aronson, 1992), p. 109. Aiken makes this statement in the context of asserting that women's prayer groups are forbidden by Jewish law. Even though she is not a rabbi, she says this quite matter-of-factly, ignoring that there *are* rabbinic authorities who *permit* women's prayer groups, such as Avraham Weiss, *Women at Prayer* (Hoboken, NJ: Ktav, 1990).

Just as Zionism is the liberation movement of the Jewish people, feminism is the liberation movement of the female people. Just as there are all kinds of Zionists—from the Kach party to Peace Now—so, too, there are all kinds of feminists. A Jew who believes in the modern state of Israel as the Jewish homeland does not stop calling him- or herself a Zionist just because there are other Zionists with whom he or she vigorously disagrees. Similarly, one can be a feminist and strongly disagree with the opinions of other women (or men) who also call themselves feminists.

The famous medieval commentator Rashi had three learned daughters, Yokheved, Miriam, and Rachel, who

> would faithfully put Rashi's thoughts down on paper, especially in his later years, and would sometimes reply in their father's name to questioners who wrote to the French sage requesting halakhic decisions. Yokheved, Miriam, and Rachel all married men who became great Torah scholars, and they and their sons, virtually all of whom distinguished themselves as brilliant students of Torah as well, formed the school of talmudic scholars known as the Tosafot.[39]

Feminism simply means that these women would not have had to hide behind their father's name; rather, they could have been known and respected as scholars in their own names and in their own right, not only in their own time but for *future generations* as well. Instead, we only hear about "Rashi and his grandsons." To begin to correct the invisibility that has been foisted upon these women because of sexism, I have included them in my definition of the Tosafot (see "Traditional Sources").

Feminism also means that we should take a serious interest in the fact that R. Yair Chaim Bachrach of seventeenth-century Germany named his major work, *Chavat Yair,* after his grandmother Chavah, *who herself wrote Torah commentaries.*[40] Where are her commentaries today? You cannot purchase a copy of them in your local Jewish bookstore. *Why have they disappeared?*

The argument that feminism is a "gentile custom" is predicated on the belief that Jewish women's dissatisfaction with their role is a result of assimilation in the modern world; in the "untainted" (ghetto) past, the argument goes, Jewish women were perfectly content with their role. That this is absolutely untrue is evident from a talmudic story about a woman named Yalta (Br. 51b).

Yalta and her husband, Rabbi Nachman, had a sage named Ulla as a dinner guest. After they said the Grace After Meals, Ulla handed a cup of wine to R. Nachman for the customary blessing. R. Nachman told him to pass it to Yalta, but Ulla objected, quoting a Torah phrase, in the masculine gender, that states that God will bless "the fruit of your belly" (Deut. 7:13). Now, most of the Torah's language is in the masculine singular because it was spoken (by God) to Moses and Moses repeated it the way it was said to him.

---

39. Michael Kaufman, *The Woman in Jewish Law and Tradition* (Northvale, NJ: Jason Aronson, 1993), p. 74.
40. Finkel, *Responsa Anthology*, p. 96.

However, Ulla misinterpreted this phrase to claim that "the fruit of a woman's belly is blessed only through the fruit of a man's belly"—is the reverse not just as true?—and twisted it into a rationale for why a woman may not make the blessing over wine after dinner! Ulla's logic would be laughable, if it were not so similar to the kind still used by many rabbis today.

Yalta, understandably, was so angry that "she got up in a passion and went to the wine cellar and broke 400 jars of wine." Her feminist indignation at Ulla's misogynist distortion of the Torah is not even the best part of the story, however. When Yalta finally calmed down and returned to the table, R. Nachman turned to Ulla and said, "Give her another cup." Imagine a modern rabbi—or any man, for that matter—being so supportive! More likely, he would call it "premenstrual syndrome" and send her to a psychiatrist, who would give her sedatives or even commit her to a mental hospital!

Because the distinction between the Torah and its distortion by rabbinic sexism is such an integral part of this book, I will not overview the latter here in the same way that I have overviewed feminist anti-Judaism. However, a few points should be emphasized so that Jews understand how truly destructive sexism is to Jewish women and, therefore, to the Jewish people as a whole.

Many Jewish women have inaccurate ideas about Judaism because of certain lackings in their Jewish education. As girls, they may have received no Jewish education at all. If they did, they probably had sexist teachers who talked about the men in the Torah while ignoring the female characters, called menstruating women "unclean," taught that God wants women to be wives and mothers but not rabbis, or refused to allow girls to perform certain rituals on the grounds of "modesty" or a misunderstanding of women's "exemption" as somehow being equivalent to a "prohibition."

Other Jewish women have become alienated from Judaism simply because they had Jewish fathers who were sexist, domineering, or even physically and/or sexually abusive. Given the family-centered nature of Judaism (it is not a "synagogue religion"), what a Jewish girl experiences in her home will greatly color her feelings about Judaism, and it will be very difficult for her to separate the two. If her family experience is positive, the result will be fine; but if her family experience is negative, the results can be devastating.

Much of Orthodoxy claims to "honor" women but actually views us in a very degrading and objectifying way. A rabbi from a prominent Orthodox organization recently published a letter in a Jewish magazine in which he referred to a woman who stands on the *bimah* (as a rabbi or Torah reader) as "putting sex before our eyes." The notion that woman equals sex is the fundamental tenet of pornography. What this rabbi is saying is that *he* cannot see a woman simply as a fellow human being; that *he* cannot look at her without having sexual fantasies. Is this a legitimate reason to prohibit women from full participation in public ritual? Is the problem in the woman or in the man's eyes and mind?

Judaism teaches men not to gaze at women's bodies for their own sexual enjoyment or as a form of pleasure or "entertainment." This is certainly a very important form of respect for women, which is sorely lacking in modern mass media culture. However, if it becomes a rationale for a man to not look a woman in the eyes when he is talking to her—or an excuse not to talk to women at all, except his wife—this totally distorts its purpose and meaning. A personal example will illustrate this point.

On *Shabbat*, I have often walked to lunch in right-wing Orthodox neighborhoods. On passing recognizably Jewish men, I used to greet them, saying, "Good *Shabbes*" or "*Shabbat Shalom*," in a plain, friendly manner. The men did not respond but rather immediately averted their eyes sideways and to the ground as they passed me. *I might as well have been a prostitute soliciting them!* Contrary to whatever rationale *they* might have for their behavior, from a female point of view, it feels like *being treated like a whore.*

Women who are raised in an environment with such men—men who have some fear of their own (inappropriate) sexual impulses, which they project onto women instead of taking responsibility for it themselves—will inevitably internalize the men's values and perpetuate them. Israeli anthropologist Tamar El-Or, who studied women's education in a Gur chasidic community in Tel Aviv, reported how the five-year-old daughter of her hostess stared at her, touched her hair (which was not covered) to see if it was a wig, and concluded, *"Zi is a pritsa!"* ("She is a loose woman!").[41]

When a little girl has already learned by the age of five that a married woman with uncovered hair is somehow immoral, what kind of positive female self-image can she develop? Whether or not she is "happy" in her role is irrelevant; people have learned to be "happy" in the most oppressive conditions, simply because they have never known anything better. The mother of this girl does not drive or even ride in a car driven by a woman because she has been taught that a car is a *kli gever,* a "male vessel."[42] This mentality is, ironically, the same as that of a gentile Saudi Arabian male—hardly that of the Torah!

While Orthodoxy perpetuates the most blatant form of sexism within Judaism, it is not the *only* form. Conservative, Reform, and Reconstructionist Judaism did not come into being because their founders were concerned about women's rights. On the contrary, even the most liberal branches of Judaism have required a great deal of confrontation to make them begin to respond to women's concerns, and much work still remains to be done.

Egalitarianism, the theoretical elimination of any sex differences, often results in a *covert* form of misogyny because the norm to which everyone is equalized is male. For instance, changing the age for *bat mitzvah* from twelve to thirteen, the same age as for *bar mitzvah,* ignores the fact that girls *really do* mature sooner than boys. (Did anyone ever propose changing *bar mitzvah* to age twelve?) Applying a male level of legal obligation to women or creating an artificial symmetry in matters of sex and reproduction (the one area where men and women really *are* different) can also work against women. There is more than a kernel of truth in the humorous slogan that "women who demand equality with men lack ambition."

---

41. Tamar El-Or, *Educated and Ignorant* (Boulder, CO: Lynne Rienner, 1994), p. 141.
42. Ibid., p. 27.

THE TORAH: ORIGIN AND TRANSMISSION

As a religious Jew, I proceed from the assumption that the Torah was revealed by God to Moses on Mount Sinai. The term *Torah* has both a broad and a specific meaning.

In the broad sense, it is used to denote the entire body of sacred Jewish literature—the Hebrew Bible (*Tanakh,* or what Christians call the Old Testament) and all the rabbinic commentaries. The Hebrew Bible is divided into three sections, called Torah, Prophets, and Writings. The first section, comprising the Five Books of Moses, is called the "written law" or "written Torah." The rabbinic commentaries are called the "oral law" or "oral Torah."

In the specific sense, *Torah* denotes only the written law, comprising the Five Books of Moses. This specific use of the term defines the scope of this book. However, the written law can only be fully understood with input from the oral law. For instance, in Deuteronomy 12:21, Moses tells the people that when they want to eat meat they must slaughter the animal "as I have commanded you." Nowhere in the written Torah are the laws of *shechitah*, or ritual slaughter, delineated. They are found only in the oral law; specifically, the talmudic tractate of *Chullin.*

How was the oral law transmitted? For forty days, Moses was like a student listening to a professor's lecture. His "notes" make up the written law. However, as in any classroom, much more was said than he was able to write down. By looking at his "notes," Moses was able to recall the rest of the content of the "Professor's" lecture. The part that Moses committed to memory is the oral law—this forms the Mishnah, which makes up a part of the Talmud.

Moses taught the Mishnah, as well as thirteen principles of Torah exegesis, to Aharon, then to Aharon's sons Elazar and Itamar, then to the elders, and then to all of Israel—men *and* women. Each time, the previously instructed people remained for the next teaching. Thus, Aharon heard it four times, Elazar and Itamar heard it three times, the elders heard it two times, and all of Israel heard it once (Er. 54b).

Maimonides, in his introduction to the *Mishneh Torah,* gives a very detailed list of how the oral law was transmitted, man to man, from the time of Moses down to Rabbi Judah. Until R. Judah, each man took notes for himself of the teachings he received, in order to enable him to teach it to others. New social conditions also necessitated new concepts in each generation. These were deduced by the thirteen principles, and not merely by "free association." R. Judah collected all the laws, teachings, explanations, and commentaries and wrote them down. This final form of the Mishnah was codified by 200 c.e. The Gemara, the main part of the Talmud, is composed of rabbinic discussions explaining the Mishnah. This was codified by 600 c.e.

The strictest Orthodox Jew believes that this entire body of work, from Torah to Talmud (and beyond), is all equivalent as "God's word." However, there are several problems with this view. First, the Rabbis are not viewed as "infallible" in Judaism, as the Pope is in Catholicism. Secondly, there are differences of opinions between the Rabbis. In the Gemara this is certainly true, but even in the Mishnah there are disagreements: for example, "Rabbi Meir says . . . but the Sages say. . . ."

Thus, even in what is generally considered to be the oral tradition from Sinai, we are already hearing different interpretations from different Rabbis. (A capital "R" refers to the Rabbis of the oral tradition, and a lowercase "r" to modern ones.) Does this indicate a difference in how a law was remembered, or does it indicate differences in the deductions made *from* a law in response to social changes?

To criticize certain interpretations of the oral law, as I do throughout this book, is not the same as rejecting the oral law as a whole. I do, indeed, accept the oral law—and, in fact, I cite it quite often. It is only the very un-Jewish concept of "rabbinic infallibility" that I reject, and which, I believe, gives me the right to disagree with a *specific* rabbinic opinion—especially considering that the Rabbis themselves disagreed with each other.

Surely, any information that is transmitted orally for over a thousand years before being written down is bound to be affected by individual nuances of understanding. (Think of the children's whispering game, "Telephone.") This is a result of imperfect human nature and does not imply that anyone *consciously* intends to change what they hear. Nonetheless, you can say the same thing to six people, yet if you ask them to repeat it back to you, you will get six different versions of your message.

For women, this dynamic is exacerbated by the fact that the official transmission was conducted totally through men. Men and women do often see things very differently—and whether this is due to social conditioning or biology is irrelevant. A body of knowledge transmitted through a male legal authority alone is very likely to ignore or undervalue subtle nuances that may be more important and more noticeable to women. We cannot, therefore, assume that women's ideas survived in the words of the men whom they influenced.

Women certainly heard the teachings themselves and taught them to their children, but they did not have the political authority of Rabbis teaching students in an academy and making decisions in a court. Most women did not gain a reputation—especially one that would last beyond their lifetime—for their ideas in their own names. Even when they did, their words generally remained orally transmitted, passed on through word of mouth (such as in conversations at the spinning wheel) and not written down in texts, like men's, as a permanent record for future generations.

There are notable exceptions, such as Ima Shalom, who was one of the greatest female scholars known in her time (she was twenty when the Second Temple was destroyed). Ima Shalom, which means "Mother Peace," is reputed to have been "irascible as well as clever, and her habit of outsmarting others might well have aggravated her husband. Stories concerning her bluntness of speech and actions are found scattered throughout the Talmud."[43]

Ima Shalom demonstrated that it is not sufficient to say that women's ideas were preserved through their men, the Rabbis. Ima Shalom was married to Rabbi Eliezer b. Hyrcanus, who is reputed for saying that a man who teaches his daughter Torah is teaching her frivolity (Sot. 3:4) and that women's wisdom is in the spinning wheel

---

43. Sondra Henry and Emily Taitz, *Written Out of History: Our Jewish Foremothers* (Fresh Meadows, NY: Biblio Press, 1983), p. 49.

(Yom. 66b). These statements actually have deeper meaning than just an apparently misogynist one, but R. Eliezer is generally understood to have been opposed to Torah study for girls and women.

A third statement attributed to him (in the Jerusalem Talmud) is that the Torah should be burned rather than studied by women. In the midst of the Hadrianic persecutions, the Romans had forbidden Jews to study Torah under penalty of death and were executing those who did by burning them to death wrapped in a Torah scroll. Thus, R. Eliezer was actually saying, better the Torah should be burned (alone), than a woman study it (and be burned to death wrapped in it).

Ima Shalom clearly studied Torah in spite of the danger, however, just as men continued to do. Not only did she not succumb to her husband's view on this, she also taught *him* a thing or two. After her brother, Gamliel II, excommunicated R. Eliezer, Ima Shalom knew that her husband's intense praying could cause her brother's death. When it did, her husband wondered how she could have known, and she replied, "All gates are locked except the gates of wounded feelings" (B.M. 59b).

The belief in divine revelation makes my book quite different from other scholarly works on women in the Bible, which are not grounded in this concept or in traditional Jewish sources but in the academic field known as "biblical criticism," which believes that the Torah was written and edited by four humans.[44]

While I have sometimes referred to such works in my research, their usefulness for my purpose was quite limited. Their references to "Yahwist authors" and "redactors" sound very strange to anyone who believes in one Author. However, that is only the least of it. Biblical critics have also created a serious time warp: They assume that the Torah was completed between 850 and 450 B.C.E., while according to the religious view based on the Jewish calendar, the Exodus and the forty years in the wilderness took place from 1313 to 1273 B.C.E. The matriarchs and the patriarchs lived even earlier.

Biblical criticism was developed by two nineteenth-century German Protestants, Karl Graf and Julius Wellhausen, who dissected the Torah into various strands and called the authors J, E, P, and D. One hundred years later, many Jews have come to accept their analysis and have added to it; indeed, one recently asserted that J was a woman!

It is difficult to understand why Jews would accept an analysis of the Torah that was created by Christians in pre-Holocaust Germany. There are many ways to destroy Judaism: killing Jewish people is one, while discrediting the foundations of the Jewish religion by ripping apart the Torah is another. (Whether this goal consciously motivated their work is irrelevant.)

However, there is a profound existential dilemma for a feminist who believes in divine revelation. If the Torah were written by men (or even three men and one woman), an apparently sexist Torah passage could simply be dismissed as anachronistic and only the meaningful passages retained. One who believes in divine revela-

---

44. The information on biblical criticism in this section is from James King West, *Introduction to the Old Testament* (New York: Macmillan, 1981), pp. 64–66.

tion, however, cannot dismiss some parts of the Torah while embracing others. It is one Torah and one God. The fabric cannot be torn apart into separate threads.

Thus, one must figure out why the same God Who liberated the Jews from Egyptian bondage allowed Jewish fathers to sell their young daughters as maidservants to other Jewish men. God, by definition, cannot be a misogynist. An all-knowing and all-perfect Creator of the Universe does not need consciousness-raising, nor are there any anachronisms in the Torah. Everything in it remains relevant, even as it has the capacity to evolve; it is we who need the consciousness-raising. Another approach must therefore be taken; the key to this is in the context.

The approach that I have developed draws largely on Maimonides' philosophy that many of the commandments (such as animal sacrifice) were intended to wean the Jews from idol worship. His assumption is that complete, sudden, drastic change would not have worked; it had to be gradual and incremental to be truly deep and effective. Such an analysis is easily applied to male attitudes and behavior toward women. My approach is also similar to the "Torah-taught" versus "Torah-tolerated" distinction made by the late Rabbi Eliezer Berkovits.

A practice that was merely tolerated by the Torah, as opposed to taught or established by it,

> derived from the mores, conditions, and circumstances of an early age, and was not essentially different from what we find in other societies in the same stage of development. Women's status in this era was nonpersonal. While it could not be changed overnight by legislation, certain limited changes were effected to indicate the direction of the kind of development the Torah desired. The second phase established women's personal status."[45]

The runaway slave (Deut. 23:16–17) serves as a model for understanding the Torah's strategy. The Torah commanded Jews to shelter and protect runaway slaves; it did not, however, command the abolition of slavery. The entire ancient world was based on slave labor; to call for the complete and immediate cessation of slavery would have, at best, been laughed at, or at worst, might have caused the collapse of entire civilizations. However, the protection of runaway slaves was *in itself* a radical concept, which paved the way for the eventual abolition of slavery by fostering the consciousness that could lead to it.

A belief in divine revelation does not necessitate legal stagnation or fossilization. As consciousness changes, so does Jewish law. One model for this is the halakhic status of deaf people, which has improved considerably as society's understanding of deafness has advanced. Unlike our medieval predecessors, we no longer believe that a deaf person is an imbecile or a lunatic just because he or she speaks in sign language rather than with a voice.

Improvements in women's social status should also be reflected in halakhic developments—and in the past, they have been. To resist this awareness today is like refusing to acknowledge that electricity has been invented and thus preferring to

---

45. Eliezer Berkovits, *Jewish Women in Time and Torah* (Hoboken, NJ: Ktav, 1990), pp. 1–2.

ignore any necessity of considering if and how it may be used on *Shabbat*, in the futile hope that the whole issue will just "go away."

TIME AND THE JEWISH CALENDAR

The dates cited in this book are given as A.M., B.C.E., or C.E.

The initials A.M. stand for Anno Mundi, "Year of the World." This is the term for the Jewish calendar, which began with the sixth day of Creation, 5,756 years ago. (Thus, 1 A.M. is equivalent to 3760 B.C.E.) Looking at Jewish events in a Jewish time frame is of the utmost importance and can be a highly mind-expanding experience for a Jewish consciousness.

The Jewish calendar, which is often mistakenly dismissed as "fanciful" by other scholars, is not inconsistent with the scientific discovery that the universe is billions of years old. Each of the first five "days" of Creation could have lasted billions of years, for the planets—whose cycles define time as we know it—were not even placed in the sky until the fourth day. A "day" on earth is equivalent to six and a half "days" on Pluto. In terms of measuring *God's* sense of time, who can say where God stands in the universe?

The initials B.C.E. stand for "Before the Common Era" (replacing B.C., "Before Christ"), and C.E., for "Common Era" (replacing A.D., for Anno Domini, "Year of Our Lord"). The Common Era is still Christian time—complete with the strange time-warp effect of dating events from before the time of Jesus *backwards*. However, the use of B.C.E. and C.E. makes a statement that Christian time is not objective, universal reality and that many people do not consider Jesus to be "their" lord.

The Gregorian calendar is simply the most recent Christian calendar. The earliest calendars used by humanity were lunar; the moon was used to set religious festivals. However, to keep a festival in its proper season (e.g., Passover in spring), the 354-day lunar year had to be aligned with the 365-day solar year. Hence, there was a need for what is called "intercalation."

The Jewish method of intercalation adds an extra, thirteenth month (*Adar* II) every third, sixth, eighth, eleventh, fourteenth, seventeenth, and nineteenth years. This pattern—three years, three years, two years; three years, three years, three years, two years—is identical to the pattern of the musical scale—whole step, whole step, half step; whole step, whole step, whole step, half step. Thus, the Jewish calendar has a cosmic rhythm, not a man-made one.

In pagan cultures, however, intercalation was "arbitrary and [done] mostly by royal decree." Rulers used it "for political purposes—extending the terms of prominent politicians or giving extra holidays."[46] The drive to make the solar calendar predominant over the lunar calendar was a phenomenon of pagan kings, emperors, and pharaohs deifying their sun gods, and hence themselves. Egypt "became the first to adopt

---

46. Frank Parise, *The Book of Calendars* (New York: Facts on File, 1982), pp. 3, 62.

a solar calendar. But the rest of the world resisted this change until Julius Caesar took a hand."[47]

The earliest Roman calendar had ten months (March to December). January and February were added in 715 B.C.E.[48] The Romans did for a while use "a lunar calendar with Hebrew intercalations. But because Roman mathematicians were not as precise as the Hebrews, their calendar [became] a hopeless mess, being 80 days behind the sun."[49] The spring equinox was now falling in December, so Caesar instituted the Julian calendar on January 1, 45 B.C.E. It was adopted by the Catholic Church as its official calendar in 325 C.E.[50]

The Julian calendar started with January 1, 4713 B.C.E., as "day one." Hence, April 9, 1994, was Julian Day 2,449,452. The Julian year is a solar one, with 365 days. In reality, however, the solar year is 365 and *one quarter* days. Caesar tried to fix this problem by adding one day (our February 29) every four years, but even this left the calendar off by about eleven minutes, so over the centuries, time again added up.[51]

By 1582 C.E., another reform was needed to keep religious festivals in their seasons, so Pope Gregory XIII simply "dropped" ten days! October 5 was decreed to be October 15, and business went on as usual. However, the Gregorian calendar is still twenty-five seconds longer than the solar year, meaning that "it will gain a full day on the sun every 3,323 years."[52]

Nor was the Gregorian calendar immediately accepted by everyone. Catholic Europe adopted it right away, but Protestant Europe did not. Great Britain and its colonies did not recognize it until 1752, while Russia only adopted it in the 1917 Revolution. Now, however, it is the standard calendar in use internationally.

For Jewish dates of events, I have relied on three sources: *The Jewish Time Line Encyclopedia*, by Mattis Kantor; *The Sequence of Events in the Old Testament*, by Eliezer Shulman; and Aryeh Kaplan's commentary in *The Living Torah*. To convert Jewish dates to the common calendar (or vice versa), I have used a computer program called Datescreen, which is available for the Macintosh computer from Jim Fremont, 6646 Alcove Ave., North Hollywood, California 91606.

I found that it is more accurate to use the Julian date rather than the Gregorian date in conversions before 1582 C.E. because astronomers still go by the Julian date to describe celestial events. Thus, the Exodus, which occurred on 15 *Nisan* 2448 A.M., corresponded to March 13, 1313 B.C.E., in the Gregorian calendar, but March 25, 1313 B.C.E., in the Julian calendar. In this calendar conversion program, March 25, and not March 13, was the full moon, as 15 *Nisan* would be.

---

47. Doris Chase Doane, *Time Changes in the U.S.A.* (San Francisco: Quarto, 1973), p. 8.
48. Parise, p. 62.
49. Doane, p. 8.
50. Parise, p. 294.
51. Doane, p. 9.
52. Ibid.

Table I-1 lists the months of the Jewish year, along with each holiday (and the date it begins). Note that the Jewish New Year falls in the seventh month, and not the first. Each month begins at the New Moon.

TABLE I-1. The Months of the Jewish Year

1. *Nisan*	Passover (15)	Mar.–Apr.; Aries
2. *Iyar*	*Sefirah*, counting *omer*	Apr.–May; Taurus
3. *Sivan*	Shavuot (6)	May–June; Gemini
4. *Tamuz*	Minor Fast (17)	June–Jul.; Cancer
5. *Av*	Tisha B'Av (9)	Jul.–Aug.; Leo
6. *Elul*	*teshuvah* and *shofar*	Aug.–Sept.; Virgo
7. *Tishre*	Rosh Hashanah (1)	Sept.–Oct.; Libra
	Yom Kippur (10)	
	Sukkot (15)	
	Shmini Atzeret (22)	
8. *Cheshvan*	(unwind from last	Oct.–Nov.; Scorpio
	month's holidays)	
9. *Kislev*	Chanukah (25)	Nov.–Dec.; Sagittarius
10. *Tevet*	Minor Fast (10)	Dec.–Jan.; Capricorn
11. *Shevat*	Tu B'Shevat (15)	Jan.–Feb.; Aquarius
12. *Adar*	Fast of Esther (13)	Feb.–Mar.; Pisces
	Purim (14)	
(13. *Adar* II)	(In leap years, Adar	
	holidays are in Adar II)	

GOD-LANGUAGE, TRANSLITERATION, AND TRANSLATION

I have tried to show through this book that it is possible—and not particularly difficult—to speak of God in genderless terminology without being redundant, grammatically clumsy, or resorting to linguistic inaccuracies. Therefore, one will not find any references to the transcendent aspect of God as He, Him, Master, Father, Lord, or King—except where I have purposely left them in somebody else's quotation or used one of these terms to make a particular point.

I have, nevertheless, retained female pronouns (She, Her) in descriptions of the Shekhinah. I consider this to be a kind of linguistic "affirmative action." Male imagery of God is so prevalent that it cannot be rectified by pure neutrality; the pendulum must first go to the other extreme in order to create balance by ending up in the middle. One frequently hears rabbis today call the transcendent aspect of God, "He," and the Shekhinah, "It."

I do not, however, make up new names for God. I use only the standard, traditional Names: Hashem (for the tetragrammaton), Elokim (with a *K* instead of an *H* to avoid pronouncing it outside of ritual purposes), the Almighty, the Eternal, Creator of the Universe, Sovereign of the Universe, the Divine, the God of Israel, and the

Holy One. I recently found a wonderful Name of God in the *Anenu* ("Answer Us") prayer of the Yom Kippur evening liturgy: Misgav Imahot, which can mean "Refuge of our Mothers" or "Refuge of the Matriarchs." There are probably many other names just waiting to be rediscovered.

In translating passages from the Torah, I use whatever Name of God appears there. Sometimes *God* is just a translation of *Elokim.* Where no Name appears but a verb is in the neuter or male gender, leading translators to insert male pronouns, I simply use *God.*

Many religious readers will wonder why I do not write *G-d.* Maimonides's list of the Seven Names of God (*Foundations of Torah* 6:2)— those that may not be erased or destroyed and are thus changed somehow in writing (like using a *K* in Elokim)— does not list *God* as one of them. *God* is simply the American English term for a deity; a small *g* indicates a pagan deity, while a capital *G* means the one God, the Creator of the Universe, Who brought Israel out of Egypt with a Strong Hand.

Gimel–Dalet in Hebrew spells *Gad* (which has the same pronunciation). *Gad* was the name Leah gave to Zilpah's first child because, she said, "good fortune has come" (Gen. 30:11). The "fortune" of Gad is *mazal,* the determination of one's fate by the constellations. That it may, therefore, be linked to idolatry is confirmed by the Talmud, where the Aramaic term *gda* means "a god," in a reference to a "god of the mountains" (Chul. 40a). R. Judah states that "Gad is none other but an idolatrous term" (Shab. 67b), and numerous other sources agree with him.[53]

Thus, not only do I see no reason to change the spelling of the name *God,* I actually consider it inappropriate to do so.

I ask the reader's indulgence in the artistic license I have taken in transliterating names. In some cases I have clearly preferred a Hebrew spelling (e.g., Avraham instead of Abraham, Rivkah instead of Rebekah or Rebecca). In some of the *J* names (Jacob, Joseph, Judah), I have preferred to retain the English forms, while in others (Yokheved, Yitro), I have not. I have spelled Aharon in its Hebrew pronunciation to keep in mind the association with his mother's pregnancy, and have rejected Moshe in favor of Moses because it *was* an Egyptian name given to him by his Egyptian mother; the Hebrew name given to him by his Jewish mother was something else entirely.

This book is not meant to be an "introduction to Judaism." It is, however, intended to be accessible to a reader unfamiliar with many Jewish concepts. A glossary thus appears at the end of this book, which defines Hebrew words, as well as other types of terms.

The Jewish concepts of *tamae* and *tahor* are basically untranslatable and so have been left untranslated in order to encourage people to stop thinking of them as meaning "defiled–undefiled" and "impure–pure."

In closing, I would like to express my thanks to Misgav Imahot, Refuge of our Mothers, for sustaining me through some difficult times, and to my own mother,

---

53. For a complete analysis, see Matityahu Glazerson, *Hebrew: Source of Languages* (Jerusalem: Raz Ot, 5748), pp. 12–19.

whose generous financial support made it possible for me to write this book on a full-time basis.

If an appreciation of the Torah is kindled in those with a feminist consciousness and the spark of feminist consciousness is kindled in those with an appreciation of the Torah, then this book will have succeeded in its purpose. Only when we have achieved both will the Messianic Era be close at hand.

Traditional Sources

The Alphabet of Ben Sira   a *midrash* containing a story of the demon Lilith as the "real" first woman, created before Chavah; attributed to Ben Sira, whose other major work, Ecclesiasticus, is part of the Apocrypha (books that were not canonized into the Hebrew Bible but did become part of the Catholic Old Testament).

Arak.   *Arakhin,* 45th tractate of the Talmud, dealing with the evaluation of persons and things dedicated to the Sanctuary.

Arama   (R. Isaac) fifteenth-century Spanish commentator, known by the name of his work, *Akedat Yitzhak.*

Ari   R. Isaac Luria, sixteenth-century kabbalist of Sfat, Israel.

Av.   *Avot,* 39th tractate of the Talmud, dealing with ethical maxims of the Rabbis.

Avot d'Rabbi Natan   a minor tractate of the Talmud that is an elaboration of the major tractate *Avot.*

A.Z.   *Avodah Zarah,* 38th tractate of the Talmud, dealing with idol worship.

B.B.   *Baba Batra,* 33rd tractate of the Talmud, dealing with property acquisition.

Bek.   *Bekhorot,* 44th tractate of the Talmud, dealing with the firstborn.

Bik.   *Bikkurim,* 11th tractate of the Talmud, dealing with firstfruit offerings.

B.K.   *Baba Kama,* 31st tractate of the Talmud, dealing with injuries and damages.

B.M.   *Baba Metzia,* 32nd tractate of the Talmud, dealing with lending, borrowing, and other financial matters.

Br.   *Brakhot,* 1st tractate of the Talmud, dealing with blessings and prayer.

Chag.   *Chagigah,* 23rd tractate of the Talmud, dealing with festivals.

Chronicles   11th book of Writings (in two parts).

Chul.   *Chullin,* 43rd tractate of the Talmud, dealing with the slaughter of animals for food.

Derekh Eretz Zuta   a minor tractate of the Talmud consisting of moral and ethical teachings.

Deut.   Deuteronomy, or *Devarim,* 5th book of the Torah.

DR   *Deuteronomy Rabbah,* 5th book of *Midrash Rabbah.*

Ecc.R.   *Ecclesiastes Rabbah,* 8th book of *Midrash Rabbah.*

Ed.   *Eduyot,* 37th tractate of the Talmud, dealing with a variety of rabbinic testi-
monies, traditions, and controversies.

Er.   *Eruvin,* 13th tractate of the Talmud, dealing with carrying on the Sabbath.

ER   *Exodus Rabbah,* 2nd book of *Midrash Rabbah.*

Esther   8th book of Writings, read on Purim.

Est.R.   *Esther Rabbah,* 9th book of *Midrash Rabbah.*

Even HaEzer   3rd section of the *Shulchan Arukh,* dealing with laws of sexuality,
marriage, and divorce.

Ex.   Exodus or *Shemot,* 2nd book of the Torah.

Ezekiel   7th book of Prophets.

Gemara   the major part of the Talmud, consisting of discussions of the Mishnah by
the Rabbis known as Amoraim; completed by 600 C.E.

Gen.   Genesis or *Bereshit,* 1st book of the Torah.

Git.   *Gittin,* 29th tractate of the Talmud, dealing with divorce.

GR   *Genesis Rabbah,* 1st book of *Midrash Rabbah.*

Hertz   (R. J. H.) early twentieth-century British commentator. *Pentateuch and
Haftorahs.* 2nd ed. London: Soncino Press, 1987.

Hirsch   (R. Samson Raphael) nineteenth-century German commentator. *The Pentateuch.* New York: Judaica Press, 1971.

Hor.   *Horayot,* 40th tractate of the Talmud, dealing with wrong decisions of authorities.

Hosea   one of Twelve Prophets, the 8th book of Prophets.

Ibn Ezra   (R. Avraham) twelfth-century Spanish commentator.

Isaiah   5th book of Prophets.

Jastrow   (Marcus) author of *Sefer Milim,* a dictionary of biblical, talmudic, and
midrashic Hebrew and Aramaic.

Jeremiah   6th book of Prophets.

Job   3rd book of Writings.

Joshua   1st book of Prophets.

Judges   2nd book of Prophets.

Judith   a book of the Apocrypha; its events occurred after the Hebrew Bible had
already been canonized.

Kallah Rabbati   a minor tractate of the Talmud consisting of a variety of rabbinic
teachings.

Kaplan   (R. Aryeh) twentieth-century American commentator. *The Living Torah.*
New York: Maznaim, 1981.

Ket.   *Ketubot,* 25th tractate of the Talmud, dealing with marriage.

Kid.   *Kiddushin,* 30th tractate of the Talmud, dealing with betrothal.

Kings   4th book of Prophets (in two parts).

Kitzur Shulchan Arukh   an abridged Code of Jewish Law, compiled by R. Solomon
Ganzfried in the nineteenth century.

Kli Yakar   R. Shlomo Efraim, seventeenth-century Polish commentator.

Kr.   *Kritot,* 47th tractate of the Talmud, dealing with *karet,* or spiritual excision.

Lamentations   6th book of Writings, read on Tisha B'Av.

Lev.   Leviticus or *Vayikra*, 3rd book of the Torah.

LR   *Leviticus Rabbah,* 3rd book of *Midrash Rabbah.*

Maimonides   R. Moses ben Maimon, twelfth-century Egyptian philosopher and codifier of Jewish law; author of

Guide of the Perplexed and

Mishneh Torah. Sections cited in this book are:

Foundations of Torah,

Talmud Torah,

Idolatry,

Circumcision,

Marriage,

Evidence, and

Kings and Their Wars.

Mak.   *Makkot,* 35th tractate of the Talmud, dealing with the punishment of flogging.

Malbim   R. Meir Leib ben Yechiel Michael, nineteenth-century Polish commentator and chief rabbi of Romania.

Meg.   *Megillah,* 21st tractate of the Talmud, dealing with Purim and the Book of Esther.

Men.   *Menachot,* 42nd tractate of the Talmud, dealing with grain-offerings.

Midrash Rabbah   homiletic exposition of various books of the Hebrew Bible, compiled up to the eleventh century.

Mishnah   oral law transmitted by the Rabbis known as Tannaim; set down in writing by 200 C.E.; a part of the Talmud.

M.K.   *Moed Katan,* 22nd tractate of the Talmud, dealing with the intermediate days of Passover and Sukkot.

Nachmanides   R. Moses ben Nachman, thirteenth-century Spanish commentator.

Naz.   *Nazir,* 27th tractate of the Talmud, dealing with the Nazirite vow.

Ned.   *Nedarim,* 26th tractate of the Talmud, dealing with vows.

Neg.   *Negaim,* 54th tractate of the Talmud, dealing with the plague of *tzaraat.*

Nid.   *Niddah,* 58th tractate of the Talmud, dealing with uterine blood.

NR   *Numbers Rabbah,* 4th book of *Midrash Rabbah.*

Num.   Numbers or *Bamidbar,* 4th book of the Torah.

Par.   *Parah,* 55th tractate of the Talmud, dealing with the Red Heifer.

Pes.   *Pesachim,* 14th tractate of the Talmud, dealing with Passover.

Proverbs   2nd book of Writings.

Psalms   1st book of Writings.

Rashi   R. Solomon ben Isaac, eleventh-century French commentator on both Torah and Gemara. His three learned daughters also wrote down his ideas and even answered halakhic questions using his name.

Redak   R. David Kimchi, thirteenth-century French commentator.

R.H.   *Rosh Hashanah,* 19th tractate of the Talmud, dealing with the Jewish New Year and *Rosh Chodesh.*

RR   *Ruth Rabbah,* 7th book of *Midrash Rabbah.*

Ruth   5th book of Writings, read on Shavuot.

Samuel   3rd book of Prophets (in two parts).

San.   *Sanhedrin,* 34th tractate of the Talmud, dealing with the courts, criminal law, and capital punishment.

Sefer Yetzirah   the oldest kabbalistic text, dealing with the mystical meaning of the Hebrew alphabet and its relationship to such phenomena as numerology and astrology.

Sforno   (R. Ovadiah), sixteenth-century Italian commentator.

Shab.   *Shabbat,* 12th tractate of the Talmud, dealing with the Sabbath.

Shevu.   *Shevuot,* 36th tractate of the Talmud, dealing with oaths.

Shulchan Arukh   the Code of Jewish Law, written in the sixteenth century by R. Joseph Caro, a Sephardic Jew. Ashkenazic customs were added by R. Moses Isserles of Cracow. This work is the standard authority of *halakhah.*

Silbermann (R.A.M.)   *Chumash With Rashi's Commentary.* 5 vols. Jerusalem: Silbermann Family, 5745. (Distributed by Feldheim in New York.)

Sifra   also known as *Torat Kohanim;* commentary on Leviticus from the third century C.E.

Sofrim   a minor tractate of the Talmud concerning scribes (writers of sacred scrolls).

Sot.   *Sotah,* 28th tractate of the Talmud, dealing with women accused of adultery by jealous husbands.

SS.R.   *Song of Songs Rabbah,* 10th book of *Midrash Rabbah.*

Suk.   *Sukkah,* 17th tractate of the Talmud, dealing with Sukkot.

SY   *Sefer haYashar,* a chronicle of biblical history once believed to be the lost book mentioned in Joshua 10:13 and 2 Samuel 1:18 but later dated to medieval times; first printed in Italy in the sixteenth century.

Ta.   *Taanit,* 20th tractate of the Talmud, dealing with public fasts.

Talmud   the Mishnah and Gemara; 63 tractates. The Babylonian Talmud, the main version, is the one used throughout this book, except where the Jerusalem Talmud is specifically cited. A colon in a talmudic source (e.g., Ket. 5:6) indicates the Mishnah, while a number with an "a" or "b" (e.g., Ket. 61b) indicates the page of Gemara.

Tam.   *Tamid,* 49th tractate of the Talmud, dealing with the daily sacrifices.

Tanya   a work explaining mystical concepts by R. Shneur Zalman, nineteenth-century Russian founder of the Chabad (Lubavitch) movement. *Likutei Amarim.* London: Kehot Publication Society, 1973.

Targum Jonathan   Aramaic translation of the Torah attributed to Jonathan ben Uzziel, first century C.E.

Tem.   *Temurah,* 46th tractate of the Talmud, dealing with substitutions for animals already dedicated for sacrifice.

Tosafot   twelfth- and thirteenth-century French and German commentary on Rashi's commentary on the Gemara by his daughters, sons-in-law, grandchildren, and students.

Yev.   *Yevamot,* 24th tractate of the Talmud, dealing with levirate marriage and forbidden sexual relations.

Yom.   *Yoma,* 16th tractate of the Talmud, dealing with Yom Kippur.

Yoreh Deah   2nd section of the *Shulchan Arukh*, dealing with a wide variety of laws, such as *kashrut,* idolatry, *niddah*, and circumcision.

Zev.   *Zevachim,* 41st tractate of the Talmud, dealing with animal sacrifice.

Zohar   the primary work of Kabbalah, originating from R. Shimon bar Yochai in the second century C.E. and published by R. Moses de Leon of Spain in the thirteenth century.

❋❋❋ ❋❋❋

The Hebrew Alphabet, Transliteration, and Gematria

There are twenty-two letters—that is, consonants—in the Hebrew alphabet. These are described below, as well as their use or combination with vowels, which are marked by dots or dashes below or above the twenty-two consonants.

Letter		Transliteration and Sound	Gematria
א	Alef	A with vowel mark (ah, ae, ee, oh, oo)	1
ב	Bet	B; v at end of a syllable	2
ג	Gimel	G	3
ד	Dalet	D	4
ה	Heh	H	5
ו	Vav	V; O or U with a vowel mark	6
ז	Zayin	Z	7
ח	Chet	Ch (as in "Chanukah")	8
ט	Tet	T	9
י	Yod	Y, I, J	10
כ	Kaf	K, C; kh at end of a syllable	11/20
ל	Lamed	L	12/30
מ	Mem	M	13/40
נ	Nun	N	14/50
ס	Samekh	S	15/60
ע	Ayin	A with vowel mark (ah, ae, ee, oh, oo)	16/70
פ	Peh	P; f/ph at end of a syllable	17/80

צ	Tzadi	tz; Z at beginning of a proper name	18/90
ק	Kuf	K, C	19/100
ר	Resh	R	20/200
ש	Shin	Sh, S	21/300
ת	Tav	T	22/400

I

Creation and Exile (Genesis/Bereshit)

Chavah:
Mother of All Life

Bereshit (1:1–6:8)

*"And do you not know that you are each an Eve? The sentence of God on this sex of
yours lives in this age; the guilt, of necessity, must live too. You are the devil's gateway."*
—Tertullian, Church father (160–230 C.E.), in an address to women

*"How does a woman help a man? . . . Does she not, then, bring light to his eyes and
put him on his feet!"*
—Talmud, Yev. 63a

The story of Chavah—or Eve, as she is called in English—has been used to rationalize the subordination of woman to man as divinely ordained. Christianity, through
its appropriation of the written Torah without the oral (rabbinic) tradition, has entirely misunderstood and distorted the meaning of Adam and Chavah's relationship.

Feminists have generally responded to this distortion in a similar way—by blaming Hebrew Scripture itself for male supremacy. When they *have* recognized patriarchal appropriation of the story as the problem, feminist critics have usually identified the appropriation itself as Jewish, maintaining that the original, authentic story
is pagan. Feminist theological critique has thus failed to understand that the Hebrew
story of Adam and Chavah is, *in and of itself,* a divine mandate for sexual equality.

Most Jews, having grown up in a Christian society, have internalized the notion
that "Jewish tradition" is to blame for male supremacy. Because they are unlearned
in traditional Jewish sources, they mistake Christian distortions of Jewish Scriptures
for authentic Jewish teachings. In this way, Christian misogyny has promoted anti-
Semitism by cultivating Jewish self-hatred.

It therefore comes as a great surprise to many people to learn that the traditional Jewish view of the story of Adam and Chavah is radically different from the Christian view and is not focused on blaming the woman. It is as different, one might say, as the name *Chavah* is from *Eve*.

A DOUBLE-FACED HERMAPHRODITE

Elokim said, "Let us make humanity in our image and likeness." . . . And Elokim created humanity in God's image, in the image of God Elokim created it, male and female God created them. (Gen. 1:26–27)

On the day that Elokim created humanity, in the likeness of God Elokim made it. Male and female God created them, and blessed them and called them *adam*. (Gen. 5:1–2)

The *adam,* or earth creature, was created as male and female joined together—an *androgynos,* or a gynandromorph or hermaphrodite, according to R. Jeremiah b. Elazar (GR 8:1; Br. 61a). R. Samuel b. Nachmani agreed that this first human being was created double-faced, split into two backs, with "one back on this side and one back on the other side." The *Zohar,* too, notes that "the *adam* of emanation was both male and female, from the side of both Father and Mother" (I:22b) and that "the word *adam* implies male and female" (47a).

This male-and-female creature was given dominion over the earth (Gen. 1:28), and it named the animals *before* it was split into two beings (2:18–20). This naming process—done by a human entity itself on the verge of being separated into male and female—divided the animals into species and also gave distinct identities to the male and female within each species, according to Nachmanides. This is why some species have different names for each gender (e.g., *bull* and *cow*).

The implication of the *androgynos* as the original mode of human existence goes beyond the inherent equality of the sexes. It also indicates that the earth was not given *to the male alone* to conquer in a macho way, but *to humanity as a whole* to take care of, to enjoy, and even to benefit from in a responsible way. Just as woman was not created for man to dominate, neither were the earth and its creatures created for humanity to exploit with impunity.

The concept of the *androgynos* was purposely distorted by the seventy-two Jewish elders who translated the Torah from Hebrew into Greek for King Ptolemy of Egypt in the third century B.C.E. *Genesis Rabbah* 8:11 and *Megillah* 9a tell us that Genesis 5:2 was one of fifteen verses they altered. They wrote "male with his apertures" instead of "male and female" in order to avoid the implication that God is of both sexes, because the pagan ruler would then think that there were two gods rather than one.

THE FORMATION OF WOMAN

And Hashem Elokim formed [*vayitzer*] the *adam* from the dust of the earth, and breathed into its nostrils the soul of life, and the *adam* became a living creature. . . . And Hashem

Elokim said, "It is not good for the *adam* to be alone. I will make an *ezer knegdo* for it."
... Hashem Elokim then made the *adam* fall into a deep state of unconsciousness, and it
slept, and God took one of its sides and closed the flesh under it. And Hashem Elokim
built [*vayiven*] the side [*tzela*] of the *adam* into a woman, and brought her to Adam. And
Adam said, "This time it is bone of my bones and flesh of my flesh. She shall be called
woman [*ishah*] because from man [*ish*] was she taken." (Gen. 2:7, 2:18, 2:21–23)

It is mistakenly asserted by scholars of biblical criticism that there are two stories
of the creation of Adam and Chavah, and that the first is "egalitarian" while the second is "sexist." In reality, the two accounts are one story, with the second, an elaboration of the first. Chapter 1 of Genesis outlines the process of Creation; chapter 2
then returns to the events of the sixth day to describe them in detail.

A kabbalistic explanation is given by Nachmanides. The first account uses the
verb *bara,* to create out of nothing, while the second account uses the verb *yitzer,* to
form from material already created. (These terms correspond to *Briyah*, the World
of Creation, and *Yetzirah*, the World of Formation—two of the Four Worlds described
in Jewish mysticism.)

Thus, Nachmanides explains: "Humanity's Creation at first was male and female,
and the soul was included in both of them. However, in the Formation, the *adam* was
formed, and then God built the woman from its side, as Scripture tells later"
(Nachmanides on Gen. 1:26). The original duality is still hinted at in the second account, by the two Yods in *yitzer* and the double Name of God (Hashem Elokim).

The *adam*'s two faces originally helped each other in the procreative process, says
Nachmanides, but God saw it was good to have them be separated and be able to join
each other at will. Rashi says there was a need to split the *adam* into two so that
humanity would not mistakenly be considered divine because of its similarity to God
in being one (Nachmanides and Rashi on Gen. 2:18).

The word *tzela,* which is frequently translated as "rib," is more accurately rendered as "side," since this same word is used in Exodus 26:20 for the wooden beams
forming the structure of the Tabernacle. To call such beams "ribs" could only be a
metaphor; clearly the term refers to the *side* of a structure (whether a human or a
building).

The formation of the woman from the side of the *adam,* which left the form of the
man, was distorted by the Church into a rationale for the subordination of woman.
Thus, the apostle Paul taught women it was their Christian duty to be submissive to
their husbands and not to teach. Woman "should be quiet," he asserted in 1 Timothy
2:12–14, "for Adam was created first, and Eve afterwards."

Similarly, Thomas Aquinas, writing in the thirteenth century (*Summa Theologica,*
Question 92), wondered if woman should even have been created, since she is "defective and misbegotten." Concluding that she is, however, needed for breeding
purposes, he considered it suitable for her to be created from man, because "woman
is naturally of less strength and dignity than man" and "the man is the head of the
woman." This view is not shared by classical Jewish commentators.

While the female portion of the *adam* developed a new identity and was called
Chavah after exile, the male portion continued to be called Adam. Why the male

maintained this continuity from the *androgynos* is unclear, but it may indicate that man remained more "earthly," more bound by his physical nature, than woman. This neuter-to-male continuity has a linguistic parallel as well: the neuter root of a word in gendered languages is also the masculine form, while the feminine gender is formed through an addition to the root.

However, this does *not* mean that the male is the "norm" and the female is "other." Creation followed a pattern of evolution from lower to higher life-forms. First, God made the elements and mineral life; then plant life; then fish and fowl, amphibians, reptiles, and mammals; and then the human. That woman was formed at the end of this process makes her the crown of Creation. While man's origin remains the mud of the earth, the woman comes from a higher source—the body of the *adam*—thus giving her a higher spiritual nature than the man. "Whatever was created after its companion has power over it" (GR 19:4).

Technically, an organism is more "highly evolved" when it has a separate structure for each function. This is why a human being is a higher life-form than an amoeba, for instance. From a purely technical definition—and not by a value judgment—female sexuality is more highly evolved than male sexuality. The woman has three separate structures for the functions of urination (urethra), sexual pleasure (clitoris), and reproduction (vagina), while the man contains all three of these functions in one structure, the penis.

That the woman is a higher evolutionary life-form than the man does not mean that society should strive toward female supremacy rather than sexual equality, but neither should the concept be distorted into chivalry, which gives the appearance of honoring women while actually keeping them down. For example, women have had doors opened for them *instead of*, rather than *in addition to*, receiving equal pay for equal work. When women demand equality, they are told they must give up such "privileges." However, such a practice is only a privilege if it is based on a foundation of equality. Having the door opened for you is only a privilege if you are *already* being treated equally to the one opening the door. Otherwise, this is not a privilege at all, but rather a compensation (and a poor one at that).

The terms *ishah* and *ish* indicate the potential for holiness or destructiveness in the male–female relationship. The root of both words is *esh*, or *fire*. A letter of God's Name is added to this root for each gender—a Yod to make *man* and a Heh to make *woman*. Without this godly presence between them, male–female relations are like fire, burning and scorching!

A major misunderstanding of the role of woman in relation to man has also been created by inaccurate translation of *ezer knegdo*. Usually rendered as "helpmate," the term has been used to say that women should be subordinate to men. Actually, however, nothing could be further from the truth. Elsewhere in the Bible, God is referred to as an *ezer* to Israel. Surely, God is not to be subordinate to the Jewish people!

Knegdo means "opposite" or "against" him: "If he is worthy, she shall be a help (*ezer*) to him; if he is unworthy, she shall oppose him (*knegdo*), to fight him" (Rashi;

Yev. 63a). This is certainly not a prescription for an obedient wife! Rather, it validates a woman's ability to accurately judge her husband's behavior and to treat him accordingly.

Another indication of the woman's spiritual level being higher than the man's and her perceptiveness in evaluating her husband's character is the word *vayiven,* which the Rabbis relate to *Binah*, the quality of Understanding. God "endowed [the woman] with more Understanding than the man" (GR 18:1; Nid. 45b).

GOOD WIVES AND BAD WIVES

"Everything comes from the woman" (GR 17:7). According to this account, two pious people divorced each other. The man remarried a wicked woman, and she made him wicked. The woman remarried a wicked man and made him righteous. "If he [a woman's husband] becomes wealthy, she rises with him. If he becomes poor, she does not descend with him" (GR 20:11).

The concept of *ezer knegdo*—that a woman knows best, bringing her husband good or bad *as he deserves*—has been difficult for men to accept. Hence, they have distorted the concept into *the wife herself* being considered good or bad. "If a man is worthy, [his wife] is like the wife of Chanina b. Chakhinai; if not, she is like the wife of R. Jose the Galilean," who "brought him misfortune" (GR 17:3).

Chanina (or Chananiah) b. Chakhinai's wife (Ket. 62b) is one of several women whose goodness is defined as encouraging their husbands to study Torah, even though it meant sacrificing his companionship for years at a time. R. Jose's wife, on the other hand, was angry when he brought his study partner home for dinner without telling her ahead of time. Perhaps to make him understand how this could have been an awkward situation for her, she told him there were only vegetables cooking in the pot when actually there was chicken. When R. Jose saw the chicken, he said, "A miracle has happened!" His disciples, however, urged him to divorce his wife, "for she does not treat you properly." When he replied that he could not afford to divorce her because her dowry (which must be returned to the wife upon divorce) was too great, the students took up a collection to enable him to do so. She remarried, but her second husband became blind and, in the end, they were both supported by R. Jose.

Another story is told (Yev. 63a): "Rav was constantly aggravated by his wife." If he wanted lentils, she would fix peas; if he wanted peas, she would fix lentils. His son Chiya used reverse psychology on his mother—asking for peas when he knew his father wanted lentils, and vice versa—which led Rav to think his wife had changed, until his son informed him of what he had done. We are then told that "R. Chiya was constantly aggravated by his wife. Nevertheless, when he obtained anything suitable, he wrapped it up in his scarf and brought it to her." When it was pointed out to him that his wife was troubling him, R. Chiya replied, "It is sufficient for us that they rear up our children and deliver us from sin."

Yevamot 63b gives several definitions of a "bad wife"—for example, "one who prepares a tray for him and has her tongue also ready for him" or "one who prepares a tray for him and turns her back on him"—and says it is a *mitzvah* to divorce her.

According to the concept of *ezer knegdo*, the woman's actions are based on *her husband's merit*. He gets what he deserves. Perhaps he *should* divorce her, because *he* is not worthy of her! However, that does not mean that *she* is a "bad wife." If a woman serves her husband dinner and gives him a tongue-lashing, he may deserve it. If she serves him dinner and walks away, she might have a good reason for her anger.

"The possession of a good wife comes to man only from God" (*Zohar* I:229a). "For God mates couples before they are born, and when a man is worthy he obtains a wife according to what he deserves. . . . Nor is it only a prudent wife who is from God. For if God has planned to bestow benefits on a man, but he goes astray . . . there shall come to him one who shall bring upon him all accusations and ills. . . . It is the man's sins which have drawn her to him."

R. Chiya seemed to understand this and appreciated what his wife did for him. R. Jose, rather than learn the lesson of consideration that his wife was trying to teach him, divorced her—but, as if to prove that one cannot escape one's fate, he ended up having to support both her *and* her new husband! Rav's "aggravation" is so benign as to be laughable: if that was his biggest problem, he had a very good life.

However, in spite of the distortion of *ezer knegdo* into the "good wife" and the "bad wife," the general rabbinic view is that a wife is good for a man. Compare this to the words of John Chrysostom (347–407 c.e.), a Church father who was a patriarch of Constantinople and wrote many biblical commentaries: "What else is woman but a foe to friendship, an inescapable punishment, a necessary evil, a natural temptation, a desirable calamity, a delectable detriment, an evil of nature, painted with fair colors?"[1]

MARRIAGE AND PROCREATION

A man shall therefore leave his father and mother and cleave to his wife, and they shall be one flesh. (Gen. 2:24)

The Rabbis say that a man who has no wife is without joy, blessing, goodness, Torah, protection, help, or peace. In fact, a man is not a complete person if he does not have a wife, and he must love her as himself and honor her more than himself (Yev. 62b–63a; GR 17:2; *Zohar* I:55b).

While a man without a woman is an incomplete person, *no analogous statement is made regarding a woman without a man.* A man must *have* a woman because he cannot *be* a woman, who is complete in herself. We can even see this reflected in the English language: *male* is an incomplete form of *female* and *man* is an incomplete

---

1. Cited in H. R. Hays, *The Dangerous Sex* (New York: Pocket, 1966), p. 142.

form of *woman*. Man is woman without the *wo(mb)*. The psychoanalyst Karen Horney (1885–1952) developed a whole theory of male psychology, which she called "womb envy," that addresses this issue.

This unegalitarian, asymmetrical view of the Torah—that men need women in a way that women do not need men—is reflected in the *mitzvah* of *pru urvu,* the commandment to marry and procreate, which is incumbent only upon men.

This is because man's nature is to conquer and subdue (Yev. 65b; Kid. 35a). The Rabbis seem to believe that, if allowed to live only on the basis of his own physical desires, a man would prefer to have a string of sexual encounters with no commitment. Sex for many men is like the hunt—they enjoy the chase and the conquest, and then they are ready to move on. Most women, on the other hand, want sex in the context of love and a committed relationship. By requiring a man to commit himself to a woman and their children, the Torah is elevating male sexuality to its highest possible expression.

While the Torah thus presumes that women will want to get married, a woman who does not (for whatever reason) has the option of remaining single. The Torah does not condone rape and forced childbearing—which is what marriage and motherhood against a woman's will amount to. Some say the Torah cannot command childbearing because it is painful and often life threatening. While a man, who is obligated to procreate, certainly needs a woman with whom to do it, the woman must be *willing,* not "commanded."

The *Zohar* gives a beautiful account of the male's lack of completeness without the female. "It is incumbent on a man to be ever 'male and female,' in order that his faith may be firm, and that the Shekhinah may never depart from him." If he must travel and be away from his wife, he should "pray to God before he starts his journey, while he is still 'male and female,' in order to draw to himself the presence of his Master. When he has offered his prayer and thanksgiving and the Shekhinah rests on him, then he can depart, for through his union with the Shekhinah he has become 'male and female' in the country as he was 'male and female' in the town" (I:49b).

While he is on his journey, he must be very careful

> in order that the celestial partner may not desert him and leave him defective, through lacking the union with the female. If this was necessary when his wife was with him, how much more so is it necessary when a heavenly partner is attached to him? . . . When he does reach home again, it is his duty to give his wife some pleasure, because it is she who procured for him this heavenly partner. . . . When a man is at home, the foundation of his house is the wife, for it is on account of her that the Shekhinah departs not from the house. (50a)

Moreover, "all females are in the shelter of the Shekhinah, and She abides with a man who has a wife, but not with a man who does not" (228b).

Nachmanides describes man's cleaving to woman in the following way: "In cattle and beast the males have no attachment to the females. Rather, the male mates with any female he finds, then they go their separate ways." However, in the case of man, "bone of his bones and flesh of his flesh" means that "he cleaves to her and she nestles in his bosom as his own flesh, and he desires to be with her always."

THE WOMAN'S ACTION

The serpent . . . asked the woman, "Did Elokim really say you may not eat of any tree in the garden?" The woman replied to the serpent, "We may eat from the fruit of the trees of the garden. But of the fruit of the tree that is in the middle of the garden, Elokim said, 'Do not eat it and do not touch it or else you will die.'" The serpent said to the woman, "You will certainly not die! For Elokim knows that on the day you eat from it, your eyes will be opened and you will be like Elokim, knowing good and evil." The woman saw that the tree was good to eat and desirable to the eyes, and that the tree was a pleasant [way to gain] enlightenment. So she took its fruit and ate, and gave it to her husband with her, and he ate. (Gen. 3:1–6)

Why did the serpent talk to Chavah rather than to Adam or to them both? The commentators resort to misogynist attitudes about women's mental capabilities to explain it. Rashi, for example, says women are "easily influenced and know how to influence their husbands" (Rashi on Gen. 3:15); Sforno attributes it to women's "weak intellect" (*sekhel chalosh*) (Sforno on Gen. 3:1).

It seems more likely that the answer is to be found in women's greater closeness to God. In other words, the serpent went "right to the top," just as a person who wants to effect change in an organization would try to speak to the president rather than the manager. We have already noted women's higher spiritual nature and her greater *Binah*, and there are other indications as well.

The name *Chavah* (Chet, Vav, Heh) contains in it the latter half of the Name of God (the Vav and the Heh), while man's name, as we have seen, remains linked to the earth. This indicates a level of Godliness in woman that is not found in man. Another clue to Chavah's greater consciousness is found in the statement that Adam was "asleep" when the serpent came along (GR 19:3). That the serpent talked to Chavah demonstrates her greater, not lesser, mental capacity. However, a greater knowledge and quest for enlightenment creates greater responsibility. Adages such as "curiosity killed the cat" and "ignorance is bliss" indicate that intellectual exploration brings with it some inherent risks and difficulties.

Chavah mistakenly added to God's prohibition of eating from the tree by saying that God also prohibited touching it. This made her vulnerable to believing the serpent's lie: when the serpent pushed her against the tree (GR 19:3) and she saw that she did not die by touching it, she then believed that she could eat from it and not die.

Chavah did not "tempt" or "seduce" her husband into eating, as Christian theology has maintained. She simply handed him some fruit to share it with him, and he followed, silently and unquestioningly, much like any man will eat the dinner his wife puts before him. Once Chavah realized she was going to die, she gave some of the fruit to her husband so that he would not remain alive and be alone or take another wife (GR 19:5). She also gave some to the animals.

Before they ate from the Tree of Knowledge of Good and Evil, Chavah was simply called "the woman" (*ha-ishah*) and Adam was referred to as "her husband" (*ha-ishah*). This indicates her primacy and the fact that when he is joined to her, he is essentially like her.

After they ate the forbidden fruit—which Jewish tradition maintains was either grapes, figs, wheat, or an *etrog,* not an apple—the couple is referred to as "Adam and his wife" (*ha-adam ve-ishto*). Then she is named Chavah, "mother of all life." The "woman and her husband" are now the "man and his wife," and her primary identity becomes "mother." Something clearly has changed in their relationship.

Chavah and Adam lost their immortality by eating the fruit. As a result, humans have to die, making us less like God. Will and desire were created by their act. Before this, sex was like eating and drinking and the erogenous zones were no different from the face or the hands. There was no need for modesty and no sense of embarrassment about nakedness until after they ate. The distinction between good and evil had been nonexistent, but now, the *yetzer hara*, or evil inclination, became an active principle in humanity.

On the other hand, we are told that both humans and snakes copulate face-to-face rather than face-to-back because the Shekhinah spoke with them (GR 20:3; Bek. 8a). Thus, the experience put them on a special level.

While Chavah is not viewed in Judaism as the "evil temptress," she does, nonetheless, hold a unique position in the garden scenario as the "middleman." The serpent *told* Chavah to eat the fruit but did not itself eat it; Adam *ate* the fruit but did not tell anyone else to eat it. Chavah both ate the fruit *and* told someone else to eat it. Thus, *Genesis Rabbah* 20:11 calls Chavah "Adam's serpent." However, while the serpent lied to Chavah, Chavah did not lie to Adam.

When God confronts them, both Adam and Chavah try to avoid responsibility for their own actions—Chavah, by blaming the snake, and Adam, by blaming Chavah (Gen. 3:11–13). Nachmanides calls Adam "ungrateful" for blaming her, and *Genesis Rabbah* 17:4 notes that woman was not created right from the beginning because "God foresaw that [Adam] would complain about her, and therefore did not create her until he requested her."

Unfortunately, this dynamic is quite familiar to us today. Throughout history, men have avoided responsibility by blaming women. The Rabbis themselves were not immune from such misogynist hostility. (See, for example, GR 17:8 and 18:2.) However, we should not confuse short-sighted rabbinic statements with the Torah itself. Judaism does not, like Christianity, believe in the infallibility of its spiritual leaders. Moreover, fortunately, God does not manifest such male hostility.

THE WOMAN'S "CURSE"

To the woman God said, "I will greatly increase your toil in child rearing [*itzvonekh*] and your pregnancy [*veheronekh*]. In painful labor [*be-etzev*] you will give birth to children. For your husband you will long [*teshucatekh*], and he will rule [*yimshal*] you." (Gen. 3:16)

This passage, more than any other, has been used to justify male dominance; hence, let us examine it very carefully. I have followed Rashi's interpretation of the Hebrew terms to mean child rearing, pregnancy, and childbirth.

The word *curse* (*arur*) is used with the snake and with the earth in relation to the man, but not with the woman. Furthermore, her decree is an "increase," and not a newly created occurrence.

The term *itzavon* is also used with Adam in relation to the earth. Here, too, it implies *toil*. In the Garden of Eden, food was ready-made for Adam and Chavah; after their exile, it became necessary to work the soil, plant and harvest crops, and remove weeds, thorns, and thistles. This explains God's decree to Adam to work "by the sweat of your brow."

God's decree to Chavah instituted the nine-month gestation period, labor pains, and a prolonged period of child rearing. With this were created the menstrual cycle and the hymen (Er. 100b). Prior to this, Chavah had given birth on the day she conceived and her children were born fully grown.

Now, both human production and reproduction changed drastically. For *both* Adam and Chavah, immediate gratification was ended. Exile meant that "labor"—in both senses of the word—would be needed to produce what had previously been done without effort.

However, despite the discomforts of pregnancy, labor pains, and child rearing, women would still have sexual desire for men. Nachmanides says the term *teshucah* is used "only in connection with sexual desire," which means that woman's "desire for her husband [will] be exceedingly great and that she should not be deterred by the pain of pregnancy and birth" or even by the fact that the man "takes possession of her like a slave" (i.e., dominates and oppresses her). Nachmanides thus disagrees with Ibn Ezra, who sees the term as a general prescription for male dominance, as well as with Rashi, who interprets it to mean that men, not women, should initiate sex.

Eruvin 100b interprets *teshucah* even more narrowly to mean that a woman will yearn for her husband when he is about to leave on a journey. Halakhically, a man is obligated to have sex with his wife, if she wants, the night before he leaves.

Thus, *at most,* the passage only refers to women's desire to have children in spite of the physical pain and the sociological difficulties they endure. It does not mean that women should obey men's orders or want to be dominated! Nor does it mean that women must passively endure painful childbirth: while the Catholic Church once used this passage to forbid the use of pain-killing drugs in childbirth, Judaism never did. Similarly, there is no prohibition on technological advances that make agriculture easier.

Unfortunately, however, many women—even those who are not economically dependent—put up with oppression and even abuse because they love, or think they need, a man. *Eruvin* 100b notes that women have been relegated to sexual passivity, confinement in the home, and covering their hair. However, this is simply a *description* of the reality of male supremacy, not a *prescription* for it.

Kabbalists have characterized the expulsion from Paradise as a descent from a higher plane to a lower one. The Messianic Era will restore us to this higher plane.

Male supremacy, far from being ordained by God, is a major indication of the imperfect state of the world in exile. The oppression of women shows how low humanity has fallen. To work against male supremacy is *tikkun olam,* the repair of the world, which we are supposed to undertake to help bring the Messiah.

With this understanding, we can see the women's liberation movement as a sign—on par with the Holocaust and the rebirth of Israel—heralding the dawning of the Messianic Era, when male–female relations will be restored from "man and his wife" to the original, perfected state of "woman and her husband."

The word that is translated as "rule" comes from the root *mashal,* and not from *malakh,* which means to rule by domination and is the root of *melekh,* or *king. Mashal* has a different connotation: it implies affinity or complementarity. It is the root used in Genesis 1:16 to say that the sun "rules" the day and the moon "rules" the night. Concerning the zodiac, it is similarly said that each planet "rules" a constellation. This use of "rule" does not mean to dominate; rather, it means to have an affinity for each other, to go together because of complementary qualities.

Mashlim in modern Hebrew means "completing" or "complementary." *Mashal* in modern Hebrew has two meanings: "example," which may mean "rule" in the sense of "to set an example for"; and "fable," an allegory. A fable is also a story one makes up—such as the myths men have created about women (beginning with Adam's excuse that "she made me do it!").

The story of Chavah lends itself to further contemplation. For instance, what does it mean when *Genesis Rabbah* 20:7 compares a woman's desire for her husband to the desire of rain for the earth and the desire of God for Israel? Surely this is not domination!

Chavah has wrongly been scapegoated for the fall of humanity, and the Torah has wrongly been blamed for giving divine license to male domination. While some *men* may claim that the message of the Garden of Eden story is that men should dominate women, *God* certainly did not say this, and it is extremely important to know the difference.

THE TWIN SISTERS OF CAYIN AND HEVEL

Cayin (Cain) and Hevel (Abel) were born to Adam and Chavah on the same day the latter were created. Because of the number of times *et* (the direct object marker in Hebrew) appears in Genesis 4:1–2, the Rabbis concluded that one twin sister was born with Cayin and two twin sisters were born with Hevel (GR 22:2).

Cayin was a farmer and Hevel was a shepherd; both made offerings to God. Hevel's animal offering was acceptable to God because it was the choicest of the firstborn of the flock; Cayin's plant offering was neither his first nor his choicest, and God rejected it. God told Cayin, "If you do not do good, sin is crouching at the door. It longs [*teshucato*] for you, but you may rule [*timshal*] it" (Gen. 4:7). Note the use of the same words as in Genesis 3:16. The *yetzer hara* yearned for Cayin as a woman longs for her husband, rain longs for the earth, and God longs for Israel (GR 20:7).

Cayin rose up in the field and killed Hevel, committing the first murder and the first instance of male rivalry over women. "An additional twin was born with Hevel, and each claimed her. The one [Cayin] claimed, 'I will have her, because I am the firstborn,' while the other [Hevel] maintained, 'I must have her, because she was born with me'" (GR 22:7). Who else could Cayin and Hevel have married but their sisters?

As punishment, Cayin was cursed and God put a mark on him. Lemekh, the inventor of weapons, was born in the seventh generation after Cayin and fulfilled God's decree of an avenger. Lemekh was blind and was led around by his son, Tuval-Cayin (Rashi). One day they were out hunting and Tuval-Cayin saw Cayin but thought he was an animal. He told his father to draw his bow and Lemekh did, killing Cayin. When Lemekh learned what he had done, he struck his hands together, accidentally hitting and killing Tuval-Cayin as well.

ADAH AND ZILLAH

Adah and Zillah, Lemekh's two wives, are discussed in Genesis 4:19–24. Lemekh's polygyny (polygamy for men) is described as a contrast to God's monogamous ideal, which was expressed in the creation of one man–woman pair.

As society degenerated from monotheism into polytheism, it also descended from monogamy into polygamy. At first this consisted of "group marriage" or "sexual communism," an exchange of men and women between two groups in which all the men of one clan married all the women of the other clan, and vice versa.[2] Thus, a man would marry a woman and all her sisters (sororal polygyny), while a woman would marry a man and all his brothers (fraternal polyandry).

Polyandry (polygamy for women) existed only with polygyny, but polygyny continued to exist even where polyandry ended. This process began as sex became linked with economics and private property, which became accumulated in the hands of men.

"Unmodified group marriage," Briffault explained, "is a practicable arrangement only so long as sexual relations remain completely independent of economic relations between associates; [as] economic factors enter into that relation the organization must of necessity break up into one or the other of its constituent aspects, into sororal polygyny or fraternal polyandry." He added that "the whole development of individualism, of individual property, and [of] personal economic interests has taken place mainly in the hands of the men and not the women, and in human societies as they exist at the present day the economic advantages are generally in favor of the men."[3]

A reference to complete polygamy (polygyny with polyandry) might be contained in Genesis 6:2, where the "sons of the gods" are said to consort with the "daughters

2. For a detailed analysis of this phenomenon, see Robert Briffault, *The Mothers* (New York: Macmillan, 1927), vol. 1, chap. 11, "Group Marriage and Sexual Communism," pp. 614–731.
3. Ibid., p. 628.

of humanity." Otherwise, the Torah's narratives begin with "post-polyandry" polygyny, that is, polygyny alone.

Adah and Zillah—who were sisters, the daughters of Kenan in the fourth generation after Adam (Gen. 5:13; SY 7)—are the first case mentioned. For a list of the
first nineteen generations, see Table 1–1. The men of the generation of the Flood had
two wives—one for childbearing and one for sexual gratification (GR 23:2; Rashi).

The childbearer lived "like a widow," without her husband's companionship,
because pregnant women were an "abomination" (*toevah*) in men's eyes (SY 7). In
this case, the childbearer was Adah (her name means to "remove" or "pass by," as
well as "pregnant"), who had two sons, Yaval and Yuval.

The sexual "playmate" was given *mashkeh akarot*, a potion to drink so she would
not conceive—this was a form of socially mandated birth control to keep her thin.
"Some of the sons of humanity made their wives drink *mashkeh akarot* to preserve
their figures so their beautiful appearance might not deteriorate" (SY 7).

Evidently then, as today, men had a fetish for thin women. Big hips and round
stomachs were despised as "fat"; no doubt, many women internalized these standards
and learned to hate themselves. Natural female roundness is positively acknowledged
in Jewish tradition: "Just as a storehouse is narrow at the top and broad at the bottom
so as to hold the produce, so a woman is narrower above and broader below so as to
hold the embryo" (Br. 61a; Er. 18a; Rashi; GR 18:3).

However, various societies have not found natural female roundness to be positive,
and entire industries have arisen around this preference, from nineteenth-century
corsets that forced the body into an "hourglass" figure to current diet and fashion
trends, which idealize broad shoulders and narrow hips—a male physique—in
women.

The generation of the Flood, however, went so far in their mania for thinness that
they even despised pregnancy. Thus, the childbearing wife lived like a widow, while
a man "cleaved" to his barren wife (SY 7), who "sat before him adorned like a harlot" (GR 23:2) or "adorned like a bride" (Rashi) and was "fed with the best food."

Zillah (who lived in Lemekh's shadow or *tzel*) was the sex-object wife. However,
her potion did not work forever. "At the end of many days and years, Zillah grew old
and Hashem opened her womb." She gave birth to Tuval-Cayin, who refined and
improved his father's weaponry by making sharp objects of copper and iron. Zillah
also bore a daughter, Naamah (Gen. 4:22).

Adah and Zillah both left Lemekh because he killed Cayin and Tuval-Cayin
(Rashi). Lemekh "pressed them to listen to him" and they returned to him when they
realized he had not purposely murdered the men. However, both women refused to
bear children who would only be destroyed in the Flood, because they knew "that
God's anger was increasing in those days against the sons of humanity" (GR 23:4;
SY 8).

Once Adam saw that his descendants were destined to die, he no longer wanted to
procreate (GR 21:9). He separated from Chavah for 130 years, during which time
"the male demons were made ardent by her and she bore, while the female demons
were inflamed by Adam, and they bore" (GR 20:11).

TABLE 1–1. The First Nineteen Generations of Humanity

Ancestral Name	Lifespan	Birth AM (BCE)	Major Event	Death AM (BCE)
1. Adam	930 yrs.	0 (6th day)	Creation and Exile from Paradise	930 (2832–31)
2. Shet	912 yrs.	130 (3632–31)		1042 (2720–19)
3. Enosh	905 yrs.	235 (3527–26)	Beginning of idolatry	1140 (2622–21)
4. Kenan	910 yrs.	325 (3437–36)		1235 (2527–26)
5. Mahalalel	895 yrs.	395 (3367–66)		1290 (2472–71)
6. Yared	962 yrs.	460 (3302–01)		1422 (2340–39)
7. Chanokh	365 yrs.	622 (3140–39)	Walked with God and was taken	987 (2775–74)
8. Metushelach	969 yrs.	687 (3075–74)		1656 (2106–05)
9. Lemekh	777 yrs.	874 (2888–87)		1651 (2111–10)
10. Noach	950 yrs.	1056 (2706–05)	Flood—1656	2006 (1756–55)
11. Shem	600 yrs.	1558 (2204–03)		2158 (1604–03)
12. Arpakhshad	438 yrs.	1658 (2104–03)		2096 (1666–65)
13. Shelach	433 yrs.	1693 (2069–68)		2126 (1636–35)
14. Ever	464 yrs.	1723 (2039–38)		2187 (1575–74)
15. Peleg	239 yrs.	1757 (2005–04)	Tower of Babel; Continental Divide—1996	1996 (1766–65)
16. Reu	239 yrs.	1787 (1975–74)		2026 (1736–35)
17. Srug	230 yrs.	1819 (1943–42)		2049 (1713–12)
18. Nachor	148 yrs.	1849 (1913–12)		1997 (1765–64)
19. Terach	205 yrs.	1878 (1884–83)	Left Ur—2018	2083 (1679–78)

Adah and Zillah caused Adam to return to Chavah. Lemekh's pressure consisted of bringing them before Adam, who advised the women to continue procreating. The women reminded him that he was not following his own advice. Thereupon, Adam returned to Chavah and "his love for her was now greater than before" (Rashi).

"Formerly [Adam] had experienced no desire when he did not see her, but now he desired her whether he saw her or not." The Rabbis used this to teach the men of their time: "This is a hint to seafarers to remember their homes and return there immediately" (GR 23:5).

LILITH

One of the most well known demons with whom Adam consorted during his separation from Chavah was Lilith. "Now in the depth of the great abyss there is a certain hot fiery female spirit named Lilith" (*Zohar* III:19a), who was one of many demons that tried to enter the *adam.*

When Lilith saw that male and female had been joined, split, and reunited through marriage, "she fled, and she is still in the cities of the seacoast trying to ensnare humanity." Lilith settles in places of desolation, as mentioned in Isaiah 34:14.

Dressed in her finery, Lilith seduces a man in his sleep, "ascends to the realms above, accuses him, obtains authority [to kill him], and descends." The man, who is called a "fool," wakes up, thinking they will have sex again, "but she takes off her finery and turns into a fierce warrior" with a sword dripping poison from its tip. "He [the warrior] kills the fool, and throws him into Gehinom" (*Zohar* I:148a–b). Thus, the seductive woman was only a mask for the angel of death—a warlike, murderous male.

The *Zohar* (I:19b, III:76b–77a) also describes Lilith as a baby killer who asphyxiates babies with croup. "She goes out into the world and seeks her little ones, and when she sees babies she cleaves to them in order to kill them and to insinuate herself into their spirits. There are, however, three holy spirits which fly in front of her and take that spirit from her and set it before the Holy One. . . . Thus they guard that child and she cannot hurt it." This only happens if a man is holy during intercourse. "But if a man is not holy [during sex] . . . she comes and makes sport with that child, and if she kills it she enters into its spirit and never leaves it."

Lilith is described in a *midrash* called *The Alphabet of Ben Sira* as a predecessor of Chavah, who insisted on equality with Adam. In this account, God created both man and woman from the earth, and when Adam insisted on lying above Lilith, she replied, "We are equal because we both come from the earth." While this story has had massive appeal among feminists, it is actually a result of the distortion and debasement of Chavah.

Ben Sira, notes Rabbi Aryeh Kaplan, was "the son of Jeremiah. Regarding his birth, there is a fascinating tradition. Jeremiah had been accosted by homosexuals in the bathhouse, and as a result, had experienced an ejaculation in the tub. His semen remained viable, and when his daughter later used the same tub, she was impregnated by it, eventually giving birth to Ben Sira. Ben Sira was therefore the son of both Jeremiah and the latter's daughter."[4]

Would Jeremiah have had an orgasm if he was raped? Could a woman really get pregnant from sperm in a pool? The story implies that Jeremiah was either a homosexual or an incest perpetrator. Even if we accept the story at face value, Ben Sira was, nonetheless, the result of a perverted conception. This event, whether consciously or unconsciously, affected his views of sexuality.

Everything written about Lilith—including the statement that "whoever sleeps in a house alone is seized by Lilith" (Shab. 151b)—indicates that she is a projection of men's discomfort with their nocturnal emissions. I once attended a Passover *seder* where a feminist suggested substituting Elijah's cup with a cup for Lilith. She might as well have proposed a toast to men's nocturnal emissions!

Lilith is only needed as the "first female" in a system where Chavah is already perceived as subordinate to Adam. In a correct view of Adam and Chavah's rela-

4. Aryeh Kaplan, *Sefer Yetzirah* (York Beach, ME: Samuel Weiser, 1990), p. xv. Jeremiah was a prophet during the destruction of the First Temple, which was destroyed because of the prevalence of murder, idolatry, and incest.

tionship, Lilith symbolizes a force gone wrong. The female who sucks the "vital fluids" out of a man is described as turning into a bloodthirsty male warrior who kills
children. Turned against herself and her own offspring, and thus perverted into a sick
reflection of her oppressor, Lilith becomes an insidious force of destruction. She is
the personification of internalized female self-hatred under male supremacy, and she
has no place in a feminist theology.

2

Naamah: Survivor of the Flood

Noach (6:9–11:32)

Naamah, the daughter of Zillah and Lemekh, married Noach and survived the Flood with their three sons and three daughters-in-law. As the mother of the one family, the eight righteous people, that God chose to save in this otherwise universal destruction, Naamah carried on Chavah's role of "mother of all life," for it was from her that all the post-Flood generations of humanity descended.

There is a conflicting tradition that Naamah, who as Lemekh's daughter was a descendant of Cayin, was a demon whose "abode [was] among the waves of the great sea" and who, like Lilith, seduced men at night, gave birth to more demons, and killed human babies (*Zohar* I:55a, III:76b–77a).

Perhaps for this reason—to remove Naamah from Cayin's lineage—*Sefer haYashar* 10 and 16 says that Noach married Naamah, the daughter of Chanokh and sister of Metushelach (Gen. 5:21–22). *Sefer haYashar* 17 adds that the three daughters-in-law were the granddaughters of Metushelach.

There is also another Naamah, an Ammonite, who is mentioned in several places in both the Talmud and the Midrash. Could it be *this* Naamah whom the Rabbis meant when they said, "There was another Naamah . . . [who] sang to the timbrel in honor of idolatry" (GR 23:3)? Naamah the Ammonite is always mentioned in conjunction with Ruth the Moabite, as examples of two women who renounced idolatry.

However, *Genesis Rabbah* 23:3 also says, "Naamah was Noach's wife, and why was she called Naamah? Because her deeds were pleasant." Indeed, Nachmanides believes that "if we say that she [Zillah's daughter] was not the woman from whom Noach begot his three sons, there is no reason for Scripture mentioning her." He adds

19

that Naamah "was famous in these generations because she was a righteous woman and she gave birth to righteous children."

That is, just as Noach was "a righteous man and perfectly unblemished [*tamim*] in his generation" (Gen. 6:9), so, too, was Naamah righteous and perfect among the women, the "daughters of humanity."

THE DAUGHTERS OF HUMANITY

> Humanity began to increase on the face of the earth, and daughters were born to them. The sons of the gods saw that the daughters of humanity were good, and they took for themselves women from whomever they chose. (Gen. 6:1–2)

In the first eighteen generations of humanity (Gen. 5:4–32, 11:11–25), we read of sons *and daughters* being born. The exception is Noach who, according to Nachmanides, was "unlike all his ancestors who begot daughters and sons." That is, no daughters are mentioned because he had none. In the nineteenth generation, Terach, we again hear only of three sons. After this we only hear about sons, even when there were daughters as well.

Genesis 6:1 equates increase with the birth of daughters, not sons. The devaluation of daughters and the rise of son-preference was a later, sociological phenomenon. When the wife of R. Shimon b. Rabbi gave birth to a daughter, he was disappointed (B.B. 16b). His father told him, based on Genesis 6:1, "Increase has come to the world." However, Bar Kappara said: "Your father has given you an empty consolation. The world cannot do without either males or females. Yet happy is he whose children are males, and alas for him whose children are females. The world cannot do without either a spice-seller or a tanner. Yet happy is he whose occupation is that of spice-seller, and alas for him whose occupation is that of tanner."

Genesis Rabbah 26:4 gives a slightly different version of the story: R. Chiya the Elder said that a daughter is a sign of blessing, and Rabbi Shimon's father responded negatively, saying: "Both wine and vinegar are needed, yet wine is more needed than vinegar. Both wheat and barley are needed, yet wheat is more needed than barley. When a man gives his daughter in marriage and incurs expense he says to her, 'May you never return here,'" meaning she should live happily ever after with her husband.

The last sentence shows the probable source of son-preference. Sons became favored over daughters with the development of patrilineal kinship and its outgrowth, patrilocal marriage: A daughter, who was generally betrothed by her father at a young age, went to live in her father-in-law's household, becoming part of *his* family and becoming lost to her own natal family.

If the daughter took with her a dowry—money or goods paid by the bride's family to the groom's family—then her natal family lost money as well as the child. On the other hand, if it had a son, the family would acquire children (daughters-in-law) *and* money. It is easy to see how sons represented gain and daughters represented loss in this kind of arrangement.

If, instead of dowry, there was bride-price—money or goods paid by the groom to the wife's family—this at least created a monetary advantage in having daughters. However, the use of the bride-price also indicates a shift from matrilocal to patrilocal marriage customs: the groom is paying the wife's family to be able to take her away. We will explore this transition later in Genesis.

That patrilocal marriage was a sociological development *not* divinely ordained by the Torah is indicated in Genesis 2:24, which instructs a man to leave *his* parents and stay with his wife and her family. This is matrilocal marriage and, along with matrilineal kinship, it is the major reason why, at this point in the Torah narrative, daughters still represent increase rather than loss.

Who are the sons of the gods? Often this is translated as "sons of God" and is taken to refer to fallen angels who copulated with human women (*Zohar* I:58a). However, R. Shimon bar Yochai saw these "sons of the gods" as human leaders. He "called them the sons of judges, and cursed all who called them the sons of God" (GR 26:5). Rashi also calls them "sons of princes and judges," and Nachmanides adds "that the judges whose duty it was to administer justice among them committed open violence without anyone interfering."

R. Shimon bar Yochai further states, "If demoralization does not proceed from the leaders, it is not real demoralization," and R. Azariah adds, "When the priests steal their gods, by what can one swear or to what can one sacrifice?" In other words, when the leaders of the people are corrupt and violent, and when they even pervert religious symbols to justify their behavior, the rest of society will follow.

This is what happened in the generation of the Flood. The "sons of princes" led the way in the degradation of women described in the story of Adah and Zillah, and the rest of the men followed. *Sefer haYashar* 15 describes the "sons of the gods" as the "sons of humanity" who "departed from the ways of Hashem. . . . And every man made himself a god, and committed robbery and violence." Each man may have made himself a statue of a god, but the more important meaning here is that each man deified himself.

What does it mean that the sons of princes "saw that the daughters of humanity were good" and took whomever they chose? Does it bear any similarity to God looking at Creation and seeing "it was good?" That is hardly the case: "They would take them forcibly" (Nachmanides on Gen. 6:2). "And their judges and officials went to all the daughters of humanity and took women for themselves by force, [even] from their husbands, from whomever they chose" (SY 15).

"When a bride was prepared for her husband, the chief [of these judges] entered and took his pleasure with her first" (GR 26:5). Official prenuptial rape was also experienced by Jewish women during the Syrian–Greek domination, which culminated in the rebellion of Chanukah.

While this could simply indicate massive arbitrary rape, it may actually refer to the practice of ritual defloration, which was common in the ancient world. The use of a stranger to deflower a girl at puberty, before her marriage, was a widespread custom, as the blood of the hymen was believed to have a certain kind of magical power. Only a "representative of the god" could avoid the "perils" of coming into contact with hymeneal blood.

Hence, this ritualized virgin-rape was frequently accomplished through "ritual defloration by a priest or prince, hierodulic prostitution in temples, [or] mechanical defloration by the image of a god."[1] Although sometimes a slave or a member of the girl's family might accomplish the defloration, in many cultures, "the rupture of the hymen had to be accomplished by the prince or chieftain."[2]

This describes the "sons of the gods" or "sons of princes" in the generation of the Flood. Ancient pagan heroes who were deified after their deaths lived during this time (Malbim on Gen. 6:4).

SEXUAL ABUSE AND VIOLENCE AS CAUSES OF THE FLOOD

The earth was being ruined [*tishachet*] before God, and the earth was filled with violence. God saw the earth, and it was destroying itself [*nishchata*]. All flesh was perverting [*hishchit*] its way on the earth. God said to Noach, "The end of all flesh is coming before Me. The earth is full of violence [*chamas*], and therefore I will destroy [*mashchitam*] them with the earth." (Gen. 6:11–13)

That sexual exploitation, abuse, perversion, and violence were rampant in the generation of the Flood—and angered God to the point of destroying all life on earth—is repeatedly described in Jewish sources. Rape, adultery, incest, promiscuity, prostitution, bestiality, sodomy, and even male masturbation are all cited as causes of the Flood. While women certainly participated in promiscuity, it is likely that then, as today, sexual abuse and violence were primarily committed by men.

The era is described as one in which men "spilled their semen upon the trees and stones," were "steeped in sexual degradation" (*znut*), and had "many women" (GR 26:4). Promiscuity was so rampant that "a woman would go out into the marketplace, see a man and desire him, whereupon she would sleep with him and give birth to a young man like him" (GR 26:7).

"The generation of the Flood was blotted out from the world because they were steeped in sexual degradation" (LR 23:9) or "because they were steeped in lewdness" (*zimah*) (LR 12:5).

"The generation of the Flood was not blotted out from the world until they composed nuptial songs for males and for animals," that is, acts of sodomy and bestiality (GR 26:5; LR 23:9). "The Holy One is long-suffering towards every offense except sexual degradation. . . . In every instance where you find licentiousness, an *andro-*

---

1. Briffault, 3:317.
2. Ottokar Nemecek, *Virginity: Prenuptial Rites and Rituals* (New York: Philosophical Library, 1958), p. 38.

lomosia [collective punishment, regardless of individual guilt or innocence] comes upon the world and kills both good and bad."

Humans not only had sex with animals but caused animals to have perverse sexual relations with each other. "The whole of the animal world had become corrupted and had mixed up their species. . . . It was the wicked among men who brought about the unnatural intercourse in the animal world, and who sought thereby to undo the work of Creation. They made the rest of Creation pervert their ways in imitation of themselves" (*Zohar* I:68a).

"Even domestic animals, wild animals, and birds did not consort with their own species" (Rashi). "All acted corruptly in the generation of the Flood. The dog [copulated] with the wolf, the fowl with the peacock. . . . Even the earth acted licentiously; wheat was sown and it produced rye" (GR 28:8). Domestic animals and fowl became predatory, and "thus they too committed violence" (Nachmanides). "Humanity began to sin first and was the first to be punished . . . but the rest [of Creation] did not escape" (NR 9:18).

Rashi adds idolatry as a cause of collective punishment but maintains, "Their fate was sealed only on account of robbery" (*gezel*). "Come and see how great is the power of violence [*chamas*], for behold, though the generation of the Flood transgressed all laws, their decree of punishment was sealed only because they stretched out their hands in robbery" (San. 108a). *Chamas* is defined as idolatry, incest and adultery, murder, and robbery (GR 31:6). The violent acts of the generation of the Flood "led to mutual hatred and contention among them" (*Zohar* I:61a).

Male masturbation is the subject of extremely strong comments. "The men of the time of the Flood committed all kinds of sin, but the measure of their guilt was not full until they wasted their [seed] upon the ground. . . . Such a one will never enter the heavenly palace nor gaze upon the Shekhinah, for by this sin the Shekhinah is repelled from the world" (*Zohar* I:56b–57a; 188a).

Similarly, "Whoever discharges his semen without purpose will never be allowed to behold the Shekhinah, and such a one is called wicked" (III:90a). Moreover, "in the generation of the Flood the measure of sin was not filled up until man became sexually perverted and destroyed its seed" (I:66b); indeed, "the sin of onanism is one by which man corrupts both himself and the earth" (I:62a).

Male masturbation is compared to murder and idolatry and is said to delay the coming of the Messiah; the man who engages in it is likened to an unmindful animal; he has no portion in the world to come, forfeits his life, is liable to the death penalty, and should even be excommunicated! (*Kallah Rabbati,* chap. 2; Nid. 13a–b).

"All the men of the generation of the Flood practiced masturbation," the Rabbis say, adding, "Whoever touches his penis while urinating is as though he brought a flood upon the world." (This latter point only applies to an unmarried man, and even then ways are described for him to touch it to urinate if he needs to. The purpose is not to make urination difficult, but to prevent him from arousing himself.) A modern consciousness, which values the development of healthy attitudes to sexuality, will naturally rebel against the notion that masturbation is bad and will, in fact, argue that its *repression* is unhealthy.

The Torah states that "the earth was being ruined *before* God." *Zohar* I:60b suggests that people "committed their sins secretly"—that is, before God, but not before other people—but then it concludes: "They finished, however, by coming out into the open [and] . . . there was not a place in the whole earth which did not witness their sins. . . . They perpetrated their crimes openly in the eyes of all."

This and the statement that men "spilled their semen upon the trees and stones" indicate that the men of the generation of the Flood masturbated *publicly*. Most, if not all, modern women have had the experience of having to deal with such a man on the telephone, in a park, on a subway car late at night, or in some other semiprivate yet public place. Imagine if the majority of men in our culture acted like that. That kind of perversity characterized the generation of the Flood.

There are also no corresponding statements concerning female masturbation. The Mishnah, in fact, makes a huge distinction between a woman who touches her genitals and a man who touches his: "Every hand that makes a frequent examination is, in the case of women, praiseworthy, but in the case of men, it should be cut off" (Nid. 13a). Granted, the reference is to a woman checking herself for menstrual blood— and men who are checking for nonseminal emissions are also regarded as praiseworthy, the Gemara hastens to add. Moreover, the recommendation that the hand be "cut off" is *only* metaphorical.

Nevertheless, a precedent is clearly set here for a different, rather than an "egalitarian," treatment of the sexes. This is due to a basic difference between male and female sexuality. A man inevitably experiences pleasure in the sex act, while a woman may not. A woman must know herself in order to be able to communicate her needs to her partner. Perhaps the Rabbis understood this complex aspect of female sexuality and hence were silent about female masturbation, which, we might add, has never posed a social threat like that posed by the exhibitionistic man in the park.

SEMEN AND WATER: THE "KARMA" OF THE FLOOD

Karma is a Hindu term that means one reaps what one sows—in other words, every action has an equal and opposite reaction. What you do to others—both good and bad actions—will definitely come back to you. Judaism has a similar concept of "tit for tat," or "measure for measure"—*midah kneged midah.* Such was the punishment of the Flood.

"With hot liquid they sinned and with hot liquid they were punished" (R.H. 12a; Zev. 113b; San. 108b), it is written, referring to semen and water, respectively. *Sanhedrin* adds, "The waters of the Flood were as hard as semen." *Zohar* I:62a notes that "the waters of the Deluge were burning hot, and caused their skins to peel off, this being a fitting punishment for the sin they committed in wasting the warm fluid [semen]. It was all measure for measure."

Similarly mentioned is the way in which men *looked* at women (Gen. 6:2)—as sex objects rather than as persons. The Flood is related to "the eyeball, which is like water" (San. 108a; NR 9:24). Finally, these latter two sources note that the generation of the Flood was haughty about all the good things God gave them, including rain. "They thought, 'Seeing that the only trouble to which we put God is to send a couple of raindrops, we do not need them. We have rivers and wells from which we can draw sufficient supplies of water.'"

The generation of the Flood was so evil that it would not participate in the resurrection of the dead, nor did its members have a share in the world to come (*Zohar* I:68b; San. 108a; GR 32:1; LR 4:1).

THE CHANGE IN HUMAN–ANIMAL RELATIONS

Midah kneged midah is also evident in the use of the Hebrew root *shachat* (Shin, Chet, Tav) to indicate both what the world was doing to itself *and* what God would do to it as a result. God's punishment was of the same essence as the crime itself: the earth was headed toward self-destruction, so God went ahead and destroyed it.

Before the Flood, humans were not allowed to eat animals. This caused a misperception that humans and animals were on the same level, which led humans to have sex with animals and even worship them.

After the Flood, it became permissible for humans to eat animal flesh—to make a very clear boundary distinguishing humans from animals, which could not be crossed again quite so easily. The only restriction made on humanity as a whole was not to tear a limb from a live animal (Gen. 9:3–4). At the same time, God created a concomitant fear of people in animals (9:2). This is when certain species became predators of humans (Rashi).

Now that humans could shed animal blood and certain animals would shed human blood, it became necessary to prohibit humans from shedding human blood. Thus, God emphasized the value of human life (9:5–6), prohibiting murder and suicide—and, some would say, abortion. What is a "person in a person" (*ha-adam ba-adam*), asks *Sanhedrin* 57b, if not a fetus?

SEXUAL SEPARATION IN THE ARK

"You will come into the ark—you, your sons, your wife, and your sons' wives." . . . Noach, his sons, his wife, and his sons' wives came into the ark. . . . God spoke to Noach, saying, "Leave the ark—you, your wife, your sons, and your sons' wives." . . . Noach, his sons, his wife, and his sons' wives left the ark. (Gen. 6:18, 7:7, 8:15, 8:18)

The word order in the preceding passage is very significant. God told the family to enter the ark separated by sex, and they did so. God also told them to leave the ark integrated by sex, but they did not. Note, however, that the monogamous ideal is again apparent: God saved four man–woman pairs on the ark, and even the animals were saved in monogamous pairs!

The men and women were "not allowed to have sexual relations since the world was living in a state of distress" (Rashi). Men are told, "When you see want and famine come to the world, regard your wife as though she were in *niddah*"—in other words, menstruating and thus sexually prohibited (GR 31:12, 34:7). Evidently, upon leaving the ark, it was difficult for them to immediately readjust to being together again.

Male and female animals were also separated in the ark. Both humans and animals needed a period of rest from sexual relations, which had gone totally awry in the generation of the Flood. Moreover, just as only "unblemished" humans were saved, so, too, only animals that had not been used for bestiality or interbreeding were taken in (Zev. 116a; San. 108b). Nevertheless, humans and animals were separated in the ark, which had three levels, with the top for humans, the middle for animals, and the bottom for excrement.

In spite of the prohibition, three pairs copulated: the dogs, the ravens, and Cham and his wife. As a result, the dog was destined to be kept on a leash, and the raven and Cham also had their unique fates. The male raven was chosen by Noach to be the first creature to go forth from the ark to see if the Flood was dissipating (Gen. 8:7)—thus putting it at risk. Because there was only one pair of ravens compared to seven pairs of some other animals, the raven felt this was unfair and became very angry.

"You hate me," he accused Noach. "Should the angel of heat or of cold strike me, will not the world lack one species? Or perhaps you desire my mate!" Noach replied, "You evil one! Even that which is permitted to me [his wife] has been forbidden; how much more so that which is [always] forbidden!" (San. 108b). Noach's revulsion to bestiality is, perhaps, a clue to his "unblemished" nature. (In addition, Nachmanides says he was not "enticed by" idolatry, and the Talmud says he rebuked people for their evil behavior.) Noach then sent out a dove, which is spoken of in both masculine and feminine terminology in Genesis 8:11 (*taraf befihah*).

Cham and his wife were the ancestors of, among others, Canaan and Mitzrayim (Egypt). After the Flood, when Noach planted a vineyard, became drunk, and passed out naked in his tent, Cham saw that Canaan had either castrated or sodomized Noach (San. 70a). The literal meaning of the verse (Gen. 9:22), however, is that Cham looked at his naked father and ridiculed him to his brothers Shem and Yafet, who then covered Noach without looking at him. Whatever actually happened, upon awakening, Noach cursed Canaan to be enslaved by Shem, ancestor of the Hebrews.

3

Sarah: First Jewess

Lekh Lekha (12:1–17:27)

It is often said that Avraham the patriarch was the first Jew—but Sarah the matriarch was also the first Jew(ess). Although the oral tradition indicates that Avraham understood the concept of monotheism at age three, we are also told that Sarah's capacity for prophecy was greater than Avraham's. The Torah portrays the couple as a team, who left Charan with "all their substance that they had gathered and the souls they had acquired" (Gen. 12:5). Avraham converted many men and Sarah converted many women to the belief in One God. How did their journey begin?

AMATLAI, SOURCE OF TRUTH AND REASON

Nimrod, a descendant of Cham, was king of Babylonia, "the first to amass power in the world" (Gen. 10:8–10). As the king, he was god, and his temple was the Tower of Babel (A.Z. 53b). Nimrod was so named because "he led all the world in rebellion" (*marad*) (Er. 53a). He was a "mighty hunter" and initiated warfare in the world.

Terach—the father of Nachor and Haran by two different wives—was the prince of Nimrod's army. His third wife, Amatlai (B.B. 91a), gave birth to Avram. When the king's astrologer predicted that this child would be greater than Nimrod, the king ordered Avram killed. Terach, however, substituted a servant's child and hid Amatlai and her baby in a cave, bringing them provisions monthly. Avram did not emerge from the cave with his mother until he was ten, when Sarah was born. His understanding of God began at age three (SY 27; GR 64:4), while he was secluded in the cave with his mother.

Her name, אמתלאי, is vocalized as Amatlai by the Jastrow dictionary, which also defines *amatla* as "something tangible; [a] plausible reason for correcting or retracting an evidence." Her name contains the word "truth" *(emet),* which in Hebrew is linguistically related to "mother" *(imah).* Avram discovered the truth about God from his mother, who taught him reasoning and logic.

When Terach told Avram that his statues had created the world, Amatlai helped her son prove the silliness of idol worship by making food for the gods to "eat" (SY 35). When he saw they could not eat, Avram angrily took a hatchet and broke all but one idol. He put the hatchet in the hand of the remaining statue and told his father that this god had destroyed the others. Walking straight into the trap of Avram's clever logic, Terach responded that the idol was not capable of doing such a deed, so Avram replied, "Then how could it have created the world?"

Terach was so angry that he exposed Avram to Nimrod and falsely accused his own child, Haran, of initiating the baby-substitution plot. Nimrod commanded that both Avram and Haran be thrown into a fiery furnace as punishment. Avram emerged from the furnace unscathed, but Haran did not, for he did not believe in God but rather had made up his mind to follow whoever prevailed, Avram or Nimrod.

Haran was the father of three children—Lot, Milkah, and Sarai. Haran's daughters each married one of his paternal brothers: Milkah married Uncle Nachor and Sarai married Uncle Avram. There is otherwise no background information on Sarai. Are we to believe that she simply followed Avram in his rebellion against idolatry, or did she have her own rebellion in becoming Sarah, the first Jew?

BABYLONIAN PRINCESS-PRIESTESS

The name of Avram's wife was Sarai. The name of Nachor's wife was Milkah, the daughter of Haran, who was the father of Milkah and the father of Yiskah. Sarai was barren; she had no children. (Gen. 11:29-30)

Sarai and Yiskah are one and the same woman (Rashi; San. 69b; Meg. 14a). She is called Yiskah because "she could see [*sokhah*] the future by *ruach hakodesh*" (divine inspiration). Yiskah also refers to "royalty" *(nesikhut),* and Sarai means "my princess." *Brakhot* 13a notes, "At first she became a princess to her own people, but later she became a princess to all the world."

As Terach's granddaughter and daughter-in-law, Sarai was a part of Babylonian royalty. Moreover, as is true for all ancient pagan societies, Babylonian royalty and priesthood were inextricably linked. Since Sarai was a princess, it is highly likely that she also was a priestess. Her role as a priestess would depend on whether her service was to a goddess or a god.

A priestess who served a goddess lived in "cloister-like buildings attached to temples in Babylon," where she would be "not free to choose her temporary partner, but under obligation not to refuse any man who offers the appointed price."[1] The

---

1. Briffault, 3:219.

rituals were "universal in Western Asia" and "observed at one time throughout Semitic lands."[2] This role has been called "sacred prostitution"; the female religious prostitute is referred to in the Torah as a *kedeshah* (holy one).

Ritual defloration thus continued after the Flood. "In Babylonia, every woman was under the obligation of proceeding once in her lifetime, most probably before her marriage, to the temple of the great goddess . . . and of waiting there until a stranger threw a piece of money into her lap. . . . She then retired with the stranger to an adjoining house, and surrendered to his embraces."[3] This description by Briffault is taken from the Greek historian Herodotus (5th cent. B.C.E.), who further explained that the woman "goes with the first man who throws [a coin] and rejects none. By having intercourse she has discharged her duty to the goddess and she goes away to her home. . . . Those women who excel in beauty and stature are soon released, but such as are ugly have to wait long before they can comply with the custom, sometimes as much as three or four years."[4]

Such a description clearly reveals the degrading nature of the practice. However, proponents of feminist spirituality have asserted that these pagan sex rites "revered" women and that it was Judaism that lowered women's status in the ancient world.[5]

In Phoenicia (what is now Lebanon), having sex with a stranger before getting married was believed to win the favor of the deity. The Amorites, one of the seven Canaanite nations, had a law that "she who was about to marry should sit in fornication seven days by the gate."[6]

A priestess who served a god, on the other hand, did not participate in this "sacred prostitution." Rather, her service was a "sacred marriage" known as the *hieros gamos*—a seasonal ritual involving a type of sympathetic magic designed to ensure the fertility of the land, in which she would have intercourse with the king, who was considered the representative of the god.

In Babylonia, such a priestess was called a *naditu*.[7] She was usually the oldest daughter from a wealthy, high-status family. Upon marriageable age, she would be dedicated to a god and economic transactions comparable to those of a marriage settlement would be carried out between the girl's family and the temple, which was a rich institution with a vast estate.

Naditus in Sippar who were dedicated to the sun god Shamash lived in a cloister. Often, there were as many as two hundred such women at a time. They were the highest-ranking *naditus*, were recruited from the wealthiest families, and were not allowed to marry. Once initiated (during puberty) with a three-day ceremony, their duties con-

---

2. Ibid., 3:214, 220.

3. Ibid., 3:219–220.

4. Harry Carter (trans.), *The Histories of Herodotus*, vol. 1 (New York: Heritage Press, 1958), p. 82.

5. See, for example, Nancy Qualls-Corbett, *The Sacred Prostitute* (Toronto: Inner City Books, 1988). The author is a Jungian analyst who believes that the sacred prostitute can and should be "a vital, functioning aspect of individual psychic processes" (p. 19).

6. Briffault, 3:220.

7. The following information is from Ulla Jeyes, "The Naditu Women of Sippar," in *Images of Women in Antiquity*, ed. Averil Cameron and Amélie Kuhrt (Detroit: Wayne State University Press, 1983), pp. 260–272.

sisted of constant attention to Shamash and his goddess, Aja—bringing offerings twice daily, plus once a month when the sun changed zodiac signs and on festivals.

Both Aja and the *naditu* were called the *kallatu* of Shamash. Like the Hebrew *kallah*, the word means "bride" or "daughter-in-law" and designated "a young girl who goes to live and be provided for in her father-in-law's house some years before the consummation of her marriage to the son of the house."[8] Thus a girl's dedication to this god was a substitute (patrilocal) marriage. When these cloistered *naditus* died, they were buried in the temple graveyard.

Other *naditus*, such as those dedicated to Marduk in Babylon and Ninurta in Nippur, were not cloistered and could marry as long as they bore no children. If they did bear a child, they were not punished or disgraced. It was, however, common for a married *naditu* to give another woman to her husband for childbearing.

SARAH AS *NADITU*

Sarah, who was married but childless and gave her female slave to her husband for childbearing, fits the description of a noncloistered *naditu*. There is more specific evidence of this in the Code of Hammurabi, the legal code of society, which was named after the sixth of eleven kings in the Old Babylonian dynasty.[9]

Table 3–1 shows that Sarah and Avraham lived in what is called the Old Babylonian Period and that Sarah would have been twelve years old, just entering puberty, when the institution of *naditu* was at its height. Furthermore, the year in which Sarah was taken to Pharaoh's palace in Egypt—2023 A.M. or 1739 B.C.E.—occurs in that period.

The status of a *naditu* is delineated in the Code of Hammurabi in laws numbers 40, 110, 127, 137, 144–147, and 178–182. The most relevant passages for our purposes are 144 through 147, which are completely descriptive of Sarah as a *naditu*, Avraham as her husband, and Hagar as her female slave.

144: If a man is married to a *naditu* who gave him a female slave to bear children in her place, he may not marry a *shugetu* [another kind of priestess].

TABLE 3–1. Events of the Old Babylonian Period

Event	Jewish Year	Common Era
Old Babylonian Period	1882–2212 A.M.	1880–1550 B.C.E.
Avraham	1948–2123 A.M.	1814–1639 B.C.E.
Sarah	1958–2085 A.M.	1804–1677 B.C.E.
Naditu's heyday	1970–2050 A.M.	1792–1712 B.C.E.
Hammurabi	2033–2075 A.M.	1728–1686 B.C.E.

---

8. Ibid., p. 265.

9. James B. Pritchard, *The Ancient Near East*, vol. 1 (Princeton, NJ: Princeton University Press, 1958), pp. 138–167.

145: If a man is married to a *naditu* who did not give him a slave for childbearing, he may marry a *shugetu* and bring her into the house, but the *shugetu* has a lower rank than the *naditu*. (Thus, Sarah gave her slave Hagar to Avraham to keep him from marrying a *shugetu*).

146: If a *naditu* gives her slave to her husband for childbearing and the slave becomes arrogant to her mistress after bearing children, the *naditu* may not sell her but may "mark her with the slave-mark and count her among the slaves." (Thus, Sarah had to evict Hagar rather than selling her in the slave market, as was usually done.)

147: A *naditu* can sell the slave if she does not become pregnant.

A *naditu*, unlike the the the average woman, could buy and sell property (law no. 40). She was, however, forbidden from opening a wine store and could be burnt at the stake for even entering one (law no. 110).

A man who falsely accused a *naditu*, or any woman, of a sexual indiscretion but had no proof, was "dragged into court and half of his hair . . . cut off" (law no. 127).

The remainder of the laws concern the Naditu's property rights. If a man divorced a *naditu* or a *shugetu* who had borne his child, he had to return the woman's dowry and half of their joint possessions as child support. After the children were grown, the woman would receive the portion of an individual heiress (law no. 137).

Laws numbers 178 through 182 discuss the control that a Naditu's brothers had over her inheritance. If she had a dowry from her father as well as his written permission to control her own inheritance, she did so. If she had a dowry but no written permission, her brothers controlled her inheritance but were required to maintain her at the level to which she was accustomed. If they did not, she could rent out her portion of the land, but she could not sell it.

A *naditu* with no dowry got the use of one-third of her father's estate in this way, but it was owned by her brothers. There are some technical differences in the use of the property by cloistered versus noncloistered *naditus*. A *shugetu*, on the other hand, got no share at all in her father's estate, whether she had a dowry or not. If she had no dowry, her brothers were supposed to give her one and marry her off (183–184).

SARAH'S REBELLION

"Why were the matriarchs barren?" *Genesis Rabbah* 45:5 asks, and then it gives three reasons: that God desired their prayers, that "the greater part of their lives would not be in servitude," and that they would be endeared to their husbands. The first two reasons are easily understandable.

The third reason means "that their husbands might derive pleasure from them, for when a woman is pregnant she is repulsive and ugly." This is pure misogyny and has nothing to do with God. However, it echoes the behavior of the men in the generation of the Flood and provides insight into why the pagan priests did not allow married Naditus to become pregnant—it was so they would always be "desirable," by male standards, for their sex-object role in the ritual.

Sarah, like Zillah, probably had to drink *mashkeh akarot* to keep herself sterile (and hence, thin). Even after she escaped the pagan priestesshood and no longer drank the potion, she remained unable to conceive. Like Zillah, Sarah was "remembered by God" in her old age. We can understand her delight at finally bearing a child at age ninety—no wonder she laughed.

Sarah's struggle in the twenty-first century A.M. may not have been totally unlike women's struggles today, as we enter the twenty-first century C.E. She may have felt sorely oppressed by the sexual objectification and exploitation of women in her society. Today, the sexual slave trade is a purely secular affair, but in her day, it was the "religion"; the pimps were the temple priests and prostitution was called "serving a god/goddess." When women were bought and sold, it was called "dedication" to the temple. Nonetheless, *naditus* were granted more financial independence than the average woman, which no doubt made the role a more attractive alternative to marriage for many women.

For Sarah, the belief in a Creator of the Universe Who was beyond gender and sexual relations must have been a liberating force indeed. While the pagan priests insisted on, and benefited from, her performance of the sexual rites, this new religion would not require her to sleep with men on command. Her service to the God of Israel was not a sexual one. Herein lay her freedom, and her own reason for "*Lekhi lakh.*"

EGYPT AND GERAR:
REJECTING THE "SACRED MARRIAGE"

Pharaoh in Egypt (Gen. 12:10–20) and Avimelekh in Gerar (20:1–18) were kings and were considered by their cultures to be representatives of gods. Sarah, as a *naditu,* would have been expected to perform the *hieros gamos*, the "sacred marriage" ceremony, with these men. Since this ritual was essentially an annual sympathetic magic intended to fertilize the earth, it would be especially important in times of famine. Given the Torah's repugnance for pagan religion, it is not surprising—indeed, it is normative—that these details are not described.

If Sarah had indeed hated the practice of *hieros gamos*, she would desperately have tried to escape her fate. This she did: with God's help, she acted very powerfully in her own defense. When Sarah went down to Egypt with Avraham, she hid in a box but was discovered by the customs officials, who praised her as being "suitable" for Pharaoh. Although her physical beauty is usually cited as the reason for this, we should note that she was sixty-five years old at the time. Thus, it was not youthful beauty but rather the dignity she commanded with her royal-religious status that was apparent to the officials who claimed her for Pharaoh.

It was customary to bring a woman to the king and slay the husband through a contrived charge, the Rabbis say, so Avraham asked Sarah to pose as his sister. Some commentators say that Avraham was confident that they could get out of Egypt safely before anything happened to Sarah, but Nachmanides reprimands Avraham, as he considers his behavior to be "a great sin." He considers it a sin that Avraham left Canaan to begin with during the famine, instead of trusting in God. Because he left, the exile to Egypt was decreed for his descendants.

Moreover, it *was* Avraham's idea to go (*Zohar* I:79a). He pleaded with Sarah and persuaded her to go with him, "for a man is not permitted to take his wife with him to another country without her consent."

When Sarah and Avraham later went to Gerar, Avraham did not even ask Sarah to pose as his sister this time but rather asserted the lie "forcibly and against her inclination" (Rashi) because he was sure she would not consent after what happened in Egypt. In both situations, Avraham's moral failing was in *abandoning* Sarah to her fate. Either way, she would have been taken for sexual purposes by these rulers, but Avraham had the choice to either suffer along with his wife or escape while she suffered alone. He chose the latter course.

In Egypt, Pharaoh lavished Avraham with gifts *before* the truth was told (Gen. 12:16). The Rabbis learn from this (B.M. 59a) that "a man must always observe the honor due to his wife, because blessings rest on his home only on account of her. . . . Honor your wives, that you may be enriched." In Gerar, Avraham only benefited materially *after* the truth was told (20:14).

SARAH'S VINDICATION

In both cases, the royal households were struck with plagues *al devar* ("by the word of") Sarah. The *Zohar* says: "The Shekhinah did not leave Sarai all that night. When Pharaoh tried to approach her, an angel came and struck him. Whenever Sarai said, 'Strike,' it would strike." Moreover, "she, as it were, gave out the order and the Holy One administered the blows" (I:82a, 111b–112a). The Midrash and Rashi also describe this.

The Midrash, saying Pharaoh was struck with a plague because he "took possession of Sarah for one night" (GR 41:1), notes that even the beams of his house were struck "because he dared to approach the shoe of such a lady" (41:2).

Avimelekh did not touch Sarah because God came to him in a dream and warned him that he would die if he did. Even so, his house was plagued with a disease that closed up all the orifices of people's bodies—wombs, excretory channels, mouths, throats, eyes, and ears—"because he dared to approach the shoe of such a lady" (GR 52:13).

In both households, the same interaction between Sarah and God is described (GR 41:2, 52:13): "All night Sarah lay prostrate on her face, crying, 'Sovereign of the Universe! Avraham went forth [from his land] on Your assurance, and I went forth on faith; Avraham is outside this prison while I am within!' Said the Holy One to her, 'All that I do, I do for your sake, and all will say, It is by the word of Sarah, Avraham's wife.'"

While this informs us that God spoke only to Avraham about leaving Babylonia— and Sarah left on faith from her husband's encounter with God—there is no reason to assume from this that Hashem is more the "God of Avraham" than the "God of

Sarah." Here, in the palaces of Pharaoh and Avimelekh, *she* cried out and God *immediately* responded, speaking to her and acting on her behalf and at her command.

Upon departing from Gerar, Avimelekh gave Avraham a thousand pieces of silver and said to Sarah, "Let it be *kesut enayim* for you and all who are with you—*nokhachat*" (Gen. 20:16).

Kesut enayim, a "covering of the eyes," indicates some form of compensation, or even vindication, for what Sarah went through. It connotes a face-saving device so that people would not look at her as if she had done something wrong. *Nokhachat* means, in modern Hebrew, to be convinced, straightforward, honest, facing, in front of, opposite, or present. Various translations of the Torah render it as "you can stand up tall" (Kaplan), "you may face everyone" (Silbermann), "you are cleared before everyone" (Jewish Publication Society), "you can come before everyone without disguise" (Hirsch), and "before all men are you righted" (Hertz). The Jerusalem Bible badly mistranslates it as "thus she was reproved."

Rashi explains:

> These will put a covering over the eyes of all who are with you so that they shall not hold you in light esteem. But had I sent you back empty-handed, they might have said, "After he abused her he sent her back"; now, however, that I have had to lavish money and to mollify you they will understand that I have sent you back against my own will by a miracle. . . . You will have an opening of the mouth [an opportunity] to defend yourself and to point to these evident facts.

In other words, just as today's victims of rape and sexual abuse are often blamed for "provoking" the deed, so, too, would Sarah's society have blamed her, thus making her easy prey for repeat abuse scenarios. The "covering of the eyes" therefore protected her both from people's reproachful looks in general and from men's lewd gazes in particular.

A number of other interpretations are given for the *kesut enayim,* including the ideas that it was a special garment or a curse that was later fulfilled by Isaac having dim vision (GR 52:12; Meg. 28a; B.K. 93a).

HAGAR

Pharaoh gave his daughter Hagar to Sarah as a *shifchah,* a female slave, in response to what God did on Sarah's behalf in his palace. Avimelekh did the same thing (GR 45:1). Both kings believed it was better for their daughters to be slaves in Sarah's household than mistresses in their own. Most likely, the women were born to each king's concubine rather than his wife, the queen. Hagar's story is told (Gen. 16:1–16, 21:1–21), but the story of the daughter of Avimelekh is not.

Avraham took Hagar when Sarah suggested it, because he "listened to [her] voice" (Gen. 16:2), meaning her *ruach hakodesh* (Rashi; GR 45:2). By giving him her female slave, Sarah prevented Avraham from bringing another pagan priestess (a *shugetu*) into her household. Moreover, by offering Hagar, she maintained control of the situation. Sarah persuaded Hagar, saying, "Happy are you to be united to such a holy man" (GR 45:3).

Sarah intended that Avraham take Hagar *as a wife, and not a concubine* (Gen. 16:3; GR 45:3). "This reflects the ethical conduct of Sarah and her respect towards her husband," Nachmanides says. It also reflects her ethical conduct and respect for the other woman. Avraham was obligated to support Hagar, and henceforth neither he nor Sarah could sell her in the slave market (GR 45:1). Hagar's status was raised from a *shifchah*—a slave or bondwoman, who was bound to unpaid service in repayment of a debt (in this case, Pharaoh's debt to Sarah)—to an *amah*, a maidservant. Hagar was freed from slavery, but she was still secondary to Sarah.

Hagar's situation should not be compared to modern "surrogate motherhood," in which a woman's womb is "rented" by a male sperm donor, who (with his wife) then takes the child. Hagar had an ongoing relationship with Avraham, and *she raised Ishmael*—she remained his mother and he, her son.

When Hagar became arrogant with Sarah and equated her barrenness to a lack of righteousness, Sarah became angry but did not cast her out as the Code of Hammurabi permitted. First she confronted Avraham: "When you prayed to the Holy One [for children], you prayed only on behalf of yourself [Gen. 15:2], whereas you should have prayed on behalf of both of us" (Rashi; GR 45:5). "Besides this, you deprive me of your words, since you hear how I am despised and yet you keep silent!"

Once again, Avraham took the easier way out. Why did the man who would later plead on behalf of the corrupt Sodomites not speak up in defense of his wife? This is the first instance in the Torah where a person is rebuked for remaining silent in the face of injustice. Avraham's lack of prayer on Sarah's behalf is equally amazing in light of the fact that he prayed for other barren women, who then conceived (GR 39:11).

However, when Sarah said to him, "Let God judge between me and you!" (Gen. 16:5), the Rabbis state: "Woe to the one who cries [for divine intervention], even more than the one against whom it is invoked! . . . Both the one who cries for divine intervention and the one against whom it is invoked come under the threat, but punishment is meted out first to the one who cries, more severely than for the one against whom justice is invoked" (B.K. 93a). "Sarah should have reached Avraham's age [at death, 175], but because she said, 'Let God judge between me and you,' her life was reduced by 48 years" (GR 45:5). "Whoever plunges eagerly into litigation does not escape from it unscathed."

However, Rashi interprets the "you" whom God should judge to refer to Hagar, saying that Sarah "cast the evil eye on Hagar so that she miscarried" her first pregnancy and only later got pregnant with Ishmael.

Avraham did nothing except tell Sarah to do whatever she wished with Hagar (Gen. 16:6). Was Avraham wrongly passive—or was Sarah right and did he once again "listen to her voice" as a husband should? Sarah began to oppress Hagar, restraining her from sexual relations, making her carry water buckets and bath towels, and even slapping her with a slipper (GR 45:6). However, when Hagar ran away, an angel told her to return and submit to Sarah. This implies that Sarah's anger, if not her behavior, was legitimate. Nachmanides, however, believes that Sarah and Avraham were both wrong.

Hagar was met by four or five angels when she ran away—more than appeared to anyone else in the Torah at one time—but she was not afraid because the members of Avraham and Sarah's household "were seers, so she was accustomed to them" (GR 45:7). Since contact with angels in itself is not prophecy, Hagar is not listed among the female prophets. She did, however, give Hashem the Name, "God of Vision" (Gen. 16:13).

When Sarah later casts Hagar out, it is because Ishmael *metzachek* (mocks or makes sport of) Isaac. Ishmael, who was nineteen years old, was shooting arrows at Isaac, who was five (SY 69). Ishmael also "was indulging in idolatrous practices. . . . [Sarah] observed him worshipping idols, and performing the practices which his mother had taught him" (*Zohar* I:118b). Ishmael brought idols in from the street, playing with and worshiping them (ER 1:1). Besides building altars and catching locusts and sacrificing them, Ishmael also committed rape and adultery, which Sarah knew about (GR 53:11).

There is reason to presume a sexual connotation with Isaac as well. The verb *letzachek* is used to describe (1) what Isaac was doing with Rivkah that made Avimelekh realize they were not brother and sister; (2) what Mrs. Potiphar said Joseph was doing at her house; and (3) what occurred at the feast of the golden calf when the people rose up to "make merry." Thus, it could imply that Ishmael was sexually abusing Isaac.

Ishmael claimed a double portion of the inheritance as the firstborn (Rashi), to which Sarah replied, "The son of this maidservant shall not inherit with my son Isaac" (Gen. 21:10). Once again, Sarah's behavior was validated by divine decree. Avraham did not want to send Ishmael away, but God instructed him, "All that Sarah says to you, listen to her voice" (Gen. 21:12).

ISHMAEL'S WIVES

In Egypt Hagar found Ishmael a wife (Gen. 21:21), whose name was Merivah (SY 70). She had four sons and two daughters, one of whom was Basmat, the wife of Esav. One day, Avraham went to visit Ishmael, but his son was not home and Merivah did not welcome him or offer him a drink. He also heard her whipping and cursing her children inside the tent.

Consequently, Ishmael divorced Merivah and married a Canaanite woman named Malkhit (SY 86). The next time Avraham went to visit and Ishmael was not home, Malkhit welcomed him and gave him food and drink, exhibiting the level of hospitality for which Avraham himself was so greatly known.

THE COVENANT

When God made a covenant with Avram (Gen. 17), promising him descendants, fruitfulness, and the land of Canaan, God also demanded a change of names. Avram became Avraham and Sarai became Sarah. That is, the letter *Yod* (with a numerical value of ten) was taken from Sarai's name and split into two *Heh*s (each of which has a numerical value of five), one for her and one for him.

"Her husband was crowned through her, but she was not crowned through her husband," says GR 47:1. Sarah was "her husband's ruler," the Rabbis agree. The letter *Yod* was "upset" at being "withdrawn from the name of that righteous woman," so God had to promise the *Yod* to use it later, in Joshua's name.

The covenant, God emphasized, must come through Sarah. It is *her* firstborn, not Avraham's, who will carry it on.

SARAH'S LAUGHTER

Avraham fell on his face and laughed. He said to himself, "Can a hundred-year-old man have children? Can Sarah, who is 90, give birth?" . . . Sarah no longer had female periods. She laughed in herself, saying, "Now that I have reached menopause, shall I be rejuvenated? And my husband is old!" . . . God said to Avraham, "Why did Sarah laugh and say, 'How can I have a child when I am so old?' Is anything too difficult for Hashem?" . . . Sarah was afraid and denied it, saying, "I did not laugh." God said, "You did laugh." (Gen. 17:17, 18:11–15)

How considerate it was of God to cater to Avraham's male ego by omitting what Sarah said about *him* being old! Why was it all right for Avraham to laugh, but not Sarah? There are two factors that appear to make Sarah's laugh *more* excusable, and not less.

1. A leap of faith was required of Sarah that was not required of Avraham. Since a man can beget children in old age while a woman cannot do so after menopause, a miracle was necessary in Sarah's body, but not in Avraham's.
2. Avraham heard the news directly from God, but Sarah heard it from three men, who she did not know were divine messengers.

Rashi explains that Avraham's laughter was rejoicing; Sarah's was more like a sneer. The verses themselves indicate that Avraham laughed out loud, while Sarah laughed inwardly. He acted happy, while she remained silent, showing no expression whatsoever of praise, thanksgiving, or joy.

In Judaism, the greater a person is, the more responsible he or she is for acting properly. A scholar is held much more accountable for a minor transgression than the average person. (This is the opposite of the secular world, where the higher up you are, the more you are allowed to get away with.)

Hence, it is precisely because Sarah's situation required *more* faith that she was held *more* accountable. Because she was a greater prophet than Avraham, she should have known better than he.

On the day that Sarah conceived (which was Rosh Hashanah), "many barren women were remembered, many sick were healed, many prayers were answered with hers, and there was great rejoicing in the world" (Rashi). The deaf regained their hearing, the blind regained their sight, and the insane regained their sanity. Even the sun and moon shined brighter on this day (GR 53:8).

Nonetheless, people derided Sarah, saying she had found Isaac on the street. As a result, when women brought their babies to Isaac's weaning banquet, Sarah's "breasts opened like two fountains and she suckled them all" (B.M. 87a). Because people continued to gossip, saying Avimelekh was the father, God made Isaac's features just like Avraham's.

THE BINDING OF ISAAC AND SARAH'S DEATH

When God told Avraham to sacrifice Isaac, Avraham agonized over what to tell Sarah and made up a lame excuse that Isaac should go away to study at the academy of Shem and Ever. Sarah agreed but wept at her separation from Isaac, saying, "I have no other son or daughter but him" (SY 76).

When Sarah heard that Isaac had been taken to be sacrificed, she died of shock. "Her soul flew from her," says Rashi. According to this view, she never learned that her son was still alive. Another version, however, says that Isaac returned home and Sarah asked him where he had been. When he told her what happened, Sarah screamed six times—which is why there are six *tekiahs* when the *shofar* is blown on Rosh Hashanah—and then died (LR 20:2). (It is hard to decide which version is sadder.) She died in *Cheshvan* (Est.R. 7:11).

Sarah's death at age 127 and her burial are recorded in great detail (Gen. 23), more so than for any other woman in the Torah. She was, in fact, buried like a queen (SY 83). "All this was to show that the likes of Sarah were not to be found among all the women of the world. . . . Sarah's death was not brought about by the tortuous serpent, which possessed no power over her as over the rest of humanity" (*Zohar* I: 124b, 125a).

Sarah lies buried in the Cave of Machpelah in Israel with Avraham, where "he lies sleeping in the arms of Sarah, [while] she is looking fondly at his head" (B.B. 58a).

✻✻✻ 4 ✻✻✻

Edith:
Pillar of Salt

Vayera (18:1–22:24)

When [the angel] led them out, it said, "Run for your life! Do not look back!" . . . But [Lot's] wife looked back behind him, and she became a pillar of salt. (Gen. 19:17, 26)

Why did Lot's wife, whose name was Edith (SY 65), turn into a pillar of salt when she looked back as she and her family fled Sodom? "It is not fitting that you should witness their doom while you yourself are escaping," Rashi states. Nachmanides also addresses "the significance of the prohibition of looking," saying: "Looking upon the atmosphere of a plague and all contagious diseases is very harmful, and they may cleave to one. Even the thought of them is harmful. . . . It was for this reason that Lot's wife turned into a pillar of salt, for the plague entered her mind when she saw the brimstone and salt which descended upon them from heaven, and it cleaved to her."

The notion that watching the violent destruction of others is harmful to oneself is illustrated in two other instances in the Torah: the ark built for the survivors of the Flood had no windows, only a skylight, so that its inhabitants would not see the mass drownings around them; similarly, the Jews were instructed to stay in their homes on the first Passover so that they should not see the slaughter of the Egyptian first-born around them.

The concept that there are certain things at which one should not look is the antithesis of acceptable behavior in our modern society, which validates voyeurism as a "normal" activity. What effect does it have on a society when people regularly watch violence and call it entertainment? These three examples from the Torah could be used to argue that what people do even "in the privacy of their homes" can affect them in ways that may, in turn, have a degenerative influence on society as a whole.

The form that Edith's punishment took was *midah kneged midah*. "By salt she had sinned and by salt she was punished" (Rashi). Edith is described as a typical Sodomite, who is hostile toward hospitality (GR 50:4, 50:6, 51:5). Lot, who had the influence of Avraham and Sarah in him, took in the angels who came to visit him as guests, but Edith said to him, "If you want to receive them, receive them in *your* part of the house."

One might argue that she was simply afraid of what the town would do to her when they found out, but had this been the case, she would not have acted in the following manner. When Lot asked her to give a little salt to the guests, she replied, "Do you want to introduce that evil practice here too?" She then went around to all her neighbors, saying, "Give me salt, as we have guests," and thus purposely making the townspeople aware of their presence. As a result, the men of the town surrounded Lot's house and demanded that the guests be brought out so they could gang-rape them.

It is understandable that Edith would feel compelled to look back at Sodom, since she had children and grandchildren remaining there. "The compassion of Edith, Lot's wife, welled up for her married daughters who were in Sodom, and she looked behind her to see if they were following her. She thereupon saw the light of the Shekhinah, and she became a pillar of salt" (Nachmanides; SY 65).

Edith's name in Hebrew, עדית, is the feminine form of the word *witness*, testifying to the fact that Edith witnessed the destruction of Sodom.

THE MEN OF SODOM

The men of Sodom were evil and sinned very much against God. (Gen. 13:13)

Like the generation of the Flood, the Sodomites are said to have no portion in the world to come. Also like the generation of the Flood, the men of Sodom greatly misused their sexuality, being abusive, exploitative, and violent. Rape, incest, and general sexual degradation were the norm, and there were no "good men" to protest it.

Sodom was the capital of a region (containing the cities of Amorrah, Admah, and Zvoyim) which shared a large valley less than a day's journey outside the city limits. Four times a year, large festivals were held there, with music and dancing, where "in the midst of their rejoicing, each man would seize the wife of his neighbor, and every man the daughter of his neighbor, the virgin daughter, and they abused [*hitallu*] them and lay with them. And every man saw his wife and his daughter in the hands of his neighbor and said nothing" (SY 58).

However, sexual violence and men's complicity in it was not all that destroyed these cities. *Sanhedrin* 109a–b and numerous sources in the Midrash describe the selfishness, greed, and robbery that also characterized the town.

The Sodomites had incredible wealth. Indeed, a gardener could pull vegetables out of the ground and find gold in the earth that clung to the roots (LR 4:1, 5:2).

"The people of Sodom only grew haughty before the Omnipresent on account of the favors which God lavished upon them" (NR 9:24).

> The Sodomites said, "Since food comes out of our land, and silver and gold come out of our land, and precious stones and pearls come out of our land, we do not need people to visit us, for they will only deprive us. Let us rise and obliterate all memory of the [visitor's] foot from our midst." The Holy One said to them, "Do you, in return for the favors I have conferred upon you, seek to obliterate all memory of the [visitor's] foot from your midst? Then I shall obliterate all memory of you from the world!"

The roads leading to the city of Sodom were flooded to make it difficult for visitors to enter. Those who managed to get in were subjected to ridicule, humiliation, robbery, rape, torture, and death. Visitors often died of hunger because no one would give them food. Moreover, there was a standard-size bed for guests to sleep in; if they were too tall for it, their feet were cut off, and if they were too short, their bodies were stretched.

"The Sodomites made an agreement among themselves that whenever a lodger came there they should force him to sodomy and take away his money" (GR 50:7). This is exactly what the men of Sodom wanted to do when they surrounded Lot's house, demanding that the guests come out. Sodom had "pride, fullness of bread, and abundance of idleness, and yet she did not strengthen the hand of the poor and the needy" (San. 104b; Ezekiel 16:49).

The intention of the Sodomites was to "stop people from coming among them . . . for they thought that because of the excellence of their land . . . many will come there, and they despised charity" (Nachmanides). "All evil practices were rampant among them. Yet their fate was sealed because of this sin—i.e., they did not strengthen the hand of the poor and needy. . . . There was none among all the nations who matched Sodom in cruelty."

However, the behavior of the Sodomites was not a state of lawlessness; it was the law itself. The Sodomite system of "justice" was based on blaming the victim and protecting the perpetrator.

- If a man raped a pregnant woman and caused a miscarriage, the judges would tell her husband to hand her over to the rapist so she could become pregnant again!
- If one person wounded another, causing bloodshed, the victim would be charged a fee for bloodletting. When Eliezer, Avraham's servant, went to Sodom, he was attacked and sentenced to pay a fee for bloodletting. He responded by throwing a rock at the judge and saying, "The fee that you owe me [for this], give to [my attacker]!"
- A Sodomite who invited a guest to a feast would be stripped naked, so once when Eliezer went to a feast no one fed him. When he was asked who had invited him, he pointed to someone sitting near him, who then left out of fear of attack. Eliezer then continued doing this until all the guests had fled and he had all the food to himself!

The Talmud names four judges of the court: Liar, Awful Liar, Forger, and Perverter of Justice. GR 50:3 names five: Falsehood, Great Liar, Chief Prevaricator, Disgrace, and Man Stealer. The Sodomites were so selfish that they would not even do a favor for someone when it cost them nothing. Hence, numerous places in the Talmud (e.g., B.B. 12b) refer to situations in which one party in a dispute is described as "acting after the manner of Sodom."

LOT

Friction developed between the herdsmen of Avram's flocks and those of Lot. . . . Avram said to Lot, "Let's not have friction between me and you. . . . All the land is before you. Why not separate from me? If you go left, I will go right; if [you go] right, I will go left." . . . Lot chose for himself the entire Jordan Plain . . . and pitched his tent in Sodom. (Gen. 13:7–11)

When Lot chose to live in Sodom, it was with full knowledge of the nature of the city and its residents. "Just because they were addicted to lust did Lot choose their locality," says Rashi, adding that Lot's shepherds used to graze his flocks in other people's fields—a form of robbery.

Lot's only saving grace was in being Sarah's brother and Avraham's nephew. He learned their sense of hospitality by being with them. However, as long as Lot was with Avraham, God kept away from the latter, which was Avraham's primary reason for separating from Lot. "Lot desired to revert to the idolatry of the inhabitants of the country" (*Zohar* I:84a–b), so Avraham separated from him. This did not change Lot's mind; he "actually did revert to idolatry."

Lot was saved from the destruction of Sodom because "God remembered Avraham" (Gen. 19:29)—not because God remembered Lot. Lot was saved because he followed Avraham from Charan on God's command; if not for Avraham, Lot would still have been in Charan and not in Sodom (Nachmanides).

Lot was not just an average citizen; he was the chief justice of the Sodomite court (GR 50:3). His moral failure as a leader was that instead of influencing the Sodomites to be like him in hospitality, he became like them in sexual immorality and idolatry.

PALTIT AND THE CRY OF SODOM

God said, "The cry of Sodom . . . is so great and their sin is so heavy. I will go down and see if they have acted according to her cry that has come to me." (Gen. 18:20–21)

"Her cry" is meant literally: the cry of Sodom was the cry of a woman, "a certain young woman whom they put to death in an unnatural manner because she had given food to a poor person" (Rashi). There were actually several women who did this and were caught.

One was Paltit, one of Lot's married daughters (SY 63; *Zohar* I:106b). Paltit used to sneak bread in her pitcher to a poor man who came to town. When he did not starve to death as other visitors did, three Sodomite men were sent to spy out the situation and Paltit was caught. They brought her to court and she was burned at the stake.

A similar event occurred in Admah when a young woman gave bread and water to a stranger. When she was caught and brought to court, she was stripped, tied up, covered with honey, and stung to death by bees (SY 64–65; San. 109b).

In another story:

> Two young women went down to draw water from a well. Said one to the other, "Why do you look sick?" "We have no more food left and are ready to die," she replied. What did she [the first one] do? She filled her pitcher with flour and they exchanged them, each taking the other's. When they [the Sodomites] discovered this, they took and burned her at the stake. (GR 49:6)

The cries of Paltit and her sister rebels being tortured evoked no compassion from the people, but God replied, saying, "Even if I wished to keep silent, justice for a certain young woman does not permit Me to keep silent." For the cry of Sodom was "the cry of the oppressed . . . begging for help from the arm of [the Sodomites'] wickedness" (Nachmanides).

God would have spared Sodom if the city had contained ten righteous people. There were eight righteous people in the generation of the Flood, yet the world was not spared on their account; only the eight were saved. The ten people of whom Avraham was thinking were Lot, Edith, their four daughters, their two sons-in-law, and two fiancés (GR 49:13, 50:9), but not even these ten were righteous.

Nevertheless, they would all have been spared, but "to [Lot's] sons-in-law, it was all a big joke" (Gen. 19:14) and they refused to leave. The cry (*tzaak*) of Sodom was to them cause for laughter (*tzachak*).

LOT'S DAUGHTERS

> Lot said, "I have two daughters who have not known a man. I will bring them out to you. Do as you please with them." (Gen. 19:8)

> The older [Bekhirah] said to the younger [Zirah], "Our father is growing old, and there is no other man left in the world to marry us in a normal manner. Come, let's get our father drunk with wine, and sleep with him. We will then survive through children from our father."
> That night, they got their father drunk with wine, and Bekhirah went and slept with her father. He was not aware that she had lain down or gotten up. . . . [The next] night, they again made their father drunk with wine. Zirah got up and she slept with him. He was not aware that she had lain down or gotten up. Lot's two daughters became pregnant from their father. (Gen. 19:31–36)

Here is a major example of the error that can be committed when one takes only the written Torah without its oral tradition, for while the written Torah indicates that the daughters (Bekhirah, the elder, and Zirah, the younger) initiated the incest, the commentaries place the blame squarely on Lot. A close reading of these commentaries, combined with a modern feminist understanding of incest, leads to the conclusion that Lot's daughters were *already* incest victims before this episode took place.

What kind of father offers his daughters to be gang-raped? Sforno tries to rationalize that Lot thought their fiancés would come to their defense and the resulting tumult would deter the crowd, but this is a weak excuse.

Nachmanides' view is more on target: "He is ready to appease the men of the city by abandoning his daughters in a free-for-all! This shows nothing but an evil heart, for the matter of prostituting women was not repugnant to him [lit., "distant from his eyes"], and he did not think he was doing a great violence [*chamas gadol*] to his daughters." He continues, "It is the custom of the world that a person [*sic*] kills or is killed for his daughters and his wife, but this one hands over his daughters to be abused! Said the Holy One to him, 'It is for yourself that you keep them.'" In other words, *Lot was an incestuous father.*

Lot "was like a man who covets his mother's dowry," meaning that he was eager for perverse sexuality (GR 41:7). This, too, brings the blame for the incest back to Lot: "Whoever is fired with immoral desire is eventually fed with his own flesh."

The reason Avraham and Sarah traveled to Gerar afterward was "to get away from Lot, who had gained an evil reputation because of his intercourse with his daughters" (Rashi; GR 52:4). Thus, Lot's incestuousness led directly to his sister Sarah being sexually endangered in the house of Avimelekh.

Lot is not excused for being drunk and "not knowing." The daughters, "whose intention it was to do right," are contrasted to their father, "whose intention it was to commit the transgression" (Naz. 23a; Hor. 10b). In response to the suggestion that perhaps Lot also intended to do right, Rabbi Jochanan cites Genesis 13:10 as an indication of Lot's "lustful character," showing how every word in the verse is used elsewhere in reference to sexual immorality. "But was he not the victim of compulsion?" the Gemara asks. It then responds that he was not, as "it was her [Bekhirah] lying down that he did not notice, but he did notice when she arose. . . . [H]e should not have drunk wine the next evening."

An objection is raised that gives us yet another reason to believe that this was not the first sexual contact between Lot and his daughters. "A woman never conceives by her first intimacy" (GR 51:9). "We would not know whether Lot lusted after his daughters or they lusted after him, except that Proverbs 18:1 says, 'One separates oneself in order to seek desire,' which means that Lot desired his daughters, and his daughters did not desire him."

The men of Sodom, like the generation of the Flood, "took for themselves women from whomever they chose." This description includes incest as a cause of the Flood (GR 52:3). Indeed, Lot should have replied to his firstborn daughter, "Shall we commit the sin for which the whole world was punished!"

Incest may have been "the sin for which the whole world was punished," but father–daughter relations were not yet a part of this definition. Father–daughter incest was normative, and not considered a perversion, in a society based purely on matrilineal descent. In matrilineal descent, heritage is determined through the mother; the uterine tie is paramount. A man is not related (uterinely) to either his wife or his children, so his "relatives" in such a system are his mother and his sister. His *sister's* children, and not his own, are his descendants and heirs.

In a matrilineal system, "incest" can only occur between men and women of the same maternal clan—in other words, between a man and his mother, his (maternal) sisters, or his (maternal) aunts. This is why Avraham's marriage to Sarah, the daughter of his *paternal* brother, was not considered incest at this time. In his reply to Avimelekh, Avraham "answered in accordance with their own views, for they permit the daughter of one's father, but forbid the daughter of one's mother" (GR 52:11).

Maimonides lists six sexual relations forbidden to Noachides (the non-Jewish world before the Torah was given), and three of them define incest: relations with a man's mother, his maternal sisters, and his father's wife (*Kings and Their Wars* 9:5). This corresponds to the matrilineal definition of incest—given the practice of sororal polygyny, the father's other wives were likely to be the mother's sisters! Relations with a married woman (polyandry) were also forbidden, as were sodomy and bestiality.

Further indications of the matrilineal definition of incest are found in the statements that "a Noachide was permitted to take his daughter" (Nachmanides) and "idolators do not recognize paternity" (GR 18:5; San. 58a). Only with the giving of the Torah at Mount Sinai did patrilineal definitions of incest become operative.

In modern America, bilineal descent (through the mother and father equally) is technically recognized, but patrilineal customs prevail—such as the notion that the father is the head of the family and giving the children the father's surname. Surnames themselves are actually patrilineal: "The ancients, since they knew their genealogy, named themselves in reference to the events [of their time]. But we who do not know our genealogy name ourselves by our fathers" (GR 37:7). R. Shimon b. Gamliel explains, "The ancients, because they could avail themselves of *ruach hakodesh* [prophecy, the holy spirit], named themselves in reference to events. But we who cannot avail ourselves of *ruach hakodesh* are named after our fathers."

In our primarily patrilineal society, one in four girls is a victim of childhood sexual abuse, mostly in the form of father–daughter incest. In many cases, the incest is accompanied by physical violence, and so the girl may realize that what is happening is abuse. In many other cases, however, the incest is not accompanied by violence. The perpetrator tells the girl that this is a normal expression of love; he is affectionate and loving *only at this time,* while he is cold and indifferent at any other. Such a man teaches his daughter that this is the price of love. A little girl in this situation will suffer serious emotional confusion. Her natural affection for her father will take on a romantic, sexual quality; she will fall in love with him and may even seek *him* out for sexual affection, since this is the only way she has learned to express her love for him. This, ironically, makes nonviolent incest more insidious than incest accompanied by violence.

Sigmund Freud saw the effects of nonviolent incest and developed the "Electra complex," which is a theory that little girls fall in love with their fathers. However, Freud erred in believing that the complex originates in the girl. Little girls *love* their fathers, but they only *fall in love* with them if the father has cultivated that state. *He* is responsible for creating this perversion in his daughter, and one of the most difficult aspects of recovery for such incest survivors is to overcome the guilt and self-blame that they incorrectly feel.

A child is *never* culpable of sexual abuse; the adult *always* is the guilty one. This is acknowledged in the Mishnah (Nid. 44b), which says about incest, "he is to be executed on her account, but she is exempt." This is because

> In relations with adults, there is no way that a child can be in control or exercise free choice. . . . Children are essentially a captive population, totally dependent upon their parents or other adults for their basic needs. Thus they will do whatever they perceive to be necessary to preserve a relationship with their caretakers. If an adult insists upon a sexual relationship with a dependent child, the child will comply. . . . Consent and choice are concepts that apply to the relationships of peers. They have no meaning in the relations of adults and children.[1]

The Rabbis were absolutely right in holding Lot accountable, even in a scenario where the act was "initiated" by the daughters. The relative ease with which Lot's daughters sought out their father on this occasion indicates a history of victimization.

MOAV AND AMMON

> Bekhirah had a son, and she named him Moav. He is the ancestor of the Moabites. Zirah also had a son, and she named him Ben-Ami. He is the ancestor of the Ammonites. (Gen. 19:37–38)

The action of Lot's daughters would not have served the purpose of continuing the human race if the whole world had been destroyed, since they had two sons. Rather, the purpose served was to bring about the Messiah. From Moav came Ruth, the great-grandmother of King David, ancestor of the Messiah.

It is one of the great enigmas of Judaism that incest—one of the three sins, along with murder and idolatry, that one is supposed to avoid to the point of death rather than commit—should be the channel for the Messiah, who will usher in an era of peace and perfection in the world. Perhaps this is further testimony to the innocence of Lot's daughters—they took control of their victimization and transformed it into a means of bringing good into the world.

---

1. Judith Lewis Herman, *Father–Daughter Incest* (Cambridge, MA: Harvard University Press, 1981), p. 27.

Later (Deut. 2:9, 2:19), God prohibits the Israelites from attacking the nations of Moav and Ammon (present-day Jordan), but the difference of one word in these verses meant that Israel could provoke fear in Moav (Num. 22:3) but not in Ammon. This is because, the Rabbis say, Moav bore the stigma of incest openly in his name (*me-av,* "from father"), whereas Ben-Ami ("son of my people") was a euphemism and spared him that stigma (GR 51:11; Naz. 23b; B.K. 38b).

✲✲✲ 5 ✲✲✲

Milkah: Sarah's Sister

Chayei Sarah (23:1–25:18)

Milkah was Haran's daughter and Sarah's (Yiskah's) sister (Gen. 11:29). As Sarah's sister, Milkah is the crucial link in establishing the lineage of the matriarchs. The matriarchs were not just the wives of the patriarchs: as a father–son lineage exists among the patriarchs, so, too, a lineage exists among the matriarchs: that of aunt–niece.

The anthropological kinship chart in Figure 5–1 illustrates these relationships. Terach had three sons by three wives. He later took a fourth wife, Pelilah (SY 74), who is not shown here. Sarah and Milkah, the daughters of Terach's one son, married his other sons, their uncles, as none of them were *maternally* related. We do not know if Sarah, Lot, and Milkah were maternal siblings.

Milkah and Nachor had eight sons (Gen. 22:20–23), as well as daughters (SY 73). The first son had a daughter named Devorah, and the last son, Betuel, had a daughter named Rivkah. Milkah was Rivkah's grandmother, and Sarah was Rivkah's great-aunt. Because Sarah was barren for so long, her child (Isaac) was in the generation of her sister's grandchildren (Rivkah).

Sarah's and Milkah's children are called "parallel cousins" in anthropology, since the related parents are of the same gender (either two sisters are the mothers or two brothers are the fathers). Because Isaac's mother and Betuel's mother were sisters, Isaac and Betuel (and, hence, Rivkah) were parallel cousins.

Rivkah's brother, Lavan, had two daughters, Rachel and Leah. Thus, as Sarah was the (great) aunt of Rivkah, Rivkah was the aunt of Rachel and Leah. Rivkah's sons, Esav and Jacob, and Lavan's daughters are "cross cousins" anthropologically, since their related parents are of the opposite gender, that is, a sister and a brother.

Chayei Sarah

Chayei Sarah 49

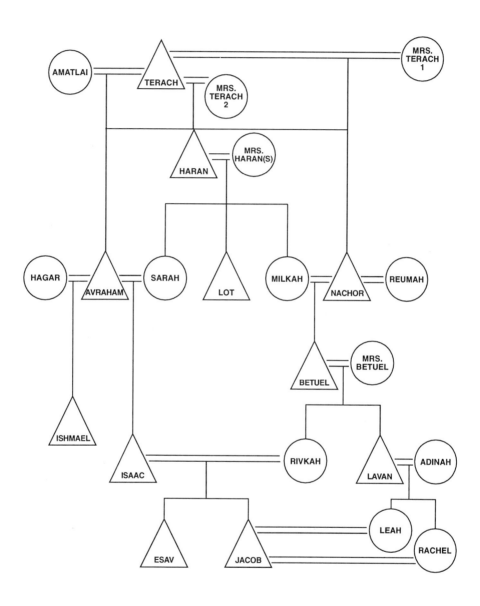

FIGURE 5-1. The lineage of the matriarchs is shown in this anthropological kinship chart, in which circles represent women, triangles represent men, double lines indicate marriage, vertical single lines indicate parent–child relationships, and horizontal single lines indicate siblings. Sarah, Milkah's sister, is thus Rivkah's great-aunt, and Rivkah is Leah's and Rachel's aunt. For the sake of simplicity, the chart omits Lot's lineage, Milkah's other children, Reumah's children, and Esav's and Ishmael's wives.

Not only is Rivkah the granddaughter of Milkah, but Milkah's name never disappears from statements of Rivkah's lineage. Rivkah is never described merely as the daughter of Betuel, the son of Nachor, as one might expect in these patrilineal lists of "begats," but always as "born to Betuel, the son of Milkah, the wife of Avraham's brother Nachor" (Gen. 24:15), "the daughter of Betuel, son of Milkah, whom she bore to Nachor" (24:24), and "daughter of Betuel, son of Nachor, whom Milkah bore to him" (24:47). Why is Milkah's name, alone among all the mothers in the Torah, retained in this way?

Nachmanides believes it is "because Nachor also had children from his concubine Reumah" and "because the girl mentioned her father's mother first . . . for such was customary among the girls." While his first reason may be valid, the second is not, or else why would other women in the Torah not have done so, too? It seems far more likely that Milkah's name continues to be mentioned because she links Rivkah to Sarah. This link is why the *parshah, Chayei Sarah,* "The Lives of Sarah," is actually about the girlhood of Rivkah.

REUMAH AND MAAKHAH

Milkah bore these eight to Avraham's brother Nachor. His concubine was named Reumah, and she also gave birth, to Tevach, Gacham, Tachash, and Maakhah. (Gen. 22:23–24)

"All these names signify chastisement" (GR 57:4)—Tevach means "slaughter," Gacham means "burn," Tachash means "silence," and Maakhah means "crush."

A concubine, in Jewish law, is a woman who has sexual relations with a man without being married to him—namely, without a *ketubah,* or marriage contract. (Some say a concubine is a woman who has relations without *kiddushin,* or betrothal, as well.) Therefore, she has no rights of maintenance during the relationship or of a monetary settlement upon dissolution of the relationship. Hence, she does not need a *get,* or divorce document. Nor does living with a man in this way create kinship between them; in other words, she could marry one of his relatives and he could marry one of hers. Any children are legitimate and can inherit from the father, at his discretion.[1]

Concubinage, in the ancient world (and where it still exists today), was "an inseparable part of slavery."[2] Since a free man could not marry a slave, the institution of concubinage gave him sexual access to her anyway. The children of such a union assumed the father's status, as free and legitimate, with equal standing among the children born of his wives. Concubinage basically meant that sex became part of the slave's "duty," along with her domestic chores. A free woman could not be taken as a concubine, but a slave could be freed and become a secondary wife.

1. Menachem Elon, *The Principles of Jewish Law* (Jerusalem: Keter, n.d.), pp. 374–376.
2. Murray Gordon, *Slavery in the Arab World* (New York: New Amsterdam Books, 1989), p. 43.

According to Sforno, Reumah and her children are mentioned to tell us that Maakhah, a daughter, "was also worthy of [Isaac] if he did not choose Rivkah, and it would not be necessary to marry from the seed of Canaan." Maakhah is mentioned elsewhere as a tribal name (Deut. 3:14; Joshua 13:13).

Nachmanides, without singling out Maakhah, agrees that "this was written in order to make known the entire genealogy of Nachor, to establish that all of them were worthy to marry the children of Avraham, and it was with reference to all of them that Avraham said to Eliezer, 'You shall go to my father's house and to my family.'"

Milkah and Reumah's childbearing pattern foreshadows the situation of Leah and Rachel and their maidservants: like Milkah, Leah and Rachel produced eight sons; like Reumah, Zilpah and Bilhah produced four (Rashi; GR 57:3). Reumah, however, remained a concubine, while Zilpah and Bilhah were freed and married.

BAKOL

Avraham was old, well-advanced in years, and God had blessed Avraham *bakol* [with everything]. (Gen. 24:1)

In GR 59:7, R. Judah b. Ilai asserts that *bakol* means that Avraham had a daughter—for if he was blessed with everything, how could he not have had a daughter? R. Nehemiah asks, how is it possible that Avraham could have had a daughter and nothing be written about her? Besides, he argues, if Avraham were blessed with everything, he did *not* have a daughter, since a daughter is a constant source of anxiety (San. 100b): "A daughter is a false treasure to her father; through anxiety on her account, he cannot sleep at night—as a minor [*ketanah*], that she be deflowered [lit., "opened"]; at puberty [*naarah*], that she be sexually degraded; as a young woman [*bogeret*], that she not get married; as a married woman [*nesuah*], that she not have children; as an old woman [*zekenah*], that she does witchcraft."

A false treasure, indeed! Although this statement is quoted in the Talmud, it comes from none other than Ben Sira (43:9–10), the *mamzer* (product of incest) who called Lilith the first woman. He seems to have had some problems with sexuality, and we should note that the Talmud quotes this passage as an example of *why it is forbidden to read* the books of Ben Sira!

R. Judah argued for daughters and R. Nehemiah, against them, for Jacob as well as Avraham. R. Judah also believed that Sarah would have borne children had she been married to a man other than Avraham; R. Nehemiah said she would not (GR 45:1).

Nachmanides explains both points of view. To not have a daughter would have been "a blessing for Avraham, for he could not have married her except to the cursed sons of Canaan. If he were to send her to his country, she would also worship the idols as they did." Even if he had a daughter, Nachmanides explains, the intent of the verse "was not merely to inform us of the name of this daughter. Far be it from them to expend the great and generalized blessing of Avraham on this matter; i.e., that Scripture is saying that God blessed him with one daughter with that name."

Calling it "a very profound matter" explained by "one of the secrets of the Torah," Nachmanides continues:

> Thus they said that the word *bakol* hints at a great matter, namely, that the Holy One has an attribute called *kol* [all], so called because it is the foundation of everything. . . . And there is another attribute called *bat* [daughter] that emanates from it, and with it God moves everything. . . . It was this attribute which was to Avraham as a daughter because he was the man of kindness, and he conducted himself in accordance with it. . . . He was blessed with an attribute called *bat* which is contained in the attribute *kol*, and is therefore also called *kol*.

Daughter in kabbalistic terms refers to *Malkhut*, the tenth and lowest of the *sefirot* (plural of *sefirah*, meaning sphere) on the Tree of Life. *Malkhut* embodies receptive power, as it is the container or vessel that receives the other nine *sefirot*. Thus, *Malkhut*, the "daughter," is described as the repository of "the collective bounty which the Creator bestows on the world" which "manifests as the general and diversified conditions affecting the existence of the nether beings. The most important nether beings are the children of Israel. Thus the feminine polarity is the true source of everything that concerns Israel, and after Israel, of everything concerning the rest of created beings who are guided after them."[3]

This concept of *daughter* is what Nachmanides was referring to. Similarly, a *bat kol* is a voice from heaven, a kind of prophecy, which is also indicative of receptivity to divine power and energy.

THE SEARCH FOR SARAH'S SUCCESSOR

> And the servant said to him, "Perhaps the woman will not want to come back with me to this land. Shall I bring your son back to the land that you left?" Avraham replied, . . . "If the woman does not want to come back with you, then you shall be absolved of my oath. But do not bring my son back there." (Gen. 24:5–6, 24:8).

Immediately after Sarah's death, Avraham sent his servant back to Padan Aram (Aram Naharayim) in Babylonia to find a daughter-in-law from among their relatives. Until then, he had thought about marrying Isaac to one of the daughters of his Amorite allies (Gen. 14:13), Aner, Eshkol, or Mamre, who, he said, "are righteous women; for what does their birth matter to me?" (GR 57:3).

However, once he heard that Milkah had children, even a righteous Canaanite woman would not suffice. Eliezer wanted his own daughter to marry Isaac, and that is why he asked the question of Avraham, who knew this and refused him (GR 59:9).

Also implied in Eliezer's question is the notion that it was not completely the custom of the place to have the woman go to her future husband's land. Rivkah's

---

3. Moses Luzzatto, *General Principles of the Kabbalah* (New York: Samuel Weiser, 1970), p. 199.

consent to *marry* Isaac is not the issue in this passage; her willingness to *leave her land*, in order to marry him, is. It indicates that matrilocal, rather than patrilocal, marriage might have been the norm in Padan Aram. Thus, Eliezer came bearing gifts—the bride-price, which allowed him to take her away. Avraham's answer indicates his awareness of the situation.

The marriage negotiations indicate the presence of a matrilineal kinship system in the process of being superseded by a patrilineal one. We saw how Rivkah's female ancestor is always named—but it is her father's mother, not her mother's mother. In a matrilineal kinship system, a woman's brother is part of her maternal group, but her father is not; he is part of his maternal group. Rivkah runs to her *mother's* house, and her *brother* comes running out (Gen. 24:28–29). It is to Rivkah and "also to her brother and mother" that Eliezer gives the "precious gifts" (24:53). It is also her "brother and mother" (24:55) who ask her if she will go immediately rather than wait a year.

Her father, interestingly, appears only to give permission for the marriage to be patrilocal. This indicates a coexistence of the two systems—while patrilocal marriage was not yet the norm, neither was it unheard of.

Rashi says Rivkah ran to tell her mother simply because "it was customary for the women to have their own house to sit in to do their work—and a daughter confides only in her mother." *Genesis Rabbah* 60:7, however, points out that Rachel ran to tell her *father* (Gen. 29:12), which seems to indicate that we are not dealing merely with a Saudi Arabian type of sex segregation here. The Midrash says Rachel did this because her mother had died but offers no source as proof.

Betuel's absence in the morning is also explained (GR 60:12) by saying that he had died during the night. While this is possible, it is equally likely that the Rabbis were not aware of matrilineal and matrilocal systems, living as they did in societies where these no longer existed.

Genesis Rabbah 60:12 derives from the "death" of Betuel the implication that "a fatherless girl may not be given in marriage without her consent." In fact, however, under Jewish law, *no* girl (or woman) can be given in marriage without her consent (Ket. 57b).

Rivkah's age at the time is a matter of dispute. In the Torah itself she is called a *naarah* (Gen. 24:16, 24:28, 24:55, 24:57), which halakhically places her in the six-month age bracket (twelve to twelve and a half years old) that is defined as the start of puberty. However, commentators either say she was three (*Sofrim* 21:87), ten (SY 85), or fourteen (Tosafot on Yev. 61b). From our modern viewpoint, any of these ages is young, but there was no concept of "adolescence" in ancient societies and girls were married off at puberty—sometimes having been betrothed in infancy—and, as we have seen, having been deflowered beforehand.

Rivkah was eager to go, whether her family allowed it or not (GR 60:12). Like her Great-Aunt Sarah before her, she was ready to leave her culture behind and begin a new life. Because she was a prophet, she could foresee that this was the appropriate opportunity.

A RIGHTEOUS WOMAN IN A LAND OF ROGUES

Rivkah was an exception among her people. Everyone in Padan Aram was deceitful (GR 63:4; LR 23:1)—although it is not clear if the wording means "everyone" or all the men. "Her father was a rogue, her brother was a rogue, and the men of her town were likewise rogues, and this righteous woman who came forth from among them might well be compared to a lily among thorns." (Rivkah, as we shall see, does possess some of this trait of deceptiveness—but she uses it only in the service of God.)

Lavan's name means *white, polished,* or *glossy,* indicating that he was "refined in wickedness" (GR 60:7; NR 10:5). When he saw Eliezer coming, he ran out to greet him because, seeing the jewelry on Rivkah, Lavan thought Eliezer was rich and planned to steal from him (Rashi). *Sanhedrin* 105a identifies Lavan as Beor (who is mentioned in Numbers 22:5 as the father of Bilam), and says he acquired this name later because he committed bestiality. Elsewhere, however, Beor is called Lavan's son (SY 105).

The men of Padan Aram sound similar to the generation of the Flood and the men of Sodom. The source that claims Rivkah was age three states a reason that also serves as another explanation for Betuel's "death": had Rivkah been any older, she would already have been deflowered by her own father, Betuel, who was prince of the land (and hence, a ritual deflowerer). However, God performed a miracle for her by causing her father to die in his sleep.

> It is customary among kings, when a daughter is born to them, to hear of it after [three years and] three days, but as her father did not hear of it, he did not defile her up to that time; and now a miracle happened to her in that her father died so that he should not defile her. For it is written that "no man had known her" [Gen. 24:16], and by "man," only her father could be meant, for such was the practice of the Arameans, to lie with their virgin daughters when they were three years of age, and then to give them away in marriage. (*Sofrim,* chap. 21)

"Betuel, the depraved ruler of Aram Naharayim, claimed first right to every girl in the country who was about to be married. When the people heard about Rivkah's betrothal, they said, 'Now we will see how he acts toward his own daughter! If he will do to her what he does to our daughters, good. If he treats her differently, we will kill him and his entire family!'"[4]

If not done by her father, Rivkah's ritual deflowering might have been done by a slave. Thus, there is a tradition that when Rivkah, Eliezer, and Isaac arrived (having met on the road when Rivkah fell off her camel), Avraham greeted them and told Isaac to take Rivkah into the tent to manually check that she was still a virgin, as she had been traveling unchaperoned with Eliezer. Isaac obeyed and found Rivkah's hymen broken. She claimed it happened when she fell off the camel, but he accused her of having been deflowered by Eliezer. Finally, Isaac believed Rivkah.[5]

---

4. Rabbi Moshe Weissman, *The Midrash Says,* vol. 1 (New York: Benei Yakov, 1980), p. 225.

5. Ibid., p. 227. See also Robert Graves and Raphael Patai, *Hebrew Myths: The Book of Genesis* (New York: McGraw-Hill, 1966), p. 185.

A comparison of the description of Rivkah's virginity (Gen. 24:16) with that of Lot's daughters (19:8) further indicates that Rivkah escaped her society's ritual abuse of pubescent girls. Of Rivkah, it is said, "no man had known her," while of Lot's daughters it is said that they "had not known a man." This subtle distinction indicates that Lot's daughters had not *initiated* any sexual activity with men but does not rule out the possibility that a man (i.e., their father) had already "known" them.

The description of Rivkah indicates that not only had she not *initiated* any sexual activity, she had not been the *object* of any, either—in other words, she had not been "known" by any man, as Lot's daughters had. "If she had lost her virginity through a physical injury, she would still be a virgin" (GR 60:5), but "no one had even made advances to her," nor had she been used anally, which technically would not affect virginity.

It was Rivkah's quality of generous hospitality that rendered her most fit for the household of Sarah and Avraham. Eliezer decided to pick the woman who, when he asked for a drink, would offer water to his ten camels as well. Because they store water in their humps, camels drink quite a bit of water, so we are not talking about just one bucket per camel. Rather, this young girl may have shlepped as many as fifty buckets of water while Eliezer sat there and watched. Rivkah's well was "none other than the well of Miriam" (*Zohar* I:132a); the water in it "ascended as soon as it saw her" (GR 60:5), just as it did later for the Israelites in the desert (Num. 21:17).

Eliezer then gave Rivkah some jewelry (Gen. 24:22), including two gold bracelets weighing ten shekels, which symbolized the two tablets with the Ten Commandments (Rashi; GR 60:6). Giving Rivkah these bracelets was the means of passing on the covenant to her, of "dubbing" her, so to speak, as the next matriarch, the foremother of the Jews who stood at Sinai.

RIVKAH'S VEIL

When Rivkah looked up and saw Isaac, she fell from the camel. She asked the servant, "Who is this man coming toward us in the field?" The servant replied, "That is my master." So she took her veil and covered herself. (Gen. 24:64–65)

"Two covered themselves with a veil and gave birth to twins," the Rabbis note in *Genesis Rabbah* 60:14, "Rivkah and Tamar." This is an interesting correlation, yet no explanation of its meaning is given. Rivkah's action is generally explained as one of modesty. That is, when she saw her future husband, she either fell off the camel because he was so good-looking or leaned over to turn her face away. Then she put on her veil.

This passage indicates that use of the veil predates Islam as a pagan custom of the ancient Near East, although Islam has been responsible for expanding its use to the point where it has become a symbol of women's seclusion in a male-dominated society. In the pre-Islamic world, however, a more limited and defined use of the veil may have had other meaning. Consider the following statement from *The Woman's Bible*, a nineteenth-century Christian feminist commentary, by Clara Bewick Colby:

It has been the judgment of masculine commentators that the veil was a sign of woman's subject condition, but even this may be disputed now that women are looking into history for themselves. The fashion of veiling a prospective bride was common to many nations, but to none where there were brutal ceremonies. The custom was sometimes carried to the extent, as in some parts of Turkey, of keeping the woman wholly covered for eight days previous to marriage, sometimes, as among the Russians, by not only veiling the bride, but putting a curtain between her and the groom at the bridal feast. In all cases the veil seems to have been worn to protect a woman from premature or unwelcome intrusion, and not to indicate her humiliated position. The veil is rather a reflection upon the habits and thoughts of men than a badge of inferiority for women.

How serenely beautiful and chaste appear the marriage customs of the Bible as compared with some that are wholly of man's invention. The Kamchatkan had to find his future wife alone and then fight with her and her female friends until every particle of clothing had been stripped from her and then the ceremony was complete. This may be called the other extreme from the veil. Something akin to this appears among our own kith and kin, so to speak, in modern times. Many instances of marriage *en chemise* are on record in England of quite recent dates, the notion being that if a man married a woman in this garment only he was not liable for any debts which she might previously have contracted. At Whitehaven, England, 1766, a woman stripped herself to her chemise in the church and in that condition stood at the altar and was married.[6]

Although some of the book's commentary is anti-Semitic, this particular writer concludes that "it is a comfort to reflect that among the Hebrews, whose records are relied on by the enemies of woman's freedom to teach her subjection, we find women holding the dignified position in the family that was held by Sarah and Rebekah."[7]

We have already noted the story of Rivkah's other "veil," namely, her hymen. There is yet another meaning to Rivkah's veil. The Rabbis say that Isaac was returning from meditating in the field, where he had just instituted the afternoon prayer (Br. 26b). In such a spiritual state, he must have been radiant—similar, perhaps, to Moses' condition when he came down from Sinai and had to put a cover over his face just so people could look at him (Ex. 34:29–35). Thus, Rivkah may have drawn her veil over her face because she was literally knocked off balance by Isaac's spiritual radiance.

THE MATRIARCHS' TENTS

Isaac brought her into his mother Sarah's tent, and he married Rivkah. She became his wife, and he loved her. Isaac was then consoled for the loss of his mother. (Gen. 24:67)

The matriarchs' lineage is referred to in *Genesis Rabbah* 58:2: "Before the Holy One allowed Sarah's sun to set, God caused Rivkah's sun to rise."

When Rivkah came to Sarah's tent, the Shekhinah returned (GR 60:5).

---

6. Stanton and the Revising Committee, pp. 49–50.
7. Ibid.

During the whole of Sarah's life the Shekhinah did not depart from it, and a light used to burn there from one Sabbath eve to the other; once lit, it lasted all the days of the week. After her death the light was extinguished, but when Rivkah came the Shekhinah returned and the light was rekindled. . . . Rivkah was in all her works a replica of Sarah [and so,] . . . although Sarah died, her image did not depart from the house. It was not, however, visible for a time, but as soon as Rivkah came it became visible again.

The Shekhinah, in the form of a cloud, returned to the entrance of the tent when Rivkah arrived, and the Sabbath lights again remained kindled (GR 60:16). "As long as Sarah lived, her doors were wide open, and at her death that wide openness ceased. But when Rivkah came, that wide openness returned." The blessing on Sarah's *challah* was also restored then.

All the matriarchs had tents and are referred to as "women in the tent" in Judges 5:24 (San. 105b; Naz. 23b; Hor. 10b). When Avraham pitched his tent (Gen. 12:8), the word for *tent* is written in the feminine gender (*ahalah*) but vocalized in the masculine (*ahalo*), leading Rashi to comment that "first he pitched a tent for his wife and afterwards one for himself."

The word for Noach's tent (Gen. 9:22) is also written in the feminine and vocalized in the masculine. Rashi tries to dismiss this example by saying that it is "an allusion to the 10 tribes who were spoken of as Samaria, which was called *ahalah*." Perhaps it was, but there is a more profound explanation: a tent has significance as a feminine abode. That is, a tent is "hers," not "his," even when a man resides in it.

In Jewish mysticism, *ohel* (אהל) is the manifestation of celestial light.[8] Composed of the same letters as *Leah*, it is linguistically related to *halo* and refers to the celestial light surrounding a person. *Ohel* is also related to *hila,* meaning shining light and brightness, and *halel,* which is an expression of praise and thanksgiving, as in "lighting up" or "throwing light on" God's greatness. From this we get *hail* and *hello* (to greet or honor someone). *Alah* (curse) has the same three letters and is an expression of the destructiveness of the basis of the celestial light.

The celestial light that surrounds and honors a person is also interpreted as one's clothing, as in Psalms 104:2, "Who covers Yourself with light as with a garment." Our clothes represent the celestial light that surrounds us: think of Sarah's garment from Avimelekh.

"The door of the tent," where Sarah listened in Genesis 18:10, represents wisdom—the gate at which the elders sit, the gate of righteousness, and an opening of the body, which is a gate to the soul (*Zohar* I:103b).

For there is door within door, level behind level, through which the glory of the Holy One is made known . . . and this is the first entrance door. Through this door a view is opened to all the other supernal doors. One who succeeds in entering this door is privileged to know both it and all the other doors, since they all repose on this one. At the present time the door remains unknown because Israel is in exile; and therefore all the other doors are removed from them, so that they cannot know or commune; but when

---

8. The following analysis is from Glazerson, pp. 22–25.

Israel returns from exile, all the supernal levels are destined to rest harmoniously upon this one. Then humans will obtain a knowledge of the precious supernal wisdom of which they knew not previously. (*Zohar* I:103b)

Sarah, who hears at the door of her tent that she will bear a child, clearly had access to such levels of wisdom. Only short-sighted misogyny permits this passage to be interpreted to mean that women should stay inside the tent out of "modesty."

KETURAH

Avraham married another woman whose name was Keturah. She bore him [six sons]. ... Avraham gave all that he owned to Isaac. To the sons of the concubines that Avraham had had, Avraham gave gifts, and sent them away from his son Isaac, while he was still alive, to the east. (Gen. 25:1–6)

Rashi, the Midrash, and the *Zohar* believe that Keturah was Hagar. "Though Hagar, when she left Avraham, went astray after the idols of her ancestors, yet in time she again attached herself to a life of virtue. Hence her name Keturah [attached]. Avraham then sent for her and took her to wife. From here we learn that a change of name acts as an atonement for sin, since that was the reason why her name was changed" (*Zohar* I:133b).

Rashi attributes her name change to the fact that "her deeds were as pleasant as incense [*ketoret*]." GR 61:4 says that "she was perfumed [*mekuteret*] with *mitzvot* and good deeds," as well as noting that she was "tied [*ketar*]," meaning that she had had no other man since Avraham.

Ibn Ezra and Nachmanides, however, say that Keturah was not Hagar. Although Sarah wanted Avraham to take Hagar as a wife, Nachmanides believes that Avraham did not follow this advice: "All his consorts were concubines to him, not as wives, since their children would not be among his heirs. Thus Hagar, Sarah's slave, was his concubine. However, Keturah he took unto himself as a wife."

Noting, therefore, that Keturah was a Canaanite, Nachmanides questions "why he did not send to his country and to his kindred as he did in the case of his son, and replies he guarded only the seed of Isaac since it was concerning him that the covenant was made." Because she was a Canaanite, the Torah "cut short her genealogy" (Nachmanides on Gen. 25:6).

The argument about whether Keturah was Hagar centers around the verse's reference to "the sons of the concubines." Who are "the concubines" (plural) if Hagar and Keturah were the same woman, who was legally married to Avraham, or even if they were different women, but both married to Avraham? Did Avraham have yet other women as concubines besides his two or three wives?

"Perhaps Keturah was called 'concubine' because she was descended from a family of slaves. And if she was a slave in his household and he came to her, Scripture would not mention her genealogy since it is not the way of writing to mention the maidservants, even as the names Zilpah and Bilhah are not elaborated" (Nachmanides).

Perhaps there was only one concubine (Rashi). The *Zohar* says the "sons of the concubines" are the sons of Keturah, "who had formerly been a concubine and was now once more a concubine," but then offers a view that the plural form of the word "must be taken literally."

There is, unfortunately, no way to resolve Keturah's blurred identity. Nor is it really possible to know if she and Hagar were legal wives, since the term used for marriage in the Torah literally means to "take a woman." (We may wonder about the meaning of "take.") The fact that Ishmael and the six sons were sent away without an inheritance, however, would imply that the women were not legal wives, for while the children of a concubine *can* inherit from their father, there is no guarantee that they *must*—especially if the woman herself is banished, as Hagar was.

❊❊❊ 6 ❊❊❊

Rivkah:
Existential Struggle

Toldot (25:19–28:9)

Like her Great-Aunt Sarah before her, Rivkah was barren at first. Like Sarah, Rivkah was a princess (her father, Betuel, was king of Padan Aram). Like Sarah, Rivkah may have been designated for a priesthood that prohibited pregnancy, and hence was a "survivor" of *mashkeh akarot*.

Unlike his father, Avraham, before him, Isaac did not just pray by and for himself to have children; rather, he prayed *with* Rivkah to have children *through* her (Gen. 25:21). Isaac never took a concubine or another wife; he was the only monogamous patriarch, as well as the only one of the three who never left the Land of Israel to go to Egypt (Gen. 26:2). Because he had been intended for a sacrifice, Isaac had the status of "a burnt-offering without blemish"; just as an animal burnt-offering became disqualified if it left the Temple area, Isaac would have become imperfect in some way by leaving Israel (Rashi; GR 64:3). Therefore, he never descended—into polygyny or into exile—from God's ideal.

Isaac and Rivkah prayed together, facing each other from opposite corners of the room (Rashi; GR 63:5). They desired to have children only with each other and no one else. *Yevamot* 64 says that Isaac was sterile, too, and that is why he prayed "opposite" rather than "for" his wife.

God responded to *Isaac's* prayer, the Torah says, "because the prayer of a righteous person [Isaac] who is the child of a righteous person is not the same as the prayer of a righteous person [Rivkah] who is the child of a wicked person" (Rashi; Yev. 64a).

Did God answer Isaac's prayer because his parents were righteous and ignore Rivkah's prayer because her parents were not? This contradicts the maxim (Br. 34b) that "in the place where penitents stand even the wholly righteous cannot stand." That is, a *baal teshuvah* (a secular Jew who becomes religious) is more righteous in some way than the Jew who was religious from birth, because the former knew sin and rejected it while the latter never experienced that struggle.

Rivkah was a *"baalat teshuvah"* and Isaac was "religious from birth." Therefore, if anything, God should have appreciated her prayer more! Remember, too, that the matriarchs were left barren for so long because God wanted their prayers (GR 45:5). God obviously "responded" to Rivkah's prayer, since her request was identical to Isaac's, but perhaps Isaac's prayer was special because he corrected his father's mistake and did not think only of himself.

Isaac did repeat another of his father's mistakes, however, when he tried to pass Rivkah off as his sister to Avimelekh (Gen. 26:7–11).

RIVKAH'S CRY AND GOD'S REPLY

The children struggled inside her, and she cried out, *"Im ken lamah zeh anokhi?"* ["If this is so, why do I exist?"] So she went to inquire of God. And God said to her, "Two nations are in your womb, and two peoples will separate from within you. One people shall become stronger than the other, and the elder shall serve the younger." And when her days of bearing were full, there were twins in her womb. The first came out all red and hairy like a cloak, and they called him Esav. After that his brother came out, his hand seizing the heel of Esav, and [God] called him Jacob. (Gen. 25:22–26)

Rivkah's cry was an existential plea. Something extraordinary was happening within her: this was no normal pregnancy. "Whenever she passed by the doors of Torah [the academy of Shem and Ever], Jacob moved convulsively in an effort to come out, and whenever she passed by the doors of idolatry [a pagan temple], Esav moved convulsively in an effort to come out" (Rashi; GR 63:6; *Zohar* I:137a). Another interpretation is that the twins were fighting each other in the womb as they would later oppose each other in life.

Therefore, Rivkah sought advice from other women, going around to their houses and asking them, "Did you suffer like this when you were pregnant?" and thinking, "If the pain of children is so great, I wish I had not become pregnant!" When the women all told her "no," she wondered, "Why am I alone in this of all women on earth?" (SY 88).

R. Nehemiah believed that "Rivkah merited that the twelve tribes should spring directly from her," deriving the number twelve from the number of people mentioned in God's reply and in the description of the birth: "Two nations" equal two; "two peoples" equal two; "one people [and] . . . the other" equal two; "the elder [and] . . . the younger" equal two; "twins" equal two; "the first" equals one; and "his brother" equals one; all of which add up to twelve.

The *gematria* (numerical value) of *zeh* is also twelve, so R. Huna claimed that Rivkah said, "If this is how I am to produce the twelve tribes, I wish I had not become pregnant!" Her prayer was answered—she did not mother the twelve tribes. In fact, she had no more children after Esav and Jacob. Her anguish was so deep that she was saying, "I wish I did not exist, that I was dead and had never been born!" She was in such pain that life was unbearable for her and she wanted to die (Nachmanides).

Although the biblical verse clearly states that Rivkah "inquire[d] of God" and "God said to her," certain commentators needed to insist that this was not so and that God spoke to her through a messenger—either the prophecy of Shem (Rashi; GR 63:6, which deduces "that to visit a sage is like visiting the Shekhinah"); Avraham (Hertz); an angel (GR 63:7); or even Shem, Ever, *and* Avraham (SY 88).

That this view might be rejected as derived from male egotism and defensiveness is further indicated by the statement: "The Holy One never engaged in speech with a woman save with that righteous woman [Sarah], and that too was due to a special cause. . . . And what a roundabout manner God sought in order to speak with her" (GR 63:7).

Why did these men need to assert that God did not speak to women? Did they feel threatened by women's spiritual power and need to constrict it to reassure themselves that male spiritual power is greater than women's? Did they forget that their male image of God is only a metaphor and not reality, and therefore think it was "immodest" for "Him" to speak to the "opposite sex"?

When God spoke to men, was it not also for "a special cause"? (Where do we ever find God making small talk?) Moreover, what was so "roundabout" in God saying to Sarah, "You did laugh," or in Sarah crying out to God in the palaces and getting a very direct and immediate response?

Fortunately, Nachmanides is a *mensch* on this issue. He disagrees that Rivkah spoke to anyone and instead says she inquired of God through prayer. "Now I have not discovered the word *drishah* [*lidrosh,* to inquire] in relation to God except in the context of prayer," he says, implicitly supporting Rivkah's *direct* contact with God.

All the matriarchs were prophets (GR 67:9), and prophecy involves a "direct line" to God. At least two instances of Rivkah's prophecy are recorded. "Although Jacob was not present when Isaac called Esav his son [for the blessing], the Shekhinah told Rivkah, who in turn told Jacob" (*Zohar* I:142a). Rivkah also knew through prophecy that Esav planned to kill Jacob (Gen. 27:42).

ESAV AND JACOB: THE ROLE OF THE JEWISH MAN

Esav became a skilled trapper, a man of the field. Jacob was a perfectly unblemished [*tam*] man who stayed in the tents. Isaac loved Esav because the trapped game was in his mouth, and Rivkah loved Jacob. (Gen. 25:27–28)

We hear a great deal these days about the "proper role" of the Jewish woman. Let us examine the characters of Jacob, progenitor of Israel, and Esav, progenitor of Rome, to see what this tells us about the proper role of the Jewish man.

Esav was a hairy, macho hunter, a "man's man," who was favored by his father for purely sensual reasons: Isaac enjoyed eating the meat his son brought home to him. Jacob was the "mama's boy" —favored by his mother, he was smooth-skinned, gentle, and domestic. He preferred to stay in the tents (a female abode), cooking and studying Torah with Shem and Ever.

The description of Esav as "a skilled trapper" and the statement that "the trapped game was in his mouth" have a metaphorical meaning as well. Esav "ensnared people by their words. . . . He was a trapper and a fieldsman, trapping at home and trapping in the field" (GR 63:10).

Esav would trap (i.e., deceive) his father by pretending to be pious and concerned with the details of religious practice. "How do you tithe salt?" he would ask him. "How do you tithe straw?" (Neither of these substances is subject to tithing.) Isaac, being lulled by his appetite for delicious meat, fell for the ruse: "There was always venison in the mouth of Isaac." "All day he would desire to eat [it]" (Nachmanides on Gen. 25:28). Esav took after Uncle Lavan in deceptiveness (Sforno). "He made himself free to all like a field" (GR 63:10)—this is a reference to his sexual behavior. Just as Esav preyed upon animals, so, too, he preyed upon women, raping some and seducing others through deception (Kli Yakar).

Esav's red hair and ruddy complexion are symbolic. An affinity exists here between Isaac and Esav (*Zohar* I:137b). In the kabbalistic Tree of Life, Isaac is associated with *Gevurah*, the quality of severity, strictness, or judgment. "And if not for [Rivkah's] gentleness, the world would not have been able to endure the severity inherent in Isaac" (*Zohar* I:137a). The color associated with *Gevurah* is red. Red, according to experts on the psychological impact of color, is hot, stimulating, and inflammatory and is associated with physical sensuality, energy, desire, passion, feverishness, excitability, impulsiveness, and aggression. Its effect on the physical senses has been exploited by bars that use red in their decor to stimulate people to drink more.

Esav's redness is linked to bloodshed—human as well as animal. "He was a highwayman who robbed and murdered people, while all the time pretending to his father that he was abroad performing his prayers" (*Zohar* I:139a). Esav is described as a rapist, murderer, adulterer, robber, and idolator, and his role as the ancestor of Rome, a symbol of the spirit of war, is alluded to (GR 63:12, 75:4): "He was red, his food red, his land red, his warriors were red, his garments were red, and his avenger will be red, clad in red." His land, Edom, literally means *red* in Hebrew.

Esav was enticed into selling his birthright by his physical appetite for a red lentil stew (Gen. 25:30). He repudiated his birthright because of his need for immediate gratification. The birthright would do him no good until his father died, and because he was in danger from the animals he hunted, he was at high risk of dying while his father was still alive (Nachmanides).

On the day that Esav sold his birthright (ER 1:1; B.B.16b), he committed five transgressions: he raped a woman, killed a man, rejected the unity of God, denied the belief in an afterlife, and wished for the death of his father so that he could kill his brother. The man that Esav killed that day was Nimrod (SY 90–91), and Esav's fear of imminent death was due to the fact that Nimrod's men were pursuing him.

In contrast to Esav's skill in trapping—on all levels—Jacob was "not expert in all these things," Rashi says, "as his heart was like his mouth [i.e., his thoughts and words matched]. One who is not ingenious in deceiving is called *tam.*"

Although Jacob was simple, honest, and gentle, he was not weak. "Notwithstanding that Jacob is designated *ish tam,* this means only that he was so in his dealings with anyone who deserved to be treated gently; but where cunning and severity were necessary, he could use these also" (*Zohar* I:139b). That is, he could defend himself when necessary. The fact that he was nice did not mean he let people walk all over him. However, he only called upon these skills for self-defense, and not for aggression.

Jacob objected to Rivkah's plan of deception to obtain the blessing for him, and she took full responsibility by saying, "Let any curse be on me" (Gen. 27:13). Her command, "Listen to my voice," is reminiscent of Avraham listening to Sarah's voice (16:2); Rivkah, too, was motivated by *ruach hakodesh.* The two goats she instructed Jacob to prepare foreshadow the two goats of the Yom Kippur service (*Zohar* I:142b), indicating that any atonement required for her deception was contained within the act itself.

Isaac was blind, literally and figuratively—from "old age" or, perhaps, because he saw the Shekhinah while he was bound on the altar or the angels cried on his eyes. However, it is also said that his eyesight weakened "because he justified the wicked" (GR 65:5–6) and "from seeing the evil of that wicked man. . . . One who raises a wicked son or a wicked disciple eventually suffers dimness of sight" (65:10). Isaac was held partially responsible for Esav's behavior because he never disciplined or chastised him for his evil deeds.

Jacob, who represents spiritual strength (the "voice of Jacob"), is the role model for the Jewish man—indeed, for *all* men. Esav, who represents physical might (the "hands of Esav"), is "malevolence" (male violence). "Whenever the voice of Jacob is interrupted, the hands of Esav are reinforced" (*Zohar* I:171a).

MALE VIOLENCE AND THE "ESAVING" OF MEN

The male hormone testosterone is responsible for male secondary sex characteristics such as hairiness, sexual drive, and aggressiveness, all of which Esav had in abundance—his was a case of "testosterone poisoning." The fact that sexual arousal and aggressiveness are biologically so closely intertwined in men is very problematic. It is the reason why many men become sexually aroused by violence, why male sexuality often takes very predatory forms, why massive raping is an integral part of warfare, and why the military has used pornographic movies to prepare fighter pilots for bombing missions.[1]

Nonetheless, biology is not destiny. Men are not helpless victims of their testosterone any more than women are powerless captives of their estrogen–progesterone

---

1. "Fighter pilots aboard the U.S.S. *John F. Kennedy* watched porno movies before their bombing missions, according to a January article in the *Washington Post.* The paper also said that the first report of this story, by the Associated Press, was censored by the military." This brief item appeared in "The Gender Gulf," *Ms.* 1:5 (Mar./Apr. 1991): 87.

cycles. The culture modifies biology and, as such, has a crucial responsibility in shaping men's behavior: it can encourage men either to be Jacobs or to be Esavs.

Modern American society, which glorifies violence—and especially sexualized violence—and feeds men a steady diet of it as "entertainment," teaches men to be Esavs. Pornography is the most extreme and direct means today for the "Esaving" of men. Many individuals who regularly consume it often decide to act out their fantasies by imitating, on real women and children, what they see in pictures. Although our society continues to act as though feeding these images to men does not affect their behavior, consider the following:

• A man convicted in the 1989 strangulation and sexual mutilation of a female employee was found to possess in his home "bondage paraphernalia, more than 100 sexually explicit videotapes, numerous sexual devices, [and] adult magazines and books." After killing the woman, he took pornographic pictures of her corpse. The judge, however, ordered the district attorney to return the collection of items to the murderer—who had also been implicated in a child pornography ring— because he (the judge) "saw no indication that [the man] intended to disseminate the magazines."[2]
• The famous 1983 "Big Dan" rape in New Bedford, Massachusetts—in which a woman went into a bar to buy a pack of cigarettes and was gang-raped on the pool table while the men who did not participate watched—occurred three months after *Hustler* magazine featured a photo spread of a young woman being gang-raped on a pool table in a working-men's bar. How do social forces shape young men's fantasies?

Pornographic imagery, which has long fed the fantasies of gang-rapists, child molesters, and serial killers, is now affecting "normal" men as well. A 1978 study in San Francisco found that 10 percent of the women in their sample answered "yes" to the question, "Have you ever been upset by anyone trying to get you to do what they'd seen in pornographic pictures, movies, or books?" That is, otherwise normal husbands and boyfriends were requesting their wives and girlfriends to experiment with activities they had seen, including sadomasochism, bondage, fellatio, sodomy, bestiality, and threesomes. While most of the women were able to avoid doing what was asked of them, some were coerced. Moreover, even in cases where the behavior was avoided, the women were often harassed or humiliated.[3]

The Esaving of men—the normalization of sexual violence in our society—has been demonstrated by three male psychologists, who found that more than half of the men in their study "do not rule out the possibility that they would engage in sexual assault if they could not be caught." The researchers concluded from this that "rape

2. Patricia Nealon, "Killer Seeks Return of His Pornography," *The Boston Globe,* Apr. 29, 1992, p. 51; Patricia Nealon, "Inmate's Erotica Ordered Returned," *The Boston Globe,* June 24, 1992, p. 29.
3. Diana E. H. Russell, "Pornography and Violence: What Does the New Research Say?" In *Take Back the Night: Women on Pornography,* ed. Laura Lederer (New York: Bantam, 1980), pp. 222–226.

is an extension of normal attitudes and socialization practices in our society rather than totally the product of a sick and aberrant mind."[4]

Media psychologists Neil Malamuth and Ed Donnerstein agree that, given certain predispositions, men who are exposed to sexually violent images show an increased acceptance and tolerance of violence against women. Even if they do not *commit* violence against women, their attitudes toward such violence tend to become more callous and desensitized.[5]

Pornography's "image pollution" is no longer marginal or socially deviant but rather has filtered down into mass media. As pornography becomes more violent and perverse, what was considered "soft-core" forty years ago, when the first *Playboy* magazine was published, is now featured on television and in mainstream movies.

Violence, whether sexualized or otherwise, is so normative, acceptable and accessible in television and movies that Esav-type movie heroes like Rambo and Dirty Harry regularly shape young boys' aspirations and images of manhood. For example, "A 16-year-old boy, apparently enthralled by the film character Rambo, killed his father, mother, and brother and wounded his sister . . . in a shooting rampage at the family's house," according to a newspaper report. The boy, about whom a neighbor said, "He didn't seem much different from other kids," had dozens of Rambo posters and magazines in his bedroom, as well as smoke grenades, ammunition pouches, a revolver, and four shotguns. When the boy was booked, he gave "Rambo" as his nickname. "I don't want to say Rambo did this, but it surely played an important role here, absolutely," said the police chief.[6]

The media, of course, is not the only culturally sanctioned means for training men to be Esavs, but in our modern technological age, it is clearly the most pervasive. Sports, military training, childhood socialization, tolerance of injuries committed in male bonding ("boys will be boys"), and other psychological and sociological factors certainly contribute to the fact that, even in this era of "gender equality," 90 percent of violence is committed by males.

At the other end of the spectrum from our society's Esaving of men is traditional Judaism, which teaches men to be Jacobs. Recognizing the potential for violence, which exists to a much greater degree in men than in women, Jewish law strictly channels and controls every aspect of men's lives, beginning with their sexual expression, to a much greater degree than women's lives. The fact that much of the fixed ritual and many of the laws in Judaism are directed at men is a result of this recognition—which is ironically misperceived as "sexist" by feminists.

---

4. Neil M. Malamuth, Scott Haber, and Seymour Feshbach, "Testing Hypotheses Regarding Rape: Exposure to Sexual Violence, Sex Differences, and the 'Normality' of Rapists," *Journal of Research in Personality* 14 (1980): 121–137.

5. Personal telephone interviews, February 1986. At that time Malamuth was at the University of California at Los Angeles and Donnerstein was at the University of Wisconsin. See also Daniel Goleman, "Violence against Women in Films," *Response*, 8:1 (Winter 1985): 21–22.

6. Lisa W. Foderaro, "Parents and a Brother Slain by Self-Styled Rambo," *The New York Times*, Mar. 23, 1989, p. B3.

Torah study and communal prayer are the major channels for male bonding in traditional Judaism—and what clever inventions they are! Historically, these activities have kept Jewish men out of fraternities, barrooms, stag parties, hunting expeditions, street gangs, gun clubs, and sports arenas. The *minyan* has elevated male bonding from the activities of a violent horde competing for a macho, self-gratifying, physical goal into a cooperative endeavor toward a holy, spiritual goal—prayer. The study of Talmud has provided a constructive, intellectual channel for men's love of battling for one-upmanship.

As a result, the traditional Jewish male has frequently been stereotyped as a "wimp" by the gentile world. Indeed, it is a label of which he should be proud! The Jewish man could (and should) be at the forefront of the feminist struggle against macho masculinity, for he has not needed bullfights and boxing matches to bolster his sense of manhood. Hunting—Esav's greatest skill—is completely forbidden in Jewish law. Alas, however, as Jewish men assimilate into the gentile culture, they incorporate the values of gentile men. Thus, we increasingly find Jewish men striving to be macho and priding themselves on developing muscular bodies instead of analytical minds and gentle souls.

The "voice of Jacob" has been interrupted, and the "hands of Esav" have been reinforced. It is time to turn the tide so that the voice of Jacob can be heard again.

ESAV'S WIVES

When Esav was 40 years old, he married Judith, daughter of Be'eri the Hittite, and Basmat, daughter of Elon the Hittite. They were a bitterness of spirit to Isaac and Rivkah. . . . Esav went to Ishmael and married Machlat, daughter of Ishmael son of Avraham, and sister of Nevayot, in addition to his other wives. (Gen. 26:34–35, 28:9)

Esav is compared to a wild pig that shows its cloven hoof in order to pretend it is kosher, and to Rome, which robs and oppresses while pretending to execute justice (Rashi; GR 65:1). "For 40 years Esav ensnared women and violated them, but when he became 40 he compared himself to his father, saying, 'As my father married at age 40, so will I.'"

The match of Esav and Judith is described as two *mamzers* who deserved and found each other (GR 65:2). Judith and Basmat, both Hittite women, were "a bitterness of spirit" to Isaac and Rivkah. "All their actions provoked anger and caused grief since they worshiped idols" (Rashi). They "sacrificed and burnt incense to the *Baalim*," and they did not "walk in the ways of Hashem, but served their father's gods of wood and stone, as their father had taught them, and they were more evil than their ancestors" (SY 96). Esav himself did not totally trust them and left certain special garments at Rivkah's house because "he knew what they worshiped" (GR 65:16).

Esav "caused *ruach hakodesh* to go away from his parents" (GR 65:4) by marrying these women. Isaac is mentioned first "because Rivkah, being the daughter of idolatrous priests, was not particular about the defilement from idolatry; whereas he was the son of holy parents and was particular." Nonetheless, Isaac never protested Esav's marriages, even though "they were as a razor and a knife which cut short the spirit in the lives of Isaac and Rivkah" (Sforno).

Esav later came to understand that Isaac was unhappy about his Hittite wives, so he married Machlat, Ishmael's daughter (his parallel cousin). Even here, however, his motives were evil: he hoped that Ishmael would want his new son-in-law to have his birthright back so much that he would kill Jacob for it. Then, Esav thought, "I will rise up against [Ishmael] as a blood kinsman and slay him [to avenge the death of Jacob], and thus become the heir of two families" (GR 67:8). However, his plan failed, for Ishmael died after Machlat's betrothal, and her brother Nevayot inherited (Meg. 17a).

Esav married all three women to increase his wealth (GR 82:2). "He added wickedness to his wickedness, for he did not divorce his first wives" after marrying Machlat (Rashi). Some say that Esav renamed his wives when he married them. Judith he called Ahalivamah, Basmat he called Adah, and Machlat he called Basmat (Gen. 36:2–3). Ahalivamah means "my tent's entrance" or "my tent's altar." Basmat was named Adah because Esav's blessing had just been "removed" from him (SY 96). Machlat means *sick*, so "because of the repugnance of her name . . . Esav called her by the honorable name of his first wife Basmat . . . because she was beloved by him since she was of his family and was not evil in the eyes of Isaac his father" (Nachmanides).

Rashi believes the name changes went the other way. Thus, Ahalivamah was named Judith by Esav, "suggesting that she had abandoned idol worship so that he might deceive his father." Adah "was called Basmat because she offered spices [*besamim*] to idols." Basmat was called Machlat because "Esav's sins were pardoned [*machal*] on his marriage to her." Others, however, believe that Ahalivamah and Adah were different women from Judith and Basmat. Judith and Basmat are said to have died childless, "perhaps as a punishment because they were a bitterness of spirit to Isaac and Rivkah," and Adah was Basmat's (paternal) sister (Nachmanides).

Judith died, agrees *Sefer HaYashar* 99, but she left two daughters: Martzit (מרצית) and Puit (פועית). Martzit married Anah, son of Zivion, and Puit married a Horite (SY 100).

ANAH AND AHALIVAMAH: EDOMITE TRIBAL CHIEFS

Ahalivamah is called "daughter of Anah, daughter of Zivion" (Gen. 36:2). Is Ahalivamah the daughter of both, or is she the daughter of Anah, who is the daughter of Zivion? There are several opinions on this.

• Ahalivamah was the daughter of both, and Anah and Zivion were both men. Anah was Zivion's son and (maternal) brother (Gen. 36:20, 36:24), a product of Zivion committing incest with his mother. Zivion then took Anah's wife, and from that union Ahalivamah was born. Zivion was Ahalivamah's biological father, but Anah, her mother's husband, was her social father (Rashi; GR 82:14; *Zohar*

I:178b). This wretched story seems a bit farfetched. Interestingly, however, Anah (meaning *violated* or *oppressed*) was the creator of the mule, the product of inter-breeding a donkey and a horse. Being himself the offspring of a forbidden sexual relation, Anah then brought about a similar relation in the animal world (Pes. 54a).
• There were two Anahs—one was Zivion's brother and one was Zivion's son (just as the name Dishon is mentioned twice in these lineages but no one says they were the same person). Ahalivamah was Anah's daughter and Zivion's granddaughter, and the relation is stated so as to make it clear that Anah, *son* of Zivion, was Ahalivamah's father, and not Anah, *brother* of Zivion (Ibn Ezra; Nachmanides).
• Anah was a woman—Ahalivamah's mother, and the daughter of Zivion (Tosafot on B.B. 115b). "According to this, [Ahalivamah's] father could indeed have been Be'eri the Hittite [making her identical to Judith]" (Kaplan). There is, however, a problem with this view: Anah the *child* of Zivion was the mule breeder and is quite clearly discussed using a masculine verb and pronouns (Gen. 36:24). He is also the Anah that Martzit is said to have married.

I suggest a fourth possibility: Anah the *sibling* of Zivion was a woman. Hence, Anah was Ahalivamah's mother and Zivion was Ahalivamah's father; as with Rivkah's lineage, both parents are mentioned. Moreover, since Zivion and Anah were *paternal* siblings, their sexual relationship was not considered incestuous at the time.
The Anah who was Zivion's sister and wife was a tribal chief (Gen. 36:20). Most male commentators would automatically assume that such a position could only be held by a man, yet, if Anah the tribal chief were a woman, her status would certainly explain why she was mentioned in this lineage when mothers generally were not.
The theory gains even more plausibility when we note that, like her mother Anah, Ahalivamah herself is described as a tribal chief, as is Timna, the concubine of Esav and Adah's son, Elifaz (Gen. 36:40–41). That Esav's people maintained a matrilineal status is also indicated by the statement that Jacob was pursued by Elifaz, who "took 10 of his mother's brothers with him" (SY 97).

THE HITTITE WOMEN

Rivkah said to Isaac, "I detest life because of the Hittite women. If Jacob marries a woman from among these Hittites, the daughters of the land, [*lamah li chaim*], why should I go on living?" (Gen. 27:46)

For the second time, Rivkah seems to be on the verge of suicide. Perhaps, as some commentators suggest, this is mere hyperbole, a clever ruse to get Isaac to send Jacob to Padan Aram to escape Esav's death threat. She has just told Jacob to go to her brother Lavan until Esav's anger subsides, saying, "Why should I lose you both on the same day?" (Gen. 27:43–45). This statement turned out to be a prophecy, for Esav was killed at Jacob's burial (Sot. 13a).
Why were the Hittite women such a source of grief to Rivkah? The Hittites, one of seven peoples of the land of Canaan, are better known in history as the founders

of an empire in Asia Minor (present-day Turkey) who engaged in a major war with Egypt more than two millennia after Rivkah's death. Known as "the nation of a thousand gods," every Hittite locale had its own deity who had to be propitiated with the aid of magic and sorcery.[7]

Hittite goddesses were served "by a multitude of armed women and eunuch priests." These women, "who danced in her honor armed with the shield and bow," were the prototype of the Amazons, the warrior women described in various Greek sources. "In ancient art the Amazons are represented as clad in the Hittite tunic and brandishing the same double-headed axe that is held in the hands of some of the Hittite deities."[8]

Such images of strong women have been enthusiastically embraced by modern feminists. However, goddess rites often included castration as well as various types of human sacrifice (e.g., kings, their firstborn sons, their widows, or other family members). The Amazons supposedly crippled male babies or sent them away. Hittite priests of a goddess were transsexuals—men who were castrated and dressed as women—because they could only serve a female deity "by renouncing their sex and assimilating themselves to women."[9]

The association of castration and human sacrifice with mother goddesses comes from the linkage of blood and fertility. Because menstrual blood was seen as the source of a woman's fertility, blood sacrifices were believed to ensure the earth's fertility. This is why mother goddesses were also goddesses of fertility, love, war, and the hunt.

"Her rites were bloody, her festivals orgiastic. . . . Everywhere blood plays a leading part in fertility ritual and human sacrifice. The great terrestrial law that there can be no life without death was early understood [and] . . . a strengthening of life can only be bought at the cost of sacrificial death. . . . Slaughter and sacrifice, dismemberment and offerings of blood, are magical guarantees of earthly fertility."[10]

"In the matriarchal phase of fertility ritual, the Great Mother predominated, and . . . bloody dismemberment of the young king guaranteed the earth's fertility."[11] In a purely matrilineal system, where the role of husband and father had little significance, a god was the son, brother, or consort of a goddess and his representative, the king, was the son, brother, or consort of the queen. Ritual enactments of dying gods, corresponding to the dry season and the dying of the crops, included actual sacrifices of the kings who represented them.

"In prehistoric times the kings themselves played the part of the god and were slain and dismembered in that character. . . . [The] kings [were] expected to regulate

---

7. Johannes Lehmann, *The Hittites: People of a Thousand Gods* (New York: Viking Press, 1977), pp. 136, 267.

8. A. H. Sayce, *The Hittites: The Story of a Forgotten Empire* (London: Religious Tract Society, 1982), pp. 78–80.

9. Briffault, 3:213.

10. Erich Neumann, *The Origins and History of Consciousness* (Princeton, NJ: Bollingen, 1954), p. 54.

11. Ibid., p. 222.

the course of nature for the good of their people and [were] punished if they failed to do so."[12] Early dynastic kings were deified at their deaths; for example, Dumuzi of Sumer (ancient Babylonia).[13]

The lists of Hittite kings are usually sacrifice lists.[14] The practice of king sacrifice was normative until "the relevance of coition to childbearing had been officially admitted"—a "turning point" in Hittite myth. "The tribal Nymph . . . chose an annual lover from her entourage of young men, a king to be sacrificed when the year ended; making him a symbol of fertility. . . . His sprinkled blood served to fructify trees, crops, and flocks, and his flesh was torn and eaten raw by the Queen's fellow nymphs—priestesses wearing the masks of bitches, mares, or sows." Her next consort then "acquired executive power only when permitted to deputize for the Queen by wearing her magical robes."[15]

An ancient king might be ritually killed in a number of ways. "He might be torn in pieces by wild women, transfixed with a sting-ray spear, felled with an axe, pricked in the heel with a poisoned arrow, flung over a cliff, burned to death on a pyre, drowned in a pool, or killed in a pre-arranged chariot crash. But die he must."[16]

As time went on, kings substituted others (often their firstborn sons). Then animals, such as a ram, began to be accepted instead.[17] "A new stage was reached when animals came to be substituted for boys at the sacrificial altar, and the king refused death after his lengthened reign ended."[18]

This information gives us a few clues, perhaps, as to why Rivkah felt such despair about her sons marrying into Hittite culture.

---

12. James Frazer, *The Golden Bough* (New York: Macmillan, 1922), pp. 439, 100.

13. Diane Wolkstein and Samuel Noah Kramer, *Inanna: Queen of Heaven and Earth* (New York: Harper and Row, 1983), p. 124.

14. I. E. S. Edwards, C. J. Gadd, and N. G. L. Hammond, eds., *Cambridge Ancient History*, vol. 1, pt. 1 (New York: Cambridge University Press, 1970), p. 202.

15. Robert Graves, *The Greek Myths*, vol. 1 (New York: Penguin, 1960), p. 14.

16. Ibid., p. 18.

17. Frazer, pp. 336–341.

18. Graves, pp. 18–19.

7

Rachel and Leah: Making Sisterhood Powerful

Vayetze (28:10–32:3)

Rachel and Leah, Lavan's daughters and Rivkah's nieces, are described as the builders of the Jewish people, resembling "two beams running from one end of the world to the other" (GR 70:15). Playing on a link between *bnot* (daughters) and *banot* (builders), the Midrash sees Rachel and Leah as the superstructure from which the entire nation of Israel was constructed.

"Each produced captains and kings. From each arose slayers of lions, prophets and judges. From each arose conquerors of countries and dividers of countries. A sacrifice of a son of each superseded the Sabbath, and a war of a son of each superseded the Sabbath. To each was given two nights."

This latter statement refers to victories; for example, the Exodus from Egypt was led by Moses, a descendant of Leah, and the victory of Purim was accomplished by Esther and Mordechai, descendants of Rachel. Here, these victories are attributed to the hero's matriarchal ancestor.

Rachel and Leah's lives are so intertwined that their story is one entity. As sisters, they were set up by their father and their society to be rivals. Sisterhood was not meant to be powerful for them or for any women in Padan Aram. However, Rachel and Leah overcame incredible odds and *made* it powerful. Such was the transformative capacity that imbued all the matriarchs.

MATRILOCAL MARRIAGE

Jacob was sent to his mother's homeland to find a wife from the family of his mother's brother, in a clear matrilocal marriage practice. He also engaged in animal *husbandry:*

72

the marriage contract required him to work for his wife's family by tending the flocks. This is the origin of the concept of a *husband* working to support his wife.

Although it is suggested that Jacob wept when he saw Rachel because he had no bride-price, having been robbed on the way to Padan Aram (GR 70:12), this is unlikely. He had no *need* of bride-price, for he was not taking his wives away from their family. Jacob's husbandry lasted twenty years—seven years each for Rachel and Leah, and six more years to earn his keep.

Matrilocal marriage was the vestige of a matriarchal system, in which the mother controlled family property and passed it on to her children. The link between sex and pregnancy—and hence, biological fatherhood—had not yet been recognized or understood. Descent was matrilineal, so a child's "father figure" was the mother's brother, and not the biological father.

However, while matrilocal marriage was "in itself a certain indication of a former matriarchal state," matrilineal descent was "quite compatible with the most completely oppressed condition of women."[1] When a woman remains with her natal family after marriage, it gives her some emotional and economic control, and "in those circumstances her status cannot be one of complete subjection." However, matrilineal descent has existed in cultures where there was little or no private property to transmit and where maternity was simply the more directly observable relationship. It does not, in itself, give women power.

As paternity became understood, patrilineal descent became important to men because they wanted to pass their property on to their own children rather than those of their sisters. (For a man with no sisters—such as Avraham, Isaac, or Jacob—this desire would be especially acute.) The matrilineal man, whose clan identity was as a son and a brother, was also confronted with a strange situation in warfare—when fighting with his natal clan, he might easily face his own sons as "enemy" soldiers. It is easy to imagine that men might rebel against this system and demand some status as husbands and fathers.

As patrilineal descent became predominant, patrilocal marriage arose. A son brought his bride home to his father's house rather than going to live with her family. Son-preference and the devaluation of daughters was a natural consequence of patrilocal marriage, especially with the practice of dowry, in which a family sent a daughter away at puberty, with money and gifts, to live in her husband's household. Patrilocal marriage thus created, consolidated, and maintained patriarchy, which means "rule by the fathers."

Where patrilocal marriage survives today, women have extremely low status, such as in India and China. Female infanticide is common, both in its crude form and in its streamlined medical form: using amniocentesis to detect female fetuses for abortion and sex selection technology to prevent females from even being conceived.[2]

---

1. Briffault, 1:309.

2. Rita Arditti, Renate Duelli Klein, and Shelley Minden, eds., *Test-Tube Women* (Pandora Press: Boston, 1984). See, in particular, Vimal Balasubrahmanyan, "Women as Targets in India's Family Planning Policy," pp. 153–164; Betty B. Hoskins and Helen Bequaert Holmes, "Technology and Prenatal

In India, young brides are often the victims of "dowry burnings" in their new homes—in the guise of a "cooking accident," the woman is set on fire by her in-laws, who may be greedy for a larger dowry payment or feel cheated because she did not bear a son.[3] In China, women known as "the marriage resisters" protest the permanent severance of relations with their natal families through a full-fledged resistance movement: they simply refuse to get married.[4]

That patrilocal marriage is as dangerous for women as warfare is stated explicitly regarding the institution in China: "A Chinese bride . . . left her natal family in the midst of a celebration designed to dramatize her permanent departure and the lasting severance of her ties with her natal family . . . [for] she could never return to her former place. Moreover, joking and informal rituals in her household prior to her wedding made it clear to her that she was about to enter enemy territory and should prepare for war."[5]

Matrilocal marriage survived for awhile within patrilineal kinship structures, however, and elements of this transition are seen in Padan Aram. We have noted mixed practices in Rivkah's case. (Avraham and Rivkah, it should be emphasized, were not necessarily invested in promoting *the institution of* patrilocal marriage. Avraham needed to continue the covenant in the Land of Israel. He sent for a wife from the land and kin of Isaac's *mother* as well as his own, and he also was quite willing to release Eliezer from his vow if the woman would not leave. Rivkah knew prophetically that something significant was happening and that she was meant to be an integral part of it.)

With Jacob we see further remnants of matrilocal marriage in a growing patrilineal kinship system: Jacob served his father-in-law and not his mother-in-law, indicating that Lavan was the head of the household. Mrs. Lavan—whose name was Adinah, עדינה (SY 93)—is never even mentioned in the Torah, while Rivkah's mother, though nameless, is mentioned throughout her daughter's marriage negotiations. Second, Jacob's husbandry was not permanent; after having children and working a number of years, he was able to take his wives and leave. Moreover, his sons were his heirs.

While daughters might still be retained by their families after marriage, son-preference was already a part of reality. This is reflected in the statement that "sons were born to Lavan on account of Jacob," indicating that Lavan was "blessed" through Jacob. Until then, Lavan had had twin daughters, Leah and Rachel, but no other

---

Femicide," pp. 237–255; Kumkum Sangari, "If You Would Be the Mother of a Son," pp. 256–265; and Viola Roggencamp, "Abortion of a Special Kind: Male Sex Selection in India," pp. 266–277. See also Susan S. Wadley, "Female Life Changes in Rural India," *Cultural Survival Quarterly* 13:2 (1989): 35–38.

3. Mary Daly, *Gyn/Ecology* (Boston: Beacon Press, 1978), pp. 114–115n, quoting a *New York Times* article of Jan. 13, 1977, documenting such a case.

4. Janice G. Raymond, *A Passion for Friends* (Boston: Beacon Press, 1986), pp. 115–147.

5. Susan Mann, "Suicide and Chastity: Visible Themes in the History of Chinese Women" (paper presented at the Sixth Berkshire Conference on the History of Women, Smith College, Northampton, MA., 1984), pp. 4–5, citing the work of Margery Wolf, *Women and the Family in Rural Taiwan* (Stanford: Stanford University Press, 1972). Cited in Raymond, p. 117.

children, because Adinah and all his other wives and concubines were barren (SY 93, 99). Sterility in women seems to have been a virtual epidemic.

RACHEL THE SHEPHERD

Rachel met Jacob at the well because she was the shepherd of her father's flocks and had to water them. The sheep had no other shepherd; even Leah never went along. Some commentators presume that had there been men to do it, Rachel would not have been permitted because of "modesty" (Rashi; Nachmanides). However, Rachel's public presence (and Leah's lack of it) constitutes an essential element of the mystical symbolism of these two matriarchs.

Leah, unlike Rachel, was not met openly at the well by Jacob because she represents the veiled world (*Zohar* I:153a, I:154a–b). Her hidden marriage to Jacob was accomplished by a veil.

In the Tree of Life (see Figure 7-1), *Binah*, the third *sefirah*, is followed by seven *sefirot*, including *Malkhut*, which we discussed in the context of Avraham's "daughter" (see chapter 5). *Binah* is likened to Leah: As Leah had six sons and one daughter, *Binah* had six "sons" (*Chesed* through *Yesod*) and one "daughter," *Malkhut*, who is likened to Rachel.

As *Binah* is Understanding, so Leah represents this inner quality of mental reasoning and discernment. She is "the origin of Israel, and most exalted. She occupies the place of the brain and is not subject to such changes as take place in Rachel. With her, union is not of chief importance. On the contrary, she is representative of the concealed world."[6]

As *Malkhut* is Sovereignty, action in this world, so Rachel represents an energy made manifest. She is "another source for Israel, which corresponds to its deeds. . . . Her conditions are constantly changing along with the changing degrees of virtue in humanity. The principal government depends on her for she is the 'mistress of the house.' The principal union takes place with her, because only Rachel can produce a renewal of bounty."[7]

Binah/Leah represents the concealed world, while *Malkhut*/Rachel represents the revealed world. The activity of *Binah*/Leah is in the upper realm, giving life to the lower realm of *Malkhut*/Rachel, which, in turn, nourishes *Binah* by its influence. Thus, their relationship is one of reciprocity. Both are symbols of the Shekhinah.

There is yet another allusion to the notion of Rachel as overt and Leah as covert. During the festival of Sukkot, Jews wave the Four Species: *etrog* (citron), *lulav* (palm branch), willow, and myrtle. These are, respectively, said to symbolize the heart, the spine, the lips, and the eyes. These Four Species are likened to the matriarchs. The *etrog* (called *hadar*) represents Sarah because God honored (*hiderah*) her with a good

---

6. Luzzatto, pp. 216–217.
7. Ibid.

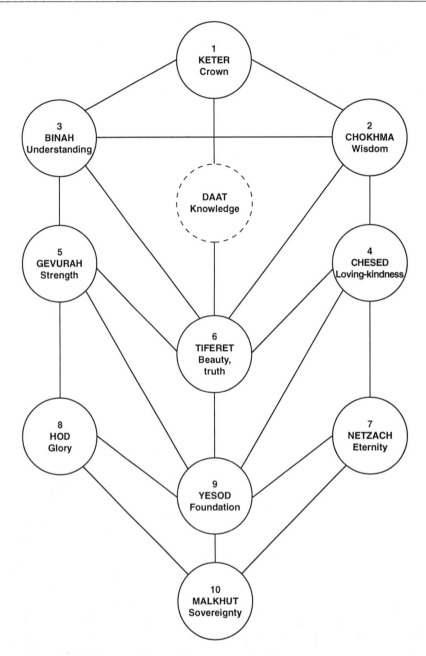

FIGURE 7-1. The Kabbalistic Tree of Life uses each *sefirah* (sphere or circle) to represent a quality of God. The patriarchs are traditionally associated with *Chesed* (Avraham), *Gevurah* (Isaac), and *Tiferet* (Jacob). Rivkah is associated with *Chesed* and Sarah with *Gevurah*. In our discussion here, Leah is associated with *Binah*, the upper world of hidden energy, and Rachel is associated with *Malkhut*, the lower world of manifest energy.

old age. The *lulav* symbolizes Rivkah because "as the palm tree contains edible fruit as well as prickly fruit, so she brought forth a righteous child and an evil child." The willow is Rachel, since "as it wilts before the others, so Rachel died before Leah." The myrtle is Leah, because as it is "crowded with leaves, so she was crowded with children" (LR 30:10).

If we combine the interpretations of the matriarchs with the body parts, we see that Sarah is the heart, opening herself up to the One God and opening her home to people in hospitality. Rivkah is the spine, the backbone of the world, birthing both the progenitors of the Jews and a large portion of the gentiles. (Furthermore, she had to have had a very strong back to endure such a difficult pregnancy!) Rachel is the lips—meaning speech, the outer manifestation, and the revealing of inner thoughts. Finally, Leah is the eyes, which see and understand from within.

LEAH'S EYES

And the eyes of Leah were *rakot*. (Gen. 29:17)

Rakot is best translated as *tender*, and we are told that Leah's eyes were puffy and sore from frequent crying. Why was she crying? Rachel and Leah were naturally considered as mates for their cross cousins, Jacob and Esav. Leah, because she was the elder twin girl, was expected to marry Esav, the elder twin boy. Upon learning what a violent man Esav was, "she wept until her eyelashes dropped out" (B.B. 123a) and prayed to God, "May it be Your will that I do not fall to the lot of that wicked man!" (GR 70:16). Her prayer successfully annulled the decree.

Later, when Leah was having children and Rachel was not, Rachel was scared that if Jacob divorced her because of her sterility, she would end up with Esav. In fact, this had already entered Esav's mind when he heard that she was childless with Jacob (Rashi).

SORORAL POLYGYNY AND LAVAN'S DECEPTION

Lavan said, "It is not done so in our country, to give the younger daughter in marriage before the elder daughter." (Gen. 29:26)

Before the Torah was given, it was permissible for a man to marry two or more sisters. It was a widespread principle in ancient polygynous cultures that "when a man marries a woman he thereby acquires marital rights over all her sisters. . . . A man has a right to all the women of the group into which he marries."[8]

In most societies practicing sororal polygyny, it was forbidden for a man to marry a younger sister before marrying her elder sister. This was due to economic consid-

---

8. Briffault, 1:614, 627.

erations—"since in primitive society girls usually marry at puberty, the younger sisters are not marriageable at the time of their elder sisters' marriage; and by that time the man's circumstances may have improved so as to enable him to maintain a larger family."[9] Lavan's deception clearly was in keeping with this custom.

When Jacob asked Rachel to marry him, "she replied, 'Yes, but my father is a deceiver, and he will outwit you.' . . . He said to her, 'What is his deception?' She replied, 'I have a sister older than I am, and he will not let me marry before her.'" Therefore, she and Jacob developed a code of secret signs (Meg. 13b; B.B. 123a). These signs—touching the right big toe, thumb, and earlobe—later became the mode of anointing Jewish priests (Ex. 29:20; Lev. 8:23–24).[10]

However, when Rachel saw Leah being led to the wedding, her love for her sister overrode her love for a man and she taught Leah the signs so that she could fool Jacob. Rachel then hid under the bed, and when Jacob spoke to Leah that night, Rachel answered. How painful it must have been for her to respond verbally for Leah, while Jacob was totally unaware of the identity of the woman to whom he was making love. (Darkness is no excuse.)

All the wedding guests knew of Lavan's deception and tried to warn Jacob of it in the words of the songs they sang, but he did not get the hint (SY 100). The next morning, when he discovered the deception, he angrily said to Leah, "What a deceiver you are, the daughter of a deceiver!" Leah, however, had a quick and clever retort: "Is there a teacher without students? Did not your father call you Esav and you answered him?" (GR 70:19). Since Jacob passed himself off as Esav, how could he possibly condemn Leah for passing herself off as Rachel?

THE CONSEQUENCES OF RACHEL'S SILENCE

Rachel, the matriarch representing speech and revealed energy, remained silent at a most crucial moment. This act had repercussions for the following generations and for the Jewish people as a whole. It is responsible for God's promise to return the Jews from exile. Because Rachel "put a ban of silence on herself when she saw her wedding presents in the hands of her sister and said nothing," so, too, "all the greatest of her descendants forced themselves to be silent" (Est.R. 6:12). Queen Esther remained quiet about being a Jew, Benjamin kept quiet about the sale of Joseph, and Saul did not tell his uncle that Samuel was making him king (1 Samuel 10:16).

While Rachel's silence led to "all her children practic[ing] concealment," Leah and her descendants (Judah, David, and Daniel) all gave thanks (GR 71:5). Thus, as Rachel took an inner role, Leah took an outer role. The significance of Rachel's silence (i.e., her loyalty to Leah) for the Jewish people as a whole is described in a commentary on *Eikhah* (Lamentations) for Tisha B'Av, the day when Jews mourn the destruction of the Temple in Jerusalem.

---

9. Ibid., p. 621.
10. Graves and Patai, p. 212.

When the First Temple was destroyed for the sins of murder, idolatry, and incest, Jerusalem was ravaged and the Jews were slaughtered and exiled to Babylonia. Avraham came before God, weeping and pleading for mercy for the Jews because he had been willing to sacrifice Isaac, but God was not moved. Isaac, too, came before God, pleading for mercy because he had been willing to be sacrificed, but again God was not moved.

Jacob then tried to arouse God's compassion because he had worked for Lavan for twenty years and risked his life in protecting his children from Esav, but God was not moved. Moses appeared and stated that he had led the Jews for forty years and did not get to see the Promised Land. Furthermore, he reminded God, mothers and children were being killed on the same day, something God had forbidden to be done even to animals! Still God was not moved.

Then Rachel came forward and spoke:

> Your servant Jacob loved me exceedingly and toiled for my father on my behalf for seven years. When those seven years were completed and the time arrived for my marriage, my father planned to substitute another for me to wed my husband for the sake of my sister. It was very hard for me, because the plot was known to me and I disclosed it to my husband; and I gave him a sign whereby he could distinguish between me and my sister, so that my father should not be able to make the substitution.
>
> After that I relented, suppressed my desire, and had pity upon my sister that she should not be exposed to shame. In the evening they substituted my sister for me with my husband, and I delivered over to my sister all the signs which I had arranged with my husband so that he should think that she was Rachel. More than that, I went beneath the bed upon which he lay with my sister; and when he spoke to her she remained silent and I made all the replies in order that he should not recognize my sister's voice. I did her a kindness, was not jealous of her, and did not expose her to shame.
>
> So if I, a creature of flesh and blood, formed of dust and ashes, was not envious of my rival and did not expose her to shame and contempt, why should You, a Ruler Who lives eternally and is merciful, be jealous of idolatry, in which there is no reality, and exile my children and let them be slain by the sword and their enemies do with them as they wish? (Lamentations, Proem 24)

God felt merciful and said, "For your sake, Rachel, I will restore Israel to its place." Consequently, "a voice is heard in Ramah, lamentation and bitter weeping, Rachel weeping for her children; she refuses to be comforted. . . . Thus says Hashem, 'Refrain your voice from weeping, and your eyes from tears [as] . . . there is hope for your future and your children shall return to their own border'" (Jeremiah 31:14–16).

The Jewish people will be restored from exile because of a woman who, in the midst of incredible rivalry, put sisterhood above all else. As the song says, there was no "mister" who could come between her and her sister. The *bnot/banot,* the daughters who built Israel, will also save it in the end.

THE RACE FOR (MALE) CHILDREN

Rachel and Leah's rivalry, however, was not over. From our modern perspective, the story of their struggle to outdo each other through bearing male children is heartrending. Pagan societies of the ancient Near East valued women as mothers of sons, and this mind-set has not disappeared in history. It is still a savage reality for women in many parts of the world, and it appears in modified form in more "enlightened" cultures.

In talmudic times, a childless woman was pitied. R. Ammi said, "Who gives a woman standing within her home? Her children [lit., sons]" (GR 71:5). Childless women are likened to prisoners—they "are bound within their homes and humiliated . . . [but] when the Holy One visits them with children [sons], they are raised up" (GR 71:1). Before a woman gives birth, her husband acts offensively to her, blaming her for things. Once she has a child (a son), the abuse "hangs on" the child—in other words, the man has somebody else to scapegoat (GR 73:5). This is an enlightening observation, indeed!

Son-preference in men was taken for granted by the Mishnah, which tells men that it is a "vain prayer" to ask God for a male child. However, the Gemara then determines a thirty-seven-day period in pregnancy during which it *is* allegedly efficacious—"from the third to the fortieth day he should pray that the child should be a male," it says, while R. Ammi's *son* teaches that a man will have male children if he puts his wife's sexual satisfaction before his own (Br. 54a, 60a).

Leah's desperation in hoping to gain her husband's love by churning out boys is understandable and sad indeed. Because she was forced on Jacob, Leah was not particularly loved by him. Because God saw that she was hated—Jacob wanted to divorce her (GR 71:2)—God gave her children and made Rachel sterile (GR 29:31).

Here we have a faint echo of polygyny at the time of the Flood: Leah, the childbearer, was hated, and lived without her husband's companionship, while Rachel, the sterile "beauty," was loved and cleaved to by her husband. By being forced into polygyny, Jacob became caught up in this misogynist dynamic. However, while polygyny flourished again after the Flood, none of the patriarchs *chose* this life-style: Avraham took Hagar at Sarah's command and did not marry Keturah until after Sarah's death, Isaac was monogamous, and Jacob wanted only Rachel but became polygynous because of Lavan's deception.

Leah "acted like those who are hated" because she was "married to a hater" and was ridiculed by society as well: "All hated her: Those across the sea hated her, those who walked in the roads hated her, and even the women who pressed grapes behind the beams hated her. And they said, 'This Leah, she hides behind an appearance of being righteous'" (GR 71:2). Notice, once again, the association of Leah with a *hidden* nature.

With each son Leah bore, she hoped to gain Jacob's affection. "See, a son!" she cried when Reuven was born. "God has seen my affliction; now my husband will love me!" At Shimon's birth she cried, "God has heard that I am hated, and has given me this also!" When Levi was born, her desperation reached a peak: "This time my husband will become joined to me, because I have borne him three sons" (Gen. 29:32–34).

Jacob did change his mind about divorcing Leah after she became the mother of his children. The security she began to feel at that point is evident in her naming of Judah, where she makes no reference to her husband at all. "This time I will praise God!" (Gen. 29:35) she exclaimed. With four sons, Leah was "ahead" of Jacob's other wives in producing the twelve tribes and thus began to transcend her despair.

RACHEL'S BARRENNESS

Rachel saw that she was not bearing any children to Jacob. She was jealous of her sister and said to Jacob, "Give me children; if not, I'll die!" Jacob became furious with Rachel. "Am I in place of Elokim?" he said. "It is God who is holding back the fruit of your womb." (Gen. 30:1–2)

Rachel was again in a relationship of envy with her sister. Her cry, which was as dramatic as those of her Aunt Rivkah, contained a threat to kill herself. Jacob seems angry because God, and not he, had closed her womb—and what could *he* do about it? Jacob was angry at Rachel for valuing herself only as a mother and not as a person, says Rabbi Isaac Arama, author of the fifteenth-century commentary *Akedat Yitzhak*. It was the culture, not Jacob, who valued women as producers of male heirs. Having children changed his mind about *divorcing* Leah, yet all the sons in the world could not have made him *prefer* Leah to Rachel.

Rachel blamed herself, seeing her barrenness as a sign that she was a bad person. She envied her sister "because of her good deeds, thinking, 'Unless she were more righteous than I am, she would not have been rewarded with children'" (Rashi).

Rachel's cry, "Give me children," was actually a reprimand of Jacob for not praying for her as Isaac did for Rivkah: "Is this how your father acted towards your mother? Did he not pray on her behalf?" she demanded (Rashi). Jacob did not pray for *them* to have children, as Isaac did, nor did he even pray only for himself, as Avraham did.

"You say that I should do as my father did," Jacob replied to Rachel. "But I am not circumstanced as my father was. My father had no children at all. I, however, have children. From *you* God has withheld children, not from me."

The selfishness of his response angered God (GR 71:7). Said the Holy One, "What a way to answer a woman in distress! By your life, your sons will in the future stand before her son"—in other words, the sons of the other mothers would stand before Joseph in Egypt to request famine relief.

Nachmanides finds it "impossible to think that Jacob did not pray on behalf of his beloved wife who was barren" and concludes that "his prayer was not accepted." Rachel "in her envy spoke improperly, thinking that because Jacob loved her he would fast, put on sackcloth, and pray until she would have children, so that she should not die of grief." Jacob's anger was kindled because she attempted to frighten him with her death, and his reply was said "to admonish and shame her" for that.

Rachel countered Jacob's selfish reply by reminding him that even though Avraham had Ishmael, he still wanted a child with Sarah. "Can you then do what my grandmother did?" Jacob challenged, reminding Rachel that Sarah had conceived only after giving Hagar to her husband.

"If that is the obstacle," Rachel replied, "here is my slave Bilhah."

Rachel never ceased being Jacob's most beloved, even though her barrenness made her "an object of reproach" to others (Rashi). The word for "barren" (*akarah*) is also the root of "chief" (*ikarah*). Hence, "she was chief of the house in compensation for Leah having children" (GR 71:4)—a far cry from the bound and humiliated woman described earlier!

"She was the chief wife of the house for whose sake Jacob had entered into relations with Lavan" (Rashi), "the main pillar of the house" (NR 14:8). In Genesis 46:19 she is called "wife" while the other women are not, because she was the mistress of the household. Even the descendants of Leah admitted this by naming her first. "All Jacob's descendants are ascribed to her" (RR 7:13).

Rachel did finally conceive, as a result of *praying for herself.* "The righteous woman Rachel, seeing that she could not rely upon Jacob's prayer, then went to pray on her own behalf" (Nachmanides). God "remembered her and heard her" (Gen. 30:22) "through many prayers" (GR 73:3), "because she had transmitted the signs to her sister" (Rashi), because of "her silence on her sister's behalf," and because she "brought a co-wife into her home" (GR 73:4). Rachel, like Sarah, conceived on Rosh Hashanah (R.H. 11a; GR 73:1).

BILHAH AND ZILPAH

Bilhah and Zilpah were Lavan's daughters through a concubine, and not by Adinah (GR 74:13, 74:14), meaning that the four women were two pairs of paternal sisters. Lavan gave Bilhah to Rachel and Zilpah to Leah, as servants upon their marriages (Gen. 29:24, 29:29). Although the custom would have been to give Bilhah, the elder slave, to Leah, the elder daughter, and Zilpah, the younger slave, to Rachel, the younger daughter, Lavan gave Zilpah to Leah as part of his plot to make Jacob think she was Rachel.

Bilhah had a son whom Rachel named Dan, "judged," as in "God has judged me and has also heard my prayer." Bilhah then gave birth to Naftali, "twisted," whom Rachel named so because "I have been intertwined with my sister through God's tortuous ways, and I have prevailed" (Gen. 30:4–8).

Not to be outdone, Leah gave Zilpah to Jacob. Because the Torah says *vatahar vateled* ("she got pregnant and gave birth") every time for Leah, Bilhah, and Rachel but only says *vateled* for Zilpah, GR 71:9 explains that "she was young and her pregnancy was not noticeable."

Leah named Zilpah's first son Gad, "fortune," because "good fortune has come" (*ba gad*). However, Rashi takes *bagad* as one word, meaning "faithless," and says that Jacob was faithless to Leah in marrying Zilpah. Because Leah was not barren, there was no justification whatsoever for using her slave in this way and Jacob should have refused her offer.

Nachmanides wonders what possible motivation Leah could have had, for "it is not natural for women to increase the number of their husbands' wives." He concludes that because the matriarchs foresaw there would be twelve tribes, Leah wanted the majority to be descended from her or Zilpah, "who was in her power, so that her sister Rachel would not prevail over her." He also hypothesizes that "Jacob wanted to have many wives in order to increase his progeny so as to inherit the Land . . . and so Leah wanted to give him her slave so that he would not wed a stranger."

Zilpah's second son, Asher, "happy," expresses Leah's sentiment upon having six sons, thus founding half the tribes.

THE MANDRAKES

Reuven took a walk during the wheat harvest and he found mandrakes in the field. He brought them to his mother, Leah. Rachel said to Leah, "Please give me some of your son's mandrakes." Leah replied, "Isn't it enough that you've taken my husband? Now you also want to take my son's mandrakes!" Rachel said, "In exchange for your son's mandrakes, [Jacob] can lie with you tonight." When Jacob came home from the field that evening, Leah went out to call him. She said to him, "You're coming to me tonight because I have hired your services with my son's mandrakes." So he slept with her that night. (Gen. 30: 14–16)

This passage is rather amusing, and it shows that Jacob's relationship with his wives was not that of a "master" and his "harem." Rather, Jacob's role was basically that of a stud. His wives negotiated who got him when, and he had nothing to say about it. The passage also teaches "how greatly [Reuven] respected his mother, for he would not taste of them until he brought them to his mother" (GR 72:2).

The mandrake (*mandragora officinarum*) has been used extensively in herbal medicine and was "at one time considered the greatest plant of all, a miracle worker that could cure anything and everything." It was considered effective as an anesthetic, an anti-inflammatory, a suppository, an emetic, a purgative, and an aphrodisiac. "It was also believed to quiet hysterics, induce sleep, and end female sterility. As a love potion, it was used to facilitate pregnancy. In 1963 a number of Indian scientists in Bombay reported that an extract from the [mandrake] consistently brought about the birth of *boy* babies in sterile women!"[11]

However, "Rachel wanted the mandrakes for delight and pleasure, for Rachel was visited with children through prayer, not by medicinal methods. Reuven brought the branches. . . . The stem, however, . . . he did not bring, and it is the stem which people say is an aid to pregnancy. . . . It is possible that Rachel wanted the mandrakes in honor of Jacob to perfume his couch" (Nachmanides), or she may have offered them as a sacrifice (Kaplan).

---

11. Brett L. Bolton, *The Secret Powers of Plants* (New York: Berkley Publishing, 1974), pp. 147–148.

"It was not the mandrakes that made Rachel bear children," but the plant was an instrument that God used and was "responsible for the birth of Yisakhar" (*Zohar* I:156b). This is because mandrakes "are a help to women who are slow in childbearing, but not barren, the latter being under the influence of *mazal* [fate]." The mandrakes helped Leah, who had stopped bearing (i.e., slowed down)—not Rachel, who had never conceived.

It was, in fact, the sister who no longer possessed the mandrakes who got pregnant on the night of the exchange! Leah gave birth to three children in succession: Yisakhar, Zevulun, and Dinah. Perhaps it was her generosity in *giving away* the mandrakes that caused God to reopen her womb.

Leah first gave birth to Yisakhar, "reward," because "God has given me my reward since I have given my slave to my husband." *Sakhar* is also the word used for "hiring" Jacob's "services." Leah then gave birth to Zevulun, "residence," for "now let my husband [permanently] reside with me." She now had a total of eight sons, or two-thirds of the tribes: six of her own and two through Zilpah. Then she had a daughter named Dinah.

"Come and see how beautiful was the negotiation of the mandrakes, for through these mandrakes there arose two great tribes in Israel—Yisakhar and Zevulun. Yisakhar studied the Torah while Zevulun went out to sea and provided Yisakhar with sustenance, so the Torah spread in Israel" (GR 72:5). Yisakhar "holds fast to the Torah more than all the other tribes"; through him, "the fragrance of the Torah ascended to the presence of the Almighty" (*Zohar* I:156b).

Rachel and Leah "each lost and each gained" (GR 72:3). Leah lost the mandrakes and gained the (two) tribes and burial with Jacob, while Rachel gained the mandrakes and lost the (two) tribes and the burial. Rachel's statement that "Jacob can lie with you" was considered an unconscious prophecy.

MATRIARCHAL PROPHECIES

"Six matriarchs" are sometimes referred to (NR 12:17; Est.R. 1:12; SS.R. 6:4-2): Sarah, Rivkah, Rachel, Leah—the *imahot*, or four matriarchs—are joined by Bilhah and Zilpah (who were freed from slavery and became *amahot*, meaning maidservants or secondary wives). Bilhah and Zilpah, like the four matriarchs, were prophets. The four wives of Jacob foresaw that he would beget twelve tribes, and they thought that each of them would have three (GR 71:4).

Rachel and Leah are said to have exercised prophecy in naming the children. We can learn something about this from how God's Name is used. God is mostly referred to by two Names in Torah: Hashem (God of Mercy) and Elokim (God of Justice). The former quality is more personal; the latter is natural law. Upon examination, the following pattern emerges.

Hashem is used in:

- Leah's conception and naming of Reuven, Shimon, and Judah; and
- Rachel's naming of Joseph.

Elokim is used in:

- Rachel's conception of Joseph;
- Rachel's naming of Bilhah's children; and
- Leah's conception and naming of Yisakhar and Zevulun.

Leah's first four children were the result of God's compassion for her being hated; her later children were simply a result of the laws of nature. (Levi is not included here, because Leah did not name him. Levi is the only child whose name is not the direct object of a feminine-gender verb ["whom *she called* —"]. Levi's name was given by a male or neuter source, which some assume was Jacob. However, Rashi says that Levi was named by the angel Gabriel, "who brought him into God's presence, called him by this name, and gave him the twenty-four gifts of the priesthood." The name *Levi* shows his connection, *lavah,* to those gifts.)

Rachel's prayer upon giving birth to Joseph was considered prophetic (GR 73:5–6), a supplication for deliverance from future calamities. Rachel *named* Joseph with the God of Mercy, but *conceived* him through the God of Justice. It felt like God's compassion to her, but perhaps it was just "fate" for her to not bear children until later in life.

Perhaps we also learn that divine compassion (the personal intervention of God) was more essential for a woman hated by her husband than for a woman who is socially unacceptable for being childless. The former suffers daily inside her home; the latter suffers only as much as she internalizes the outside society's view. (This is yet another Leah–inner and Rachel–outer link.)

Rachel called on Elokim in naming Bilhah's children, but God was not mentioned in Bilhah's and Zilpah's pregnancies, nor in Leah's namings of Zilpah's babies. The absence of a Divine Name on the part of the maidservants may be due to their initial state of slavery. Holiness cannot prevail when a free man has sexual relations with enslaved women. Moreover, Leah did not need to use Zilpah this way. The lack of God's Name with Levi and Dinah indicates a subtle linkage, which we will explore later.

TERAFIM AND TENTS

When Jacob could no longer stand Lavan's shady dealings, he wanted to leave, but he first consulted Rachel and Leah to gain their permission (Gen. 31:4–16).

Upon leaving, "Rachel stole her father's *terafim*" (Gen. 31:19), idol statues serving as household gods. Her intention was "to wean her father from idol worship" (Rashi). The *terafim* were frequently made from the shrunken heads of firstborn sons who had been sacrificed (SY 103; *Targum Jonathan*). The hair was removed, the head was salted and oiled, and a small tablet of copper or gold with a name written on it was placed under the tongue. The worshiper or diviner would then light candles in front of it and bow down to it. The head would respond to any questions asked of it "through the power of the name that was written on it."

Thus Rachel took the *terafim* for practical, safety reasons as well—so that Lavan could not use divination to discover her whereabouts or curse Jacob. "Not all *terafim* were for the purpose of worship. . . . [Some] are vessels to receive a knowledge of the hours, and they divine with them in order to gain knowledge of future events. . . . People of little faith set them up for themselves as gods . . . [and] their deeds are guided by divination revealed to them by the *terafim*. . . . Lavan was a diviner and an enchanter. . . . His country, too, was a land of diviners" (Nachmanides).

"Lavan was a great sorcerer who practiced all kinds of magical arts, and it was by such means that he learned all he wished to know" (*Zohar* I:164b). Without the *terafim,* it took three days for Lavan to find out that Jacob and his family were gone for good (Gen. 31:22). The *Zohar,* which says these particular *terafim* depicted a male and female image, notes that by sitting on the *terafim,* Rachel prevented them from speaking.

The astrological basis of the *terafim* created a delay in making new ones, as one had to wait for certain auspicious times: "They were derived from a close observance of the times and moments for striking and for holding off," the *Zohar* (I:164b) continues. "For when the craftsman was making [them], one who knew the proper seconds and hours stood over him, saying now 'strike' and now 'stay.' There is no other work which requires to be timed in this way."

Rachel was not really "stealing" in taking the *terafim;* they were rightfully hers. Because their father had cheated them out of the profits made from Jacob's labor, Rachel and Leah believed that Lavan's property was really theirs. "Is there still a portion and an inheritance for us in our father's house?" the sisters asked rhetorically. "He treats us like strangers! He has sold us and devoured our money! All the wealth that God has taken from our father actually belongs to us and our children!" (Gen. 31:14–16).

When Lavan finally caught up with them, he searched for the *terafim* by going "into the tent of Jacob, the tent of Leah, and the tent of the two maidservants. . . . When he left Leah's tent he went into Rachel's" (Gen. 31:33). The first tent mentioned "was Rachel's tent also, for Jacob was constantly with her" (Rashi; GR 74:9). Lavan went to Rachel's tent twice because he knew that she liked to touch the *terafim.*

Lavan appears to have gone to Leah's tent twice. However, Jacob had a tent of his own and Lavan went to each tent once (Ibn Ezra; Nachmanides). Rachel's is mentioned last because that is where the *terafim* were.

"It is true that there were separate tents for all of the wives," including each of the maidservants (Nachmanides). From our previous exploration of "tents," we realize the mystical significance of that statement. Nachmanides, however, attributes the phenomenon to "modesty . . . so that one [wife] should not know when he came to the other." (However, as we saw with the mandrakes, not only did the other wives know, they probably controlled it!) Jacob's tent was shared at mealtime with his children and his servants.

Rachel hid the *terafim* in the cushion on which she was sitting and told Lavan that she could not get up because she had her period. "I do not understand what kind of excuse this is," Nachmanides says, clearly puzzled. "Do women in that condition not rise or stand?" Perhaps she had menstrual cramps, he concludes. The excuse was much more purposeful than that, however—due to menstrual taboos Rachel could be sure that Lavan would not touch her *or* the cushion on which she sat.

Because Jacob had been so consistently defrauded by Lavan, on everything from wives to wages, Lavan's accusation that someone in Jacob's party had stolen the *terafim* angered him immensely. He did not realize that Rachel had taken them, so when he stated, "If you find your gods here, let [that person] not live!" (Gen. 31:32), he did not realize that he had just put a dreadful curse on his beloved Rachel.

❊❊❊ 8 ❊❊❊

Dinah: Rape Victim

Vayishlach (32:4–36:43)

Dinah's birth is recorded in Genesis 30:21. Ibn Ezra says she was Zevulun's twin, while *Baba Batra* 123a says that Dinah herself had a twin sister.

The majority of commentaries (Br. 60a; GR 72:6; Rashi) say Dinah was origi-nally Rachel's fetus and Joseph was Leah's fetus, but "Leah passed judgment on herself" (*danah Leah din*). Because tribal affiliation was patrilineal and Leah knew prophetically that there would be twelve tribes, she realized that if she bore the elev-enth son, Rachel could only bear one and would not even be equivalent with the maidservants, who had each borne two. Consequently, Leah prayed to have a girl, and God switched the fetuses.

This is the origin of Dinah's name, which means "judgment." *Genesis Rabbah* 72:6 relates her name to *dayenu,* "enough," because "the matriarchs were prophets. . . . All the matriarchs [i.e., Leah, Rachel, Bilhah, and Zilpah] assembled and prayed, 'We have enough males! Let this one [Rachel] be remembered.'"

Perhaps there are more esoteric and woman-positive reasons why Leah yearned for a daughter and why the mothers of all boys collectively exclaimed to God, "Enough males!" Such possibilities remain potent material for feminist musings.

The fetus-switching story establishes a link between Dinah and Joseph, which comes up again with Shechem—the city where Dinah was raped and Joseph was sold into slavery and buried. This link becomes more significant as time passes.

PROTECTING WOMEN FROM ESAV

Jacob looked up and saw Esav coming with 400 men. He divided the children with Leah, with Rachel, and with the two slavewomen. He put the slavewomen and their children first, Leah and her children behind them, and Rachel and Joseph last, and he

88

went ahead of them. . . . The slavewomen approached with their children and bowed down; Leah also approached with her children and bowed down. Then Joseph and Rachel approached and bowed down. (Gen. 33:1–3, 33:6–7)

This arrangement is explained as "the farther behind, the more beloved" (Rashi; GR 78:8). That is, the maidservants were put first because they were valued least by Jacob. Leah was next, and Rachel, whom he loved most, came last. Jacob's motivation is also explained in another way: "The Shekhinah never departed from the tent of Leah nor from the tent of Rachel. Jacob knew, therefore, that they were protected by the Almighty, so he put the maidservants and their children foremost." Regarding Rachel and Leah, Jacob thought, "I have no fear, since the Shekhinah is with them" (*Zohar* I:168b).

Joseph, however, feared for his mother. While the other women preceded their children, Joseph preceded Rachel. Feeling afraid that Esav would rape Rachel if he saw her, Joseph walked in front of her to block her from Esav's vision (Rashi; GR 78:10)—yet Joseph was only a little boy at the time! For using his "greatness"—his alleged height—like this, Joseph was later blessed with another type of greatness— a high position in Egypt.

Jacob went ahead of his entire party because he thought, "If that wicked man [Esav] comes to fight, let him fight me first" (Rashi). He is called "the most compassionate of the patriarchs" for his willingness to bear whatever harm Esav might inflict (GR 78:8). Jacob's sensitivity is also illustrated by the fact that he let the pace of the children and even the animals determine his speed (Gen. 33:13–14).

If the adult women were vulnerable, how much more so were female children! Hence, Jacob put Dinah "in a chest and locked her in so that Esav should not set his fancy on her" (Rashi). While this certainly seems like a wise precaution, given what we know about Esav, Rashi nevertheless asserts that Dinah was raped by Shechem as God's punishment of Jacob for hiding her. Claiming that Dinah's influence as Esav's wife would have led him to good behavior, he offers no evidence for this leap of faith, nor does he consider what the cost would have been to Dinah, had this even been possible. Was it not enough that Leah had wept so profusely in fear of marrying Esav? Should her daughter then be condemned to that fate?

Later, Rashi says that Dinah's rape was a punishment of Jacob for delaying the fulfillment of his vow (Gen. 28:20) to sacrifice to God. Either way, by viewing the rape as *a punishment of Jacob* rather than as *a crime against Dinah,* Rashi is expressing a common misogynist notion—that rape is an offense that one man commits against *another man* to hurt him through "his" woman.

This sentiment was graphically acted out by Black Power leader Eldridge Cleaver, who raped white women as "an insurrectionary act. It delighted me that I was defying and trampling upon the white man's law. . . . I was very resentful over the historical fact of how the white man has used the black woman. I felt I was getting revenge." The hypocrisy of his alleged concern for black women, however, is clear. "To refine my technique and *modus operandi,*" he notes, "I started out by practicing on black girls in the ghetto . . . and when I considered myself smooth enough, I crossed the tracks and sought out white prey."[1]

To suggest, as Rashi does, that God would punish a man by having his daughter raped is repugnant, for it presumes that God thinks and acts like a misogynist man. Instead, Jacob should be praised for protecting his daughter as he did.

DINAH GOES OUT

> Dinah, the daughter of Leah born to Jacob, went out to see the daughters of the land. Shechem, the son of Chamor the Hivite, a prince of the land, saw her and took her. He lay with her and violated her. Then his soul cleaved to Dinah, the daughter of Jacob, and he loved the girl [naarah], and spoke sweetly to [lit.,"to the heart of"] the girl. Shechem said to Chamor, his father, "get me this girl [yaldah] as a wife." (Gen. 34:1–4).

Much rabbinic commentary on Dinah's rape is sexist. Like modern rape victims, Dinah is blamed for "provoking" it, and the crime against her is used to justify women's seclusion from the public sphere. Dinah was raped because "her arm became exposed." She was like "a pound of meat" that "a bird swooped down and snatched away" (GR 80:5).

Dinah "brought upon herself her violation by Shechem" because she went out "while her father and brothers were sitting in the house of study" (Ecc.R. 10: 7-1). If men had allowed women to study, she would have been in the *bet midrash* with them!

"Like the daughter, so is the mother" (GR 80:1). Dinah's "going out" is related to Leah "going out" to Jacob (Gen. 30:16)—Leah "went out to call him adorned like a whore." That both women liked to "go out" is the reason why Dinah is specifically identified as the daughter of Leah in this passage (Rashi).

Women who initiate sex with their husbands, as Leah did, were also condemned as whores by Rabbi Solomon Ganzfried in his nineteenth-century *Kitzur Shulchan Arukh,* an abridged code of Jewish law. This book, which sometimes contains misogynist statements not found in the sixteenth-century *Shulchan Arukh* (Code of Jewish Law), from which it is mostly drawn, states: "When a man sees that his wife is coquetting and primping and trying to please him, he is bound to visit her even if it is not the appointed time, and from such a union will come worthy children. However, if she demands it openly, she is a brazen woman, and is considered like a whore, with whom he must not live together" (chap. 150, no. 8).

This view of Leah and other sexually aggressive wives is not found in other rabbinic sources, however. Leah's going out "appears to be immodest, but is really a proof of Leah's modesty that she said nothing in the presence of her sister, but went out to meet Jacob, and there told him in a low tone that, though he properly belonged to Rachel," he was to be with Leah that night (*Zohar* I:157a).

---

1. Eldridge Cleaver, *Soul on Ice* (New York: Dell-Delta/Ramparts, 1968), p. 14.

Leah also told Jacob that she

> obtained permission from Rachel; and in order that he might not become confused in the sight of Rachel, she spoke to him outside and not in the house. Moreover, one door of Leah's tent faced the road, and she brought him in by that door before he could enter into the tent of Rachel, so that she should not say anything in the presence of Rachel, which would have been immodest. She further reflected that once Jacob entered Rachel's tent, it would not be right for her to make him leave it; she therefore intercepted him outside. Leah went to all this trouble because *ruach hakodesh* stirred within her.

The Talmud is even more laudatory. "A woman who solicits her husband to sexual relations will have children the like of whom did not exist even in the generation of Moses." The people of the tribe of Yisakhar—the result of Leah's solicitation of Jacob—are called "men of understanding" (Er. 100b; Ned. 20b).

We have noted that Leah and Rachel have mystical significance as "inner" and "outer" energy, respectively. When Rachel departed from her normative manifest role and became "inner"—that is, remained silent rather than speaking—it had great positive consequences for the Jewish people. Now we can surmise that when Leah departed from her normative hidden role and "went out," that, too, had great positive results. Her action is, in fact, reflected in the halakhic norm that sexual relations in a Jewish marriage are determined by the woman, and not the man.

Misogynist interpretations of the creation of woman label Dinah a "gadabout" (GR 18:2, 80:5). Proceeding from the misbegotten notion that the original human was a male and that the woman was created from his rib, the Midrash claims that God pondered what part of Adam's body to use to create Chavah. If the head, she would have a proud bearing; the eye, she would be flirtatious; the ear, she would be an eavesdropper; the mouth, she would be a gossip; the heart, she would be jealous; the hand, she would be a thief; the foot, she would be a gadabout. However, in spite of not coming from these parts, women turned out to have all these traits anyway, the Midrash laments! The daughters of Zion (Isaiah 3:16) were haughty and flirtatious; Sarah was an eavesdropper, listening at the tent door; Rachel was jealous of her sister and stole the *terafim;* and "Dinah went out," the proof that women constantly wander around for no good reason.

Similarly, "women are said to possess four traits" (GR 45:5): greed (Chavah takes the fruit from the tree), eavesdropping (Sarah), laziness (Avraham tells Sarah to hurry and make cakes), and jealousy (Rachel). Other Rabbis add that they are talkative (Miriam speaking against Moses), thieves (Rachel), and gadabouts (Dinah).

Imagine if an all-female rabbinate sat around thinking up such vicious commentary on men, concluding that the actions of *one* man in *one* particular set of circumstances is indicative of *all* men at *all* times. This is what it would sound like. Men possess six traits: they are cowards (Adam blamed Chavah), liars (Avraham said Sarah was his sister), cheaters (Jacob pretended to be Esav), gang-rapists (the men of Benjamin—Judges 19), adulterers, and murderers (King David slept with Batsheva and then had her husband killed) (2 Sam. 11:2–17).

THE SECLUSION OF WOMEN

Male dominance and female seclusion are rationalized from Dinah's rape. Regarding Genesis 1:28, where *vekivshuah* refers to human stewardship of the earth (a feminine-gender noun), Rashi interprets (misinterprets) it to mean that the man should subdue the woman "in order that she not become a gadabout." He cites *Genesis Rabbah* 8:12: "The man subdues his wife so that she does not go out to the marketplace, for every woman who goes out to the marketplace will eventually come to disgrace. Whence do we know it? From Dinah, as it is written, 'And Dinah went out.'"

Rashi blames rape victims for being in public (Deut. 22:23): "A man found her in the city and therefore lay with her. A breach invites the thief. If she had stayed at home, this would not have happened to her." In other words, any woman who has the *chutzpah* to presume she has the right to some freedom of movement in her life makes herself fair game for rape!

Freedom of movement was all Dinah wanted:

> Lest one say here that Dinah was guilty of loose behavior, the narrative stresses that in no way was she at fault. . . . She was not in the habit of venturing forth for boys, but only "to see the daughters of the land," and to observe their ways. Nor should one say that she had already entered into promiscuous relationship with Shechem, as in fact he "saw her" for the first time and "took her" by force—and that is unmitigated robbery. . . . [Thus,] as she did not yield to him, it was rape, considered as inflicting torture upon her, which means that he was also guilty of robbery against her private person. (Malbim)

In fact, Dinah went out with Rachel, Leah, and *all* the women of Jacob's household, "to dance and rejoice" at a festival. Shechem saw her, had her kidnapped, and raped her at his house (SY 113).

Maimonides urges the virtual imprisonment of women while pretending that he does not:

> For every woman has the right to leave her home and go to her father's house in order to visit him or to a house of mourning or to a wedding as an act of loving-kindness to her friends and relatives, so that they may also come and visit her. She is not like a prisoner that she should neither come nor go. But it is shameful for a woman to leave her home continually, at times outside her house and at other times walking in the streets. A husband should prevent his wife from doing this. He should not allow her to leave the house more than once or twice a month, according to the need. For the beauty of a woman consists in her sitting in a corner of her home. (*Marriage* 13:11)

We should feel sorry for Mrs. Maimonides!

In ancient traditional societies, a woman on the street or in the marketplace—the public sphere—was assumed to be a prostitute. "Good" women stayed at home. Leah and Dinah both defied this custom, which modern societies reject but that still survives today in Islamic countries like Saudi Arabia and Iran. Where female seclusion is the norm, women must be veiled when they do go out; they have few, if any, political rights, and wife beating is considered normal "discipline." Even in twentieth-century America, many battered wives are not allowed to leave their homes without their husbands.

While such seclusion of women is not practiced in the modern Jewish world, the attitude that women are to blame if they are raped is still very prevalent among modern men. At one point in her early political career in Israel, Golda Meir was the only woman in the legislature. When the men proposed putting a curfew on Israeli women to "protect" them from rape, Meir replied, "It's the men who are doing the raping—put the curfew on them!"

Controlling men by confining women remains the logic of Orthodox rabbis today who, while not going so far as to seclude women in the home, still restrict their participation in the public sphere because of the possibility of male sexual arousal. If *a man* might become aroused, *the woman* must limit her behavior accordingly. Thus, if a man is aroused by a woman's voice, she should not sing, while if he is aroused by her hair, she should cover it.

It is one thing to require reasonable standards of modest dress, for both women *and* men, but it is quite another to say, as did Rav Kook, the first chief rabbi of Israel, that it is "an abomination" of the Torah to allow women to vote or hold public office! The Israeli rabbinate today still opposes women serving on political bodies such as town councils, and most of the halakhic restrictions on women regarding participation in synagogue ritual and serving as witnesses in a Jewish court of law also stem from the notion that women must be "protected" from (male) public view.

FEMINIST REVISIONISM

However, if rabbinic sexism regarding Dinah is disturbing, the "feminist retellings" of the story are even worse, as they deny that Dinah was raped and assert that "she wanted it"!

Deena Metzger's novel, *What Dinah Thought,* which was excerpted in *Lilith* magazine as "Transforming a Tale of Patriarchal Gore," is truly perverse. In "recasting the rape of the biblical Dinah by Shechem as a love story," Metzger mistakenly asserts it would have been "customary under the circumstances" for Dinah to have been killed by her brother. (However, it is Arab men, and not Jews, who kill their sisters or daughters for bringing "shame" on the family.) Metzger compares the slaughter of the Hivites with the massacres of Palestinians at Sabra and Shatila. However, the most sickening aspect of her tale is that she has Dinah engaging in necrophilia with Shechem, licking his circumcision wound, and dancing a striptease for her father![2] Rabbinic sexism is much more palatable by comparison!

Ita Sheres's book, *Dinah's Rebellion,* shares the same political agenda—an anal-

---

2. "What Dinah Thought," *Lilith*, 15:2 (Spring 1990): 8–12.

ogy between the Hivites and the Palestinians. Her analysis, proceeding from the assumptions of biblical criticism, asserts that Dinah's story was "rewritten" by "redactors" who made up the rape in order "to poison the readers' impressions of the young woman and her 'prince.'"[3]

"The story," writes Sheres, a university professor of Judaic studies, "is that of innocent love between two young people who were ready to merge culturally, politically, and religiously. . . . Dinah and Shechem must be seen as a man and a woman who accidently met and, in a rather romantic vein (not too different from Romeo and Juliet), committed themselves to each other."[4] In a strange twist of logic, Sheres sees Shechem as the good guy and Jacob and his sons as the bad guys. "Shechem is the only person in the tale that is sympathetic to Dinah," she maintains.[5]

Shechem's behavior after the rape does not indicate remorse or "love." A man cannot love a woman he has just raped. The Torah describes what he may have *thought* he felt, but it was not objective reality. Shechem's behavior is best explained by comparing it to this woman's description of her Harvard University fraternity party rapist. "He started asking if he could have my phone number," the woman said. "We had been talking earlier about going out and he reminded me that I hadn't given it to him and he needed it. I've since discovered that's really normal—these kinds of guys don't think they did anything wrong, in this kind of rape. If they've made a date with you earlier, they remind you. That's when I really got scared—that showed me what a freak he was. He didn't think there was a problem."[6]

For some men, a woman is there for the taking and it is his prerogative to take her. He may even believe that when a woman struggles and says "no," she really means "yes." Such a man accepts as a matter of course that women exist for the fulfillment of his pleasure, and it does not even occur to him to wonder what the woman wants; he believes her will is merely to do his will.

Shechem would be particularly likely to have this mentality; as a member of his society's ruling class—the city is even named after him—he was used to taking and having whatever he wanted. (Perhaps, as prince, he was used to "ritually deflowering" all the virgins!) Dinah must have been terrified by his psychopathic personality.

The so-called "sweet-talk" in which he engaged after the attack was purely financial: Shechem tried to bribe Dinah. "Your father has one little plot of a field, and see how much money he has put into it! I will marry you and then you will own the city and all its fields" (Rashi). While Rashi thinks that these were "words that would appeal to her heart," they are certainly not the average *woman's* idea of romantic conversation!

Dinah was indeed raped—and sodomized (GR 80:5). Nachmanides describes the attack: "The girl did not consent to him and she steadily protested and cried." However, he disagrees that she was sodomized: "There is no need for this, for all forced sexual connection is called 'violation.' . . . Scripture thus tells—in Dinah's praise—

3. Ita Sheres, *Dinah's Rebellion* (New York: Crossroad, 1990), p. 87.
4. Ibid., pp. 89–90.
5. Ibid., p. 137.
6. Adrian Walker, "Fighting Rape's Stigma," *The Boston Globe,* Apr. 17, 1991, pp. 1, 18.

that she was forced and she did not consent to the prince of the country." *That* is the feminist version of the story.

SHIMON AND LEVI'S REVENGE

Dinah was held captive in Shechem's house while his father, Chamor ("ass"), tried to acquire her permanently through marriage negotiations with Jacob and his sons. Dinah's maternal brothers plotted to rescue and avenge her. This is the real reason why Dinah was called the "daughter of Leah," to emphasize her link with the *sons of Leah* who came to her rescue (Nachmanides).

Demanding that the Hivite men be circumcised if they wished to intermarry with Jacob's clan, Shimon and Levi then attacked them while they were recovering. The brothers killed all the men, rescued Dinah from Shechem's house, and took at least eighty-five Hivite virgin girls (if not all the women) and forty-seven boys as captives. The captives threw out their idols, changed their clothes (i.e., immersed themselves in a *mikvah*), and became slaves in Jacob's household. One little girl (a *naarah ketanah*) named Bunah was taken by Shimon as a wife (SY 119; Gen. 35:2, 35:4).

Had Shimon and Levi only killed Shechem, their action would have fulfilled every rape survivor's fantasy. In their massive plundering, however, they subscribed to the notion, which is still common today, that the solution to male violence is more male violence. They also subjected the captured Hivite females to a fate not much better than Dinah's—especially Bunah, for marriage-by-abduction is certainly akin to rape.

Jacob was angry with Shimon and Levi "because they killed the men of the city who had committed no sin. . . . They should have killed Shechem alone. . . . Shimon and Levi killed them without cause, for they had done them no evil at all" (Nachmanides).

Shimon and Levi did not consult Jacob before acting (Rashi; GR 80:10). The Canaanites had a tradition that they would fall by the hands of Jacob's sons; thus, Jacob was afraid that they would now (mistakenly) think that the conquest of Canaan had begun and unite against him. When Jacob admonished his two sons for endangering him in this way, Shimon and Levi indignantly replied, "Should he be able to treat our sister like a whore?"

Shimon and Levi's propensity to commit violence as a pair is further indicated by the tradition that it was they who plotted against Joseph (Gen. 37:19) and Shimon who cast Joseph into the pit (GR 84:16). Shimon was later imprisoned by Joseph (Gen. 42:24) to separate him from Levi, lest the two again conspire to kill him (GR 91:6).

Thus, when Jacob blessed his sons on his deathbed, he said of Shimon and Levi, "Instruments of violence are their wares. . . . Cursed be their anger, for it was fierce, and their wrath, for it was cruel. I will . . . scatter them in Israel" (Gen. 49:5–7). Levi received no land at all in Israel, and Shimon's land was contained within Judah's portion.

On the other hand, rescuing Dinah from the prince's palace would certainly have provoked a war with the entire (male) nation. Moreover, citing the Noachide requirement that gentiles set up courts, Maimonides asserts that "all the men of Shechem were liable for the death penalty. For Shechem robbed, and they saw it and knew it and did not judge him" (*Kings and Their Wars* 9:14).

"Shechem would never have done this if it had not been considered acceptable, common practice for the leaders of the city to take the daughters of the people without their consent" (Sforno). Shimon and Levi acted reasonably (GR 80:2), and Shimon was even rewarded; because he "had been zealous to avenge the sexual degradation of his sister in Shechem," he was "privileged to present his offering" after Reuven at the dedication of the Tabernacle in the desert (NR 13:19). His offering paralleled the Tabernacle's structure because "it afforded an analogy to the action of Shimon [who] had been zealous to punish sexual degradation and had slain all the men of Shechem for having violated his sister, Dinah."

This link with God's House is also found in the prayer recited by Judith as she prepared herself to kill Holofernes, the Syrian-Greek general who carried out the prenuptial rape of Jewish women during the oppression that led to the rebellion of Chanukah. "Hashem, God of my forefather Shimon!" Judith invoked:

"You put in his hand a sword to take vengeance on those who stripped off a virgin's veil to defile her, uncovered her thighs to shame her, and polluted her womb to dishonor her! . . . Now hear a widow's prayer. . . . You see the Syrians assembled in their strength. . . . Shatter their strength by Your power and crush their might in Your anger. For they have planned to desecrate Your sanctuary, to pollute the dwelling place of Your glorious Name, and to strike down the horns of Your altar with the sword. Mark their arrogance, pour Your wrath on their hands, and give to me, widow as I am, the strength to achieve my end. . . . Shatter their pride by a woman's hand." (Judith, chap. 9).

In her struggle against the rape of Jewish women, Judith compared the Syrian-Greeks' plundering of the Temple to the rape of Dinah. That is, a woman's body is a temple and her sexual and reproductive organs are the holy of holies. Like the Holy of Holies in the Temple—which was covered by a veil, or hymen—God's Presence dwells there and man must not desecrate this sacred space.

We noted that God's Name was not mentioned in the namings of either Levi or Dinah. Levi (the passive partner in the Shimon–Levi duo) became the tribe that took care of the Temple service. Here we see that Dinah is the Temple itself. Perhaps because of this link with God's House, no (further) mention of God was required.

WHATEVER HAPPENED TO DINAH?

Dinah did not want to leave Shechem's house, so Shimon and Levi had to drag her out (GR 80:11). "When a woman is intimate with an uncircumcised man, she finds it hard to tear herself away," R. Huna surmises. How would he know—and are we to believe that Dinah "enjoyed" her rape because the rapist had a foreskin?

However, R. Huna continues. "She pleaded, 'And I, where shall I carry my shame?' [the words of another rape victim in 2 Samuel 13:13] until Shimon swore that he would lift her up [*notlah*]." Shimon promised to exalt her, to lift her out of her shame. Some translators think that this means he married her, but that seems unlikely, given that they were maternal siblings and that such a marriage was considered incestuous, even by the pagans.

Rather, it seems that Dinah was pregnant from the rape, and Shimon promised to adopt the child. Thus, when Genesis 46:10 refers to Shaul, a son of Shimon by "the Canaanite woman," the Midrash asserts that this phrase is a euphemism for Dinah, and that Shaul, her son, was adopted by Shimon.

That Shimon took Dinah to live with him indicates that the rape rendered her "unmarriageable." In contrast to the notion that a virgin must be ritually deflowered before marriage, we now see the development of the idea that a girl must be a virgin to be married; otherwise she is "damaged goods" and no man will want her. This reality is reflected by the command (Deut. 22:28–29) that a rapist must marry his victim if she demands it and may never divorce her. This may have acted to curb the practice of "hit-and-run" defloration by a stranger, but it also shows how oppressed these women were, when marrying their rapists "protected" them from an even worse fate.

The Moslem world provides a modern example of this custom. In the 1971 war in Bangladesh, more than 200,000 women were raped by Pakistani soldiers. Bangladeshi men, fighting for the liberation of their country, would not extend the politics of liberation to taking back the raped women, whose only possible future consisted of life as a beggar, prostitute, or suicide victim.[7]

Dinah could only have married Shechem, but Jacob's family would not give Dinah to him. Rape was "an obscenity in Israel" (Gen. 34:7), whereas in Canaan it was not. (Rashi specifically defines the obscenity as "violation of a virgin," lending credence to the notion that ritual defloration is referred to here.)

Had "the nations of the world learned to guard themselves against sexual immorality as a consequence of the Flood" (Rashi; GR 80:6)? "I do not know this, for the Canaanites were immersed in sexual immorality with women, beasts, and males . . . and they did not begin such practices in that generation; even in the days of Avraham and Isaac the patriarchs feared lest they kill them in order to take their wives. . . . This is why it said 'in Israel,' for it was not an obscenity among the Canaanites" (Nachmanides).

There is a tradition that Dinah married Job (GR 19:12, 57:4, 76:9, 80:4), but Nachmanides agrees that she lived in Shimon's house as a widow:

> Shimon took her, and upon her death, he buried her in the land of Canaan. . . . She was with him in his house as a widow, she went down with them to Egypt, and there she died, but was buried in the Land of Israel.
>
> Her grave is known to this day as being in the city of Arbel with the grave of Nitai the Arbelite [leader of the Sanhedrin in the early days of the Hasmoneans]. It is possible that Shimon brought up her remains from Egypt out of compassion for her while

---

7. Susan Brownmiller, *Against Our Will* (New York: Simon and Schuster, 1975), pp. 78–86.

the Israelites were still in Egypt, or that the children of Israel brought them up together with the bones of her brothers, all the tribes.

DEVORAH

Devorah, Rivkah's nurse, died, and she was buried in Beth-El, under the oak. He [Jacob] called its name Alon Bakhut ["weeping oak"]. (Gen. 35:8)

Devorah, the daughter of Milkah's firstborn son, was Rivkah's cousin and nurse and accompanied Rivkah when she went to Canaan with Eliezer. Rivkah sent her back to Padan Aram after Jacob had been there fourteen years to tell him it was safe to come home. However, Jacob could not yet get away from Lavan, so while the other members of her party returned to Canaan, Devorah stayed with Jacob for his last six years in Padan Aram (SY 101–102; Rashi).

However, "the weeping and anguish could not have been such for the passing of the old nurse that the place would have been named on account of it. Instead, Jacob wept and mourned for his righteous mother who had loved him and sent him to Padan Aram and who was not privileged to see him when he returned" (Nachmanides). Because *alon* is Greek for *another* (Rashi), Devorah's death was thus an allusion to another death—Rivkah's.

THE DEATHS OF RIVKAH AND RACHEL

"Because the time of [Rivkah's] death was kept secret in order that people might not curse the one who gave birth to Esav, Scripture does not publicize it" (Rashi). However, neither is the death of Leah mentioned, while Esav's presence at Isaac's burial is. Rivkah's death is not mentioned because it "lacked honor, for Jacob was not there, and Esav hated her and would not attend. Isaac's eyes were too dim to see, and he did not leave his house. Therefore, Scripture did not want to mention that she was buried by the Hittites" at night so no one would know (Nachmanides).

How sadly ironic it is that Rivkah was buried by the very people whose culture she had hated so much! Assuming that she was 14 at her marriage, Rivkah was 133 years old when she died.[8]

No sooner did Jacob learn he had lost his mother than he lost his wife: Rachel died giving birth to Benjamin (Gen. 35:16–20). One source says that she was thirty-six years old,[9] and another, that she was forty-five (SY 124). The date was 11

8. Eliezer Shulman, *The Sequence of Events in the Old Testament* (Israel: Bank Hapoalim and Israel Ministry of Defense, 1987), p. 25.
9. Ibid., p. 24.

Cheshvan 2207 A.M. (1555 B.C.E.), a *Shabbat.*[10] Leah died in 2216 A.M. (1546 B.C.E.), when Joseph was sold into slavery; she was either forty-five years old[11] or fifty-one (SY 145). (See Table 8–1.)

Jacob said, "The death of Rachel is more grievous to me than all the calamities which have befallen me" (RR 2:7). Was this perhaps because he had caused it by his inadvertent curse on her?

It has also been suggested that Rachel died then because the Torah's (later) prohibition of a man marrying two sisters cast its aura on Jacob once he entered the Land of Israel. For this reason, also, Jacob could not be buried with more than one wife at the Cave of Machpelah, "for he would be embarrassed before his ancestors. Now Leah was the one he married first, and thus her marriage was permissible" (Nachmanides). Therefore, Rachel was buried on the road to Efrat, outside Bethlehem.

Jacob foresaw that the Jewish captives exiled to Babylonia would pass by that site, so he buried her there that she might pray for mercy for them, in fulfillment of the prophecy that she would weep for her children. Her voice would be "heard in Ramah"—in Benjamin's portion (Rashi; GR 82:10).

Table 8–1. The Matriarchs and Patriarchs

Name	Lifespan	Birth A.M. (B.C.E.)	Events	Death A.M. (B.C.E.)
Avraham	175 yrs.	1948 (1814–13)	• Left Ur—2018 • Left Charan—2023	2123 (1639–38)
Sarah	127 yrs.	1958 (1804–3)	• To Pharaoh—2023 • Hagar bore Ishmael —2034	2085 (1677–76) *Cheshvan*
Isaac	180 yrs.	2048 (1714–13)	• Binding—2085 • Blessed Jacob—2171	2228 (1534–33)
Rivkah	133 yrs.*	2074 (1688–87)	• Married Isaac—2088	2207 (1555–54)
Jacob	147 yrs.	2108 (1654–53)		2255 (1507–6)
Rachel	36 yrs.**	2171 (1591–90)	• Married Jacob—2192 • Gave Bilhah to Jacob —2195	2207 (1555–54) 11 *Cheshvan*
Leah	45 yrs.**	2171 (1591–90)	• Married Jacob—2192 • Gave Zilpah to Jacob —2196	2216 (1546–45)
Joseph	110 yrs.	2199 (1563-62)	• Sold into slavery—2216 • Put in prison—2217 • Viceroy—2229	2309 (1453–52)

* According to the view that she was age 14 at her marriage.
** According to Eliezer Shulman.

---

10. The date of the month is given by Eliyahu Kitov, *The Book of Our Heritage,* vol. 1 (New York: Feldheim, 1978), p. 265. The year is given by Shulman.

11. Shulman, p. 24.

There is also a more practical reason why Rachel was buried there. She died suddenly; how could Jacob "leave his children and his flocks on the road and hurry with her body to the Cave of Machpelah? And where could he find doctors and medicines to embalm her? . . . Even though the Cave of Machpelah is but a half-day's distance from the place of her death, Jacob was heavily laden with much cattle and family, and he would not arrive there for many days . . . 'The bier of a woman may never be set down, out of respect' [M.K. 27a]" (Nachmanides). Again we can see the symbolism of Rachel as manifest energy and Leah as hidden energy, for "Rachel's death and burial place are recorded, but neither the death nor the burial place of Leah is recorded" (*Zohar* I:175a).

Although Rachel named the baby Benoni ("son of my oppression") in reference to her dying, Jacob changed his name to Benjamin, meaning "son of the south"—the only one born in Canaan—or "son of his days"—referring to Jacob's old age (Rashi). Jacob misunderstood Benoni to mean "son of my power" and did not intend to change the meaning by calling him Benjamin, "son of my right hand" (a symbol of power). "Jacob wanted to call him by the name his mother had called him, for all his children were called by the names their mothers had called them" (Nachmanides).

REUVEN AND BILHAH

After Rachel's death, "Reuven went and lay with Bilhah, the concubine of his father" (Gen. 35:22). Is this another case of rape, or did Bilhah consent, making it an act of incest and adultery? According to the Rabbis, it was neither. "Whoever maintains that Reuven sinned is mistaken" (Shab. 55b). The real meaning is that "he upset his father's bed" because "he resented his mother's humiliation." It was bad enough, in his view, that Leah's own (maternal) sister had to be her rival; should Rachel's maidservant—her paternal sister and a former slave—now be her rival as well? Once Rachel died, Jacob put his bed in Bilhah's tent, making his primary residence with her. Reuven moved his father's bed out of Bilhah's tent and into Leah's.

However, R. Shimon b. Elazar's statement, "That righteous man was saved from that sin and that deed did not come to his hand," seems to imply that Reuven might have been *tempted* to sleep with her—in order to make it impossible for her to continue a sexual relationship with Jacob, according to the laws of adultery—but he did not succumb to the impulse.

The Talmud also says he upset *her* bed. "Others say he upset two beds," it explains, "the Shekhinah's and his father's." Rashi here notes that "Jacob set a bed for the Shekhinah in the tents of each of his wives, and where the Shekhinah came to rest, there he spent the night."

Zohar I:175b, presuming that Leah had also died by this time, maintains:

In spite of the words of the text, we are not to suppose that Reuven really lay with Bilhah. . . . During the lives of Leah and Rachel the Shekhinah hovered over them; and now that they had died, the Shekhinah never departed from the house, but took up Her abode in the tent of Bilhah. She would not have been found there had not Jacob formed a new union of male and female. But Reuven, in his displeasure at seeing Bilhah filling his mother's place, came and upset the bed; and because the Shekhinah rested on it, it is written, 'And he lay with Bilhah.' . . . Reuven laid himself down to sleep on that bed, thus showing disrespect to the Shekhinah.

Reuven was afraid that Jacob would beget more children with Bilhah and replace the twelve tribes with them. "What he did was to prevent her from having sexual relations with his father, and this was the object of upsetting his father's bed; moreover, he did it in the presence of the Shekhinah, for the Shekhinah is always present whenever marital intercourse is performed as a religious duty. Whoever obstructs such a performance causes the Shekhinah to depart from the world" (*Zohar* I:176a).

The Ari says that Menasheh and Efraim were meant to be fathered by Jacob on that night (instead of later by Joseph), and Reuven's action prevented this. As Leah's *and* Jacob's firstborn, Reuven would have received a double portion of the inheritance, and he did not want it reduced by Jacob having more heirs—especially from the "Rachel side of the family." Because he did this, it was *midah kneged midah* that Jacob gave the birthright to Joseph, Rachel's firstborn, instead (Nachmanides; Gen. 49:4).

The Rabbis believe that had Reuven actually slept with Bilhah, he would not have been included in the twelve tribes at all and his descendants certainly would not have been allowed to stand on Mount Ebal and put a curse on men who lie with their fathers' wives (Deut. 27:13, 27:20).

TIMNA

Timna was the concubine of Elifaz, the son of Esav, and she bore, to Elifaz, Amalek. . . . Lotan's sister was Timna. . . . These are the names of the tribes of Esav: . . . the tribe of Timna." (Gen. 36:12, 36:22, 36:40)

Timna was "a princess [lit., "daughter of kings,"] . . . an uncrowned ruler. Desiring to convert, she went to Avraham, Isaac, and Jacob, but they did not accept her. So she went and became a concubine to Elifaz, the son of Esav, saying, 'It is better to be a slave of this people than a mistress of another people.' From her descended Amalek, who afflicted Israel [Ex. 17:8]. Why so? Because they should not have rejected her" (San. 99b).

"This tells you how important Avraham was, how eager people were to attach themselves to his seed. . . . She said [to Elifaz], 'If I am not worthy to marry you, let me be your concubine!'" (Rashi).

The story of Timna teaches the dangers of rejecting sincere converts. Amalek was the progenitor of many oppressors of the Jews—Haman and even Adolf Hitler are said to be his descendants. Had Timna been accepted by the patriarchs, she would not have joined Esav's family. That she did shows that even a remote connection to the patriarchs was more preferable to her than none at all. Perhaps her ascendancy to tribal chief in Esav's clan was her reward for being willing to reduce herself from a Horite princess to a slave in the house of Isaac's son. Who knows how Timna's son might have turned out had she been accepted among the Jewish people?

MEHEITAVEL

His [a king of Edom's] wife's name was Meheitavel, daughter of Matred, daughter of Mei Zahav. (Gen. 36:39)

This description is similar to "Ahalivamah, daughter of Anah, daughter of Zivion," and similar questions are asked. Is Meheitavel the daughter of Matred (her father), who is the son of Mei Zahav (*his* father), or is Meheitavel the daughter of *both* Matred and Mei Zahav—her mother and her father? With Ahalivamah, the mother was mentioned first. In this case, Mei Zahav is the mother (Ibn Ezra). Their names are explained as follows (GR 83:4).

Meheitavel, the Edomite queen: "They adorned [*metivei*] their gods," "they adorned themselves for idolatry," and "they adorned women."

Matred, Meheitavel's father: "They erected towers [*maamidin turiot*] for idolatry," and "after adorning a woman for her husband, they drove her away [*tordin*] from her husband."

Mei Zahav, Meheitavel's mother: "When they became wealthy, they used to say, 'What is gold [*mah zahav*]'" That is, they took their wealth for granted.

This family is in a long list of lineages, comprising passages in the Torah that are not usually pondered for deep meaning or inspiration. However,

Did not R. Jochanan evolve 300 legal decisions through esoteric allusions from the verse, "His wife's name was Meheitavel, the daughter of Matred, the daughter of Mei Zahav"—decisions which he revealed only to R. Elazar? This shows that each incident recorded in the Torah contains a multitude of deep significations, and each word is itself an expression of wisdom and the doctrine of truth. The words of the Torah, then, are all sacred, revealing wondrous things. (*Zohar* I:145b)

What these three hundred legal decisions were, we will never know.

✧✧✧ 9 ✧✧✧

Tamar: Widow–Prostitute

Vayeshev (37:1–40:23)

Tamar's story (Gen. 38:6–30) is told in the midst of the account of Joseph's sale into slavery and his rise to viceroy of Egypt. Judah's sexual behavior—in going to a "prostitute"—is interjected in contrast to Joseph's resistance of sexual temptation in Potiphar's house.

Tamar married Judah's eldest son, Er, who practiced anal sex because—like the men of the generation of the Flood—he did not want his wife to become pregnant and "lose her beauty" (Yev. 34b; GR 85:4). For viewing Tamar as a sex object and denying her pleasure by perverting sex in this way, Er was considered evil by God and was killed.

Because Er died childless, Tamar had the status of a *yevamah*—a widow obligated to marry her deceased husband's brother in order to "raise up seed" for the dead man. That is, any child born to the *yevamah* and her brother-in-law (the *yavam*) would be considered the dead man's progeny for purposes of name and inheritance.

The *yavam* here was Onan, Judah's second son, but Onan was not interested in fathering a child who would not be considered his. Therefore, although he married Tamar as required, he practiced coitus interruptus, and God killed him, too. From this the Rabbis derived the halakhic prohibitions against male masturbation and any form of male birth control entailing the "spilling of seed," such as withdrawal or condoms.

Again a *yevamah*, Tamar had to wait for the third brother, Shelah, to grow up. None of these boys was even twelve years old (Nachmanides), so we can presume that Tamar was even younger. Judah had no intention of letting the third marriage occur, because he thought that Tamar was a *katlanit*, a woman who has "caused" two husbands to die and is thus prohibited from remarrying (Ket. 43b; Yev. 64a; Nid. 64a).

Tamar returned to her parents' house, living as a widow-in-waiting for several years. Because of *yibum*, or levirate marriage, she was not allowed to marry anyone outside her first husband's family. Seeing Shelah as grown-up (though he was not yet ten) and believing that Judah had tricked her, Tamar devised a plan to accomplish *yibum* with her father-in-law.

Did Judah institute *yibum* (GR 85:5)? Nachmanides calls it "one of the great secrets of the Torah concerning human procreation," hinting that the practice relates to reincarnation, and states cryptically, "The enlightened person will understand." (By this he means one who studies Kabbalah.)

> "The ancient Sages prior to the Torah knew there is great benefit in *yibum* by the brother. He is the one who takes precedence in it, and his next of kin after him, for any remaining relative who would inherit his legacy would benefit from it. And it was customary for the wife of the dead man to be married by the brother, or the father, or the nearest relative in the family. We do not know if this was an ancient custom before Judah. . . . Since he had received the secret from his ancestors he was quick to fulfill it." (Nachmanides on Gen. 38:8)

LEVIRATE MARRIAGE AND POLYANDRY

Levirate marriage was indeed "an ancient custom before Judah," which was not only common in the ancient pagan world but occurs in modern tribal societies as well.[1] According to Briffault, the (pagan) levirate was a vestige of fraternal polyandry— namely, whereas a woman once married several brothers *at a time,* later she only married them *in succession.* (Sororal polygyny also had a vestige, the sororate, in which a widower would marry his dead wife's sister.)

We have noted that polygyny continued to exist even where polyandry ended. Polygyny without polyandry—that is, a man's right to have several wives who must each be monogamous with him—certainly creates a male supremacist, sexual double standard. However, polyandry did not create the reverse situation for women, for it never existed without polygyny. At no time or place has a woman been allowed to have several husbands *who each had to be monogamous with her.* Polyandry, like polygyny, is a form of male sexual prerogative. Only mutual monogamy limits this prerogative.

In polyandry, men share the same woman in "a bond of brotherhood"; it is "part of the relation of tribal brotherhood" designed to "promote good fellowship among brothers."[2] A woman was acquired in marriage, not for an individual man, but for an entire household. The eldest brother in the household contracted marriages; his wives were then shared by his younger brothers—and sometimes by his father and uncles as well. If the elder brother divorced a wife, she was automatically divorced from the rest of the men, too.

---

1. Briffault, 1:767–771.
2. Ibid., pp. 633, 635, 678.

Polyandry was thus bound up with "the communal undivided household, in which all brothers remain in one family and share alike. . . . With the rise of individual economic interests, and the consequent breaking up of the communal fraternal household, polyandrous marriage is necessarily also broken up."[3] Polyandry indicates a form of male supremacy that we might call *fratriarchy* (preceding *patriarchy*, rule by the *fathers*), because biological paternity was uncertain and often irrelevant. Children either were considered the offspring of the eldest brother, were assigned fathers in rotation, or had their paternity decided by their mother.[4]

Polyandry today is mostly found in parts of Tibet, Nepal, and India. Among the Nyimba people of northwest Nepal:

> Several brothers share one, sometimes two, wives. The oldest brother, who heads the future household, chooses the first wife. She is often much younger than him and must wait to live with her future family. When she reaches puberty, she moves into the household of her father-in-law, where she takes on her duties as the wife of several men. Each brother has equal rights to sleep with the wife, who keeps peace by avoiding sexual favoritism.
>
> The importance of paternity differs among Nyimba villages. In one report, the first-born male was designated the child of the oldest brother, the secondborn of the second brother, and so on until each brother had someone to care for him in old age. In another instance, the family members carefully determined actual paternity for each child.[5]

This brotherly "sharing of wives" is the root of the custom of "hospitality prostitution," in which a man's generosity to his male guests includes offering his wife to them. In a society where a man is either a "tribal brother" or a stranger and potential enemy, the act of offering one's wife is "a necessary pledge that the guest is a friend and not an enemy"—a way of making a stranger into a "brother." For the guest to refuse is tantamount to a rejection of this bond and, hence, a declaration of war.[6] Modern forms of "wife-swapping" are a remnant of this as well.

In this light, we can see another level of significance in the fact that Sarah stayed "in the tent" while Avraham separately entertained his three guests: his hospitality did not include sharing his wife.

The progression from polyandry to the pagan levirate is illustrated by several points:

* In some cultures, the dead husband's brother was already a sexual partner of the woman, and his levirate obligation merely created an economic responsibility to her.

---

3. Ibid., p. 671.
4. Ibid., p. 659 n. 4.
5. "The People of 'Millennium'," *Cultural Survival Quarterly* 16:2 (Spring 1992): 68.
6. Briffault, 1:636.

• In polyandry, a younger brother had access to the wives acquired by his elder brother, but not vice versa. In the (pagan) levirate, usually the younger brother was obligated to the elder brother, but not vice versa.
• As a polyandrous wife was the communal property of her (primary) husband's family or household, so, too, was the levirate widow forever a part of her husband's family or household.

Sometimes the widow passed to the deceased man's father instead of his brother (as Nachmanides mentioned and as Tamar plotted). Some cultures required that the woman do a ceremony of "divorce" with the husband's corpse, while others released the widow after a temporary levirate—that is, she had to have sex with her husband's brother as a "purification rite" designed to avert the anger of her husband's ghost.[7]

LEVIRATE MARRIAGE IN THE TORAH

Given the origins of the levirate, why is *yibum* a *mitzvah* commanded by God in the Torah (Deut. 25:5–6)? Is this not simply maintaining a male supremacist practice? First of all, the Torah *limited* the practice. *Yibum* was required only under the following circumstances:[8]

• if the dead man had no children or grandchildren of either gender—even if the child was born after he died, and even if the child died;
• if the dead man had no children by any other wife, or even an illegitimate child by a woman forbidden to him. If *yibum* was done with one wife, it exempted any others to whom the man had been married;
• if the dead man had a brother living during his lifetime. Any brother born *after* the man's death was not permitted to marry the widow;
• if the brother was paternally, and not just maternally, related to the dead man;
• if the widow was capable of childbearing; or
• if the dead man had been capable of begetting children (i.e., he was not a eunuch).

The Torah limited the custom to the *brother's* wife. A man could no longer marry the childless widow of his father, his son, or his uncle (Nachmanides). Thus, Tamar was clearly following *pagan* levirate customs in having sexual relations with Judah— by Torah law it was incest. "It was only in the case of a brother . . . and the benefit is likely with him and not with the others. . . . Now it was considered to be very cruel when a brother did not want to do *yibum*" (Nachmanides).

Second, besides limiting *yibum*, the Torah also immediately provided a way to avoid it: *chalitzah* (Deut. 25:7–10), a ritual that releases the widow from her dead husband's brothers. The *yevamah* declares that the *yavam* refuses to do his duty,

7. Ibid., pp. 772–780.
8. This list is compiled from Elon, pp. 403–404, as well as from Rashi on Deut. 25:5–6.

removes his right shoe, and spits in (or toward) his face. This description assumes that the *yevamah* wants the *yavam* to marry her; that it is *he* who wants out and that he deserves to be humiliated by her for shirking his responsibility.

This view becomes understandable after examining the status of widows in the ancient world. As with the rape victim, the Torah law is meant to protect the woman from a worse fate. In this case, that fate could be murder, often by immolation on her husband's funeral pyre. This practice, called suttee, is still incumbent upon Hindu widows in India today, although it was *technically* outlawed in 1829.

Although labeled suicide, widow-sacrifice is clearly murder: "If she was so ill-mannered as to hesitate to do so, the husband's relatives used gentle pressure to compel her."[9] Then again, death may be preferable to a life of torture: "Fijian women, who are among the most brutally treated, insist upon being killed on the graves of their husbands."[10]

The Torah's admonitions on behalf of widows (Ex. 22:21–22; Deut. 24:17) are significant in this light. That widows are still sorely oppressed in much of today's world is demonstrated by this 1990 appeal from Africa:

> Among the Yako tribe in Cameroon a widow has no claim to her husband's property and no right to remain in her husband's compound after the funeral rites have been completed. The story is the same among the Ibos of Nigeria. Occasionally, in a polygamous family, the widow is married off to the deceased husband's first son by another wife.
>
> It is not only this deprivation of property that is appalling, but also the confinement and oppression to which widows are subjected. In many societies the widow is restricted to her late husband's compound during the traditional mourning period, and made to sleep on a mat on the floor. She is not allowed to bathe or comb her hair. If the husband was a titled chief, the daughters of the husband's clan may confine the widow for up to 21 days, during which she can't wash or change clothes. At the end of the mourning period, the widow scrapes her hair, washes, and puts on sackcloth black attire for one year. Although this confinement is no longer acceptable to educated women, when they object, they are often accused of being responsible for their husband's death. Therefore, in their bid to exonerate themselves, many widows still allow themselves to be subjected to the rigors of this tradition.
>
> How can a widow so dispossessed start a new life? What happens to the children of a widow whose husband's kindred have mismanaged and squandered the wealth? What fate befalls widowed homemakers who have been economically dependent all their lives? They face poverty, loneliness, feelings of inadequacy, insufficiency of income, and lack of health care. At times they are depressed, and their depression is taken for senility.[11]

Biblical law (written Torah) represents the first stage of lifting the widow out of her slave status in the pagan world. Rabbinic law (oral Torah), which has historically remained flexible in order to retain its relevance in the face of changing social

---

9. Briffault, 2:329.

10. Ibid., 1:133.

11. Hannah Edemikpong, "Nigeria: A Direct Appeal," *Ms.* 1:3 (Nov./Dec. 1990): 10.

conditions, continued that process. As a widow's social status improved, *chalitzah* was given an increasing priority over *yibum*, until eventually (among Ashkenazi Jews and in Israel), *yibum* was, in effect, legally canceled out of existence.

TAMAR'S RUSE

Tamar successfully accomplished *yibum* with Judah by disguising herself as a prostitute and sitting at a crossroads that she knew he would pass, as she had heard he was going to the sheep-shearing festival after completing the mourning period for his wife's death. When Judah saw her, he came over. Obtaining his seal, his cord, and his staff as a pledge for the goat that he would later try to send as payment, Tamar returned home pregnant and dressed again as a widow.

When Judah heard that his daughter-in-law was pregnant, he ordered her to be executed for adultery, since she was technically "married" to Shelah. When she produced the three items, stating, "I am pregnant by the man who owns these articles," Judah declared, "She is more righteous than I am." Tamar not only averted her death sentence, she also gave birth to twins, one of whom was the ancestor of the House of David and, hence, the Messiah.

The Rabbis have nothing but praise for Tamar. Her act was "based on a deeper knowledge" (*Zohar* I:188a–b), and she was operating with *ruach hakodesh* (GR 85:9). She did not even despair at being sentenced to death, "for her heart was like the heart of a lion" (Sforno). Her tact in exposing Judah was considered a model for all humanity: "It is better for a person to cast oneself into a fiery furnace than to put another to shame in public. Whence do we know this? From Tamar" (Br. 43b; Sot. 10b).

Even the fact that she was committing incest and adultery under Jewish law did not earn the Rabbis' condemnation. "Tamar committed adultery and gave birth to kings and prophets. . . . A transgression performed with good intention is better than a precept performed with evil [or no] intention" (Naz. 23b; Hor. 10b).

Judah, too, is praised for being a *mensch* in the end (Meg. 25b). Significantly, his fellow judges on the Court of Shem, which decreed the death sentence on Tamar (A.Z. 36b), did their best to overlook the truth of the matter. "Isaac and Jacob and all his [Judah's] brothers sat there covering up [*mechapin*] for him" (ER 30:19). When confronted with the evidence of the seal, cord, and staff, they tried to excuse Judah by saying he must have *lost* them! However, in spite of this male collaboration, which could have easily gotten him off the hook, Judah was big enough to admit his wrongdoing. For dealing justly with Tamar and not allowing her to be burned at the stake to save his own reputation, Judah was rewarded with the ancestry of the House of David.

Judah's sexual behavior in going to a prostitute is especially significant because the local people thought she was a *kedeshah* (Gen. 38:21–22), a "sacred," religious prostitute. Judah assumed she was a *zonah* (38:15), a "common" prostitute, whose body was used for sex with no pretense of religious significance. For a Jewish man to sleep with a *zonah* was a sexual offense, but to have sex with a *kedeshah* was idolatry!

The Rabbis, who were accustomed to associating the veil with "modesty," were confused that Tamar veiled herself for prostitution. Thus, one view states that she had covered her face with a veil *before*—while in Judah's house, as the wife of Er and then Onan—and so *now* he did not recognize her when she sat in the street (Meg. 10b; Sot. 10b). Hence, "a person [*sic*] should take heed of his wife's sister and his female relatives, so as not to stumble into sin with any of them" (GR 35:8).

However, the literal meaning is actually correct. Tamar veiled herself because

> it was the way of the *zonah* to sit at the crossroads wrapped in a veil that covered part of the hair and face, deceiving with the eyes and the lips, and exposing the throat and the front of the neck. Since she would speak to the passerby impudently, grab him and kiss him, she therefore covered part of her face. Also, the *kedeshot* [pl. of *kedeshah*] sitting by the roadside, who commit harlotry even with relatives, cover their faces. The *kedeshim* [male religious prostitutes] still do it to this day in their countries, and when they return to the city they remain anonymous. (Nachmanides)

Tamar's victory over Judah was *midah kneged midah*. What she said to Judah, *Haker-na*, "Identify this, please" (Gen. 38:25) is precisely what Judah said to Jacob in deceiving him with Joseph's blood-stained coat (37:32). Moreover, just as Jacob was deceived by (the blood of) a goat, so, too, Jacob had deceived Isaac by (the skin of) a goat. What goes around comes around.

ZELIKHAH

Potiphar's wife was named Zelikhah, זליכה (SY 158). Her story (Gen. 39:7–19) is juxtaposed to that of Tamar, for "just as that one acted for the sake of heaven, so too this one acted for the sake of heaven, for she saw through her astrological calculations that she was destined to produce children by him [Joseph], but she did not know whether from her or from her daughter" (Rashi; GR 85:2). Joseph later married Zelikhah's daughter.

Joseph is described as *yefeh-toar* and *yefeh mareh*, "well-built and handsome" (Gen. 39:6). Avraham called Sarah a *yefat-mareh* when he worried that Pharaoh would take her (Gen. 12:11). Rachel is described as *yefat-toar* and *yefat mareh* when Jacob falls in love with her at first sight (Gen. 29:17). Esther is called *yefat-toar* and *tovat mareh* when Persian King Achashverosh rounds up all the virgins in town and picks the one he likes best—Esther (Esther 2:7). *Yefat-toar* is the term used for a woman who is captured by a soldier in warfare (Deut. 21:11). The term thus indicates sexual objectification—a person's looks are all that matter in that moment.

Joseph "used to pay great attention to his personal appearance" (*Zohar* I:189b). He was "like a man who stood in the marketplace, making up his eyes, curling his hair, and lifting his heel" (GR 87:3; Rashi). Joseph had a lot of sex appeal, to men as well as to women. This made him very vulnerable. When Joseph's brothers went down to Egypt, looking for him, they went first to the prostitutes' quarter, for they thought, "Our brother Joseph is well-built and handsome; maybe he is in a brothel [as a male prostitute]" (GR 91:6).

Potiphar, Pharaoh's chief officer (*saris*, which also means *eunuch*), bought Joseph from the slave market to use for sodomy, so God punished Potiphar by castrating him (GR 86:3; Sot. 13b). However, Pharaoh's chief butler and baker were eunuchs, too (Gen. 40:2). Any man who was a "harem guard" or worked in the women's quarters of the palace was castrated to prevent his sexual involvement with the women. Judah is even said to have accused Joseph of keeping Benjamin (Gen. 44:18) because "as Pharaoh has a passion for males, so do you!" (GR 93:6).

Joseph's ultimate sexual struggle was with Potiphar's wife. Zelikhah, who was married to a eunuch, certainly had reason to be swept away by the presence of such a gorgeous man in her house. She was so desperately lovesick for Joseph that all the Egyptian women who visited her asked what was wrong. She made a banquet for them and, giving them knives to peel their fruit, had Joseph come in. "All the women looked at Joseph, and could not take their eyes off of him, and they all cut their hands with the knives, and all the citrons in their hands were filled with their blood. And they did not know what they had done, but continued to look at Joseph's beauty and did not turn their eyelids from him." When Zelikhah asked them what happened, "all the women saw their hands were full of blood, and their blood flowed down upon their clothes, and they said to her, 'This slave in your house has overcome us, and we could not turn our eyelids from him on account of his beauty.' 'If this happened to you in one moment,' Zelikhah responded, 'imagine what it's like for me, seeing him day after day!'" (SY 159–60).

As Potiphar's personal servant, Joseph was master servant of the household—yet he was, nevertheless, a servant. As mistress of the household, Zelikhah could order him to do tasks that would put him in close proximity to her. "She brought him from room to room and from chamber to chamber, until she brought him to her bed"— above which there was an idol with its face covered—but he would not even get close to her (GR 87:5–6). She constantly changed her clothes to try to attract him, and she even threatened him and tried to bribe him with money (Yom. 35b), but nothing worked. Joseph was tested in this way because he had insulted the sons of Bilhah and Zilpah by calling them slaves and had falsely accused them of casting their eyes on the daughters of the land (*Zohar* I:182b; GR 87:3). Thus, a "bear" (Zelikhah) was set upon him.

One festival day, when the Egyptians were all celebrating at the Nile, Zelikhah pretended to be ill and stayed home so that she could be alone with Joseph. R. Jochanan believed that "both had the intention of acting immorally," but that Jacob's image came to Joseph and "his erection subsided. . . . He stuck his hands in the ground and his semen came out from between his fingernails" (Sot. 36b; GR 87:7).

Zelikhah falsely accused Joseph of attempted rape. She told this to Potiphar while they were having "sex" (GR 87:9; Rashi)—so although he was a eunuch, they still had a sexual relationship. Potiphar knew that Joseph was innocent after examining the location of the tear in the coat (SY 163), but he imprisoned Joseph nonetheless to avoid any stigma on their children. Had Potiphar really believed he was guilty, he would have had him executed. A servant—even a valued one—does not sleep with his master's wife and get away with it. Had anything really happened, a rape charge would have saved Zelikhah, but not Joseph, from the death penalty for adultery.

Even with Joseph in prison, Zelikhah did not give up but rather visited him and continued threatening and trying to bribe him. "She went so far as to place an iron fork under his neck so that he should have to lift up his eyes and look at her. Yet in spite of that he would not look at her" (GR 87:10). Joseph feared Zelikhah, but he feared God more (Nachmanides).

THE TRIBAL MOTHERS

All [Jacob's] sons and daughters tried to console him. (Gen. 37:35).

His sons and his sons' sons were with him. His daughters and his sons' daughters, and all his seed, came with him to Egypt. . . . The number of people who came to Egypt with Jacob, who came from his thigh, except for the wives of Jacob, was 66. (Gen. 46:7, 46:26)

Who were Jacob's daughters? The only one we know of is Dinah. R. Nehemiah, who argued that Avraham was blessed by *not* having a daughter, asks: "How many daughters did he [Jacob] then have? One, and would that he had not known her!" The term *daughters* refers to Jacob's daughters-in-law, he says, who were Canaanite women (GR 84:21).

Ibn Ezra says that Genesis 37:35 refers to Jacob's granddaughters. Presumably, this would include the wives of Jacob's grandsons, such as Tamar. Nachmanides says that Genesis 37:35 refers to Dinah and to Jacob's granddaughter, Serach, the daughter of Asher, as well as being "an expression of love" for the daughters-in-law, while Rashi says that 46:7 refers to Serach and Yokheved, the daughter of Levi. Jacob's sons did not marry Canaanite women, Nachmanides emphasizes, but women who came to Canaan from Egypt, Ammon, Moav, and from Ishmael and Keturah.

However, R. Judah, who believed that Avraham was blessed with a daughter, disputes R. Nehemiah again by saying that each of the twelve sons had a twin sister and each son married a paternal sister. Benjamin had two twin sisters (GR 82:8).

Nachmanides, who had just finished explaining R. Nehemiah's view, now explains R. Judah's! Disagreeing with Rashi, who states that the twin sisters must have died before they went down to Egypt because they were not enumerated in Genesis 46, Nachmanides asserts:

There is no necessity for this conclusion. . . . These twin sisters were thus the wives of Jacob's sons. . . . R. Judah arrived at this opinion on the basis of this verse [Gen. 46:26], since if it refers to Canaanite women, what reason is there to say "except for the wives of Jacob" after it had already said "who came from his thigh"? It is only because his sons' wives were also of those "who came from his thigh" that Scripture refers to them. It does not, however, divulge them here, just as it did not mention them explicitly when they were born together with Jacob's sons.

If there were thirteen sisters besides Dinah, we will never know. If the twin-sister theory is true, it means that Jacob retained his daughters as his daughters-in-law, rather than sending them away in patrilocal marriages. That would have been a coup. However, given that his descendants are described as "his sons' sons and his sons' daughters"—in other words, only as the children of his sons—it seems likely that *daughters* really does refer to his patrilineal female descendants (i.e., his daughters-in-law and sons' daughters). Any biological daughters that Jacob may have had besides Dinah were probably lost to patrilocal marriage and patrilineal descent. This is alluded to by R. Judah, ironically, when he notes, "Sons' daughters are like your own children, but daughters' sons are not" (GR 94:6). (The same man who sees daughters as a blessing to a man nevertheless admits that her children are not considered his grandchildren!)

An actual lineage of tribal mothers is given (SY 165–66), which supports the view that the majority were not native Canaanites but rather the descendants of Shem and Ever; Terach, Milkah, and Nachor (Padan Aram); Ishmael (Egypt); Keturah (Midian and the "land of the east"); and Moav (Lot's son and grandson). The women's names are given in the following list, along with their tribal name, number of sons, father's name, place of origin, and any other available information.

1. אליורם, Eliyoram—Reuven (four sons). Daughter of Avi, a Canaanite from Timnah.

2. בונה, Bunah—Shimon (six sons). A Hivite captive of Shechem, "the Canaanite woman" who was mother of Shaul. She became Dinah's maidservant. The mother of Shimon's other five sons may have been Bunah, or possibly a Canaanite woman named Adivah or an Aramaean woman (Kaplan).

3. עלית, Aliyat—Judah (three sons, two of whom died). Also called Bat-Shua, Aliyat is briefly profiled in Genesis 38:2–5; she died (at the "turning of the year") in verse 12. She was the daughter of Shua, a Canaanite man who settled in Adulam. Judah met her through a business colleague, a merchant named Chirah who was foreman of his shepherds (Kaplan).

Ibn Ezra says that Er and Onan died because Judah married a Canaanite woman, but Nachmanides reminds us that Er died for his own sin, and not as a punishment to Judah for taking a leading role among the brothers in selling Joseph into slavery.

Judah married Aliyat because of her father (Nachmanides). Aliyat named her second son Onan ("mourner") because she had a very difficult labor, "for it is customary for women to name their children after such an experience" (Nachmanides)—as, for example, Benoni, the name Rachel gave to Benjamin as she died.

Judah named Er, and Aliyat named Shelah, whose place of birth, Kheziv, is mentioned either because that is where she stopped bearing children (Rashi) or because all three sons were born there (Ibn Ezra). Tamar, Aliyat's daughter-in-law, was also "the daughter of one of the strangers living in the land, not the daughter of a man who was a Canaanite by descent" (Nachmanides). Tamar is described elsewhere as a "daughter" of Shem (GR 85:10)—that is, the daughter of Shem's son, Elam.

4. עדינה, Adinah—Levi (three sons). First daughter of Yovav, son of Yaktan, son of Ever, in "the land of the east."

5. ארידה, Aridah—Yisakhar (four sons). Second daughter of Yovav.

6. אפללת, Aflelet—Dan (one son), after being barren and "remembered" by Elokim. Daughter of Chamudan of Moav.

7. מרימת, Merimat—Naftali (four sons). First daughter of Amuram, son of Utz, firstborn son of Milkah and Nachor of Charan. Merimat was thus Devorah's niece.

8. עוצית, Utzit—Gad (seven sons). Second daughter of Amuram, so she, too, was Devorah's niece.

9. עדון, Idon—Asher. Daughter of Aflal, son of Chadad, son of Ishmael. She died. Asher then married הדורה, Hadorah (four sons, one daughter). She was the daughter of Avimael, son of Ever.

10. מרושה, Merushah—Zevulun (three sons). Daughter of Molad, son of Avida, son of Midian.

11. מחליא, Machalia—Benjamin (five sons). Daughter of Aram, son of Zoba, son of Terach. Benjamin was ten years old when he married her. At age eighteen he also married ערבת, Aravat (five sons), daughter of Shomron, son of Avraham.

❊❊❊ 10 ❊❊❊

Asnat: Joseph's Wife

Miketz (41:1–44:17)

Pharaoh gave Joseph the name Zaphnat-Paneach. He gave him Asnat, daughter of Potifera, the priest of On, as a wife. (Gen. 41:45)

After Joseph interpreted Pharaoh's dreams and was made viceroy of Egypt, he received an Egyptian name that in Hebrew means "revealer of hidden things." In Egyptian it had a similar meaning: "Nut speaks life." Nut was an Egyptian goddess; her name is contained in both Joseph's Egyptian name, Zaphnat, and in *Asnat*. "Nut speaks life" described Joseph's gift of dream interpretation. The goddess, according to Pharaoh, had spoken through Joseph.

Asnat, in Egyptian, meant "belonging to Nut." In Hebrew, her name means "bush" *(sneh)*, because that is where she was found as a child (after which she was taken to Potifera's house). The bush and her upbringing in a royal household of Egypt immediately call to mind Moses, to whom God spoke at a burning bush and who was raised in Pharaoh's household. Asnat was thus a forerunner of Moses in being an Egyptian-raised Hebrew. Her bush may not have been "burning," but the reason why she was found there certainly is!

DINAH'S DAUGHTER

Asnat was Dinah's daughter from the rape *(Targum Jonathan; Sofrim,* chap. 21) who was driven out of Jacob's house after he tied a disk around her neck to indicate that she was of his family. Joseph saw the disk and hid it, so that her identity would not be discovered. Thus, Joseph's name is also said to have meant, "you have come to reveal the one who was hidden here" (GR 90:4).

That Dinah's child from the rape was a girl confirms that Bunah, and not Dinah, was "the Canaanite woman" who was the mother of Shaul (unless, perhaps, we want to suggest another twin-sister theory). Nor did Shimon adopt the child. Instead, Dinah's brothers wished to kill the baby.[1] Jacob prevented this but was unable to stop them from disposing of her another way—they abandoned her in a basket under a bush.

That Jacob did not want to get rid of Asnat is evident from the "name tag" he put on her—indicating that he was afraid of losing her. Given that his ten sons had thrown an *adult man* into a pit full of snakes and scorpions and then sold him into slavery, their cruelty to an *infant girl,* who signified shame to them, is not at all astonishing. It is a vicious validation of patrilineal descent that Dinah's daughter was not considered an Israelite by them, and it is to Jacob's credit that he *did* see his granddaughter's true identity.

Asnat must have been abandoned soon after her birth. Her Egyptian father, Potifera, is identified as Potiphar, Zelikhah's eunuch husband and Pharaoh's chief officer (Rashi; GR 89:2; Sot. 13b). When Zelikhah accused Joseph of rape, an eleven-month-old child in the household spoke up and told Potiphar that Zelikhah was lying. That child, some say, was Asnat,[2] who was adopted by Potiphar and Zelikhah. Others, however, say the eleven-month-old was a boy and that Asnat was the youngest daughter (SY 180).

Sarah, the first matriarch, descended to Egypt in fear of rape and came out victorious. Joseph descended to Egypt in slavery—thanks to his brothers—and also emerged victorious. Dinah, the last matriarch, was raped and her daughter was exiled to Egypt—again thanks to the brothers. Asnat's exile to Egypt turned to victory with her marriage to Joseph, which completed the Dinah–Joseph link. Now, however, with Asnat and Joseph in Egypt, the entire Jewish people was about to descend. Asnat's and Joseph's exile thus represents the beginning of Jewish exile.

EGYPT IN THE TIME OF JOSEPH

In order to reconstruct the life of Asnat as well as the setting in which the Jewish people were enslaved, I need to discuss some Egyptian deities and rituals in detail. My exploration of these matters proceeds from an assumption that these mythological creatures were in no way "deities." Rather, they are legends of past heroes—pagan kings and queens who were deified and worshiped after their deaths. A knowledge of their significance is important if we are to understand Egyptian society and religion.

Some general introductory historical information is also needed. Egyptologists, while disagreeing on specific dates, divide ancient Egyptian history into approximate periods (see Table 10–1).

The end of pharaonic rule was with the Thirtieth Dynasty, around 340 B.C.E. After this, Egypt was ruled by the Greeks (Ptolemy) and then the Romans.

---

1. Graves and Patai, p. 237.
2. Ibid., p. 261; Weissman, p. 377.

TABLE 10–1. Periods of Ancient Egyptian History

	Dynasties	B.C.E.	A.M.
Old Kingdom	1st to 11th	3000–2000	762–1762
Middle Kingdom	12th to 17th	2000–1600	1762–2162
New Kingdom	18th to 20th	1600–1100	2162–2662

Sarah was taken to Pharaoh's palace at the time of the Thirteenth or Fourteenth Dynasty. Joseph was sold in Egypt in the Eighteenth Dynasty, which is also when Jacob's family came down to Egypt and Miriam was born. The enslavement and Exodus of the Jews took place during the Nineteenth Dynasty. The New Kingdom era—when the Jews were in Egypt and immediately after they left—was, significantly, the "golden age" of Egyptian monarchy. (For a detailed time line of major Jewish events during this era, see Table 10–2.)

Joseph was sold into slavery at age 17. This was in 1546 B.C.E., the early part of the Eighteenth Dynasty. Pharaoh, at that time, was probably Amenophis I. Joseph became viceroy at age 30, in 1533 B.C.E. The pharaoh at that time was either Amenophis I or Tutmoses I. When Joseph died at 110 in 1453 B.C.E., Tutmoses III was pharaoh. What is interesting about all of this for our purposes is the queen mother, Hatshepsut, of the Tutmoses era.

Hatshepsut was the daughter of Tutmoses I and both the sister and wife of Tutmoses II. Because of the matriarchal nature of Egyptian royalty—it was transmitted from mother to daughter—a prince had to marry his maternal sister to maintain his royal link, for only by marrying his maternal sister could he make his *patrilineal* heir—his son—also his *matrilineal* heir—his sister's son.

The change from matrilineal to patrilineal descent was thus begun by men marrying their maternal sisters. A frequency of brother–sister marriage in a culture indicates that it is undergoing a transition from matrilineal to patrilineal descent. This was the case among Egypt's royal class, particularly at the time the Jews were there. "In the XVIIIth Dynasty, seven kings married their sisters; in the XIXth Dynasty all but three are known to have done so; in the XXth Dynasty every king married his sister. Kings married their sisters in the XVIIth, XIIIth, XIIth, and as early as the IVth Dynasty."[3]

Hatshepsut and her brother–husband, Tutmoses II, were not the parents of Tutmoses III. Tutmoses III was the son of Tutmoses II and his common (nonroyal) wife, Aset. However, the power of succession to the throne lay with Hatshepsut, and not with Tutmoses II. Hatshepsut brought Tutmoses III to the throne by marrying him to *her* daughter, the real (matrilineal) heir. "Any commoner might reign as king provided he married a royal princess."[4]

---

3. Briffault, 3:42 n. 2. See also 1:222.
4. Ibid., 3:37.

TABLE 10–2. The Jews in Egypt

Event (Pharaoh)	Lifespan	A.M.	B.C.E.
New Kingdom	500 yrs.	2162–2662	1600–1100
18th Dynasty			
(Amoses)			1580–1560
(Amenophis I)			1560–1530
Joseph as slave		2216	1546/45
Joseph as viceroy		2229	1533/32
(Tutmoses I)			1530–1520
Jacob to Egypt; Yokheved born	Levi, 43 yrs. old	2238	1524/23
(Tutmoses II)			1520–1485
Amram born; Jacob dies		2255	1507/6
(Hatshepsut)			
(Tutmoses III)			1500–1450
Joseph dies	110 yrs. old	2309	1453/52
(Amenophis II)			1450–1425
Levi dies; Jews enslaved	137 yrs. old	2332	1429
		16 Nisan	April 16
(Tutmoses IV)			1425–1410
(Amenophis III)			1410–1375
Miriam born		2361	1401/00
Aharon born		2365	1397/96
Moses born		2368	1393
		7 Adar	March 1
(Akhnaten)	(Henotheistic sun worship)		1375–1355
[Amenophis IV]			
Amram dies	137 yrs. old	2392	1370/69
(Tutankhamen)			1355–1340
(Ay)			1340–1335
(Horemheb)	(Died childless)		1335–1315
19th Dynasty			1315–1200
Exodus from Egypt		2448	1313
		15 Nisan	March 25
(Ramses I [appointed by Horemheb])	(May have ruled for only a year)		1315–1310
(Sety I)	(son of Ramses I)		1310–1300
(Ramses II)	(son of Sety)		1300–1235
(Merneptah)			1235–1225

Note: Professional Egyptologists have a wide variety of dating systems for the periods of pharaonic rule. No two are exactly alike. The Egyptian dates given in this table, compiled from seven such lists, have been rounded off into five-year periods for simplicity.

Tutmoses III was only a boy when Hatshepsut—his stepmother, aunt, and mother-in-law all in one—put him on the throne. This in itself was not unusual; there were several queen mothers who ruled as regents for their sons until the boy-kings reached majority. What made Hatshepsut different from the average queen mother was that in the seventh year of her son's reign, she herself took the throne and ruled as king, dressing in male attire and even wearing the pharaoh's artificial beard. She dared to make her power direct, taking on the role of the nation's "god."

"The great queen, who was associated with her father, Tutmoses I, reigned supreme for 33 years, and it is significant that, although her nephew, Tutmoses III, proved after her death one of the most brilliant and aggressive kings of Egypt, he was, during the period of his official association with her, entirely eclipsed by Queen Hatshepsut."[5]

These events all took place within the eighty years during which Joseph was "prime minister" of Egypt. Interestingly, when Joseph wanted to leave Egypt to bury his father in Canaan. he spoke to the queen's hairdresser, who in turn spoke to the queen. The Rabbis say that she spoke to the king because, as a mourner, Joseph could not enter the king's palace (GR 100:4). However, this is an unnecessary concoction that simply tries to ignore the fact that the *queen* was the real power.

"BELONGING TO NUT"

After being emasculated, Potiphar "was embarrassed and retired from his office. He then entered a temple of idol worship and became a priest in it, for such was the custom among the nobility, and it is possible that On was the name of his idol" (Nachmanides). On was actually the Egyptian city of Heliopolis, a major site of the worship of Osiris and his mother, Nut. Potifera was high priest (Malbim).

Unlike Joseph, who began his Egyptian life as a slave, Asnat began hers as the daughter of the royal high priest and dedicated to the goddess Nut. That Nut was a major deity of Pharaoh, and not just Potifera himself, is evident from Pharaoh's naming of Joseph. Nut, Net, and Neith were all the same deity.[6] Nut was the goddess of death and rebirth; hence, her image was often found on sarcophagus bottoms. Nut represented the sky, and her image on coffin linings was sometimes accompanied by the zodiac. Nut was also depicted as a cow, a pig, a rabbit, and a tree.

Net or Neith was the "lady of the west . . . the goddess of Sais. . . . Her cult was already ancient in the first dynasty [and] . . . her matriarchal character is more distinct than that of any other Egyptian goddess." She was the goddess of magic and weaving. "In very early times Net was the personification of the eternal female principle of life which was self-sustaining and self-existent and was secret and unknown and all-pervading. . . . Thus Net was the prototype of parthenogenesis."[7]

In ancient times, Net was a goddess of war and was "especially honored by women."[8] She is also called "one of the most prominent deities of the conquered kingdom" of the Fifth Dynasty, who was "an integral element of the state pantheon with a sanctuary at Memphis."[9]

The Fifth Dynasty marked the ascendancy of the sun god Ra. "No Egyptian king

5. Ibid., 3:40.
6. Erich Neumann, *The Great Mother* (Princeton, NJ: Bollingen, 1955), p. 221.
7. Ibid., pp. 220–222.
8. Neumann, *Origins,* p. 55.
9. George Hart, *A Dictionary of Egyptian Gods and Goddesses* (London: Routledge and Kegan Paul, 1986), pp. 131–134.

claims descent from Ra" before the Fifth Dynasty, which "is marked by its priestly character from the first."[10] Before this time, Pharaoh's emblem had been a hawk, a symbol of Nut's son, Horus. When Pharaoh died, he was called "Osiris," another son of Nut who was "the personification of dead kingship."[11] However, even after the political-religious conquest by Ra, Nut survived and had a national temple.

Nut's son Osiris also continued to be "the most popular of all Egyptian deities. . . . The worship of the other gods was overshadowed by that of Osiris."[12] His cult "was the most conservative form of Egyptian religion and successfully withstood the persistent efforts to merge it into the official cult of Ra. . . . The result of all this was to create a perpetual contest between the two great priesthoods of Egypt, namely, those of Ra and Osiris. In the end the doctrine of Osiris prevailed."[13]

Nut had five children altogether: Osiris; Horus; another son, Seth; and two daughters, Isis and Nephthys. Osiris married Isis and Seth married Nephthys.

ISIS AND OSIRIS: LAMENTING THE GRAIN

Osiris was probably a sacred king who was ritually sacrificed and deified after his death for, as elsewhere, "in ancient Egypt the sacred kings were blamed for the failure of the crops."[14] A king of Egypt named (in Hebrew) Osviros began the institution of pharaoh (SY 49–50). King Osiris appears to have brought the Egyptians out of barbarism and cannibalism by teaching them to plant and eat crops.[15]

Thus, the "goddess" Isis is said to have discovered grain (wheat and barley), and the "god" Osiris introduced its cultivation in Egypt and elsewhere. Because corn was the staple grain in Egypt, Osiris was represented as a cornstalk and Isis, as the "green goddess," the field of corn (or wheat or barley) itself.

In Egyptian mythology, Seth killed Osiris by trapping him in a wooden box and throwing him into the Nile. Isis recovered his body, and she and Nephthys sat down with it and uttered a lament that became the prototype of all Egyptian lamentations for the dead. Seth rediscovered the body and hacked it into fourteen pieces, which he scattered throughout Egypt. This is reminiscent of the "widespread practice of dismembering the body of a king or magician and burying the pieces in different parts of the country in order to ensure the fertility of the ground and also the fecundity of man and beast."[16]

Isis recovered all the body parts except for the penis, which had been eaten by the fish, so she made an artificial one for him, "around which the Egyptians established

10. Briffault, 2:764.
11. Hart, pp. 154, 155.
12. Frazer, pp. 420, 443.
13. Briffault, 2:783, 774.
14. Frazer, p. 100.
15. Ibid., pp. 421, 426.
16. Ibid., p. 440.

a cult and festival."[17] This also echoes the rituals of the sacred king, for one particular part of his body was not buried but instead kept as a sacred relic. "In all probability the phallus of the dismembered king was mummified as a symbol of male potency until the death of his successor."[18] Is this the origin of the king's sceptre? Since castration was part of this "sacred dismemberment," Potifera/Potiphar could have been a eunuch as part of his priestly service to Nut and Osiris.

The sisters, with the help of three gods, "pieced together the broken body of the murdered god . . . and observed all the other rites which the Egyptians were wont to perform" over the dead.[19] From Osiris came the Egyptians' methods of preservation and burial of the body.

Osiris, the first mummy, became the god of death and resurrection—"a god who thus fed his people with his own broken body in this life, and who held out to them a promise of a blissful eternity."[20] As Osiris died and was reborn, so all Egyptians hoped to achieve immortality. As lord of the underworld, he controlled their fate after death.

Osiris's two identities—as cornstalk and mummy—were thus combined in his worship as a vegetation god who annually died and was reborn. In the spring harvest season, Egyptian corn reapers would "beat their breasts and lament over the first sheaf cut," while calling on Isis. In the autumn sowing season, the priests would bury effigies of Osiris made of earth and corn.[21] These burial rites, which were observed for eighteen days throughout Egypt, were accompanied by

> the pretense of finding the god's body, and probably of restoring it to life. [It] was a great event in the festal year of the Egyptians . . . [who], with shorn heads, annually lamented over a buried idol of Osiris, smiting their breasts, slashing their shoulders, ripping open their old wounds, until, after several days of mourning, they professed to find the mangled remains of the god, at which they rejoiced.[22]

While Osiris (the crops) died annually, Isis (the field) did not. Her festival was in the summer, at the Egyptian New Year, when the waters of the Nile rise up and inundate the land. This, and not rainfall, determines whether Egypt will have feast or famine. The annual inundation of the Nile was characterized as Isis mourning for Osiris and her tears filling up the Nile. This festival—which occurred on the day when Zelikhah stayed home "sick" —is the occasion of the ceremonial cutting of the dam, which unleashes the water into the canals and fields.

---

17. Hart, p. 167.
18. Neumann, *Origins*, p. 224.
19. Frazer, p. 425.
20. Ibid., pp. 426, 443. See also Bob Brier, *Ancient Egyptian Magic* (New York: Quill, 1981), pp. 68–69.
21. Frazer, pp. 431, 437.
22. Ibid., p. 435.

In ancient Egypt, this Isis festival was celebrated with human sacrifice. "Tradition runs that the old custom was to deck a young virgin in gay apparel and throw her into the river as a sacrifice to obtain a plentiful inundation."[23] A twentieth-century Egyptian feminist notes: "Since ancient times, the waters of the Nile, source of life to Egyptians, have been propitiated. . . . Before Islam a young woman dressed as a bride was sacrificed to the river; afterwards an effigy was substituted."[24]

Thus, we can understand the assertion that "the ambivalent character of the great Mother Goddess . . . is seen most clearly in Egypt, where the great goddesses . . . are not only nourishing goddesses who give and sustain life, but goddesses of savagery, blood-lust, and destruction."[25]

Isis and Osiris were also symbolized as a cow and a bull, respectively, "since these animals above all others had helped the discoverers of corn in sowing the seed and procuring the universal benefits of agriculture."[26] A ceremony called "driving the calves," which was meant to encourage an abundant harvest, consisted of "the hooves of calves threshing grain on a floor sacred to the god [while] . . . the calves, by trampling over the threshing floor, now symbolizing the grave of Osiris, hid the spot from the god's enemies."[27]

Bulls also pulled plows, and hence, the bull was linked with the worship of the phallus, a fertility symbol akin to a plow. The worship of Osiris included mourning his lost penis, and Isis's lament for "the loss of the 'living phallus' . . . is why the symbol of the pillar, the *djed,* emblem of Osiris, is found in conjunction with the bull."[28]

We can only shudder at the thought of Asnat's "dedication" to Nut and her daughter Isis. That she did not end up as a Nile sacrifice was a blessing. Her participation in the phallic rites of Osiris, which we will discuss in chapter 12, is likely, given that her father was the eunuch high priest of that god. Since Nut was associated with the zodiac and since Asnat's Egyptian mother, Zelikhah, practiced astrology, we can assume that Asnat was well schooled in that art. Joseph was not the only diviner in the family!

Moreover, like any other pagan princess, Asnat would have undergone ritual defloration as a *kedeshah.* In Egypt "every girl of a noble family was, before marriage, and indeed, before the age of puberty, appointed to serve for a period in the temple of the god, and gave herself to any stranger who paid the required amount into the temple treasury. That promiscuous intercourse ceased when the first menstruation appeared, and the young woman was then married as befitted her station."[29]

---

23. Ibid., p. 430.
24. Huda Shaarawi, *Harem Years,* trans. by Margot Badran (New York: Feminist Press, 1987), p. 141 n. 12.
25. Neumann, *Origins,* p. 55.
26. Frazer, p. 424.
27. Hart, pp. 158–159.
28. Neumann, *Origins,* p. 222.
29. Briffault, 3:220

ASNAT AND JOSEPH: PROVIDING THE GRAIN

Joseph accumulated so much grain, it was like the sand of the sea. They had to give up counting it, since there was too much to count. Joseph had two sons before the famine years came, borne to him by Asnat, daughter of Potifera, priest of On. Joseph named the firstborn Menasheh, "because Elokim made me forget [*nashani*] all my troubles, and even my father's house." He named his second son Efraim, "because Elokim made me fruitful [*hifrani*] in the land of my suffering." (Gen. 41:49–52)

Asnat bore two sons, the "double portion" that was given to Joseph rather than Reuven, who prevented their originally intended conception by Bilhah and Jacob. Jacob changed the order of Menasheh and Efraim when he blessed them, and he blessed them *before* he blessed the other tribes (Gen. 48:17).

Efraim and Menasheh were born before the seven years of famine, which Joseph had predicted to Pharaoh and then prepared for during the seven years of plenty. Joseph and Asnat had other children, but not until after the famine, since "a person is forbidden to reproduce in times of famine" (Nachmanides; *Ta.* 11a; *Zohar* I:204a–b). They seem to have had some daughters (GR 86:3).

Pharaoh dreamed of seven cows and seven ears of corn—Isis and Osiris symbols. Each year of famine indicated to the Egyptians that their gods were dead: Osiris was not reappearing annually any more, and Isis' tears were not watering the fields. However, where the Egyptian gods failed, Joseph prevailed. This master magician, who had interpreted the dreams of Pharaoh, his cupbearer, and his baker, was now planning and maintaining the country's grain supply in a time of famine in such a way that he had enough to sell to outsiders! Joseph must indeed have seemed like a god to the Egyptians.

"The land was preserved through Joseph in conjunction with Pharaoh's dreams. . . . Joseph was himself the river by means of which the whole of Egypt was blessed." In fact, "it was Joseph who restored the one [the cupbearer] to his office, and hanged the other [the baker], through the medium of his interpretation" (*Zohar* I:193b–194b).

As Joseph eclipsed the power of Osiris over grain, so, too, Asnat eclipsed the power of Isis, for in Aramaic (*isna* or *usna*), Asnat means "storehouse" or "granary." Asnat was the repository for the accumulated grain, the "kernel of truth" that Joseph shared with the Egyptians during the seven years of their despair: belief in a God who truly is immortal and does not die annually.

✵✵✵ 11 ✵✵

Serach:
Daughter of Asher

Vayigash (44:18–47:27)

The sons of Asher: Yimnah, Yishvah, Yishvi, Briah. And Serach, their sister. (Gen. 46:17)

And the name of the daughter of Asher was Serach. (Num. 26:46)

Serach, "the daughter of Asher," was actually Hadorah's daughter from a previous marriage. Before marrying Asher, Hadorah had been married to Malkiel, the son of Shem's firstborn son, Elam (Gen. 10:22). (This Malkiel should not be confused with Asher's grandson Malkiel.)

After Idon, Asher's first wife, died, he married Hadorah and adopted Serach, who was three at the time. Serach "walked in the ways of the sons of Jacob, the holy ones. She lacked nothing, and God gave her wisdom and common sense" (SY 166). Thus, as one daughter, Asnat, was sent away from Jacob's house, another, Serach, was brought in.

Serach was "a daughter who possessed an inheritance, and therefore Scripture mentions her [in Numbers] just as it mentions the daughters of Zelophechad. . . . Had she been the daughter of Asher himself, she would not have inherited [a portion in the land], since he had male children. But she was the daughter of his wife from another man, who did not have a son; therefore his inheritance passed to his daughter" (Nachmanides).

REVIVING JACOB'S SPIRIT

Jacob's ten sons (of Leah, Bilhah, and Zilpah) went down to Egypt to buy grain from the government (from Joseph), for the famine was affecting Canaan. Joseph accused

123

them of being spies and held Shimon hostage, telling the other brothers that they must bring Benjamin to prove their identities. Jacob was enraged when his sons returned and told him this, and the sons themselves were scared because they found all their money returned in their bags.

After fourteen months, Jacob's family ran out of food and again had to go to Joseph. Judah pledged himself to Jacob so that nothing should happen to Benjamin. Jacob wrote a letter to the Egyptian leader (not knowing it was Joseph), urging him to take care of Benjamin (or else): "Do you not know what God did to Pharaoh when he took Sarah, my mother, and to Avimelekh, king of the Philistines, on account of her? . . . And also what my two sons Shimon and Levi did . . . on account of their sister, Dinah?" (SY 190).

Joseph welcomed his brothers lavishly, giving them a feast at which he sat Benjamin next to him and gave him five times the amount of food and drink as the others. Through astrology, Benjamin realized that this was Joseph (SY 193), who then planted his divining cup in Benjamin's bag, sent the brothers on their way, and had his men capture them. Joseph took Benjamin as a slave in punishment for the "theft" and let the others go.

Judah pleaded with Joseph and even warred against him until his shrieking "caused all of Egypt to quake, and the walls of Egypt and Goshen fell in from the shaking of the earth. . . . All the pregnant women of Egypt and Goshen miscarried when they heard the noise of the shaking" (SY 198). Pharaoh told Joseph to release the "thief" and stop the strife or else go with the men. Joseph finally revealed his identity to his brothers, and all of Egypt rejoiced with Joseph that he was reunited with his family (SY 200).

The brothers then returned to Canaan to tell their father that Joseph was still alive. Joseph sent them back laden with gifts, which included clothing, incense, and jewelry for the tribal mothers from the wardrobe of the queen and Pharaoh's other wives. It specifically included "garments of silver and gold, and frankincense and myrrh, and aloes and jewelry in great plenty" for Dinah and for Benjamin's two wives (SY 203).

How were the brothers to tell Jacob? Joseph warned them not to give Jacob the news too suddenly, so they had Serach tell him through a song. This time—unlike at his wedding—he understood.

They went along until they came to their houses, and they found Serach, the daughter of Asher, going out to meet them. The girl was very good and wise, and knew how to play the harp. And they called her and she came to them and kissed them, and they took her and gave her a harp and said to her, "Please go before our father, and sit in front of him, and speak to him on the harp these words." And they commanded her to go to their house, and she took the harp and hurried before them, and she came and sat near Jacob.

And she played the harp well and sang the pleasing words, "Joseph, my uncle, is alive, and he rules the whole land of Egypt and is not dead." And she continued to sing these words, and Jacob heard them and was pleased by them. He heard her words again twice and three times, and joy entered the heart of Jacob at the pleasantness of her words. The spirit of God was upon him, and he knew all her words were correct.

And Jacob blessed Serach when she spoke these words before him, saying, "My daughter, may death never rule over you, for you have revived my spirit. Only speak to me again like you have spoken to me, for you have made me happy with your words." And she continued to sing these words, and Jacob heard and it pleased him and made him happy, and the spirit of God was upon him. (SY 203)

Note that Jacob did not observe *kol ishah,* the halakhic prohibition of a man hearing a woman sing. He listened quite readily to Serach's soothing musical message, and did not seem to have any problem of sexual arousal with it. It did, however, arouse (revive) his spirit (Gen. 45:27). If our ancestors really did observe all the *mitzvah*s given at Sinai whenever they were in the Land of Israel, then *kol ishah* is clearly not *Torah miSinai* (a law given by God).

Serach restored Jacob (*Targum Jonathan*). This means that she brought the Shekhinah back to him (Rashi). "Jacob was different, because the Shekhinah was closely attached to him" (*Zohar* I:226a), but She left him when Joseph was sold—that is, "when the brothers made Her a party to the oath of secrecy regarding the sale of Joseph. But now that the Shekhinah returned he rose to the higher degree symbolized by Israel" (210b). "The Shekhinah does not rest on a place which is defective or disturbed, but only in a place properly prepared, a place of joyfulness. Hence all the years that Joseph was away and Jacob was in sadness, the Shekhinah did not rest on him" (216b). Instead, She was with Joseph in Egypt (GR 86:2, 86:5).

Once Jacob learned that Joseph was still alive, all the Canaanites celebrated his good fortune and their kings feasted with him for three days. When Jacob came down to Egypt, Joseph decreed that all of Egypt come out to greet him (SY 204). Jacob lived happily and prosperously in Goshen for seventeen years. When he died, all of Egypt and Canaan came to mourn for him, and all the Egyptian women mourned with Asnat (SY 209).

RECOGNIZING MOSES' PROPHECY

The Jews enslaved in Egypt knew that Moses was a true prophet even before he showed them the signs God had given him (ER 5:13). There was

a tradition from Jacob, Jacob having handed down the secret to Joseph, and Joseph to his brothers, while Asher, the son of Jacob, had handed down the secret to his daughter Serach, who was still alive. This is what he told her: "Any redeemer that will come and say to my children, *Pakod pakadti,* 'I will surely visit you,' shall be regarded as a deliverer of truth." When, therefore, Moses came and said these words [Ex. 3:16, 4:29–31], the people believed him at once. They believed him as soon as they heard the password.

Moreover, they knew the password because of Serach.

Pakad means to "visit" in the sense of "remember" or "decree upon." It is the verb used when God "remembered" Sarah with Isaac (Gen. 21:1), but not when God "remembered" (*yizkor*) Rachel with Joseph (Gen. 30:22). This is because "Rachel was still dependent on *mazal*," or astrological timing, but Sarah's pregnancy "was a process taking place on high, above *mazal* " (*Zohar* I:159b). *Pakad* thus implies divine intervention, above and beyond any laws or cycles of nature.

RECOVERING JOSEPH'S COFFIN

Serach also found Joseph's coffin for Moses so that the Jews could leave Egypt. God became concerned with the burial of Moses because Moses busied himself with finding Joseph's coffin before leaving Egypt (DR 11:7). While the rest of the Jews were asking their Egyptian neighbors for gold and silver, Moses spent three days and three nights looking for Joseph's sarcophagus. The children of Israel could not leave Egypt without it, because he had bound them by an oath—*pakod yifkod*—at his death (Gen. 50:24–25; Ex. 13:19). Moses became tired of searching, at which point "a *segulah* met him" who "is elsewhere referred to as Serach, the daughter of Asher" (ER 20:19).

When Moses explained what he was looking for, Serach took him to the Nile and said: "In this place have the magicians and astrologers made for him a coffin of 500 talents in weight and cast it into the river, and thus have they spoken to Pharaoh, 'If it is your wish that this people should never leave this place, then as long as they do not find the bones of Joseph, they will be unable to leave.'"

Moses stood on the riverbank and, invoking *pakod yifkod,* called out to Joseph to "give honor to the God of Israel and do not hold up the redemption of Israel; you have good deeds to your credit, intercede then with your Creator and come up from the depths." Joseph's coffin immediately rose to the surface of the water (Sot. 13a).

ACHIEVING IMMORTALITY

Serach "had a large family which was called by her name [!] and which was included in the tally of the families of Asher's descendants" given in Numbers 26:47 (Nachmanides). She was still alive in the time of King David (GR 94:9), and is "the wise woman from the city" referred to in 2 Samuel 20:16–22.

Serach not only lived a long life on earth, she never died. She is one of several righteous people who are said to have entered Gan Eden—Paradise, or "heaven"—alive (*Targum Jonathan; Kallah Rabbati,* chap. 3; *Derekh Eretz Zuta,* chap. 1).

❈❈❈ 12 ❈❈❈

The Daughters of Egypt

Vayechi (47:28–50:26)

Ben porat Yosef ben porat alei-ayin bnot tzaadah alei-shur. (Gen. 49:22)

"A son of cows [*parot*] is Joseph, a son of cows on the eyes of the daughters climbing the wall" is how I would translate this verse, which is part of Jacob's blessing of Joseph on his deathbed. It can then be explained in light of Joseph's replacement of Osiris as the "corn god" of Egypt, Joseph's sex appeal to women, and Osiris's connection with bull and phallus worship. *Shur,* "wall," can also be read as *shor,* "ox."

First, let us notice what translators usually do with this verse. "Joseph is a fruitful vine, a fruitful vine by the fountain, with branches running over the wall" is the most common translation—linking *par* (young bull) with *pri* (fruit). Given the bull's link with fertility, "a fruitful vine" works well as a metaphorical translation.

Some translations leave "daughters" in the latter part of the verse, saying, "Joseph is a son of fruitfulness, a son of fruitfulness by a well; daughters climb on the wall." Either way, "branches" or "daughters" is interpreted to refer to the five daughters of Zelophechad (Num. 27), who succeeded in inheriting a portion of the Land of Israel and whom Joseph was privileged to have as his descendants (his "fruitfulness").

Porat has been interpreted as *prat,* "broken," indicating that Joseph "broke" with his brothers by slandering them to Jacob, his brothers "broke" with him by selling him, he "broke" away from Zelikhah, and Zelikhah "broke" him by having him imprisoned (GR 98:18).

Porat also means "graceful" in Aramaic. "His gracefulness attracts the eye that looks at him. The daughters of Egypt used to climb up on the wall to look at his beauty." Although this was done by "many daughters, each one individually climbed to a place from which she could see him" (Rashi).

127

THE EYES OF THE DAUGHTERS

"When Joseph went out to rule over Egypt, daughters of kings used to squeeze between the window lattices and throw bracelets, necklaces, earrings, and finger-rings at him, so that he might lift up his eyes and look at them; yet he did not look at them" (GR 98:18). Such a description of royal Egyptian women evokes the impression that they were secluded, the bars on the windows connoting a prisonlike environment.

The common Egyptian woman's situation was different. "All the women and adolescent girls went up on the roofs and filled the streets, playing and rejoicing with Joseph, and gazed at the appearance of Joseph and his beauty" (SY 178). Similarly, upon Jacob's arrival, "all the women of Egypt went upon the roofs of Egypt and upon the walls to meet Jacob, and they played timbrels and danced in a circle" (SY 204).

From the start Joseph's fate involved the eyes—and people gazing at him. Jacob "cast his eyes" upon Joseph, favoring him as Rachel's child by giving him a colorful coat—which would certainly draw people's eyes. The envy this created in Joseph's brothers was exacerbated by Joseph's false accusations that they "cast their eyes" on the women of the land. Joseph was then sold into slavery by these brothers and ended up working for Potiphar and Zelikhah, who each "cast their eyes" on him. Ever since, Joseph had to learn to avoid the gaze of those who were mesmerized by his beauty.

"Said the Holy One to him: 'You did not lift up your eyes and look at them [the Egyptian women]. By your life, I will give your [Zelophechad's] daughters a place in the Torah'" (GR 98:18). The Talmud repeatedly states that "the evil eye has no power over the seed of Joseph" (Br. 20a, 55b; Sot. 36b; B.M. 84a; B.B. 118b). This is because "Joseph did not cast his eyes upon her [Zelikhah], nor, when he became ruler, upon the other Egyptian women" (NR 14:6). Joseph's greatness also lay in having protected his mother Rachel from Esav's eyes (GR 78:10, 90:4).

A SON OF COWS: JOSEPH AND EGYPTIAN BULL WORSHIP

These last two sources note that "through cows Joseph became great," referring to his interpretation of Pharaoh's dream of seven fat cows and seven thin cows. There are several other significant calves or cows in the Torah: the golden calf (Ex. 32), the Red Heifer (Num. 19), and the calf that was to be decapitated by a river by the elders of a city when a corpse was found and no one knew who the murderer was (Deut. 21:1–4). The latter two calves must never have been yoked or put to work for humans.

Joseph was studying the laws of this last calf with his father when they were separated (*Zohar* I:210b)—ironic, indeed, given that his brothers left him in a pit and he could have ended up as such a corpse himself! Egypt itself is referred to here as a "calf" (*egel*). This is particularly interesting in light of the fact that in Egypt "there were four bulls which were worshiped in the primitive periods: Apis of Memphis,

Mnevis of Heliopolis, Buchis of Hermonthis, and the Golden Bull of Canopus. Apis was the most famous of the four. . . . The cult of Apis, the bull of Memphis, is of very early date."[1]

Apis and Mnevis were different breeds of bulls, but both "were dedicated to Osiris, and it was ordained that they should be worshiped as gods in common by all the Egyptians."[2] "Mnevis was entirely black . . . [and] was a heavily built animal with such high shoulders as to be almost humped like the zebu. He was the incarnation of the sun god [and although he was worshiped by several pharaohs], he never entered into the popular worship like Apis."[3]

An Apis bull, says Herodotus, was "the calf of a cow that is not allowed to bear another. The Egyptians say that a flash of light from heaven falls on the cow, and this causes her to give birth to Apis. This calf, Apis, is black and is known by these markings: he has a triangular white spot on his forehead and the likeness of an eagle on his back; the hairs of his tail are double and he has a 'beetle' under the tongue."[4]

Apis was

> so closely connected with Osiris as to be called the incarnate Soul of Osiris. As the Soul of God was in him, he was worshiped as God, and suffered the same fate as the human incarnation of the divine Spirit. He was not allowed to die of old age, but was ceremonially killed and a new bull installed in his place. . . . When the new bull was identified, the old bull seems to have been drowned, and there is some evidence to show that the flesh was eaten at a ritual feast; the skin, bones, and some parts of the body were mummified and then buried with royal honors. The drowning, the dismemberment, and the royal burial show the close connection with Osiris.[5]

Each Apis bull was given his own sarcophagus and burial chamber, beginning in the Eighteenth Dynasty, and each had a tablet listing the reigning years of his particular pharaoh. These have been of great value to Egyptologists in determining the sequence and length of the pharaohs' reigns.

Apis was worshiped with massive celebrations. "At his appearance the people put on their richest clothes and made a holiday."[6] We are also told that "at his festival women used to go about the villages singing songs in his praise and carrying obscene images of him which they set in motion by means of strings."[7] His worship by women was actually orgiastic. "During the first forty days after his installation in his temple at Memphis, the women stood before him and, raising their clothes, exposed their persons." (This gives credence to translating the latter part of the biblical verse

---

1. Margaret A. Murray, *The Splendor That Was Egypt* (New York: Hawthorn, 1963), p. 162.
2. Frazer, p. 424.
3. Murray, *Splendor*, p. 163.
4. Carter, p. 178.
5. Murray, *Splendor*, p. 162.
6. Carter, p. 178.
7. Frazer, p. 442.

as "daughters climbing the ox"!) "Egyptian princesses were assimilated to cows. . . .
In one tomb a large mummified phallus, apparently that of a bull, was found with the
body of the princess."[8]

Osiris and Apis were later fused into Serapis, and "Serapis alludes to Joseph" (A.Z.
43a). By continually producing grain where Osiris could not, Joseph was elevated in
the eyes of the Egyptians to a god—specifically, to their major bull god. Without
Joseph, Egypt would have starved to death.

Now we can understand more clearly the meaning of Jacob's blessing, "A son of
cows is Joseph, a son of cows on the eyes of the daughters climbing the wall [or ox]."
When Moses blessed Joseph (Deut. 33:17), he also referred to him as a bull: "The
firstborn of his ox is a glory to him [and] . . . he shall gore nations to the end of the
earth."

It was not simply Joseph's good looks that made women climb the walls to see
him. He was the (phallic) fertility god who had come to save their lives, and they
welcomed him as such. They welcomed their new god's father, too. This is why Jacob
did not want to be buried in Egypt—so "that the Egyptians should not make a god of
him" (*Zohar* I:222a). Jacob and Joseph were both mummified in the custom of Egyptian pharaoh gods (Gen. 50:2, 50:26). Both, however, also had their coffins taken
out of Egypt and buried in the Land of Israel. Moreover, if Joseph's request was
honored, Asnat, too, was buried in Israel—in Rachel's tomb.[9]

CLIMBING THE WALLS

That Egyptian women were "climbing the walls" can be taken as a pun—that is, they
were emotionally "climbing the walls," which implies boredom, entrapment, and
going crazy. What did an upper-class Egyptian woman of the Eighteenth Dynasty
do all day? Gazing at a handsome man like Joseph might have been a pleasant
distraction.

Any book on ancient Egypt spends at least an entire chapter discussing the makeup,
jewelry, hairstyles, and clothing of Egyptian women. That upper-class women put
so much time and effort into their looks indicates that their major function in society
was to be decorative, pretty, and entertaining for men. This appears to be exactly the
case. The royal harem was called "the house of the secluded," and was "strictly
guarded. It was the duty of the inmates to cheer Pharaoh by songs, and the ladies of
the private harems had also to be skilled in similar accomplishments." Women and
children in an Eighteenth Dynasty priest's harem spent their days "eating, dancing,
playing music, or dressing each other's hair; the storerooms behind were evidently
full of harps, lutes, mirrors, and boxes for clothes."[10]

---

8. Briffault, 3:189.
9. Graves and Patai, p. 278.
10. Adolf Erman, *Life in Ancient Egypt* (New York: Dover, 1971), pp. 152, 153.

Only four professions were open to women: temple attendant, midwife, professional mourner, and dancer. The temple attendants

> entered the profession when quite young and learned to dance the sacred dances and sing the sacred songs. Midwives must have been held in some esteem, for according to the legend the great goddesses had once acted in that capacity. . . . Professional mourners began as young girls; they are shown in company with the grown women with their arms upraised and apparently shrieking as loudly as they could. Dancers were trained from very early childhood, so young that they are still represented nude, in contrast to the apprentice mourners, who are always shown fully clothed. . . . Allied to the dancers were the acrobats, girls who turned somersaults, either singly or in groups.[11]

> The professions were not open to [women], nor were any of the crafts except those which were traditionally feminine. They were not carpenters or sculptors or scribes—although some, at least, of the royal women did know how to read and write. They were not priests, either, although each temple had its corps of women attendants. The commonest title of the temple women was "singer"; they formed a choir of singers and dancers, who performed for the god's amusement and accompanied themselves on the rattle-like sistra. . . . Women might be singers, dancers, or musicians and in these capacities they are depicted entertaining guests at private banquets. But the girls—most of whom were young and pretty—may not have been professionals who worked for pay; they may have been household servants or slaves.[12]

Female entertainers, like female slaves, were usually nude for the sake of male enjoyment. "Professional female musicians . . . often wore no clothes at all and only a little jewelry. . . . The young servant-girls, who are often difficult to distinguish from the children, went about their work naked, especially when their master had guests, and displayed their lissom and graceful bodies to admiring eyes without embarrassment."[13]

Despite this male author's annoyingly smug assumption that the girls enjoyed being objects of voyeurism, this passage nevertheless tells us a great deal about the privilege of the well-to-do Egyptian male and the function that females—whether free women or slaves—fulfilled in his household. All the women were "his," to do with as he pleased.

> As a rule, one woman is the legitimate wife and the mistress of the house; at the same time the man may, if his fortune allow it, keep other women, and it is generally considered that the slaves of the household belong to him. . . . Such were the views of marriage which were held in ancient Egypt. One woman alone was the legitimate wife of the husband . . . yet when we obtain a glimpse into the interior of a well-to-do household, we find also "beautiful singers" and other attendants in the "house of the women."[14]

---

11. Murray, *Splendor*, p. 104.

12. Barbara Mertz, *Red Land, Black Land* (New York: Peter Bedrick, 1990), pp. 55–56.

13. Pierre Montet, *Everyday Life in Ancient Egypt* (Philadelphia: University of Pennsylvania, 1981), p. 74.

14. Erman, pp. 150–151.

While men could be polygynous, women's adultery was a capital offense.[15] However—perhaps in more ancient times—Egyptian men "set up bazaars where they stole each other's women" (GR 37:5), reminding us of the Sodomites' quarterly festivals. Men were also allowed to beat women: "In a country in which the stick played so large a part, a husband had the right to beat his wife and a brother to beat his sister, provided that they did not go too far."[16] We can only speculate on the definition of "too far."

Sons were preferred over daughters,[17] and virgin girls were ritually deflowered. "In ancient Egypt a girl had to be deflowered by promiscuous intercourse before the age of puberty; on the appearance of menstruation such relations ceased."[18] While we have already noted this practice for royal girls, it appears that common girls underwent the same thing with no pretense of religious ritual.

Incest was a normative experience for Egyptian girls, at least royal ones.

> A Pharaoh safeguarded himself from abdication by marrying every heiress without any regard to consanguinity; so that if the chief heiress died, he was already married to the next in succession and thus retained the sovereignty. The age of the heiress was of no account, she might be a grandmother or a newborn infant. As long as she was the heiress or likely to be the heiress later on, she was married off to the king, and when the king died his successor married all the heiresses also.[19]

In other words, Pharaoh ruled by virtue of his marriage to the queen. When they had a daughter, who would be the queen's heir, Pharaoh would marry the girl to guarantee his continued right to rule should his wife die. If Pharaoh died, his son would marry his father's wives—including his own mother and sisters—to assure his succession to the throne.

This practice was not always restricted to the royal harem but was once found in any household in which property descended through the female line. Thus, an example is given of a "small official in charge of a government storehouse" in the Twelfth Dynasty. (See Figure 12–1.) The official, whom I shall designate as A, had a mother, B, and a maternal grandmother, C. A also had two sisters: D and E. However, D was the daughter of C, making D the maternal *aunt* of A. E was the daughter of D and hence A's maternal *cousin*. The only way in which D and E could be *sisters* of A is if they all had the same father. This means that Dad (F) not only married Mom (B), but Grandma (C) and Aunt D, as well! F, this unnamed husband of all the women in the family, was not even nobility, but "probably a person of inferior status, not worth considering."[20]

---

15. Mertz, p. 59; Montet, p. 54.
16. Montet, p. 55.
17. Ibid., p. 57.
18. Briffault, 3:317.
19. Murray, *Splendor*, pp. 100–101.
20. Ibid., p. 101.

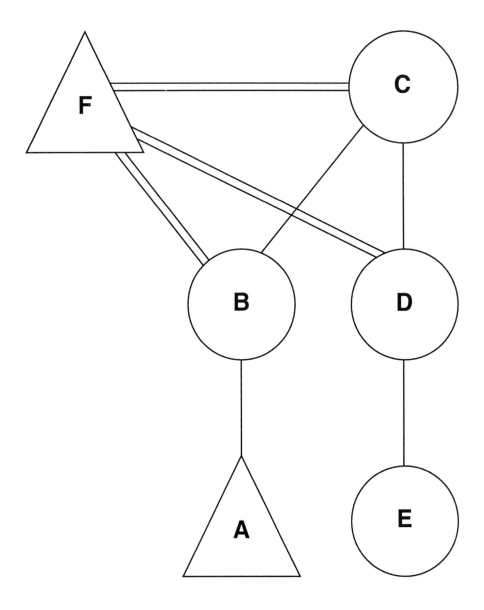

FIGURE 12–1. The common Egyptian family pattern: *A*, *D*, and *E* could only be siblings by having the same father. Since *B* and *D* are daughters of *C*, and *E* is the daughter of *D*, this means that *F* slept with a woman *and* their two daughters (as indicated by the equal signs).

Although it might be inappropriate to assume that the psychological damage done by incest was the same for ancient Egyptian girls as it is for modern American girls, there is evidence that at least some women in ancient Egypt experienced it as oppressive and tried to escape their fate. Descent through the female line—which on the surface appears to empower women—simply meant that heiresses were taken, with or without their consent, by male relatives who wanted the throne.

An example is Ankhesenamun, a daughter of Nefertiti, who was married at the age of ten or twelve to Tutankhamun, the boy-king popularly known in museum exhibits as King Tut. When Tut died, Ankhesenamun, who was not yet twenty, wrote to the Hittite king asking for one of his sons in marriage. She did this because seventy days after Tut's death she would be required to marry Ay—her maternal grandfather. That such a marriage would be repugnant to her comes as no surprise to us today. Unfortunately, the son sent by the Hittite king was killed by Ay, who then succeeded in marrying his granddaughter and installing himself as pharaoh.[21]

It is no wonder that the daughters of Egypt were "climbing the walls." By fostering a "slave mentality" in its own women, a society naturally paves the way for the acceptance of a more overt and brutal enslavement of other peoples. Consider, for example, the status of the Southern white woman at the time of black slavery in the United States. Similarly, Egypt's enslavement of the Jews was made possible by its more subtle enslavement of Egyptian women.

---

21. Lehmann, pp. 13–15.

II

Liberation from Bondage
(*Exodus*/Shemot)

✼✼✼ 13 ✼✼✼

Yokheved and Miriam

Shemot (1:1–6:1)

A man of the house of Levi went and took Levi's daughter [as a wife]. (Ex. 2:1)

Amram took his aunt Yokheved for a wife, and she bore to him Aharon and Moses. (Ex. 6:20)

Kehat [a son of Levi] begat Amram. The name of Amram's wife was Yokheved, the daughter of Levi that Otah bore to Levi in Egypt, and she bore to Amram Aharon, Moses, and Miriam, their sister. (Num. 26:58–59)

Yokheved was conceived in Canaan but was born just as Jacob's family crossed the border into Egypt (Sot. 12a; BB. 120a, 123b; NR 13:20; Rashi).

Yokheved was Levi's daughter and Amram was Levi's grandson; Yokheved was, therefore, Amram's aunt. However, she was his *paternal* aunt (San. 58b), which was not a forbidden relationship prior to the Torah. Levi's wife Adinah was the mother of his three sons, but not of his daughter Yokheved.

A woman named Otah was Yokheved's mother; this is evident from a close examination of the verse from Numbers (26:58–59). Although it is usually translated as "the daughter of Levi that *was born* to Levi in Egypt," this is incorrect because the verb (*yaldah*) is in the active, and not the passive, voice, and *otah*, the direct object "her," makes no sense in this context. Hence, Otah is a proper name (Kaplan; Malbim).

Yokheved and Amram had their first child, Miriam, after thirty years of Jewish enslavement (see Table 10–2). The name Miriam, which means "bitter sea," reflects this harsh reality.

Nearly four years later, Yokheved had a son, Aharon, whose name means "I will be pregnant" (*aheron*), indicating her determination to have the child in spite of Pharaoh's order to the midwives to kill Jewish boys at birth (SY 238). Three years after Aharon's birth, Yokheved conceived a third child, whom she named Yekutiel, "hope of God" (SY 243), but he came to be known by his Egyptian name, Moses. In Yokheved's third month of pregnancy, Pharaoh decreed that all baby boys be thrown into the Nile.

THE HEBREW WOMEN

The Israelites were fruitful and prolific and they multiplied, greatly increasing themselves until the land was filled with them. (Ex. 1:7)

At this time, Jewish women were bearing sextuplets as a normal occurrence (Rashi). Because "prolific" (*sharatz*) is linguistically related to "reptile" (*sheretz*), the women are compared to the scorpion, which "gives birth to 60" offspring at once (ER 1:8). Some women even bore a dozen children at a time. These babies, who must have been tiny, were not even weak at birth but rather strong and healthy. Pharaoh, who was threatened by the Jews' population growth and afraid of them becoming a fifth column in warfare, decided to enslave them. This happened after Levi, the last of Jacob's twelve sons, died.

However, although the Hebrew women are praised for their fertility and for their vigor in childbearing, they are primarily regarded as a model for righteousness and rebellion. "On account of the righteous women of that generation was Israel redeemed from Egypt" (ER 1:12; Sot. 11b). What did they do to merit this reward?

The Jews were oppressed through slave labor. As a result, the men were continually exhausted and had little interest in sex. Sometimes they were not even allowed to go home at night. All this was done to keep them from reproducing. However, the women, who also must have been exhausted from their slave labor, saved the day. When their husbands were not allowed to come home at night, the women went out to them.

When they went to draw water, the Holy One arranged that little fish should enter their pitchers, which they drew up half full of water and half full of fishes. They then set two pots on the fire, one for hot water and the other for the fish, which they carried to their husbands in the field, and washed, anointed, fed, gave them to drink, and had sex with them between the mounds in the field [i.e., discreetly, so each couple could not be seen by the others]. . . .

After the women had conceived they returned to their homes, and when the time of childbirth arrived, they went and were delivered in the field beneath the apple tree. . . . When the Egyptians noticed them, they came to kill them, but a miracle was done for them and they were swallowed in the ground. [The Egyptians] brought oxen and plowed over them. . . . After they had departed, [the women and their babies] burst forth and came out like the grass of the field." (ER 1:12; Sot. 11b)

The oppressiveness of the Israelites' labor also consisted of giving "men's work to women and women's work to men" (ER 1:11, 1:27, 18:9; Sot. 11b). This might be an observation of Egyptian culture in general, for Herodotus tells us that "the customs and laws of the Egyptians are contrary to those of other people in almost all respects. Among them the women go to market and do business; the men stay at home and weave. . . . Men carry burdens on their heads, women on their shoulders. The women urinate standing, the men crouching."[1]

Evidently, not all Jewish women were at home having sextuplets. Many of them must have been out building the cities of Pitom and Raamses, while many of the men were probably domestic slaves. "The buildings in primitive Egypt were constructions of reeds and plastered mud, identical with those erected by the women in every part of Africa. Even at the present day, a great deal of the building is done in Egypt by the women, and the assistants of a master builder are inevitably girls, not men."[2] This adds another dimension to the nature of the Hebrew women's strength and heroism.

Before the Israelites left Egypt, God instructed every Jewish woman to "borrow" silver, gold, and clothing from her Egyptian neighbors, in order to drain Egypt of its wealth (Ex. 3:22). As reparation for a century of slavery, "Israel was privileged to despoil Egypt" because the women had maintained enough dignity to lie with their husbands "between the mounds," where they would not be seen (Sot. 11b).

THE DECREE AGAINST BOYS

Pharaoh first plotted to have the midwives secretly kill all Jewish male babies as they delivered them, before the infants had even fully emerged, in order to make them appear to be stillbirths so that even the mothers would not know (Ex. 1:16; Nachmanides). He gave the midwives a sign: "If its face is turned downward, it is a male; but if its face is turned upward, it is a female" (ER 1:14; Sot. 11b; Nid. 31a).

Although girls were spared so that Egyptian men could use them for sexual purposes (ER 1:18), there was also a more specific reason: Pharaoh's astrologers had told him that a *son* would be born who would become the deliverer of the Jews. However, they could not predict if this redeemer would be born of an Egyptian or an Israelite; all they could see was that he had already been conceived and that he would ultimately suffer misfortune through water—a reference to Moses' later experience with the waters of Merivah. Pharaoh, however, decided that this meant the Nile and issued a public decree that *all* boys—Egyptian as well as Jewish—be drowned. He was not afraid of divine retribution because God had promised Noach never to destroy the world again with water (Ex. 1:22; Rashi; ER 1:18; Sot. 12a; San. 101a).

Pharaoh's decree had a significant psychological effect on his people. In an attempt to save their own sons, the Egyptian nation as a whole became quite zealous in ferreting out Jewish boys. Egyptian soldiers would search Jews' houses at night, Gestapo-like, and take away any male infant they found (Nachmanides). Egyptian

---

1. Carter, pp. 105–106.
2. Briffault, 1:481.

women collaborated by bringing their babies to Jewish women's houses for visits; when the Egyptian babies began to cry, the hidden Jewish babies also began to cry and the Egyptian women reported them to Pharaoh (SY 242; ER 1:20; Sot. 12a).

This pharaoh, whose death is recorded in Ex. 2:23, is said to have bathed in the blood of Jewish children in an attempt to cure his skin disease (Rashi).

SHIFRAH AND PUAH

Not only did the midwives, Shifrah and Puah, refuse to kill any babies, they also collected food and water for poor mothers to prevent any newborns from dying of malnutrition. They prayed that no child would be born disabled so they would not be falsely accused of having caused it while attempting to kill them. They also success-fully resisted Pharaoh's sexual advances (ER 1:15; Sot. 11b).

When Pharaoh demanded to know why they were not carrying out his orders, Shifrah and Puah told him, "The Hebrew women are not like the Egyptian women. They are wild animals. Before the midwife can come to them, they have given birth" (Ex. 1:19). This comparison with animals is not unusual; it is found frequently in descriptions of the tribes and indicates positive qualities such as strength or grace—for example, Judah (lion), Dan (serpent), Naftali (deer), Yisakhar (donkey), Joseph (ox), and Benjamin (wolf). Here the comparison is meant to show the vigor with which Jewish women underwent natural childbirth (ER 1:16; Sot. 11b).

Who were Shifrah and Puah? They may have been Egyptians who were midwives for Jewish women: Shifrah prepared the mother and delivered the child, while Puah cut the umbilical cord and cared for the baby (Malbim). Alternately, they may have been Jews themselves.

Like Keturah with Hagar, many commentators choose to merge the identities of Shifrah and Puah with Yokheved and Miriam—or, in one opinion, Yokheved and her daughter-in-law, Elisheva (ER 1:13; Sot. 11b). If this is true, it explains how Yokheved knew during her pregnancy with Aharon that he was threatened—some-thing only the midwives would have known at that point.

Yokheved was called Shifrah because she cleaned and fixed up (*meshaperet*) the babies when they were born, because Israel multiplied (*sheparu*) a great deal because of her, and because she smoothed over (*meshaperet*) her daughter's words and paci-fied Pharaoh in an incident in which Miriam had brazenly told him that God would punish him for his decree. (Yokheved explained it away by telling Pharaoh, "She's just a child; she doesn't know what she's saying.")

Miriam was called Puah because she blew bubbles before the babies to entertain them while Shifrah took care of the mother, because she rebuked first Pharaoh and then her father, and because she cried out to the babies to bring them forth and cried with *ruach hakodesh* in predicting Moses' destiny. (All of these phrases use the verb *pa'ah*.)

Because of their fear of God, Elokim "made houses for them" (Ex. 1:21). Yokheved—whose name, *Yah kaved*, means "God honors"—was blessed with Moses and became foremother of the *kehunah* (the Jewish priesthood) and the Levites. Miriam was blessed with Betzalel (architect of the Tabernacle) and became foremother of Jewish royalty, the House of David, through her marriage into the tribe of Judah.

MIRIAM'S PROPHECY

When Pharaoh's decree was announced, Amram ceased having sexual relations with Yokheved and divorced her, saying it was useless for the Israelites to have any more children. Because he was a leader of the Jews, the rest of the men followed his example and divorced their wives.

Miriam, having already reproached Pharaoh, who then wanted to kill her until Yokheved smoothed things over, certainly was not about to stand by silently with her own father! "Your decree is worse than Pharaoh's," she accused him, "for Pharaoh only decreed against boys, but you decree against both boys and girls. Pharaoh's decree concerns this world, but your decree concerns this world and the world to come. Besides, since Pharaoh is wicked, his decree may not be fulfilled, but since you are righteous, your decree will certainly be fulfilled" (ER 1:13; Sot. 12a). When Amram heard the logic of his five-year-old daughter, he remarried Yokheved, and all the Jewish men again followed his example and returned to their wives.

Yokheved was 130 years old when Moses was born; Miriam, age 6, assisted her. Since Sarah giving birth at age 90 was a cause for wonder, why is Yokheved's bearing of *three* children after age 120 not the subject of more discussion? "There is in the matter of Yokheved a great wonder of the hidden miracles which are the foundation of the Torah. . . . Why should Scripture mention them? All the foundations of the Torah are hidden miracles! In all the Torah there are only miracles, no natural law or custom. All the Torah's statements of fact are signs and wonders" (Nachmanides).

Yokheved was able to keep Moses hidden for three months before the Egyptian soldiers came looking for him. This was because she gave birth six months after remarrying Amram, having been—possibly unknown to him—three months pregnant when he left her. The Egyptians did not know this (either) and only came to check up on her nine months after her remarriage.

At this time, Yokheved cast Moses into the water in a basket, rather than leaving him in a field, so that the astrologers would get a mental image that the redeemer of the Jews had been cast into the Nile and Pharaoh would end his decree. The ploy worked (ER 1:20, 1:21; Sot. 12a, 12b).

Miriam had prophesied, "My mother is destined to give birth to a son who will save Israel." When Moses was born circumcised and the house was then flooded with light, her father stood up and kissed her head, saying, "My daughter, your prophecy has been fulfilled." However, when Yokheved cast Moses into the Nile, Amram took his anger out on Miriam—he slapped her and said, "Where is your prophecy now?" (Sot. 13a; Meg. 14a; ER 1:22 [which changes the story to have Yokheved slapping her]).

Thus, Miriam—who was no doubt frightened from such physical abuse—stood at a distance from the river to see what indeed would be the outcome of her prophecy. Because Miriam had waited to see what would happen to Moses, all of Israel later waited for her when she was sick (Sot. 9b).

Miriam is not named at all at this point. She is simply called *achoto,* "his sister." Moses' sister is not identified as Miriam until the wilderness. In Exodus 15:20 she is called "Miriam the prophet, the sister of Aharon." This is either because Miriam prophesied when she was only Aharon's sister, before Moses was born (ER 1:22; Sot. 12b) or because Aharon was especially devoted to her and prayed for her recovery when she was sick (GR 80:10).

BATYAH

Pharaoh's daughter (Ex. 2:5–10) is called Batyah or Bityah (ER 1:26, 1:30; San. 19b, 31b). Having repudiated idolatry, Batyah went down to the Nile to immerse and "cleanse herself of her father's filth"—namely, his idols (ER 1:23; Sot. 12b; Meg. 13a).

She saw the basket containing Moses and told her servant to fetch it, but the latter refused. Batyah reached out for him herself, and as she did so, her arm increased several cubits in length to reach him (Rashi; ER 1:23; Sot. 12b; Meg. 15b). She saw that he was a Jewish boy and, as he began to cry, she took pity on him and decided to adopt him.

Moses would not suckle from any of the Egyptian women who tried to nurse him, so Miriam, observing all this, came forward and offered to find a Hebrew woman to nurse the child. Through this clever scheme, Miriam enabled Yokheved to get her baby back and keep him for two years, until he was weaned. Batyah's instructions to Yokheved to take *her* child were an unconscious prophecy (Rashi; ER 1:25; Sot. 12b).

Moses was thus raised in the royal house of Egypt. Although he had several other names, he was always called by the Egyptian name that Batyah gave him. Moreover, because she called him her son—in other words, saved him and raised him as her own—God called her "God's daughter," *bat-Yah* (LR 1:3). Batyah, who had no biological children of her own, was a loving mother to Moses. "She used to kiss and hug him, and loved him as if he were her own son. She would not allow him out of the royal palace. . . . So did the daughter of Pharaoh bring up him who was destined to exact retribution from her father" (ER 1:26).

It is commonly asserted that Ramses II was the pharaoh of Jewish oppression. This may not be the case, given that Jewish tradition dates the Exodus as 1313 B.C.E. and Ramses II ruled later (see Table 10–2). On the other hand, as the Egyptian calendar was not linear—that is, it did not count years—historians' estimates of yearly dates of Egyptian events *are* only estimates, and could be slightly inaccurate.

Whether Ramses II was the pharaoh in question, it is nevertheless interesting to examine his daughter Bint-Anat as a prototype of an Egyptian royal daughter. Given that Anat was the name of a Canaanite goddess also worshiped in Egypt, there is a definite structural similarity between the names *Bint-Anat* and *Bityah*. (The idol's name is substituted with *Yah*, one of God's Names.)

Bint-Anat, like most Egyptian princesses, was an incest victim by Torah—but not by matrilineal—standards. She was the firstborn daughter of Queen Istnafert by Ramses II. Ramses II, in order to maintain his right to rule, married Bint-Anat, who was naturally her mother's heir. Bint-Anat, significantly, is said to have died child-less. Ramses II also had another queen-wife, Nefertari, and he married two of their daughters as well.[3]

This information gives added meaning to Batyah's desire to "cleanse herself of her father's filth." It was not just the worship of stone and wooden gods she was discarding, but the sexual practices of idolatry as well. Many incest survivors today change their names as a way of healing themselves and disassociating themselves from their perpetrators. Perhaps this is the reason that Bint-Anat became Bityah and then Batyah—to be the daughter of God instead of the daughter of Pharaoh, his false gods, and his decadent culture.

Bint-Anat's position as firstborn adds to the notion that she could have been the woman who raised Moses, for Batyah was Pharaoh's firstborn. She was spared from the plague of the killing of the firstborn (which included girls) because she had saved Moses. For the same reason, Batyah was the only woman besides Serach who entered Gan Eden alive (ER 18:3, 20:4; *Kallah Rabbati,* chap. 3; *Derekh Eretz Zuta,* chap. 1).

SHLOMIT

He [Moses] saw an Egyptian man beating a Hebrew man. . . . He killed the Egyptian and hid him in the sand. (Ex. 2:11–12)

The son of an Israelite woman and an Egyptian man went out and quarreled in the camp with an Israelite man. The son of the Israelite woman blasphemed God's Name in a curse, so they brought him to Moses. His mother's name was Shlomit, daughter of Divri, of the tribe of Dan. (Lev. 24:10–11)

The Egyptian man in these passages was a taskmaster in charge of overseeing ten kapos, Jewish officers who did the oppressor's dirty work by overseeing ten slave laborers each. The taskmasters would go to the kapos' houses early in the morning to drag them to work by dawn. This Egyptian taskmaster noticed Shlomit, the wife of a Jewish officer named Datan. After dragging Datan to work, the Egyptian returned to his house and raped Shlomit, who became pregnant. When Datan confronted the Egyptian taskmaster, the latter beat Datan, trying to kill him. However, Moses saw this happening and killed the Egyptian (ER 1:28; Rashi).

Shlomit's son from the rape is the subject of the second passage; he was later stoned to death. The subject of the quarrel was his matrilineal descent: he went to pitch his

---

3. Murray, *Splendor,* p. 102.

tent with the tribe of Dan and was told by an Israelite man that he had no right to be there because tribal descent was patrilineal. Shlomit's son took his case to Moses, who judged that he was wrong (Rashi). No wonder he was so angry! He was Jewish, because his mother was, but the Israelites rejected him—as Dinah's brothers had rejected Asnat—because his Jewishness was not patrilineal.

Shlomit's rape is the subject of much less commentary than Dinah's, but the blame-the-victim message is unfortunately the same: "She was talkative in greeting"—namely, she dared to speak to men!—and "she brought death to her son" (LR 32:5). "She alone [of all Israelite women] was a whore. She continually babbled, inquiring after everyone's health. . . . She talked with every person, and therefore came to ruin" (Rashi).

The most sympathetic commentary says that Shlomit mistook the Egyptian for her husband (ER 1:28). This is not only hard to believe, it also says a lot about how rough and insensitive "normal" sex with her husband must have been!

ZIPPORAH

Zipporah's story is told in Exodus 2:16–22 and 4:24–26. After killing the Egyptian, Moses fled to Midian and sat near a well. When seven sisters, daughters of the priest of Midian, came to draw water for their sheep, the male shepherds tried to chase them away. Moses came to their aid, defending them and watering their sheep.

Their father, Yitro, had abandoned idol worship and resigned from its priesthood because he saw it was false. As a result, he was banished from the community, no one would be seen with him or work for him, and his daughters were harassed. The daughters, of whom Zipporah was the firstborn, used to arrive early at the well on account of their fear of the shepherds, who came that particular day with the intention of raping the girls. They did not succeed at this, but they did throw them into the well, whereupon Moses pulled them out (ER 1:32).

When the seven sisters told their father what had happened, he urged them to bring their rescuer home. "Immediately, Zipporah ran after him like a bird [tzipor] and brought him home. Why was her name Zipporah? Because she purified the house like a bird." That is, like a sacrificial bird offered as atonement for sin, she had a purifying effect in ridding her father's house of idolatry.

Moses stayed and married Zipporah, and they had two sons, Gershom and Eliezer. After seeing the burning bush, Moses returned to Egypt, bringing his family with him because he had faith that they would not be staying (Nachmanides). On the way, "Hashem confronted Moses and wanted to kill him" (Ex. 4:24). How could this possibly occur when God had just told Moses to lead the Jews out of slavery?

Zipporah took a sharp stone and circumcised their son. There are conflicting opinions as to whether this son was Gershom or Eliezer. Some commentators say that Moses had listened to his father-in-law's advice not to circumcise Gershom (SY 265; *Targum Jonathan*). The more likely opinion, however, says that Moses delayed circumcising the newborn Eliezer because of the journey but that even after they had arrived, he concerned himself first with food, drink, and accommodations instead of circumcising the baby (Rashi; ER 5:8; Ned. 31b–32a).

Zipporah understood that Moses' failure to perform this *mitzvah* was the reason for God's anger—she saw a vision of an angel try to swallow Moses, but it could not go any further than his sexual organ. Hence "she recognized the great power of circumcision" (ER 5:8). Then—in what has to be the most enigmatic verse in the Torah—Zipporah threw the foreskin down at "his" feet, saying, "For you are a bridegroom of blood to me, . . . a bridegroom of blood for circumcision" (Ex. 4:25–26). Again there are conflicting opinions: did she throw the foreskin down at the feet of Moses, the child, or the angel of death, and to whom was she talking? Rashi says it was Moses' feet and that she was telling the child that her husband was nearly killed (i.e., had his blood shed) because of him. Sforno says she was reminding Moses that he married her on the condition that they would observe circumcision, and she was also telling the angel this in Moses' defense.

One thing, however, is definitely clear: through her quick thinking and action, Zipporah saved Moses' life. Without women like Zipporah, Batyah, and Miriam—two of whom were gentiles—there would have been no Moses, no Exodus, and no Jewish people.

When Moses met up with Aharon on his way back to Egypt, Aharon said it was enough to bring out the Jews who were already in Egypt; why add more? Therefore, Moses sent Zipporah and their sons back to Midian; they later returned to Moses in the wilderness with Yitro (Ex. 18:2).

✳✳ 14 ✳✳

Elisheva

Vaera (6:2–9:35)

Aharon took Elisheva, daughter of Aminadav, sister of Nachshon, for a wife, and she gave birth to Nadav, Avihu, Elazar, and Itamar. (Ex. 6:23)

"Elisheva, daughter of Aminadav, did not enjoy happiness in the world, even though she saw five crowns in one day" (LR 20:2). The "five crowns" were the five men in her life:

1. Her brother, Nachshon, was prince of the tribe of Judah in the wilderness (Num. 1:7, 2:3);
2. Her husband, Aharon, was high priest;
3. Her brother-in-law, Moses, was leader of the Jewish people;
4. Her son, Elazar, was the *segan*, or assistant high priest; and
5. Her grandson, Pinchas, was the "war priest," who was specifically anointed to spiritually prepare the people for battle (Deut. 20:2).

Elisheva is thus said to have had "five joys more than the other daughters of Israel" (Zev. 102a). However, when Nadav and Avihu were killed by God for offering "strange fire" (Lev. 10:1–2), Elisheva's joy turned into mourning.

Elisheva's father, Aminadav, was the fifth generation from Tamar and Judah, a patrilineal descendant of their son Peretz. Thus, Elisheva and Nachshon were the sixth generation. Nachshon was the first of the twelve tribal princes to make a dedication offering to the Tabernacle (Num. 7:12). He was rewarded in this way for his faith at the Red Sea. Pursued from behind by the Egyptians, the Jews were confronted and apparently trapped by the vast sea before them. Everyone was afraid to jump in, but Nachshon fearlessly took the first plunge, trusting in God's providence. Nachshon is

146

mentioned in Elisheva's lineage to teach that "all who marry a woman should investigate who her brothers are" because "most sons resemble the mother's brothers" (Rashi; B.B. 110a; ER 7:5). This belief is an obvious vestige of matrilineal descent.

Nachshon had a grandson named Boaz, who was the man who did his duty as a *yavam* to Ruth; they were the eighth generation from Tamar. King David was the eleventh generation (Ruth 4:18–22). Tamar, Elisheva, and Ruth were thus all women of the tribe of Judah—Elisheva as a daughter, and Tamar and Ruth as daughters-in-law. Women were not so much "lost" through patrilineal tribal descent as they were "exchanged."

Elisheva, a "daughter" of Judah on her father's side (we do not know who her mother was), married into the tribe of Levi. Miriam, a "daughter" of Levi both maternally and paternally, married Calev, a "son" of Judah. Thus, her children were Judeans, as was Miriam after her marriage. Daughter-in-law replaced daughter: Miriam went, tribally, from Levi to Judah, while Elisheva went from Judah to Levi. This exchange of Miriam and Elisheva might have even been a specific marriage barter between Amram and Aminadav.

Elisheva might have had four twin daughters with her sons, given the numerical occurrence of the direct object marker *et,* the method used to determine the existence of Cayin and Hevel's sisters (see chapter 1). Each of Elisheva's daughters, as well as her sons' daughters, was a *bat-kohen*: a *kohenet* (priestly woman) by virtue of being the daughter of a *kohen* (priest). Daughters' daughters did not continue the line.

Elisheva and her daughters-in-law, the wives of her sons, were each an *eshet-kohen*, a *kohenet* by virtue of *marrying* a *kohen*. The *kehunah* was formed by patrilineal descent; hence women's positions in it, relative to men, are as daughter and wife, contrary to matrilineal descent, in which women's positions vis-à-vis men are as mother and sister.

There were three "classes" of Jews: *kohen* (a descendant of Aharon), *levi* (a descendant of Moses), and Israel (the other eleven tribes). These were not economic classes but distinctions in religious duties regarding the care of the Tabernacle and the execution of its daily services and offerings. *Kohen* and *levi* were not landowners but were supported by tithes from Israel.

Kohen, *levi*, and Israel also functioned as marriage classes; there are special laws governing marriage between them. An Israelite man who married a *kohenet* was called a *zar* ("stranger"); he did not enter the *kehunah* by marriage and so could not participate in any priestly privileges, such as eating the tithes or the sacrificial food. An Israelite woman who married a *kohen*, however, did become a *kohenet* by marriage and participated in all female priestly privileges, the eating of the sacred foods. Thus, women could enter the *kehunah* through birth or by marriage, but men entered only through birth.

BAT-PUTIEL

Elazar, son of Aharon, took from the daughters of Putiel for a wife. She gave birth to Pinchas. (Ex. 6:25)

Elazar was the older of the two surviving sons of Elisheva and Aharon. The other, Itamar, was in charge of keeping the accounts of the Tabernacle and of transporting it (Ex. 38:21; Num. 4:28, 4:33). Elazar succeeded Aharon as high priest, and his son Pinchas later succeeded him.

Bat-Putiel may have been one of Zipporah's sisters, for she was a descendant of Joseph on her mother's side and Yitro on her father's side (San. 82b). Some believe Putiel was Yitro himself, which would make Bat-Putiel one of the seven sisters. Her father's name, Putiel, is related to Yitro's "fattening calves for idolatry" as well as Joseph's "overcoming his passion" (Sot. 43a; B.B. 109b–110a).

Bat-Putiel is said to be mentioned because of the importance of Pinchas. "In the case of kings, it is the customary way of Scripture to mention the names of their mothers"—another obvious matrilineal vestige. Putiel had many daughters, and the one who was the mother of Pinchas may even have been a granddaughter rather than a literal "daughter" (Nachmanides).

THE TEN PLAGUES: DEFEAT OF
EGYPTIAN GODS AND GODDESSES

The Egyptians had as many as two thousand deities. As Egyptian religion developed over the millennia, these deities evolved from pure animal imagery to humans with animal heads. For instance, the god Horus was first represented as a falcon, and Pharaoh was his incarnation. Later, Horus was depicted as a man's body with a falcon's head. Such anthropomorphism represented development toward a higher stage of imagining the divine. Now it was time to understand that God is suprahuman.

Each of the plagues that God cast upon Egypt attacked one or more deities. Hence, the God of Israel demonstrated the ultimate powerlessness of Egyptian gods and goddesses: "By your life, Israel will not leave here until they slaughter the gods of Egypt before their eyes, so that I will show them that their gods are nothing" (ER 16:3). This was very psychologically and spiritually liberating for the Jewish slaves, who had "despaired of escaping on account of the magical arts with which the Egyptians held fast their prisoners" (*Zohar* II:25a).

Each plague was *midah kneged midah* for the ways in which the Egyptians had oppressed the Jews; each was intended to make the Egyptians feel for themselves what it meant to be alien, enslaved, and oppressed. Each plague lasted one week and was preceded by a three-week warning (Rashi; ER 9:12), but every third plague had no warning at all.

Aharon brought about three plagues, Moses brought about three, God brought about three, and all three parties together brought about one (ER 12:4). Each plague is listed in Table 14–1, along with its Hebrew name and its initiator.

We will now examine the first seven plagues and the gods they represented.

TABLE 14–1. The Ten Plagues

Plague	Hebrew Name	Initiator
1. Blood	*Dam*	Aharon
2. Frogs	*Tzefardea*	Aharon
3. Insects	*Kenim*	Aharon
4. Wild Beasts	*Arov*	God
5. Pestilence	*Dever*	God
6. Boils	*Shechin*	All three
7. Hail	*Barad*	Moses
8. Locusts	*Arbeh*	Moses
9. Darkness	*Choshek*	Moses
10. Killing of the Firstborn	*Makat Bekhorot*	God

Blood

The Nile River was and is the source of life for Egypt. The river, and not rainfall, determines feast or famine for the Egyptian people. Thus, it determines not only the agricultural cycle, but the calendar and the people's sense of time itself. Being so central to Egyptian life, the Nile's various phases were deified into a number of entities.[1]

"As Egypt's supramundane power was centered in the Nile, the Holy One enforced [God's] will first on that principality, so that—the Nile being one of their divinities—their highest power might first of all be humbled. From the lesser idols also blood gushed out. . . . Pharaoh was the ruler of the waters. . . . For that reason the turning of his river into blood was the first plague" (*Zohar* II:29a). "Because rain does not fall in Egypt but the Nile rises and irrigates the land and thus the Egyptians worshiped the Nile, therefore God first struck their god and afterwards struck them" (Rashi).

The New Year occurs with the rising of the star Sirius, just before sunrise around July 21. Sirius was personified as the goddess Sothis or Sopdet. The three main seasons of Egypt then follow:

• Akhet, or Inundation, when the Nile overflows its banks and floods the land (July–November). It was mythologized as Isis weeping for Osiris. It is celebrated with a ceremony of cutting the dam to let the waters gush forth; a virgin dressed as a bride was drowned as a sacrifice. This is the season in which pyramid builders were conscripted. The Nile flooding, Isis's tears, became personified as the god Hapy. "Thousands of miniature figures of Hapy were manufactured in every sort of material, among them gold and silver, copper, lead, turquoise, lapis lazuli . . . , besides seals, pendants, and statuettes of his consort, Repit. When the floods were due to rise, these were offered to the god in large numbers of temples."[2] These

---

1. All information in this and the next chapter about Egyptian deities, unless otherwise noted, is taken from Hart.

2. Montet, p. 32.

idols, along with the "books of the Nile" (books of fate or oracular papyruses) were cast into the lake of a particular temple in a form of sympathetic magic (so the idol would provide protection from an unfavorable prediction). The ritual was repeated two months later, in September, when the floods reached their peak.

• Proyet, or Emergence, when the land reappears and the waters recede. Crops are sown at this time (November–March). Tatenen was a god of the emerging Nile silt after the waters of the inundation had receded.

• Shomu, or Summer, the harvest season (March–July).

Other deities included Nun, a god personifying the primeval waters, and Satis and Anukis, mother-and-daughter Nile goddesses.

The Nile turned to blood in repayment for Pharaoh's mass murder of baby boys and for his preventing Jewish women from ritual immersion after menstruation. Because the Egyptians sought to curb the Jewish population in these ways, the fish (a fertility symbol because they were so prolific) died, something that had not even happened in the Flood.

This plague struck the creatures of the Nile as well: Hatmehyt, the preeminent fish goddess; Sobek, a crocodile god; Khnum, "lord of the crocodiles"; Taweret, hippopotamus goddess, divine midwife, and protector of women in childbirth; and Ipy, a hippopotamus goddess.

The Egyptians dug around the river, but all they found was blood. "Even their saliva became blood" (ER 9:10). Furthermore, if an Egyptian and an Israelite drew water from the same source, the Egyptian would get blood but the Israelite would get water. Consequently, the Israelites became rich by selling water to the Egyptians. All the rivers, streams, and pools were filled with blood; so were the wooden and stone idols, vessels, altars, and public baths (ER 9:11).

Frogs

The Nile returned to normal, but God was not yet done with it. Now, frogs emerged out of the river. Actually, one frog emerged and either "bred prolifically and filled the land" or "croaked for the others and they came" (San. 67b). This was Heket, the frog goddess whose image was worn on amulets by women for protection in child-birth, as well as on ivory knives to defend the home and ward off threats to families. These latter amulets, at least, no longer worked—Egyptian homes were invaded by the very being that was supposed to protect them.

Why were frogs chosen? "The Egyptians, in enslaving Israel, ordered them to bring reptiles and creeping things; in retaliation did God bring frogs upon them. When-ever they filled a cup, it was full of frogs" (ER 10:4).

All households were affected. "Whenever an Egyptian woman was kneading dough, or heating her oven, frogs would come into the dough, eat it and then go down into the oven, cool it, and cleave to the bread. . . . Whenever there was a little earth and a drop of water touched it, it would become a frog" (ER 10:2–3). This plague even settled a border dispute between Egypt and Ethiopia.

"Through the croakings of the frogs no one in Egypt could converse with his or her neighbor [and] . . . babies and young children hid from the chatter." For every frog an Egyptian killed, six more came forth from its belly, so people stopped trying to kill them (*Zohar* II:30a).

The frogs even got inside the Egyptians' bodies. "Bad as was the havoc wrought by the frogs, their raucous noises were even worse to the Egyptians than their touch, for they used to enter their bodies and croak from within." The frogs died and their carcasses piled up and stank. "Because Israel smelled bad from the beatings of the Egyptians, God retaliated in kind upon them" (ER 10:6). The frogs even emasculated men (ER 10:3, 15:27).

The biggest frogs were in the house of Pharaoh. As soon as Pharaoh drank, the liquid would become a frog that stayed wedged in him. Pharaoh was hit particularly hard by this plague because the pharaoh in Sarah's time had had her picture painted on his bedroom wall, as well as on a wooden image he took to bed with him. "Each successive pharaoh used to similarly feast his eyes on that picture. For that reason, Pharaoh was punished more severely than his subjects, the frogs entering even into his bed" (*Zohar* II:30a).

Insects

This plague, which was generally thought to consist of lice or gnats coming up out of the dust, was the first plague that Pharaoh's magicians could not reproduce (Ex. 8:14). Why were insects chosen? "Because they made Israel the streetcleaners, therefore their dust became insects, so when they dug, cubit by cubit, there was no dust" (ER 10:7).

The insects were most likely scarabs, beetles that emerge from within balls of dirt that they themselves roll up and move across the ground. The scarab was worshiped as the god Khepri and

> was held in special regard [because] ancient Egyptians believed that the beetle had offspring without the union of male and female. . . . After fertilization the female deposits her eggs in a piece of dung and rolls it into a ball, so that when they hatch, the newborn will be provided with food. Since this was the only part of the reproductive cycle the Egyptians saw, they assumed the beetle was somewhat like the god Atum who begot children without a female partner.[3]

Scarab amulets were common, and "scarab beetles were themselves mummified, so it is almost certain that they were sacred. Their magical powers can be assumed from several of their uses: Parts of the body and the wings were used to make an ointment for stiff joints; the wing cases were used in an unguent to facilitate child delivery; and evil spells were undone when a large beetle was beheaded, its wings removed, and the body burned."[4]

---

3. Brier, p. 146.
4. Ibid., p. 150.

Wild Beasts

This plague of wild beasts was a mixture of flies, scorpions, snakes, birds, and mammals, as well as the "mingling of a perverse and hybrid kind" (*Zohar* II:30b). Their carcasses disappeared at death so that the Egyptians could not benefit from their meat or skin.

Why were wild animals chosen? This occurred because the Egyptians "used to say to Israel, 'Go and bring us bears, lions, and tigers' in order to vex them," to send them out into the wild and keep them from their homes (ER 11:3). In addition, "because of their [sexual] confusion, one man sleeping with 10 women, and 10 men sleeping with one woman, therefore God struck them with a motley crew" (ER 15:27).

Many wild animals were worshiped by the Egyptians as gods and goddesses, including the falcon, hawk, vulture, ibis, heron, pelican, jackal, lion, panther, baboon, snake, and scorpion. From this we can deduce the composition of the "motley crew."

Pestilence

Pestilence killed all the cattle and other domestic livestock owned by the Egyptians. No beast owned by an Israelite died, even if it was in the hands of an Egyptian, so this plague settled ownership disputes. Why was pestilence chosen? It was "because they had made the Israelites shepherds of their herds and flocks, and had scattered their cattle over hills and desert places, in order to prevent Israel from being fruitful and multiplying" (ER 11:4).

We have noted the prevalence of bull worship in Egypt, mostly symbolizing Osiris, and that both Nut and Isis were represented as cows. Other cow goddesses included the Seven Hathors, whose role was to determine a child's destiny at birth; Bat, cow goddess of upper Egypt; Hesat, who gave birth to Pharaoh in the form of a golden calf; and Mehet-Weret, a cow goddess of the sky, like Nut.

Pestilence is later defined by the Talmud as being caused by corrupt or delayed judgments (Shab. 33a) and by ignoring one's responsibilities to the poor (Av. 5:9).

Boils

The plague of boils was created by furnace soot that was thrown up in the air and settled as dust on all of Egypt. Why were boils chosen? It was "because they had ordered the Israelites to heat for them what was [already] hot and to chill for them what was cold" (ER 11:5). Boils made the Egyptians unable to stand either hot or cold on their bodies.

"A wound caused by wood or stone, or olive peat, or the hot springs of Tiberias, or anything that does not come from the heat of light, including a wound caused by lead just taken from the mine, is a boil" (Chul. 8a). The Talmud contains an incantation for healing boils (Shab. 67a), which are considered so serious that a man who has them can be compelled to divorce his wife (Ket. 77a), and a *yevamah* is not obliged to marry a *yavam* if he has boils (Yev. 4a).

This plague is said to have struck "the celestial patron" of Pharaoh's magicians, "so that they should have no power" (ER 15:27). It also struck right at the heart of the Egyptians' obsession with their bodies—their vain cult of beauty and the rituals, such as embalming and mummification, which preserved the body even after death.

Hail

The hail was ice with fire inside it. "In order to do the will of their Creator, they [fire and water] made peace between them" (Rashi). This hail killed every Egyptian person, animal, and plant that was outdoors, but in Goshen, where the Jews lived, there was none. Why was hail chosen? "Because they had made the Israelites planters of their vineyards, gardens, orchards, and trees, so hail destroyed all these plantations" (ER 12:3).

Flax and barley were destroyed, but wheat and spelt, which were late in sprouting, were not (Ex. 9:31–32). This plague targeted grain and earth gods such as Geb, from whose ribs barley grew. It also targeted Baal, god of the sky and storms, who was known as "he who rides on the clouds" and whose voice was thunder. The Talmud names a "prince of hail" among the angels (Pes. 118a).

The plague was supposed to only affect the produce, but many Egyptians did not heed the warning to bring the cattle inside (ER 12:2). Many did, however, and as a result, Moses would not pray in the city because it was full of idols (Ex. 9:29; Rashi; ER 12:5).

❀❀❀ 15 ❀❀❀

Firstborn Daughters

Bo (10:1–13:16)

The last three plagues on Egypt—Locusts, Darkness, and Killing the Firstborn—were God's way of attacking the related idolatrous cults of the sun and the son.

Son-preference was prevalent in the ancient world and continues in modern times. Although it diminishes somewhat with economic development and modernization, it has never disappeared entirely, for son-preference is not restricted to wanting a son *instead of* a daughter; it also consists of wanting *mostly* sons or even simply a *firstborn* son. Most American couples today want children of both sexes, but two out of three would choose a son first;[1] among American Jews, the figure is said to be 92 percent.[2] The phenomenon of firstborn-son idolization is the focus of this chapter.

A PRIESTHOOD OF FIRSTBORN SONS

The eighth plague, of locusts, was brought upon the Egyptians because Pharaoh was willing to let the Israelite men, *but not the women,* leave Egypt to travel three days in the wilderness to worship God (Ex. 10:11). Pharaoh could not understand why women and children had to go worship. Even letting *all* the adult men go was a concession. The democratic notion of religious worship proposed by Moses was a totally foreign concept to the king of Egypt, for "priests were nearly always the sons of priests," with firstborn sons holding the most elite positions.[3]

---

1. John Leo, "Baby Boys, to Order," *U.S. News and World Report,* Jan. 9, 1989, p. 59. See also Gena Corea, *The Mother Machine* (New York: Harper and Row, 1979), p. 191.
2. Letty Cottin Pogrebin, *Deborah, Golda, and Me* (New York: Crown, 1991), p. 237.
3. Montet, p. 279.

Women were, by definition, excluded from a father–son priesthood. "No woman is a minister of any deity, whether male or female; all are served by men," Herodotus states in his observations of Egypt.[4] However, in earlier millennia of Egyptian history,

> there were many important orders of priestesses under the Old and Middle Kingdom. . . . During the first dynasties the names of the women exercising the full functions of priestesses are exceedingly numerous. After the XIIth Dynasty, apart from the sacerdotal functions exercised *ex officio* by princesses of the royal family, and the secondary religious offices commonly held by women, there is not a single example of a priestess to be found.[5]

By the Eighteenth and Nineteenth Dynasties—the time of Jewish descent, slavery, and Exodus—women had not served as Egyptian priestesses for at least two hundred years. Religious worship in the New Kingdom was purely a royal, elite, and lavishly corrupt affair. "The main preoccupation of every king was the creation of new shrines, and the enlargement and embellishment of those that already existed."[6]

Originally, the king served as high priest. "The Egyptian king had always to play a religious part. In the same way as each Egyptian of high standing exercised a kind of priestly office in the temple of his god, so the king was considered the priest of all the gods. Whenever we enter an Egyptian temple, we see the king represented offering his sacrifice to the gods."[7] The priesthood later rose in power as a separate institution, rivaling the kings, "and indeed at last entirely thrust them aside. . . . At that period religion undermined and stifled the energies of the nation; kings exhausted their resources in building gigantic temples, or in giving the booty of towns to the god Amon. . . . It was natural that the priesthood should thrive on the religious fanaticism of a decaying nation."[8]

> The activity of the state . . . that of the king for the gods, was so excessive, particularly under the New Kingdom, that the state must be regarded as really maintaining the religion of the country. The state and the priesthood are alone responsible for its prosperity. . . . The king builds the temple; the king bestows treasure, the long lists of offerings are said to be royal gifts; scarcely anything worth mentioning comes from private individuals. . . . It is the king who is always represented in the temple, and it is the king for whom prayers are offered in the temple. No mention is made of pious worshipers. The temple services appear to have been of a strictly official character.[9]

The king started the day by assisting at the morning sacrifice in the temple, where the high priest prayed for the god's blessing on the king. The king "alone with the

---

4. Carter, p. 106.
5. Briffault, 2:515 1:387.
6. Montet, p. 275.
7. Erman, p. 67.
8. Ibid., p. 105.
9. Ibid., p. 273.

high priest might enter the holy of holies in the temples, he alone might open the doors of the inner sanctuary and 'see his father the god.'"[10]

The Egyptian public could not go beyond the temple courtyard and mostly worshiped at sacred groves or at home with "household gods," miniature replicas of a temple god's image. Once a year, the temple image would be brought out for a public procession and festival. However, "the daily rites performed in all Egyptian temples, in the king's name and at his expense, were conducted in the innermost shrine and in secret. The public [was] debarred from all participation."[11]

Under such circumstances, women's role as "temple musicians" was clearly a subordinate one, like that of any harem entertainer for her master. "Dressed in long transparent clothes, and with tambourine or castanets in their hands they turn round and round in quick time, bending their bodies in a coquettish manner. The old Egyptians took no . . . offense at these questionable movements of the dancers [and, indeed,] . . . it was a favorite amusement to look on at this dancing, and at social parties dancers were invited for the entertainment of the guests."[12]

Royal temple rites were simply the most lavish party of all.

The god was . . . regarded as an earthly prince, and the singers, who made music in his presence, were the beautiful singers, the inmates of the house of women. The singers formed the harem of the god, and they held various degrees of rank as in an earthly harem. . . . At public worship their duty was to play the sistrum before the god; probably there was not much more for them to do in their official capacity, for we find that a child could be invested with this high rank.[13]

The role of the "harem of the god" was clearly a sexual one:

It is sometimes suggested that the members of this divine harem formed a kind of corps of sacred prostitutes such as is known to have existed in Byblos, a town steeped in the traditions of Egyptian civilization. . . . The behavior of the singers of [the god] Amon was sometimes distinctly forward and they were not always over-particular about where they went, but it would no doubt be quite unfair to assume that all the singers of Amon behaved like this on the evidence of the only example preserved in a papyrus now in Turin. It could not in any case prove that women attached to the temple were obliged to follow the example of the women of Byblos during the feast of [the god] Adonis, namely, to give themselves to strangers and to hand over any resulting profits to the temple treasury.[14]

The Jewish prohibition of female musicians and singers at the Temple in Jerusalem makes sense as a response to the exploitation of female sensuality in pagan religious rites. *Kol ishah,* as practiced today in Orthodox communities, is a vestige of

10. Ibid., pp. 67, 68.
11. Montet, p. 280.
12. Erman, pp. 249–250.
13. Ibid., pp. 295–296.
14. Montet, p. 279.

that practice, as it continues to keep men who observe it from using women's singing and dancing as entertainment, much less "religious worship." However, the religious context today is no longer paganism, but Christianity, which combined the Jewish rejection of pagan sexual rites with a *much more extensive* repression of women's voices, demanding that women be silent in teaching and preaching as well as in song.

LOCUSTS AND SUN GODS

The locusts destroyed the wheat (which had been spared by the hail). Because the Egyptians "made Israel sowers of wheat," . . . the locusts "devoured all that the Israelites had sown for them." At first the Egyptians rejoiced and gathered the locusts, salting them to preserve as food, but even those that had been pickled in pots and barrels flew away (ER 13:6). Like the frogs, the locusts served to settle a border dispute with Ethiopia (ER 13:4).

Locust plagues were not unusual in the Middle East, but this was the worst to ever occur, both then and ever after (Ex. 10:14). A plague of *arbeh*—red locusts, which are kosher (Kaplan; Lev. 11:22; Chul. 65a)—was generally accompanied by pestilence. In talmudic times, a fast was proclaimed in response to a plague of *arbeh*, and the *shofar* was sounded (Ta. 19a, 22a).

Because the locusts "darkened the land" (Ex. 10:13), they worked in conjunction with the next plague, darkness, in targeting the Egyptian sun gods. The locusts came into Egypt by an east wind, the direction of sunrise, striking Sopedu, "lord of the east," and Khepri, the scarab beetle, who represented "the sun god at dawn on the eastern horizon."[15]

Sun gods were the highest of Egyptian deities and were always male. Since the Fifth Dynasty, "the quintessence of all manifestations of the sun god" was Ra (or Re), whose "supremacy was the basis of Pharaoh's own security and power, governing Egypt in accordance with the universal order. . . . Deviation from the sun god's dictates rendered a monarch unworthy of divine kingship." The sun god was "traditional father of the Egyptian pharaoh,"[16] while Pharaoh himself was called "the living sun."[17]

Sun gods, like the scarab (which was thought to reproduce alone), were worshiped as male creators of the universe. Atum, a sun god called "the father of the king of Egypt," was believed to have arisen "self-engendered out of the primeval water" and to have created the universe through an act of masturbation.[18]

The Theban sun god Amon became the prominent royal deity in the Eighteenth Dynasty under his namesake pharaohs, the Amenophises. "A woman slept in the

<hr>

15. Hart, pp. 205, 108.
16. Ibid., pp. 179, 180–181, 53.
17. Neumann, *Origins*, p. 149.
18. Hart, pp. 47–48.

temple of Amon as the consort of the god. . . . Usually she was no less a personage than the Queen of Egypt herself. For according to the Egyptians, their monarchs were actually begotten by the god Amon."[19] Pharaoh was thus "the sun's son."

Under Akhnaten (Amenophis IV), the "solar disk" of Aten was briefly declared the exclusive god of Egypt. This henotheism—the worship of one god while still believing that others exist—was the closest that ancient Egypt ever came to monotheism. It occurred while Moses was growing up in the Egyptian royal household (see Table 10–2). Although the movement was destroyed by its own fanatic zeal and failed to make any lasting religious reformation, it is nevertheless quite conceivable that the spark of revolution stemmed from Moses' influence on Akhnaten, as they had grown up together as boys in the house of Amenophis III.

THE PLAGUE OF DARKNESS

The ninth plague continued the attack on Egyptian sun gods. It lasted a week but took part in two phases. For the first three days, "people could not see each other"; for the next three days, "no one left their place"; in other words, no one could stand up, sit down, or move in any way (Rashi; Ex. 10:22–23).

Only about 20 percent of Jacob's descendants actually left Egypt. Those who were so far "gone" into the slave mentality—who did not even despise their slavery enough to yearn for freedom—were destroyed. "There were, among the Israelites of that generation, evil ones who did not want to leave. They died during the first three days, so the Egyptians could not see their destruction and think the Israelites were being struck too" (Rashi).

During the second three days, the Jews entered the Egyptians' houses and saw their jewelry; thus, when the Jewish women later asked their Egyptian neighbors if they could "borrow" their silver and gold, if an Egyptian said she had nothing, the Jew could say what she had seen and where. The Egyptian, however, thought, "If she wanted to deceive me, she would have taken it then." Since the Jews did not steal the goods in the dark, the Egyptians believed that they really would return them later and so willingly lent them (Rashi; ER 14:3).

The Jews in Goshen had light in their houses; wherever a Jew went in Egypt, there was light. The Egyptians' "light itself came from darkness"—all their advances and success had come from sorcery (ER 14:2). Enslavement to the mind-set of magic had created the need for a physical and spiritual Exodus, and Israel was chosen as the nation "for whose sake the knots of magic were loosened . . . because only at night does the Holy One exercise judgment, therefore it was night when the knots of sorcery were loosened and the bonds of darkness rent in two" (*Zohar* II:38a).

For this reason, the firstborn of Egypt were slaughtered in the darkness of midnight, but the Jews left Egypt in the light of day so that all could see.

---

19. Frazer, p. 164.

KILLING THE RAM GODS

The tenth and final plague, killing the firstborn, contained within it a subplague: killing rams (male lambs) at the solar month of Aries (March 21–April 19). Aries is the first constellation of the zodiac and is symbolized by a ram; it represents initiative, leadership, and other "firstborn" traits. The month was given to Israel at this time as *Nisan*, the first *Rosh Chodesh* and head month of the Jewish year.

The ram was sacred to the sun god Amon. "The Thebans and all other Egyptians who worshiped the Theban god Amon held rams to be sacred, and would not sacrifice them. But once a year at the festival of Amon they killed a ram, skinned it, and clothed the image of the god in the skin. Then they mourned over the ram and buried it in a sacred tomb. . . . The ram was Amon himself."[20]

Other ram gods were also linked to the sun. Heryshaf of middle Egypt wore the sun disk on his horns. Khnum was considered the "soul of the sun god," and rams sacred to him "have been discovered on Elephantine Island, mummified, adorned with gilded head-pieces and buried in stone sarcophagi."[21] Khepri, the scarab sun god, was sometimes represented as a *ram-headed* beetle.

While the sun god succeeded the hawk of Horus as the emblem of Pharaoh's ancestry—his spiritual "father"—the ram symbolized Pharaoh himself, the god's "firstborn." The ram cult symbolized an emphasis on Pharaoh's "divine" patrilineal heritage, to the exclusion of his human matrilineal right to the throne. This emphasis is indicated in the myths of the "self-engendered" male, who not only was *created* without a female but was able to *create* a whole universe without a female, through a lone act of masturbation!

The Jews were instructed to kill this patriarchal ram god, spread its blood on their doorways, eat its flesh roasted in fire rather than boiled in water, and burn any leftovers. The burning left the bones intact, "so the dogs might drag them about and the Egyptians be made to realize the nothingness of that which they worshiped" (*Zohar* II:41b).

The blood was painted on each doorway in the shape of a Heh (ה), "the design of the Holy Name." Bunches of hyssop were used as paintbrushes (Ex. 12:22) because "all the streets and marketplaces of the Egyptians were filled with idols, and all their houses with implements of magic. . . . Therefore it was necessary to purge the doors with the hyssop, in order that these powers might be exorcised" (*Zohar* II:35b–36a).

One of hyssop's uses in herbal medicine is as an emmenagogue, "an agent that promotes menstrual flow."[22] The blood on the two doorposts of each Jewish house in Egypt has been said to represent the blood of the ram and the blood of circumcision—the circumcision having been done en masse at that time by gentile male servants and Jewish men who had ignored it, as a requirement for attendance at the *seder*.

---

20. Ibid., p. 580.
21. Hart, pp. 110–111.
22. John Lust, *The Herb Book* (New York: Bantam, 1974), pp. 236, 54.

A doorway, however, consists of two doorposts and a lintel, indicating a three-fold symbolism to the blood. It makes no sense to say that the blood of a ram sym-bolizes the blood of a ram. Considering the feminine nature of a "doorway" and the shape of the letter *Heh*, which represents the birth canal and is a "feminine" letter in God's Name and in Hebrew grammar, it is more accurate to say the ram's blood symbolizes the threefold blood of menstruation, childbirth, and circumcision. The first two represent the strength of Jewish women in the face of Pharaoh's mass mur-der program of population control.

KILLING THE FIRSTBORN OF EGYPT

"Every firstborn in Egypt will die, from the firstborn of Pharaoh sitting on this throne, to the firstborn of the slavewoman behind the millstones, and every firstborn animal."
... And Hashem struck every firstborn in the land of Egypt, from the firstborn of Pharaoh sitting on his throne, to the firstborn of the prisoner in the dungeon, and every first-born animal. (Ex. 11:5, 12:29)

The plague was democratic: Pharaoh had no more privilege than a female pris-oner or war captive. It included every household's firstborn child, whether a son or daughter; we are told, for instance, that Batyah, Pharaoh's daughter, was spared (ER 18:3) and that there was not a single house where someone did not die (Rashi). Pha-raoh himself was a "spared firstborn," but he was saved only in order to be drowned in the Red Sea later.

The firstborn of other nations in Egypt at that time were killed, and the firstborn of prisoners were killed because "they rejoiced at the misfortune of the Israelites," and so they would not think it was their gods who punished the Egyptians. Egyptian firstborns in the care of Jews died, but Jewish firstborns in the care of Egyptians did not. Pregnant Egyptian women about to give birth miscarried and then themselves died (Rashi; ER 17:5, 18:2).

God punished the firstborn "because Israel is God's firstborn" (ER 15:27). The plague was based on a matrilineal definition of firstborn: the firstborn of every *woman* was killed (Nachmanides). With polygyny, a man thus had as many firstborns as he had wives and concubines. Bint-Anat, for example, was the firstborn of Queen Istnafert, but her father, Ramses II, had other firstborns from other wives and concu-bines.

Rashi, mistakenly believing the definition to be patrilineal (meaning the firstborn of every *man*), came up with the misogynist distortion that "Egyptian women were unfaithful to their husbands and bore children from young unmarried men and thus Egyptian men had many firstborn—sometimes there were five to one woman, each being the firstborn to its father." The matrilineal definition includes the firstborn of *both* women and men, in most cases; the patrilineal definition includes only the first-born of men. For example, Reuven and Joseph were both matrilineal firstborns of Jacob; one was the firstborn of Leah and the other was the firstborn of Rachel. By a patrilineal definition, however, only Reuven was Jacob's firstborn. Jacob's favoring of Joseph can thus be seen as an attempt to preserve the matrilineal definition of the firstborn, and Joseph's supersession of Reuven is evidence that he succeeded.

Killing the firstborn was the grand finale in God's destruction of the Egyptian deities. Idols made of wood rotted, and those made of metal melted. "They took their children and hid them in the temples of their idols. . . . What caused them to be smitten by such a succession of plagues? The fact that they trusted their idols. So what did God do? Struck their deities together with them." (ER 15:15).

THE SACRIFICE OF FIRSTBORN SONS

God made the death of Egypt's firstborn a plague because firstborn sons were an Egyptian cult idol, like frogs, beetles, rams, bulls, and the sun. By striking *all* the firstborn—male and female, royal and slave, human and animal—God was demonstrating the equal value of sons and daughters as well as a universal power far superior to that of any Egyptian deity. Although an Egyptian deity might demand the ritual sacrifice of a firstborn son, the scope and undiscriminating nature of God's plague made it clear that this was not the current situation.

The ritual sacrifice of firstborn sons was part of a wider system of human sacrifice in the ancient world, which consisted of "sacrifice of the one for the many—to make the seed sprout—and of the many for the one—to attend the dead king."[23]

Sacrifice of "the many for the one" consisted of slaughtering *masses* of people with *low* social value, such as war captives, widows, servants, and concubines. War captives were often sacrificed by a king to thank his god for the victory. Amenophis II, the pharaoh around the time of Joseph's death, "slew seven chiefs with his own club and hung their bodies head downwards at the bows of his boat" as an offering to Amon.[24]

Widows and concubines of the king were sacrificed to accompany their "lord and master" to the grave. It was a "sacred duty" to follow him "to the next world, as part of a sumptuous ritual."[25] Tombs have been discovered from 2100–2000 B.C.E. in Ur (less than three hundred years before the time of Sarah and Avraham), "in which many bodies of attendants were found slain with their masters." The tomb of Amenophis II contained "two women laid out on the floor [who] had either also been strangled or committed suicide." Larger groups of women have been found in such tombs as well; for example, "ten women carefully arranged in two rows, with no tomb furnishings of their own . . . because they themselves were part of the tomb furnishing of their king."

One royal tomb was found with "sixty-four court ladies" in it. "It is possible that the Queen, in common with the rest of the great retinue, was herself a victim. . . . The

---

23. Nigel Davies, *Human Sacrifice* (New York: Morrow, 1981), p. 17.
24. Ibid., p. 36.
25. This and the following, see ibid., pp. 28–31, 36–37.

customs of wives accompanying their husbands into the next world is ancient and almost universal."

Sacrifice of "the one for the many" consisted of slaughtering one *individual* person of *high* social value. In ancient times this meant the king, as we discussed in chapter 6. King sacrifice dates back to around 2800 B.C.E.—a full millennium before the births of Avraham and Sarah in Ur and the time of the early Old Kingdom in Egypt. It was, understandably, not too popular with kings, who eventually succeeded in gaining the right to rule permanently. They began to accomplish this by substituting some other "valued" person at the ritual execution.

For instance, one account tells that a red-headed man was sacrificed by Egyptian kings as a summer precaution against drought and pestilence. They burned him at the grave of Osiris and then scattered his ashes with a winnowing fan. His red hair, which was a rarity in Egypt, symbolized the ruddy grain whose growth the sacrifice was supposed to promote.[26]

Children often served as sacrifices of "one for the many." Virgins, including kings' daughters, were drowned to honor a river god (as in the Nile inundation festival) or some other kind of water spirit in the form of a large serpent or dragon.[27] Infants were buried alive in the foundations of new buildings or city gates to dedicate and protect the new edifices. Given kings' love of building, this must have been frequent. "Foundation sacrifice springs from a primitive fear of anything new or of doing an act for the first time."[28] Infants have been discovered in foundations of Egyptian buildings as late as the Twenty-second Dynasty.[29] The Hebrew Bible itself recounts that "in his days Hiel of Beth-El rebuilt Jericho. Laying its foundations cost him his eldest son Aviram, and the setting up of its gates cost him Seguv, his youngest son" (1 Kings 16:34).

Firstborn sons were the most valued children in society and hence made "good sacrifices," precisely *because they were so valued.* "If one sacrificed his son to the idol, the priest said to him, 'You have offered a most precious gift to it'" (San. 63b). Their heads, as we noted in chapter 7, were sometimes made into *terafim* and used for divination.

Kings thus naturally shifted their fatal destiny onto their firstborn sons:

When the king first succeeded in getting the life of another accepted as a sacrifice instead of his own, he would have to show that the death of that other would serve the purpose quite as well as his own would have done. . . . The substitute who died for him had to be invested, at least for the occasion, with the divine attributes of the king. . . . No one could so well represent the king in his divine character as his son. . . . No one, therefore, could so appropriately die for the king and, through him, for the whole people, as the king's son. . . . [In ancient Greece there was] at least one kingly house of great

---

26. Davies, p. 36; Frazer, pp. 438–440.
27. Davies, p. 17; Frazer, p. 169.
28. Davies, p. 21.
29. Ibid., p. 37.

antiquity of which the eldest sons were always liable to be sacrificed in [place] of their royal sires.[30]

Later kings had other reasons for placating the gods with their sons, such as war or famine. "Among the Semites of Western Asia the king, in a time of national danger, sometimes gave his own son to die as a sacrifice for the people."[31] For instance, "when the king of Moav saw that the battle was too hard for him . . . he took his eldest son, who would have ruled after him, and offered him up as a burnt-offering upon the wall" (2 Kings 3:26–27).

There were other reasons for sacrificing firstborn sons as well. One anthropologist relates the practice to an "irreconcilable conflict" between men in a transition from matrilineal to patrilineal descent. "Redemptive sacrifice is a ritual offering to redeem a blood debt. Its central feature is the killing of the firstborn son. . . . It had begun as a transaction between men—between mothers' brothers and fathers—in an effort to change the line of blood kinship and descent and achieve a one-father family."[32]

Firstborn sons have also been sacrificed by fathers in the belief that this would get them *more* sons. "If a wife had one son and wanted more, the firstborn son was slain on the supposition that the gods would then provide a series of children to take his place."[33]

> Even royal infants were sometimes offered as single victims to ensure that a copious flow of offspring would follow. The tale is told of King Somaka in northern India who for some time could not get a single son out of his cohort of a hundred wives. Finally one boy was born but the king wanted not one son but a hundred, and the family priest [advised him to sacrifice his son]. The son was sacrificed; the wives smelt the smell of the burnt-offering, all of them became pregnant, and when ten months had passed one hundred sons were born to Somaka. . . .

In Bengal as late as the 1860s,

> barren women would promise their firstborn son to the God of Destruction . . . in the hope of being given others. The mother would rear this first child and then tell him of his fate when he reached puberty. From that moment he was pledged to the god, and at his annual festival would cast himself from a rock five hundred feet high.[34]

This latter example illuminates the *akedah*, the binding of Isaac. As the firstborn son of his previously barren mother, Isaac could have been sacrificed, according to the pagan worldview, to make Sarah have more sons. Avraham did not appear shocked by God's request; he may have been puzzled by God's apparent "change of mind" about child sacrifice, but *the practice itself* was certainly not unfamiliar to him.

---

30. Frazer, p. 337.
31. Ibid., p. 340.
32. Evelyn Reed, *Woman's Evolution* (New York: Pathfinder Press, 1975), pp. 398, 402.
33. Davies, p. 22.
34. Ibid., p. 77.

The *akedah* illustrates God's rejection of human sacrifice as a means of divine "worship." That the incident specifically relates to the pagan sacrifice of firstborn sons is symbolized by Avraham finding a *ram* in the bush, because "as time went on, the cruel custom was so far mitigated that a ram was accepted as a vicarious sacrifice."[35] Thus, the ram was linked to the firstborn plague in Egypt, and the redemption of a firstborn donkey had to be done with a lamb.

THE REDEMPTION OF FIRSTBORN SONS

Hashem spoke to Moses, saying, "Sanctify to Me every firstborn that opens the womb from the children of Israel. From human and from beast, it is Mine." (Ex. 13:1)

You will bring everything that opens the womb to Hashem, even the premature first birth of an animal that is yours; the males belong to Hashem. Every firstborn donkey shall be redeemed with a sheep and if it is not redeemed, it must have its head cut off. Every firstborn of human sons shall be redeemed.

In the future your [firstborn] son will ask you, "What is this?" and you should answer him, "With a strong hand Hashem brought us out of Egypt, from the house of slavery. When Pharaoh was stubborn in sending us out, Hashem killed every firstborn in the land of Egypt, from the firstborn of humans through animals. Therefore I offer to Hashem the firstborn of males and every firstborn son I redeem." (Ex. 13:12–15)

Not only will a firstborn son be likely to ask why he had to be redeemed for five shekels when he was a month old (Num. 18:16). A firstborn daughter is also likely to ask why she did not have to be redeemed in this way, for if this ritual, *pidyon haben*, is a direct consequence of the slaughter of Egypt's firstborn, then daughters, who were also slain, would need to be "bought back" from God, too. However, *pidyon haben* is a remembrance of the plague in Egypt, which was itself a consequence of firstborn-son sacrifice. *Pidyon haben* is ultimately a response to—and a compensation for—firstborn-son sacrifice. Thus it applies to all (i.e., matrilineal) firstborn sons.

Under Jewish law, only the patrilineal firstborn son receives a double portion of his father's estate. This is a separate issue from *pidyon haben*. Primogeniture—the inheritance privileges of a man's first son—is a universal patriarchal phenomenon that had become firmly entrenched by the time of the Torah. The Torah (Deut. 21:15–17) does not command primogeniture but does discuss it as a given, and it addresses a case in which a man's patrilineal firstborn is a *ben-hasnuah,* "son of a hated wife." The father is not permitted to revoke this son's birthright and give it to the firstborn son of a loved wife (as Jacob did with Reuven and Joseph). The Torah's decree is concerned with the injustice of taking out one's hatred of one's spouse on the children; it may not necessarily imply divine support for primogeniture itself, although male commentators have unanimously assumed that it does.

---

35. Frazer, p. 340.

God, however, *rejected* primogeniture as the means of transmitting the covenant with Israel, which never once went through a man's firstborn: Isaac was chosen over Ishmael, Jacob received Esav's birthright and blessing, Joseph superseded Reuven, and Efraim got the firstborn blessing instead of Menasheh. Peretz, the progenitor of the House of David, was technically born first, but his twin brother had already stuck his hand out and pulled it back in (Gen. 38:28–29). Peretz is thus similar to Jacob except that he usurped his "red" twin brother *at* birth rather than after. Moses was a youngest son, as were Gideon, Saul, and David. Aharon's firstborn son was killed, and his thirdborn, Elazar, became high priest instead.

Were the covenant man-made, it would surely have followed primogeniture. That it did not may be the clearest proof yet of the divine origin of the Torah.

THE REDEMPTION OF FIRSTBORN DAUGHTERS

The statistics cited at the beginning of this chapter regarding firstborn-son preference among modern Americans may seem benign, unless one understands the extent to which medical research has advanced the accuracy and accessibility of sex-selection technology in the last fifteen years.[36]

Son-preference is now an issue of sexual eugenics and poses the same ethical dilemmas and risks as racial eugenics. The limited use of the available methods of sex selection has already been disastrous to the female sex in societies where women are valued only as mothers of sons, such as India or China. However, even in America, sexual eugenics would be a threat. Given "reproductive choice," two out of three Americans might promote dominant social prejudices by planning a blond-haired, blue-eyed firstborn son—representing the "master" race and the "master" gender. Jews might not as often opt for blonds, but they would still overwhelmingly make firstborn sons.

A planned society of firstborn sons and secondborn daughters would psychologically consolidate male supremacy, fostering boys' initiative and leadership while promoting female habituation to following an older male. Firstborns learn to take responsibility and authority, which cultivates intelligence, self-confidence, ambition, and success. They usually receive more individual attention and nurturance from their parents, being the "only child" in their early years of life, according to psychologists who have studied the effect of sibling placement in the family.

Firstborn daughters have as much potential for initiative and leadership in the world as their male counterparts. However, their strength is often channeled into maternal responsibilities for their younger siblings, a duty that is rarely, if ever, placed on a firstborn son. Nor have firstborn daughters received the traditional education, career, and inheritance privileges accorded to firstborn sons; on the contrary, they have had to overcome additional obstacles.

---

36. See Corea, pp. 188–212; Betsy A. Lehman, "Upping the Odds That 'It's a Boy!,'" *The Boston Globe,* Nov. 18, 1985, p. 42; "If a Boy Is What You Want," *Parade,* Jan. 8, 1984, p. 8.

Firstborn daughters have been especially vulnerable to sexual abuse. In one study of incest survivors, 80 percent

> were the oldest or the only daughters in their families. Before the age of 10, almost half (45%) had been pressed into service as "little mothers" within the family. They cared for their younger sisters and brothers and took on responsibility for major household tasks. . . . Whether or not they were obliged to take on household responsibilities, most of the daughters were assigned a special duty to 'keep Daddy happy.'"[37]

Firstborn daughters can only be valued in a society that accords women the same human worth, dignity, opportunity, and civil rights as men. "The degree to which parents in a given society tend to value sons more than daughters provides a measure of the extent to which women's rights are denied and suppressed. . . . Whatever status [women] may gain as the mothers of sons will be contingent upon the society's underlying contempt for females."[38]

The Jewish overvaluation of sons may not have misogynist origins. Rather, it may have arisen as compensation for losing all the boys in Pharaoh's "gendercide"—*his* "sex selection," after all, favored baby girls! The preference for a firstborn son has, nevertheless, been maintained in traditional Jewish life by the plethora of ceremonies for boys and the corresponding lack of them for girls—circumcision, *shalom zakhor*, *bar mitzvah*, *pidyon haben*, fast of the firstborn on *Erev Pesach*—as well as the practice of allowing sons, but not daughters, to say *kaddish* for a deceased parent.

This inequity has only begun to be remedied. We have a long way to go in "redeeming" our firstborn daughters from the ways in which they have been "sacrificed." Many of them, such as Miriam, Batyah, and Zipporah, have overcome incredible obstacles to become our finest leaders. To "select" them out of existence in our "brave new world" would be sad indeed.

---

37. Herman, p. 79.
38. Mary Anne Warren, *Gendercide: The Implications of Sex Selection* (Totowa, NJ: Rowman and Allanheld, 1985), pp. 14, 41.

✻✻✻ 16 ✻✻✻

The Shekhinah

Beshalach (13:17–17:16)

And Hashem went before them by day as a pillar of cloud to guide them on the way, and by night as a pillar of fire to light the way for them. (Ex. 13:21)

"What was this pillar of cloud? . . . It was the cloud which is always seen with the Shekhinah, . . . the pillar of cloud by day represented *Chesed* [Mercy], and the pillar of fire by night *Gevurah* [Judgment], both attributes being united in the Shekhinah" (*Zohar* II:51b). Thus, it was actually one pillar that changed form, from cloud to fire and back again (Rashi). "The cloud of the Shekhinah looked like smoke because the fire which Avraham and his son Isaac kindled clung to it and never left it, and by reason of that fire it ascended both as cloud and smoke" (*Zohar* I:176b).

God's manifest presence is called the Shekhinah (from שכן, *dwell*), or the Divine Presence. While the transcendent aspect of the divine is characterized in Jewish tradition as masculine, divine immanence is characterized as feminine. Whenever God is immanent—that is, able to be perceived through the physical senses—this is the Shekhinah. The Strong Hand that brought the Jews out of Egypt (Ex. 13:16) was the Shekhinah. *Chesed* and *Gevurah* were unified then, as with the pillar, because "the same power which exercised Judgment on the Egyptians was the agent of Mercy to Israel" (*Zohar* II:36a).

The burning bush and the Revelation at Sinai are other examples of the Shekhinah. "When the smoke came out of Mt. Sinai a fire ascended. . . . It was the Shekhinah who manifested Herself thus at the giving of the Law. . . . The 'I' in the first commandment represents the Shekhinah. . . . What stands above Mt. Sinai? Surely the Shekhinah" (*Zohar* II:84a, 85a, 86a). If this is the case, why is God's booming voice always cast as a male?

THE SHEKHINAH AND THE FEMININE

The Shekhinah, we saw in chapter 1, inherently dwells within women but comes to men only through marriage. That women are an embodiment of Her is beautifully illustrated by the following statement: "When R. Joseph heard his mother's footsteps he would say, 'I will arise before the approaching Shekhinah'" (Kid. 31b).

The Shekhinah resided in the matriarchs' tents during their lifetimes. She left Sarah's tent at her death, but returned with the arrival of Rivkah (see chapter 5). Thus, their Sabbath lights never went out and their *challah* never became stale. The Jews later made a replica of Sarah's tent in the wilderness—a portable tabernacle where the Shekhinah could dwell (Ex. 25:8, 40:35), containing an eternally burning light and a table of eternally fresh *challah*. It is called the *mishkan*, grammatically indicating its purpose as the Shekhinah's tent. Since the Shekhinah dwells in the west (B.B. 25a), the Divine Presence hovered above the ark in the Holy of Holies, the westernmost part of the Tabernacle.

The marriage *chuppah* is also the Shekhinah's tent. "Therefore must the bride below have a canopy, all beautiful with decorations prepared for her in order to honor the Bride above, who comes to be present to participate in the joy of the bride below" (*Zohar* II:169a).

The tent is a feminine symbol; its entrance is a gateway from the inner to the outer world. On a physical level, this is the birth canal, the gateway from the other world into this one. The tent itself is the warm, secure uterine environment traditionally made by women and called a "home." The Torah thus sometimes describes tents in the feminine gender even when they belong to a man, such as Avraham, Noach, Yitro (Ex. 18:7), and Moses (Ex. 33:8).

On a metaphysical level, the door of the tent represents the gates of *Binah*, or Understanding. *Binah* is the quality that the Rabbis said God gave more of to women at Creation. *Binah* is also the name of the *sefirah* associated with Leah. *Binah* is characterized as a palace with fifty gates, and Wisdom (*Chokhmah*) as the key that opened them. Out of the palace came the *sefirot* and the Hebrew letters (*Zohar* II:175b).

"In this palace there are hidden treasures, one greater than the other. The palace is provided with fifty mystic gates, forty-nine of which are on the four sides. The one remaining gate is on none of its sides, and it is not known whether it is above or below. Consequently this gate is hidden" (*Zohar* I:3b). Similarly, "fifty gates of understanding were created in the world, and all but one were given to Moses" (Ned. 38a). The hidden, fiftieth gate is symbolized by the Jubilee (fiftieth) Year, when slaves were freed, debts were canceled, and property reverted to its original owner. *Binah* is thus "the source of all release and redemption."[1]

Binah is called the "upper Shekhinah"; *Malkhut*, the *sefirah* associated with Rachel, is called the "lower Shekhinah. . . . The name 'Shekhinah' is assigned first to *Malkhut*,

---

1. Isaiah Tishby, *The Wisdom of the Zohar,* vol. 1 (New York: Oxford University Press, 1989), p. 355 n. 489.

and from there it is transferred to *Binah*. . . . The activity of *Binah* in the upper worlds is similar to the activity of *Malkhut* in the lower worlds."[2]

As divine immanence, the Shekhinah links the upper and lower worlds, the heavens and the earth. As "lower Shekhinah," She is the supernal Daughter, receiving and manifesting the flow of celestial energy; as "upper Shekhinah," She is the supernal Mother, "the very beginning and highest point, assuming the role of mother and ruler of the world" below.[3]

The Shekhinah is also called Sister, as well as Mother and Daughter. "And She is indeed all these. One who penetrates into this mystery has imbibed precious wisdom. . . . But such a veiled mystery ought not to be disclosed" (*Zohar* II:100b).

THE SHEKHINAH AND ISRAEL

The Shekhinah's specific "residence" in the upper world is among the stars and the angels; in the lower world, it is among Israel. The Shekhinah represents the Community of Israel whose fate is linked to the Land of Israel.

> The Shekhinah on high abides in the twelve holy chariots and the twelve supernal *chayot*; the lower Shekhinah is among the twelve holy tribes, and thus the upper Shekhinah and the lower Shekhinah are intertwined, and operate together simultaneously. When Israel is in exile, the upper Shekhinah is not complete because the lower Shekhinah is not complete, and that is what is meant by the Shekhinah being in exile when Israel is in exile. (*Zohar* I:159b)

With the death of Rachel at the birth of Benjamin, "the Shekhinah was equipped with the full 12 tribes, and with him the kingdom of heaven began to be made manifest on earth. . . . When the Shekhinah was about to assume Her rightful place and to take over the house, the doom fell upon Rachel" (*Zohar* I:174a).

The Shekhinah stayed with the twelve tribes until Leah died and the brothers sold Joseph into slavery—at which point She accompanied *him.* She was restored to Jacob through Serach and reunited with all twelve tribes when Jacob went down to Egypt. Joseph "was in the relation of a brother towards the Shekhinah." He "was the symbol of the heavenly covenant, and so long as he was alive the covenant of the Shekhinah remained with Israel in perfect harmony, but as soon as Joseph departed, the covenant of the Shekhinah together with Israel was plunged into captivity" (*Zohar* I:184a). The Exodus from Egypt "set Her free" (*Zohar* II:216b). The bitter herbs of the Passover *seder* "signify the Shekhinah's exile with Israel in all their bitter afflictions in Egypt" (*Zohar* II:41b), and *matzah* is called "the bread which emanates from Her" (*Zohar* II:40a).

In the later Babylonian exile, the Shekhinah was also with the Jews. "When Israel sinned and burned incense to other gods in the Holy Land, the Shekhinah was driven

---

2. Ibid., p. 372.
3. Ibid.

from its place" (*Zohar* I:84b). In fact, wherever the Jews have been exiled, the Shekhinah has gone with them, and She will accompany them in their future redemption (Meg. 29a; ER 23:5; *Zohar* II:2b).

Symbols of the Shekhinah have included the moon (*Zohar* II:51b), a rainbow (*Zohar* II:66b), the Garden of Eden (*Zohar* I:26a), the Tree of Life (*Zohar* II:2a), a rose and a lily (*Zohar* I:1a, I:221a), a wall (*Zohar* I:228b), the gates of righteousness (*Zohar* I:7b), the "door of the tent" (*Zohar* I:103b), a female deer (*Zohar* III:249a–b), a well and a field (*Zohar* I:151b–152a), a woman of valor (*Zohar* III:97a), and the continual burnt-offering in the Temple (*Zohar* III:256b).

The righteous people of a generation are called "the face of the Shekhinah, because in them is the Shekhinah hidden; She is hidden in them and they reveal Her. For they who are the friends of the Shekhinah and are near to Her are regarded as Her 'face'" (*Zohar* II:163b). The Torah is the Shekhinah's robe or gown; keeping the commandments is like clothing Her, while sin "strips" Her. Had God not created the Torah, "the Shekhinah would have been without a vestment like a beggar" (*Zohar* I:23b).

Sin—especially men's misuse of their sexuality—drives the Shekhinah from the world (*Zohar* I:57a, I:61a, I:68b, II:3a–b). Marital sexual relations performed in holiness (*Zohar* I:176a), as well as Torah study, bring Her back. "Even a single person who sits and studies the Torah has the Shekhinah for a companion. . . . When the Torah forms a crown over a person's head, the Shekhinah does not depart. . . . Whenever the Torah is studied earnestly, the Shekhinah comes and joins, and all the more so on the road" (*Zohar* I:72a, I:76a, I:115b).

The Shekhinah "is in charge of the blessings of the world, and from Her flow blessings for all" (*Zohar* I:70b). Escorting one's guests draws the Shekhinah to accompany them on their way as protection (*Zohar* I:104b). Where the Shekhinah is present, and Mercy and Judgment are thus united, a person takes a more lenient, rather than a harsher, view of another's conduct (Br. 31b). In a court of law, "a judge who delivers a judgment in perfect truth causes the Shekhinah to dwell in Israel. . . . And one who does not deliver judgments in perfect truth causes the Shekhinah to depart from the midst of Israel" (San. 7a). Four kinds of people do not receive the Shekhinah's presence: scoffers, liars, hypocrites, and slanderers (San. 103a).

CROSSING THE RED SEA

The splitting of the sea was another manifestation of the Divine Presence. *Chesed* and *Gevurah* were united as the Jews were saved and the Egyptians drowned.

The passageway between the walls of the sea was like a birth canal, through which the Jews were born into freedom. They were given whatever they needed while crossing the sea as soon as they thought of it, and they did not even have to speak. "A daughter of Israel passed through the sea with her child in hand, and when it cried, she would stretch out her hand and pluck an apple or a pomegranate from within the sea and give it to the child" (ER 21:10).

The Egyptian army—six hundred chariots of men—was drowned, *midah kneged midah,* in return for all the Jewish boys *they* had drowned (ER 22:1). The most wicked were tossed about, while the best of them died immediately (Rashi).

Halakhically, Pharaoh and his soldiers constituted a *rodef,* or "pursuer." According to Jewish law, if someone comes to kill you or rape you, you not only have the *right,* but the *obligation,* to kill them in order to stop them. Any third-party bystander must do the same (San. 73a). God, in this case, was the "bystander" stopping the *rodef.* Might God have stopped the Egyptians *without* killing them? Evidently God could not; based on Pharaoh's previous behavior, it is clear the ruler would never have given up.

Many feminists have expressed great discomfort with God being likened to a "warrior" (Ex. 15:3). It is not just the usual maleness of the image that is considered objectionable, but "the notion of God as dominating Other" that "evoke[s] a troubled response. In depicting God's power as domination, the tradition draws on symbols of political authority that are not only foreign to citizens in a democracy but also morally repugnant."[4]

Their sympathies are misplaced. If we identify with the *victim,* there should be nothing troubling or repugnant in the fact that God destroyed armed men in chariots pursuing a bunch of runaway slaves on foot! On the contrary, "Hashem"—God's aspect of Mercy—is used in the account, for *drowning the Egyptians was a merciful act.* It is the *victim* who deserves the mercy; being merciful to the perpetrator is being cruel to the victim. Even in war, God "retains the attribute of compassion for all creatures, feeding the inhabitants of the world" (Rashi).

MIRIAM'S SONG

And Miriam the prophet, sister of Aharon, took the timbrel in her hand, and all the women went out after her, with timbrels and with dancing. And Miriam led them in response, "Sing to Hashem, Who is highly exalted; the horse and its rider God has thrown into the sea." (Ex. 15:20–21)

"The righteous women of that generation trusted that God would do miracles for them, so they brought timbrels from Egypt." Moses sang to the men and they answered; Miriam sang to the women and they answered (Rashi). Every woman "saw at the sea what even the prophets never saw" (Rashi), and all sang in praise of God. The Song at the Sea has been called the "Song of the Shekhinah" (*Zohar* II:54b) and is considered feminine—a *shirah* rather than a *shir.* "All the songs ever sung [by Israel] were feminine, as if to say, 'As this female conceives and gives birth again and again, so too troubles came upon them,' and they sang their songs in the feminine form" (ER 23:11).

---

4. Judith Plaskow, *Standing Again at Sinai* (San Francisco: Harper and Row, 1990), pp. 131–132.

A baby lay on its mother's knees and an infant suckled at its mother's breast; when they beheld the Shekhinah, the baby raised its neck and the infant released the nipple from its mouth, and they exclaimed, "This is my God Whom I will glorify." . . . Even the embryos in their mothers' wombs uttered a song. . . . The abdomen became for them like a window of light and they could see. (Sot. 30b; *Zohar* II:55b)

The Jews were filled with such awe that they did not want to leave. "They all beheld the divine glory eye to eye, and when their singing was ended their souls were so filled with joy and ecstasy that they refused to continue on their journey, desiring yet more perfect revelations of that glorious mystery." Therefore, God "hid the divine glory" and the Shekhinah was not disclosed to the Israelites again until they were in the wilderness (*Zohar* II:60a).

The Song at the Sea is one instance in the Torah where women gather separately from men at a time of spiritual intensity. How interesting that Jewish women's first act of freedom was to celebrate separately from men! During their enslavement in Egypt, the women were focused on keeping up their husbands' morale. Separation from men was no doubt a respite for women at this point, a form of freedom in and of itself.

Thus, rather than being an oppressive, enforced *segregation,* this "separate and equal" celebration was a strong affirmation of female bonding. Any woman who has ever lived or worked in an all-female environment knows that the energy is different from that of a mixed group. Women in all-female groups have more freedom to express themselves in a self-defined way, rather than assimilating with men. In mixed groups, women adapt to men much more than men adapt to women,[5] because men as a group strive for domination in ways that women as a group do not. Thus, women who value themselves and other women enjoy, and often prefer, all-female groups.

Equality and self-determination are essential if same-sex groups are to be separatist rather than segregationist. The Song at the Sea serves as a model of "separate and equal." A school that separates boys and girls and has a different curriculum for each is not equal. Similarly, separate seating in a synagogue where only men get to read from the Torah is not equal. Finally, a women's yeshiva with a male leader and male teachers is not separate *or* self-determined.

MIRIAM'S WELL AND "BITTER WATER"

For three days the Israelites traveled in the desert without water, until they came to Marah, where the water was too bitter to drink (Ex. 15:23). God then showed Moses a piece of wood that, when thrown into the water, made it drinkable. Finally, Israel arrived at Elim, where there were twelve springs of water (Ex. 15:27).

5. See Deborah Tannen, *You Just Don't Understand: Men and Women in Conversation* (New York: William Morrow, 1990), for an analysis of how male–female groups usually take on the qualities of male rather than female communication styles.

Later, at Rephidim, the people again were without water and they began to quarrel with Moses. He pleaded with God and was told to strike a certain rock to make water flow out of it. Moses named the place Masa u-Merivah ("Testing and Argument") because the people had argued and tested God (Ex. 17:7).

The Hebrew word for "bitter water" *(marim)* is identical to "Miriam" (מרים), whose name, we noted, embodied the condition of Israel at the time of her birth. The first incident of bitter water in the wilderness is told immediately after Miriam's song. The second incident marks the establishment of Miriam's Well, which accompanied and sustained the Israelites in the wilderness during her lifetime (Nachmanides; Ta. 9a; *Zohar* II:190b).

The well—a symbol of the Shekhinah—was present due to the merit of Miriam. "How was the well constructed? It was rock-shaped like a kind of beehive, and wherever they journeyed it rolled along and came with them" (NR 1:2). The well had been created by God at twilight on the first *Erev Shabbat*, the sixth day of Creation (Pes. 54a).

THE MANNA

Once the Jews ran out of provisions, they complained about the lack of food, stating that they preferred to die with full stomachs as slaves in Egypt rather than starve to death in the wilderness (Ex. 16:3). After all the miracles God had performed for them, their lack of faith was indeed astonishing. Instead of again quarreling with Moses, they should have simply told him that there was no more food (ER 25:4).

God sent bread (manna) in the mornings and meat (quails) at night. While bread is necessary for sustenance, meat is not, and a lesson is taught in the wording of Exodus 16:8 that "one should not eat meat to satiety" (Rashi). The manna tasted like whatever each person desired. Again the people's needs were filled just by thinking, without even speaking (ER 25:4). The manna was another symbol of the Shekhinah, for through it, the Israelites saw "God's glory" (Ex. 16:7). Like Miriam's Well, the manna was created at twilight on the first *Erev Shabbat* (Pes. 54a).

THE SABBATH

Sabbath observance was first commanded to the Jews at this time, in the context of the manna. The people were given a double portion on Friday so that they would not have to gather it on Saturday (although some tried anyway). Two Sabbath prohibitions are mentioned here: cooking (Ex. 16:23) and traveling beyond a certain distance (Ex. 16:29). Other prohibited activities are defined later by the work necessary to build the Tabernacle (Ex. 35:1–3).

The Sabbath, like the Shekhinah, is a feminine entity. It has been called God's only Daughter (*Zohar* II:94b), indicating its preciousness. Elsewhere it is characterized as the divine Queen and Bride, and "the union of the King with the Shekhinah" takes place on Friday nights (*Zohar* II:63b).

The Queen symbolizes the sovereignty of the Sabbath through observance of its laws. The Bride symbolizes the joy and ecstasy—the taste of Paradise—that such observance brings. A heightened sense of spirituality is achieved through the sanctification of time. By prohibiting everyday, mundane activities, space is made for spiritual activities, creating a virtual oasis in time. Sabbath observance is an acknowledgement by humans that we—*creators* in God's image, who are capable of manipulating and dominating nature—are also part of God's *creation.*

The Sabbath "celebrates the freedom and unification of the Shekhinah." Because of this "the precept of kindling the Sabbath light is the woman's prerogative."[6]

The burning bush, the Strong Hand, the splitting of the sea, the Revelation at Sinai, the pillar of cloud and fire, Miriam's Well, the manna, and even the Tabernacle were all *temporary* manifestations of the Divine Presence. The Sabbath is the Shekhinah's *permanent* dwelling among Israel.

---

6. Tishby, 3:1225, 1233.

✸✸✸ 17 ✸✸✸

The House of Jacob

Yitro (18:1–20:23)

Moses went up to Elokim. Hashem called to him from the mountain to say [le'emor], *"Thus say* [tomar] *to the house of Jacob and tell* [taged] *the children of Israel."* (Ex. 19:3)

Three dualities appear in this verse: two Names of God, two categories of people, and two manners of speaking. What do they mean and how are they related?

The two Names of God symbolize two different aspects of the Sovereign of the Universe. "Hashem" is God as a personal, merciful being motivated by compassion for the individual; "Elokim," on the other hand, is God as the indiscriminate laws and forces of nature, striking through fate and acting in judgment.

The name Hashem is said to be "the heritage of the one particular people. . . . [It] belongs only to Israel." The name Elokim "spreads and separates itself towards many diverse ways and paths," including the "ministering angels who guide other nations" and "all the principalities and powers appointed over the nations. . . . This Name signifies even the objects of pagan worship" (*Zohar* II:96a). "Elokim" can mean a demigod or a judge (Gen. 6:2). It is used to describe Moses' function with the Jewish people (Ex. 4:16), and it is what the golden calf was called by those who demanded it (Ex. 32:1).

Elokim created the universe, including humanity, but Hashem Elokim formed humanity into male and female. "Hashem Elokim" is the *full* Name of God; it literally means "Hashem is God," and it makes up the most basic declaration of Jewish faith—"*Shma Israel, Hashem Elokeinu, Hashem Echad,*" or, "Hear, Israel, Hashem is our God, Hashem is one."

The Shekhinah, in uniting Mercy and Judgment, unites the two aspects of God. The Shekhinah rests "on the head of one who recites the *Shma,*" for the prayer

175

"declares the unity of the Name" and "unites the above and below" (*Zohar* II:160b). To know that Hashem *is* Elokim—that is, to unite God's Name—is the whole purpose of human existence.

"The only aim and object of the Holy One in sending humanity into this world is to know and understand that Hashem is Elokim. This is the sum of the whole mystery of the faith, of the whole Torah, of all that is above and below, of the written and oral Torah, all together forming one unity. The essence of the mystery of faith is to know that this is a complete Name. This knowledge that Hashem is one with Elokim is indeed the synthesis of the whole Torah" (*Zohar* II:161b).

The two categories of people in the verse are women and men—"house of Jacob" means women, while "children of Israel" means men. The verb *le'emor* (*to say*) is used with the women—and with Moses—but *lehagid* (*to tell*) is used with the men. *Le'emor* implies a kinder form of speech, while *lehagid* is harsher. The women received a general overview of the commandments, while the men were instructed in the details and warned about the punishments for disobeying (Rashi; ER 28:2; *Zohar* II:79b).

The all-encompassing "structure" of the law given to the women is indeed like a *house,* which provides the "foundation" for the "family" (the Jewish people). The men, on the other hand, were like *children* who need extensive instruction and discipline. These dual modes of relating to the sexes bear some correspondence to the two aspects of God.

Le'emor is linked to God's aspect of Mercy, for after the Jews built the golden calf, "the Holy One began to give Moses paths to ask for mercy for them." This is derived from the use of *vayomer* in Exodus 32:9, which is "a softer expression, as when a person has offended a friend and wishes to become reconciled. . . . As soon as Moses heard tender words from the Holy One, he began to ask for mercy for them" (ER 42:2).

Hence, in giving the Torah to the Jews, God chose to relate to women with more kindness or mercy, but to treat men with more severity or judgment. In order to have these different encounters with God, women and men had to be separate.

SEXUAL SEPARATION AT SINAI

And Hashem said to Moses, "Go to the people and sanctify them today and tomorrow, and have them wash their clothes. And be ready for the third day, for on the third day Hashem will come down before the eyes of all the people on Mount Sinai." . . . And Moses went down from the mountain to the people and sanctified the people, and they washed their clothes. And he said to the people, "Be ready for the third day; do not go near a woman." (Ex. 19:10–11, 19:14–15).

What is going on here? Is Moses like a bad journalist misquoting his source? God does not speak in sexist language, but Moses does. God wanted men *and women* to separate *from each other* and immerse in a *mikvah,* but Moses apparently spoke only to the men. Surely he was not prohibiting *the women* from going near a woman!

We might assume that Moses spoke to the men, and Miriam (briefed by Moses) spoke to the women. Given the unique level of Moses' prophecy, this explanation seems more likely than the possibility that he misquoted God, for that would have been incredibly arrogant, and Moses was chosen by God precisely because he was the *humblest* of men. Due to a speech impediment acquired as an infant (ER 1:26), Moses felt inadequate to be Israel's spokesman, but God insisted. Therefore, let us give Moses the benefit of the doubt and assert that, as Moses instructed the men not to go near a woman, Miriam instructed the women not to go near a man (or, perhaps, not to *allow* a man to come near *them*).

Thus, like crossing the Red Sea, receiving the Torah at Mount Sinai was an extremely intense, spiritual experience at which men and women were separate. This time, however, due to the difference in communication styles, it was not "separate and equal," if equality means sameness; but does it? Is it "equality" to educate a precocious child in the same way as an average child, or an average child in the same way as one with a learning disability? Equality of opportunity actually requires that education be individually geared to each child's capacity. This is precisely what happened at Sinai.

Not only were the experiences of the sexes different, but each *individual's* encounter with God varied according to his or her personal capacity. God's Voice is said to have come down to each person according to his or her strength (ER 5:9), and "everyone received according to his or her level of perception" (*Zohar* II:94a). "The souls of all Israel—past, present, and future, born and unborn—were present there" (*Zohar* II: 83b).

RECEIVING THE TORAH

The revelation of the Torah to Israel changed the entire world from a vast wilderness into a fortified place (ER 24:4).

> At that hour all the mysteries of the Torah, all the hidden things of heaven and earth, were unfolded before them and revealed to their eyes, for they saw eye to eye the splendor of the glory of their God. Never before, since the Holy One created the world, had such a revelation of the Divine Glory taken place. Even the crossing of the Red Sea . . . was not so wonderful as this. . . . Creation had no proper basis before Israel received the Torah. . . . But once Israel received the Torah on Mt. Sinai the world was duly and completely established, and heaven and earth received a proper foundation. (*Zohar* II:93b–94a)

The Revelation at Sinai is traditionally viewed as a marriage between God and the Jewish people, with the mountain as the *chuppah,* or wedding canopy. "We will do and we will hear," the Jews said (Ex. 24:7), pledging to have no other gods, while God promised to make them "a precious treasure" (Rashi; Ex. 19:5).

There is another tradition, however, that God *forced* the Torah on the Jews, "overturn[ing] the mountain upon them" and saying, "If you accept the Torah, fine; if not, it will be your burial" (Shab. 88a). Such a "forced marriage" is nothing more than rape. "From this we have a protest [against the Torah]," R. Acha b. Jacob rightly notes. The answer is given that the Jews later reaccepted the Torah willingly. Continuing the nuptial analogy, however, this would mean that the "victim" later began to love her "rapist"—clearly an inadequate explanation.

There must, therefore, be some other way to reconcile the dichotomy of coercion versus willingness in acceptance of the Torah. Perhaps the coercion refers to the extreme terror that the Jews felt in God's presence, so that after hearing the first two commandments, they asked Moses to hear the rest by himself and tell them later! Thus, for the remaining commandments they heard only the *sound* of God's Voice, and not its *content.* God knew that this would happen but had consented to speak directly to the people at first anyway, so that later they could not excuse the making of the golden calf by claiming they had had no direct experience of God (ER 41:3).

A better explanation, however, goes back to the different approaches that God took with men and women. For the women, the experience at Sinai was like a marriage with God because they were ready and willing to accept the Torah. However, the men's experience was at least *somewhat* coercive, since their acceptance relied on the threat of punishment.

WHY WOMEN RECEIVED THE TORAH FIRST

Not only did God have different ways of giving the Torah to men and women, but women received the Torah first. Three reasons are cited for this (ER 28:2):

1. They are prompt in the fulfillment of the commandments. This implies that women have an eagerness to receive God's laws that men do not. It is why receiving the Torah was like a "marriage" for them and why God saw fit to use nicer language with women than with men.
2. They should introduce their children to the Torah. Women were, and still are, the primary caretakers of children. Fathers may participate more in child rearing than they used to, but their lack of capacity for childbearing and nursing means that mothers will continue to be the first and earliest influence on their children.
3. If women are not given the Torah first, they will be the first to reject it. According to R. Tachlifa of Caesarea, God said, "When I created the world, I only commanded Adam first, and then Chavah, too, was commanded, with the result that she transgressed and upset the world. If I do not now call to the women first, they will nullify the Torah."

God's permission to eat from every tree in the Garden of Eden except one was given to the *adam* before it was split into male and female. R. Tachlifa's statement presumes that the *adam* was a male who had to pass the commandment on later to the not-yet-created female. If we were to accept this view, we should place even *more* responsibility on Adam, whose lame excuse of blaming Chavah would thus be even *more* reprehensible! However, if we reject his explanation and maintain that the *adam* was a hermaphrodite, there is still significance in the notion that women must receive the Torah first.

Centuries of sexism in Jewish education and exclusively male God-language have had the effect of "giving the Torah to boys first," and the results are evident in the number of Jewish women who have rejected Judaism and sought spiritual fulfillment elsewhere. Others, while not actually leaving Judaism, have developed distorted and mistaken notions about its teachings. Most of these women believe that the sexism they experienced as girls is Torah-based rather than sociological.

Such sexism only creates a massive ignorance that boomerangs back to the Jewish world and hurts Judaism. For instance, some feminists question whether women were even present at Sinai! One claims that "the men heard the revelation at Sinai, and entered the Promised Land. . . . But Jewish women are still wandering in the desert, awaiting inclusion in the covenant, awaiting their Sinai."[1] Another feminist says that women must stand *again* at Sinai (and "reshape Torah," which she calls a "male text") because we were "invisible" the first time.[2]

These authors must be unaware that Jewish tradition says that women received the Torah first. Perhaps their brothers were given a better Jewish education than they—if they, as girls, got any Jewish education at all. Perhaps they did have a "good" Jewish education, but even a "good" education consisted of sexist instructors who did not teach such things. Alternately, maybe they *are* aware of it but find it meaningless because it has played only a minimal role in shaping Jewish life.

At Sinai, God knew the importance of "calling to the women first." The price of not doing so since then has been steep indeed.

THE TEN COMMANDMENTS

There are 613 commandments of the Torah—248 positive and 365 negative—which are incumbent on the Jewish people as "a kingdom of priests and a holy nation" (Ex. 19:6).

The Ten Commandments (Ex. 20) are symbolically inclusive of all 613. For example, the commandment against adultery includes incest and other sexual prohibitions explicitly defined in Leviticus. The commandment against stealing comprises kidnapping, theft, robbery, not returning a borrowed object, and not attempting to locate the owner of a lost object that one has found.

"Every word contained all manner of legal implications and derivations, as well as all mysteries and hidden aspects; for each word was indeed like a treasurehouse,

---

1. Pogrebin, p. 113.
2. Plaskow, pp. 25–28

full of precious things. And though when one word was uttered it sounded only like itself, yet . . . seventy different aspects were revealed in it" (*Zohar* II:83b). This, perhaps, is what is meant by the statement that there are "seventy who are always attendant on the Shekhinah, there being seventy thrones around the Shekhinah" (*Zohar* I:173b).

While Jews were given the Torah with its 613 commandments, gentiles continued to be obligated to the seven Noachide laws, commandments that date from the time of Adam and Chavah through the generation of Noach. The Noachide laws prohibit idolatry, blasphemy, murder, sexual immorality, robbery, and tearing the limb off a live animal, as well as requiring courts of law to be established. The Noachide laws were an attempt to create basic civilized behavior in pagan societies; they also set the stage for later Torah law. For example, the Torah could not prohibit "bearing false witness" in a court of law until such courts had been established.

Christianity took on the Ten Commandments, but with a different numbering. The gentile pagans converting to Christianity had not come out of Egypt, and the Catholic Church wanted to retain the pagan practice of using images and statues. Consequently, the first and second commandments were reduced and combined, and each successive commandment was moved up by one. Thus, honoring one's parents is the fifth commandment in Judaism but the fourth commandment in Christianity. The Church split the tenth commandment in two; coveting a wife became their ninth commandment, while coveting property remained the tenth.

That the Jews were "chosen" by God to obey more commandments than gentiles does not mean that Jews are morally superior. Such a notion is pure chauvinism. Being "chosen" does not confer more privilege but only added responsibility. It means, for example, that a gentile can eat shrimp but a Jew cannot. Gentiles, who are part of God's Creation and equal recipients of divine love, have greater freedom and flexibility than do Jews. Jews who think "chosen" means "superior" should pause to remember that it was their "stiff-necked" (Ex. 33:5), stubborn behavior that made it necessary for God to give the Jews so many laws to begin with.

WOMEN'S EXEMPTION FROM CERTAIN COMMANDMENTS

Within Judaism itself, a similar misunderstanding persists. Because men are obligated to more commandments than women, it is assumed that men are "superior" or somehow favored by God, but if anything, the reverse is true.

Women, like men, are obligated to keep all the negative commandments. Women are also obligated to keep most of the positive commandments, except for those that must be done *at a certain time* of day or season. These positive, time-bound commandments (Kid. 29a, 33b–34a) consist of:

1. Saying the *Shma* morning and evening.
2. Putting on *tefillin* in the morning for davening.
3. Wearing *tzitzit*, ritual fringes, which must be seen by day.

4. Sitting in the *sukkah* during Sukkot.
5. Waving the Four Species during Sukkot.
6. Hearing the *shofar* on Rosh Hashanah.
7. Counting the *Omer*, the fifty days between Passover and Shavuot (Maimonides).

Women are *obligated to pray,* but not at fixed times or with fixed content as men are. This gives a woman greater flexibility because her day is not regimented like a man's. She does not need to be told when or how to pray. She can pray alone, and her own words are perfectly acceptable. A man does not have this option. Neither mode is "better" than the other: "All are equal before God—women, slaves, poor, and rich. . . . Before God all are equal in prayer" (ER 21:4).

However, women's greater flexibility brings a concomitant limitation: a woman cannot be counted in a men's fixed-prayer *minyan* or serve as a cantor for one. This is only one kind of *minyan*; women are definitely counted in others where they are obligated, such as the *minyan* required for *Kiddush Hashem*. (A Jew, male or female, must accept death rather than commit certain sins; this is true only if there is a *minyan* present.)

Women are not required—but may if they wish—sit in the *sukkah*, wave the Four Species, and count the *omer*. It is actually quite routine for women today to do these things, as well as to say the *Shma* and other fixed prayers at fixed times if they want. Women historically took on the obligation of hearing *shofar*, to the point where it is now taken for granted that they *should* hear it.

There has been no rabbinic resistance to women doing these *mitzvot*, but a woman cannot fulfill a man's obligation for him *when their obligation levels differ.* A woman cannot serve as a cantor for men, because for *her* to say prayers that she is not obligated to say cannot replace *his* obligation to say them. On the other hand, a woman who makes *kiddush* on the Sabbath fulfills a man's obligation to hear it, because she has an identical obligation. Thus, having only male cantors for male prayer is not misogynist, but allowing only men to make *kiddush* is. Unfortunately, such distinctions have been completely ignored by *all* branches of Judaism, which take all-or-nothing stances regarding women's role in ritual.

There *has* been rabbinic resistance to women wearing *tefillin* or *tzitzit*. These two *mitzvot* have been treated differently than the others because they are viewed by some authorities as "male clothing" and Jews are not allowed to cross-dress.

Such a view is by no means absolute: R. Judah believed that the custom of *tzitzit* is not time-bound, and so he obligated the women of his household to wear them. In fact, the Sages included women in the obligation of *tzitzit,* but R. Shimon's view that it is time-bound (and, hence, that women are exempt) won out in the end (Men. 43a). Similarly, Michal, Saul's daughter, wore *tefillin,* "and the Sages did not attempt to prevent her" (Er. 96a). Rashi's three daughters, Miriam, Rachel, and Yokheved, wore them, too.

Why are women exempt from positive time-bound commandments? The usual explanation involves the demands of a home and children. That this is not the reason, however, is indicated by two proofs:

1. *All* women, and not just wives and mothers, are exempt. Even societies that married girls off at puberty had a significant proportion of women who were widows, divorced, or childless.

2. If, in a modern marriage, the woman goes out to work and the man stays home with the children, he does not become exempt, nor does she become obligated.

A woman's exemption is thus not due to her role in society, but to something specific about her female nature. Rabbi Emanuel Rackman has suggested that men are obligated to perform positive time-bound *mitzvot* because they do not menstruate.[3] A woman's natural periodicity makes her aware of the sanctity of the cyclical nature of time. Because a man has no "built-in apparatus" for this, he must be given *mitzvot* governed by a calendar and a clock.

Thus, as the woman's menstrual cycle correlates to the monthly lunar cycle, the schedule of prayer imposed upon men correlates to the daily solar cycle. This and other time-bound obligations, such as the festival pilgrimages where "all your males shall be seen" (Deut. 16:16), enable men to learn to *remember*, for cyclical time, by its very nature, maintains a link with the past, whereas linear time simply forges ahead. This issue explains why "male" (*zakhar*) and "remember" (*zakhor*) have the same root in Hebrew.

The duality we have been exploring in this chapter may also be a reason for the different obligation levels. Women needed only general instruction because they were eager to receive the Torah, but men had to have the details spelled out for them in language that contained the threat of punishment. Consequently, men had to be obligated to perform certain activities at certain times, while women did not. One does not need to stipulate how and when an activity must be done to those who are eager to do it; their freedom of choice and enthusiasm can be relied upon. It is those who are reluctant or even resistant who need a fixed structure to guide and motivate them—like children who need to be told what time to go to bed.

There are also some positive commandments *not* bound by time from which women are exempt. Women are not, we noted in chapter 1, obligated to marry and procreate. Nor is it incumbent on a mother to circumcise or redeem her son; if the father does not do these things, the obligation falls upon the *bet din* or, later, on the boy himself. However, even though Zipporah was not *obligated* to circumcise her son, there was nothing to *prohibit* her from doing so.

Furthermore, there are positive time-bound commandments to which women are *obligated:*

1. Those whose instructions in the Torah explicitly cite women, such as rejoicing on festivals (Deut. 16:14) and gathering for the Eighth Year Torah Assembly (Deut. 31:12).

2. Those that are linked to a corresponding prohibition or negative commandment: women are obligated to eat *matzah* on the first night of Passover because

---

3. Emanuel Rackman, *One Man's Judaism* (New York: Philosophical Library, 1970), p. 330.

they are also prohibited from eating *chametz*. Women must light candles and hear *kiddush* on the Sabbath because they, too, must refrain from the prohibited forms of work. Festival rejoicing also has a negative corollary in work prohibitions. There is no corresponding prohibition *specific to* Sukkot or Rosh Hashanah, so women are exempt from the positive commandments unique to those days.

3. Those of rabbinic origin, not commanded by the Torah itself: postbiblical holiday observances, such as hearing *Megillat Esther* on Purim and lighting Chanukah candles, are examples. Drinking four cups of wine and reciting *Hallel* on Passover were also rabbinically instituted (as were Sabbath candle lighting and *kiddush*).

Fasting on Yom Kippur, which is cited by some as a positive time-bound commandment, is actually a negative commandment, as food and drink are forbidden.

EXEMPTION VERSUS PROHIBITION

Two things become readily apparent about women's exemption. First, the range of exemption is really quite narrow. Second, *exempt* does not mean *prohibited*, although it has frequently been misused this way. This distortion of the concept may be more prevalent today than in ancient times, if the following talmudic discussion is any indication. The Rabbis ask whether a woman may perform *smikhah*, the laying of hands on a sacrificial animal that one brought to the Temple. *Smikhah* is one of eight practices associated with sacrifices that the Mishnah says only men were obligated to do (Kid. 36a–b) because the Torah specifically cited "children of Israel."

However, the Rabbis agreed that women were certainly *allowed* to do Smikha, if they chose, *for the sake of their own spiritual satisfaction* (Chag. 16b). If rabbis today were all liberal enough to consider women's "spiritual satisfaction" to be of primary importance, there would be no conflict over women's prayer services and Torah readings.

While "children of Israel" may mean men in relation to "house of Jacob," it is problematic, if not impossible, to interpret it as "men only" in *all* situations. If that were so, then Jewish women could eat shellfish (see Lev. 11:2)! A strict interpretation of *ben* as "son" rather than "child" (Deut. 6:7, 11:19) is at the root of the notion that women do not have the obligation of Torah study that men do. This is very important, for out of the *mitzvah* of Torah study come the privileges of *aliyah* (being called up to the Torah in synagogue) and rabbinic ordination (which includes the ability to be a judge in a Jewish court).

Anyone may be called to the Torah, "even a minor and a woman, only the Sages said that a woman should not read from the Torah out of honor for the congregation" (Meg. 23a). While some scholars have suggested that "honor" refers to preventing the sexual distraction of men, the stronger opinion is that it refers to protecting men from the "shame" of a woman being more Torah-educated or literate than they. (Note that, in either case, *congregation* means "men.")

"In normal cases a congregation that allowed women to read the Torah would cast doubt on the piety of its male members. . . . One would think that in a congregation where women are given *aliyot* the men are too ignorant to read the Torah."[4] (Women used to hide their intelligence and lose on purpose at tennis because of this same misogynist logic in the secular world.)

Torah study is not a time-bound *mitzvah.* Although men are supposed to study every day, there is no fixed time when they must do so and no fixed content. They can learn what they want and should do it as often as possible. Women, too, should study Torah as often as possible. Some men have argued that women do not *need* to study the books; they already have the knowledge in them, because women are on a higher spiritual plane. This is absolutely true—but the men who say this *do not really believe it.* If they did, they would be humble enough to recognize that they—as beings from the "lower spiritual plane"—have no business telling those from the "higher spiritual plane" what they should or should not study.

The most blatant evidence of their hypocrisy is their continuing resistance to women in the rabbinate. Why would anyone believe that only members of the "spiritually lower" class should be the community's leaders and legal experts? Those who really *do* believe in women's greater Binah (spiritual understanding) not only encourage women's Torah study, but yearn for the day when the "house of Jacob" will take her rightful place in the house of study *and* the courts of law.

---

4. Rachel Biale, *Women and Jewish Law* (New York: Schocken, 1984), p. 28.

✳✳✳ 18 ✳✳✳

Female Servitude

Mishpatim (21:1–24:18)

*P*arshat Mishpatim contains laws from Sinai that define minimal standards of justice in human relationships. These were a first in the ancient Near East, as a comparison with pagan practices will show.

Women and men were equal under biblical law in the honor due to them as parents (Ex. 21:15–17) and in matters of bodily harm, such as murder, kidnapping, and being gored by an ox (Rashi, Ex. 21:12, 21:16, 21:28–32); children's lives were also of equal worth. "Women are equal to men in all laws of damages in the Torah. So that one not think that liability is only in the case of an adult man or woman, Scripture therefore says . . . liability is for minors as for adults" (Nachmanides).

Justice for the poor, the enslaved, the accused criminal, and even for animals was in all cases defined in a way that surpassed standards of kindness in surrounding societies. An animal in distress could not be ignored simply because the owner was one's enemy (Ex. 23:5). A baby animal could no longer be boiled in its mother's milk—a pagan practice to propitiate their gods for an increase in crops (Ex. 23:19; Sforno).

We will examine six of the seven categories of women about whom laws are defined. (For a discussion of widows, see chapter 9.)

1. Canaanite slave;
2. Jewish maidservant;
3. wife;
4. pregnant woman (and the status of her fetus);
5. seduced girl;
6. sorceress;
7. widow (and her children).

Such women are the poorest, most vulnerable, and most oppressed members of a male-dominated society. Except for the sorceress (for reasons we shall see), all were protected in new ways by Torah legislation and experienced a significant upgrading of status. The measures needed to improve women's status in fourteenth-century B.C.E. Canaan or Egypt were not identical to the measures needed in the modern world. However, by showing how the Torah improved women's status at *that* time, we are furnishing evidence of its continuing mandate to do so in *this* time.

One might naturally question why the Torah did not simply *abolish* slavery, polygyny, sex discrimination, or child-marriage. The answer lies in the "weaning" theory of Maimonides (*Guide of the Perplexed* III:32). In the context of Temple services and animal sacrifice, Maimonides explains that pagan ritual had to be *transformed* rather than *eliminated;* given the people's attachment to the practices, the latter was highly unlikely. "For a sudden transition from one opposite to another is impossible. And therefore human nature is not capable of abandoning suddenly all to which it is accustomed." God did not "give us a law prescribing the rejection, abandonment, and abolition" of these things because "one could not then conceive the acceptance of such, considering human nature."

The Torah was given in a sociological milieu in which slavery and the subjection of women were absolute foundations of society. However, just because God *chose to work* within the confines of a society where prepubescent girls were sold by their fathers to husbands or masters does not mean that God *wants* prepubescent girls to be sold in this way! Nor does it mean that the Torah, which reflects these social conditions, is inherently sexist and should be "rewritten."

SLAVERY IN THE ANCIENT NEAR EAST

Chattel slavery, in which one human being is owned as property by another, was universal, normative, and morally unquestioned in the ancient world. Slave labor *built* the empires of the ancient Near East; it was "the means by which Babylonia and many other countries in the ancient world were enabled to become so prosperous."[1]

Slaves were generally war captives, foreigners imported and sold by merchants, or native residents who were heavily in debt who sold themselves or their children to their creditors. Children were particularly vulnerable to slavery—usually through sale by their parents, although young girls were also sold by their brothers. Children were sometimes kidnapped and sold. Even adoption was merely a form of sale which, "though serving primarily family and economic purposes, was also, in a restricted sense, a source of slavery."[2]

Children abandoned to infanticide were sometimes rescued and raised as slaves—

---

1. Georges Contenau, *Everyday Life in Babylon and Assyria* (New York: St. Martin's Press, 1954), p. 24.

2. Isaac Mendelsohn, *Slavery in the Ancient Near East* (Westport, CT: Greenwood Press, 1949), pp. 1–5, 10, 19–21.

"girls and children who were not wanted, or who . . . could not be reared by their parents, were cast into pits, or thrown out into the desert to be devoured by jackals and wild beasts, or . . . laid in little reed-chests and committed to the river."[3] (The stories of Asnat, Joseph, and Moses contain remnants of these practices.)

War captives became the king's slaves and were used to build roads, temples, irrigation systems, and military fortifications and till state-owned land. They might also be dedicated to temple service, which could mean being immediately sacrificed to the god in thanks for the victory.[4]

Besides the king's war captives, temple slaves were acquired through private dedications by a master at his death, as well as freeborn children—orphans and poor children dedicated by parents who could not support them. Temple slaves had a harsher status than "secular" slaves. Their "caste character" meant that their treatment was "more severe and exacting than that accorded to their brothers [sic] owned by private persons. . . . The mistreatment of the temple slaves is reflected in the very large number of fugitives from their ranks."[5]

Most privately owned slaves were domestic or agricultural laborers. Houseborn slaves were more valuable than purchased slaves. Some domestic slaves became trusted assistants to their masters—such as Eliezer with Avraham, Joseph with Potiphar. A slave could even manage property, control money, or run the master's business.[6] However, this did not change the slave's status as the master's property. In Egypt runaway slaves were pursued,[7] and Babylonia's Code of Hammurabi (15–20) prescribed the death penalty for any freeman who helped a slave escape or hid one in his home.

The Torah's command to shelter a slave seeking refuge (Deut. 23:16–17) thus "stands unparalleled in the slave legislation of the ancient Near East. It is a most extraordinary law and its application in life would have spelled the end of slavery" in Canaan.[8] Equally revolutionary were the Torah's laws avenging a slave's murder (Ex. 21:20–21) and freeing the slave whose master caused the loss of an eye, a tooth, or other injuries that the Rabbis added (Ex. 21:26–27; Kid. 23b–25a).

A slave's "head was generally shaved in a peculiar way."[9] He or she was branded with a hot iron like a beast of burden, usually on the wrist; a slavemark could only be removed by cutting it out. The brand might be the name of the owner or a symbol—for example, temple slaves of the goddess Ishtar were branded with a star. Runaway slaves received an additional brand, usually on the forehead. Slaves might also be labeled with tags (like that put on Asnat's neck when she was abandoned); they were frequently beaten by their masters.[10]

---

3. E. A. Wallis Budge, *Babylonian Life and History* (New York: Dorset Press, 1992), p. 165.
4. Contenau, p. 22; Joan Oates, *Babylon* (London: Thames and Hudson, 1979), p. 70.
5. Mendelsohn, pp. 101–105.
6. Contenau., p. 22–23; Mendelsohn, pp. 57, 66, 68; Oates, p. 70.
7. Montet, p. 62.
8. Mendelsohn, p. 63.
9. Budge, p. 161.
10. Mendelsohn, pp. 42–49, 65.

Like cocks or bulls, male state-owned slaves were put in a ring to fight for the master's entertainment. In their numerous military campaigns, the Egyptians took "spoils" who "immediately on capture were branded like cattle, stamped with the king's name, sorted into squads and subjected to discipline on the Egyptian model. Training took the form of route marches and single combat. The king liked to watch the fights and competitions."[11]

Many of Egypt's slaves came from Libya, Nubia (Sudan), Ethiopia, and Somalia. "There had always been slaves in Egypt's history, but their numbers greatly increased in the age of the New Kingdom, when foreign conquests brought in prisoners of war."[12] Canaan, a narrow corridor of land between vast empires, had always been a "middleman in traffic, in war and peace, diplomacy, trade, and culture between Mesopotamia and Egypt."[13] However, around the time of Joseph's death, Canaanite cities became vassals of Egypt, through Tutmoses III's conquest of Megiddo and further campaigns by his successor, Amenophis II. The Canaanite peasantry was reduced to bondmen and bondwomen holding and working Egyptian-owned land. Amenophis III and IV (Akhnaten) continued this rule, suppressing Canaanite rebellions fomented by the Hittites in the north.

The pharaohs of the Nineteenth Dynasty (the Exodus era) continued in "great efforts to secure Egyptian domination over the land of Canaan," well into the time of Jewish settlement there.[14] Given Canaan's small size and strategic location, its population was thus particularly vulnerable to war, captivity, and enslavement in the time of the Torah.

THE CANAANITE SLAVEWOMAN

If his master gives him [a Hebrew male slave] a [Canaanite slave] woman, and she bears sons or daughters, the woman and her children will belong to her master, and he [the Hebrew slave] leaves alone. (Ex. 21:4)

Women in the pagan world were primarily enslaved through captivity in war or through sale by destitute fathers, husbands (Code of Hammurabi, 117), and sometimes brothers. Slavery for women of any age automatically included sexual servicing of the master, especially if his legal wife was childless. "A female slave was under obligation to give her purchaser not only her labor but also herself. . . . He could indeed actually give her over to prostitution. Even when she became her purchaser's concubine, and she had children by him, nonetheless she still remained a slave."[15]

---

11. Montet, p. 228.

12. Lionel Casson, *Ancient Egypt* (Alexandria, VA: Time-Life, 1965), p. 102.

13. John Gray, *The Canaanites* (London: Thames and Hudson, 1964), p. 17.

14. Yohanan Aharoni and Michael Avi-Yonah, *The Macmillan Bible Atlas* (New York: Macmillan, 1968), pp. 32–35, 38–39.

15. Contenau, pp. 21–22.

Wealthy Babylonians like Lavan gave slavewomen to their daughters as wedding presents. "To safeguard for their daughters the status of a first wife, wealthy parents presented them with one or two maids as part of their dowry. In case of sterility or incurable illness, such a maid was handed over to the husband to bear him children and thus prevent him from taking a second wife."[16]

"The highest position a female slave could achieve was to become a childbearing concubine for her master, and the lowest, to be used as a professional prostitute. . . . The practice of using female slaves for the sexual satisfaction of their master and of the male members of his household led, in some cases, to the practice of employing them as professional prostitutes." This included breeding her with "a successive number of his male slaves" or selling her while pregnant.[17]

Not only did a master have complete sexual rights to his female slaves (a concept that was still accepted during the period of black slavery in America), but any children she bore were *his* property. The master thus gratified himself physically, bred a large number of servants for himself, and caused "the frequent occurrence of large families. These enhanced the importance of the head of the family, who was for all practical purposes the ruler of a community. . . . [Thus,] the family was able to grow in size more rapidly than it could have done by natural means."[18]

The Torah made several significant improvements in the situation of female slaves. First, no adult Jewish woman (over twelve years old) could be sold into slavery. A destitute Jewish man could sell himself but not his wife; a Jewish court could sell a male thief, but not a female thief, who had no way of making restitution—but only to a Jewish master. A Jew who sold himself to a gentile had to be immediately redeemed by relatives (Lev. 25:47–55). A Jewish slave worked a *maximum* of six years and was released with a share of the master's flocks and produce as a gift (Deut. 15:12–14).

A Jewish wife who accompanied her husband into a master's household could work in exchange for food and support—as a hired worker—but she was free to decline the support and refuse to work. She and her labor were not the master's by absolute right (Nachmanides), and he certainly had no sexual prerogative over her.

The Torah did not give a Jewish master *personal* sexual rights to his Canaanite female slave, but he was still allowed to "give" her to a Jewish male slave, who served as the master's "stud" to breed additional slaves. However, unlike the promiscuous breeding of slaves in the pagan world, the Torah required the *monogamous pairing* of slaves. This was meant to be *like* a marriage—for while only a freewoman can be "betrothed" (Kid. 68a), the female slave was "designated" to one man sexually (Git. 43a). This reduction of sexual exploitation was a vast improvement for her—she was no longer public property and no longer available to any man, free or slave, who would take her.

---

16. Mendelsohn, pp. 4, 50, 119.
17. Ibid., pp. 50, 52, 54.
18. Contenau, p. 25.

Not all Jewish masters followed the Torah's ideal. In talmudic times, Samuel designated his female slaves to individual husbands but R. Nachman interchanged his. R. Sheshet entrusted the care of his slavewomen to Arabs and, although he told the men not to touch them, he did not concern himself with the consequences (Nid. 47a).

The Torah allowed for a Jewish male slave to become emotionally attached to his Canaanite "wife" and children, and he did not have to leave them when his time was up. If he chose to stay, his master had to take him to court and pierce his ear in the doorway (Ex. 21:5–6). This was a symbol of "the ear that heard at Sinai" not to steal and did so anyway (the court-sold slave) or not to serve any master but God and did so anyway (the self-sold slave). The doorway recalled the flight from slavery in Egypt, for now this Jew was *choosing to remain* in slavery (Rashi; Kid. 22b).

Although a Jewish master was given the right to "put to stud" his male slave, he could take no other sexual license with him. A Jewish master could not sodomize his male slaves (the reason why Potiphar bought Joseph) or castrate them (like eunuch harem guards). The use of a male slave *only* as a stud was thus yet another restriction of a master's sexual prerogative.

THE JEWISH MAIDSERVANT

If a man sells his daughter as a maidservant, she does not go out as the male slaves go out. If she be evil in the eyes of her master, who has not designated her [as a wife], he must cause her to be redeemed. He shall have no power to sell her to an alien people, for he has treated her contemptuously. If he designates her for his son, she has the legal status of a daughter. . . . If none of the three are done, she shall be released without liability or payment. (Ex. 21:7–9, 21:11)

Although no adult Jewish woman could be sold by her husband, the Torah permitted a minor daughter (up to the age of twelve) to be sold by her father as a domestic servant. Like the Jewish male slave, the Jewish maidservant could not be sold to a gentile and she had to be released, with gifts, after six years of servitude or in the Jubilee Year (the fiftieth year in the land's cycle), whichever came first.

Unlike the Jewish male slave, the Jewish maidservant had additional ways out:

1. She was automatically released at puberty.
2. She was released if her father died, for "if puberty, which does not free her from her father's authority, frees her from her master, how much more so that [the father's] death, which does free her from her father's authority, should free her from her master!" (Kid. 16a).
3. She was released if her master died, while a Jewish male slave continued his term in service to the master's son (Kid. 17b).

The maidservant could never choose to remain in slavery and have her ear pierced. She could only stay on as a wife, which meant as a freewoman.

A wife, a maidservant, a Jewish slave, a Canaanite slave, and immovable property (i.e., land) all shared the quality of being acquired by a man through money *(kesef)* and deed *(shtar)*. In addition, taking a wife included "sexual connection" *(biah)*. Taking a Canaanite slave included "possession" *(chazakah)*, a quality of the *combination* of movable and immovable property (i.e., an estate). Canaanite slaves were inherited with a father's estate (Kid. 1:1–5; Lev. 25:44–46).

A father thus exchanged his daughter for money, whether he was betrothing her to a husband or selling her to a master. In the ancient world, "there were scarcely any limits to a father's rights over his children. . . . In certain legal documents he was even described as 'master' or 'owner' of his child. . . . A father had equally complete authority in the matter of a daughter's marriage . . . [and he] was free to settle her in marriage exactly as he thought fit."[19]

The Torah only allowed a father to *sell* his minor daughter if he had never *betrothed* her, for he could only bring her up in status, not down. Hence, he could betroth her to a husband after having sold her to a master but could not sell her to a master after having once betrothed her to a husband. Nor could he resell her from one master to another (Kid. 18a).

Her father had no right to resell her to a second master because he had "treated her contemptuously" *(bagad)* (Jastrow) by selling her the first time (Rashi). His own behavior was to blame for him having had to sell her at all (ER 30:16), and he was obligated to redeem her as soon as he could afford it. Her family was obligated to redeem her even against the father's will; however, it was not so obligated with a son, who could simply be resold by the father (Kid. 18a).

Her master, by paying the purchase price, was supposed to be contracting an eventual marriage as well as buying a temporary domestic servant. *Yiud* (designation) was a *mitzvah* incumbent on the master (Rashi), either for himself or his son, but *not* for his Jewish male slave. Marriage, like puberty, freed the maidservant. If she was not designated, the master was considered to have "treated her contemptuously," and was therefore required to do everything possible to release her—even making it easy for her to be redeemed by calculating the monetary value of her work (purchase price divided by six years equals one year's value) and treating her as a hired worker who is owed back pay (Rashi). If the master designated her but then changed his mind, he still could not resell her but had to divorce her, as a freewoman (Kid. 18a, 18b).

Thus, all paths led to freedom for the Jewish maidservant. Unlike the Canaanite slavewoman, the Jewish maidservant could not be used *in any sexual way as a servant,* not even by a Jewish male slave. A Jewish freeman could *marry* her, as he could any freewoman, but he could not "mate" her with male slaves to make slave babies.

This separation of domestic labor from sexual slavery formed the essential distinction between an *amah*, the Jewish maidservant, and a *shifchah*, the pagan female slave. Even a *shifchah* might be called an *amah*, however (Ex. 23:12). As the "wife" of one Jewish male slave, the Canaanite woman rose above the normative sexual

---

19. Ibid., pp. 18, 15.

slavery of *shifchut*. Any Canaanite slave, male or female, who was owned by a Jew had to immerse in a *mikvah* (Yev. 46a) and keep most of the commandments (except those that were positive time-bound or marriage-related) while living in a Jewish household. Male slaves, in addition, had to be circumcised to be present at the Passover *seder*. Because of this intermediate status of a Canaanite slave in a Jewish household, the Canaanite woman rose to a position of domestic laborer without sexual servitude. She could also be set free by her Jewish master, and sexual abuse was argued to be grounds for automatic emancipation (Git. 38a).

Thus, the Torah's laws, while significantly *improving* the Canaanite slave's life under a Jewish master, went even further within Jewish society itself, legislating the sexual enslavement of women out of existence and preventing any kind of permanent slave caste from emerging among the Jewish people. "For they are My slaves whom I brought out of Egypt, and they shall not be sold in the marketplace. Do not dominate or break [their] spirit" (Lev. 25:42–43).

MARRIAGE: A WIFE'S RIGHTS

If he takes another wife, he may not reduce her [the first wife's] sustenance, clothing, or conjugal rights. (Ex. 21:10)

At this point in human sexual evolution, humanity—having descended from monogamy to polygamy—needed a turning point to get back on the road to monogamy. Polyandry had declined, but polygyny was still in full swing. Enter the Torah: the fact that it lists the obligations of a husband to his wife in the midst of the obligations of a master to his maidservant is not accidental. The status of marriage was meant to lift women even further out of sexual slavery. The laws of acquiring a slave, significantly, are found in *Kiddushin,* the talmudic tractate on betrothal, while the laws of emancipating a slave are found in *Gittin,* the tractate on divorce.

In the ancient world, even in areas where monogamy was theoretically practiced, concubinage as an established institution made the concept of one "legal wife" irrelevant, for if a man slept with one wife and two slaves, he was hardly being "monogamous."[20]

First, the Torah had to legislate that women could only be taken sexually as wives and not as slaves, so concubines had to be freed. The second step was to insure that each wife received her just due, so the husband would not try to keep "two for the price of one."

The three biblically ordained duties of a husband to a wife are *she'er*, *kesut*, and *onah*. To this the Rabbis added seven others: *ketubah*, medical costs, ransom from captives, burial, support and residence in her widowhood, support of their minor daughters until betrothal, and inheritance by their sons of her *ketubah* and his estate.[21]

---

20. Ibid.
21. Elon, p. 379.

We will examine only the biblical duties in order to understand the foundation of the wife's legal rights.

She'er: Translated as "sustenance," "food," or "maintenance," this refers to a wife's right to economic support. Because the literal meaning of *she'er* is "flesh," it also refers to close bodily contact; a woman's husband "may not treat her in the manner of the Persians who perform their conjugal duties in their clothes," and he may even be forced to divorce her if he will only have sex with his clothes on (Ket. 48a).

Kesut: This means "covering"—as in *kesut enayim,* the "covering of the eyes," Sarah's article of compensation or vindication from Avimelekh. *Kesut* is usually translated as "clothing" but refers to lodging—the "cover" over her head—as well. Nachmanides calls it "the cover of her bed."

Onah: The term for "conjugal rights," it literally means "due season or period" (Jastrow), and refers to a husband's duty to have sex with his wife at certain intervals. Nachmanides calls it "her time of love"; he sees all three duties as a means by which a man becomes "one flesh" with his wife and will be unable to treat her like a concubine or a whore.

The Mishnah gives men guidelines for their "obligation" in terms of their profession: "men of independent means, every day; workmen, twice a week; ass-drivers, once a week; camel-drivers, once in 30 days; sailors, once in six months" (Ket. 5:6 or 61b). A man must also carry out his "duty" on the night his wife goes to the *mikvah* and before he goes on a journey. Moreover, a newly married man is exempt from military service for a year because he is supposed to focus on making his wife happy (Deut. 24:5).

Sexual pleasure, in the Jewish view of marriage, is the woman's right and the man's duty.[22] That "conjugal rights" are defined as the *woman's* rather than the *man's* rights makes the Jewish marriage contract unique in that it does not legitimize rape in marriage. In traditional Christian, Anglo-Saxon, and Islamic legal systems, "conjugal rights" have always been defined as a *man's* right to sex (in addition to housework) from his wife, in exchange for his economic support. In these systems, marital rape is legal because he is only claiming what is "rightfully his."

Christian wives were biblically commanded to "be subject to your husbands as to the Lord, for the man is the head of the woman, just as Christ also is head of the church. . . . Just as the church is subject to Christ, so must women be to their husbands in everything" (Ephesians 5:22–24). Although husbands were instructed to love their wives, this merely taught them to be benevolent masters; it did not take away their right to *be* masters. Until recently, Christian wedding vows for a woman consisted of a promise to "love, honor, and *obey* ," while a man had to promise to "love, honor, and cherish." In such a contract, marital rape is at least *covertly* permissible.

Anglo-Saxon law *overtly* permitted marital rape. According to Sir Matthew Hale, writing in the 1700s, "The husband cannot be guilty of a rape committed by himself

---

22. David M. Feldman, *Marital Relations, Birth Control, and Abortion in Jewish Law* (New York: Schocken Books, 1974), pp. 64, 69.

upon his lawful wife, for by their mutual matrimonial consent and contract the wife hath given up herself in this kind unto her husband, which she cannot retract."[23] Up until just a century ago (1891), husbands in Britain were allowed to forcibly imprison their wives in their homes to obtain their "rights."[24] The marital rape exemption law was not invalidated by a British court of appeals until March 1991.[25]

In the United States, marital rape was legal in every state until the late 1970s, when feminist pressure began to have some effect. In 1977, marital rape was legal in forty-seven states; by 1985, this had decreased somewhat, to forty; and as of June 1991, it was still legal in thirty-one states. Of these thirty-one, twenty-seven allowed the prosecution of a husband for rape *if* he threatened his wife with a gun or a knife and *if* the wife had had the opportunity to consent—in other words, not if she was raped while drunk, asleep, unconscious, or comatose. The other four states allowed no prosecution at all.[26]

Under Islamic law, a husband is obligated to maintain his wife and "she is bound to cohabit with her husband unless she cannot do so for no fault of her own, such as sickness, imprisonment, and so on."[27] The Koran itself states, "Men have authority over women because Allah has made the one superior to the other, and because they spend their wealth to maintain them. Good women are obedient. . . . As for those from whom you fear disobedience, admonish them and send them to beds apart and beat them" (4:34).[28]

In a notable example, which contrasts Islamic law to modern Israeli law, a Beersheva court sentenced a forty-two-year-old Bedouin man who pleaded guilty to forcing his sixteen-year-old wife to have sex. The girl had been betrothed by her father against her will. After the wedding, her husband "beat her repeatedly and threatened to kill her if she refused to submit to him sexually. She stated that during the first months of their marriage she often ran away from her husband after being forced into sexual relations." She even ran back to her family, but they returned her to him.

The husband's lawyer did not dispute the girl's testimony but rather based his defense on the premise that in Islamic law, "the husband's wishes must be honored. . . . The *Koran* obligates her to sleep with him even if she does not want to." Nonetheless, the Israeli judge ruled that "a woman has the full right to refuse sex to any man, including her husband, and under no circumstances does he have the right to force himself on her." However, because this concept was so foreign to the husband, who had no idea he had done anything wrong, the judge sentenced him to

23. Quoted in Carole Pateman, *The Sexual Contract* (Stanford, CA: Stanford University Press, 1988), p. 123.
24. Ibid.
25. Helen Benedict, *Virgin or Vamp: How the Press Covers Sex Crimes* (New York: Oxford University Press, 1992), p. 44.
26. Ibid., p. 43; and Susan Estrich, *Real Rape* (Cambridge, MA: Harvard University Press, 1987), p. 74.
27. Alfred Guillaume, *Islam* (Harmondsworth, England: Penguin, 1956), p. 173.
28. N. J. Dawood (trans.), The Koran (Harmondsworth, England: Penguin, 1974), p. 370.

only a year in prison but noted that subsequent rulings would be "much more severe."[29]

Thus, Judaism stands in a class by itself. While certain reforms have occurred in these other traditions, Judaism's prohibition of marital rape is *not the result of reform but rather the original law itself.*

"A man should not have intercourse with his wife unless she has a desire for it, but not otherwise, and certainly he is forbidden to force her. Nor should he have intercourse with his wife if he hates her, or if she hates him and she tells him that she does not want his attention, even if she consents to having sex" (*Kitzur Shulchan Arukh* 150:13). Thus, not only is coercion forbidden, but even pressure or exploitation are prohibited! A man may also not have sex with his wife while she is asleep or while either of them is intoxicated.

Not only is sexual activity defined in terms of the *wife's* right in the Jewish marriage contract, it is also completely unrelated to the exchange of housework for economic support. A man has a right to certain domestic tasks from his wife in exchange for his duty of supporting her. *Her* right to maintenance, however, takes precedence over *his* right to housework: He must maintain her even when she cannot work, but she need not work unless he is actually maintaining her. *She* may waive her right to support and earn her own income instead, whereupon he will have no claim to her housework. *He,* however, cannot waive his right to housework in order to avoid supporting her. Nor may he compel her to earn her own income.[30]

If a woman brings servants with her into the marriage, her domestic tasks are delegated to them until, if she has four, she can "sit in a high-backed chair" all day—that is, be financially supported yet not required to do any housework (Ket. 5:5 or 59b). A woman cannot be made to do any kind of work that was not done by women of her family, and if her husband is of a higher class background, she cannot be made to do any work not done by the women of *his* family. Thus, a wife can only go up, not down, in her standard of living.[31]

All of this does not deny that throughout history, many Jewish women have been wrongly dominated and mistreated by their husbands. However, it must be made clear that the Torah is not to blame for sociological problems that, even when committed by Jewish individuals, clearly contravene Jewish law.

THE STATUS OF A FETUS AND REPRODUCTIVE SLAVERY

When two men fight and harm a pregnant woman, causing her to miscarry, but there is no fatal injury, [the offender] must be punished with a fine imposed on him by the husband of the woman through the court. But if there is fatal injury, he shall give life for life, an eye for an eye, a tooth for a tooth. (Ex. 21:22–24).

---

29. "The Koran, Israeli Law, and Women's Rights," *The Jerusalem Post,* June 27, 1987, p. 17.
30. Elon, p. 385.
31. Ibid., p. 384.

The fine was determined by estimating the woman's slave market value and adding on a percentage for the fetus (Rashi). If the woman was permanently injured, the culprit had to pay in like—which the Rabbis defined as monetary compensation rather than as poking out the eye or knocking out the tooth of the guilty man.

If the woman died, the guilty man had to pay "full compensation." The Code of Hammurabi (209–14), which also charged a fee for the fetus based on the woman's social status, legislated that if the woman died, the guilty man's *daughter* must be put to death!

The meaning of "full compensation" has been cited in support of both pro and con positions on capital punishment. However, in the "accidental" scenario described here, the woman's death would be manslaughter (punishable by exile to a city of refuge), and not murder. There is a definite sense of euphemism to the entire description. What is the likelihood of a pregnant woman intervening between two fighting men? More pregnant women are hit by men on purpose than by accident. Interestingly, the term *ason,* "fatal injury," is defined by Jastrow as "accident"—rendering the verse; "causing her to miscarry, and it was no accident." Nonetheless, even if it *is* only describing an accident, we can nevertheless learn *how much more so* would be the penalty in an intentional case.

The verse is significant as the source of Jewish legal attitudes toward abortion, which can best be summed up as: Abortion is not murder, but neither is the fetus simply a piece of tissue. Abortion may be performed under Jewish law when the physical or mental health of the mother is at stake. "Mental health" will be interpreted as liberally as the tendencies of the rabbi who is doing the interpreting. Historically, "the tradition of humaneness and compassion for 'that poor woman' motivated the entire thrust of Jewish law," and the Rabbis sought "whatever legal leniencies" they could on her behalf.[32]

Maternal, and not fetal, indicators are significant halakhically. Thus, if a fetus is believed to be deformed, Jewish law would not permit an abortion on the grounds of concern for the possible *future* happiness of the *child.* It would only permit the abortion if the *mother* was *currently* in a state of anguish over the situation.[33]

If a pregnant slave was freed, her child would then be free as well, because "a fetus is [considered as] the thigh of its mother" (Tem. 25b). Thus, just as amputating one's leg is a serious matter that is only undertaken as a last resort, so, too, is terminating a pregnancy. However, terminating a pregnancy is not considered equivalent to murdering a viable human being. Abortion is not on par with infanticide or euthanasia.

To kill a slave is worse than destroying a fetus, Nachmanides asserts, deriving this from the Torah's list of laws in "proper sequence and order," from most to least serious. The murder of a slave is listed *before* injury to human limbs. The verse itself makes the connection of fetus-as-limb, for the law in its entirety deals with, first, injury to a fetus; then, injury to (another) limb of the woman's body; and finally, injury to the woman as a whole (i.e., she dies).

32. Feldman, p. 302.
33. Ibid., pp. 291–292.

The fact that the fetus is given any status at all in the Torah, "though the child [has] not seen the light, being still in the mother's womb," is due to the fact that "the Torah gives precautions to Israel on everything" (ER 30:6). No form of life—slave, fetus, or animal—is inconsequential.

A woman's body is a temple, and her reproductive organs are its holy of holies. Procreation—the ability of human beings to engender other human beings—is a power akin to God's own creative force—or, to put it more succinctly, "women giving birth ... makes the divine image explicit."[34]

This sacredness, however, has been interpreted by many male religious leaders as cause to prohibit even birth control. Birth control is a tool that lifts women out of reproductive slavery, the condition in which women are *able* to control how often they get pregnant but are not *allowed* to do so. The Torah's juxtaposition of the fetus's status with those of slaves and wives is significant because "no woman is morally obligated to have as many children as she possibly can."[35]

That women need not submit completely to their biological processes, but may regulate them through tools created by God-given human talent, is not a radical idea. Birth control is like any other scientific advance that allows humanity to gain some measure of control over nature and its processes. However, this particular process— unlike agriculture or disease, for instance—is *completely under the province of women* because it occurs within a woman's body. Herein lies the source of male religious resistance.

The accessibility to safe and effective birth control for women is a major way to reduce the need for abortion.[36] Social, professional, and economic conditions conducive to single mothers are another. Finally, reducing the sexual abuse and exploitation of women would greatly help. (Prostitutes, for example, are at extremely high risk for repeated abortions.)

Judaism teaches that our bodies belong to God and we are only the custodians. This forms the foundation of most medical ethics decisions in Jewish law. However, it really does mean that *we*—not the U.S. Senate, Supreme Court, or president—are the "custodians."

To safeguard Judaism (which permits abortion in circumstances where Christianity does not) as a minority religion, abortion must be legally accessible in the United States. To support the *legal availability* of abortion in this country does not necessarily mean that one must agree with the *morality* of every abortion that is performed. Judaism's view of abortion could, if allowed, provide a much-needed "middle path" of wisdom in the American debate on the subject and perhaps even break the deadlock between the "pro-choice" and "right-to-life" factions.

---

34. Charles Mopsik, "The Body of Engenderment in the Hebrew Bible, the Rabbinic Tradition, and the Kabbalah," in *Fragments for a History of the Human Body*, ed. Michel Feher (Cambridge, MA: MIT Press, 1989), p. 54.

35. Warren, p. 23.

36. For a discussion of the halakhic problems with birth control for men, see Feldman, pp. 109–131, 229–230.

THE SEDUCTION OF GIRLS AND
THE CONCEPT OF BETROTHAL

If a man entices a virgin who is not betrothed and lies with her, he shall pay the *mohar* [bride-price] for her as a wife. If her father absolutely refuses to give her to him, then he pays the *mohar* for a virgin. (Ex. 22:15–16)

The Torah is here discussing the *seduction* of a not-yet-betrothed girl. The *rape* of a not-yet-betrothed girl, as well as the rape and the seduction of a betrothed girl, are discussed in Deuteronomy. A "virgin," *betulah*, is the term used for a *ketanah* (a minor up to the age of twelve) and a *naarah*. Unlike boys, who pass immediately from minorhood to adulthood under Jewish law, girls had an "in-between" stage called *naarut*—a six-month period, from twelve to twelve and a half, whereupon they attained puberty and were betrothed for marriage. After twelve and a half, a girl was a *bogeret*. *Bagrut* was full adulthood and freed the girl from her father's control.

Although a father could not contract a marriage for a minor son, he could contract one for his daughter as a *ketanah* and a *naarah* so that men would not "treat her as ownerless property," that is, sexually use her and then abandon her (Yev. 112b). A *naarah* could not contract a marriage without her father's consent (Kid. 43b–44b). A father was not supposed to betroth his daughter as a *ketanah* but rather wait "until she grows up and says about someone, 'I want [him]'" (Kid. 41a). If she was betrothed as a *ketanah*, under certain circumstances a girl had the right to repudiate the marriage upon coming of age and have it dissolved without a divorce, in a procedure called *miun*.

If a *ketanah* or a *naarah* was either seduced or raped, the perpetrator paid the following fines:

1. *Knas*, or fifty shekels. R. Meir believed that *knas* was only paid for a *naarah* and not a *ketanah*, but the Sages overruled him and said it was for both (Ket. 40b). In the case of seduction, this fine was only paid if the couple did not get married.
2. *Boshet*, payment for disgrace and indignity—"an indictable insult without physical injury," such as spitting in someone's face (Jastrow). The amount was determined by each party's social status.
3. *Pgam*, payment for "blemish" or "deterioration," here referring to the fact that the girl would command a lower bride-price now that she was no longer a virgin. The amount was determined by the girl's slave market value.

A rapist paid an additional fourth fee, *tzaar*, for the pain he inflicted.

Seduction, as opposed to rape, is a situation in which the girl willingly participates. The Torah, however, foreshadowed the concept of statutory rape in its understanding that even a girl's willingness is at times insufficient, especially with an older man. Like a slave who cannot truly "consent" to sex with her master, neither can a child truly "consent" to sex with an adult, for even where such consent appears to exist, the power inequity involved belies it. The seducer may simply be exploiting a girl's emotional need for love, affection, and attention.

This thin line between seduction and rape is noted by the commentators. In explaining seduction, Rashi echoes the description of Dinah's rape: the man "speaks sweetly to her [lit., 'to her heart'] until she surrenders to him." Nachmanides says a man "bends her will to his desire by words of falsehood. . . . He will attempt by devious means to invest the virgin with a sense of trust in him, by many ruses, until she submits to him. . . . Seduction may be achieved in many ways—sometimes with words, sometimes with money, sometimes by falsehood to mislead her, and sometimes even by truth, as when he really wishes to marry her."

The deception of young women by men, regardless of the age difference, is a major concern of the oral tradition. The Mishnah spends a good two chapters (Kid. 3, 4) delineating ways in which men might deceive women into betrothal and ruling that such betrothals are invalid. Although R. Shimon believed the betrothal could be valid if the deception was to the woman's advantage (e.g., the man said he was poor but he really was rich), the Sages overruled this, deciding that *any* deception invalidates a betrothal.

Deception by the woman also invalidates a betrothal, but this is only briefly mentioned. The focus on men's deception indicates that the Rabbis saw male lies as either more common, more dangerous, or, perhaps, both. This relates to the rabbinic view that male sexuality is linked to a desire to conquer and subdue, and so must be duly harnessed (see chapter 1).

Betrothal itself is called *kiddushin*. The man *mekadesh,* "sanctifies"; while the woman *mitkadeshet,* "becomes sanctified." This does not mean that the woman is a passive object but rather that a man has to invest sexual relations with holiness through his seriousness of purpose. He has to make a permanent commitment to care for her *before* he can have sex with her. He cannot sow his wild oats just to put another notch in his belt and be able to brag to his friends.

The concept of a wedding developed for this reason. Marriage ceremonies in the ancient world were virtually nonexistent, consisting of nothing more than the delivery of the wife to her husband.[37] In Egypt, the marriage ceremony "was unimpressive, if indeed it existed. Perhaps a man simply built a house and invited a woman to share it; when she moved in, the couple was married. Some sort of legal settlement may have been drawn up, but there are no traces of religious rites."[38] In Babylonia, a woman was brought to her husband's house veiled, whereupon, in the presence of relatives and friends he declared, "This woman is my wife."[39]

The Torah's law concerning seduction was clearly meant to protect a young woman from sexual exploitation. At the same time, it also helped to free her from the *absolute* paternal authority over her betrothal that was customary in the ancient world. The law thus represents yet another step in freeing girls and women from sexual slavery.

---

37. Contenau, p. 16; Montet, p. 48.
38. Mertz, p. 58.
39. Budge, p. 167.

SORCERY AND POWER

A sorceress (*mekhashefah*) you shall not sustain. (Ex. 22:17)

Sorcery continues the theme of this chapter, for it is both seductive and (mentally) enslaving. "Fools are easily enticed" by sorcery; those who practice it "cause many to become ensnared" (Nachmanides).

Kishuf (pl., *keshufim*), meaning "sorcery," is a very specific term. The Torah uses other Hebrew words for divination, astrology, omens, snake charming, and necromancy. Webster's dictionary defines *sorcery* as "the use of magic power derived from evil spirits."

The law against sorcery applies equally to men and women, yet the Torah puts the prohibition in the feminine gender because "women are excellent at sorcery" (Rashi). The Talmud notes that the daughters of Israel freely engaged in *keshufim* in postbiblical times and cites the burning of incense as part of the practice (Br. 53a; Er. 64b). It asserts that when two women sit at a crossroad, on opposite sides facing each other (interestingly, the way in which Isaac and Rivkah prayed), "it is certainly *keshufim* they are engaged in" (Pes. 111a). Amemar, a Babylonian Sage of the fourth century C.E., describes a protective formula taught to him by "the head of the sorceresses" (Pes. 110a–b).

The link between women and sorcery stems from witchcraft, women's historical antidote to political powerlessness. Where women have lacked direct political power, they have used the only means of control available to them—"that of pronouncing curses, of casting spells. . . . Women's traditional weapon [was] the tongue; and the dread which she inspired was chiefly associated with her faculty of uttering curses [and] . . . of bewitching and performing incantations. It was a dreaded power. The curse of a woman is accounted far more potent than the curse of a man."[40] This may explain the link in Hebrew between "sorcery" and "to whisper; to think, devise" (Jastrow).

Male sorcerers arose to counteract women's witchcraft and succeeded in gaining a monopoly over magical practices.[41] The nature and dynamic of such practices was completely transformed, eventually coming to bear little or no relationship to women's intuitive wisdom or power to protect themselves. Magic was no longer a tool of the underdog, the powerless, and the disenfranchised but a weapon of the socially powerful and the esoteric knowledge of an elite priesthood, whose members in turn persecuted women who were thought to be "witches."

The Hindus and the Arabs, for example, developed "a simple means of depriving a sorceress of the power to do harm; they extract her front teeth so that she is unable to sing or articulate distinctly."[42] (This, no doubt, is the source of the witch's image as a toothless old woman.)

---

40. Briffault, 2:560–561.
41. Ibid., 2:561–562.
42. Ibid., 1:19.

This biblical verse was translated by King James I as "Thou shalt not suffer a witch to live" and then used by him and his ecclesiastical cronies throughout medieval Europe as a rationale for burning women at the stake. However, the Church's *use of the Torah,* to justify the Inquisition's torture and extermination of social deviants, midwives, herbalists, "heretics," and other vulnerable people, is a gross misinterpretation of the Torah's prohibition of sorcery. The witch-hunters *themselves* were actually more akin to sorcerers: King James, for instance, wrote a comprehensive book on demonology and is said to have retained certain (male) magicians and wizards in his service.[43]

The most famous practitioner of sorcery in Jewish tradition appears to have been a man named Jesus of Nazareth. The unexpunged version of the Talmud[44] relates that Jesus was condemned to death by the Jewish court "because he practiced sorcery [*keshufim*] and enticed Israel to apostasy" (San. 43a–b). His "apostasy" lay in claiming to be the "son of God" and persuading people to worship him as such; his "sorcery" consisted of his miracles—for example, walking on water, changing water into wine, and multiplying the number of loaves and fishes.

Kishuf, unlike most of the other occult practices described by the Torah, was punishable by death—but only if it *actually was magic* (San. 53a)—because the power was derived from an idol. *Kishuf* was not punishable—although it was still forbidden—if the practitioner merely *created an illusion* (San. 67a), because such activity did not have the power of an idol behind it. Thus, modern stage magicians are not real "sorcerers."

The Torah's objection to sorcery, regardless of the gender of the practitioner, is rooted in the following description. "The driving force behind black magic is hunger for power. . . . Carried to its furthest extreme, the black magician's ambition is to wield supreme power over the entire universe, to make himself a god."[45]

Even a simple fortuneteller will create fear in people to extort money (e.g., Susan Sarandon's character in the movie *King of the Gypsies*). The sorcerer or sorceress goes way beyond this and uses willpower to *exert influence over others through magic.* Common tools include names of gods, angels, and demons; wax images of the person to be influenced, or body parts such as hair and nail clippings. Common goals of sorcery include harming an enemy or causing a particular person to fall in love with the practitioner. Examples of sorcery in ancient Egypt included spells to achieve fame, become a god, have power over wind or fire, seduce a married woman, make a man blind, cause skin disease, make a man die, and avoid execution or decapitation.[46]

Kishuf was considered by the Rabbis to "diminish the heavenly council." Although R. Chanina argued that *not even kishuf* could do this—and offered his own success

---

43. Kurt Seligmann, *Magic, Supernaturalism, and Religion* (New York: Pantheon Books, 1948), pp. 192–193.

44. See the Soncino English translation for a restoration of the paragraphs which were removed because of the extreme danger for Jews of pogroms motivated by accusations of "Christ killing."

45. Richard Cavendish, *The Black Arts* (New York: G. P. Putnam's Sons, 1967), pp. 1, 3.

46. Brier, pp. 287–291.

in overcoming a sorceress's curse to prove it—his opinion was attributed by the Gemara to the fact that he "was in a different category due to his merit" (Chul. 7b).

However, precisely because *kishuf* was prohibited (for gentiles as well as for Jews) (San. 56b), it was considered essential knowledge for a Rabbi! To qualify as a judge on the Sanhedrin (Jewish court), a man had to have "stature, wisdom, good looks, old age, a knowledge of *keshufim*, and be conversant with the seventy languages of humanity so the court does not need an interpreter" (San. 17a). A judge had to be able to recognize sorcery—and the distinction between real magic and illusion—in order to accurately pass sentence on someone accused of it.

Sorcery is distinguished from what is called "practical Kabbalah." The former derives its power from demons or idols, while the latter derives its power from God. Kabbalists were able to manipulate reality through the use of permutations of God's Name, the use of angels' names, and other techniques taken from a mystical work known as the *Sefer Yetzirah*. R. Chanina and R. Oshaia are said to have "spent every Sabbath eve studying the laws of Creation, by means of which they created a calf and ate it" (San. 67b). The Ari and others are said to have exorcised demons.[47]

However, even the Rabbis who distinguished between the *sources* of magical power—the "Side of Holiness" versus the "Side of Impurity"—warned against the use of practical Kabbalah by anyone but the most evolved in character, deed, and Torah knowledge. It is considered virtually impossible for anyone today to be on such a high level.[48] Practical Kabbalah has, in recent history, been adapted in a perverted form by non-Jewish Western occultists, such as the Order of the Golden Dawn; one of its most famous leaders was Aleister Crowley, who was known as "the wickedest man in the world."[49]

Sorcery is a strongly egotistical attempt to gain control over another person's psyche. Even where this power is allegedly used to benefit someone, it is still considered dangerous. Like the deceptive *kiddushin,* which benefits the woman but is still forbidden because its essence is deception, so, too, "white magic," though potentially beneficial, is nevertheless forbidden because its essence is still psychic control.

The command against sorcery is followed by prohibitions on bestiality, sacrificing to idols, and afflicting strangers, widows, orphans, and the poor. This juxtaposition enhances the notion that sorcery is essentially an ego-trip that is destructive to society. Not only must a practitioner of sorcery be stopped; the oppressive social conditions that foster vulnerability to enticement by such individuals must not even be allowed to take root. This is the meaning of the command to not "sustain" a sorceress or sorcerer.

---

47. Rabbi Yaakov Hillel, *Faith and Folly: The Occult in Torah Perspective* (Jerusalem: Feldheim, 1990), p. 69.

48. Ibid., pp. 31–49.

49. Graham Weaver, *A to Z of the Occult* (London: Everest Books, 1975), p. 52.

*** 19 ***

The Tabernacle

Trumah (25:1–27:19) and Tetzaveh (27:20–30:10)

The Tabernacle, or *mishkan*, was built as the dwelling place for the Shekhinah and maintained the cosmic purpose of the matriarchs' tents through the symbols of bread, blood, and light. These substances are the focus of three *mitzvot*, known as ChaNaH, that have special spiritual significance for women: *challah, niddah,* and *hadlikat nerot*—making bread, observing menstrual laws, and lighting the Sabbath and festival lights.

Their significance for women stems from the link between the Tabernacle and the matriarchs, for "the earthly Tabernacle represents the Shekhinah, who is the celestial Tabernacle," and the celestial Tabernacle is Binah.[1] As the Shekhinah's presence with the matriarchs was evident through their ever-burning lights and ever-fresh *challah*, so, too, the Tabernacle contained an eternal light and a table of showbread.

As the matriarchs observed ritual around bloodshed, through the menstrual laws, so, too, the Tabernacle ritualized bloodshed, through animal sacrifice. The sacrificial altar, a symbol of *Malkhut*, is said to have shed tears whenever a man divorced his first wife because "all women stand in the image and form of the altar" (*Zohar* II:102b).

Feminine symbolism pervades the descriptions of the Tabernacle. "What did the Tabernacle resemble? A woman who goes in the street and her skirts trail after her" (Shab. 98b). This refers to the overhanging curtain in the back, while the overhanging curtain at the entrance was compared to "a modest bride with a veil covering her face" (Rashi). The curtains sewn together are described as being attached like "a woman to her sister" (Ex. 26:3, 26:5). The poles of the ark pressed into the *parokhet,*

---

1. Tishby, 3:870–871.

the veil covering the Holy of Holies, which therefore "protruded like the two breasts of a woman" (Yom. 54a).

The reason for the Tabernacle is explained midrashically as a kind of antidote to patrilocal marriage. A king's only daughter was married to another king who intended to return to his country with her. The father of the bride could not bear to part with his daughter, yet he could not prevent her husband from taking her away. Consequently, the father told the husband, "Wherever you live, have a chamber ready for me that I may dwell with you, for I cannot leave my daughter." The "father" in this parable is God, the "husband" is the Jewish people, the "only daughter" is the Torah, and the "chamber" is the Tabernacle (ER 33:1).

Beyond its feminine symbolism, the Tabernacle also was "a testimony to the whole world that there is forgiveness for Israel" after the sin of the golden calf (ER 51:4). "God was indulgent to them . . . for the Shekhinah dwelled among them" (Rashi). Hence, the Tabernacle was built with gold, for "with earrings they sinned and with earrings they became reconciled to God" (ER 48:5, 48:6; *Zohar* II:224a).

The Tabernacle had other cosmic significance and also served the more mundane function of weaning the Jews from idol worship, but first let us examine its physical structure.[2]

ELEMENTAL COMPONENTS

There were thirteen materials needed to make the Tabernacle (Rashi).

1. Gold.
2. Silver.
3. Copper: although this is sometimes translated as "bronze" or "brass," copper—like silver and gold—is an elemental metal. Bronze is an alloy of copper and tin; brass is an alloy of copper and zinc. Thus, "copper" cannot possibly be an *incorrect* translation.
4. Sheep's wool: this was of three colors, indigo blue, purple (or perhaps violet), and crimson. Indigo blue is the color of sapphire and of the sky sometimes at dawn and twilight. Crimson is a purplish red, like maroon; it is not scarlet, which is red on the orange side of the spectrum.
5. Linen (white).
6. Goat's wool (the animal's natural color).
7. Ram's skins (dyed red).
8. *Tachash* skins: translated as leather, ermine, or sealskin, the *tachash* was actually a multicolored unicorn that existed in the wilderness only at that time. "It came to Moses' hand just for the occasion, and he made the Tabernacle, and then it was hidden" (Shab. 28b).

---

2. I recommend Moshe Levin, *The Tabernacle* (Tel Aviv: Soncino, 1969), for his illustrations of the Tabernacle's structural imagery, but *not* for his rendition of the colors in the weavings.

9. Acacia wood.
10. Plain olive oil for lighting.
11. Spiced olive oil for anointing.
12. Incense: this was made from eleven different spices, three of which were also components of the anointing oil. Its precise mixture later became a secret of the priestly family of Avtinas. None of the Avtinas *kohanot* (women who were born *or* married into the family) ever wore perfume, lest they be accused of making the incense for personal use (Yom. 38a).
13. Gemstones.

We recall that when the Jews left Egypt, the women "borrowed" their neighbors' valuables. However, the Jews are said to have gotten more booty in the Red Sea, from the ornaments of the drowned horses of the Egyptians, than they themselves brought out of Egypt (Rashi).

PHYSICAL STRUCTURE

The Tabernacle, which is shown drawn to scale in Figure 19–1, was a rectangular structure three times longer than it was wide. It sat in the back half of a courtyard that was two times longer than it was wide.

The Courtyard

The courtyard was made of white linen curtains on wooden pillars decorated with silver and set apart from each other in copper sockets—with twenty on each long side and ten on each short side. An entrance screen was woven from blue, purple, and crimson wool and white linen, and it had a pattern of cherubs (winged creatures with children's faces). The courtyard, which might be entered by any Israelite, contained the sacrificial altar and the laver, both of which were made of copper.

The altar was a copper hollow casing filled with earth. Built with a ramp rather than stairs to preserve the modesty of the priests mounting it (Ex. 20:23), the altar also had a parapet to keep the priests from falling and a ledge to catch any sacrificial spillage. A sewage system facilitated the drainage of blood. The altar had copper utensils—pots, scoops, basins, flesh pokers, and fire pans—and rings and poles for carrying it through the wilderness.

The laver, or copper washstand, stood between the altar and the Tabernacle. A priest had to wash before offering a sacrifice or entering the Tabernacle. First he washed his right hand and foot simultaneously, and then his left hand and foot (Rashi).

The Tabernacle

The Tabernacle's walls were gilded wood (acacia beams overlayed with gold), joined together and set in silver sockets—twenty on each long side, six in back, and five in

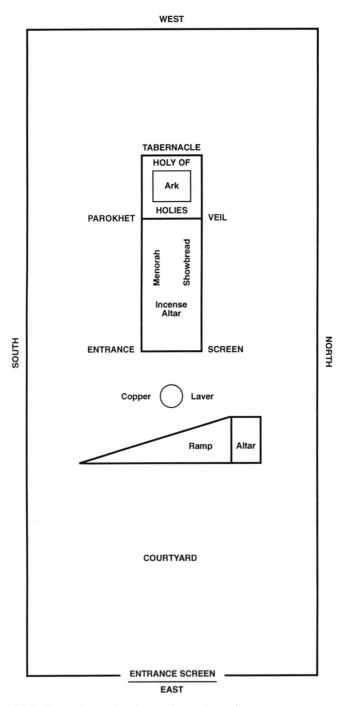

FIGURE 19-1. The Tabernacle, shown drawn to scale.

front, where there was a woven entrance screen like that in the courtyard. This structure then had four layers of fabrics draped over it.

1. The *mishkan*, the curtain that was visible from the inside as the ceiling, was made of ten tapestries sewn together, each of which was seven times longer than it was wide. These tapestries were weavings of the same blue, purple, and crimson wool, linen, and cherub pattern as the entrance screens. Two groups of five were joined in the middle by fifty blue loops and fifty gold buttons.
2. Over this was the *ohel*, a tent made of eleven tapestries of goat's wool. These, too, were sewn together into two pieces joined by fifty loops and fifty copper buttons. The *ohel*, because it was one tapestry wider than the *mishkan* and three feet longer, hung beyond it, trailing on the ground like "a woman's skirt."
3. These two layers were then covered by the *mikseh*, a roof made of ram and *tachash* skins. It is disputed whether one skin was on top of the other or if the two pieces were on the same level.

The Tabernacle is called, in Hebrew, either *mishkan* or *ohel moed* ("Tent of Meeting"). It was divided into two sections separated by the *parokhet*, a veil of the same tricolored wool, linen, and cherub combination. The back third of the Tabernacle was the Holy of Holies (*Kodesh Kadashim*); the front two-thirds was the Sanctuary (*Kodesh*).

The Tabernacle contained four items, one in the Holy of Holies and three in the Sanctuary. The Holy of Holies contained the ark, which housed the second set of tablets from Sinai. The Sanctuary contained a seven-branched *menorah* (candelabra) along the southern wall, a table of twelve loaves of bread on the northern wall, and an incense altar in front center.

The Holy of Holies

The ark containing the Torah was, like the Tabernacle walls, essentially of gilded wood: it consisted of a gold box inside a larger wooden one inside a still larger gold one. It was about four feet by two feet by two feet. The outer box had a crown around it, into which fit a pure gold cover called the *kaporet*. On top of the *kaporet*, and formed from the same piece of gold, were the *kruvim*—two cherubs, a girl and a boy, depicted facing each other. The ark, like the altar, had rings and poles to carry it. However, "it was not the priests who carried it; rather, it carried them" (ER 36:4).

The Holy of Holies was entered only once a year, on Yom Kippur, by one person, the high priest. Anyone else who entered it would be zapped, and the high priest himself was zapped if he made the slightest mistake in the Yom Kippur service. Clearly, it was an intense place, for here the Shekhinah actually dwelled. God told Moses, "I will meet with you there, speaking to you above the ark cover, from between the two cherubs that are on the ark of the covenant" (Ex. 25:22).

The ark and its cover were lost after the Babylonian destruction of the First Temple in Jerusalem. This seems to have lent a certain vulnerability to the Second Temple.

Having no *kruvim*, it was "susceptible," in a way, to defilement by a golden winged creature of idolatry—a Roman eagle placed over the entrance by Herod I.[3]

The Sanctuary

The Sanctuary could only be entered by a priest. Inside was an incense altar, a *menorah*, and a table with twelve loaves of bread. The table was made of gilded wood and had rings and poles for carrying. It was three feet long, one and half feet wide, and two feet high. The table had gold breadpans, frames, and dividers so that it could hold two stacks of six loaves each. Two dishes of frankincense were burned on the table with the *challah,* which was thick *matzah* (unleavened bread) that was baked and placed on the table every Friday and replaced the following Friday. Because it was U-shaped, each loaf had two sides, was visible from both directions, and hence was called *lechem panim*—"bread of faces" or showbread.

The *menorah*, like the *kaporet*, was made of *zahav tahor*—"complete gold," and fashioned from one original piece. With a central shaft and three branches on each side, the *menorah*'s design contained twenty-two cups, eleven spheres, and nine flowers. It was over four feet tall, and each of the seven lamps held almost seven ounces of oil.

There is a dispute as to whether the *menorah* was placed along the wall or if it spanned across the room, facing the person entering. In either case, one lamp was the "western light" and burned continuously. From it the other lights were lit every evening. In the morning, the lamps that had burned out were cleaned and relit from those that had not burned out. The latter were then extinguished, cleaned, and relit from the former (Nachmanides; Tam. 3:9).

The incense altar, like the Tabernacle walls, ark, and table, was made of gilded wood. It was perfectly square—one and a half feet long, wide, and high—and, like the altar, ark, and table, it had rings and poles for carrying. Incense was burned every evening and morning by the priest who cared for the *menorah*. No "strange incense" might be burned on it, nor could it be used for any animal sacrifice, grain offering, or libation. The incense effected atonement for *lashon hara* (gossip) spoken privately (Zev. 88b).

THE PRIESTLY VESTMENTS

We will discuss the priesthood itself in chapter 23. Now we will simply describe the priestly vestments: there were four for a common priest and four for the high priest. The saying that "the clothes make the man" could have its origin here, for it was the priestly garments themselves that invested the priest with his priesthood. Any priest who entered the Tabernacle or offered a sacrifice without being dressed in these clothes was zapped (Ex. 28:43).

---

3. Mattis Kantor, *The Jewish Time Line Encyclopedia* (Northvale, NJ: Jason Aronson, 1992), p. 92.

The significance of the vestments lies in a mystery of the Hebrew alphabet. Of the twenty-two letters, three are called mother letters, seven are called double letters, and twelve are called simple or elemental letters. The seven double letters are Bet, Gimel, Dalet, and Kaf, Peh, Resh, Tav, which spell BeGeD KaPoReT, meaning "clothing of atonement." Each vestment effected atonement for a particular thing (Zev. 88b).

All priests wore a linen tunic, linen pants, a linen and tricolored wool sash, and a turban. The tunic atoned for sins of bloodshed where the murderer was known but could not be brought to justice because there were no witnesses—like Joseph's brothers, who brought his coat dipped in blood. The pants atoned for sexual sins, the sash for sins of the heart, and the turban for sins of arrogance and haughtiness, as in holding the head too high. The common priest's turban was pointed, while the high priest's turban was round.

In addition to these vestments, the high priest wore a gold headband, a robe, an ephod (an apron-like garment), and a breastplate of twelve gemstones. The headband had "Holy to God" embossed on it and was fastened near the turban with blue wool. The high priest wore it "only at the time of the sacrificial service" (Rashi). It atoned for brazenness and sins of being headstrong.

The robe was made completely of blue wool, with an opening for the head. Along its hem were seventy-two gold bells and seventy-two pomegranate-shaped balls made of tricolored wool. Some accounts say that the bells and balls alternated, while others say that the bells were inside the balls. Aharon had to wear this robe to enter the Tabernacle or he would be zapped (Ex. 28:35). Nachmanides likens the bells to the honor bestowed upon a king of announcing one's arrival before entering the palace. The sound of the bells atoned for *lashon hara* spoken publicly, which is a sin of sound.

The ephod was made of tricolored wool, linen, and gold thread. It atoned for idolatry, and particularly the use of *terafim*. It had shoulder straps and a belt to which was attached, with gold chains and blue wool, a breastplate woven of the same materials. Set in the breastplate were twelve stones set in four rows of three, amounting to one for each tribe. The breastplate atoned for the lack of fair judgment stemming from a neglect of civil laws. A tribe's stone would dim when it sinned (e.g., Joshua 7:14). There is a dispute as to whether the stones were set in tribal birth order (Rashi) or whether all the Leahite tribes came first (ER 38:8–9).

The tribal names, and other names that were included in order to complete the Hebrew alphabet, were carved into the stones and lit up to spell words when they were consulted by the high priest. The breastplate was doubled over; in its fold were the *urim* and *tumim*, parchment scrolls on which were written "the holy Names of God, and it was by virtue of the power residing in these Names that the letters inscribed upon the stones of the breastplate would light up before the eyes of the priest who inquired of their judgment" (Nachmanides). The knowledge of how to combine the letters that lit up into words required a level of *ruach hakodesh* that no longer existed after the destruction of the First Temple.

THE PAGAN TEMPLE

The structure and purpose of the pagan temple illustrates how the Tabernacle functioned to wean Jews from idol worship. Pagan temples were rich, lavish, powerful
estates of the king, which were maintained by his selected cadre of priest-magicians.
In a world where kings were gods, God had to be a "king"—that is, Israel had to be
reeducated to understand that rich and powerful men were *not* deities.

In Babylonia the king "was absolute lord and master of the country and of all who
lived in it, and in some capacities he was held to be 'like God.' He and his governors
and nobles formed a small class by themselves and possessed great power."[4] Kings
built and dedicated temples to the god whose "incarnation" they were. These temples
were "immensely wealthy, the city god himself being one of the chief landowners of
the state."[5] The king and his temple owned a large number of slaves, and hence, "cultivated extensive holdings by means of sharecroppers or client labor."[6]

Egyptian temples, we have noted, were completely the province of Pharaoh and
his priests during the New Kingdom. The pyramids were a complex of mortuary
buildings and temples, designed to glorify Pharaoh in the afterlife.

The pagan temple was the house of the god, as the royal palace was the house of
the king. The temple housed the god's image, usually made of gilded wood.

> The deity was considered present in its image; thus when the image was carried off in
> war, the deity remained absent until its return. . . . Most temple images were made of
> precious wood, covered with garments plated with gold, adorned with pectorals and
> crowned with tiaras. They were fashioned and repaired in special workshops and had
> to undergo an elaborate and highly secret ritual of consecration which endowed them
> with "life." The image stood on a pedestal in the cella of the temple; here the god "lived"
> with his family, and was served, like the king, in courtly fashion.[7]

The image was kept in an inner chamber of the temple called the holy of holies
which—at least in the temple of the chief Babylonian god, Marduk—lay to the west.
The idol sat "on a golden throne, supported on a base of gold, with a golden table
standing beside it. . . . To make all this more than 22 tons of gold were used. Outside
the temple is a golden altar, and there is another, not of gold, but of great size. . . . The
Chaldeans offered some two and a half tons of frankincense every year at [Marduk's]
festival."[8]

Annually, at the Babylonian New Year (celebrated from 1 through 11 *Nisan*), the
king's royal insignia was removed by the high priest so the king could enter the holy
of holies. "He was then humiliated by having his cheek slapped and his ears pulled,
and then had to crouch down before Marduk and assure the god that during the year

---

4. Budge, p. 160.
5. Sir Leonard Wooley, *Ur 'of the Chaldees'* (Ithaca, NY: Cornell University Press, 1982), p. 211.
6. Budge, p. 162; Oates, p. 26.
7. Oates, p. 174.
8. Quote of Herodotus, cited in Oates, p. 157.

he had not committed any sins." The priest then restored the king's insignia, and later that evening, the king participated in the ceremonial sacrifice of a white bull.[9]

Egyptian temples normally had three areas: an open court for commoners, a roofed area for nobility, and a holy of holies reserved for the priesthood.

> The temple design was intended to impress upon a visitor that, as he walked farther and farther into the temple, he was nearing a mysterious, sacred place. . . . In the holy of holies were kept oracles—cult statues used for forecasting the future and obtaining divine guidance. . . . These statues were kept in shrines of stone and were carried about in shrines made of gilded wood. . . . These portable shrines rested on two long wooden poles, so that they could be carried about on the shoulders of the priests during religious ceremonies.[10]

Hittite temples stood in the center of a "holy city" and also "consisted of an outer court and an inner sanctuary, which again contained a holy of holies, entered only by the high priest and those of his companions who were 'nearest the gods.' The temple was . . . brilliant with gold," while the holy of holies was separated with a veil. In the outer court was a brass altar. "Oxen, horses, eagles, bears, and lions were kept in the court, as being sacred to the deities worshiped within."[11]

> [Inside were] the statues of various divinities, among others the wonder-working image of a god who was believed to deliver oracles and prophecies. At times, it was said, the image moved of its own accord, and if not lifted up at once by the priests, it began to perspire. When the priests took it in their hands, it led them from one part of the temple to the other, until the high priest, standing before it, asked it questions, which it answered by driving its bearers forward.[12]

Egyptian idols, which might be as small as two feet high, were kept in a wooden ark which sat in the temple's holy of holies. This wooden ark was carried around in public procession on the god's festivals.[13] The oracle statues were believed to be able to "nod their heads and even talk. . . . Oracles could also act as judges in courts of law. . . . Oracle statues not only gave advice, but could also perform miraculous cures. . . . These statues could heal the sick, solve crimes, settle legal disputes, and send prophetic dreams."[14]

The deity, like the king, was cared for, fed, and clothed by his servants.

> The image was fed, in a ceremonial fashion accompanied by music, from offerings and the produce of temple land and flocks. When the god was "eating," he was, at least in later times, hidden from human view, even the priests', by linen curtains surrounding

---

9. Ibid., p. 176.
10. Brier, p. 205.
11. Sayce, pp. 104–105.
12. Ibid., p. 105.
13. Erman, p. 275.
14. Brier, pp. 205–213.

the image and his table. When the meal was done, the curtains were removed, but they were drawn again to enable the god to wash his fingers. . . . When the god had "eaten," the dishes from his meal were sent to the king for consumption. What was not destined for the table of the main deity, his consort, his children, or the servant gods was distributed among the temple administrators and craftsmen.[15]

Each temple required a different number of ceremonies for its god. A typical scenario consisted of the following:

The god was roused in the morning by the singing of a hymn of praise; then followed his morning toilet, the perfuming with incense or other scents, the decking with robes and crowns; after which came the first meal of the day, . . . the morning sacrifice. That finished, the god was brought out with chants and hymns into the main part of the temple to transact business by receiving petitions, giving judgment in difficult cases, receiving and acknowledging offerings; in the afternoon he retired to his private apartments, where he either rested or was entertained with music and dancing girls; in the evening he appeared again and had his evening meal (the evening sacrifice), then retired for the night, the robes and crown were removed, incense was burnt before him, the evening hymn was sung, the shrine doors were shut upon him, and he was left to pass the night in peace.[16]

The God of Israel had no image and no dancing girls. Jews were not to place their faith in talking or sweating statues, and certainly not to seek judgment from them. The tablets of the Law in the ark and the invisible Presence of God between the cherubs on the ark cover served as substitutes for an image, while gilded wood was still overwhelmingly present—in the walls, the ark, and the table. Moses took over the function of lawgiver and judge. Aharon with his breastplate was able to obtain oracles—but through Names of God, not an image of God.

Only the barest outline of pagan worship remained: "feeding" God through regular sacrifices, offerings, and libations; burning incense; and praising God through song (which was deeroticized). Such a *structure* gave this group of emancipated slaves something familiar to hold on to in the midst of a radical, sweeping change in *content* —the worship of an invisible "King."

---

15. Oates, p. 175.
16. Murray, *Splendor*, pp. 183–184.

✸✸✸ 20 ✸✸✸

The Golden Calf

Ki Tisa (30:11–34:35)

Moses went up Mount Sinai three times (see Table 20–1). Before his first ascent, he promised he would return in forty days. The people, however, mistakenly counted the day he left as day one and so expected his return on 16 *Tamuz* (Rashi). When Moses did not appear on that day, they assumed he was not coming back.

THE DEMAND FOR AN IMAGE

The people, feeling panicky at their supposed loss of Moses, gathered around Aharon and demanded that he make an *elohim* to lead them (Ex. 32:1). There is a debate as to whether the Jews really descended into wholehearted idolatry by demanding another god or whether they simply wanted a substitute for Moses, their leader, for while *elohim* is God or a pagan god, it also means "judge," the role of Moses with the Jewish people, while Aharon was the "mouth" (Ex. 4:16).

Moses sat at the entrance of his tent—and later, the Tabernacle—every day so that people could come to him "to inquire of God" (Ex. 18:15, 33:7). In this role, he functioned to wean the people from pagan reliance on the "judgments" of inanimate statues. The people clearly had a great need for something visible to turn to. Moses' workload became so overwhelming that Yitro had to teach him how to delegate responsibility, and thus the Jewish court was born.

"These are your *elohim*, Israel," the makers of the golden calf announced when it was completed (Ex. 32:4). The plurality of "these," *eleh*, indicates that the calf was not a *replacement* for God but an "assistant" to God (ER 42:3; San. 63a). "There is no fool in the world who would think that this gold which was in their ears brought them up out of the land of Egypt" (Nachmanides).

TABLE 20–1. The Forty Years in the Wilderness (Including the Forty-two Campsites)

1st Year		A.M.	B.C.E.	
Passover	**Exodus**	**2448**	**1313**	
Yetziat Mitzrayim	Leave Egypt	15 *Nisan*	Mar. 25	Tues.
1. Ramses				
Sefirah **Begins**	Count *omer*	16 *Nisan*	Mar. 26	Weds.
2. Sukkot	Forty-nine days			
3. Etam	or seven weeks			
4. Pi HaChirot				
Yam Suf	**Cross Red Sea**	21 *Nisan*	Mar. 31	Mon.
5. Marah	Bitter water	24 *Nisan*	Apr. 3	Weds.
6. Elim	Twelve springs			
7. By Red Sea				
8. Sin Desert				
9. Dafkah				
10. Alush	Manna			
11. Rephidim	Water from rock	23 *Iyar*	May 2	Fri.
12. Sinai		1 *Sivan*	May 9	Fri.
Sefirah **Ends**		5 *Sivan*	May 13	Tues.
Shavuot	**Revelation**	6 *Sivan*	May 14	Weds.
Fiftieth day	at Mt. Sinai			
Moses up Sinai no. 1	First tablets	7 *Sivan*	May 15	Thurs.
Fast of *Tamuz*	**Golden Calf**	17 *Tamuz*	June 24	Tues.
First descent	Tablets shattered			
Moses up Sinai no. 2	Prays for mercy	19 *Tamuz*	June 26	Thurs.
Second descent		29 *Av*	Aug. 4	Mon.
Rosh Chodesh:	*Shofar* blown each	30 *Av*–1 *Elul*	Aug. 5–6	Tues.–Wed.
New Moon *Elul*	morning			
Moses up Sinai no. 3	Second tablets			
Rosh Hashanah		**2449**		
Yom Kippur	**Atonement**	10 *Tishre*	Sept. 13	*Shabbat*
Tabernacle begun	Moses starts	11 *Tishre*	Sept. 14	Sun.
Census no. 1	teaching elders			
2nd Year			**1312**	
Tabernacle set up		1 *Nisan*	Mar. 29	Sun.
First Red Heifer	Death Tumah	2 *Nisan*	Mar. 30	Mon.
Passover	First anniversary	15 *Nisan*	April 12	Sun.
Census no. 2		1 *Iyar*	April 28	Tues.
Begin travels again		20 *Iyar*	May 17	Sun.
13. Kivrot HaTavah	Quails			
14. Chatzerot	**Miriam secluded**	22 *Sivan*	June 17	Weds.
15. Ritmah	Spies sent out	29 *Sivan*	June 24	Weds.
Tisha B'Av	**Decree on men**	9 *Av*	Aug. 2	Sun.
Next 38 Years	No communication			
	of God with Moses			
16. Rimon Peretz				
17. Livnah				
18. Risah				
19. Kehelatah				
20. Mt. Shafer				
21. Charadah				

TABLE 20–1. (*continued*)

Next 38 Years		A.M.	B.C.E.	
22. Mak'helot				
23. Tachat				
24. Tarach				
25. Mitkah				
26. Chashmonah				
27. Moserot				
28. Bnei Yaakan				
29. Chor HaGidgad				
30. Yatvatah				
31. Avronah				
32. Etzion Gaver				
40th Year		**2487**	**1274**	
33. Kadesh				
Death of Miriam	126 years old	10 *Nisan* "Lamb day"	Apr. 8	Mon.
34. Mt. Hor				
Rosh Chodesh Av				
Death of Aharon	123 years old	1 *Av*	July 26	Fri.
35. Zalmonah				
36. Punon	Snake plague			
37. Ovot				
38. Iyei HaAvarim				
39. Divon Gad	**Decree ends**	15 *Av*	Aug. 9	Fri.
40. Almon Divlataim				
41. Mt. Avarim				
42. Plains of Moav	**Baal-Peor** Census no. 3 War versus Midian			
		2488	**1273**	
Moses reviews Torah with Israel	**Daughters of Zelophechad**	1 *Shevat* to 6 *Adar*	Jan. 18 to Feb. 22	*Shabbat* *Shabbat*
Death of Moses	120 years old	7 *Adar*	Feb. 23	Sun.

Moses used this argument in his prayers for God's forgiveness, suggesting that this "assistant" could look after the sun, moon, stars, dew, winds, rains, and plant growth—that is, take over the functions of the God of Nature, Elokim. When God reminded Moses of the emptiness of the concept that the Creator of the Universe needs an "assistant," Moses cleverly replied, "If there's nothing to it, then why are You so angry?" (ER 43:6).

Moses also accused God of being partly to blame for the people making a calf, because it was God who had had them enslaved in Egypt (ER 43:7). Having spent their entire lives in that culture, they turned to the only symbolism they knew. Moses was God's "assistant" in this new religion; his apparent loss led the people to seek a substitute in the symbol of an Egyptian god's "assistant." Major objects of Egyptian worship included the Golden Bull of Canopis[1] and a cow goddess named Hesat who "gave birth to the king in the form of a golden calf."[2] Golden bulls, like red ones, were probably associated with Egyptian worship and sacrifices geared toward "the express purpose of making the corn turn red or golden."[3]

WHO MADE THE CALF?

And Aharon said to them, "Take the gold earrings from your wives, your sons, and your daughters and bring them to me." All the people removed their gold earrings and brought them to Aharon. He took it from their hands and formed it by chiseling, and they made it a molten calf, and they said, "These are your *elohim*, Israel, that brought you up from the land of Egypt." And Aharon saw this, and built an altar before it. Aharon announced, "Tomorrow will be a festival to Hashem." (Ex. 32:2–5)

Aharon is clearly speaking here to men, which lets us assume that it was men who "gathered around" him complaining of Moses' loss and demanding a substitute. Though the Torah says that *kol ha-am,* "all the people," removed their earrings, the oral tradition tells us that the women refused to do so but the men eagerly donated their own. Because the women stood fast in their refusal, they were rewarded by God with a special observance of *Rosh Chodesh.* Although the New Moon was a holiday for everyone, it was more so for women, who were required to refrain from work while men were not (NR 21:10; Tosafot on Meg. 22b).

Not all the men were involved in demanding an image. The impetus to make a calf is attributed to the *erev rav,* the "mixed multitude" that left Egypt with the Jews (Ex. 12:38; ER 42:6). "It was the mixed multitude which came up from Egypt that gathered themselves together against Aharon, and it was they who made it and afterwards led Israel astray after it" (Rashi). This explains the unspecified *they* in the biblical passage. The *Zohar* (II:191a) also describes the sin as one that the "mixed multitude committed, and in which the holy people participated."

At first this appears to be no more than a convenient scapegoating of converts, for the *erev rav* is originally defined as "worthy" Egyptians, the minority who "made Passover with Israel and left with them" (ER 18:10). In the following quotation, the actual guilty party is more specifically identified: the sorcerers of Egypt—led, according to the *Zohar,* by two grandsons of Lavan. "The mixed multitude consisted entirely of one people, all the members of which spoke one language: namely, all the sorcerers of Egypt and all its magicians. . . . They consisted of all the levels of the Egyptian magicians, at their head being Yainis and Yimbres" (*Zohar* II:191a). The levels of sorcery that they practiced are described in detail further in this passage, as is the notion that God tried to stop Moses from taking these people with him.

---

1. Murray, *Splendor*, p. 162.
2. Hart, p. 87.
3. Frazer, p. 552.

They wanted to oppose the wonderful works of the Holy One. When they beheld the signs and the wonders which Moses wrought in Egypt they came to Moses to be converted. Said the Holy One to Moses, "Do not receive them!" Moses, however, replied, "Sovereign of the Universe, now that they have seen Your power they desire to accept our faith; let them see Your power every day and they will learn that there is no God like You." And Moses accepted them.

According to Rashi, the head sorcerer was a man named Micah who "had the Divine Name in his hand and a plate upon which Moses had written, 'Come up, ox, come up, ox!' in order to raise the coffin of Joseph out of the Nile. He cast it into the smelting pot and the calf came out."

AHARON'S ROLE

Aharon himself is exonerated for his role in making the calf because all his actions were intended to stall the people. Because he knew that the women would not give up their earrings, he ordered the making of the calf precisely to give Moses more time to arrive. "But the men did not wait and took off their own jewelry" (Rashi). Aharon also proclaimed a festival for the following day instead of immediately, in hopes that Moses would return in the meantime.

Aharon was terrified because his nephew, Chur, had been killed for trying to stop the men from making the calf (Rashi; ER 41:7, 48:3; San. 7a). Chur was Miriam's son (ER 40:4). He is first mentioned in the battle with Amalek, in which Aharon and Chur held up Moses' arms so that Joshua and the Jews would win (Ex. 17:10–12).

Aharon saw Chur slaughtered by the mob and acted out of fear that the same thing would happen to him. Rather than oppose the people, he tried to *appear* to placate them while actually working to restrain them. However, even Moses did not understand his motives at first. When he came down from the mountain, he saw Aharon beating the calf with a hammer. Aharon was doing this as a last resort, to convince the people that the calf was not yet ready for worship, but Moses thought Aharon was a partner in their crime and was angry with him. God therefore told Moses, "I know that Aharon's intention was very good." Later, when Aharon was to be consecrated as high priest, he felt unworthy of the role because of the part he had played in making the calf and Moses reassured him by telling him what God had said (ER 37:2).

However, Aharon also failed to properly "guard himself against the two magicians who were the head of that 'mixed multitude.' One of these stood in front of him, and the other busied himself with his sorcery. After the two magicians had hatched their plan they took the gold, one two-thirds and the other one-third, this being the method of that kind of magic" (*Zohar* II:192a). Aharon made two major mistakes. First, he took the gold directly from the sorcerers' hands instead of telling them to put it on the ground and picking it up from there, and second, he put the gold into a bag.

Had he only taken the gold from the ground, all the magicians of the world could not have succeeded in their designs. . . . Had he, even after taking it from their hands, thrown it on the ground, even if he had picked it up afterwards, this evil operation would not have succeeded; but what he did was to put all of the gold into a bag, thus keeping it hidden from view. This made the sorcery effective . . . for in their lore it is taught that anything which is to be made a public show of must first be covered up and hidden away; and conversely, what has to be hidden afterwards must first be shown to view. (*Zohar* II: 192b)

WHO WORSHIPED THE CALF?

They got up early the next morning and offered burnt-offerings and peace-offerings. The people sat down to eat and drink, and then rose up to make merry. (Ex. 32:6)

The actual "worship" of the calf consisted of animal sacrifices and the burning of incense. This was performed by firstborn sons, for they were the priests at this time among Israel, as in the pagan world. The *immediate* result of their action was that three thousand of them were slain by the Levites at Moses' command (Ex. 32:26–29). Some of those slain were the Levites' own maternal brothers, uncles, and grand-fathers, as well as their grandsons (their daughters' sons by non-Levitical men). The *permanent* result of their action was that the priesthood was forever taken away from firstborn sons and given to the Levites, specifically Aharon and his sons (NR 6:2; Rashi; Yom. 66b).

The festive atmosphere accompanying the worship consisted of feasting and "making merry." This latter term, *letzachek*, as we have noted in its previous uses, has a sexual connotation. It also indicates bloodshed, and indeed, Miriam's son Chur was a virtual human sacrifice (Rashi; ER 42:1).

Embracing and kissing the image of a calf as a form of worship by those who offer human sacrifices is mentioned in the Talmud (San. 63b; Hosea 13:2). Those who embraced and kissed the golden calf died in a plague from God *after* God prom-ised Moses to forgive the rest of the people (Ex. 32:35; Yom. 66b).

"Most of the people shared in the sin of the calf," but the number of those killed by the Levites and the plague was relatively small, because "most shared in the sin only in their evil thoughts" (Nachmanides). This third category of people died from Moses' "bitter waters," a concoction he made by burning the calf, grinding it into a fine powder, and adding it to water. He then made everyone drink some (Ex. 32:20), and "whoever had rejoiced in one's heart"—though not actively participating in the festivities—died from the potion (Yom. 66b).

Thus, there were various levels of involvement with the calf and various levels of accountability for it. Many men brought their gold, but only some men made the calf and only some men worshiped it. Some men may have done all three things. Only the women and the Levites did none of these.

We do not know the extent of the women's participation in the feasting and sexual activity or the physical fondling of the image, nor do we know whether any woman died from the potion for "rejoicing in her heart." However, women as well as men—and Levites as well as Israelites—are obligated to fast on 17 *Tamuz*, the day the calf worship took place and Moses returned, and on Yom Kippur, the day Moses returned with a second set of tablets and forgiveness from God. No one was completely innocent.

The fact that atonement for the sin was granted on Yom Kippur teaches that *teshuvah* (repentance) is always possible. "The Israelites made the calf only in order to place a good argument in the mouth of penitents" (A.Z. 4b)—in other words, if that sin could be forgiven, any sin can be. It is said that no retribution ever comes upon Israel in which there is not a particle stemming from the sin of the golden calf (San. 102a; ER 43:2).

Thus, the golden calf continues to be atoned for and forgiven *every* Yom Kippur. For this reason, gold jewelry is not worn on that day. Nor did the high priest even wear his gold-threaded vestments into the Holy of Holies then, "because the accuser may not act as defender" (R.H. 26a).

The people stopped wearing jewelry after the golden calf (Ex. 33:4, 33:6). Could this be the point when earrings became "women's apparel," no longer to be worn by men?

MOSES AND THE SHEKHINAH

Meanwhile, back at the mountain, Moses was engaged in the most cosmic experience known to humanity: "face-to-face" communication with God (Ex. 33:11). Moses had just received the sapphire tablets of the Law inscribed by the Finger of God when the firstborn sons began offering sacrifices and incense to the calf. At this point, God told Moses to go down from the mountain (Nachmanides). Had he not already received the tablets, Moses would not have brought them down at all (ER 41:5). He only shattered them once he saw the idol worship with his own eyes (46:1).

Moses broke the tablets so that Israel would be judged as having sinned unintentionally and could not be said to have known what was written on the tablets: that the punishment for sacrificing to other gods was destruction. This act is compared to a king who sent a marriage broker to betroth a particular woman to him. While the marriage broker was on his way, the woman slept with another man. The broker tore up the betrothal certificate, saying, "It is better that she be judged as an unmarried woman than as a married woman" (ER 43:1).

As the covenant at Sinai was like a marriage of God and the Jewish people, the golden calf was the Jewish people's "adultery." Moses' potion was analogous to the "bitter waters" given to a suspected adulteress. The Jews' unfaithfulness to God was forgiven, and the "marriage" was restored through Moses' prayers (ER 42:1, 44:1, 44:2).

The "marriage mediator" himself, however, had his own domestic problems. On his own initiative, Moses separated from Zipporah, and although God did not command this, God did agree with it. Moses reasoned, "If to the Israelites, with whom the Shekhinah spoke only for a while and for whom a definite time was fixed, the Torah nevertheless said [to men], 'Come not near a woman,' how much more so to me, who is liable to be spoken to at any moment and for whom no definite time has been fixed" (Yev. 62a; ER 46:3).

On Sinai, Moses needed no food or drink, for he was "nourished by the splendor of the Shekhinah" (ER 47:5, 47:7). Indeed, he was "united with a supernal sphere of holiness" (*Zohar* II:65b, 69b). Moses' relationship with God was so intimate that they even calmed each other's anger (ER 45:2).

The Shekhinah "became, as it were, Moses' bride. As soon as She was united with Moses, She descended to this world and united Herself with it, and She became firmly established in this world, as never before" (*Zohar* II:145a). In between Moses' trips up the mountain, the Shekhinah hung out at his tent as the pillar of cloud. "When Israel beheld the pillar of cloud, they realized that the Shekhinah had revealed Herself to Moses" (Ex. 33:9, ER 45:4).

Moses requested, and was granted, a vision of God's divine glory (Ex. 33:17–23). When he came down from Sinai the last time, his face was so luminous from his contact with God that the people were afraid to look at him. Like the Holy of Holies, he needed a veil to cover the manifestation of the Divine Presence.

ATONEMENT FOR MIRIAM'S SON

Because Chur, Miriam's son, was slaughtered when he tried to stop the making of the calf, the task of overseeing the Tabernacle's construction was entrusted to his grandson, Betzalel (Ex. 31:2, 35:30). Betzalel's name means "in the shadow of God," referring to the inner wisdom he possessed in fathoming the nuances of meaning within God's instructions. Moses told him to make the vessels first and then the structure, but Betzalel, who was only thirteen years old, pointed out that the structure should be made first so as to have a place to put the vessels as soon as they were made (Br. 55a; San. 69b).

"He had a knowledge of the various permutations of the [Hebrew] letters, by the power of which heaven and earth were created. Without such knowledge Betzalel could not have accomplished the work of the Tabernacle. . . . Betzalel was [also] skilled in the various permutations of the Divine Name" (*Zohar* II:234b). He merited all this wisdom because of his great-grandmother, Miriam (ER 40:1, 48:4). "And so, through him, full atonement was made for the sin of the golden calf" (*Zohar* II:223b).

✵✵ 21 ✵✵

Women's Wisdom

Vayak'hel (35:1–38:20) and *Pekudei* (38:21–40:38)

$\mathbf{W}$e have so far seen two instances of women's enthusiasm for the God of Israel being greater than men's. First, at Sinai, women were eager for the Torah and received it first. They did not need to be given time-bound activities or threats of punishment, as men did.

Later, men eagerly donated their gold jewelry for the calf, while women refused to give theirs at all. This, too, resulted in obligation for men and freedom of choice for women, for in building a Tabernacle of gold to atone for the calf, men were *required* to make certain contributions, while women's gifts were determined solely by the dictates of their own hearts.

DONATIONS FOR THE TABERNACLE

God spoke to Moses, saying, "Speak to the Israelites and have them take *trumah* for me. From every person [*ish*] whose heart is willing, you shall take *trumah*. And this is the *trumah* that you shall take from them." (Ex. 25:1–3)

Trumah, a term later used for the priestly tithe, means "elevated offering." It refers here to something set apart from one's possessions as a voluntary gift. The word is mentioned three times in this verse to indicate that it was the third type of offering involved in making the Tabernacle, the other two being mandatory contributions from men which were taken by census (Rashi).

The first census was taken at the beginning of the Tabernacle's construction on 11 *Tishre* (see Table 20–1). It required half a shekel from every male over twenty years old, no matter how rich or poor he was (Ex. 30:12–15, 38:25–27). These coins were used to make the silver sockets for the Tabernacle. The second census (Num. 1), taken on the first of *Iyar*, a month after the Tabernacle was set up, collected another half shekel from every male over twenty, this time for the purchase of animals for communal sacrifices.

Both censuses recorded 603,550 males over age twenty. How did the number remained so exact from *Tishre* to *Iyar*? The answer is that although twenty thousand Levites were not counted in the second census, twenty thousand Israelite men had turned twenty in those seven months (Nachmanides).

The third offering, *trumah*, consisted of voluntary donations. That *ish* means "person" and not "man" here is evident from the word's inclusive use elsewhere in the Torah. If *ish* only meant "man," then women could cook and travel on the Sabbath (Ex. 16:29), touch Mount Sinai (Ex. 19:13), or commit murder and manslaughter (Ex. 21:12)! No one, of course, would argue such a view.

The voluntary donations came in so thick and fast that Moses had to give orders to stop: "Let no man or woman do any more work for the *trumah* of holiness" (Ex. 36:6). This in itself was atonement for the calf, for there, too, the contributors of the gold had to be told, "Enough!" (ER 51:8).

WOMEN'S OFFERINGS

Each person whose heart was uplifted and whose spirit was willing came and brought *trumat Hashem* [gifts to God] to make the Tabernacle, its implements, and its sacred vestments. The men came with the women; all who were prompted in their hearts brought bracelets, earrings, rings, and body ornaments [*kumaz*], all vessels of gold. (Ex. 35:21–22)

The men came with the women and *smukhin* (Rashi), a term that means "in support of" them as well as "closely following" them. "The women were there first, while the men joined them later" (Nachmanides). Once again we see that women's eagerness led the way. Nonetheless, misogynist commentaries attempt to deny women's leadership by saying that the men came with the women "to approve of their offerings . . . since we do not receive from women except for lesser things" (Sforno).

Of particular significance is the *kumaz,* the body ornament. The Gemara defines it as a metallic cast of *bet harechem* ("house of the womb") and treats the term as an acronym for *kan makom zimah*—"here is the place of lust" (Shab. 64a). It also notes that the Targum translates it as *machok* because it leads to *gichuk* ("laughter and lewdness").

Rashi calls *kumaz* "a vessel of gold worn against the place of woman" *(makom le-ishah)*. Jastrow defines it as "an opprobrious name for an ornament bearing the impress of the female breast or pudenda," and describes *machok* as "gold hooks over the female bosom" in addition to its meaning of "laughter and lewdness." Since the Gemara gives another term, *agil*, for a cast of the female breasts, we might presume that *kumaz* was most commonly a type of girdle, a golden encasement worn around the female genitals. Such "virgin girdles of antiquity," which were also made of cloth or leather, were used to prevent sexual activity. "Certain of the customs clustering around the use of these sashes suggest ideas allied to the notion of a forcible closure of the private parts. Indeed the adoption of a belt or even a more elaborate form of dress has long been indicative of a desire to preserve chastity, and such devices are found distributed in many parts of the world."[1] The belt was, in some cultures, "worn until marriage, on the night of which the bridegroom cuts it with a sharp dagger, a proceeding which, it is reported, is not infrequently attended with some danger."[2]

The *kumaz* was actually a mild form of sexual control compared to the cruel and barbaric practice of infibulation (sewing the labia). *Fibula* is the Latin term for "clasp," and indeed, "female slaves in ancient Rome had one or more rings put through their labia majora to prevent their becoming pregnant." However, "there is sufficient evidence to assume that infibulation was practiced in ancient Egypt, and that it was perhaps there that the custom originated."[3] Indeed, the Sudanese still call it "pharaonic circumcision."

Clitoridectomy, or excision, "was practiced already in ancient Egypt by the ruling class. . . . It is reported that women in ancient Egypt could not inherit unless they were circumcised."[4] Infibulation and excision are still practiced today in parts of Africa, including Egypt, and along the southern coast of the Arabian peninsula (Oman and South Yemen).

The *kumaz* of the ancient Near East, a "civilized" step up from body mutilation, was itself the prototype of the metal, padlocked chastity belt brought into Europe by Crusaders in the twelfth century. Here, in the midst of Christian medieval attitudes about women and sex, its use flourished for five hundred years. A French account from 1881 tells of a jealous husband who informed his wife on their wedding night "of certain girdles of chastity with which he became acquainted during a pilgrimage to Jerusalem. He procured three or four of these belts and brought them back with him," putting one on his wife while she was under the influence of a narcotic.[5]

While infibulation, where it existed in Europe, was a lower-class phenomenon, chastity belts were supplied "to the upper classes, who [could] afford such luxuries, and who [were] aware that bodily cruelty is punished more heavily than the imposition of mental torture."[6] However, it was not simply *mental* torture to have to be unlocked by one's husband before being able to defecate, as was frequently the case.

The *kumaz* thus serves as a potent symbol of female sexual oppression, despite its relative "humaneness" compared to its Roman, European, African, and Arab coun-

1. Eric John Dingwall, *The Girdle of Chastity: A History of the Chastity Belt* (New York: Dorset Press, 1992), pp. 10–11.

2. Ibid., pp. 11–12.

3. Scilla McLean and Stella Efua Graham, *Female Circumcision, Excision and Infibulation,* Report no. 47 (London: Minority Rights Group, 1983), p. 6.

4. See Fran P. Hosken, *Female Sexual Mutilations* (Lexington, MA: Women's International Network News, 1980), p. 55.

5. Dingwall, p. 102.

6. Ibid., p. 13.

terparts. Once in the wilderness, the women could remove these gold girdles and give them over to be melted down. This in itself says much about their newly acquired freedom from slavery, but even more, it says that the Tabernacle walls and sacred vessels built from these items were *themselves* a form of atonement for sexual oppression, exploitation, and degradation.

"Why did the Israelites of that generation need atonement? Because they "gratified [*znu*] their eyes with nakedness [*ervah*] " (Shab. 64b). Men needed to atone for the consequences of their sexual objectification of women. "Whoever looks at the little finger of a woman is as if he has looked at the place of the pudenda," the Gemara concludes. The point here is not the *woman's body,* but the *men's eyes.* They are told not to gaze at even a woman's *little finger*—a nonsexual body part—but to keep their eyes to themselves. Men's erotic gazing is considered to be a force requiring restriction.

THE COPPER MIRRORS

He [Betzalel] made the copper washstand and its copper base from the mirrors of the hosts of women [*tzovot*] who assembled [*tzavu*] at the entrance of the *ohel moed.* (Ex. 38:8)

"The daughters of Israel had mirrors that they looked into to adorn themselves," Rashi explains.

Even these they did not hesitate to bring as a donation to the Tabernacle. Now Moses was about to reject them since they were made for the *yetzer hara* [to arouse sexual desire] but the Holy One said to him, "Accept them, for they are dearer to Me than everything else, because through them the women produced huge hosts in Egypt." For when their husbands were weary from crushing labor, they used to come and induce them to eat and drink. Then they would take the mirrors, and each looked at herself in her mirror with her husband, saying endearingly to him, "I am better-looking than you!" Thus, they awakened their husbands' desire, slept with them, became pregnant, and gave birth to children there. (Rashi)

The mirrors were thus the direct symbol of Jewish women's heroism and resistance under Egyptian bondage. The women donated them eagerly because they knew the washstand would be used for *sotah,* a ritual for women accused of unfaithfulness by jealous husbands. The laver promoted domestic peace by "affording [a woman] an opportunity to prove her innocence" (Rashi). Women thus "accepted the law [of *sotah*] upon themselves with joy, and offered to give all their mirrors" (Nachmanides).

If Moses wanted to reject the mirrors because of their association with sexuality, why did he accept the *kumaz* so readily? The *kumaz* was mixed in with other items and melted down with them, and the gold was used for a variety of purposes. In this case, however, the copper from *the mirrors alone* was being used to make *the laver alone.* "Therefore Moses did not consent at first until he was told to do so by the Almighty" (Nachmanides).

THE HOSTS OF WOMEN

Who were the *tzovot,* the hosts of women who assembled *(tzavu)* at the *ohel moed?* (Before the Tabernacle was built, the *ohel moed* meant Moses' tent). *Tzava* (צבא), "host," is a term used to denote both an army of men and a camp of angels. Similarly, the "hosts of heaven" are the planets and the stars. Hence, one of God's Names, Hashem Tzevaot (usually translated as "Lord of Hosts"), refers to the Creator's sovereignty over angelic activity and planetary motion.

A *tzava* is thus a large group of individual entities assembled into an association of some kind in order to achieve a common purpose. Some form of service is involved—for example, being a soldier in the Israeli army, orbiting around the sun, or performing a round of duty in the Temple. The second census of men over age twenty is described as being for *tzava* (Num. 1:3), which has been interpreted as either military conscription or a more general kind of communal service.

The large group of women who gathered at the entrance of the *ohel moed* formed such an association. This sisterhood of women was eager to worship the God of Israel, for this was a deity Who did not require them to be sexual or seductive in the name of "service," as pagan gods and priesthoods did. Under Egyptian slavery, Jewish women's resistance consisted largely of using their sexuality. The enticement of their spiritually demoralized husbands enabled the women to thwart the population-control campaign against the Jews. However, this, too, demanded that they focus on their physical attractiveness and act in "bewitching" and seductive ways.

Now, after liberation, the women of Israel could abandon sexual objectification, which is a form of slavery, and move on to human dignity and personhood, which is the essence of freedom. They had no further inclination to sit in front of a mirror decorating themselves but chose instead to focus on their spiritual and intellectual development.

> It was an ordinance among women to beautify themselves by looking at their faces every morning in copper mirrors or glass to fix adornments on their heads. They are remembered in the book of Isaiah because it was a custom of Israel, like the custom of Ishmael, until today. But there were in Israel women who served Hashem by weakening their desires in this world, and they gave their mirrors willingly because they no longer needed them to beautify themselves. They came every day to the entrance of the Tabernacle to pray and to listen to teachings about the *mitzvot.* These are the ones who came to the entrance of the Tabernacle. For there were a large number of them. But they are not mentioned in Scripture except for the law of the washstand. (Ibn Ezra)

That this association of women is not mentioned elsewhere in the Torah leaves us with frustratingly few clues about the group's specific activities. However, this lack of information about their *activities* should not lead us to mistakenly devalue their *existence.* The "serving women that did service" at the Tabernacle consisted of "women who resolved to be in attendance there and afterwards were" (Hertz).

What that "attendance" consisted of we can only surmise. Perhaps the women were skilled in meditation techniques. Their mirrors may have facilitated their intuition or psychic development, for "prophecy and vision must always come through . . . a mirror or a lens. Although the initiate actually perceives God's Glory, it is not seen directly, but must be reflected through . . . an angel or some other transcendental being. . . . The angel is serving as the lens or mirror for the vision, or as God's spokesman."[7] The mirror, in its function of reflection, is also the quintessential symbol of women's greater *Binah*, which is an understanding based on the capacity to receive and reflect back.[8]

Another aspect of the *tzovot* relates to the fact that, throughout the vast majority of cultures and historical periods, women have been considered the repository of the spiritual mysteries symbolized by spinning and weaving.

WOMEN AND WEAVING

Every woman wise of heart in her hands spun and brought yarn of blue, purple, and red wool, and white linen. And all the women whose hearts uplifted them in wisdom spun the goats. (Ex. 35:25–26)

Women wove the tricolored wool fabrics for the Tabernacle's structure and the priestly garments: the *mishkan* curtain, the *parokhet* veil, the two entrance screens, and the priestly sash; the high priest's ephod, breastplate, and the pomegranate balls hanging from his robe. (The ephod and breastplate were woven with gold thread as well as white linen.) The high priest's robe itself was woven completely of blue wool, as were the attachments of the breastplate to the ephod, and the headband to the turban.

Women also wove the *ohel*, the goatskin tent that was draped like a woman's skirt. The weaving of the *ohel* was acknowledged by the Rabbis to be a special skill, for the women "spun it directly off the backs of the goats" (Rashi; Shab. 74b).

Spinning and weaving, traditional female tasks, are not just physical activities but also basic, primordial symbols of time, fate, destiny, and the interconnectedness of all life. Women have universally been considered the archetypal weavers of the web of life, the spinners of the threads of fate; these "mundane" activities are therefore full of spiritual significance. "From menstruation . . . the woman is regulated by and dependent on time; so it is she who determines time—to a far greater extent than the male, with his tendency toward the conquest of time, toward timelessness and eternity. . . . All such activities as plaiting, weaving, and knotting belong to the fate-governing activity of the woman."[9]

An allusion to weaving as a symbol of women's wisdom is found in the Talmud. When a "wise woman" asked R. Eliezer why the death penalty was not the same for

---

7. Aryeh Kaplan, *Meditation and Kabbalah* (York Beach, ME: Samuel Weiser, 1982), p. 36.

8. The notion of Binah as receptivity and reflection comes from Tzippora Heller, a teacher at Neve Yerushalayim in Israel.

9. Neumann, *The Great Mother*, pp. 226–227.

everyone associated with the golden calf, he cryptically replied, "All wisdom of women is in the spinning wheel" (Yom. 66b).

Spinning, weaving, and related tasks such as embroidery have even "formed the chief purpose of a kind of 'secret society' from which men were excluded."[10] Perhaps it was men's jealousy of such exclusion that led to the social denigration of the "spinster"; originally meaning *one who spins,* the term later became a derogatory epithet for a woman who does not get married.

Among the Maori women of New Zealand, initiation to the craft was "conducted as a religious ceremony; a consecrated workshop . . . was reserved for the work, and if a man entered the precincts all work was stopped and put aside." Interestingly, these women wove twelve styles of mats, and "each was the specialty of the women of a particular tribe."[11]

A talmudic proverb states, "While a woman talks she spins" (Meg. 14b). R. Joshua uses the discussions of "the women spinning yarn by moonlight" as a legal criterion (Sot. 6:1). "Spinning a yarn" is an idiom for telling a story, while "spinster associations" no doubt served as a means for women to develop and pass on their own oral traditions. The oral traditions of men are given lofty titles such as "ethics of the fathers" and "wisdom of the Sages." The oral traditions of women, however, have generally been devalued as "gossip" and "old wives' tales." Sewing circles and knitting clubs are hardly centers of social and spiritual power in the modern world.

Among many Native American cultures, however, women's traditions have been recorded and preserved through the actual patterns woven into their baskets, rugs, shawls, tapestries, and so forth. The designs, which are believed to hold spiritual powers, are often symbolic, inspired by the women's dreams, which they attribute to a spider deity.[12] "Their artistic labors were carried out as an almost religious function, and were subject to all manner of ritual rules."[13]

A similar spiritual significance characterized the "deft needlework wrought with gorgeous dye materials for which the women of Tyre [Lebanon] were famous."[14] Therefore, it is not fantastic to assert that, a little further south, the Jewish women who wove the tapestries and priestly garments for the Tabernacle might have had some knowledge that they were transmitting sacred spiritual mysteries—and there were indeed sacred spiritual mysteries in these weavings. The curtain, the veil, and both entrance screens had *kruvim* woven into them. On the entrance screens, the cherubs were in the image of lions and were visible from both sides of the fabric. On the curtain and the veil, however, the cherubs were seen as a lion from one side of the fabric and as an eagle from the other side (Rashi).

---

10. Briffault, 1:462.
11. Ibid., p. 466.
12. John Upton Terrell and Donna M. Terrell, *Indian Women of the Western Morning* (New York: Anchor, 1976), p. 90.
13. Briffault, 1:462.
14. Ibid., 1:463.

These figures are found in the prophet Ezekiel's mystical vision of God's "Chariot" or Throne of Glory. Holding it up were four creatures called *chayot*, which each had four faces: a human and a lion on the right side, and an ox and an eagle on the left side (Ezekiel 1:4–13). Later, these creatures are called *kruvim* (Ezekiel 10). The wheels of the Chariot are called *ofanim*.

According to Maimonides, *chayot*, *ofanim*, and *kruvim* are three of ten levels of angels (*Foundations of Torah* 2:7). Yet another level, the *serafim*, was symbolized by the beams of the Tabernacle (*Zohar* II:139a, II:147b, II:170a, II:171a, II:233b).

The four faces—ox, lion, eagle, and human—will be recognized by those familiar with the zodiac as the symbols of the four fixed signs of Taurus, Leo, Scorpio, and Aquarius, respectively. The Talmud explains their symbolism as follows: "The king of wild animals is the lion; the king of domestic beasts is the ox; the king of the birds is the eagle; humanity is exalted over them; and the Holy One is exalted over all of them and over the whole world" (Chag. 13b).

The human and lion faces, because they appeared on the right side of Ezekiel's vision, represent *Chesed* (Mercy), while the ox and eagle faces, appearing on the left side, represent *Gevurah* (Judgment). The ox as a symbol of the left side of Judgment is described by the *Zohar* (II:193b, II:236b).

In the second account of the vision, the ox face is replaced by the face of a cherub (Ezek. 10:14). The ox is omitted because of the sin of the golden calf, which was "a sin against the Holy Mother, the Shekhinah. . . . The design of the Mother which is outwardly discernible follows the four prototypes—human, lion, ox, and eagle—in the Supernal Chariot" (*Zohar* II:191a, II:73b).

"Ezekiel entreated concerning [the ox face] and changed it into a cherub. He said to God, 'Sovereign of the Universe! Shall an accuser become an advocate?'" (Chag. 13b). Likewise, in the Tabernacle, the *kruvim* in the fabrics had faces of lions and eagles and the *kruvim* on the *kaporet* had faces of humans; no oxen were represented. However, the *kaporet* itself was so named because it made atonement *(kaparah)* for the golden calf (ER 50:4), for "gold indicates the attribute of Judgment" (Nachmanides).

The *kruvim* on the *kaporet* also represented the two aspects of God, Hashem and Elokim. When God acted with Mercy, the *kruvim* faced each other and embraced; when God acted in Judgment, the *kruvim* turned away from each other. Interestingly, at the time of the destruction of the First Temple, the *kruvim* were embracing (Yom. 54b).

The mysteries symbolized by the Chariot with its four-faced creatures make up a form of Jewish mysticism known as *Maaseh Merkavah*. While an explanation of these mysteries is far beyond the scope of this book and the capacity of its author, it is nevertheless clear that the Tabernacle was a living symbol of this wisdom. The women who wove it must have had some inkling of what they were doing. This is what is meant by, "every woman [who was] wise of heart in her hands." It is also alluded to in the statement that "the least of their women was like Ezekiel" (Nachmanides on Num. 20:1).

THE COSMIC SIGNIFICANCE OF THE TABERNACLE

The Tabernacle was a microcosm of the universe. "Everything was made with a mystic significance, so that all things should bear the supernal pattern. . . . All the works of the universe were contained in the equipment of the Tabernacle" (*Zohar* II:229a, II:232a). The 13 materials required to make the Tabernacle correspond to the "13 channels of flow from the superconscious source to the beginning of consciousness."[15]

Figure 19–1 illustrates the multilayered structure of the Tabernacle, symbolizing "worlds within worlds," or the various levels of reality. The ark, which is composed of a box within a box within a box, was itself a box within the Holy of Holies, which was a box within the Tabernacle, which was, in turn, a box within the courtyard.

The metals also reflect a layered progression. The inner vessels were gold, while the outer vessels were copper; similarly, the inner beams were gold with silver sockets, while the outer beams were silver with copper sockets. Iron could not be used at all in the Tabernacle; nor could stones cut by a sword be used to build an altar (Ex. 20:22; Deut. 27:5). This is because the Tabernacle represented *sukkat shalom,* a shelter of peace, while iron represented violence and warfare. "A sword is made of iron and is the destroyer of the world. . . . With them Esav's might is shown—therefore it must not be brought into the House of God" (Nachmanides).

The ten tapestries forming the *mishkan* symbolized the ten firmaments of heaven (*Zohar* II:164b), and the gold buttons joining the two pieces together were like the stars glittering in the night sky (II:172a, II:229a; ER 35:6; Shab. 99a). "The colors below were of the colors above, and drew down the Shekhinah" (*Zohar* II:147a). Blue represented the spiritual plane; red, the physical plane; and purple, the union of the two realms.

The ark, table, and altar were each called a "crown": the ark was the crown of Torah; the table, the crown of *Malkhut,* or royalty; and the altar, the crown of *kehunah,* the priesthood (ER 34:2). The ark symbolized the Torah itself as spiritual wealth (gold) and a tree of life (wood), while the *menorah* symbolized the Torah's wisdom, the teachings that give light to the world (*Zohar* II:167a; ER 36:3).

The table was "the medium through which the blessing of nourishment flowed to the entire world" and was therefore never allowed to be empty, for God's blessing is said to rest only on substantial matter and not in an empty place. (This is the reason that bread should be left on one's table when one says *Birkat Hamazon,* the Grace After Meals.) The showbread was celestial food—"upon it rested the blessing, and from it came abundance to all Israel," says Nachmanides, who recommends pondering the term *lefanai* ("before Me," or "to My Face") to understand the "name and secret" of *lechem panim.*

---

15. Rabbi Yitzchak Ginsburgh, *The Alef-Beit: Jewish Thought Revealed through the Hebrew Letters* (Northvale, NJ: Jason Aronson, 1991), p. 194.

The Tabernacle was not only a microcosm of the universe, it was a macrocosm of the human body. "As the human body possesses many organs, higher and lower, some internal and not visible, others external and visible, and yet they all form one body, so also was it with the Tabernacle" (*Zohar* II:162b).

In this symbolism, the ark is the heart, the *kruvim* are the lungs, the table is the stomach, the *menorah* is the mind, the incense is the sense of smell, the laver is bodily fluids, the *ohel* is the skin, and the beams are the ribs.[16] Hence, "the structure of the Tabernacle corresponds to the structure of heaven and earth" (*Zohar* II:149a). The building of an earthly Tabernacle not only mirrored the process of Creation, it also produced a corresponding celestial Tabernacle. "When Moses set up the Tabernacle in the wilderness, another such was raised in the heavenly spheres" (*Zohar* II:143a, II:159a). All our earthly actions are believed to have consequences on the heavenly plane.

------

16. Weissman, p. 244.

III

Freedom to Worship
(Leviticus/Vayikra)

Animal Sacrifice

Vayikra (1:1–5:26)

The soul [nefesh] *of the flesh* [basar] *is in the blood* [dam]; *I have given it to you upon the altar to make atonement for your souls, for it is the blood in the soul that will atone.* (Lev. 17:11)

The blood contains the *nefesh,* the soul or spiritual life force of an animal. Sprinkling it on the altar in the Tabernacle effected atonement for humans because *nefesh* is also the lowest of the five levels of the human soul. Hence, the animal's blood represents our own animal instincts.

Animal sacrifice was practiced as early as the time of Cayin and Hevel, and some even say that Adam offered a bull (LR 2:10). While Cayin brought a *minchah,* or grain-offering, Hevel offered the fattest firstborn of his flock (Gen. 4:4). Noach sacrificed several mammals and birds upon leaving the ark, and God was appeased (Gen. 8:20–21). Similarly, God's covenant with Avraham was made through a heifer, a goat, a ram, a dove, and a pigeon (Gen. 15:9).

As the ancient world descended into idolatry, however, "men and animals were offered together on the same altar, to the same god, to obtain the same favors."[1] Human sacrifice began in the generation of the Flood, resumed after the Flood, and, by Avraham's time, once again became common. The *akedah* represents its rejection and replacement by animal sacrifice. Animal sacrifice thus predated human sacrifice and coexisted with it for quite a while before eventually replacing it in most parts of the world. Some pagan traditions, such as Greek mythology, bear tales indicating such a transition.[2]

---

1. Davies, p. 20.
2. Ibid., pp. 55–57.

"Ritual purification" of the animal instincts of eating and sex is the primary subject of Leviticus. It has been said that getting the Jews out of Egypt was nothing compared to getting Egypt out of the Jews. Forty years' wandering in the wilderness was needed for this band of newly freed runaway slaves to develop a more sanctified approach to both human and animal life.

BLOOD RITES OF THE ANCIENT WORLD

The sacrificial system of the Torah was designed to combat the bloody rituals of the "Great Goddess" religions of the ancient Near East. Throughout western Asia, a goddess was worshiped with a vegetation god who was her son or brother as well as her lover. In Egypt, this was Isis and Osiris. In Asia Minor, it was Cybele and Attis; in Babylonia, Ishtar and Tamuz (in earlier Sumeria, Inanna and Dumuzi); in Syria and Phoenicia, Astarte and Adonis; and in Canaan, Asherah (mother) or Anat (sister) and Baal. Later, in Greece, Aphrodite and Dionysus were such a pair, while on the island of Cyprus, they were called Aphrodite and Adonis.

She was the earth and he was the grain. Sowing and harvest festivals consisted of ritual enactments of his death, her mourning for him, and his subsequent resurrection. These ceremonies, which lasted for several days, began with a sacrifice accompanied by mourning practices, and culminated in "a wild outburst of glee. . . . the celebration took the form of a carnival."[3] Feasting and merrymaking included the music of flutes, drums, and timbrels, as well as orgiastic sexual activity meant to function as fertility magic.

> The fertility ritual was originally performed between the Great Mother and her son-lover, and culminated in his sacrifice. . . . In ancient times a human victim, whether god, king, or priest, was always offered up to ensure the fertility of the earth. Originally the victim was the male, the fertilizing agent, since fertilization is only possible through libations of blood in which life is stored. The female earth needs the fertilizing blood-seed of the male. . . . Blood is dew and rain for the earth, which must drink blood in order to be fruitful.[4]

The sacrificial victim was dismembered, his limbs buried in various places, and his blood sprinkled throughout the land. (In an animal sacrifice, however, some of the limbs would be eaten rather than buried.) The phallus of the victim—whether king (chapter 10), priest, or bull (chapter 12)—was preserved and held sacred. In the spring harvest festival of Cybele and Attis, severed male genitalia "were carried in solemn procession in baskets on the heads of priestesses, taken to the innermost shrine, the bridal chamber of Cybele, washed, anointed, sometimes even gilded, and then buried."[5]

3. Frazer, p. 407.
4. Neumann, *Origins*, pp. 57, 74, 77.
5. Wolfgang Lederer, *The Fear of Women* (New York: Harcourt Brace Jovanovich, 1968), p. 144.

The sacrifice of the goddess's human male consort was eventually replaced by the sacrifice of a horned (and potent) male animal, such as the bull, which became a primary, universal object of fertility worship. Bull worship in the ancient world was particularly prominent among the pagan Semites.[6] The labyris, a double-edged axe, was carried by the priestesses of the bull cult on the island of Crete because it was "the sacred sacrificial implement" used in his slaughter. It was also "the instrument of sacramental castration."[7]

"In later times, the sacrifice, castration, and dismemberment were no longer performed on a human victim, but on an animal. . . . The decapitation of the bull subsequently replaced the sacrifice of the phallus, and in the same way his horns became phallic symbols." In Egypt, the head of Osiris's Apis bull could not be eaten but was thrown into the Nile, corresponding to the part of the myth where Osiris's phallus is lost after his dismemberment. The bull's head thus became a substitute for the human phallus.[8]

Initiation into Attis's death rites required the individual to be "baptized" in bull's blood. The devotee stood in a pit covered with a grate called a Taurobolium.

> A bull, adorned with garlands of flowers, its forehead glittering with gold leaf, was then driven on to the grating and there stabbed to death with a consecrated spear. Its hot reeking blood poured in torrents through the apertures and was received with devout eagerness by the worshiper on every part of his person and garments, till he emerged from the pit, drenched, dripping, and scarlet from head to foot . . . as one who had been born again to eternal life and had washed away his sins in the blood of the bull. . . . The testicles as well as the blood of the bull played an important part in the ceremonies.[9]

Ritual bloodshed not only ensured fertility and made atonement, it also provided protection from disaster or evil powers and was a means of communion with a deity. It "reestablish[ed] a lost alliance between the sacred and the profane. . . . To sacrifice is to render sacred."[10]

The ritual use of blood often extended to ingesting it. The blood of an animal or a human was drunk to acquire a quality of the deceased, such as courage, or by worshipers as the blood of their god in an act of communion with him.[11] In some cultures it was "regarded as a delicacy. Even peoples whose habitual diet is entirely vegetarian will miss no opportunity of indulging in a draught of warm blood. . . . There is no instance known of blood, in general, being regarded with horror by any [primitive] people."[12] Drinking blood was not necessarily connected to eating the meat of a sacrifice. "The flesh diet of Egyptian kings was restricted to veal and goose. In

6. Briffault, Vol. 3, "The Divine Bull," pp. 191–195.
7. Neumann, *Origins*, pp. 76–77.
8. Ibid., p. 77.
9. Frazer, pp. 408–409; Lederer, p. 146.
10. Davies, pp. 24–26.
11. Frazer, p. 576.
12. Briffault, 2:398–399.

antiquity many priests and many kings of barbarous peoples abstained wholly from a flesh diet," yet even a vegetarian priest might ritually drink fresh blood.[13]

In ancient Greece, inspiration was believed to come from "sucking the fresh blood of a sacrificed victim. In the temple of Apollo Diradiotes at Argos, a lamb was sacrificed by night once a month; a woman, who had to observe a rule of chastity, tasted the blood of the lamb, and thus being inspired by the god she prophesied or divined. At Aegira in Achaia the priestess of Earth drank the fresh blood of a bull before she descended into the cave to prophesy."[14] Nor was this practice unique to the Mediterranean world.

> In Southern India, the goddess Kali is believed to descend upon the priest, and he gives oracular replies after sucking the blood which streams from the cut throat of a goat. At a festival of the Alfoors of Minahassa, in Northern Celebes [near Indonesia], after a pig has been killed, the priest rushes furiously at it, thrusts his head into the carcass, and drinks of the blood . . . whereupon he begins to prophesy how the rice crop will turn out that year.[15]

Blood was sprinkled in rain-making ceremonies and smeared for protection. Worshipers smeared the blood of their god on themselves, or on the woodwork of their houses to "propitiate the forest spirits who may still be in the timber." Hunters smeared the blood of an animal on themselves and their weapons "to calm their souls and hinder them from fleeing away."[16]

THE TORAH'S SACRIFICIAL SYSTEM

Maimonides' statement that "the eating of blood led to a certain kind of idolatry" *(Guide of the Perplexed* III:46)[17] is easily understood in light of what we have just learned. He cites an example—one much more benign than those above—where the worshipers did not drink the blood but would "slaughter an animal, collect its blood in a vessel or in a ditch, and eat the flesh of this slaughtered animal close by its blood." Spirits supposedly drank the blood while the worshipers ate the flesh, and as a result would "come to them in dreams, inform them of secret things, and be useful to them."

The Torah prohibited Jews, not only from ingesting blood, but also from smearing it on themselves, bathing in it, or making any use of it whatsoever. In voluntary sacrifices, the blood of a mammal was collected in a vessel and spilled on the northeast and southwest corners of the altar, while the blood of a bird was squeezed on the southeast corner. In obligatory sacrifices, the high priest entered the Tabernacle, dipped his finger into the vessel of blood, and sprinkled it towards the *parokhet* seven

---

13. Frazer, p. 277.
14. Ibid., p. 109.
15. Ibid.
16. Ibid., pp. 74–75, 135, 257, 620.
17. All references to Maimonides in this chapter are to this source.

times. Sometimes (depending on the sacrifice), he anointed the horns of the incense altar with it, or sometimes, the horns of the sacrificial altar. He then spilled the rest of the blood at the base of the sacrificial altar, which had a built-in drainage system.

The Torah also limited the quantity of sacrifices. In Babylonia, "the quantities of food involved could be enormous: . . . a daily total of over 500 kg. [1,100 pounds] of bread, 40 sheep, 2 bulls, 1 bullock, 8 lambs, 70 birds and ducks, 4 wild boars, 3 ostrich eggs, dates, figs, raisins and 54 containers of beer and wine."[18]

One moderately rich Egyptian templet received 3,220 loaves of bread, 24 cakes, 144 jugs of beer, 32 geese, and several jars of wine in a day's offerings, in addition to honey, flowers, and incense. On the New Moon and the sixth of the month, the temple got an extra 356 loaves of bread, 14 cakes, 34 jugs of beer, 1 ox, 16 birds, and 23 jars of wine. On another six festive days of the month, the stipulated additional offering was 83 loaves of bread, 15 jugs of beer, 6 birds, and 1 jar of wine.[19] In a thirty-one-year time span, Egyptian temples "are said to have received 514,968 head of cattle and 680,714 geese."[20]

The Tabernacle's daily sacrifice consisted of one sheep *(keves)* in the morning and one sheep in the evening. (A sheep, as opposed to a lamb, is at least a year old.) The sheep had to be a male that was *tamim* (or *tam*)—the term used to describe Noach and Jacob—meaning whole, perfect, and unblemished. Each sheep was offered with eight cups (four pounds) of wheat flour mixed with a quart of olive oil and a quart of wine, as a libation (Num. 28:3–7). All sacrifices had to be salted, and no leaven, honey, or other sweetener could be used (Lev. 2:11–13). Frankincense accompanied the grain-offerings.

On the Sabbath, an additional two sheep and eight pounds of wheat flour with oil were offered. On the New Moon, one goat, two young bulls, one ram *(ayil),* and seven sheep were offered with sixty pounds of wheat flour with oil and three gallons of wine, as a libation (Num. 28:9–15).

Thus, even if we add a moderate number of daily individual sacrifices of both a voluntary and an obligatory nature, the Tabernacle's quantitative intake was still minuscule compared to that of a pagan temple. These quantities also applied to the Temples in Jerusalem.

Maimonides' view that the three mammals permissible as sacrifices in Judaism— cattle, sheep, and goats—were those most worshiped by idolaters has much evidence to support it. Bulls and their cow-mothers certainly were "held . . . in very great esteem" by the vast majority of the pagan world, as we have seen; the Hindu "sacred cow" is but a vestige of this.

The Pesach sacrifice (chapter 15) illustrates that the male sheep, the ram, was also a major god. "Egyptians used to worship the constellation of Aries," Maimonides notes. The ram was forbidden to be slaughtered at any time but on the festival of Aries, which would have been the vernal equinox, March 21. The Passover sacri-

18. Oates, p. 175.
19. Erman, p. 277.
20. Ibid., p. 443.

fice, whose bones were left for the dogs to drag around so the Egyptians could see
how stupid it was to worship sheep, was eaten by the Jews at midnight on March 25,
just prior to their flight. By killing and eating rams "out of season," four days after
the solar festival of Aries, Jews were flaunting their complete and utter disdain for
the ram gods of Egypt.

The goat was the third species worshiped throughout the pagan world. "Certain
sects of the Sabians worshiped the jinn and believed they assumed the outward forms
of goats." Maimonides, living in medieval Egypt, used the Moslem term for spirits
or demons. However, the satyr, which was a goat god, was found throughout pagan
Greece, Rome, and pre-Christian Europe as well. Pan, the European goat god, provided the image for the Christian devil, Satan, whose name is derived from the *satan,*
Jewish mysticism's "prosecuting angel." Jews blow the *shofar* every morning of the
month of *Elul* (except the last, the day before Rosh Hashanah) in order to "confuse"
this *satan,* who is waiting for the slightest opportunity to argue against each individual to God.

Goat worship was common throughout the ancient Near East. "The worship of
the goat, accompanied by the foulest rites, prevailed in lower Egypt. This was familiar to the Israelites, and God decided to wean them from it" (Hertz). The Yom Kippur service, with its two goats, was an attempt to transform satyr worship into a form
of atonement: "And they will no longer sacrifice to the *seirim* [goats] who seduce
[*zonim*] them" (Lev. 17:7).

"Thus it was in order to erase these incorrect opinions that we have been ordered
by the Law to sacrifice only these three species of mammals," Maimonides states.
"In this way an action considered by them [the pagans] as an extreme act of disobedience was the one through which one came near to God and sought forgiveness for
one's sins. These wrong ideas, which are diseases of the human soul, are cured by
their contrary, found at the opposite extreme."

Nachmanides disputes the possibility that the Torah's sacrificial system could have
cured the false spiritual notions that Maimonides describes. "It would only add to
the problem," he maintains. He agrees that pagans did not eat rams and bulls because
they worshiped the constellations of Aries and Taurus. However, if Jews sacrificed
these animals to Hashem, he asserts, this would have *promoted* idolatry, not prevented
it, because the pagans, too, sacrificed these animals to gods other than the ones they
represented.

The views of Maimonides and Nachmanides appear to conflict, but they are easily reconciled. Both are missing the following information. "The primitive worship
of animals conforms to two types. . . . On the one hand, animals are worshiped, and
are therefore neither killed nor eaten. On the other hand, animals are worshiped
because they are habitually killed and eaten."[21]

Maimonides thinks the pagans *never* sacrificed bulls, rams, and goats, while
Nachmanides thinks that they *frequently* did so. Maimonides seems not to have known
that animal deities were sacrificed and eaten on their annual festivals. Since there

21. Frazer, p. 617.

were many Egyptian gods who were represented as bulls and rams, there could have been a number of sacrifices of these in one year.

However, while *fertile* bulls and rams were worshiped and only sacrificed on annual festivals, perhaps animals that had been neutered for agricultural purposes could be offered throughout the year. For example, perhaps an ox (an adult castrated bull) could be sacrificed when a bull could not. This would add insight to Nachmanides' view. However, since writers routinely use "ox" as a synonym for "bull," it is difficult to tell.

That castrated male animals were a frequent sacrifice in the pagan world would be a very good reason for the Torah's repeated stipulation of *tamim* animals—namely, sexually whole and not neutered. While pagans may have kept other body parts and fetishized them (e.g., a rabbit's foot or a sow's ear), a phallus would have been considered the most sacred of all.

Thus, Maimonides' view that these three mammals were chosen by the Torah as a rebellion against idol worship does not contradict Nachmanides, the *Zohar*, and other Jewish mystics who see deeper levels of meaning to the sacrifices. "Far be it that they should have no other purpose and intention except the elimination of idolatrous opinions from the minds of fools!" (Nachmanides).

THE ELEMENTS OF SACRIFICE

Any person could offer a sacrifice, as indicated by the term *adam* (Lev. 1:2). Unlike pagan temples, where offerings came completely from the king, any man, woman, or slave could bring an offering to the Tabernacle. Offerings atoned for (1) the unintentional violation of a negative commandment or (2) the neglect of a positive commandment. Neither of these could be punished by a Jewish court. There were four basic types of sacrifices.

1. *Olah*, or burnt-offering: a bull, ram, male goat, adult turtledove, or baby pigeon. A voluntary sacrifice, this atoned for neglecting a positive commandment, or transgressing a negative commandment that was repaired with a succeeding act, such as stealing an object and then returning it (Rashi). The *olah* was also said to atone for "thoughts which are in the recesses of one's heart" (*Zohar* III:11b).

2. *Chatat*, or sin-offering. This was an obligatory sacrifice that atoned for unintentional violations of sins that, when committed intentionally, were punishable by *karet* (excision). There are thirty-six of these: fifteen sexual prohibitions; ten related to Tabernacle service, including the eating of sacrifices; four prohibitions on the eating of common (nonsacrificial) food—internal fat *(chelev)*, blood, *chametz* during Passover, and eating common food on Yom Kippur; and three concerning idolatry. The rest are blasphemy, Sabbath violation, working on Yom Kippur, and neglecting circumcision (Kr. 2a).

A *chatat* was differentiated by whether the sin was committed by a common individual (ewe or female goat), a king or Sanhedrin leader (male goat), or a high priest (bull). The Sanhedrin that unanimously made an erroneous decision that caused the community to sin also had a bull *chatat*—for example, if they made a mistake in setting the calendar, and the community ended up fasting on the wrong day and eating on the actual Yom Kippur. Such an occurrence was probably quite rare, and the individual *chatat* was thus the norm.

A *chatat* based on an individual's income (ewe or female goat, pair of birds, or grain-offering) was also required for an unintentional false oath, breaking an oath to testify in court, or transgressing the laws of *tumah*, a condition in which one may not enter the Tabernacle or eat sacrificial food.

3. *Asham*, or guilt-offering: a ram. This obligatory offering atoned for *uncertain* violations of a sin punishable by *karet*. If the violation were later found to be certain (but unintentional), a *chatat* had to be brought. For example, suppose you think two pieces of meat are kosher (blood-free) and you eat one. Later you find out that only one piece was kosher, but you do not know which one. Because you *might* have eaten the one with blood in it, you have to bring an *asham*. If you later establish with certainty that the unkosher piece was indeed the one you ate, then you have to bring a *chatat*.

An *asham* was also required of someone who made personal use of Tabernacle vessels or animals, or who withheld another's money or property and denied this with a false oath when confronted by the victim.

4. *Shlamim*, or peace-offering: a bull or cow, a ram or ewe, or a male or female goat. This voluntary offering "makes peace between higher and lower, and between the various quarters of the world. Therefore the bringer also eats of them and has a share in them. Of all the offerings, none are so well beloved to God as the peace-offering . . . [they] spread peace everywhere and allay strife and wrangling" (*Zohar* III:11b). A person who is not at peace—for example, a mourner—could not offer a *shlamim* (LR 9:8).

The *shlamim* was the only way in which a Jew could slaughter a mammal for meat in the wilderness (Maimonides); thus, it sanctified meat eating. It was the only sacrifice in which the owner received a portion. The *olah* was totally burned and none was eaten at all, while the *chatat* (with rare exceptions) and the *asham* were partly burned and partly eaten, but only by the priests within the Tabernacle courtyard. The *shlamim* could be eaten anywhere in Jerusalem. The breast and right leg went to the priests, while the skin and the rest of the meat went to the owner. The *shlamim* is said to be the only sacrifice that will exist in the Messianic Era (LR 9:7).

Only a domesticated animal was permitted as a sacrifice because it "is reared on the crib of its master and eats neither indiscriminately nor from that obtained by robbery and by violence." However, bird-offerings had to have their digestive systems removed because a bird "flies about and swoops throughout the world, and eats indiscriminately; it eats food obtained by robbery and by violence" (LR 3:4).

Bird-Offerings

A person too poor to bring a **mammal** for an *olah* could bring an adult turtledove (after maturation, as indicated by a change to gold-colored plumage around the neck) or a baby pigeon (before this change). Both were domesticated birds. Like wild animals, birds of prey were forbidden as sacrifices. The feathers of a bird sacrifice were burned in spite of the bad smell "in order that the altar may be enhanced by the sacrifice of a poor person" (LR 3:5).

Turtledoves *(torim)* and pigeons *(yonah)* are "accessible and can be more easily caught," but it is their sexual habits that are most significant—an especially interesting concept in light of the dove's sacredness to Aphrodite.[22] Adult turtledoves "attach themselves only to their mates, and once they lose their companions they never associate with others" (Nachmanides on Lev. 1:14). Likewise, Israel cleaves to God. "Pigeons, on the other hand, are very jealous and as a result of their jealousy they part and take on other mates." Hence, only baby ones, who have not yet begun to mate, may be offered, "for as long as the pigeon is young it is attached with greater love to the nest where it is reared than are all other fowls." While other birds will not return to a nest touched by a human, "the pigeon never abandons it under any condition." Likewise, Israel never abandons God.

The chicken and the turkey, although domesticated, were not permitted as sacrifices. God "did not choose cocks because of their inclination to lewdness." Nachmanides also asserts that the birds chosen had special qualities as food: "For turtledoves have a propensity to sharpening the mind, and young pigeons have a propensity to benefit greatly those who are not fully matured physically."

Grain-Offerings

Those who could not afford even a bird brought a *minchah*, or grain-offering. Either the owner or the priest could mix the flour and oil. A handful of the dough was scooped out by a priest and burned on the altar, and the rest was eaten by the priests. *Kemitzah*, the scooping of the handful, was analogous to draining the blood in an animal sacrifice. There were many kinds of *menachot*, including obligatory community offerings such as the firstfruits of the barley harvest.

God was satisfied with whatever one could offer. "It is the same whether a person offers much or little, so long as one directs one's heart to heaven" (Men. 110a). "Once a woman brought a handful of fine flour, and the priest despised her, saying, 'See what she offers! What is there in this to eat? What is there in this to offer up?' It was shown to him in a dream: 'Do not despise her! It is regarded as if she had sacrificed her own life'" (LR 3:5).

Leaven and honey could not be used in a *minchah* because pagans used them (Maimonides). Pagan grain-offerings were thus bread and sweet cakes, while Jewish grain-offerings were thick *matzah*.

Salt

Salt had to be used on all offerings, meat or grain, because pagans did not use it (Maimonides). A saltless offering is called a mark of contempt (Ibn Ezra). Rashi states that God established a covenant with salt during the six days of Creation, "for the

---

22. Neumann, *Origins*, p. 76.

lower waters [the oceans] were promised that they would be offered upon the altar in the form of salt, and at the water libation on Sukkot," in compensation for not being in the heavens like the upper waters.

Salt is important to preserve and flavor food, but its overuse can be destructive. "Thus salt is like the covenant . . . for the covenant is 'the salt of the world,' and by virtue of it the world exists or may be destroyed " (Nachmanides).

Mammals

The procedure for offering a mammal began with the owner bringing the designated animal to the north side of the altar. Here, one laid one's hands on the animal's head and confessed one's sin (this step was obligatory for men and optional for women). The animal was then slaughtered. This could be done by the priest, the owner, or any qualified layperson (Rashi).

Everything from this point on had to be done by a priest. The blood was received in a vessel, taken to the altar, and thrown on it. The animal was skinned and cut up, the parts were rinsed off, and the innards (the internal fat, the kidneys, and the liver lobe) were salted and burned on the altar. In the case of a bull, the head was specially prepared by covering the bloody area with some fat and burning it separately. In the case of a lamb or goat, the fatty part of the tail was burned with the innards. The Torah no doubt stipulated the burning of animal livers and entrails because of the common Babylonian practice of using them for divination.[23]

"The essence of the offering is that it is analogous to the sinner." The sacrifice is "heated in the same way as one heated one's flesh and blood with evil passions and set all one's limbs on fire" (*Zohar* III:9b). Hence, the person is offering one's own (animal) desires and passions to God. Fasting is the modern-day equivalent of "burning fat" in an offering to God.

Every aspect of the procedure was a substitute for a part of the person. The innards of the animal were burned "because they are the instruments of thought and desire in the human being," while the confession represented speech and the laying on of hands represented deed (Nachmanides). The legs of the animal represented "the hands and feet of a person, which do all one's work." The animal blood was a substitute for human blood.

> All these acts are performed in order that when they are done, humans *(adam)* should realize that they sinned against God with body and soul, and that their blood should really be spilled and their bodies burned, were it not for the Mercy of the Creator, Who took a substitute. This sacrifice atones so that its blood stands for their blood, its life stands for their life, and its major limbs stand for their major limbs. (Nachmanides)

COSMIC MEANING OF THE SACRIFICES

The Hebrew word for "sacrifice," *korban,* is of the same root as *karav,* "to approach or come near." Sacrifice connected the lower worlds with the upper ones (*Zohar*

---

23. Budge, p. 151; Oates, p. 178.

III:8a), a function that is mostly filled in post-Temple times by prayer. The morning and evening sheep sacrifices, which are said to have reminded God of the ram substituted for Isaac (LR 2:11), correspond to *Shachrit* and *Minchah-Maariv*, the daily Jewish prayers at sunrise and sundown. Avraham instituted *Shachrit*, Isaac instituted *Minchah*, and Jacob instituted *Maariv* (Br. 26b).

Sacrifice "refers to those holy crowns which are all knit together and drawn to one another until they constitute a perfect unity to make whole the Holy Name so that Mercy should be shown to all worlds, and rigor should not be aroused" (*Zohar* III:5a). Thus, only Hashem, and not Elokim, is used as God's Name in offering sacrifices. This also makes it clear that the sacrifice is to the One God, "in order not to give an opponent an occasion for a point of attack"—in other words, so no one could say it was this or that pagan god who commanded the sacrifice (Nachmanides; Men. 110a).

Sacrifices were made to "Hashem" because they were meant to invoke the Mercy of the Creator, to turn divine anger (red) into forgiveness (white). This is the reverse of pagan symbolism, in which the white becomes red: Aphrodite, hastening to her wounded lover Adonis, trods on a bush of white roses; "the cruel thorns tore her tender flesh, and her sacred blood dyed the white roses forever red."[24] Similarly, the priests of Baal cut their (white) skin till the (red) blood gushed forth (*Zohar* II:20b). The Jewish view, however, *stops* the blood, and so red yields to white and not vice versa.

The priest brings the offering "to the fire, which is red; around the altar he sprinkles blood, which is red; the attribute of Judgment is red. The smoke ascending to heaven is white. Thus the red is turned into white. The attribute of Judgment (*Gevurah*) is turned into Mercy (*Chesed*). Red is indeed the symbol of rigorous justice" (*Zohar* II:20b).

Red and white is also interpreted here as the blood and the internal fat *(chelev,* which is linguistically related to *chalav,* meaning *milk*). "Red and white are offered for sacrifice, and the scent rises from both. The spices of incense are in part red and in part white—frankincense is white, pure myrrh is red—and the odor ascends from red and white. . . . It is fire alone which turns a sacrifice into something entirely white. Similarly, one who fasts and offers one's own fat and blood turns white because of fire."

The fire on the altar burned constantly, never going out (Lev. 6:6). In relation to the offerings, the fire is not called *esh,* but rather a feminized form of the word—*isheh* (אשה), which is merely a different vocalization of the word *ishah,* "woman." It is so called because the offering "is in the attribute of justice" (Nachmanides).

"Fire always symbolizes Judgment, whereas the priest is from the right side and is far away from Judgment. . . . Yet here he has to kindle the fire of judgment in the world." Sin is "burning oneself in the flame of the evil inclination"; the priest's purpose is to keep the fire burning so that "judgments may be subdued and prevented from arising in the world" (*Zohar* III:27a–b).

Right and left refer to the pillars of the Tree of Life. Hence, Mercy (*Chesed*) is

---

24. Frazer, p. 390.

from the right side and Judgment (*Gevurah*) is from the left side. The *olah, chatat,* and *asham* had to be slaughtered on the north side of the altar because north—as one walked *out* of the Tabernacle—was on the left, "the side of *Gevurah*, which is designated Elokim, the purpose being to soften and break the spirit of severity, so that Mercy may obtain the upper hand" (*Zohar* III:5a).

Judgment (*Gevurah*) emanates "from the side of the Mother" (*Binah*). When atonement is made for a sin, "punishment is mitigated and removed, and Mercy is awakened and prevails over the evil which arose from stern judgment, and then there is joy and consolation. . . . When Judgment is mitigated, all the crowns return to their places and the keys are restored to the Mother, and this is called repentance [*teshuvah*], and the world is forgiven, since the Mother is in perfect joy" (*Zohar* III:15b).

GENDER, SPECIES, AND SEXUALITY

"When God wants to, God calls for a female . . . and when God wants to, God calls for a male" (ER 38:3). The gender of the animals offered for sacrifice was significant, as was the species chosen. The *olah* had to be a male of any of the three mammals, while the *asham* had to be a male of one particular species. The occasional *chatat* (of the rulers) was a specific male animal, while the normative *chatat* (of the individual) was a female of two of the species. The *shlamim* could be either gender of any of the three species. Gender did not matter in bird-offerings.

Maimonides is no help at all in explaining the gender distinctions.

Know that the greater the sin that had been committed, the more defective was the species from which the sacrifice offered up for it was taken. Therefore only a female goat is offered up for an act of idolatry committed inadvertently, and other sins of a private individual require a ewe or a female goat. *For a female is in all species more defective than the male,* and there is no sin greater than idolatry, and no kind more defective than a female goat. Because of the king's distinguished rank, the sacrifice required for his inadvertent transgression is a male goat. . . . Do you not see that the sex of the *olah*, which is entirely consecrated to God, has distinction, for it may only be male? [emphasis mine]

The gender specifications are not due to notions of male supremacy. The *olah* is not "better" than other sacrifices. Indeed, we have been told that the *shlamim*—which used both genders—was the most "beloved to God," and is the only sacrifice that will exist in the Messianic Era!

Maimonides *could* have fallen back on his own theory of rebellion against idol worship. He might have surmised that the *olah* was male because the ram, and not the ewe, is the symbol of Aries. The bull, and not the cow, is the symbol of Taurus. Satyrs were also by definition male. This goes back to the fact that it was the god, not the goddess, who had to be sacrificed.

The *olah*, which is unique among the sacrifices in that it was totally burnt up and not enjoyed as food, represented the *total destruction of these specific gods.* However, in spite of the Torah's delight in burning up animal *representatives* of deities, no animal that had *itself* been worshiped as a deity (*ne'evad*), or had *itself* been dedicated as a sacrifice to a deity (*muktzah*), could be offered in the Tabernacle.

Maimonides' comments on the species are more insightful. The high priest had a bull *chatat* in memory of Aharon's role in the golden calf. Goats were offered on the festivals, the New Moon, Yom Kippur, and as a commoner's *chatat* for unintentional idolatry because "their [Jews'] greatest act of disobedience consisted at that time in sacrificing to the satyrs." The community is frequently atoned for with goats because "the whole congregation of Israel committed their first act of disobedience with the help of a goat," referring to the sale of Joseph.

The gender specifications of the sacrifices relate to the mystical concepts discussed in the last section. As the fire is the "female" from the left side of Judgment, and the priest is the "male" from the right side of Mercy, each sacrifice had to be of the gender that maintained this balance.

The *olah*, which was totally consumed by this female fire, had to be totally male in order for perfect unity. Thus,

> the female element must not be parted from the male, which is offered through it, so that the two are united. It was right for Noach to bring an *olah*, since God had set him in the place of a male in relation to the ark. . . . The left side is joined with the female (since the female is from the left side and the male from the right side) through the clinging of one to the other. Hence the female is called *isheh,* indicating the bond of love in which the left side is joined to her, so as to mount with her on high and be united with her there. Hence the words *olah isheh,* "a burnt-offering, a fire offering," indicate the bond of the male and the female. (*Zohar* I:70a)

Before the Tabernacle (and later, the Temple) was built, individuals were allowed to make offerings on a private altar called a *bamah*, built on a high place or hill. There an *olah* could be female (see 1 Samuel 6:14, 7:9); nor did one need a priest to sacrifice there (Zev. 113a). The two are related. Maleness was not cosmically needed in the priest *or* the animal, because the fire on a *bamah* did not hold the sanctity—that is, the cosmic femaleness—of the fire in the Tabernacle. This is because the Shekhinah, Who unifies Mercy and Judgment, dwelled only in the Tabernacle and was not present on the individual *bamot*.

The *chatat* and the *asham* were both partially consumed by the (female) fire and partially consumed by the (male) priests. The normative *chatat* was female, and the *asham* was male. Both were from the flock and not the cattle. Hence, they balanced each other. The *shlamim*, which was a celebratory rather than an atonement offering, harmonized opposites in itself, and so was taken from either gender.

All sacrificial animals, male or female, had to be *tamim*. This excluded (in terms of sexuality) a castrated male, a spayed female, a *tumtum* (a creature of indeterminate sex), and a hermaphrodite. However, in addition to being complete and distinct in its gender, the animal must also have never been "sexually abused."

Both bestiality and interbreeding come under this heading. A female animal used for bestiality by a man is called a *nirbah*. A male animal used for bestiality with a woman is called a *rovea*. The root of both—Resh, Bet, Ayin—also forms words meaning "to fructify the ground" and "to inundate for the sake of improving the soil" (Jastrow). Thus, bestiality was most likely another pagan fertility practice. In Aramaic, the same root forms the word for "to copulate animals, to hybridize."

An animal of mixed breed was forbidden because such purposeful manipulation of animal sexuality goes against God's Creation and the animals' natural instincts. Forcing or enticing animals to have sex with other animal species is as perverse, in the Torah view, as forcing or enticing them to have sex with the human species. Hence, the hybrid of a ewe and a male goat or the hybrid of a deer and a male goat are forbidden as a sacrifice, whether known for sure or only suspected (Bek. 12a).

Bestiality was apparently not uncommon in the pagan world. "A *behemah* (domestic animal) may not be left at inns of idolators because they are suspected of bestiality" (A.Z. 22a). Not only are female and male animals not to be left with a pagan man, or a male animal with a pagan woman, but even female animals are not to be left with pagan women. Why was this so? "Because idolators frequent their neighbors' wives, and should one by chance not find her in, and find the animal there, he might use it immorally. . . . Even if he should find her in he might use the animal, [for] idolators prefer the cattle of Israelites to their own wives" (A.Z. 22b).

R. Eliezer held the view that an animal bought from an idolator could not be used for a sacrifice, on the suspicion that it was sexually abused. Furthermore, a pregnant *nirbah* was not only forbidden herself as a sacrifice, but her offspring was forbidden as well, since the fetus was considered to have been abused along with its mother (A.Z. 24a).

Thus, we see that the Torah's notion of the sanctity of sex extended even to its transformation of animal sacrifice.

❉❉❉ 23 ❉❉❉

The Priesthood

Tzav (6:1–8:36)

You shall be a kingdom of priests and a holy nation to Me. (Ex. 19:6)

Just as Israel was sanctified among the nations through a stricter moral code, the *kehunah* (the Jewish priesthood) was sanctified among Israel. The priesthood was given to Aharon because of his role in making the golden calf (LR 7:1).

All of the Levites were rewarded with Tabernacle service for not worshiping the calf, but the *kehunah* itself only went to Aharon's part of the tribe. Moses was jealous of this until God reminded him, "I gave you the Torah" (ER 37:4).

Aharon was "the starting point of the priesthood because God chose him to make peace in the world, his conduct having entitled him to this distinction. Since all his days he strove to promote peace in the world, God appointed him to bring peace to the celestial family also" (*Zohar* III:88a).

It was precisely this peacemaking tendency that got Aharon in trouble with the golden calf. Someone with a less patient and tolerant personality would have *confronted* and *refused* the crowd's demand for a graven image. Chur did, and he was murdered. Aharon's strategy was to *pacify* by pretending to help, and then use every delay tactic possible. His cleverness in this regard was certainly appreciated by God, but the reverse side—his skill at duplicity—was nothing of which to be proud. The priesthood was, therefore, both a reward for Aharon's peacemaking personality *and* an atonement for the negative consequences of that same trait.

Because the priesthood was an atonement for Aharon's role in the golden calf, it was fitting that his *sons* should assist him, for it was *men* who assisted Aharon in making the calf by donating their gold. It was also men (the firstborn sons) who sacrificed and burned incense to the image. Women had nothing for which to atone in either regard (see chapter 20). Because the priesthood was an atonement for Aharon's role in the golden calf, his sin-offering—and that of every high priest after him—was always a calf.

Aharon hesitated to approach the altar at his installation because he felt unworthy. During the first seven days of the priestly installation, the Shekhinah had not rested upon the Tabernacle and the Israelites were upset because they had done all this ceremony "so the Shekhinah would be with us and we would know that atonement has been made for us for the sin of the calf." Aharon was afraid it was his fault the Shekhinah had not come down, so he and Moses prayed (Rashi on Lev. 9:7, 9:23).

On the eighth day of installation, when the Shekhinah did descend, "upper and lower beings reached their perfection, and there was peace everywhere in the joy of heaven and earth. . . . On that day the sin of the golden calf was wiped out, and the priests and people were cleansed of it" (*Zohar* III:37b).

HOW THE JEWISH PRIESTHOOD WAS DIFFERENT

The *kehunah* was quite different from other priesthoods. The Jewish priesthood, unlike its pagan counterpart, was not a landowning class. Even when Joseph bought up all the land of Egypt, he did not acquire what was owned by the Egyptian priesthood (Gen. 47:22).

The Jewish priesthood, coming from the line of Levi, was not connected to royalty, which came from the line of Judah. Pagan priesthoods, on the other hand, were literally the king's men. The role of an Egyptian priest was "to be a stand-in for the pharaoh."[1] Ancient Egypt was a theocracy; its ruler was a god and the priests were his trained magicians. They formed "a tremendous bureaucracy numbering thousands of men," but "only a select few of the priests were permitted to enter each temple's holy of holies and care for the oracle."[2] Priestly offices were hereditary, from father to son.

At the top of this priesthood was the high priest, "an extremely learned man, an elder of the temple, a man with considerable administrative ability and political sense . . . in charge of seeing that the temple and all its holdings ran smoothly, and officiating at the most important ceremonies. While normally such a man would have risen to his position through the ranks, it was the pharaoh's prerogative to place whomever he wanted in that office."[3]

Beneath the high priest were cadres of specialists—scribes, horologers and astrologers, dream interpreters, and readers of sacred texts. The high priest of Heliopolis (Potifera was one) served as the city's chief astronomer, and was called "he who is great in regarding," "he who sees the secrets of heaven," and "chief of the secrets of heaven."[4]

---

1. Brier, p. 34.
2. Ibid., p. 35.
3. Ibid., p. 41.
4. Erman, p. 290.

The most powerful priests of Egypt were the learned men of the House of Life, temple libraries that contained books on such topics as spells, charms, dream interpretation, astrology, amulets, and incantations. Such books were kept secret and believed to be dangerous in the hands of the laity. These priests "were entrusted with the responsibility of protecting the king by magic, warding off malevolent forces, protecting fishermen from crocodiles, and numerous other functions."[5] These magician-priests were the *chartumim* upon whom Pharaoh called to challenge Moses and Aharon in turning staffs into snakes and the Nile into blood. By virtue of his position, Pharaoh was the most powerful magician of all.

There are three other major ways in which the Jewish priesthood differed fundamentally from pagan priesthoods. Jewish priests could not serve while intoxicated (Lev. 10:9). Hence, there would be no more drunken revelries among the Jews like that of the golden calf. In addition, a man who was maimed could not serve as a priest, and priests were to have no contact with the dead.

THE PROHIBITION OF MAIMED MEN

Every man that is maimed [*mum*] from the seed of Aharon the priest shall not approach the fires [*ishei*] of Hashem to make an offering. As long as he is maimed he may not approach to offer God's bread. But he may eat God's bread [sacrificial food], from the holiest and from the holy. He may not come to the *parokhet* and he may not approach the altar because he is maimed. He shall not profane [*chalel*] the sacred things because I am Hashem, Who sanctifies them. (Lev. 21:21–23)

Just as a sacrificial animal had to be *tamim*, whole and "unblemished," so did a priest. While a maimed animal could not be offered as a sacrifice, it could be donated as a gift to the Tabernacle (Lev. 22:21–25). Similarly, a maimed priest could not enter the Tabernacle or approach the altar, but he could eat sacrificial food of any type.

What is a "maimed" priest? Leviticus 21:18–21 lists twelve conditions: blind, lame, deformed nose, misshapen limb, crippled leg, crippled hand, hunchback, dwarf, eye abnormality, eczema, ringworm, and crushed testicles. The oral tradition elaborates on these, thus defining many more conditions considered "maimed" (Bek., chap. 7). No distinction is made between a natal condition and an acquired one. As long as the *mum* remains, the priest cannot serve.

This may, at first, appear to be discrimination against men with physical disabilities, but a *mum* is not a "disability." One is not "disabled" by being bald or having a flat nose, no eyebrows or eyelashes, one eyebrow or extremely bushy eyebrows, or a head that is narrower at the top than at the bottom (or vice versa). Nonetheless, all of these are listed as *mum* by the Mishnah. Apparently, the priest had to be good-looking, and even a mere asymmetry of the body could disqualify him. Priests of pagan goddesses had to be youths of striking "beauty and loveliness . . . [who]

---

5. Brier, p. 45.

please the amorous goddess by their physical beauty."[6] There the similarity ends, however.

A maimed man was disqualified from the Jewish priesthood for the same reason a maimed animal was disqualified from the Jewish altar. The mutilation of men, like that of animals, was common in the goddess religions. Castration was certainly the most important kind, due to the phallus's role in fertility magic, but other body parts have also been regarded as potent charms. The use of the head, the heart, and even the skin have been cited in the sacrifice of human victims.[7]

However, body parts of living people were also employed for religious purposes. "The amputation of children's fingers was thought to be an excellent means of moving the gods to cure the ailments of a nobleman" in one part of the world,[8] and the Egyptians dedicated severed hands of war captives to their god Amon.[9] Thus, there must have been a significant number of mutilated people living in the pagan world. Skin gashing and flagellation, which were often practiced at religious rites, could also cause permanent mutilation. In the Torah's attempt to stop all this, it did not distinguish between, for example, a priest who was missing a finger from birth and one who had had a finger cut off. There could be no room for doubt in the minds of those who saw him functioning in service to Hashem.

Priestly castration was no anomaly. Entire sects of eunuch priests existed in western Asia. The most well known are the Galli, the priests of Cybele and Attis. We have already cited two practices of Cybele–Attis worship: the initiate's baptism in bull's blood, and the burial of baskets of gilded phalluses in Cybele's bridal chamber by her priestesses.

If the activity of Cybele's priestesses leaves much to be desired as a role for women in religion, then even more dismal was the role of Cybele's priests, "who regularly castrated themselves on entering the service of the goddess."[10] The following account describes the six-day spring festival of the death and resurrection of Attis as it was observed in Roman times, around 200 B.C.E., but the Galli were by no means a new phenomenon then. Several centuries later, "in the days of Augustine, her effeminate priests still paraded the streets and squares of Carthage with whitened faces, scented hair, and mincing gait." The only "Roman" aspect of this festival account is the substitution of an effigy for a human sacrifice.

On March 22, an effigy of Attis was tied to the trunk of a pine tree that had been cut down and brought into Cybele's sanctuary and "treated as a great divinity." On March 23, trumpets were blown. March 24 was called the Day of Blood. The "high priest drew blood from his arms and presented it as an offering. Nor was he alone in making this bloody sacrifice." Stirred by the music of cymbals, drums, horns, and flutes, the other priests danced themselves into a frenzy of excitement until, insensi-

---

6. Neumann, *Origins,* p. 50.
7. Davies, pp. 33, 50, 265.
8. Ibid., p. 186.
9. Casson, p. 68.
10. Here and following, see Frazer, pp. 403–414.

tive to pain, "they gashed their bodies with potsherds or slashed them with knives in order to bespatter the altar and the sacred tree with their flowing blood."

It was on the Day of Blood "and for the same purposes that the novices sacrificed their virility. Wrought up to the highest pitch of religious excitement, they dashed the severed portions of themselves against the image of the cruel goddess. These broken instruments of fertility were afterwards reverently wrapped up and buried in the earth or in subterranean chambers sacred to Cybele."

After the dead god was "mourned" in this way, the effigy was buried and the worshipers refrained from eating bread until the following day, March 25. This Festival of Joy (the Hilaria) was reckoned as the vernal equinox and celebrated as the divine resurrection with feasting, music, dancing, and sexual merrymaking (like the *letzachek* of the golden calf). "A universal license prevailed. Every man might say and do what he pleased."

March 26 was a day of rest after frolicking, and on March 27, the festival closed with a procession, in which a statue of Cybele was drawn in a wagon to a body of water, where the high priest immersed her and other sacred objects.

"Other Asiatic goddesses of fertility were served in like manner by eunuch priests," including Artemis of Ephesus and Astarte of Hierapolis. Astarte's "greatest festival of the year at Hierapolis fell at the beginning of spring, when multitudes thronged to the sanctuary from Syria and the regions about. While the flutes played, the drums beat, and the eunuch priests slashed themselves with knives, the religious excitement gradually spread like a wave among the crowd of onlookers."

A eunuch priest lived as a transvestite. "Then he ran through the city, holding the bloody pieces in his hand, till he threw them into one of the houses which he passed in his mad career. The household thus honored had to furnish him with a suit of female attire and female ornaments, which he wore for the rest of his life."

Similarly, "offerings to Artemis include phalli and all species of animals and fruits, for she was the protector of all life. . . . Mutilated beasts, from which 'a member was cut off,' were sacrificed to Artemis in Boeotia, Euboea, and Attica."[11] Artemis Orthia of Sparta was worshiped with the flagellation of boys.[12] The priests of Baal "cut themselves after their manner with knives and lancets, till the blood gushed out upon them."[13]

Not all of the goddess-god cults were quite as bloody as that of Cybele and Attis, but they were nevertheless all "phallus cults . . . invariably solemnized by women. . . . The orgiastic element does not occur only in the sex festivals, which are fertility festivals. Women also celebrated orgiastic rites among themselves."[14] The Talmud itself tells us that Maakhah, the queen mother of King Asa, carried around a phallus, which she used every day (A.Z. 44a; 1 Kings 15:13).

11. Gimbutas, Marija, *The Goddesses and Gods of Old Europe* (Los Angeles: University of California Press, 1982), p. 199.

12. Neumann, *Origins*, p. 84; Davies, p. 56.

13. Sayce, p. 106.

14. Neumann, *Origins*, pp. 52, 58.

We noted in the story of Sarah a distinction between a priestess who served a god and a priestess who served a goddess. The priestess of a god engaged in a ritual "sacred marriage" with the king on certain occasions. The priestess of a goddess, the *kedeshah*, was dedicated to a temple and had to have sex with the first man who came and paid the required price; hence she is called a "sacred prostitute." Nachmanides, in discussing Tamar, described the *kedeshah* as partially veiled. A secular source calls the veil "the symbol of *kedeshah*, the harlot. She is 'unknown,' anonymous."[15] In the case of the priestess serving a god, it is the king who embodies the god. In the case of the priestess serving the goddess, however, it is the priestess herself who embodies the goddess.

A distinction can also be made between a priest who served a god (alone) and a priest who served a goddess (with a god consort). The priest of a god had no sexual service to perform. The priest of a goddess became a eunuch and a transvestite—perhaps because men were "secondary introductions in the cult of goddesses who originally were served exclusively by women."[16] The castration of a priest was, in later times, a substitute for his actual sacrifice.[17]

The priests of the goddess often served as male prostitutes for men, a sexual function similar to that of the goddess's priestesses.

> Not only is the male sacrificed to the Great Mother, but he becomes her representative, a female wearing her dress. Whether he sacrifices his masculinity in castration or in male prostitution is only a variant. The eunuchs are, as priests, also sacred prostitutes, for the *kedeshim*, like the *kedeshot* or female sacred prostitutes, are representatives of the goddess whose orgiastic sexual character excels her fertility character. . . . The male votaries of the Great Goddess who prostituted themselves in her name were called *kelavim*, "dogs," and wore women's clothing.[18]

The Torah prohibited Jews from having a *kadesh* or a *kedeshah* in their religious rites, as well as from using as Temple donations the earnings of a common prostitute (*zonah*) or the "price of a dog" (Deut. 23:18–19). The "price of a dog" clearly refers to the earnings of a male prostitute.

The prohibition was not adhered to completely throughout Jewish history, however. "The *kadesh* was in the land" during the reigns of Rechavam and his son, Aviyam (1 Kings 14:24) and was driven out under Asa (1 Kings 15:12) and Jehoshafat (1 Kings 22:47). A "house of *kedeshim*" was even attached to the First Temple as part of the idolatrous worship promoted by King Menasheh, and was demolished by King Josiah (2 Kings 23:7). *Kedeshim* apparently died at a young age (Job 36:14).

The prevalence of eunuch priests in goddess worship was not just the reason for prohibiting maimed priests in Judaism, it was also the root of the prohibitions of

---

15. Ibid., p. 53.
16. Briffault, 3:213.
17. Neumann, p. 53.
18. Ibid., pp. 59, 61.

transvestism (Deut. 22:5) and of *any* castrated man entering "the assembly of Hashem" (Deut. 23:2).

The God of Israel may have developed into a father image precisely to get the Jewish priesthood away from the practices of priesthoods associated with the mother goddess and her boy-lover. Because the priest of a god was the only type of pagan service with *no sexual role,* the Torah had to use an all-male priesthood serving a *symbolically* male (without a phallus) God in order to eliminate sexuality from religious rites. There was no service for priestesses in Judaism because removing sex from religious ritual meant eliminating *all* the religious roles there were for women at that time. Even the Temple musicians, the Levites, were all-male because of paganism's complete eroticization of female singers.

THE CULT OF THE DEAD

> Let them [priests] not make bald patches on their heads. Let them not shave the edges of their beards nor gouge their flesh. They must be holy to their God and not profane the Name of their God. Since they bring the fire-offerings [*ishei*] of Hashem, the food of their God, they must be holy. (Lev. 21:5–6)

> You are children of Hashem your God. Do not make gashes in your skin and do not put a bald patch on your head [lit., "between your eyes"] for the dead. For you are a nation sanctified to Hashem your God. God has chosen you as a treasured nation from all the nations on the face of the earth. (Deut. 14:1–2)

Mourning and lamenting the death of the vegetation god spawned a massive death cult. The rejection of this death worship was the core of both the Jews' "chosenness" (their sanctification among the nations) and the priests' "holiness" (their sanctification among the Jews).

Osiris, whose burial served as the foundation of Egyptian lamentations and mummification rites, was mourned by worshipers who shaved their heads and gashed their skins (see chapter 10). Adonis of Byblos "was annually mourned, with a bitter wailing, chiefly by women," and by worshipers who "shaved their heads as the Egyptians did on the death of the divine bull Apis." Women who refused to do so "had to give themselves up to strangers on a certain day of the festival" and dedicate the earnings to Astarte.[19] Women's lamentations for the midsummer death of Tamuz of Babylonia took place even at the Temple in Jerusalem (Ezekiel 8:14).

Growing a long lock of hair which was then cut as an offering to a god is cited as a pagan (male) practice by the Midrash (DR 2:18). Egyptian priests "are always depicted as shaven-headed" and had to shave off all body hair as well.[20] "The sacrifice of men's hair is an ancient mark of priesthood. . . . Hairlessness is always associated with sexual abstinence and celibacy, that is, with symbolic self-castration. The

---

19. Frazer, pp. 384–385, 389–390.
20. Brier, p. 37.

shaving of the head played this part officially in the cult of the Great Mother. . . . The priests of Isis were shaved, and in some way not known to us, barbers were among the attendants of Astarte."[21]

Death worship reached its height in Egypt with the cult of the cadaver. The Egyptians believed the body had to be preserved intact in order to attain immortality in the afterlife. This life was simply a preparation for the life to come. Thus, a great deal of energy was put into preparation of one's tomb during one's lifetime, as well as into preservation of the body through a cult of youth and vanity whose main goal was to delay the aging process.

Mummification was important to preserve the corpse. Embalming procedures lasted for seventy days. In each phase of the process, certain spells were uttered and certain rituals performed. There is "some circumstantial evidence" that necrophilia was involved.[22] The fingers and toes of the wealthy were often encased in gold.[23]

The burial rite that finally took place was a lavish festival that sent the deceased off to the afterlife supplied with food and drink. Animals were sometimes mutilated rather than slaughtered for this purpose. "Numerous tomb reliefs and paintings show that one offering of food for the deceased was the foreleg of a calf, amputated while the animal was still alive. Exactly why it was crucial to perform a live amputation we do not know, but perhaps the ancient Egyptians insisted on an almost-live offering so that the deceased would be nourished by the living."[24]

Here we see the Torah's motivation for the Noachide law of *ever min hachai*, the prohibition of tearing the limb off a live animal. The high priest touched the mouth of the mummy with the leg of the bull and uttered an incantation to facilitate entry into the afterlife.

Royal tombs were fully furnished with couches, chairs, beds, boats, weapons, games, vessels, and clothing, jewelry, pictures, ornaments, amulets, ritual objects, and mementos. Professional mourners, mostly women, were hired to weep at funerals; they tore their clothes, "groaned and struck their heads incessantly."[25]

In reaction to the pagan priesthoods' obsession with death, the Jewish priesthood was to have *no contact* with the dead. A *kohen* could only be involved in the burial of his seven closest relatives: mother, father, sister, brother, son, daughter, and wife. The high priest could not even do these (Lev. 21:1–4, 21:11). Aharon, Elazar, and Itamar were not allowed to engage in any mourning—by growing their hair or tearing their clothing—for Nadav and Avihu (Lev. 10:6).

Ironically, however, the Jewish priesthood was "always side by side with death," for death was the penalty for transgressing even the most minute of the priestly regulations (LR 10:4). One mistake and he would be zapped.

---

21. Neumann, *Origins*, p. 59.

22. A. T. Sandison, "The Use of Natron in Mummification in Ancient Egypt," *Journal of Near Eastern Studies,* no. 22 (1963):259.

23. Brier, p. 82.

24. Ibid., p. 86.

25. Montet, pp. 310, 317, and 318.

PRIESTLY SERVICE AND THE FEMININE

The Jewish priesthood may have been exclusively male, but the realms in which it operated—the Tabernacle and the sacrificial altar—were both feminine in their symbolism. Furthermore, in order to enter the Tabernacle or approach the altar, a priest first had to wash his hands and feet in the laver made from copper mirrors, the instruments of women's self-reflection.

The Tabernacle's feminine imagery was described in chapter 19. We also noted, in reference to Dinah (chapter 8), an analogy between the Holy of Holies, where the Shekhinah dwells, and a woman's sexual and reproductive organs. The *parokhet*, the veil covering it, is thus a symbolic "hymen." The destruction of both Temples, in which pagan rulers ripped open the veil and invaded the Holy of Holies, is akin to the rape of a woman. Both involve the desecration of a "sacred vessel."

The Jewish ritual requirement that the Holy of Holies be entered only by the high priest once a year has its parallel in the sanctity attributed by Judaism to sexual relations: A woman is to be "entered" only by one man, within marriage, at the appropriate time(s). Both priest and woman immerse in a *mikvah* (ritual bath) before engaging in the consecrated activity. Also of interest in our analogy is the requirement in some sacrifices that the high priest sprinkle blood toward the *parokhet*—calling to mind the hymeneal blood of defloration.

The other realm in which the priests operated, the sacrificial altar, is also feminine. We have learned that "all women stand in the image and form of the altar" (chapter 19) and that the fire on this altar is *isheh* rather than *esh* (masculine). The blood of the sacrificial animals was poured at the *yesod,* or foundation, of the altar (Lev. 4:7, 4:18). *Yesod*, in the Tree of Life's symbolism of the human body, represents the genitals. Thus, as the blood sprinkled on the *parokhet* (inside the Tabernacle) is symbolic of hymeneal blood, the blood dashed at the base of the altar (outside the Tabernacle) might be said to represent menstrual blood.

The Tabernacle's feminine imagery—with its homebaked bread, the warm glow of the *menorah*'s light, and the sensual aroma of incense—is very nourishing and maternal. The fire on the altar is also feminine in essence, but not in a maternal sense. Fire is passionate, ecstatic, bold and brazen; it burns, scorches, and consumes. It is said to be punishment for those who are boastful, haughty, and overbearing (LR 7:6). The altar's fire symbolizes a more active, sexual aspect of female energy. It was the obligation of the male priests to keep this fire burning and never let it go out.

NADAV AND AVIHU

Fire came forth from before God and consumed the *olah* and the fat on the altar. All the people saw this and became ecstatic and fell on their faces. Aharon's [two oldest] sons, Nadav and Avihu, each took his fire pan and put fire and incense on it. They offered before God a strange fire which was not commanded of them. Fire came forth from before God and consumed them, and they died before God. (Lev. 9:24–10:2)

A number of reasons are given for why Nadav and Avihu were zapped (like the *olah* before them) for offering "strange fire" that was not commanded by God. One view is that they simply offered their incense at the wrong time. Others suggest that they entered the Tabernacle intoxicated, without washing, or without wearing the priestly vestments. Two other opinions are particularly compelling, however, because they relate to the essence of the fire, as discussed in the previous section.

- Although fire was going to come down from heaven (as it did in consuming the *olah*), Nadav and Avihu decided that the priests should add more fire to the altar themselves. Regardless of whether they were right or wrong, they had the arrogance to render a legal decision in Moses' presence instead of deferring to him as their teacher. Their brazenness even extended to desiring the deaths of Moses and Aharon so that they might succeed them as leaders. Because of this haughtiness, they met their death through fire, *midah kneged midah* (Rashi; Er. 63a; San. 52a).
- They were not married (*Zohar* III:5b). While men in general are considered incomplete if unmarried (chapter 1), this was accentuated for a priest. It was an absolutely essential requirement for a *kohen* to be married. (We will see why in chapter 29, where we discuss the *kohenet*.) Given the fire's symbolism of active, female sexual energy—which the priest has the duty to "keep burning"—the need for him to be married is obvious, at least on the metaphorical level.

The priestly installation united the masculine and feminine aspects of the Divine, but "Nadav and Avihu rose up and spoiled the general joy. . . . They came and linked all the others together and left Her outside. . . . Therefore a priest should not enter the sanctuary till he is married, in order that he may have a share in the union of the Community of Israel" (*Zohar* III:37b).

Nadav and Avihu purposely renounced marriage. "They were arrogant. Many women remained unmarried waiting for them, but they said, 'Our father's brother is a king, our mother's brother is a prince, our father is high priest, and we are both assistant high priests. What woman is worthy of us?'" (LR 20:10).

"While they gave up Woman completely, it was only to identify more strongly with the more spiritual feminine part of themselves that only God could fulfill," says one modern author. "They may consciously have been giving up relations with Woman as the Other only because theirs was a homosexual relationship to start with. In their attitude to God, they wanted to make themselves into the censers of the fire they carried, to act the part of pure Vessel, notably a woman's role."[26]

The notion that these two biological brothers had a sexual relationship with each other seems rather farfetched, but the point is again made clear that male without female is considered incomplete. Like the *olah*, which had to be male, Nadav and Avihu's total male energy was completely consumed by the female fire. Only their souls were burnt, however; their bodies and their clothing remained intact (San. 52a). Their deaths are said to have been "an atonement for Israel" (*Zohar* III:56b).

---

26. Freema Gottlieb, *The Lamp of God* (Northvale, NJ: Jason Aronson, 1989), p. 366.

*** 24 ***

Food and Sanctification

Shemini (9:1–11:47)

$\mathbf{F}$ood in Judaism is divided into the sacred (sacrificial) and the secular (nonsacrificial). Sacred food is called *kadashim*; it was the food from those sacrifices that were partially burned and partially eaten. Secular food is called *chullin*; it is common, everyday food, which was not offered as a sacrifice. Hence all food in post-Temple times is *chullin*.

There were two types of *kadashim*, defined by (1) where the food could be eaten and (2) who could eat it. Any person eligible to eat *kadashim* also had to be "*tahor*," which for now we will simply define as "ritually fit."

- *Makom kadosh,* "holy place," was the *mikdash*, the area contained within the Tabernacle courtyard. Any priest, even a maimed one, could eat this food, which came from a *minchah*, a *chatat*, or an *asham* (Lev. 6:9, 6:19; 17:6).
- *Makom tahor*, meaning "ritually fit place," was the camp in the wilderness, or the city of Jerusalem in Temple times. Any priest or layperson could eat this food, which came from a *shlamim*. The priest and the owner split the meat. The owner's portion, like the priest's, could be shared with others (Rashi).

The priest's portion, the breast and right leg, was called *trumah*. In the peace-offering, the breast, the leg, and the fat were taken by priest and owner together, ritually waved in the four directions, and then elevated up and down (as Jews today wave the Four Species at Sukkot). Technically, the "wave-offering" was called *tnufah*, while the "elevated-offering" was called *trumah*. *Tnufah* was "symbolic of preventing misfortune and bad winds," while *trumah* was "symbolic of keeping away evil dews" (Rashi).

Trumah, however, is used as a collective term not only for both of these portions, but for the priest's portion of *any* kind of offering, as well as for the priestly tithe of annual crops. The *kohanim* automatically received a small percentage of every Jewish farmer's harvest since they owned no land to farm for themselves. Thus, *trumah* was the priestly food that was "taken home," as opposed to the priestly food that had to be eaten "at work."

The right to eat *trumah* was the basic defining principle of the *kehunah.* Both *kohanim* (male priests) and *kohanot* (priestly women) ate *trumah*—as did their Canaanite slaves, who were owned as permanent household "possessions." No Levite or Israelite of either gender could eat *trumah*—not even Hebrew slaves and hired workers of priestly families, whose labor was merely a temporary acquisition.

KODESH AND CHOL

Kadashim and *chullin,* sacred and secular food, are examples of the sacred-secular *(kodesh-chol)* dichotomy in other realms as well. *Kodesh*—Kuf, Dalet, Shin (קדש)—is something sanctified through separation, its use being rare and precious. K-D-SH is the root of *kedushah* (sanctity), *kiddush* (sanctification of wine), *kaddish* (sanctification of the dead), *kiddushin* (sanctification of sex), the *mikdash* (the sanctified area of the Tabernacle and its courtyard), and *kadashim* (sanctified food). It is also the root of the "sacred" prostitute (*kadesh* and *kedeshah*).

Chol—Chet, Lamed (חל)—means "everyday," as in *chullin* and *chol hamoed,* an intermediate day of a weeklong festival (Passover and Sukkot). *Chol hamoed* possesses less *kedushah* than *yom tov,* the first and last days of a festival.

CH-L is the root of *chilel,* to "profane," meaning to "secularize" something sacred and precious through common everyday use. A *chalal* is a *kohen* who has lost his priestly status, which means he simply has the status of a regular Israelite male. *Chilul Hashem* is the desecration (desacralizing) of God's Name, and *chilul habat* is the desecration of one's daughter. In all these cases, something that should be consecrated—set aside as precious—is made common through everyday use.

TUMAH AND TAHARAH

> You shall distinguish between the sacred [*kodesh*] and the secular [*chol*], and between the *tamae* and the *tahor.* (Lev. 10:10)

Tamae (טמא) and *tahor* (טהור) are difficult and challenging concepts to understand. Here, *tamae* is parallel to the sacred and *tahor* is parallel to the secular, contradicting the usual association of *tamae* with the nonsacred and *tahor* with the sacred. This is because a person who is *tamae,* or in a state of *tumah,* may not enter the *mikdash* or eat *kadashim.* A person who is *tahor,* or in a state of *taharah, may* enter or eat. *Tumah* and *taharah* together form a cycle that affected every Jew on a regular basis during Tabernacle and Temple times.

Thus, we can see an interesting dichotomy. *Tamae*, which is linguistically parallel to K-D-SH in the verse, is the state in which one must *stay away from* K-D-SH. Since K-D-SH involves sanctity through separation, any *further* separation, such as this state of *tumah*, must surely only *add* holiness.

Tamae and *tahor* are Hebrew words that have become severely distorted through translation into English. *Tamae* has been translated as "unclean," "defiled," or "impure," while *tahor* has been translated as "clean" or "pure." These terms have no relation whatsoever to physical cleanliness or dirt. Putting "ritually" in front of any of the English words does nothing, unfortunately, to clarify the Hebrew words. In order to fully explore their meanings and avoid any preconceived notions, I do not attempt to translate them.

Taharah

The Torah has so far used *tahor* in reference to gold, incense, the sky, and animals.

- *Zahav tahor,* "pure gold," was used to make certain items in the Tabernacle (Ex. 25); it means "complete" gold as opposed to gold-plated or an alloy.
- The incense is called *tahor kodesh* (Ex. 30:35). Here, too, the meaning of "complete" is possible, since the context is the mixture of individual spices. Their combination is "holy"—that is, they form a whole that is greater than the sum of its parts.
- The sky is called *tohar* (Ex. 24:10), which means clear and (completely) blue—the perfect sky on a bright, sunny, cloudless day.
- Animals on the ark are categorized as *"tahor"* and *"not tahor"* (Gen. 7:2; 7:8). This corresponds to the kosher and nonkosher species, respectively. The notion of completeness is again present, for *"tahor"* is spelled fully, with a Vav, and *"not tahor"* is spelled without the Vav.

    Tahor as "complete" takes on yet another dimension when Noach offers sacrifices from all of (completely from) the birds, but only some of (partly from) the beasts (Gen. 8:20). Even though all the animals are *tahor*, the birds are *tahor* with a Vav and the beasts are *tahor* without a Vav.
- The Hivite women and children taken as captives in Shechem had to *hitaher,* "become *tahor*," in order to enter Jacob's household. They did so by throwing away their idols and immersing themselves in a *mikvah* (Gen. 35:2).

Tumah

The Torah has, until Leviticus, used *tamae* in only one instance: the rape of Dinah. The prince of Shechem *timae* Dinah by raping her, and the city of Shechem *timu* Dinah by not bringing him to justice (Gen. 34:5, 34:13, 34:27). *Tumah*, the state in which one may not enter the Tabernacle, is in this case used to refer to the entry of a woman against her will. Thus, we can again see the Dinah–Tabernacle analogy.

Tumah is not mentioned at all in Exodus, even though Egypt (and idolatry in general) was considered a major source of *tumah*. In Leviticus, *tumah* starts to be used to describe what has, until then, only been called "not *tahor*"—namely, the nonkosher animals.

Nonkosher animals are those species that may not be eaten by Jews. Gentiles, however, may eat them. The only Torah law for a gentile regarding the eating of meat is to not tear a limb off a living animal. A gentile may even eat blood in meat.

KASHRUT: THE DIETARY LAWS

You shall distinguish between the *tamae* and the *tahor*, and between the animal that may be eaten and the animal you may not eat. (Lev. 11:47)

This verse parallels Lev. 10:10 (cited above), which was spoken to the priests; this one was spoken to all of Israel. The parallel indicates that a Jew's body is sanctified through *kashrut* just as the Tabernacle is sanctified through *tumah* and *taharah*. Both the body and the Tabernacle can only be "entered" by what is *tahor*.

Kashrut, the set of dietary laws incumbent upon a Jew, consists of four major principles: three concerning the consumption of animal flesh, and the fourth comprising regulations concerning wine, cheese, oil, and bread. Judaism views the desire to eat animal flesh as a human weakness to which God conceded after the Flood but that will end in the Messianic Era (except, perhaps, for a feast of the Leviathan, a whale-type fish).

The three meat principles are the following.

Permitted animals: Certain animals may be eaten, while others may not. The distinction between kosher and nonkosher animals occurs at all levels—mammals, birds, reptiles, amphibians, and fish. Species on each level that are carnivorous or predatory or that eat waste matter are forbidden "on account of their cruel nature" (Nachmanides). The permitted species on each level are herbivorous.

Ritual slaughter: Mammals and birds permitted to be eaten must be slaughtered "ritually," that is, by a method called *shechitah*. *Shechitah* itself involves a vast body of laws, specifying everything down to the very sharpness of the knife. It is designed to be the most painless way possible of slaughtering an animal. The animal's blood is completely drained out. A kosher animal that dies on its own or is killed any way besides *shechitah* may not be eaten. A Jew, therefore, may not hunt animals for meat, eat *nevelah* (carrion, or an animal carcass), or eat *trefah* (an animal that dies from a fatal organic flaw). The latter term is the source of *treif* as slang for nonkosher.

Separation of meat and milk: After a permitted animal has been ritually slaughtered and its blood has been drained, the meat may then be eaten—but not in any combination with dairy products. The prohibition comes from the Torah's literal admonition against boiling a baby *goat* in its *mother's* milk (Ex. 23:19, 34:26; Deut. 14:21). It refers to the practice of cooking the meat of any mammal in the fluid of its mammary glands, for if one may not cook an animal in its mother's milk, how much more so may one not cook an animal in its own milk!

The separation of meat and milk legally extends to eating *any* warm-blooded animal flesh with milk—even birds, which do not have mammary glands. Nor does the "mother–child" nature of the prohibition extend to other species; hence, one may eat eggs with chicken. The laws of meat and milk form the basis for the "kosher kitchen"—the practice of keeping separate dishes, cups, pots, utensils, dishpans, sponges, dish-drainers, dishwashers, counters, and even ovens for meat and dairy foods.

Fish and eggs, although animal, are considered *pareve*, neither meat nor milk, and may be eaten with either one. While eating fish with a meat meal is permissible, observant Jews nevertheless use a different plate and fork for it. This practice of distinguishing fish from meat ever so slightly is a symbolic reminder that cold-blooded and warm-blooded creatures are not quite the same.

TUMAH AND ANIMALS

Let us now return to the first principle, permitted animals. Kosher mammals have two traits: their hooves are split and they chew their cud. Split hooves and chewing its cud are not the *reasons* an animal is permitted but are simply the *signs* by which one may be recognized (Maimonides, *Guide of the Perplexed* III:48).

While most nonkosher mammals *neither* have split hooves *nor* chew their cud, four mammals are specifically named because they have one trait but not the other: The camel, hyrax, and hare chew their cud but have toes or paws; the pig has split hooves but does not chew its cud. Nonkosher mammals are called "*tamae*": not only may they not be eaten, but a person who touches their carcasses becomes *tamae* and may not enter the *mikdash* or eat *kadashim* (Lev. 5:2, 11:4–8, 11:24–28).

The *tumah* conveyed by touching an animal carcass is called *nevelah*, and applies to the carcass of a kosher as well as a nonkosher mammal. Thus, unless a kosher mammal is sacrificed and eaten as *kadashim* or ritually slaughtered and eaten as *chullin*, its carcass, too, is *nevelah* (Lev. 11:39–40).

Forbidden fish, birds of prey, and insects are categorized as *sheketz,* to be "shunned" or "avoided" (Lev. 11:9–23). (The feminine form of this word, *shiktzah,* is the Jewish slang term for a gentile woman.) They are not called *tamae*, however, because although forbidden as food, their carcasses do not convey *tumah*.

Another eight animals—a combination of mammals and reptiles that burrow underground and live *in* the earth, including weasels, moles, mice, lizards, chameleons, and snails—form a category called *sheretz,* or "creepy-crawlies." Contact with their carcasses conveyed the *tumah* called *sheretz* (Lev. 11:29–38).

A person who was *tamae nevelah* or *tamae sheretz* had to immerse in a *mikvah* and wait until sundown to become *tahor*. Touching the carcass was a "milder" form of *tumah* than lifting the carcass, which meant that one's clothes had to be washed as well. This state of being "*tamae* for a day," until evening, is called *tumat erev* (Lev. 11:24–28).

Nor did only people become *tamae* through animal death. Any article of wood, cloth, or leather became *tamae* from touching a carcass; it, too, had to be immersed in a *mikvah* and could not be used until sundown. A clay vessel that became *tamae* could not be made *tahor*, and it had to be broken. Moist food and water itself could become *tamae*, but the waters of a *mikvah* always remained *tahor* (Lev. 11:32–36). *Kadashim* that touched something or someone *tamae* could not be eaten and had to be burned (Lev. 7:19–21).

TUMAH AND BODILY MORTALITY

While animal carcasses were two major sources of *tumah*, a corpse (human carcass) conveyed the greatest *tumah* of all, the *tumah* of *met*. While contact with an animal carcass made a person *tamae* for a day, contact with a corpse made one *tamae* for a week, which is called *tumat shivah*. Anyone who touched a *tamae met* person also became *tamae*, but only for a day (Num. 19:11, 19:22).

The three sources of *tumah* we have named so far—*met*, *nevelah*, and *sheretz*—all come from contact with the dead. An Israelite was prohibited from entering the Tabernacle or eating *kadashim* after such contact; a *kohen*, however, was prohibited from even having such contact. The only exceptions, we have noted, were his seven closest relatives, and for the high priest, not even these were exempt. Since a *kohen* could not make himself *tamae* to bury a person, he certainly could not do so to bury an animal. Any *kohen*, however (even the high priest), had to become *tamae met* if he came upon a corpse with no one attending to its burial.

The other sources of *tumah*, those that do not come from dead bodies, are nevertheless connected to human mortality and concern a number of bodily fluids. Indeed, *tumah* may best be explained as *a condition affecting those forms of life that take on bodies and later shed them*—in other words, that undergo birth and death.

Creation, according to Maimonides (*Foundations of Torah* 2:3), takes three forms (*tzurot*) in relation to matter (*golem*). "Form" is an entity on the astral plane, just below the spiritual plane and just above the physical plane—it is the "shape" or "image" of the soul, like the image in a photograph. All three forms are alive, and each recognizes and knows its Creator according to its own level (ibid. 2:8, 3:9). The three are:

* Form with no matter—the angels, bodies of light, individual entities that do not have physical bodies.
* Form with fixed matter—the planets and stars, which have physical bodies but do not *change* those bodies—hence, they are not "born" and do not "die." Mars will always be Mars; it will not die and be reborn as another planet. Although we say that stars (including our own sun) "die" by exploding after billions of years, this is not "death" as the term is meant here. The stars and planets are called *tahor* (*Foundations of Torah* 3:1).
* Form with variable matter—humans, animals, plants, and minerals, which enter and leave physical bodies at birth and death. They do not leave their bodies by exploding in one big bang, but rather through gradual, stinking decay—decomposition into the elements from which they are composed. This type of form enters and leaves *a number of* physical bodies—in other words, it "reincarnates."

The *Zohar* (III:88a–b) discusses reincarnation as the reason a corpse should be buried by sundown:

> Before a person dies one beholds the Shekhinah, towards which the soul goes out in great yearning. . . . After the soul has left the body and the body remains without breath, it is forbidden to keep it unburied. For a dead body which is left unburied for 24 hours causes a weakness in the limbs of the Chariot and prevents God's design from being fulfilled.
>
> For perhaps God decreed that [the deceased] should undergo a transmigration at once on the day of death, which would be better [for the deceased]. But as long as the body is not buried the soul cannot go into the presence of the Holy One nor be transferred into another body. For a soul cannot enter a second body until the first is buried, just as a man should not take a second wife until the first is buried.
>
> Another reason why the body should be buried on the same day is that when the soul departs from the body it cannot enter the other world until it is invested with another body formed of light. . . . So long as the body remains unburied the soul suffers pain and the spirit of *tumah* rests upon the body, and therefore the body should not be kept overnight, because by night the spirit of *tumah* spreads over the earth, looking for a body without a soul to make it more *tamae*. . . . The body without the spirit is *tamae*.

That *tumah* is a condition affecting forms whose bodies decompose makes it readily apparent why *tumah* would be conveyed by a carcass, human or animal. It also provides a reason why carnivorous animals are not kosher—they *contain tumah*, the animal remains within their digestive systems. In addition, *tahor* now makes sense as meaning *complete*—it is body–spirit unity, which begins at birth and ends at death.

✻✻✻ 25 ✻✻✻

Childbirth

Tazria (12:1–13:59)

And God spoke to Moses, saying, "When a woman conceives and gives birth to a male, she is tamae *for seven days, as in the days of her menstrual flow she is* tamae. *On the eighth day the flesh of his foreskin shall be circumcised. For 33 days she sits in* [be-] *the blood of* taharah. *She may not touch any* kodesh, *and she may not come into the* mikdash *until the days of her* taharah *are fulfilled. If she gives birth to a female, she is* tamae *for two weeks as if menstruating. For 66 days she sits on* [al] *the blood of* taharah.

And when her days of taharah *are fulfilled for a son or a daughter, she shall bring a sheep in its first year for an* olah, *and a pigeon or a turtledove for a* chatat, *to the priest at the entrance of the Tabernacle. He shall offer it before Hashem and will bring atonement upon her, and she will become* tahor *from the fountain of her blood* [mekor damehah].*This is the law of the* yoledet [*a woman who gives birth*], *for a male or a female.*

If she cannot afford a lamb, she should take two turtledoves or two pigeons, one for an olah *and one for a* chatat, *and the priest will bring atonement upon her and she will become* tahor. (Lev. 12:1–8)

The *yoledet*, a woman after childbirth, goes through a complete cycle of *tumah* and *taharah*—forty days for a boy and eighty days for a girl. Why is the cycle of double length when the baby is a girl? Why does the circumcision of a baby boy occur at the woman's transition point from *tumah* into *taharah*? Why do women have to bring sacrifices after birth, especially sin-offerings? What does it mean for a woman to be "*tahor* from the fountain of her blood"? What, indeed, is the "fountain of her blood"?

TUMAH, TAHARAH, AND BIRTH

We have begun to understand *tumah* and *taharah* as a cycle pertaining to forms of life that acquire bodies at birth and shed them at death. *Taharah* is a state of completeness, of body–soul unity. *Tumah* is the state of the body without the soul, and it is even said to "rest" upon a corpse prior to its burial. Three kinds of *tumah* come from death, when the body *loses* its soul: *met* (human), *nevelah* (mammal), and *sheretz* (creepy-crawlies). However, it is the person *in contact with* the entity who becomes *tamae*.

Another kind of *tumah*, *yoledet*, comes from birth, when the body *acquires* its soul. Unlike death *tumah*, birth *tumah* only comes from *human* birth. Like death *tumah*, it is the person *in contact with* the entity who becomes *tamae*. Hence, the mother, but not the baby, is *tamae* in birth *tumah*. A child comes into the world with no "original sin." Nor is the *tumah* of the mother in any way related to "original sin," although it has certainly been misunderstood as such.

A process has taken place within the *yoledet*'s body, of which birth is only the culmination. That *tumah* affects the birth *giver* appears to indicate that the soul enters the body at some time during pregnancy—not necessarily at the moment of conception, as Catholicism asserts, but not at the last moment (when leaving the womb), either.

The Catholic idea that the soul enters the body immediately at conception is the inevitable result of an overemphasis on the spiritual role of the sperm. Aristotelian philosophers believed that the sperm alone formed the baby, while the mother was simply the fertile field. A fertile field provides nutrients to a seed, but it does not otherwise contribute to its essence (its genetic code). Now, of course, we know that that analogy of biological motherhood is completely inaccurate.

The father's biological influence on the child *begins and ends* at conception, while the mother's biological influence continues throughout pregnancy (and even after birth, if she breastfeeds). Every emotion that is registered in her body is also transmitted to the fetus. The soul enters at some point or points during the nine-month period—whatever that means. The Torah has indicated, in discussing animals, that the blood is the medium for the soul, so it makes sense to suppose that the human soul enters the body through the mother's bloodstream during pregnancy.

We have no way of determining, predicting, or controlling such a phenomenon, nor should science even try. This is the mystery and the sacredness of the beginnings of life, as well as of the spiritual power inherent in femaleness. This is *mekor damehah*, "the fountain of her blood." It is the woman's "holy of holies," the source of life itself.

The *yoledet* is in a state of *tumah* for one week after the birth of a boy and two weeks after the birth of a girl. During this time her status is the same as when she is in *niddah*, or menstruating (the subject of chapter 26). In this period of *tumah*, she may not enter the *mikdash* or eat *kadashim*, nor may she have sex with her husband.

The *yoledet* immerses in a *mikvah* after this period, and she then spends another thirty-three or sixty-six days in the "blood of *taharah*," which is often translated as "blood of purity" or "blood of purification." Her blood is "purifying,"—becoming *tahor*—in the sense of completing, healing, repairing, and returning to being a self-sufficient circulatory system once again; in other words, to serving her body alone and no longer forming another entity as well.

During these days of *taharah*, the *yoledet* may still not enter the *mikdash* or eat *kadashim*, but she *may* have sex with her husband, according to biblical law, because "her husband is *chullin*" (Chul. 31a). Sexual relations are thus *chol*—common and everyday—while the periods of separation during menstruation and childbirth are *kodesh*—a form of sanctification through separation.

There were actually three distinct phases for a *yoledet* (Yev. 74b; Zev. 33b; Neg. 14:3):

- *tumah*, seven or fourteen days, after which she could have sex;
- *taharah*, thirty-three or sixty-six days, after which she could eat *trumah* if she was a *kohenet*; and
- offering the sacrifice, after which she could eat *kadashim* (e.g., the Pesach sacrifice).

Although sex was biblically forbidden only during the one to two weeks of *tumah*, it became rabbinically forbidden in the one or two months of *taharah* as well (Pes. 113b; Chul. 109b; *Yoreh Deah* 194:1). In practice, then, a *yoledet* may not resume sexual relations until forty days after the birth of a boy or eighty days after the birth of a girl.

If the baby was a hermaphrodite, the mother was *tamae* for fourteen days and *tahor* until the end of the fortieth day, thus combining the female and male time periods (Bik. 4:2, 4:3; Nid. 21a, 29a; B.B. 127a). The existence of hermaphrodites was taken for granted in the Talmud. It is only due to the surgical knife that society can forget that God does indeed create such people.

POSTPARTUM PEACE

The Arab women of Oman have a saying, "Out goes the baby and in goes the man," to refer to the immediate resumption of sexual intercourse after childbirth. The Baluchi, an ethnic minority of Oman, abstain from intercourse from the sixth month of pregnancy on, and the men "show patience" by waiting another forty days after the birth. On the other hand, "Arab husbands demand their right up to the last day," and, according to the women's slogan, as soon as possible after birth.[1]

Recovery after childbirth is both physical and emotional. The more tranquility a woman can provide herself and her new baby, the easier the postpartum period will be for her.

When a woman gives birth, there is a vaginal discharge from her uterus, similar to menstruation, that lasts for ten to twenty days and gradually changes from red blood to white mucus. This is called lochia, and it consists of the remaining cells of the

---

1. Unni Wikan, *Behind the Veil in Arabia: Women in Oman* (Chicago: University of Chicago Press, 1991), p. 41.

placental site and the uterine lining.[2] During this time, it is absolutely essential that nothing enter the vagina, due to the risk of pelvic infection. Tampons as well as penises are forbidden. Medical doctors have traditionally recommended a six-week period of abstention from intercourse.

Six weeks is also the time required for the involution (return to normal size) of the abdominal cavity and wall. Menstruation returns in six to ten weeks in mothers who are not breastfeeding, and later in those who are. Hormonal fluctuations are much greater after pregnancy than menstruation. These are just some of the *physical* changes that a new mother undergoes.

The emotional changes last even longer. Postpartum depression has been medically defined as occurring in three stages: the first ten days, the next three months, and a final three months. However, women's experiences indicate that the medical definition is conservative; postpartum depression often lasts beyond six months, and even as long as two years. Postpartum depression is a common phenomenon, ranging from 60 to 85 percent among first-time mothers, "with statistics slightly higher for women having a second child."[3]

Most women have a decreased interest in sexual activity during the early postpartum period, if for no other reason than sheer fatigue. Getting a full night's sleep is a much greater pleasure than sex at this point. The physical contact of mother and child, especially during breastfeeding, satisfies many of the woman's needs for closeness and physical intimacy while excluding her husband, even if he is a highly involved father. He may even feel jealous about no longer being the sole object of his wife's nurturance, and indeed, some new fathers act more like children who have lost a mother than adults who have had a child.

To provide the opportunity for physical and emotional recovery for a woman after childbirth is extremely important, especially in cultures where a husband can "demand" his sexual "rights." Even in cultures shaped by Torah values, where sex is not the husband's right and the woman's duty, there is still a need to release women from any guilt they might feel for "depriving" their husbands.

One male childbirth educator suggests that the traditional medical six-week ban on intercourse "is really a matter of convention and is falling by the wayside. Four-week checkups are the rule in some practices. The French suggest waiting three weeks. . . . Three weeks seems to be about average."[4] In our sex-obsessed culture, where abstinence may be viewed as "unhealthy"—and "French" is often used as a synonym for "erotic"—pressure on a woman to be sexual soon after childbirth is perhaps greater than ever. This is just one result of the "sexual revolution," which liberated male sexuality from previous restraints imposed by religious authority. The sexual revo-

---

2. Boston Women's Health Book Collective, *Our Bodies, Ourselves* (New York: Simon and Schuster, 1973), p. 205; Diane Lynch-Fraser, *The Complete Postpartum Guide* (New York: Harper and Row, 1983), p. 48.

3. Lynch-Fraser, pp. 10, 16–17.

4. Carl Jones, *After the Baby Is Born* (New York: Dodd, Mead and Co., 1986), pp. 157–158.

lution did not really liberate female sexuality, however, but only made it more available for common use, so that it became like *chullin*.[5]

The male author cited here is certainly *not* advocating that male sexual needs take priority over those of women. "Lower maternal sexual desire is common for several weeks, and perhaps even for a few months," he notes, suggesting that the "best way to get through this period" is for both partners to be open and sensitive to each other— "the woman generous, the man understanding."[6] His view is very egalitarian, but the reality is illustrated by an accompanying quote from a woman who says that she would feel guilty if she denied her husband's sexual needs just because her own have declined.

The Torah's view, on the other hand, is not egalitarian but unabashedly prowoman: women do not have to be "generous"; a period of postpartum recovery *free from sexual pressure* has been legislated for them. If a husband is "understanding," all the better—but even if he is not, he still must obey the law.

Why should the *tumah–taharah* cycle be twice as long for a daughter as for a son? Since *tumah* has been mistakenly defined as "defilement," feminists have seen "double time for a daughter" as just more evidence that the Torah is innately misogynist—in other words, a female baby makes the mother "doubly dirty." However, this is not the case. Instead, a postpartum sexual taboo gives the woman space to focus on bonding with her baby, without having to divide her bodily affection between her baby and her husband. The Torah gives her twice as long with a daughter as with a son.

Studies have been reported that indicate that mothers pay more attention to baby boys than baby girls, picking them up and talking to them more as well as breastfeeding them longer. This may be a result of boy babies being more aggressive and fussy—in other words, the squeaky wheel gets the grease. Perhaps, however, it is one of the more insidious results of male supremacy—that women themselves internalize the value of male superiority and end up perpetuating it, often quite unconsciously, through different ways of relating to sons and daughters. (Similar research has also demonstrated that favoritism is shown to boys by teachers in classrooms and nurses in maternity wards.) Being a woman does not automatically make one prowoman, anymore than being a Jew automatically makes one pro-Jewish.

The Torah gives mothers twice as long to bond exclusively with a daughter than a son because the daughter needs it. Both girls and boys need healthy bonding with the mother in order to form stable, sane identities. However, the boy eventually must switch his sense of gender identification to the male (ideally his father). The daughter's gender identification, however, remains with the mother and therefore requires a firmer foundation. The Torah, in its infinite wisdom, provides the opportunity for this.

Since circumcision of a boy is done on the eighth day, after the mother's seven days of *niddah*, mothers of girls might want to consider holding a *simchat bat*—a

---

5. For the classic analysis of the differences between "sexual liberation" philosophy and feminism, see Anselma Dell'Olio, "The Sexual Revolution Wasn't Our War," *Ms.*, Spring 1972, pp. 104–110.

6. Jones, p. 160.

ritual that has been developed to celebrate the birth of a daughter—on the fifteenth day, after the mother's fourteen days of *niddah*. To do so instead of holding it on the eighth day, in imitation of a son's ritual, would make the ceremony more uniquely female.

CHILDBIRTH, SANCTITY, AND SEPARATION

A *yoledet* may not enter the *mikdash* or eat *kadashim*, even during her days of being *tahor*. This is somewhat perplexing, since separation from *kodesh* is the basic definition of being *tamae*, and *tahor* has been the opposite. Here the *entire cycle* of *tumah* and *taharah* is defined by separation from K-D-SH.

The separation from K-D-SH that characterizes *tumah* has mistakenly been viewed as due to a defilement or lack of holiness. Actually, *tumah* is an accentuated state of holiness. An unburied corpse is sacred (even though it rots and stinks physically); that is why it conveys *tumah*.

Similarly, a woman who is *tamae* through childbirth or menstruation, which are normal physiological functions, is in a state of *kodesh*; when she is *tahor* and having sex with her husband, she is in *chol,* or common, everyday life. The reason why a woman may not touch *kodesh* while she is *kodesh* may be similar to why you do not have a wedding on a Jewish holiday—you should not mix two religious celebrations, festivities, or kinds of holiness.

The woman bleeding from her internal fountain is as sacred as the Holy of Holies is for 364 days of the year, and neither may be entered at these times. If a baby has been delivered through a Caesarean section, the mother is not *tamae* because birth did not occur "through the normal passage" (Mak. 14b; Nid. 40a). If a *tamae* person enters the Tabernacle through the roof, there is no culpability, for that is also not "the normal passage" (Shevu. 17b).

THE SACRIFICES

The *yoledet* must bring an *olah* and a *chatat* to the Tabernacle on the 41st or 81st day, after the entire *tumah–taharah* cycle is complete.

The *chatat* is required because sometimes a woman, screaming in the agony of labor pains, swears she will never have sex again. (Who can blame her?) She usually feels differently after the birth is over, but because she has "fluttered in her heart" and made a vow she will not keep, she must bring a bird-offering to atone for its unintentional violation (GR 20:7; Nid. 31a).

If a husband at any time vows not to have sex with his wife, she must consent to it for one week (Hillel) or two weeks (Shammai); then he must either give up his vow or divorce her (Ket. 61b; Ed. 4:10). The time period given for the husband's vow is based on the *tamae* period of the woman after birth, with Hillel opting for the "boy time" while Shammai holds by "girl time."

The reason for the *olah* is not so clear. One source suggests that it is offered in gratitude for a safe delivery,[7] yet one would expect a *todah*—a *shlamim* offered in thanks for rescue from grave peril—to be used in such a case. Furthermore, if the woman offered a *chatat* and then died, her heirs had to bring her *olah*, while if she brought an *olah* and died, they did not bring her *chatat* (Kid. 13b; Men. 4b).

Clearly, a woman needs nothing to nullify an unfulfilled vow if she is dead, but if she is dead, why would an *olah* need to be brought if its purpose is to give thanks for a safe delivery? That would be an irony that no one mourning the woman would fail to notice. The *olah*, the completely burnt-offering, simply represents the completion of her cycle. Its purpose of atoning for the neglect of positive commandments is also relevant here, as a woman in labor on *Shabbat*, for instance, might not have time to light candles or hear *kiddush*.

A woman may bring two birds if she cannot afford a sheep and a bird. Her husband, however, must give her to bring whatever he is capable of giving. "A husband must bring a sacrifice of the rich for his wife, and likewise for every obligatory sacrifice of hers," for he undertakes such liabilities in the *ketubah* (B.M. 104a).

CIRCUMCISION AND WOMEN'S BLOOD

A boy must be circumcised on the eighth day after birth, when his mother passes from *tumah* into *taharah*. Circumcision is required only of *Jewish* males, just as *tumah* and *taharah* apply only to Jews and not to gentiles (Ed. 5:1).

The definition of a newborn Jewish male includes a gentile baby boy adopted by Jewish parents, as well as an adult male gentile who converts to Judaism. Both must have a symbolic blood-pricking even if they are already circumcised. Thus, it is *the shedding of the blood,* not the physical absence of the foreskin itself, that is the key factor (Shab. 135a).

Although the command to circumcise boys on the eighth day was given by God to Avraham, it was given again at Sinai in the midst of the laws of childbirth. This is not coincidental. Drawing blood from the male genitals is placed in the midst of the commands regarding a woman's blood in childbirth because circumcision is a kind of *tikkun*—a repair, an atonement, or a compensation for female bloodshed and its accompanying biological pain.

Women deal with pain and bleeding *on a regular basis* in their reproductive organs, through menstruation and childbirth. Men have to experience pain and bleeding in their reproductive organs *just this once*. Opponents of circumcision who fear traumatic consequences from "pain to the baby" should understand that this is not even 1 percent of the pain routinely experienced by women in labor or even in menstrual cramps. Nonetheless, no one worries that those forms of pain might be permanently traumatizing.

"In this world a woman bears children in pain," but in the Messianic Era she will not (LR 14:9). The foreskin was created at the time of exile from the Garden of Eden

---

7. Weissman, 3:115.

along with the hymen, menstruation, and labor—the three sources of female blood. The fingernail-like sheaths over Adam and Chavah's bodies fell off, leaving only a foreskin covering him and a hymen covering her. Circumcision thus bears some analogy to female defloration.

Circumcision is mystically described as perfecting men spiritually, as symbolized by the letter Heh that was added to Avraham's name at the time of his circumcision. "Before a man is circumcised he is not attached to the Name of God, but when he is circumcised he enters into the Name and is attached to it." Avraham attained higher levels of vision with God after being circumcised (*Zohar* I:89a). He "became associated with the letter Heh, and the Shekhinah rested on him" (*Zohar* I:93a). Before circumcision, "Avram" (without the Heh) was "defective" (*Zohar* I:200b). However, the "defect" was spiritual, not physical. The penis is, in some symbolic way, "defective morally. The bodily pain caused to that member is the real purpose of circumcision." In this view of Maimonides (*Guide of the Perplexed* III:49), circumcision diminishes male sexual arousal without destroying it. It is just one example of how the Torah harnesses male sexual energy and contains its expression within certain boundaries or limits.

The argument as to whether circumcision has any medical or health benefits is, from this spiritual view, basically irrelevant. It is certainly not damaging or permanently traumatizing, for God does not command people to be self-destructive. However, neither can it be explained solely in terms of physical benefits, any more than the meaning of the dietary laws can be reduced to potential physical health benefits. There is a spiritual element in both that has nothing to do with physical effects.

Circumcision does something to a boy to bring him *up to the level* of *women*. This is indicated by the fact that women are considered in Judaism to be "already circumcised," for one who is uncircumcised may not participate in eating the Pesach sacrifice, and this does not refer to women (Ex. 12:48). This should make it clear that any attempt to use circumcision to exclude women or to imply that men have an exclusive covenant with God is a grand fallacy. Assertions by male Jews, for example, that "one must have a member to be a member"[8] or have a penis to be a part of the covenant are absolutely invalid from an authentic Torah point of view and reduce circumcision to some kind of Jewish tribal phallic rite.

MALE INITIATION RITES

Jewish circumcision is not a phallic male initiation rite. It can, however, be distorted into a kind of crude phallus worship when it is used as an excuse to celebrate the birth of boys more lavishly than the birth of girls or when it is the only Jewish ritual that a person practices.

---

8. Howard Eilberg-Schwartz, "Why Not the Earlobe?" *Moment* 17:1 (Feb. 1992):28–33. The primary fault of his analysis is that he seeks to *assimilate* Jewish circumcision to pagan phallic tribal rites, when what he should be doing is *distinguishing* it.

The latter was well illustrated on the television show *thirtysomething,* in which a Jewish man, Michael Steadman, was married to a gentile woman, Hope. When their second child, a son, was born, Michael agonized over whether to circumcise him. Suddenly he began to question what being Jewish really meant. Although Michael carried on no other Jewish traditions in his life, it seemed to him that this one should not be broken, for it linked him to his forefathers in a gut-level way unlike anything else.

Hope, as a result, thought this all very sexist. After all, Michael had not gone through a similar agony about his Jewish identity when their daughter, Janey, was born. He did not wonder if she *was* Jewish or if she *should* be, because such a decision did not have to be expressed on her body. *His entire sense of Jewishness came from his son's penis.* Unfortunately, Judaism takes the rap for being "sexist" in a situation like this, when actually it is a combination of assimilation and male supremacy that *reduces* Jewish observance to a ritual penis-clipping.

Most cultures have some form of initiation rite in which an adolescent male "becomes a man," through differentiation from women. Oddly, however, many of the rituals to accomplish this transition are *imitative* of women. Men's simulation of birth is called couvade, and their simulation of menstruation is known as saignade.[9]

In some societies there is a male lodge, set totally off limits to women, to which a boy goes at a certain age to live with the older men. From this "male womb" he is reborn, often through rituals that shed his blood supposedly as women shed theirs. For instance, men who have been subincised (have had the underside of the penis slit) must urinate squatting, like women; "the subincised penis is called *vagina* in sacred songs; blood squirting from the penis is described by words that mean 'women' or 'milk.'"[10]

Women's bleeding is natural, nonviolent, and occurs in a lifegiving context. Male bleeding—through subincision, scarification, flagellation, incision, or tattooing—is induced through slashing, gashing, sadism, and mutilation. This is what it has meant "to make a man out of" someone. If the boy is unable to endure this, he is a "sissy," which means woman-like or effeminate. This is also the root of the misogynist view of the female genitals as a "gash" or "wound."

"The basic theme of the initiatory cult . . . is that women, by virtue of their ability to make children, hold the secrets of life. Men's role is uncertain, undefined, and perhaps unnecessary. By a great effort man has hit upon a method of compensating himself for his basic inferiority. . . . Women, it is true, make human beings, but only men can make men."[11]

Male initiation ceremonies "serve to punctuate a growth-sequence that is inherently unpunctuated." While menarche, defloration, pregnancy, childbirth, lactation, and menopause are all clear physical demarcations of female stages of growth, "to

---

9. See Hays. pp. 53–58; Janice Delaney, Mary Jane Upton, and Emily Toth, *The Curse: A Cultural History of Menstruation* (New York: New American Library, 1977), pp. 205–211.

10. Delaney, Upton, and Toth, p. 209.

11. Margaret Mead, *Male and Female* (New York: William Morrow and Co., 1975), pp. 102–103.

achieve comparably dramatic sequences in a man's life, either something may be done to his body . . . or the society must itself introduce artificial social distinctions."[12]

While menarche was an individual rite, male initiation rites were conducted in groups.[13] A girl's menarche *was* her *bat mitzvah*, or puberty rite. *Bar mitzvah*, on the other hand, was a social invention required as a civilized substitute for bloody male group rites. Modern secular male initiation rites, such as military training or fraternity hazing, may involve less *actual* male bloodshed but are characterized by the same sadism and violence.

Jewish circumcision, occurring as it does at birth rather than puberty, is *not* this type of male coming-of-age ceremony. Penis-cutting has been removed from the realm of "making boys into men" and redefined.

BOYS AND FRUIT TREES

"Happy are Israel who bring an offering willingly to the Holy One, for they bring their sons on the eighth day as an offering" (*Zohar* I:93a). A boy is circumcised at eight days old, just as an animal may not be sacrificed until it is eight days old (Ex. 22:29).

The wisdom of eight days is reflected in the fact that newborn infants tend to have a deficiency of Vitamin K, which is responsible for blood clotting. This deficiency only lasts for up to a week. Hence, circumcision was legislated to be done just at the time that the baby developed the means to deal with it.

The comparison of boys with sacrificial animals echoes several themes that we have discussed—*pidyon haben*, the substitution of animal sacrifices for human sacrifices, the similar mutilations of men and animals in pagan rites, and circumcision as an "atonement" for the mother's blood. The real symbolism of circumcision, however, lies not in animals but in fruit.

Orlah, which means "foreskin" and "uncircumcised," refers to any kind of sheath or cover. The fruit of a fruit tree is *orlah* for three years, *kadashim* in the fourth, and *chullin* in the fifth (Lev. 19:23–25). The link between fruit trees and circumcision is reflected in the practice of not cutting a baby boy's hair for three years. That, too, is *orlah*.

Those who circumcise their sons on the eighth day are likened to "a branch of those shoots which God planted in the Garden of Eden" (*Zohar* I:93a). Avraham was said to be "pruned" through circumcision in order to bring forth the "blossoms" (*Zohar* 97b). "Before Avraham was circumcised he was, as it were, covered over, but as soon as he was circumcised he became completely exposed to the influence of the Shekhinah, which therefore rested on him in full and perfect measure" (*Zohar* 98b).

Isaac was born only after Avraham was circumcised to show how much God loved Avraham, for "in this way it was made certain that his seed should be holy. . . . For

---

12. Ibid., pp. 175, 180.
13. Delaney, Upton, and Toth, p. 209.

had Avraham begotten before he was circumcised, his seed would not have been holy, as it would have issued from the state of *orlah*" (*Zohar* 103b).

Orlah as a "covering" that desensitizes is what is meant by "uncircumcised ears" (Jeremiah 6:10), which are stopped up and cannot hear, or an "uncircumcised heart" (Jer. 9:25), which is closed and cannot understand. Moses pleaded with God not to make him the spokesman of the Jews because he had "uncircumcised lips," a speech defect (Ex. 6:12, 6:30). *Milah,* "circumcision," also means "word."

However, if an "uncircumcised" organ has a cover that desensitizes it, this is the *opposite* of Maimonides's claim that *circumcision* desensitizes male sexual desire. On the contrary, circumcision must *sensitize* the penis—but on a level of spiritual receptivity rather than mere physical sensation.

THE IMPORTANCE OF CIRCUMCISION

The duty of circumcising male babies, which is surely the most "male" *mitzvah* of the Torah, devolves only upon men. The father, not the mother, is obligated to have a boy circumcised (Kid. 1:7). If he neglects his duty, it falls upon the Jewish court or, eventually, the boy himself, who is subject to *karet* for failure to perform the *mitzvah* (Maimonides, *Circumcision* 1:1). Circumcision even supersedes the Sabbath when the latter is on the eighth day (Shab. 131b–132a).

Circumcision is one of only two positive commandments that receive *karet* for ignoring them. The other is eating the Pesach sacrifice (and a male had to be circumcised in order to do so). Usually there is no penalty for ignoring a positive command, and *karet* is otherwise given only for the violation of a prohibition.

The importance of circumcision was illustrated when Zipporah saved Moses' life by circumcising their son. The *Zohar* describes how "heaven and earth go on in their appointed course" as long as Jewish men observe this *mitzvah.* "But if Israel neglects this covenant, then heaven and earth are disturbed, and blessing is not granted to the world. Now in the time of the Judges the gentiles gained power over Israel only because they neglected this covenant" until Deborah brought them back to it (93b).

Circumcision was ridiculed and labeled "barbaric" by cultures that glorified the phallus, such as classical Greece. The pharaoh who arose in Egypt after Joseph's death did not permit circumcision (ER 1:8). Consequently, Jewish men in Egypt, except for the Levites, ignored the *mitzvah* and had to have a "mass circumcision" at the time of the slaughter of the Pesach ram (ER 19:5).

Although circumcision is not incumbent upon the mother, Jewish women have often been as zealous about it as Zipporah. If a son dies from circumcision, his brothers need not be circumcised. However, R. Nathan tells of two different women who each brought their *third* sons to be circumcised after the first *two* had died (Shab. 134a). Maimonides stipulates that such a woman should wait more than eight days to circumcise the third son (*Circumcision* 2:18).

Jewish women have died rather than repudiate the practice. In the days of Syrian-Greek oppression, Jews were forbidden to observe the Sabbath, *Rosh Chodesh*, and circumcision:

> So drastic was the king's edict that when a man was discovered to have circumcised his son, he and his wife were hanged along with the child. A woman gave birth to a son after her husband's death and had him circumcised when he was eight days old. With the child in her arms, she went up on top of the wall of Jerusalem and cried out, "We say to you, wicked Bagris [the governor]: This covenant of our fathers which you intend to destroy shall never cease from us nor from our children's children." She cast her son down to the ground and flung herself after him so that they died together. Many Israelites of that period did the same, refusing to renounce the covenant of their fathers.[14]

The same pagan rulers who considered circumcision to be mutilating and cruel did not hesitate to plunder Jerusalem and slaughter its inhabitants. Pain is indeed in the eye of the beholder.

---

14. "The Scroll of the Hasmoneans," in Philip Birnbaum, *Daily Prayer Book* (New York: Hebrew Publishing Co., 1977), pp. 718–720.

✳✳ 26 ✳✳

Menstruation

Metzora (14:1–15:33)

There are three sources of "death *tumah*"—*met*, *nevelah*, and *sheretz*—and three sources of "procreative *tumah*"—birth (*yoledet*), menstruation (*niddah*), and ejaculation or seminal emission (*shikhvat zera*).

Shikhvat zera affects both the man who has the seminal emission and the woman who receives it; both are *tamae* for a day (Lev. 15:16–18). Similarly, a man who has sexual relations with a *niddah* (menstruating woman) is considered a recipient of her blood and is called a *boel niddah*. Both are equal sources of *tumah* (Rashi); each is *tamae* for a week, while anyone who touches them or their beds is *tamae* for a day.

There are also three kinds of "sickness *tumah*," a category that reminds the afflicted person of his or her bodily mortality. It includes the *metzora*, a person with the skin disease *tzaraat*; the *zav*, a man with a nonseminal genital emission (Lev. 15:1–15); and the *zavah*, a woman with a nonmenstrual genital emission (Lev. 15:25–30).

The emission of a *zavah* had to be blood, not white mucus (Nachmanides). The laws of *tumah* applying to a *zavah* (and a *zav*) were the same as for a *niddah*, but the *zavah*'s flux was abnormal, a sign that something was wrong, so she had to bring a sacrifice of two birds on the eighth day. A *niddah*'s flux was normal, a sign that her body was working properly, so she did not bring a sacrifice. The *zav* and the *metzora* also brought sacrifices.

That procreation, bodily secretions, and death all convey *tumah* indicates that it is inaccurate to categorize *tumah* as "death" and *taharah* as "life," for *tumah* itself comprises both life and death.

THE FOUNTAIN OF HER BLOOD

If a woman has blood emerging from her flesh, for seven days she is in her *niddah* [period of separation], and anyone who touches her becomes *tamae* until evening. . . .

Anyone who touches her bed or sits on her seat must wash his clothes and bathe in water and is *tamae* until evening. . . . If a man lies with her and her *niddah* is upon him, he is *tamae* for seven days and the bed on which he lies becomes *tamae*. (Lev. 15:19–24)

Do not approach a woman in her menstrual separation of *tumah* to uncover her nakedness. (Lev. 18:19)

If a man lies with a woman who has her period and uncovers her nakedness, he has stimulated her fountain. She has uncovered the fountain of her blood. Both of them shall be cut off from among their people. (Lev. 20:18)

The Torah legislated seven days of *niddah*. *Niddah* is a period of *tumah* that comprises the actual "red" days of menstruation and some additional nonbleeding "white" days. Although *tumah* is no longer applicable, because there is no *mikdash* to enter and no *kadashim* to eat, the sexual restriction of *niddah* remains.

According to Nachmanides, the seven biblically proscribed days *included* the woman's days of flow. R. Simlai, however, maintained that they were *additional:* "The Holy One gave a great hardship to woman, for after she observes [*meshameret*] the days of her flow, she sits and observes seven days of separation" (LR 19:5). The observance of *niddah* as seven days *in addition to* menstruation (rather than inclusive of it) is said to be a rabbinic decree in response to a practice collectively initiated by women (Nid. 66a). Hence a woman who menstruates for five days is now considered to be "in *niddah*" for twelve days, after which she goes to the *mikvah*. A woman in *niddah* is herself called a *niddah*.

To "sit"—the same terminology used for the *yoledet* in the blood of *taharah*— refers to the custom of the menstrual hut (Nachmanides). The "observing" that a woman does in *niddah* is *shomeret*—keeping and guarding something sacred, as in being *shomer Shabbat* (Sabbath-observant) or serving as a *shomeret* for a corpse (sitting with it so it is not left alone before burial).

The *kohanim* and Levites were divided into twenty-four "watches," or *mishmarot,* for Tabernacle service; each *mishmar* officiated for one week. On the Sabbath, there was double "guard duty"—both the *mishmar* of the week just finishing and of the week about to begin were on call.

Mishmeret is thus a sacred duty involving watchfulness, observance, keeping, guarding, and preserving. The Sabbath, the Tabernacle, and a woman's fountain were all carefully observed, or vigilantly guarded, to preserve their sanctity. A *meshameret* is also a filter or strainer (Jastrow), and thus an instrument of refinement.

WOMEN'S BLOOD AND MEN'S SEED

Menstruation has been inaccurately associated with death by male philosophers and scientists who have viewed it solely as the indication of a *failure* to conceive. A recent study shows how medical textbooks have described menstruation—the shedding of the uterine lining—in terms of breakdown, degeneration, and deterioration, while the shedding of the lining of the stomach or of the seminal duct at ejaculation are described in more positive terms of secretion, regeneration, and renewal.[1]

The notion that menstruation indicates something "wrong"—that is, the "failure" to achieve fertilization—reached its zenith in the nineteenth century, when "writers were extremely prone to stress the debilitating nature of menstruation and its adverse impact on the lives and activities of women. Medical images of menstruation as pathological were remarkably vivid by the end of the century." Medical students used to be taught that "menstruation is the uterus crying for lack of a baby."[2]

This is clearly the "fetal view" of menstruation, not the woman's view. Menstruation is one part of a woman's entire reproductive cycle and is intimately bound up with sexuality and childbirth, not death and degeneration. Women who have experienced relief at not being pregnant are especially unlikely to simplistically characterize ovulation as "life" and menstruation as "death."

The "fetal view" of menstruation is essentially a male view because it stems from a focus on the fate of the male seed to the exclusion of the "vessel" hosting it. Nachmanides associates male ejaculation with death "even though it is in the nature of procreation . . . because the fountain can destroy [the sperm]; thus the ejaculator does not know whether his seed will be destroyed or a child will be formed from it."

Chavel, translating Nachmanides in 1974, renders "the fountain can destroy" as "the womb can be malfunctioning."[3] Thus, a rabbi in late twentieth-century America is still promoting the notion that *female anatomy is working improperly if an egg is not fertilized.* (Why not bemoan the "malfunctioning" sperm?) Nachmanides himself is right, however, that a man does not know the fate of his seed. Male obsession with the viability of sperm inside a woman has been explained by Karen Horney, the psychoanalyst who formulated the theory of "womb envy."

Horney noted that "during intercourse the male has to entrust his genitals to the female body, that he presents her with his semen and interprets this as a surrender of vital strength to the woman, similar to his experiencing the subsiding of erection after intercourse as evidence of having been weakened by the woman." She concludes, "Are love and death more closely bound up with one another for the male than for the female, in whom sexual union potentially produces a new life?"[4]

Among the medieval Jewish commentators, Nachmanides understood that menstruation is natural, and took issue with Rashi and Ibn Ezra for defining *devotah* (Lev. 12:2) as "her sickness." Rather, menstruation is more like "plague and pain," he said, "an affliction upon the woman even though it is natural." (No one who has ever had menstrual cramps would argue with that.)

However, even men who realized that menstruation is natural lacked an accurate understanding of where menstrual blood "goes" during pregnancy. We now know

1. Emily Martin, *The Woman in the Body* (Boston: Beacon Press, 1989), pp. 44–51.
2. Ibid., pp. 35, 45.
3. Chavel, 3:208.
4. Karen Horney, *Feminine Psychology* (New York: W. W. Norton and Co., 1967), pp. 116–117, 138.

that menstrual blood is from the endometrium, the uterine lining that builds up to nourish a fetus. The medieval European view of menstrual blood, however, was that it was the matter to which the semen supplied form and that any "excess menstrual blood was retained in the womb, providing the basis for lactation at parturition."[5]

R. Meir expressed this view with a male supremacist twist: "All the nine months that a woman does not see blood, she really should see it; but what does the Holy One do? Directs it upward to her breasts and turns it into milk, so that the fetus may come forth and have food, the more of it if it be a male" (LR 14:3).

Nachmanides, stating that "the whole child or the greater part of it is formed out of the woman's blood," nevertheless emphasized that this was *not* menstrual blood, which he claimed could *harm* a fetus. (The reader should bear in mind that Nachmanides was a physician in thirteenth-century Spain.) He explained:

> From the blood of menstruation it is not formed at all. How could a fetus be formed out of that, since it is a deadly poison, causing the death of any creature that drinks it or eats it! If this is most of the blood in the womb, she cannot become pregnant, as this blood does not give form. Even if she becomes pregnant from other blood, if it [the fetus] derives nourishment from this [menstrual blood], it will die.

Nachmanides' beliefs were the prevailing medical views of his time, if we take his word for it (and there is no apparent reason why we should not). "Physicians have already mentioned that if the fetus derives its nourishment from the best blood, . . . but if it is mixed with menstrual blood, it will ferment. This produces a child with sores and pustules. . . . Even if a little remains in its body, it produces a *metzora*." The Rabbis thought that a newborn would be a *metzora* if the mother did not observe the laws of *niddah*; hence, the proximity of these topics in the Torah (LR 15:5).

Nachmanides relates another bit of menstrual folklore from his fellow doctors:

> If a menstruating woman at the beginning of her flow gazes into a mirror with prolonged concentration, she will see in the mirror red drops like drops of blood, especially in an iron mirror that shines, for the evil nature of the demon ["damager"] bears a certain stigma and *rua ha-avir* ["the tremulous sound of space" or "the shaking of the atmosphere"] cleaves to the mirror. It is like a viper that kills with its gaze, and damages one who comes near to lie with her.

It is unfortunate that women really do not have all the powers that men have attributed to us. For example, "If a menstruating woman passes between two [men], if it is at the beginning of her period she will kill one of them, and if it is at the end of her period she will cause strife between them" (Pes. 111a). What a handy self-defense technique that would make!

---

5. Thomas Buckley and Alma Gottlieb, *Blood Magic: The Anthropology of Menstruation* (Berkeley: University of California Press, 1988), p. 38.

THE ORIGIN OF MENSTRUAL TABOOS

Women are not the only female mammals who menstruate. "Old World monkeys and apes menstruate too, though none with as marked a flow of blood as the human female."[6] Female mammals other than humans and higher apes, however, have what is called an estrous cycle. "Estrous and menstrual cycles are really expressions of the same process, with emphasis at a different stage."[7] In the estrous cycle, the female goes through *anestrus*, when she has no interest in sex; *proestrus*, a preparatory phase during which her eggs begin to grow; *estrus*, the hours or days surrounding ovulation, when she is highly interested in sexual activity and often becomes sexually aggressive; and *met estrus*, when the egg has moved out of the ovary into the fallopian tube and again her interest in sex declines.

"Among all animals the female admits the male at such times only as she is prepared for the exercise of his function. At other times she repels him, and her attitude towards him is generally one of positive hostility."[8] Male animals do not rape; if the female is not in her period of sexual activity, the males will stay away.

Among herbivorous animals, "the females, as soon as they are pregnant, retire from the company of the males to seek either complete seclusion and solitude, or to collect in herds from which the males are excluded." Male sexual instincts adapt to the female in a yearly breeding season. Among carnivorous animals, whose food supply is not based on agricultural seasons, "there is no definite yearly periodicity in the female" and hence, "no exact adjustment of the male instincts to that function." The male's sexual readiness is constant, but the female's is still intermittent.[9]

Menstrual taboos are simply the human female's version of the animal female's estrous cycle, reflecting a pattern of intermittent sexual relations based on male adaptation to the female cycle. "Had the primitive human female admitted the male during menstruation, pregnancy, and lactation she would have departed from all biological precedents; her behavior would have constituted an abnormality."[10]

With the loss of the estrous cycle, *rape* became possible because female *choice* became the modus operandi of sexual relations. With the human female's potential for continual sexual readiness, new limits were needed. This explains the development of menstrual taboos. Menstrual and postpartum taboos both served as the basis of the entire notion of "taboo," which is similar to *tamae* and *kodesh* in that the "concepts of holy and forbidden are inseparable."[11]

"The women, it appears from most accounts, segregate themselves of their own accord; they isolate themselves without consulting the men; they warn the latter not

---

6. Bettyann Kevles, *Females of the Species* (Cambridge, MA: Harvard University Press, 1986), p. 87.

7. Ibid, p. 89.

8. Briffault, 2:400.

9. Ibid., 2:401–403.

10. Ibid., 2:401.

11. Buckley and Gottlieb, p. 8.

to approach them." Menstrual taboos were a "veto originally laid by women on the exercise of the sexual instincts of the male" and were similar to taboos put upon sacred priests and kings.[12]

Men's fears of what will happen to them if they touch a menstruating woman may therefore have been instilled *by women themselves,* to keep men away from them. (This does not preclude men's ability to use these fears against women or to create more of their own.)

The psychology of women in teaching men in this way is not difficult to understand. For example, a mother may tell her little boy not to go near a pit because a big monster will come out and grab him. The purpose is to make the child afraid to even approach the pit so that he will not get close and fall in. Using "reason" with this child, however, would not yet work because he is too young.

Similarly, telling men to leave women alone physically when they are crampy and bloody is "reasonable" but would not have worked in the ancient world. It would have been viewed as a big joke. Modern men who feel offended by this analysis of male sexuality should remember that they have already been influenced by Torah values enough to take for granted the woman's right to say no. Therefore, like children too young to appeal to through reason, men learned "not to touch" by being told that their hunting, fishing, war making, or any other major male activity would be impaired if they did.

"Although the taboos and rules of avoidance were instituted by women for their convenience, these also furnished protection to those men who abided by the rules and stayed away from women and children whenever they were tabooed."[13] The idea that women instituted menstrual taboos to set limits with men enables us to understand more clearly why God would command such taboos at Sinai—they were intended to set limits to human sexuality and, hence, to sanctify it.

The taboos also served to curb *men's* (but not women's) ritual use of menstrual blood. Pliny reported accounts of Roman men using menstrual blood to ensure the fidelity of their wives, increase the fecundity of their wheat fields, and treat a number of medical conditions. Menstrual blood has also been used in fertility rites in conjunction with human sacrifice.[14]

Knowing what menstruation means to men really tells us nothing about what it means to women. A distorted view of menstrual taboos has been created by a double male bias, as "the descriptions of male anthropologists [are] based on the testimony of primarily male consultants. . . . It is men who have by and large defined menstruating as polluting, and the typical ethnography rarely tells us what the women of the culture at hand think of their own menstrual periods, and those of other women."[15]

Male domination has certainly made women vulnerable to internalizing notions of pollution and contamination, and to developing a self-loathing of natural bodily

12. Briffault, 2:403–412.
13. Reed, p. 98.
14. Buckley and Gottlieb, pp. 21, 35–36.
15. Ibid., pp. 193, 31.

functions as a result. That many women have done so is undeniable, as is the fact that the Torah itself has even been misused in this regard. However, a negative attitude of women toward their own cycles—a phenomenon that is particularly prevalent in postindustrial Europe and America—should not be assumed to be the experience of all women in all times and places. Indeed, there is plenty of evidence to the contrary.

THE MENSTRUAL HUT

One of the most blatant distortions of the double male bias can be found in descriptions that women are "isolated" or "secluded" in menstrual huts. Reports of male anthropologists have been like the story of the man who approaches a woman sitting in a bar with her three girlfriends and asks, "Are you alone?" The woman's female companions are irrelevant; he is only concerned with whether she is with a man and feels that if she is not, she is "alone."

A menstruating woman goes somewhere that *men may not,* but this does not mean that she stays in *solitude.* There might be fifty menstruating women in a hut! In fact, the menstrual hut seems to have functioned as the original women's center, ensuring women's autonomy and enabling them to enjoy a "break from their normal labors and spend the time happily talking or weaving."[16] Menarche celebrations in particular involved "large exchanges of food, splash parties in the lagoons, good times among the women, and the exclusion of men."[17]

In an analysis of how many symptoms of premenstrual syndrome (PMS) "seem to focus on intolerance for the kind of work discipline required by late industrial societies," anthropologist Emily Martin discusses the premenstrual experience many women have of being "klutzy"—dropping things, bumping into things, or cutting and burning themselves more than usual.[18] "A woman who drops things, cuts or burns herself or the food in this kind of environment has to adjust to an altogether different level of demand on her time and energy than, say, Beng women in Ivory Coast." Menstruating Beng women may not enter the forest, farm, chop wood, or carry water—women's normal daily chores. Instead:

> they are free to indulge in things they usually have no time for, such as cooking a special dish made by cooking palm nuts for a long time. This dish, highly prized for its taste, takes hours of slow tending and cooking and is normally eaten only by menstruating women and their close friends and kinswomen. Whatever the differing demands on Beng as opposed to Western women, Beng social convention requires a cyclic reduction in women's usual activities. Perhaps Beng women have fewer burned fingers.[19]

---

16. Ibid., pp. 7, 12.
17. Delaney, Upton, and Toth, p. 28. See also Buckley and Gottlieb, p. 37; and Mead, p. 176.
18. In Buckley and Gottlieb, pp. 161–181.
19. Ibid., p. 168.

The "medical condition" of PMS—and the receptivity to such a concept even among feminists—is a reaction to generations of doctors telling women their symptoms were "in their heads." There is relief in finally having real physical feelings validated as truth. However, the experience that is called PMS in medicalized, industrialized America functions very differently in a society based on women's rhythms. Many modern women find that they simply need quiet and privacy during their periods. Some even report increased emotional energy and psychic sensitivity, which can be channeled into creative work.

Unfortunately, however, privacy and creative space are not easily accessible to women with small children *or* to those who must adapt their biological clocks to an industrial timeclock. Extrasensitive abilities are then likely to be channeled into crying spells. "What in the right context might be released as powerful creativity or deep self-knowledge becomes, in the context of women's everyday lives in our societies, maladaptive discontent."[20]

The menstrual hut was thus its own kind of sanctuary, releasing a woman from her daily labors and her husband's demands so that she could simply sit around and *be*. Virginia Woolf said that every woman needs a room of her own; the menstrual hut, however, gave every woman a house of her own, one week a month.

"MOONTIME"

A correlation between the lunar cycle and the reproductive cycles of many forms of life, including the menstrual cycle of women, has been amply documented.[21] Light, and in particular the full moon, has been shown to trigger ovulation. Lunaception, a method by which women can regulate their hormonal cycles through controlling light exposure during sleep on a cyclical basis, has even been used as an effective means of natural birth control by some women.

Lunar–menstrual synchronicity is indeed remarkable. When combined with women's menstrual synchronicity—the phenomenon that women who live together tend to menstruate together[22]—it creates a very powerful collective female energy, which can even govern an entire culture's cyclical rhythms.

The occurrence of "lunar phase-locked menstrual synchron[icit]y"[23] has been described among the Yurok Indians of northwestern California in precontact times. The following is the ethnographer's description of a modern Yurok woman's account of "moontime," which is the Yurok term for menstrual separation:

---

20. Ibid., p. 172.
21. See Louise Lacey, *Lunaception* (New York: Warner, 1976); Briffault, 2:429–431, 583–592; E. L. Abel, *Moon Madness* (Greenwich, CT: Fawcett, 1976), pp. 73–91; and Buckley and Gottlieb, p. 203.
22. Buckley and Gottlieb, pp. 46, 199.
23. Ibid., p. 184.

A menstruating woman should isolate herself because this is the time when she is at the height of her powers. Thus the time should not be wasted in mundane tasks and social distractions, nor should one's concentration be broken by concerns with the opposite sex. Rather, all of one's energies should be applied in concentrated meditation "to find out the purpose of your life," and toward the "accumulation" of spiritual energy. . . . The blood that flows serves to "purify" the woman, preparing her for spiritual accomplishment.[24]

Like the *mikvah* for Jewish women and the lagoon-splashing mentioned earlier, here too there was a "'sacred moontime pond' where in the old days menstruating women went to bathe and to perform rituals that brought spiritual benefits. . . . Many girls performed these rites only at the time of their first menstruation, but aristocratic women went to the pond every month until menopause."[25]

Thus, the Jewish practice of women going to a *mikvah* every month can be seen as an "aristocratic" practice by this standard. Indeed, the relationship between the moon, menstrual blood, and the regenerative property of the element of water are the key to understanding why Jewish women immerse themselves in a *mikvah*—a natural body of water—after every monthly period. It has nothing to do with "cleaning" or "washing" in any "hygienic" sense.

All of a Yurok household's fertile women who were not pregnant menstruated at the same time and practiced the bathing rituals at the same time. This corresponded to ten days around the New Moon. Husbands and wives did not eat or sleep together during this period. Nor could men hunt or fight; instead, they maintained their own activities, consisting of intensive physical training in a men's sweat lodge.

The entire Yurok village thus functioned on a cycle determined by women's collective bodily rhythms in sync with the moon. For one-third of each month, a significant portion of the population was engaged in intensive, inward spiritual pursuits. Postmenopausal women and premenarcheal girls attended the menstruating women and also prepared food for the men in the sweathouse. Food intake was significantly decreased at this time, for women did not cook or gather and men did not hunt. Community festivals were specifically held during the nonmenstrual times of the month— around the full moon. Menarche itself was sometimes a synchronized experience for groups of girls.

Individual menstrual synchronicity with the moon has been set askew by artificial lighting. Electricity, as well as the custom of living in nuclear families, certainly prevents any *collective* synchronicity with the moon. However, such a phenomenon may have once been more common than we know. In 1898, a study charting the menstrual periods of Swedish women found that the number of occurrences of the onset of menstruation peaked on the evening before the New Moon.[26] Indeed, we may have here the *real* origin of *Rosh Chodesh* as a "women's holiday."

---

24. Ibid., p. 190.
25. Ibid.
26. Lacey, p. 108.

NIDDAH AS "MOONTIME"

Thus, far from devaluing themselves as "contaminating," women who observe menstrual taboos may see this time as "a powerful, positive phenomenon with esoteric significance" and "a context for spiritual training."[27]

Niddah is Jewish "moontime." We do not know if Jewish women lived together in menstrual huts or had any collective menstrual-lunar synchronicity that set the rhythms of Jewish culture. (By talmudic times, at least, that women did *not* live separately from their husbands during their periods is evident from *Ketubot* 61a).

It may be significant, however, that the major Jewish festivals of Passover and Sukkot fall at the full moon, the "nonmenstrual" lunar phase. The Pesach sacrifice could not be eaten by menstruating women, so having it at the full moon would have enabled the most number of women to eat it. Similarly, Sukkot is observed by dwelling in huts, so having that holiday at the full moon would ensure that the practice did not overlap with dwelling in menstrual huts. It would be very interesting to conduct a study to see if *mikvahs* today are more crowded at the full moon.

We noted in chapter 17 that, just as women's menstrual cycle correlates to the monthly lunar cycle, Jewish men's prayer obligations correlate to the daily solar cycle. The symbolic association of woman–moon and man–sun is found in many cultures and is also evident in *niddah*. Like the sun and the moon, a husband and wife are two "bodies" that have a cyclical relationship to each other—a phase of togetherness and a phase of separation. Just as the moon separates from the sun for about two weeks before beginning to approach it again, a husband and wife separate from each other sexually for about two weeks before approaching each other again.

Women who observe the laws of *niddah* describe its benefits in terms of synchronization of the couple's sexual desire, female autonomy within marriage, decreased perception of the woman as a sex object, and enhancement of verbal communication between partners. *Niddah* is a time when a married woman can focus on herself and her female friends. However, because there is no menstrual hut in Judaism today, the couple continues to relate as platonic companions, thus building a strong non-physical foundation to their relationship. Moreover, disputes cannot be "settled" or glossed over through sex.

Menstruation has been a very integral part of Jewish women's spiritual lives. Rather than seeing "contamination" as the reason a menstruating woman could not enter the Tabernacle or eat sacred food, we might instead posit that women's spiritual activities were simply dichotomous and that the menstrual rites were on par—but not to be mixed—with the sacrificial rites. That is, when women were shedding the blood of life, they were not to involve themselves with the male shedding of the blood of death.

Menstruation required women to be much more involved with the process in the past than it does today. Disposable sanitary napkins were developed and marketed

---

27. Buckley and Gottlieb, pp.194, 208.

in 1921, and tampons first appeared in 1933.[28] For most of history, a menstruating woman simply used rags—turning one over and over until it was full, then using a different one and washing out the first one. If she were rich she might have a lot of rags or servants to wash them. However, for the average woman, menstruation must have required an incredible amount of attention to one's body and to washing—somewhat like having a baby in (cloth) diapers.

Menstruation was thus an experience that occupied a woman continuously for several days. One did not simply take a pill and forget about it for a few hours. Modern attempts to mask menstrual ups and downs have actually *decreased* women's awareness of their bodily functions. The feminist movement began to reclaim this awareness twenty-five years ago through self-help health care classes for women, complete with pelvic exams conducted by the women themselves using plastic speculums.

Jewish women observing *niddah* never lost this awareness. They know their own menstrual cycles like clockwork. The Talmud instructed them to examine themselves with rags twice a day—*shachrit ve-aravit,* "morning and evening," the same times when men were to attend the *bet midrash*—thus emphasizing, once again, the parallelism between menstruation and men's prayer obligations (Nid. 4b).[29] Such examinations have given observant Jewish women a certain comfort and ease in touching themselves. Unlike many modern women, they do not need tampons with cardboard or plastic applicators because of squeamishness about inserting a finger.

There is some evidence that menstruation has not always been as frequent or as long as it is now. Women who practice lunaception have found that menstruation "tends to be of much shorter duration and may be heavier."[30] Athletic training has been found to delay menarche as well as to reduce the frequency of periods.[31]

Although monthly menstruation is medically defined as normal and anything else as abnormal, "'normal' monthly periods are probably not that at all, historically and cross-culturally, but rather are most likely biologically anomalous products of particular cultural systems at specific historical conjunctions."[32]

Indeed, the misogynist assertion that women should be kept "barefoot, pregnant, and in the kitchen" reflects the reality that physically immobile women menstruate more often because their estrogen levels rise. Thus, keeping women sedentary means they will get pregnant more often. Pastoral nomadic women (such as the !Kung San of Africa) menstruate rarely, in comparison with women of settled agricultural societies. Industrialism, which replaces physical exertion with pushing buttons, would therefore increase menstrual frequency even more.[33]

---

28. Delaney, Upton, and Toth, p. 109.
29. Birnbaum, *Daily Prayer Book,* p. 15.
30. Lacey, p. 116.
31. "Researchers Study the Relation between Exercise and Menstrual Irregularities," *Harvard Gazette,* Jan. 25, 1980, p. 5.
32. Buckley and Gottlieb, p. 44.
33. Ibid., p. 45.

Thus, Jewish women may not have been in *niddah* as often or for as long as they are today. The more rare menstruation was, the more profound it must have seemed.

THE WOMAN'S BLESSING

"Blessed are You, God, Sovereign of the Universe, for making me *kirtzono.*" This is the blessing said by traditional Jewish women in their morning davening. It is the parallel prayer (said simultaneously) to men saying, "Blessed are You, God, Sovereign of the Universe, for not making me a woman."

A woman thanks God for making her *kirtzono*. A man thanks God for making him a nonwoman. Both also thank God for making them not gentiles and not slaves, and even a convert to Judaism says the "nongentile" blessing because it is not an issue of "race."

The man's blessing can easily be understood from the perspective of womb envy—that women have something men do not (the capacity to give birth to a life that has grown inside them). Men have to learn to accept their lack without being envious, hostile, or trying to compensate through the domination and devaluation of women. Ironically, the blessing sounds as if the man saying it *devalues* women, but its function—in theory, at least—is precisely the opposite. Whether men actually say it with the proper *kavanah* (intention) of humility toward women is another matter, but that is something only the individual can judge.

What does the woman's blessing mean? *Kirtzono* means "according to (God's) Will," which can certainly be twisted into justifying women's subordination, if that is perceived as "God's Will." However, this is not its true meaning. Women are made in accordance with divine will in a way that men are not, and a clue to *how* this was accomplished is revealed through another use of *kirtzono*. In the evening davening, we acknowledge God's rulership of the planets, stars, and seasons: "With Wisdom You open the gates of heaven, and with Understanding You change the times and cause the seasons to alternate. You arrange the stars in their courses in the sky according to Your will [*kirtzono*]." God's quality of *Binah* thus regulates the cyclical nature of time.

In both cases, *kirtzono* refers to cycles—the planetary orbits and the female cycle. The blessing said by women thanks God for making us with menstrual cycles. It is a vibrant feminist affirmation in a society where all aspects of the female sexual cycle—menstruation, childbirth, and menopause—have been turned into "syndromes" requiring medical intervention.

✿✿✿ 27 ✿✿✿

Sexuality

Achrei Mot (16:1–18:30)

Sexual boundaries are as essential for human society as laws against killing and stealing. Modern sexual ethics—ushered in by Dr. Alfred Kinsey and his researchers, who evaluated sex through a quantitative count of orgasms—hold that any activity is permissible as long as it occurs between "consenting adults" and does not "hurt" anyone. This presumes that human reason can always be depended upon to know what is *ultimately* harmful.

The inaccuracy of this view is painfully evident in the 1990s. No one in 1970, at the height of the "sexual revolution," could have predicted the phenomenon of AIDS, or the common plight of many women who cannot get the men they love to commit themselves, or the increased sexual unfaithfulness, exploitation, and violence that are now normative in our entertainment media.

Certainly the double standard of sexual morality was wrong and needed to be eradicated. However, it was changed in the wrong direction: instead of giving women the "right" to become as promiscuous and emotionally detached as men were allowed to be, we should have demanded that men become as emotionally involved and faithful as women were required to be. Sexual repression was replaced with sexual license; true liberation is yet to be found.

ERVAT GILAH: THE VIOLATION OF SEXUAL BOUNDARIES

The Torah sets very clear sexual boundaries in Leviticus 18 and repeats most of the prohibited activities in Leviticus 20, along with the penalties for committing them. The violation of sexual boundaries is called *legalot ervah*, "to uncover nakedness." The root of the verb is the same as *galut*, or *exile*; hence, "to exile nakedness" means, in effect, to pervert sexuality (Kaplan). The noun form, *ervat gilah*, can be translated as "sexual offense" or "sexual prohibition."

The Torah speaks in the plural, to both men and women, in the general commands preceding and following the individualized list of sexual offenses (Lev. 18:6, 18:29; Rashi). Each individual prohibition, however, is in the singular and addressed specifically to the (adult) male. This reflects the social reality that sexual violations are overwhelmingly initiated by men. Most of Jewish law concerning sexuality comes down to telling a man where he may put his penis and when. The purpose is to take the aggressiveness of male sexuality, harness its potential for violence, and channel it into its highest possible expression.

Most of the Torah's sexual prohibitions concern incest (Lev. 18:7–17; 20:11–12, 20:14, 20:17, 20:19–21). A man is prohibited from marriage and/or sexual relations with his:

1. mother—whether or not she is his father's wife;
2. stepmother—any wife of his father;
3. sister—the daughter of his father or his mother;
4. granddaughter—the daughter of his son or his daughter;
5. half-sister—the daughter of his father and his stepmother (his stepsister, the stepmother's daughter from a previous marriage, is not prohibited);
6. aunt—the sister of his father or his mother, as well as the wife of his father's brother (the wife of his mother's brother was not biblically included but was added rabbinically);
7. daughter-in-law—this biblically refers only to the legal wife of a man's son. A woman sexually connected to his son through rape or premarital sex was rabbinically prohibited.
8. sister-in-law—the wife of his brother. This woman, unlike any other forbidden relation, not only became *permitted* if his brother died childless, she became *obligated* through *yibum,* unless released by *chalitzah* (see chapter 9); and
9. daughter, stepdaughter, and mother-in-law—these three relatives are included in one prohibition, "a woman and her daughter" (Lev. 18:17), which is later repeated as "a woman and her mother" (20:14). Both ways of saying it define the same three relationships.

The Rabbis also extended the biblical definitions of incest to include the grandmother, great-grandmother, grandfather's wife, great-granddaughter, great-aunt, and so on, all the way up and down through the generations (*Even HaEzer* 28a–29b).

Besides incest, a man is also prohibited from sex and/or marriage with:

10. sisters in their lifetime—in polygamous times this prohibited sororal polygyny, so that women would never again be subjected to the kind of intense jealousies that Rachel and Leah endured. When monogamy was made mandatory for men (1000 c.e.), this prohibition prevented a divorced man from marrying his ex-wife's sister in the ex-wife's lifetime (Lev. 18:18);

11. a menstruating woman—the only sexual prohibition that is obviously not a forbidden *marriage* (Lev. 18:19, 20:18);

12. a married woman—polyandry. No woman may have more than one husband or sexual partner. Today we would simply call this "adultery" (Lev. 18:20, 20:10);

13. a male—sodomy. Sexual intercourse between males, whether anal, oral, manual, or "intercrural"[1] (Lev. 18:22, 20:13); and

14. an animal—bestiality (Lev. 18:23, 20:15–16). This prohibition, unlike any of the others, contains a parallel statement that is explicitly directed at women as well.

In the nine incest prohibitions, both the converse (the *same* relationship from the woman's viewpoint) and the inverse (the *corresponding* relationship from the woman's viewpoint) are also prohibited. For example, the first prohibition is a son with his mother. The converse is a mother with her son, while the inverse is a daughter with her father.

Hence, a woman may not have sex with (and/or marry) her:

1. son	1. father
2. stepson	2. stepfather
3. brother	3. brother
4. grandfather	4. grandson
5. half-brother	5. half-brother
6. nephew	6. uncle
7. father-in-law	7. son-in-law
8. brother-in-law	8. brother-in-law
9. father, stepfather, son-in-law	9. son, stepson, father-in-law

Basically, the converse and inverse prohibitions end up forbidding the same relationships, only through different means. However, both lists are needed to prohibit the grandfather *and* the grandson, the uncle *and* the nephew.

In the four human nonincest prohibitions, the converse and inverse for a woman are:

10. her (living) sister's ex-husband	10. her (living) ex-husband's brother
11. a man during her period	11. no inverse
12. any man besides her husband	12. a married man—polygyny
13. no converse	13. a woman—lesbianism

While the converse applies completely, the inverse is not so absolutely equivalent. R. Jose, for instance, was married to his niece (GR 17:3). Polygyny continued to be permitted for a long time after the Revelation at Sinai. Today this is adultery by

---

1. This means "between the thighs." See Eva C. Keuls, *The Reign of the Phallus: Sexual Politics in Ancient Athens* (Berkeley: University of California Press, 1985), p. 274.

a married man, which does not have as serious halakhic consequences as adultery by a married woman. (The child of a married man and a single woman is not a *mamzer*, while the child of a married woman and a single man is.)

Similarly, lesbianism does not have as serious halakhic consequences as sodomy. Feminists have mistakenly assumed that this indicates a devaluation of female sexuality. On the contrary, it recognizes that male homosexuality (male sexuality "doubled") and lesbianism (female sexuality "doubled") are at *opposite* ends of the sexual spectrum, with heterosexuality (male and female sexuality blended together) in the middle. Gay men and lesbians, as we shall see, have very little in common aside from the demand for civil rights.

Ervat gilah made the land *tamae*, so God chose to "vomit" the Canaanites out of Israel and give the land to the Jews. However, Jews, too, will be "vomited" out of Israel if they commit these offenses (Lev. 18:24–30).

THE DEFINITION OF INCEST

The Torah has been wrongly perceived by some feminists as not prohibiting father–daughter incest. "The biblical injunction against incest omits any specific reference to sexual relations between father and daughter," claims a feminist author who is one of the foremost psychiatric experts on incest. "The patriarchal God sees fit to pass over father–daughter incest in silence."[2] What a sad irony her statement is. God is not at all silent; but whether people can hear is a different matter. The father–daughter prohibition is subtle because it is enclosed in the three-in-one prohibition noted previously.

Why is father–daughter incest described in this way? Is there really any man who wants to sleep with his mother-in-law? Why does God tell adult men not to sleep with their mothers instead of telling mothers not to molest their little boys? The Torah's style of presentation was dictated by the social structure of the time, in which incest was defined purely in matrilineal terms (see chapter 4). Before the Torah was given, *only maternal relatives were prohibited as incestuous.* Thus, a man could not have sexual relations with his mother, his maternal sisters, or his maternal aunts (who, in sororal polygyny, would also be his father's other wives).

The only exception to this seems to have been Egyptian royalty (see chapters 10 and 12). Because the throne was matriarchal, passing from the queen to her daughter, a man became king only by marriage to the queen. Hence, a prince would have to marry his own mother or his maternal sister in order to succeed his father on the throne.

Most of the ancient world did observe a matrilineal taboo, but there was as yet no patrilineal taboo. Hence, it was normal for a king to marry his own daughter so that he could keep the throne when the queen died. The king's son by a woman other than the queen could also marry the queen's daughter (who was his half-sister) because

2. Herman, pp. 60–61.

paternal brothers and sisters of different mothers—a common phenomenon in a polygynous society—were not considered related.

Feminists, in viewing purely matrilineal descent as a positive and powerful phenomenon for women, have ironically ignored the fact that in such societies, *father–daughter incest is not a crime.* From the stories of Lot's daughters and Rivkah we saw that a father might even be his daughter's "deflowerer." Sarah could marry Avraham because he was her *paternal* uncle, and Amram could marry Yokheved because she was his *paternal* aunt. After Sinai these relations, too, became incestuous.

That Isaac, Miriam, Aharon, and Moses came from relationships that we now rightly view as incestuous is startling, but no more so than the fact that Lot's incest with his daughters generated the lineage that will culminate in the Messiah.

Feminists should therefore champion, rather than criticize as "male-dominated," the Torah's emphasis on patrilineal descent, for the lack of a patrilineal incest taboo in the ancient world is precisely *why* the Levitical sexual code placed so much emphasis on the father—not because a "patriarchal God" sought to validate male ownership of women.

A man had to be taught that sex with his mother is an offense against his father as well as against her, and that sleeping with *any* wife of his father is wrong. A girl is his sister, whether she is the daughter of his mother *or* his father, whether she is born in the same house or abroad (which means a daughter of his mother or of another woman by his father). Besides learning that women of his *father's* line were forbidden, a man had to be trained that all other women of his *wife's* line were also forbidden: hence the grouping of his wife's daughters with his wife's mother.

INCEST AND CHILD SEXUAL ABUSE

It would be a mistake to assert that the Torah's prohibition of incest was equivalent to a prohibition of child sexual abuse. The latter is a modern concept, like repugnance toward corporal punishment and slavery. The Torah paved the way for such a consciousness to evolve, but it did not command it. The marriage of young girls to older men was not forbidden, so the adult–child power dynamic was clearly not the agenda here.

Even in talmudic times, a girl could be betrothed at three years old, and a boy at nine years old. The same Mishnah that condemns an incest perpetrator to death while proclaiming the total innocence of the victim nevertheless states that if the girl is under three years old, "intercourse with her is like putting a finger in the eye"—referring to a belief that her hymen would heal. The notion of psychological trauma was completely foreign to human consciousness, although it certainly must have been a reality to the baby girls who had to endure the prerogative of male penetration. Similarly, sodomy with a boy under nine was also not punishable (Nid. 44b–45a; San. 54b).

While human consciousness (including Jewish law) has indeed evolved enough to prohibit child *marriages* in most societies—with notable exceptions, such as India and parts of the Moslem Arab world—*sex* with children continues to flourish even in "enlightened" societies. Jews, unfortunately, are no exception.

The prevalence of father–daughter incest in nineteenth-century Vienna was discovered by Sigmund Freud in his work with "hysterical," upper-class assimilated Jewish women. At first, he lent a sympathetic ear and formulated the "seduction theory"—that incest was the cause of hysteria—but later he abandoned it and replaced it with the "Oedipus complex" and began to dismiss women's accounts of childhood molestation as "fantasy."[3]

Realizing that all hysterics were incest survivors but that all incest survivors did not become hysterics, Freud refused to face the reality of the prevalence of sexual abuse. "Surely such widespread perversions against children are not very probable," he protested to his colleague Wilhelm Fliess. His findings had come a little too close to home, since his brother and several younger sisters were all hysterics. "The frequency of this circumstance often makes me wonder," he wrote at first, but he later stopped wondering when he realized "that in all cases, the father, *not excluding my own,* had to be accused of being perverse" (emphasis mine).[4]

One might hope that Kinsey's research would have been a little more courageous, yet in his 1948 study of male sexuality, Kinsey "never asked the subjects whether there was any history of sexual assault in their backgrounds."[5] In his 1953 study of female sexuality, Kinsey's focus on counting orgasms led him to report that only 1 percent of women who had had childhood "sexual contacts" with adults experienced orgasm. However, his "objective" scientific method did not allow him to question the moral responsibility of adults in the situation or even to speculate whether physical pleasure might nevertheless coexist with psychological damage.

Although Kinsey then reported that 80 percent of these women "had been emotionally upset or frightened by their contacts with adults" as children, he *dismissed* the feelings of the child (whom he consistently refers to as "it" rather than "she") as being akin to a fear of insects or spiders. "If a child were not culturally conditioned, it is doubtful if it [*sic*] would be disturbed by sexual approaches of the sort. . . . It is difficult to understand why a child, except for its [*sic*] cultural conditioning, should be disturbed at having its [*sic*] genitalia touched, or disturbed at seeing the genitalia of other persons, or disturbed at even more specific sexual contacts," he maintained. He concluded that the real problem was the "hysterical" emotional reaction of adults, which he claimed "may disturb the child more seriously than the sexual contacts themselves." Only "physical damage" caused any harm, in Kinsey's view.[6]

---

3. See Jeffrey Moussaiff Masson, *The Assault on Truth* (New York: Penguin Books, 1984); Marianne Krüll, *Freud and His Father* (London: Hutchinson, 1986); and Florence Rush, *The Best-Kept Secret: Sexual Abuse of Children* (Blue Ridge Summit, PA: Tab, 1980), pp. 80–104.

4. Jeffrey Moussaiff Masson, *The Complete Letters of Sigmund Freud to Wilhelm Fliess 1887–1904* (Cambridge, MA: Harvard University Press, 1985), pp. 231, 264.

5. Mic Hunter, *Abused Boys: The Neglected Victims of Sexual Abuse* (New York: Fawcett, 1990), p. 26.

6. Alfred C. Kinsey, Wardell B. Pomeroy, Clyde E. Martin, and Paul H. Gebhard, *Sexual Behavior in the Human Female* (Philadelphia: W. B. Saunders, 1953), pp. 120–122.

Today, it is estimated that one out of every three or four girls, *in the United States alone,* is sexually abused; estimates of boys range from one out of seven to one in ten.[7] These statistics are, if anything, conservative, due to the shame and terror that inhibit children from speaking about the experience. Most sexual abuse of children is incest—that is, it occurs *within* the family, and not by strangers. Even the perpetrator who is not a relative is usually a known and trusted caretaker, such as a babysitter, neighbor, doctor, teacher, or family friend.

Men are overwhelmingly the perpetrators—constituting 95 percent of the molesters of girls and 80 percent of the molesters of boys. (Most of these men are heterosexual, and many molest both girls and boys. A man who molests boys is *not* necessarily homosexual.)[8] Even though women are the perpetrators in 5 percent of girls' cases and 20 percent of boys' cases, more girls than boys are molested by women, because 5 percent of a large number is greater than 20 percent of a small number. Boys experience more nonincest ("extrafamilial") abuse than do girls, but even when boys are molested by a parent, it is usually the father, not the mother.[9]

Finkelhor offers ten reasons men abuse children so much more than women do, even though women have more opportunity to do so given their closer physical and emotional proximity to children as mothers. Most of these reasons have to do with the nature of male sexuality as well as male dominance in society. He also found that men are less likely than women to view any given incident as sexual abuse, and hypothesizes: "This may well be the influence of a long history of subtle toleration of this kind of behavior in the male subculture. It may be the result of pornographic media which have tended to legitimize such behavior. It may also be that males, who are less frequently sexually victimized than women, are thus less alarmed and take the problem less seriously."[10]

We can see such male oblivion in Nachmanides' medieval view. "What harm would there be if a man would marry his daughter?" he asks seriously. "What could be more fitting for a person [*sic*] than to give his daughter in marriage to his eldest son, so they would inherit his possessions and be fruitful and multiply in his house?"

The harm, we now know, includes a wide range of effects on the incest survivor's capacity for sexual intimacy and trust, as well as drug and alcohol addiction, depression, suicide, eating disorders, prostitution, multiple personality disorder, self-mutilation, juvenile delinquency, and a great vulnerability to repeat-abuse situations as adults.[11] Furthermore, most, if not all, child abusers were themselves abused as chil-

---

7. While a number of excellent books exist on child sexual abuse, the psychological damage it causes, and strategies for recovery by adult survivors, the best *statistical* studies on the subject are David Finkelhor, *Child Sexual Abuse: New Theory and Research* (New York: Free Press, 1984), and Diana E. H. Russell, *The Secret Trauma: Incest in the Lives of Girls and Women* (New York: Basic Books, 1986).

8. Hunter, p. 22.

9. Finkelhor, pp. 12, 158–160, 165, 174, 184.

10. Ibid., pp. 120–128, 182–183.

11. Russell, *Secret Trauma*, pp. 12, 191–203; E. Sue Blume, *Secret Survivors: Uncovering Incest and Its Aftereffects in Women* (New York: John Wiley and Sons, 1990).

dren (but most abused children do not become abusers). *The sexual abuse of children may very well be the primary underlying cause of the vast majority of our social problems.*

Nachmanides might be excused for not knowing better because he lived so long ago, but what are we to make of the view, expressed in 1976 by Kinsey researcher Ward Pomeroy, that "incest between adults and younger children can also prove to be a satisfying and enriching experience"?[12] Satisfying and enriching *for whom?*

BESTIALITY, SATYRS, AND AZAZEL

Bestiality is the only form of *ervat gilah* in which a prohibition is *explicitly* stated for women as well as for men. The reason for this might be that women's copulation with animals was a prevalent part of pagan fertility rites, as we saw, for example, in Egyptian phallic bull worship (chapter 12). The goat was often used in this way:

> When the Egyptians desired to consort with the demons, they used to go out to certain high mountains and offer sacrifices and make trenches in the ground and pour some of the blood around the trenches and the rest into them and put flesh over it, and bring offerings to the demons. Then the demons used to collect and consort with them on the mountain. Israel, being subject to the Egyptians, learned their ways and went astray after them. . . . The demons used to appear to them in the form of he-goats. (*Zohar* III:70a)

"At Mendes [in lower Egypt] a living goat was kept as the image of the generative power, to whom the women presented themselves naked, and had the honor of being publicly enjoyed by him."[13] Herodotus noted the practice in the fifth century B.C.E.: "The Mendesians regard all goats as sacred, but the males more so than the females. . . . In my time a marvel happened in this province: a goat had intercourse with a woman in public, and the thing was common knowledge."[14]

Connected to phallic goat worship was the satyr, "one of a class of riotous, lascivious woodland deities . . . represented as part human and part goat," according to the Random House dictionary. The term also means a man who has satyriasis, which is "abnormal, uncontrollable sexual desire in men." Satyrs had sex with men, women, animals—anything and everything.

The satyr—apparently a man in costume acting as representative of the goat god[15]—is usually associated with the orgiastic worship of the Greek god Dionysus

---

12. Ward Pomeroy, "A New Look at Incest," *Forum* (Nov. 1976):10. Quoted in Russell, *Secret Trauma*, p. 8. Pornography continues to be the biggest promoter of men's use of children for sexual gratification.

13. Richard Payne Knight and Thomas Wright, *A History of Phallic Worship* (New York: Dorset Press, 1992), p. 61; see also Briffault, 3:189–190.

14. Carter, p. 111.

15. Keuls, pp. 357–371.

or Bacchus but was evidently found in the ancient Near East as well. The "perennial satyr's attribute" was "a huge erect penis, which . . . to the Greeks was a sign not of manhood but of bestiality."[16]

Seir, the Hebrew word for "goat," "satyr," or "demon," also means "hairy"—the description of Esav (Gen. 25:25, 27:11), whose licentious behavior might be described as satyriac. Seir was also the name of the place where Esav eventually settled (Gen. 36:8).

This connection of goats, satyrs, and bestiality is why the Torah section on *ervat gilah* opens with the Yom Kippur service, in which one goat was sacrificed as a sin-offering and another goat was sent off "to Azazel," into the wilderness (Lev. 16:8, 16:10, 16:21–22). The Azazel goat, *which had to be a male,* was pushed off a cliff (Yom. 67a) to atone for the people's sins—hence the origin of the term *scapegoat.* The man who did the pushing also died within the year.[17]

Bestiality no longer has any "religious" connotation, but it still exists in the modern world, where it is primarily employed as a form of torture of women by the most sadistic of men. The Nazis, for instance, trained dogs to rape women. Klaus Barbie, the "butcher of Lyons," had an Alsatian (German shepherd) named Wolf which he used for this purpose. It may be no coincidence that the Alsatian was Hitler's favorite type of dog; that he, too, had one named Wolf; and that he called the Schutzstaffel (SS) "my pack of wolves."[18]

Pornographers also train dogs to rape women and then film the act. Linda Lovelace, who was held captive for two years by her boyfriend-pimp and forced to do many horrible and degrading things, writes about a time when she was held at gunpoint and ordered to submit to a dog. Her statement gives insight into why the Torah's death penalty for the woman as well as the animal (Lev. 20:16) is not really as cruel as it might at first seem:

> If I could have foreseen how bad it was going to be, I wouldn't have surrendered. I would have chosen the possibility of death. I am able to handle almost everything that has happened to me in my life . . . but I'm still not able to handle that day. . . . There were no greater humiliations left for me. The memory of that day and that dog does not fade the way other memories do. The overwhelming sadness that I felt on that day is with me at this moment, stronger than ever.[19]

Evidently there are still men who like to gratify themselves with animals. We might presume that most of these men are heavily involved in, and influenced by, the many

16. Ibid., p. 360.

17. Weissman, 3:191.

18. Edwin Eytan, "Barbie Ordered Back to Courtroom for Witnesses' Identification," *The Jewish Advocate,* May 28, 1987, p. 3; Jerome Grossman, "U.S. Shares in Barbie's Guilt," *The Jewish Advocate,* Aug. 6, 1987, p. 2; Robert G. L. Waite, *The Psychopathic God: Adolf Hitler* (New York: Basic Books, 1977), p. 26.

19. Linda Lovelace, *Ordeal* (New York: Berkley Books, 1981), pp. 109–110, 113. This book has always been difficult to find in bookstores. The most ardent defenders of pornography as "free speech" are usually the first to silence women who try to speak out about its harm.

perversities promoted by pornography. However, they do not necessarily fit the stereotype of the "sleazy pervert." For example, a "respectable" clinical psychologist writes: "Moralists condemn sex with animals as disgusting, immoral, and generally horrible. Fortunately it's no longer a crime in a great many places, and nowhere in the United States is it a capital crime. We disagree with the moralists."[20]

This psychologist, Dr. Charles Silverstein, was instrumental in getting the American Psychiatric Association to remove homosexuality from its list of mental disorders, which it did in 1973. The American Psychological Association honored him for his work by elevating him to the status of Fellow of the association.

SODOMY

Sodomy and bestiality are often discussed together in Jewish sources because both human males and animals of either gender are considered improper receptacles for a man's penis.

The Code of Jewish Law states

> Israel is not suspected of sodomy and bestiality. Therefore it is not forbidden to be alone with [other men and animals]. But if a man removes himself anyway from seclusion with a man or an animal, this is praiseworthy. The greatest of the Sages distanced themselves from animals in order not to be alone with them. In generations of great licentiousness, those who removed themselves from seclusion with [another] male were praised. (*Even HaEzer* 59a)

Lesbianism is not mentioned, nor are women "praised" for avoiding seclusion with other women and animals.

Sodomy is called *toevah* (Lev. 18:22), which is a term used throughout Deuteronomy to describe various kinds of idol worship (Deut. 7:25–26, 12:31, 13:15, 17:4), eating forbidden foods (14:3), the sacrifice of a maimed animal (17:1), a number of magical techniques (18:9, 18:12), and the return of an adulteress to her husband (24:4). It basically includes any "strange practice" that provokes divine jealousy (32:16).

Toevah is also the term used by Joseph to describe the status of shepherds in Egypt to his brothers (Gen. 46:34), as well as the reason why Moses pleaded with Pharaoh to let the Jews leave Egypt—because their sacrifice of a sacred animal would be *toevah* to the Egyptians (Ex. 8:22). Eating with Jews was *toevah* to the Egyptians (Gen. 43:32). The term basically means "repugnant," and it is often translated as "abomination."

The prohibition against sodomy is worded as "a man [*ish*] shall not lie with a male [*zakhar*]." The Talmud explains that this wording was necessary to make it clear that an adult man may not lie with either a man *or* a boy (San. 54a)—something that evidently needed to be explicitly spelled out for men.

---

20. Charles Silverstein and Felice Picano, *The New Joy of Gay Sex* (New York: HarperCollins, 1992), p. 171.

While the sexual abuse of children is overwhelmingly committed by heterosexual men and gay men should not be scapegoated for it, nevertheless, such behavior appears to be more *overtly* accepted by the gay male community than by the mainstream straight world. There is, for instance, a publication called the *Journal of Paedophilia,* which has had a medical doctor on its board, and an organization called the North American Man-Boy Love Association (NAMBLA), which seeks the repeal of all age-of-consent laws and marches openly in gay pride parades every year.

Notwithstanding the preponderance of men who have sex with girls, there is, nevertheless, no *Journal of Father–Daughter Incest* and no Man–Girl Love Association whose members march in public parades with banners proudly proclaiming what they are. Heterosexual child molesters, at least, still have to *hide* what they do (except perhaps in the pornography subculture).

The Torah's admonition not to commit *ervat gilah* with one's father or mother (Lev. 18:7) is interpreted literally by some commentators to mean that sodomy with one's father is prohibited along with intercourse with one's mother (San. 54a); others, however, find that somewhat outrageous and interpret the verse to mean that intercourse with one's mother is also an offense against the father (Rashi; Nachmanides).

However, Silverstein and Picano's book contains a section called "Daddy–Son Fantasies," which describes "the sexual interest some gay boys have in their fathers; some boys [masturbate] to fantasies of having sex with them. Occasionally, boys even attempt to seduce their fathers."[21] This sounds like a Freudian reversal of father–son molestation. Nevertheless, a major study of the gay community includes comments from about twenty men who reported having had sexual feelings for their fathers, sons, uncles, and nephews and even long-term sexual activity with their brothers. Many of these men saw nothing wrong with incest.[22]

The Torah does not prohibit deep love relationships between men (e.g., David and Jonathan), but it does forbid such love to become sexualized. Societies that have encouraged and celebrated male homosexuality have traditionally been extremely male supremacist and phallus worshiping—a fact that is further evidenced by the lack of status these same cultures gave to prevailing lesbian relationships. Women, girls, boys, and slaves existed simply to serve the free man in all his desires. There was no such thing as a separate gay "identity"; it was an activity indulged in by any man.[23]

Silverstein and Picano's manual of "normal" gay sex indicates that gay men, as a group, must have an incredibly high tolerance level for pain and subjugation. Besides anal penetration (a fairly standard activity), sadomasochism, "bondage and discipline," fetishism (e.g., boot-licking), "fisting," piercing of the most sensitive body parts, and sexual arousal from urine and feces are described as if they were pleasurable. Aversion for intimacy is indicated by anonymous sex, orgies, mutual mastur-

21. Ibid., p. 48.

22. Karla Jay and Allen Young, *The Gay Report* (New York: Summit Books, 1977), pp. 99–104.

23. See Keuls; also K. J. Dover, *Greek Homosexuality* (Cambridge, MA: Harvard University Press, 1978); and John Boswell, *Christianity, Social Tolerance, and Homosexuality* (Chicago: University of Chicago Press, 1980), pp. 61–87, for explorations of male homosexuality in ancient Greece and Rome.

bation clubs, and something called "sleazy sex," which is described as a reaction against "Mama's middle-class morality."[24]

This high tolerance level for pain and the avoidance of intimacy shed light on the Talmud's association of sodomy with the rape of a woman whose cries for help are ignored—both are said to be reasons why God makes solar eclipses (Suk. 29a). The male version of crying out, in a culture that defines masculinity as unemotional toughness, consists of putting his fist through the wall or keeping a stiff upper lip as he grins and bears the pain. Perhaps the gay man is exhibiting a "cry for help" that we have not yet learned to recognize as such.

LESBIANISM

> You shall not act according to the deeds of the land of Egypt where you lived. And you shall not act according to the deeds of the land of Canaan to which I will bring you. Do not walk in the ways of their statutes. (Lev. 18:3)

Contrary to popular perception, the rabbinic prohibition of lesbianism is not derived from the Torah's prohibition of sodomy. A law with one level of punishment cannot be derived from a law with a different level of punishment. Sodomy ranks with the most serious sexual violations—incest, adultery, and bestiality—and was a capital crime, punishable by stoning, while lesbianism was punishable "merely" by flogging—the most minor penalty in the days of corporal punishment. Hence, the prohibition of the former cannot be the source for the prohibition of the latter.

Lesbianism ranks only with certain improper heterosexual behaviors, such as public sex or inappropriate advances by men toward women:

> There are several prohibited acts which do not amount to punishable offenses, but which may render the perpetrator liable to flogging by way of admonition and rebuke: e.g., indecent gestures or suggestions to women with whom intercourse is prohibited; lesbian conduct among women; sexual intercourse with one's wife in public; being secluded with a woman with whom intercourse is prohibited.[25]

The prohibition of lesbianism is derived from the verse quoted above, according to the author of *Sifra* (also known as *Torat Kohanim*), a rabbinic commentary on Leviticus dating from the early third century c.e. "And what are these deeds [of Egypt and Canaan]? The man marries the man and the woman marries the woman; the man marries a woman and her daughter, and the woman is married to two men" (*Sifra* 8:8). Unlike the written Torah, this commentary seems to equate sodomy with lesbianism and father–daughter incest with polyandry.

The Talmud offers several interpretations of the "deeds" referred to in this verse,

24. Silverstein and Picano, p. 185.
25. Elon, p. 486.

none of which has to do with lesbianism. "Walking in the ways of their statutes" is interpreted as burning articles or mutilating an animal at a king's funeral (A.Z. 11a); beheading a criminal with a sword, which R. Judah claims is a Roman custom (he recommends using an axe instead) (San. 52b); and a long list of Amorite practices, such as "she who urinates before her pot in order that it should be quickly cooked," imposing silence for lentils or cries for beans (to benefit food preparations), or one who "breaks eggs on a wall in front of fledglings" (Shab. 67a–b).

The Talmud calls lesbianism *pritzuta be-alma,* "mere obscenity"; women who *mesulelot* (commit lewdness) with each other, are not, however, committing *ervat gilah* (Yev. 76a; Shab. 65a). *Mesulelot* is also used to describe a woman's sexual activity with a prepubescent boy (San. 69b).

This illustrates, once again, that *it is phallic penetration that is the target of the prohibitions known as ervat gilah.* This is not because the penis is considered more "important," but because it is viewed as more in need of control.

Consider the following findings of a major study of American couples—heterosexual, gay, and lesbian. Women are more monogamous than men. Even when they are not monogamous, they have only a few outside partners and tend to be emotionally involved with them. Lesbians have fewer outside partners than do straight women. Nonmonogamous men have more outside partners than nonmonogamous women and are less likely to become emotionally involved with them. Gay men have the most outside partners—sometimes in the hundreds—and these are usually casual or even anonymous encounters. Only a minority of gay men (unlike the other two types of couples) are monogamous.[26]

The tempering effect of female sexuality on male sexuality is obvious. Male sexuality without the female runs amuck; female sexuality without the male does not.

GAY RIGHTS AND JUDAISM

It would be extremely difficult to rationalize, from a Torah point of view, "gay marriages" or anything else that seeks to put homosexual relationships on par with heterosexual marriage. That an individual should have the legal right to name whomever he or she chooses as "next of kin" (for inheritance, medical power of attorney, etc.) is a separate issue. However, to make bisexuality a societal norm would erase a significant boundary. On the other hand, deep, *nonerotic*, same-sex friendships are very devalued in our society and need to be encouraged.

However, while a Torah-observant society cannot encourage homosexuality as an "equal alternative," it may also be argued that there is no halakhic basis for discriminating against gay men and lesbians in basic civil rights, such as renting an apartment or being hired for a job. Accepting the Torah's boundaries also does not negate the importance—indeed, the responsibility—of speaking out against gay-

26. Philip Blumstein and Pepper Schwartz, *American Couples* (New York: William Morrow and Co., 1983), pp. 272–279.

bashing, the violence committed against men and women *perceived* as gay by macho straight men such as the neo-Nazi Skinheads.

A questionable double standard exists in Jewish religious practice.[27] Male homosexuality is an offense on par with violating the Sabbath, eating blood (nonkosher meat), eating *chametz* during Passover, or working and eating on Yom Kippur. Lesbianism is much less serious than any of these—it is on par with eating lobster, for instance.

Observant Jews (except for a minority of men in Israel who throw stones at cars on the Sabbath) do not harass, castigate, exclude, or banish Jews for not keeping kosher or observing the Sabbath. Lobster-eaters do not have to form synagogues of their own, and even though "special" (i.e., Conservative) synagogues have been formed for people who drive on the Sabbath or want mixed seating, these halakhic deviations do not make the individuals who practice them unwelcome at an Orthodox synagogue. Gay and lesbian Jews, however, are not treated like any other "halakhic deviation."

Orthodox Jews participate in Jewish community events with all kinds of Jews, from Conservatives to atheists and the intermarried. However, in New York City, in 1993, Orthodox Jews threatened to boycott the annual Salute to Israel parade if a gay synagogue was allowed to participate.[28] This is halakhically inconsistent.

Similarly, should any branch of Judaism that ordains rabbis who eat nonkosher meat or drive on the Sabbath refuse to ordain gay rabbis? The most traditional forces in the Conservative movement oppose allowing gay and lesbian Jews to be synagogue board members or educators or be called to the Torah.[29] If the same standard were applied to Jews across the board halakhically, there would probably be few "qualified" people left to fill these roles. It might be argued that a sexual violation is different—that, for example, no one would call a known incest perpetrator up to the Torah or ordain him as a rabbi. This is not necessarily true, however. "Jewish law disqualifies one who openly desecrates the Sabbath, or commits idolatry, from slaughtering animals for 'kosher' consumption. But not in the case of a person guilty of any other particular transgression, including incest" (*Tanya*).[30]

Furthermore, homosexuality should perhaps be perceived as more akin to incest *victimization* than *perpetration*, for evidence exists that incest may play a significant role in the development of gay and lesbian sexual preferences. Finkelhor found that "boys victimized by older men were over *four times* more likely to be currently engaged in homosexual activity than were nonvictims. Close to half the male respon-

---

27. Here I primarily refer to the Orthodox and Conservative movements, which both maintain that halakhic observance is central to Jewish life. The Reform and Reconstructionist *movements* do not, although certain *individuals* within them may.

28. "Gays Not Permitted Banner in Parade," *Weekly News Digest* (Jewish Telegraphic Agency), Apr. 1, 1993, p. 3.

29. Yosef I. Abramowitz, "Conservative Movement Begins to Struggle with Homosexuality," *The Jewish Advocate,* Dec. 13–19, 1991, p. 10.

30. *Likutei Amarim* (Kehot Publication Society: London, 1973), p. 103 n. 19.

dents who had had a childhood sexual experience with an older man were currently involved in homosexual activity." He emphasizes that this finding "should not be used to increase our culture's already intense fear of homosexuals."[31]

A psychotherapist who runs groups for male incest survivors notes that sexual abuse "almost always leads the survivor to have confused feelings about his sexuality. . . . The victimized male wonders and worries about what the abuse has turned him into. Believing that he is no longer an adequate man, he may see himself as a child, a woman, gay, or less than human—an irreparably damaged freak."[32]

Russell states: "Some research suggests that a relationship exists between child sexual abuse and homosexuality. . . . One response to the trauma of incest is to turn away from heterosexuality and to embrace a lesbian orientation and lifestyle. . . . Whether or not this outcome is viewed positively or negatively, however, is a matter of opinion."[33] A lesbian psychotherapist who views the outcome positively believes that the key factor is not so much the damage done by the father, but the loss of the mother inherent in the situation:

> Damage to the mother–child bond, which always occurs following the seductive interest in the child by the father, may be a significant contributing factor in the development of lesbianism as a sexual preference in the adult father–daughter incest survivor. . . . I observe in my practice that virtually all of the lesbian father–daughter incest survivors reveal an intense longing for a nurturing, positive relationship with a woman, . . . a distinctly separate issue from the survivor's anger at and difficulties with men.[34]

Every year at *Parshat Achrei Mot*, many rabbis take the opportunity to preach to their congregations against homosexuality. Unfortunately, some of these same rabbis *never* speak out against incest. "People know incest is wrong, but they think homosexuality is all right," a rabbi once stated in his own defense when challenged on this. However, only one out of ten girls will become a lesbian (and recent studies indicate this is too high an estimate), while one out of three or four girls is an incest victim. It should be clear which issue is more urgent.

---

31. Finkelhor, pp. 195–196.

32. Mike Lew, *Victims No Longer* (New York: HarperCollins, 1988), pp. 41, 55.

33. Russell, pp. 199–200.

34. Eileen Starzecpyzel, "The Persephone Complex: Incest Dynamics and the Lesbian Preference," in *Lesbian Psychologies,* ed. by the Boston Lesbian Psychologies Collective (Urbana: University of Illinois, 1987), p. 263.

✱✱✱ 28 ✱✱✱

Holiness

Kedoshim (19:1–20:27)

The Torah portion containing the holiness code (*Kedoshim*) follows the portion on forbidden sexual relations (*Achrei Mot*) "to teach you that in every place where you find sexual boundaries, you find holiness" (LR 24:6).

Judaism views the body as a sacred vessel and sex as a sanctified activity. Modesty is an important aspect of human dignity, which is designed to make sex *private,* not *shameful.* Even mere voyeurism is to be avoided. Sexual sins are said to drive the Shekhinah from the world, but "one who happens to see a naked part of the body and does not feed his eyes on it is worthy to greet the Shekhinah" (LR 23:13).

Kedoshim, like *Mishpatim,* contains a list of laws setting boundaries for human behavior. Some are social ordinances like respecting one's parents and the elderly, taking care of the poor, making fair judgments in a court of law, avoiding gossip, admonishing others rather than holding grudges against them, paying a worker's wages on time, treating the convert equally, and dealing in honest weights and measures. Others are statutes such as to not eat blood; mix breeds of animals, seeds, or fabrics; cut a man's sideburns or beard in a certain way; gash the skin in mourning; or eat the fruit of a fruit tree during its first three years.

ZNUT: SEXUAL DEGRADATION

Three prohibitions employ the word *znut,* or "sexual degradation": *chilul habat,* or "desecration of the daughter," worship of the god Molekh, and consulting an *ov* or *yidoni* (certain kinds of mediums and oracles). We will only discuss *chilul habat* and Molekh now and will leave the *ov* and *yidoni* for Deuteronomy (part 5).

Znut, or sexual degradation, includes prostitution but is not limited to the paid profession. All promiscuity is included. "Prostitution," "whoredom," "harlotry," and "licentiousness" are all included in the term *znut,* but each of these English words fails to convey the Hebrew word's broader meaning and true implications. Translating *znut* as "sexual degradation" makes the point that something sacred has been secularized. A *zonah* is a woman who has been sexually degraded through common use—a harlot, whore, or prostitute is simply the most extreme case.

Rashi interprets *znut* to include giving one's daughter away without *kiddushin.* "If you do this, the land will degrade [*mezaneh*] its fruits, producing them in other places but not in your land." The earth's reproduction system is thus affected by how humans use theirs. A clue to this may lie in the fact that in Aramaic, the root *zan, zen,* or *zna* is equivalent to the Hebrew *min,* meaning "quality, nature, kind, species" (Jastrow).

Nachmanides takes issue with Rashi that *znut* includes premarital sex, noting that the Sages *overruled* the minority view that "an unmarried man who had intercourse with an unmarried woman, with no matrimonial intent, renders her a *zonah*" (Yev. 61b). Rather, *znut* can only apply to a married or a betrothed woman. Additionally, he states, it may apply to a father giving his daughter to a man whom she cannot legally marry, such as a relative, a slave, or a gentile. *Znut* therefore includes incest.

Znut is why men (but not women) are commanded to wear *tzitzit* (fringes)—it is a means by which men are to discipline their eyes. "When you see them, you will remember Hashem's commandments and do them. You will not follow your heart and your eyes with which you *zonim*" (Num. 15:39).

One can degrade oneself (*liznot*), make degradation or be degraded (*lezanot*), or cause the degradation of another (*lehaznot*). The first term is used to describe what people do in worshiping an idol, the second is used of the earth's refusal to yield its fruits, and the third is used to describe what fathers may not do to their daughters.

CHILUL HABAT: DESECRATION OF THE DAUGHTER

> Do not desecrate[*techalel*] your daughter by sexually degrading her [*lehaznotah*], lest the land become degraded [*tizneh*] and the land be filled with *zimah.* (Lev. 19:29)

The Rabbis interpreted this verse to include incest, "giving over of one's daughter for sex with no matrimonial intent," marrying one's young daughter to an old man, and delaying the marriage of an adult daughter in order to benefit from her labor. A father who did the last act is called "a subtly wicked poor man" (San. 76a–b; Yom. 18b).

Nachmanides defines *zimah* ("lewdness") as "*znut* that is thought of in secret." Another view sees *zimah* as an acronym for *zu mah hi,* "who is she," a reference to the unknown paternity that results (Ned. 51a). However, only two things are actually called *zimah* in the Torah: father–daughter incest (Lev. 18:17, 20:14) and *chilul habat.* We have already noted that father–daughter incest was normative in the ancient world. It was also not unusual for fathers to sell their daughters into prostitution. This usually took a religious form, that is, dedicating the daughter to a temple. However, secular prostitution existed as well. Herodotus tells a long story of an ancient Egyptian king who was trying to discover the identity of the man who stole a thief's body from the gallows. "He is supposed to have made his daughter sit among the prostitutes and receive all men without exception; telling her before she lay with any to oblige him to confess to her what was the cleverest and the wickedest thing he had done in his life. Then, if any confessed to her about the thief, she was to hold him and not let him go. The girl did as her father told her."[1]

He also tells of another king named Cheops (who is known in Egyptian chronologies as Khufru). "The wickedness of Cheops reached such a pitch, that being in want of money, he prostituted his daughter and ordered her to make a certain sum of money. . . . This she did."[2]

There are many parts of the rural Third World today where men sell their daughters into prostitution out of poverty, sometimes for as little as seventy-five dollars.[3] However, pimping his daughter is only the most extreme way a man can violate the prohibition of desecrating her. By giving her over as a commodity in marriage to a man she does not want, he degrades her as well. By using his daughter's sexuality for himself *in any way,* he sets her up for continued degradation the rest of her life. This is *zimah.*

ZIMAH: FROM INCEST TO PROSTITUTION

It is highly significant that God does not tell women *not to be* prostitutes but instead tells men *not to make* their daughters *into* prostitutes. Father–daughter incest is indeed the major cause of women entering a life of prostitution. "The father, in effect, forces the daughter to pay with her body for affection and care which should be freely given. In so doing, he destroys the protective bond between parent and child and initiates his daughter into prostitution."[4]

A girl whose body has been repeatedly invaded against her will by a known and trusted male caretaker does not get the chance to develop a sense of boundaries or normal mechanisms for self-protection. Saying "no" has never stopped unwanted activity in the past, so there is no reason it should be expected to in the future. The sense of powerlessness instilled in the victim is matched by "an impaired ability to correctly judge the trustworthiness of others."[5]

1. Carter, p. 138.
2. Ibid., p. 141.
3. See, for instance, Steven Erlanger, "Thriving Sex Industry in Bangkok Is Raising Fears of an AIDS Epidemic," *The New York Times,* Mar. 30, 1989, p. A3, on Thailand; and Kathleen Barry, *Female Sexual Slavery* (New York: Avon Books, 1979), pp. 68–69, on Paraguay.
4. Herman, p. 4.
5. Russell, *Secret Trauma,* p. 168.

Incest thus sets the stage for revictimization. Sexual predators "can sense a target to victimize. They can tell by the person's carriage, body language, facial expression. They can sense the fear, the helplessness, the passivity," as well as pick up cues of "a low self-image or a strong but unsatisfied need for affection, approval, and attention."[6] Understanding how victims are easily revictimized should *not* be confused with blaming the victim, nor should it be used as an excuse to do so.

Russell's study found that 82 percent of the incest survivors had experienced some form of sexual assault in their later lives, compared to 48 percent of the women who had never been abused as children. (All child sexual abuse, and not just incest, correlated in this way, although the correlation for incest was slightly higher.) Three times as many incest survivors as nonvictimized women reported having been raped in marriage. More than twice as many reported physical violence from a husband, as well as unwanted sexual advances from a doctor, teacher, employer, clergyman, or therapist.[7]

While some incest survivors may develop an aversion to sex, others

> respond to their earlier traumatic sexualization by becoming promiscuous as adolescents or adults. Some of these women see sexuality as a commodity—something they can use to gain money, favors, or rewards of some kind. Incestuous abuse can serve as a perfect training ground for prostitutes in this way—particularly when combined with economic pressures it may alienate the victim from her sexuality and train her to expect to be bribed in one way or another in exchange for sexual submission.[8]

To put it simply, "many incest survivors feel that as long as they are obligated to have sex with men, 'they might as well get paid for it.'"[9] Others, who may have become used to feeling powerless in sexual encounters, find the manipulation and control that a prostitute can exert over a client to be a form of power. Because they do not expect sex to ever be separated from exploitation, such women experience prostitution as *a step up* because at least they can take control over *how* they will be exploited.

Children and young teenagers who run away from home to escape sexual abuse (and/or physical violence) are the population most vulnerable to repeat-abuse situations. In the United States, one-third of them

> are lured into selling their bodies within two days of leaving home. . . . Runaway kids run away from abuse in the home and attach to pimps—or are abducted by pimps—

---

6. Blume, p. 179; Russell, *Secret Trauma*, p. 171.

7. Russell, *Secret Trauma*, pp. 158–160. See also "Tie Found between Risk of Adult Rape and Being Raped as a Child," *The New York Times,* Aug. 17, 1992, p. A17, for a study by Jacquelyn White at the University of North Carolina which found that women who had experienced family violence or sexual abuse before age fourteen had 244 percent more chance of adolescent rape or attempted rape than women who did not.

8. Russell, *Secret Trauma*, p. 167.

9. Blume, p. 182.

because pimps offer them something familiar: the illusion of nurturing and protection, the use of their bodies, the marketing of their souls. The girls swear that these pimps, who give them abuse, entrapment, and violation, along with care and attention, are their boyfriends.[10]

The sex industry relies on the damage done by incest to provide it with a crop of "workers." According to some estimates, 92 percent of teenage prostitutes are incest survivors. In one study, "60% of the adult prostitutes had been sexually abused by an average of two males each, some having been molested by up to 11 different males; 90% knew their abusers. But most prostitutes were not adults: 60% were 16 or under, many were younger than 13, and almost 80% had become prostitutes before age 18."[11]

The incest survivors in Russell's study were more than twice as likely to have been asked to pose for pornography, while father–daughter incest survivors in particular were *four times* more likely to have been asked, not only to pose, but to enact it. Incest victims of multiple perpetrators were three or four times more likely to report such experiences. "Men appear to be selecting previously victimized females for further pornography-related victimization," Russell concludes. "They are females who may have particular difficulty in handling such experiences."[12]

Society has dealt badly with prostitution, preferring to blame the woman for being "loose" and "immoral" rather than punish the buyers and sellers and address the circumstances that cause women to become involved. Even many women who call themselves feminists defend prostitution as a "victimless crime" and pornography as "free speech." The civil libertarian argument chooses to ignore the most salient factor: a lucrative sexual slave trade in women and children continues to flourish throughout the world. What we see of this in America is only a very small tip of the iceberg.

To believe that women freely "choose" a life of prostitution ignores the reality that two million Thai women are sold to men on "specifically designed sex tours, popular in West Germany and Japan,"[13] that women and girls have died in brothel fires because they were chained to the beds,[14] or that the military and the tourism industries are the biggest pimps worldwide. Why, for example, are French brothels called *maisons d'abattage* ("houses of slaughter")?[15]

To assert that prostitutes are "independent" women who have rejected being the "private property" of a man in marriage ignores the fact that being public property is hardly less degrading. It ignores the reality that prostitutes are usually "owned" by pimps who beat them if they get "out of line" or try to escape. It also ignores the fact

---

10. Ibid., p. 180.
11. Ibid., p. 181.
12. Russell, *Secret Trauma*, pp. 160–161, 173.
13. Erlanger, p. A3. The figure of two million is cited in Margot Hornblower, "The Skin Trade," *Time*, June 21, 1993, p. 46. Anyone who believes that prostitution is a "victimless crime" should read this article.
14. Barbara Crossette, "As Thai Sex Trade Increases, So Do Abuses," *The New York Times,* Oct. 6, 1986, p. A10.
15. Barry, pp. 3–4.

that prostitutes exist to gratify male sexual desires that a wife or girlfriend cannot, or will not, fulfill, such as sadomasochistic or excretory practices or the compulsive acting out of sexual traumas.[16]

Girls and women are "purchased, kidnapped, drawn in through syndicates or organized crime, or fraudulently recruited by fronting agencies which offer jobs, positions with dance companies, or marriage contracts that don't exist. . . . Conning a girl or young woman by feigning friendship or love is undoubtedly the easiest and most frequently employed tactic, . . . and it is the most effective."[17]

It is the most effective tactic because a woman's history of incest will make her vulnerable to mistaking the predator's initial kindness for love. Thus, to make the prostitute a criminal only entrenches her in the life-style; so, too, does legalized regulation of the trade, which simply makes the government the pimp under the guise of protecting "public health." The only constructive way to help prostitutes get out of the life without punishing them for being there is by criminalizing *the buying and selling of a woman's body* while decriminalizing the activity of the woman herself.

Punishing men who buy girls' and women's bodies has never been taken seriously as a solution, however, because it would mean putting many of our most "respectable" doctors, lawyers, and businessmen behind bars. Policemen and judges who patronize prostitutes would certainly rather put the woman in jail than be put there themselves!

Society also seems to be extremely willing, if not eager, to ignore the degree to which incest, pornography, and prostitution are interrelated. Perhaps this is because it thrives so much on the acting (and acting out) of previously abused women for "entertainment." Hollywood is indeed the first cousin of the sex industry. Consider, for example, Marilyn Monroe, who was "left in foster homes, raped in one of them, . . . vulnerable all her life to father figures . . . [and] encouraged by Hollywood to play roles that perpetuated her deepest fear: that she was valueless except for sex"; Rita Hayworth, who escaped a violent and incestuous father only to marry a man who "not only lived off her salary and supervised every dress and hairdo, but also promised and delivered her sexual services to men who might help with movie roles"; or Hedy Lamarr, who also went from child abuse to wife abuse and was the actress used to film "the first female orgasm on screen"—the camera focused on her face "while the director repeatedly plunged a large pin into her bare buttocks."[18]

If it is acceptable for men to be entertained by the psychological damage done by incest, society cannot truly be said to be "against" such abuse. We need to take a good, hard look at the social denial that allows us to continue sacrificing our children.

16. See Lovelace, pp. 45–48, for examples.
17. Barry, pp. 4–5.
18. Gloria Steinem, "Women in the Dark: Of Sex Goddesses, Abuse, and Dreams," *Ms.* 1:4 (Jan./ Feb. 1991):36–37.

MOLEKH AND CHILD SACRIFICE

Every man, from the children of Israel or from the converts that live in Israel, who gives his seed to Molekh shall be put to death. The people of the land shall pelt him with stones. I will set My Face against that man and cut him off from among his people, because he gave his seed to Molekh and therefore made My *mikdash tamae* and desecrated My holy Name. And if the people of the land avert their eyes from this man giving his seed to Molekh, and do not put him to death, I will set My Face against that man and his family, and I will cut off him and all the *zonim* after him, who *liznot* after Molekh, from among their people. (Lev. 20:2–5)

Giving one's "seed"—that is, one's child—to Molekh is one of the thirty-six sins punishable by *karet*, or divine excision. Nevertheless, society had the responsibility to rid itself of men who did this to their children. The Jewish court was supposed to put the man to death, but if for some reason it did not, *the people themselves* had to kill him (Rashi). If society chose to ignore or deny what was going on, then even the members of the man's *family* would be punished by God as collaborators, in addition to anyone else who degraded themselves by worshiping Molekh.

Social denial is complicity, and it is rapidly self-perpetuating. "If they conceal one thing, in the end they will conceal many things; if the Small Sanhedrin [of 23 judges] conceals, in the end the Great Sanhedrin [of 71 judges] will conceal" (Rashi).

Who was Molekh and what did it mean for a man to "give his seed" to him? Molekh has the same root as *melekh*, "king," reflecting the pagan reality that where the king is god, the god is king. *Molekh* may have been a generic name for any god worshiped with this particular rite, for "the same law applies to whatever they proclaimed as their king, even a pebble or a splinter" (San. 64a). There were two phases of the rite—handing the child over and causing it to pass through the fire. A Jewish man was culpable only if he completed both phases. The law applied to any of his grandchildren or illegitimate offspring as well (San. 64b).

Molekh was "well-known to [the Jews] from Egypt," according to Nachmanides, but is also said to be the Ammonite god Milkom (1 Kings 11:5, 11:7). Molekh is described throughout Prophets as being worshiped in *gei ben hinom,* the Valley of the Son of Hinom (south of Jerusalem), and he is sometimes linked to the Canaanite god Baal, as well as something called Tophet (Joshua 15:8; 2 Kings 16:3, 17:17, 21:6, 23:10; Jeremiah 7:31–33, 19:4–6; Ezekiel 23:37–39). Adramelekh and Anamelekh, other gods to whom children were offered, may also have been "Molekhs," as indicated by the word *melekh* in their names (2 Kings 17:31).

Some commentators believe that offering a child to Molekh was merely an initiation rite for the child that consecrated him or her to Molekh. The father "handed his child over to the priests. They lit two large piles of wood and made the child pass on foot between the two fires" (Rashi). "There was a loose pile of bricks in the middle, and fire on either side of it. . . . It was like the children's leaping [over a bonfire] on Purim" (San. 64b).

"How was it done?" asks Maimonides.

One lights a big fire, and takes some of his seed and delivers it to the priests who serve the fire. After it is delivered into their hands, the priests give the child [back] to its father to pass it in the fire with his permission. The father of the child is the one who passes his child upon the fire, with the priests' permission. He passes it while walking from one side to the other side in the midst of the flames. He does not burn it [the child] to Molekh as sons and daughters are burned in other idol worship. (*Idolatry* 6:3)

Nachmanides, however (supported by several verses in Prophets cited earlier in this section), asserts that the child was actually sacrificed by being burned in the fire. "They made the child pass through the flame many times, until he [or she] died in the burning fire." Molekh worship may have differed from child sacrifice to other deities only in the details of how the burning was done. Alternately, the burning to Molekh may have been a form of sorcery, used for divination and prophecy.

Secular sources confirm Nachmanides' view that the child was indeed sacrificed:

In order to renew the solar fires, human victims may have been sacrificed to the idol by being roasted in its hollow body or placed on its sloping hands and allowed to roll into a pit of fire. It was in the latter fashion that the Carthaginians sacrificed their offspring to Molekh. The children were laid on the hands of a calf-headed image of bronze, from which they slid into a fiery oven, while the people danced to the music of flutes and timbrels to drown the shrieks of the burning victims.[19]

This explains the name *Tophet* associated with Molekh, for *toph* is the Hebrew word for timbrel. Another account echoes this description.

In Carthage we find that the sacrifice of children was performed at a great image with a bull's head and human body. The image was of metal, and made hot by a fire kindled within it, and the children laid in its arms, rolled from them into the fiery lap below. Rabbi Simeon says, in speaking of the statue of Molekh outside Jerusalem: "It was a statue with the head of an ox, and the hands stretched out as a man's who opens his hands to receive something from another. It was hollow within. . . . The child was placed before the idol, and a fire made under it till it became red-hot. Then the priest took the child, and put him into the glowing hands of Molekh, and, lest the parents should hear his cries, they beat drums to drown the noise."[20]

Yet a third account says;

Child sacrifice was a specialty of the Carthaginians, inherited from their Phoenician and Canaanite ancestors. In honor of Baal, who was both sun god and god of fire, the

---

19. Frazer, p. 327.

20. Elford Higgens, *Hebrew Idolatry and Superstition* (New York: Kennikat Press, 1983), pp. 38–39.

children were rolled down into a fiery pit in the shape of the image of the god; the image was itself known as Molekh. In a site near modern Tunis 6,000 urns containing the charred remains of infants were found. . . . In earlier times, Baal had demanded the sons of nobles but the latter-day Carthaginians secretly bought and bred poor children for the purpose.[21]

The urns that have been found contained mostly cremated infants (under age two), but also some remains of children up to age twelve. "Here for the first time sufficient evidence accumulated to show conclusively that the ancient stories of Phoenician and Canaanite infant sacrifice to Molekh were only too true. . . . It is now clear that other peoples' detestation of the Phoenicians for such a practice was founded on fact."[22]

These secular sources are in turn confirmed by a "lost Midrash,"[23] which reads as follows:

Although all the pagan shrines were in Jerusalem, the Molekh was outside Jerusalem. It was made as a hollow idol within seven rooms. If one would sacrifice fine flour, they would open one room for him. If he would sacrifice turtledoves or young pigeons, they would open two rooms for him. If he would sacrifice a lamb, they would open three rooms for him. If he would sacrifice a ram, they would open four rooms for him. If he would sacrifice a calf, they would open five rooms for him. If he would sacrifice an ox, they would open six rooms for him. If he sacrificed his son, they would open all seven rooms for him. Its face was like that of a calf. Its hands were extended as one does to receive something from his friend. They would heat it with fire. Then the priests would take the child and place him in the hands of the Molekh, where he would let out his soul.

Gei ben hinom, the Valley of the Son of Hinom, is also called the "Valley of Slaughter." Usually this area—which today lies south of Mount Zion and west of Silwan—is simply called the Valley of Hinom, or Gehinom. *Gehinom* (or sometimes *Gehenna*) is the Jewish term for what Christianity calls "hell," and the "prince of Gehenna" (Shab. 104a) is the *satan,* the prosecuting angel who was combined with the pagan satyr to form the Christian devil, Satan. Thus, the image of hellfire is rooted in the revulsion toward pagan child sacrifice.

There is one Jewish view that the totally righteous inherit eternal life, the totally wicked are "doomed" to Gehenna, and those in between "will go down to Gehinom and squeal and rise" (R.H. 16b–17a). For the most part, however, Judaism rejects the concept of eternal damnation. After death, even a wicked soul is believed to spend only a year in Gehinom, becoming "purified" through fire before it ascends to "heaven," which is Gan Eden or paradise (Shab. 33b; B.M. 58b; Ed. 2:10). Fire is said to be a one-sixtieth part of Gehinom (Br. 57b). The entrance to Gehenna con-

---

21. Davies, p. 51.
22. Donald Harden, *The Phoenicians* (New York: Praeger, 1962), p. 95.
23. See commentary to 2 Kings 23:10 in the Judaica Press translation (New York, 1989), p. 417.

sists of "two palm trees in the Valley of Hinom, between which there ascends smoke" (Suk. 32b).

While some biblical verses refer to "sons and daughters" being passed through the flames, others simply say "sons," which of course could be generic for "children." However, it is highly likely that the worship of Molekh frequently consisted of a father's sacrifice of his firstborn son. As we noted in chapter 15, firstborn-son sacrifice was common in the ancient world for a number of reasons, such as a belief that offering the firstborn would cause a man to father many more sons.

An interesting account of a young female victim by Herodotus may or may not be actual Molekh worship, but the resemblance is certainly unmistakable. The Egyptian king Mycerinus (or Menkaure) "lusted after his daughter and lay with her against her will, upon which the girl strangled herself for grief. . . . Grievously afflicted by what had befallen *him*, and desirous of giving his daughter a burial of surpassing splendor, he made a hollow wooden cow and covered it all over with gold, and in this he entombed her" (emphasis mine).[24] Surely, this girl can be said to have been "sacrificed" by her father, even though she *technically* killed herself.

Here can be seen a link between incest and idolatry that is also found in Jewish sources. "The Israelites knew that there is no reality in idolatry, but they worshiped idols because it allowed them to publicly commit the sexual prohibitions" (San. 63b). This is why the term *znut* is used for both sexual degradation *and* idol worship.

Furthermore, the Mishnah (Meg. 4:9) demands that two kinds of people should be "silenced"—those who "speak in euphemisms about the sexual prohibitions," and those who render "You shall not give your seed to pass over to Molekh" as "You shall not give your seed to impregnate a gentile woman" (thus creating a child who will be raised in idolatry).

Interestingly, before Freud abandoned his seduction theory, he linked Molekh worship with incest. "I am beginning to grasp an idea," he wrote to Fliess in January 1897. "It is as though in the perversions, of which hysteria is the negative, we have before us a remnant of a primeval sexual cult, which once was—perhaps still is—a religion in the Semitic East (Molekh, Astarte)."[25]

---

24. Carter, p. 142.
25. Masson, *Complete Letters*, p. 227.

✻✻✻ 29 ✻✻✻

The Kohenet

Emor (21:1–24:23)

Awoman of the *kehunah*, the Jewish priesthood, is called a *kohenet*. Since the priesthood was maintained through patrilineal descent (from father to son), a woman was a *kohenet* by birth—being the daughter of a priest (*bat-kohen*); or she was a *kohenet* by marriage—becoming the wife of a priest (*eshet-kohen*). The significance of being a *kohenet* as opposed to an Israelite (or Levite) woman centered on sacred food (*trumah*) and sacred sex (a higher level of "obligation" regarding menstruation and marriage).

A *bat-kohen* did not necessarily become an *eshet-kohen*, nor was an *eshet-kohen* necessarily a *bat-kohen*. If a *bat-kohen* did not marry a *kohen*, her Israelite husband was called a *zar*, or "stranger." Upon betrothal to a *zar*, the *kohenet* by birth forfeited her priestly privilege of eating *trumah* (Yev. 67b–68a), and her husband did not acquire this privilege.

An Israelite woman, on the other hand, could marry a *kohen* and become an *eshet-kohen*, by which she acquired priestly privilege. Although biblically this occurred at betrothal, rabbinically it was delayed until the actual marriage, out of fear that while still living in her Israelite father's house, she would inadvertently give some *trumah* to her siblings (Kid. 58b; Ket. 57b).

Even if she became widowed or divorced from the priest, the *kohenet* by marriage continued to eat *trumah* as long as she had *any* descendants by her husband. If she was pregnant but had no other descendants, however, the fetus did not count as a born child in this regard (Yev. 67a–b).

Upon becoming widowed or divorced from a *zar*, the *kohenet* by birth resumed eating *trumah* in her father's house if she had *no* descendants by her husband (Lev. 22:12–13; Kid. 4a). In this case, a fetus *did* have the same effect as a born child—that is, of disqualifying her from returning to her original premarital status. The opinion is also expressed that the widowed or divorced (but childless) *bat-kohen* only resumed eating tithe *trumah* and not sacrificial *trumah* (Yev. 68b, 74b, 87a).

A *bat-kohen* who married a *kohen* experienced no change in status; the priestly privilege she had as a daughter continued during her marriage, as well as after it, if the marriage ended. The ideal situation was thus for a *bat-kohen* to marry a *kohen* and for a *kohen* to marry a *bat-kohen*.

THE PRIEST'S DAUGHTER

Before marrying a *bat-kohen*, a *kohen* was supposed to investigate her lineage through four generations of foremothers—that is, "her four mothers, who are actually eight" (Kid. 4:4). The use of *arbah imahot* in this *mishnah* brings to mind the Four Matriarchs.

These eight foremothers are: a woman's mother, her two grandmothers, three of her four great-grandmothers, and two of her four great-great grandmothers. The great-grandmother who does *not* have to be checked out is the *kohenet*'s mother's mother's mother—that is, the purely maternal line. The two great-great grandmothers who do not need to be checked out are the continuation of this maternal line (see Figure 29–1).

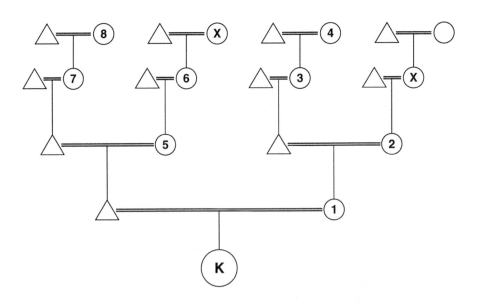

FIGURE 29-1. The priestly foremothers: the *kohenet*'s (K) "four mothers, who are actually eight," are to be checked into by any priestly man who wishes to marry her. If he marries an Israelite woman (a nonpriestly woman), he must check into two additional foremothers ("x") as well. The purely maternal line is the least checked in both cases.

A priest who married an Israelite woman rather than a *bat-kohen* was also advised to check out the same eight foremothers, as well as the fourth great-grandmother and one more great-great grandmother.

Although a *bat-kohen* could marry a man who was not a priest, "their union will not be auspicious. How? R. Chisda said, 'She will either be widowed or divorced or childless.' In a *baraita* it was taught: He will bury her or she will bury him, or she will reduce him to poverty. But that is not so, for R. Jochanan said, 'One who wants to become wealthy should cleave in his seed to that of Aharon, for the Torah and the priesthood will enrich them'" (Pes. 49a). "Them" is in the feminine plural, referring to the daughters of Aharon.

This Gemara then gives examples of the fates of Israelite men who married *kohanot*:

> R. Joshua married a *bat-kohen*. When he became weak, he said, "Aharon is not pleased that I should cleave to his seed and he possesses a son-in-law like myself." R. Idi b. Avin married a *bat-kohen*, and there came forth from him two ordained sons—R. Sheshet, the son of R. Idi, and R. Joshua, the son of R. Idi. R. Papa said, "Had I not married a *bat-kohen*, I would not have become wealthy." R. Kahana said, "Had I not married a *bat-kohen*, I would not have gone into exile."

However, he was reminded by his colleagues that his exile was "to a place of Torah."

Although an Israelite man did not theoretically gain the right to eat *trumah* by marrying a *bat-kohen*, it appears that in some cases he actually did so and that some scholars considered this halakhically correct (Rashi on Chul. 132a). According to R. Nissim, "the giving of the priestly dues to the husband of a priest's daughter is a proper fulfillment of the obligation."[1]

"R. Kahana used to eat [*trumah*] on account of his wife. R. Papa used to eat them on account of his wife. R. Yemar used to eat them on account of his wife. R. Idi b. Avin used to eat them on account of his wife." The rabbinic logic allowing this is "a limitation following a limitation, and the purpose of a double limitation is to extend the law" (Chul. 132a). In Deuteronomy 18:3, first *kohanim* and then *kohen* is used to exclude *kohanot*. However, the result of two sequential exclusions is inclusion—"the successive limitations actually amplify the scope of the law and include the priest's daughter."[2]

The *Zohar* sees the *kohenet* as an example of the esoteric significance of the Torah, in which "every word contains hidden seeds of wisdom, comprehensible only to the wise who are familiar with the ways of the Torah. For truly the words of the Torah are not mere dreams. And even dreams have to be interpreted according to certain rules" (II:95a).

The *bat-kohen* is said to symbolize

---

1. Soncino translation of *Chullin*, p. 746 n. 4.
2. Ibid. n. 3.

the celestial soul, the daughter of our father Avraham, the first proselyte, who drew this soul from a supernal region. . . . This is the *neshamah,* which emanates from a supernal region and enters into the hidden part of the Tree of Life. And when the breath of the supernal priest breathes souls into that Tree, they fly away from there and enter a treasurehouse. (*Zohar* II:95b)

The *zar* symbolizes the *yetzer hara.* The *bat-kohen* who marries a *zar* is like the soul that enters a body controlled by the individual's evil inclination. When the *neshamah* "flies down and finds the edifice of a *zar,*" the soul is ruled by the body rather than being its ruler. "So she does not achieve perfection in this world. And when she leaves him 'she shall not eat *trumah,*' as do the other souls, which reach perfection in this world." *Trumah* itself symbolizes "the Feminine realm" and was eaten at night. *Kodesh kadashim,* the sacrificial food eaten only by male priests within the Tabernacle courtyard, "belongs to the world of Masculinity [and] may be eaten only during the day" (*Zohar* III:101b).

FIRE, SEXUALITY, AND THE *BAT-KOHEN*

A *bat-kohen* who desecrates [herself] with sexual degradation desecrates her father [as well]; she shall be burned in fire. (Lev. 21:9)

The activity described in this verse is only adultery (after betrothal), and not pre-marital sex (Rashi). The normal penalty for the adultery of an Israelite woman was stoning, for both the adulteress and the adulterer, if the young woman was a betrothed *naarah* (Deut. 22:23–24). If she committed adultery when she was older and already married, the penalty was strangulation.

Although there are different rabbinic views on the order of severity of the four methods of execution—stoning, burning, decapitation, and strangulation (San. 50a–b, 66b), one opinion is that the *kohenet* was burned because her adultery was a more serious offense than that of an Israelite woman. "She desecrates and makes light of his [her priestly father's] honor, so that people say, 'Cursed be he who begot this one, cursed be he who raised this one'" (Rashi).

The distinction applied even to a *kohenet* who was married to a maimed priest or to a *zar* (San. 51a–b). Thus, it was related to *her* priestly status and not her husband's. Nor was it based on a sexual relationship with him, since "maimed" could include castrated and other genitally damaged men.

Differentiating a priestly woman's adultery from that of a nonpriestly woman may have been a reaction to the extremely sexual nature of pagan priesthoods. Such a woman's menstruation was also differentiated in that she conducted examinations before and after eating *trumah,* in addition to morning and evening examinations and before and after intercourse (Nid. 1:7 or 11a).

The Torah emphasized that the priestess in Judaism was to have no public sexual role, which was considered degrading, yet her private sexual activity was to be sanctified—but in a much different way from the pagan definition of *holy.* Separating the *kohenet* from *znut* was similar to separating the *kohen* from contact with the dead. The pagan cadaver cult was associated only with *male* priests; hence, the *kohenet* had no such prohibition placed upon her (Sot. 23a).

As the Tabernacle (and later the Temple) was a "feminine vessel" entered by the priest only under the conditions of utmost sanctity, so too was the Jewish priestess. The *kohenet*, like the Holy of Holies, was the dwelling place of the Shekhinah—she was the channel through which divine energy was made manifest on earth. That the misuse of her sexuality was punishable by fire may relate more to the female sexual symbolism of the fire on the altar than to any evaluation that burning is more "severe" than being stoned or strangled to death!

A link between the altar fire and the *bat-kohen* is evident in the distinction made in her *minchah*. A grain-offering brought by a *bat-kohen* was eaten after burning a handful, while the *minchah* of a *kohen* or even an *eshet-kohen* was completely burned (Chul. 131b; Sot. 23a).

There is some question as to what it actually meant to "burn" someone as a form of execution under Jewish law. Because of the Jewish prohibition on cremation of the body, as well as the story of Nadav and Avihu being burned spiritually while remaining physically intact, it is said that those executed by burning actually had molten lead poured down their throats. However, the Talmud records that a *bat-kohen* named Imarta bat Tali committed adultery, and "thereupon R. Chama b. Toviah had her surrounded by bundles of branches and burned." Nonetheless, this is said to have been done only "because the *bet din* at that time was not well versed in the law" (San. 52b).

ESHET-KOHEN AND FORBIDDEN PRIESTLY MARRIAGES

They [the priests] may not marry a woman who is a *zonah* or a *chalalah*, and they may not marry a woman who is divorced from her husband, because he [the priest] is sanctified to his God. (Lev. 21:7)

While the *bat-kohen* was free to marry whomever she wanted because "fit women were not admonished against marriage to the unfit" (Kid. 72b–73a; Yev. 84b–85a), a *kohen* was prohibited from marrying a divorcee, a *chalalah*, or a *zonah*. Included in the definition of a divorcee is a *chalutzah*, a woman who has released her brother-in-law from *yibum* (Yev. 24a). A *chalalah* is the daughter of a forbidden priestly union, such as the marriage of a priest and a divorcee (Kid. 77a). A daughter of the marriage was herself disqualified from the priesthood, as was a son, a *chalal*.

A *zonah* is a woman who has had any of the forbidden sexual relations with men defined as *ervat gilah*—that is, incest or adultery. An incest survivor victimized solely *before* the age of three was not disqualified, however. Such a woman once inquired of R. Akiva whether she could marry a *kohen*, and he replied that she could (Nid. 45a).

In terms of disqualification from the priesthood, a *zonah* also includes a convert to Judaism over age three, a freed slavewoman, and a Jewish woman who has had sexual relations with a slave or a gentile (Yev. 60b, 61a; Sot. 26b; Kid. 78a). The inclusion of a convert as a *zonah* seems to contradict God's command that "the foreigner who becomes a proselyte must be exactly like one who is native-born among you" (Lev. 19:34), that "there shall be one Torah and one law for you and for the proselyte who lives with you" (Num. 15:16). Is marriage supposed to be an exception?

The premarital sex of a Jewish woman with a Jewish man she could marry does not, in the majority rabbinic opinion, render her a *zonah*, as we noted in chapter 28. Thus, a priest *can* marry such a woman. A priest can also marry a woman who has been a lesbian. Although R. Huna asserted that he could not, the majority opinion was that a woman can be rendered a *zonah* only by sex with a (forbidden) *man*. Samuel's father did not permit his daughters to sleep together, and the question was asked whether this does not support R. Huna. The Rabbis disagree and reply that instead "it was in order that they should not become accustomed to a foreign body" (Shab. 65a–b; Yev. 76a).

A priest can even marry a woman who has had sex with an animal.

> R. Shimi b. Chiya stated: "A woman who had intercourse with a beast is eligible for the priesthood." Likewise it was taught: A woman who had intercourse with that which is not a man [*ish*], though she is consequently subject to the penalty of stoning [if there are witnesses], is nevertheless eligible for the priesthood [if there are no witnesses and she cannot be executed]. When R. Dimi arrived he said: "It once happened at Haitalu that while a woman was sweeping the house, a village dog covered her from the rear, and Rabbi declared her eligible for the priesthood." Samuel said: "Even [to marry] a high priest." . . . There is no *znut* with a beast. (Yev. 59b)

Thus, it appears that the prohibition on a priest marrying a divorcée, a *zonah*, or a *chalalah* does not stem from any belief that these women's sexual activities have defiled them—for what could be more defiling than bestiality? Rather, in order to function at the utmost level of holiness, a priest must have a wife *who has not been emotionally damaged by a man through sex.*

The damage of incest is clear. The damage done by adultery and divorce may consist of the possibility that the woman continues to love a man she no longer has (the adulterer or the ex-husband). A *chalalah* is simply the daughter of such a woman; the logic here might be that what applies to the mother also applies to her daughter.

This interpretation helps to make sense of the law that a raped *kohenet* cannot return to her *kohen* husband, something that is not true for the raped Israelite wife in general (Ket. 51b) or the *kohenet* married to a *zar* (Yev. 35a). How could God be so cruel? To be raped is bad enough; to be rejected by one's husband for being raped simply blames the victim. It is inconceivable that God could have such motives. The Torah law, however, does not concern a *kohen* husband *rejecting* his raped wife, for it makes him divorce her *regardless of what he wants.*

Granted, it also makes him divorce her regardless of what *she* wants, and herein lies the apparent cruelty. However, many rape survivors do find it difficult, if not impossible, to have heterosexual sex again without experiencing memories of the attack that interfere with the present situation. Many marriages have broken up because of the results of this painful phenomenon. If the raped woman no longer wants to have sex or responds to her husband's genuine expressions of love with fear and revulsion, this can destroy their sex life and ultimately their marriage.

While any Jewish marriage would somehow have to come to terms with this problem, in the case of a priestly marriage the Torah dictated the solution: the couple must divorce. However, even a slave's testimony was accepted in order to prevent the occurrence of such a situation (Ket. 2:9).

The solution of the raped *kohenet* is consistent with every other rule about priestly marriages: the woman must have the potential for unequivocal happiness in the marriage, meaning that she must never be emotionally damaged by a man through sex. If she has been so damaged, she cannot stay married to a priest.

THE HIGH PRIESTESS AND THE "HOUSE" OF ISRAEL

He [the high priest] must marry a woman in her virginity. He may not marry a widow, a divorcee, a *chalalah*, or a *zonah*, but only a virgin from his people. He shall not desecrate his seed among his people because I am Hashem Who sanctifies him. (Lev. 21:13–15)

In addition to the marital prohibitions placed upon a priest, the high priest was subject to even further restrictions. He could not marry a widow; in fact, he could only marry a virgin. For while the priest "should always have a shining, happy face, more than any other person, as a result of his crown. . . . The high priest should always present a face bright and shining and more joyful than others, seeing that he symbolizes the higher level" (*Zohar* III:8a, III:89b).

Joy meant being happily married. The importance of a high priestess is indicated by the fact that on Yom Kippur, another woman was waiting in the wings to marry the high priest in case his wife should die, for he could not perform the service if he was not married. He had to make atonement for his "house," and he had no house if he had no wife. However, he could not have two "houses," and a wedding could not be performed on Yom Kippur. Hence, there were many complexities involved in how he could have a second, "conditional" wife while the first was still alive (Yom. 2a, 13a–b; LR 5:6).

The logic we applied to forbidden priestly marriages is carried even further with the high priest. Not only could a high priest not marry a woman who had been emotionally *damaged* by a man through sex, he could not marry a woman who had been emotionally *connected,* even happily, to a man through sex.

A widow may always mourn her first husband, for she did not end her marriage by choice (as a divorcee might have). Many widows report seeing apparitions of their deceased husbands. The *Zohar* describes this spiritual phenomenon:

The spirit of a man is left in the woman who was his wife. . . . When the second husband's spirit enters into the body of the woman, the spirit of the first husband contends with it, and they cannot dwell in peace together, so that the woman is never altogether happy with the second husband, because the spirit of the first one is always pricking her, his memory is always with her, causing her to weep and sigh over him. In fact, his spirit writhes within her like a serpent. And so it goes on for a long time. If the second spirit prevails over the first one, then the latter goes out. But if, as sometimes happens, the first conquers the second, it means the death of the second husband. (II:101b–102a)

Thus, a high priest could never do *yibum* and was required to submit to *chalitzah* (San. 2:1; Yev. 6:4). He could be flogged for marrying a widow and compelled to divorce her (Ket. 77a), but as long as he was married to her he had to ransom her if she were taken captive (Ket. 51b). She was also entitled to a *ketubah* (Ket. 100b). A widow named Marta bat Boetus is cited as an example of a case where a regular priest betrothed a widow and only then was appointed high priest. The marriage happened nevertheless.

The definition of a virgin in terms of marriageability to a high priest is discussed at length by the Rabbis (Ket. 97b–98a; Yev. 53b, 59a). She could be a *naarah* or a *bogeret*. Anal sex or the initial stage of normal intercourse disqualified her, as did *miun*, the repudiation of a (previous) marriage by her as a minor. A widow from betrothal, who had never actually been married, was disqualified, even though she was still technically a virgin. The Rabbis also discuss the possibility of a technical virgin being pregnant and whether a high priest may marry her (Chag. 14b–15a). A high priest may not marry a woman whom he himself has seduced or raped (Yev. 59b–60a).

The emphasis of having a "whole-soul" connection to a woman in marriage was required of the high priest, in particular, in order to effect atonement at Yom Kippur. It was, however, important for *all kohanim* because of their role in blessing the people.

THE PRIESTLY BLESSING

Hashem spoke to Moses, saying, "Tell Aharon and his sons that thus you will bless the Israelites. Say to them: 'May Hashem bless you and keep you. May Hashem's Face shine upon you and be gracious unto you. May Hashem's Face lift up to you and grant you peace.' They [the priests] will put My Name upon the Israelites and I will bless them." (Num. 6:22–27)

Birkat Kohanim, the priestly blessing, was part of the daily service in the Tabernacle and Temple. Today, in the diaspora, *Birkat Kohanim* is done only on festivals. Facing the congregation, with their backs to the ark, the priests cover their faces with their prayer shawls, lift up their hands in a certain pattern, and recite the blessing.

Birkat Kohanim was foreshadowed in the Torah when Moses had to keep his hands raised to be victorious over Amalek (Ex. 17:22). "Moses lifted his 10 fingers to the height of heaven in order to allude to the 10 *sefirot* and to cleave firmly to the One Who fights for Israel. Here is explained the matter of the uplifting of hands during the priestly blessing, and its secret" (Nachmanides). The blessing was first done by Aharon at the initiation rite following the construction of the Tabernacle (Lev. 9:22).

The meaning of "Hashem's Face" is explained mystically in terms of the *sefirot* (*Zohar* II:122b–123a). The shining of God's Face upon us is an indication of good favor. "This is a reference to the light of the Shekhinah" (Nachmanides; NR 11:5).

The lifting up of God's Face toward us indicates approval; in divine anger, God's Face is hidden from, or even set against, us (Lev. 17:10, 20:3–6, 26:17; Deut. 31:17–18, 32:20). This "privation of providence leaves one abandoned and a target to all that may happen and come about, so that one's ill- and well-being come about according to chance" (Maimonides, *Guide of the Perplexed* I:23). However, while God's Face led the Jews through the wilderness, no human—not even Moses—could *see* God's Face and survive (Ex. 33:14, 33:20).

The congregation is not supposed to look at the priests as they bless the people because the light of the Shekhinah is transmitted through them:

> One who gazes at a rainbow gazes, as it were, at the Shekhinah. For the same reason it is not right to look at the fingers of the priests when they spread their hands out to bless the people—the Shekhinah "showing herself through the lattice," that is, through the priests' fingers. . . . When the priest spreads his hands at the time he blesses the people, the Shekhinah comes and hovers over him and endows him with power. (*Zohar* II:66b, II:225a)

At one time a priest could only do *Birkat Kohanim* if he was married. This is because the Shekhinah, the Divine Presence, resides only with women and with *married* men. Only a *kohen in unity with a kohenet* had the power to transmit a true blessing. The current practice of allowing single men to participate in *Birkat Kohanim* mistakenly ignores this vital (if invisible) female role.

"All blessings issue from male and female together," the *Zohar* states, explaining, "it is written, 'May Hashem bless you and keep you'—'bless' from the male, and 'keep' from the female" (I:248a).

❋❋❋ 30 ❋❋❋

Mother Nature

Behar (25:1–26:2) and *Bechukotai* (26:3–27:34)

Throughout Leviticus, we have seen how the Torah attempted to transform spiritual values concerning blood, food, and sexuality. In the pagan worldview, human as well as animal bloodshed was required, along with various sex rites, to propitiate the earth so that crops would grow and a bountiful harvest would ensue.

The link between divine approval of human behavior and crop growth did not change with the Torah; only the standards for what *received* divine approval changed. The earth—specifically, the Land of Israel—was still the feminine mother, and the fruit of the tree was, on a symbolic level, still her son.

DIVINE SOVEREIGNTY, MOTHER EARTH, AND THE LAND OF ISRAEL

Carry out My statutes and keep My ordinances. If you carry them out, you will live securely in the Land. The Land will yield her fruit, and you will eat to satisfaction, and you will live securely in her. (Lev. 25:18–19)

If you follow My statutes and keep My commandments and do them, I will give your rains in their season and the Land will yield her produce [*yevulah*], and the tree of the field will yield his fruit. (Lev. 26:3–4)

If you do not listen to Me and do not keep My commandments . . . you will plant your seed in vain, for your enemies will eat it. I will turn My Face against you so that you will be defeated by your enemies, and those who hate you will descend upon you. You will flee even when no one is pursuing you. . . . Your Land will not yield her produce and the tree of the Land will not yield his fruit. (Lev. 26:14, 26:16-17, 26:20)

"The Land," with a capital *L*, means Israel. "The land," with a small *l*, means the earth. The Jews' relation to the Land of Israel can serve as a prototype for the gentile nations' relation to the lands on which they live. That is, the sensitivity of the Promised Land to Jewish behavior might be seen as a kind of role model for the ecological sensitivity of the earth to the behavior of all its inhabitants.

The Torah opens with the verse, "In the beginning God created the heavens and the earth" (Gen. 1:1). Rashi wonders why the Torah did not begin with *Rosh Chodesh* (Ex. 12:1), which was the first commandment to Israel *as a nation.* The answer is that Israel's right as a nation to *that piece* of the earth could not be established until God's ownership of the *entire* earth was first established.

"For if the nations of the world say to Israel, 'You are robbers, because you conquered the lands of the seven nations [of Canaan],' Israel can reply to them, 'All the earth belongs to the Holy One, Who created it and gave it to whom [God] pleased. When God wanted, God gave it to them, and when God wanted it, God took it from them and gave it to us'"(Rashi).

Indigenous peoples in many parts of the world still have a fundamental understanding of their sacred relationship with the land on which they dwell—that they do not own it, but only "rent" it from its Creator. Humanity is simply the caretaker of the earth, as Adam and Chavah were meant to be the caretakers of Eden. The latter two were expelled when they failed to fulfill that function.

Jews have a fundamental indigenous relationship to a small strip of land on the eastern shore of the Mediterranean between Mesopotamia and Egypt. The Jews' modern claim to Israel, after having been twice expelled from it (most recently in 70 c.e.), can serve as a model for all indigenous land claims and reclamation attempts, in spite of propaganda attempts to the contrary by later conquerors who portray themselves as the original indigenous inhabitants.

Jews' right to the Land is not based on any innate superior "racial" qualities. Indeed, their tendency toward "stiff-necked" behavior made God threaten to "do to you what I was going to do to them" if Jews imitated pagan ways (Num. 33:56). Nor is the Jewish claim to Israel based on military might, for it was only through *spiritual* power that the descendants of a group of runaway slaves could "expel nations greater and stronger than [themselves]" (Deut. 11:23). Only if Jews obey the laws of God do they merit the Land, just as Adam and Chavah only merited Eden while they lived in accordance with divine law. Similarly, the nations of the world are learning that they must honor the laws of ecological balance if they want to continue to merit the earth.

While the earth's fecundity is dependent on human behavior, the power of a king is dependent on the earth's fecundity. "'A king is a servant to the field.' Even though he is king and holds power from one end of the world to the other, he is 'a servant to the field.' If the earth yields produce, he can accomplish something; if the earth does not yield, he is of no use whatsoever" (LR 22:1). The Torah never called for the annual sacrifice of the king to ensure a good harvest, but the link between the two remained symbolically intact.

FERTILITY, FAMINE, AND WOMEN

> There will be no woman who miscarries and no barren woman in your land; I will fulfill the number of your days. (Ex. 23:26)

> When I break off your food supply ["staff of bread"], so that 10 women bake your bread in one oven, they shall deliver your bread in a weight. You will eat but you will not be satisfied. (Lev. 26:26)

The divine blessing of fertility applied to women as well as to the earth. However, the Torah transformed the pagan meaning of this, for it ended the requirement that women engage in ritual sex, just as it ended the need to "nourish" the earth with human blood.

Similarly, the Torah mentions women in connection to famine: ten women (a *"minyan"*!) will bake their bread together in one oven instead of individually in their own ovens. However, the essence of the curse is not really that the women *bake together*. Rather, it is that they must then *measure out the result into ten separate parts* (Rashi; Men. 87b). If there were no famine, there would be no need for deliberate, exact measurement into separate parts—everyone could simply eat according to individual need without regard for quantity.

SHMITAH: THE LAND'S SABBATH

> When you come to the Land that I am giving you, the Land must rest in a Sabbath to Hashem. Six years you will plant your field, and six years you will prune your vineyard and gather her crops. In the seventh year there will be a *Shabbat Shabbaton* for the Land, a Sabbath of Hashem. (Lev. 25:2–4)

> I will command My blessing to you in the sixth year, and the Land will produce crops for three years. You will plant in the eighth year but will eat from the old crops until the ninth year. (Lev. 25:21–22)

Every seventh year the Land had to have a Sabbath, just as every seventh day the Jews had to have a Sabbath. Furthermore, enough food would be produced in the sixth year to last until the ninth year, just as the double portion of manna given in the wilderness on the sixth day lasted through the Sabbath.

Just as refraining from working at our jobs on the Sabbath requires faith that God will provide enough income for us, so too the observance of *Shmitah* requires faith that God will provide enough food. On a purely physical level, *Shmitah* allows the land to regenerate itself by lying fallow for a year; on a spiritual level, *Shmitah* affirms that the land belongs to God and may not be subjected to unlimited human exploitation. Similarly, the Sabbath allows us to regenerate ourselves by "lying fallow" for a day, and affirms that our creative endeavors also ultimately belong to God.

That the Jews found it difficult to have such faith is indicated in Leviticus 26:34–35. Because *Shmitah* was not observed, the Jews were exiled. Only through desolation was the Land of Israel given the rest it needed. The seventy years of Babylonian exile are said to correspond to the seventy Sabbatical Years that the Jews neglected to observe (Rashi). The term *"Shabbat Shabbaton,"* which is also used to describe Yom Kippur (Lev. 16:31; 23:32), implies a relationship between *Shmitah* and atonement. *Shmitah* is still observed today in Israel (it is not required in the diaspora). While the chief rabbinate has enacted a practice in which farmers can "sell" their land to a gentile so that it is no longer technically "owned" by a Jew (similar to "selling" one's *chametz* at Passover), extremely observant Jews do not accept this ruling.

YOVEL: THE JUBILEE YEAR

You shall count seven Sabbatical Years, seven times seven years. The period of the seven Sabbatical Years shall be 49 years. . . . You shall sanctify the 50th year, and proclaim freedom throughout the Land for all the inhabitants. It will be a *Yovel* [Jubilee Year] for you; you shall return everyone to his inheritance and everyone to his family. (Lev. 25:8, 25:10)

After seven Sabbatical Years, the fiftieth year was observed as the Yovel, or Jubilee Year. The *shofar* was blown on Yom Kippur (the tenth day of the Jubilee Year), all landed property reverted to it original owner, all debts were canceled, and all Hebrew slaves (males who had had their ears bored and remained with their masters beyond six years) were set free. As with *Shmitah*, crops could not be sown or harvested in the *Yovel*.

As the seventh year, *Shmitah*, corresponds to the seventh day, the Sabbath, so too the fiftieth year, *Yovel*, corresponds to the fifty days of the *Omer*, the period between Passover and Shavuot:

R. Judah said: "Fifty days elapsed between the Exodus and the giving of the Law. Why was this? In order that the number of days should correspond to the number of years of the Jubilee" . . . R. Shimon remarked that it was the Jubilee which led Israel out from Egypt; that is to say, the divine liberation emanated from the side of Jubilee, and from the same side was Judgment stirred up against the Egyptians. For this reason the deliverance from Egypt is mentioned 50 times in the Torah. (*Zohar* II:83b)

The *Zohar* here calls *Yovel* "the Mother." *Yovel* is associated with *Binah* (the "upper Shekhinah") because of its "fifty gates" (see chapter 16). Similarly, *Shmitah* is associated with *Malkhut* (the "lower Shekhinah") because that is the seventh *sefirah* emanating from Binah.

"They are two transcendent Mothers, the *Yovel* and the *Shmitah*. The desire of the *Yovel* [*Binah*] is to crown him [*Tiferet*] and to spread blessings upon him, and to pour sweet fountains over him. . . . The desire of the *Shmitah* [*Malkhut*] is to be blessed and illumined by him [*Tiferet*]" (*Zohar* II:22a).

The *sefirah* of Tiferet is traditionally associated with Jacob. *Binah* and *Malkhut*, as we learned in chapter 7, are, respectively, associated with Leah and Rachel, the hidden and the manifest worlds. Thus, the *Zohar* tells us that Jacob served seven years for Rachel "in order to join himself to the Sabbatical Year. . . . The Jubilee Year, wherever mentioned, symbolizes that which is undisclosed, whereas the Sabbatical Year symbolizes the disclosed." Jacob's deception by a veiled Leah joined him to the Jubilee Year, "for those which are veiled and undisclosed are from the category of the Jubilee Year." This happened "in order that he should make a beginning from the highest world. . . . And after the years symbolic of the Jubilee cycle, which is undisclosed, had passed, he served the years of the Sabbatical septennate which are disclosed. He was thus crowned with the two worlds and laid hold of both of them" (*Zohar* I:153b).

ENDING TEMPLE SLAVERY

We noted in chapter 18 how the Torah, while not abolishing slavery outright, did in fact set the stage for it, especially *within* Jewish society itself. That Hebrew slaves were automatically freed in the *Yovel*, the fiftieth year, is another example of this phenomenon, for in the pagan world, "service under contract for fifty years meant in fact sale into slavery for life."[1]

Another difference made by the Torah was the prohibition of any kind of Jewish "temple slaves." In the pagan world,

> temple slaves were recruited from two main sources: prisoners of war and dedications by individuals. . . . This practice of presenting war captives to temples prevailed throughout the long history of Babylonia. . . . A third source of recruits for temple slavery was the dedication of freeborn children. Orphans who had no one to care for them and poor children whose parents could not support them were sometimes dedicated to a sanctuary as slaves.[2]

Whether a king dedicated war captives or an individual master dedicated a household slave, the purpose was to secure favor from the gods. A man might dedicate his personal slave to a temple in his will, so that the term of service only began with the master's death. Temple slavery was a caste system; those who were dedicated, and their children, could never buy their way out or be ransomed by relatives.

Many priestesses serving the goddess were simply temple slaves.

> The Neo-Babylonian temple slaves were, as a rule, though not exclusively, marked with a star, the symbol of the goddess Ishtar. . . . Similarly, animals belonging to the temple were also marked with a star. . . . [In one case] a man marked his female slave with a star and then dedicated her to a temple. After his death his heir refused to hand her over to the proper authorities. But the female slave apparently preferred the temple to her newly acquired master. She went to the temple authorities and showed them her

---

1. Mendelsohn, p. 32.
2. Ibid., pp. 101, 103.

star mark. That proved the case. Her owner was allowed to keep her in his service until
his death and afterwards she was to be handed over to the temple.[3]

In Egypt, temple slaves "were really organized in a military manner, and were
reckoned as part of the army. . . . They formed part of the property of the crown or of
the temple as much as the land or the cattle. . . . These slaves were despised by the
scribes."[4]

Jewish slaves could not be "dedicated" to Tabernacle service in any such way. A
Jew could only make a vow to donate to the Tabernacle the "endowment valuation"
of a person (oneself or another). This corresponded to the price the person would
command in the slave market (San. 15a).

These values, which were based on age and gender, are listed in Leviticus 27:3–7:

20- to 60-year-old male	50 shekels
20- to 60-year-old female	30 shekels
5- to 20-year-old male	20 shekels
5- to 20-year-old female	10 shekels
1-month- to 5-year-old male	5 shekels
1-month- to 5-year-old female	3 shekels
60 years and older male	15 shekels
60 years and older female	10 shekels

A person had to be definitively male or female to be the object of such a valuation;
thus a *tumtum* and a hermaphrodite could not have any such value placed upon them
(Arak. 2a).

The age distinctions are self-evident in terms of the ability to do hard labor. In the
slave market, twenty- to sixty-year-olds have the most "value" because they can do
the most work. Infants have little value in this way, and the elderly have less value as
slaves than do children and adolescents. Interestingly, the Talmud tells us that "an
old man in the house is a burden in the house; an old woman in the house is a treasure in the house" (Arak. 19a).

The disturbing feature of the list, on the surface, is that the Torah seems to be
supporting a misogynist notion that women are of less value than men. On the contrary, however, the underlying reality is quite different: the lower prices for women
reflect the Torah's prohibition of sexual slavery. Where female slaves are *officially*
used for sex as well as labor—that is, kept in harems as concubines—they are in
greater demand than male slaves and thus command a *higher* price. (The only male
exception is eunuchs, who also served in dual roles, as sexual slaves and harem
guards.)

In the Moslem Arab slave trade, for example, "the marketplace confirmed the high
value attached to the sexual aspects of slavery. Eunuchs commanded the highest prices

---

3. Ibid., pp. 47–48.
4. Erman, p. 128.

among slaves, followed by young and pretty white women. . . . From the end of the seventeenth to the middle of the nineteenth century, the average price of a white female slave was four to six times greater than that of a comparable black woman slave," and both were more expensive than uncastrated male slaves.[5] (In the European-American slave trade of Africans, where black women were more often than not raped by their white masters but were not "officially" sold for sex—that is, to form legal harems—male slaves seem to have commanded higher prices than females.)[6]

Thus, we see that the Torah cannot always be judged by surface appearances. Its true significance and wisdom are often deeper than meets the eye.

------

5. Gordon, pp. 80, 82.

6. Basil Davidson, *The African Slave Trade* (Boston: Little, Brown and Co., 1980), pp. 106–108. See also Bell Hooks, "Sexism and the Black Female Slave Experience," *Ain't I a Woman: Black Women and Feminism* (Boston: South End Press, 1981), p. 15.

IV

In the Wilderness
(*Numbers*/Bamidbar)

❀❀❀ 31 ❀❀❀

The Leviah

Bamidbar (1:1–4:20)

The Levites were the tribe of Israel who were put in charge of caring for the Tabernacle and its vessels. In the Temple, they also played music and sang psalms. A male Levite is called a *Levi*; a female Levite is called a *Leviah*.

Levi was the third son of Jacob and Leah. He was the only child of Jacob's four wives who was not named by his mother. Rashi states that he was named by the angel Gabriel, who gave Levi the twenty-four gifts of the priesthood: ten in the Sanctuary, ten in the Land of Israel, and four in Jerusalem (NR 5:1).

Levi had three sons: Gershon, Kehat, and Merari. Levi also had a daughter, Yokheved, who married her paternal nephew Amram, a son of Kehat (Num. 3:19). Yokheved and Amram produced Miriam, Aharon, and Moses. Miriam married into the tribe of Judah, while Elisheva of Judah married Aharon and thus became a Leviah.

Aharon and Elisheva's patrilineal descendants are the *kohanim*, a subgroup of the Levites. The rest of the Levites comprise the patrilineal descendants of Moses and Zipporah, of Gershon and Merari with their unnamed wives, and of Amram's three brothers and their wives.

The Levites are equated with the poor and the needy—poor in number and poor in inheritance (NR 5:2). "Poor in inheritance" refers to the fact that the Levites owned no land and depended on tithing for their food. They received their tithe, known as *maaser*, as "wages" for their duty of caring for the Tabernacle.

This care was incumbent upon all Israel, but the Levites served as representatives of the people in this regard (Rashi). The Levites' official duty is called *mishmeret,* the same term used for women's watchfulness over their menstrual cycles (see chapter 26). "Any post to which a person is appointed and must carry out is called *mishmeret* in all of Scripture and in the language of the Mishnah" (Rashi on Numbers 3:7; Num. 1:53).

A popular feminist-theological interpretation of *maaser* mistakes it for some kind of fat-cat privilege. "The general picture rendered," claims Merlin Stone, "is not one of monastic priests or ascetic gurus, but rather a well-clothed, well-fed, well-housed, well-transported, perfumed aristocracy, who ruled with supreme authority over the other Hebrew people."[1]

While it is certainly true that the Levites cannot be compared to celibate Catholic priests, monks who take vows of poverty, or the gurus of Eastern religions, Stone's basic thesis contains echoes of Nordic supremacy: she asserts that the Levites were actually an Indo-European (read, Aryan) ruling class of "other" (i.e., Semitic) Hebrew people. This in itself should make Jewish readers extremely wary of her perspective.

A TRIBE WITH FEW MALES

"Poor in number" refers to the fact that even the smallest tribe, Menasheh, had 32,200 men between twenty and sixty years old. There were also more males under age twenty and also over age sixty. Levi, however, had only 22,300 males *older than one month* (not including the *kohanim*)—7,500 Gershonites, 8,600 Kehatites, and 6,200 Merarites (Num. 3:22, 3:28, 3:34). To count them, Moses approached each tent but did not enter. Rather, the Shekhinah went before him and a *bat kol* (divine voice) issued from each tent telling him the correct number (Rashi).

The Levites were counted separately from the other tribes and numbered from one month old, so that they would not be included in the decree made later against the men numbered from twenty years old (NR 1:12, 2:19, 3:7). Furthermore, God was "accustomed to number this tribe on all occasions while they are still young, . . . even while they are still in their mother's womb"—a reference to Yokheved being counted in the number of Jacob's descendants going down to Egypt even though she was conceived in Canaan and born in Egypt (NR 3:8).

This census was the second and was taken on the first of *Iyar*, a year after the Exodus and a month after setting up the Tabernacle. Only Israelite males ages twenty to sixty were counted because: (1) they had to make mandatory contributions to the Tabernacle due to their role in the golden calf (women's contributions were quite plentiful on a voluntary basis); (2) knowledge of patrilineal ancestry was emphasized by the Torah to encourage male responsibility to women and children and to outlaw previously legal forms of incest; and (3) the census also served as a count of soldiers for military duty.

Of the 22,300 Levite males, 8,580 were between the ages of thirty and fifty, the years of service to the Tabernacle—2,630 Gershonites, 2,750 Kehatites, and 3,200 Merarites (Num. 4:36, 4:40, 4:44, 4:48).

Only 22,000 Levite males are recorded, however, because the other 300 were first-borns and a firstborn Levite male could not be used to redeem a firstborn Israelite male. This redemption was another major reason for taking a separate census of the

---

1. Stone, p. 120.

Levites. Firstborn sons had to be redeemed because of their idolatrous status in the ancient world (see chapter 15). The Levites replaced them in priestly service because the Levites did not participate in the worship of the golden calf, while the firstborn sons, being the priesthood at that time, did (see chapter 20).

The *total* number of Levite males was only equivalent to the *firstborn* male population *of the rest of Israel*—22,273. The surplus 273 firstborn Israelite males were redeemed through a five-shekel payment (Num. 3:39, 3:43–48). Nachmanides believes that the tribe of Levi was very small because of its experience in Egypt: Slavery was not imposed upon Israel until Levi, the longest-living of Jacob's sons, had died. Even then, however, Pharaoh did not subject the tribe of Levi to enslavement because they were the teachers and elders of Israel. Since God multiplied the Jewish population in Egypt *because* it had been diminished through oppression, Levi's exemption from this oppression also exempted them from God's miraculous multiplication methods. Hence, the tribe merely "reproduced and increased in a normal way, and therefore did not become as numerous as the other tribes."

Nachmanides also suggests an alternative view: that Levi became a small tribe because of Jacob's anger with Shimon and Levi for their violence in Shechem, for Shimon's numbers also decreased—from 59,300 to 22,200 (Num. 1:23, 26:14)—while most of the other tribes either increased or decreased only slightly.

There is, however, a much simpler explanation. *Levi could have been a predominantly female tribe.* Perhaps, for some reason, the tribe simply consisted of many more daughters than sons. This possibility (which does not even occur to male commentators) would also shed light on the "women and Levites" linkage in the resistance to the golden calf.

There is a "women and Levites" linkage in the Exodus as well. Israel is said to have been redeemed from Egyptian slavery because of the righteousness of the women, and because of the righteousness of the Levites, "for though the rest of Israel served idols in Egypt, the tribe of Levi served the Holy One and circumcised themselves" (NR 3:6).

If "women and Levites" are special, then the woman who *is* a Levite is in a class by herself. Unlike other Jewish women, the *Leviah retains her status regardless of whom she marries.* While a *bat-kohen* lost the right to eat *trumah* if she married an Israelite man or a gentile, the *Leviah* retained her right to eat *maaser* in such circumstances. Furthermore, if the *Leviah*'s husband is an Israelite man or a gentile, their firstborn son is exempt from *pidyon haben* because *she* is a Levite (Bek. 47a). This is a notable exception in a tribal system which otherwise always goes by the father.

THE FAMILIES OF KEHAT

Do not cause the Kehatites to be cut off from among the Levites. This is what you must do so that they live and do not die. (Num. 4:18–19)

Kehat—no doubt because of his ancestry of Miriam, Aharon, and Moses, although this is not explicitly stated in the Torah—was the most significant of the three branches of Levites. The Kehat clan carried the vessels of the Tabernacle: the ark, showbread table, *menorah*, two altars, and utensils. The Gershons carried the fabrics: the screens, roofs, and curtains—while the Meraris carried the structure: the boards, bars, pillars, and sockets.

"The tribe of Levi was superior to all the other tribes. And superior among the tribe of Levi was the family of Kehat. . . . Their spirit was not haughty within them, but they were subdued before the ark. . . . Although the family of Kehat were nobility, when they came to carry the ark they carried it like slaves" (NR 5:8). In other words, they had great humility.

Kehat's male population decreased while Gershon's and Merari's increased. Taking the numbers cited above, the Midrash notes that Gershon's thirty- to fifty-year-old male population was more than a third of its entire male population, Merari's was more than half of its population, but Kehat's was only less than a third.

This depletion occurred, in one view, because "when Israel was on its journeys, two sparks of fire would emerge from the two staves of the ark to strike their enemies. . . . Now when the sparks came out the fire grazed those that bore the ark and so they were burned and reduced in numbers." As a result, "they would all flee from the ark because it inflicted damage upon them, and so it seemed as though the ark was being slighted, whereupon the Holy One was angry with them and they were again consumed." An alternate view states that protective measures had to be instituted because the Kehat families quarreled among themselves as to who should have the privilege of carrying the ark (NR 5:1).

Another opinion is that they were consumed because they entered the Holy of Holies, gazed upon the ark and made uncalled-for remarks (NR 5:9). Therefore, specific individuals were given specific tasks, and the *kohanim* were told to take down the *parokhet* and cover the ark before the Kehatites picked it up. The analogy we have been making between the Tabernacle and the female body again comes to mind here—reverence and respect for something sacred requires that it not be subjected to voyeurism and crude comments.

Those who were close to the sacred objects, but not careful enough regarding them, were struck by "the attribute of justice [*din*]" (NR 5:2). "In order, therefore, that the attribute of justice might not strike them all, the Holy One took half of the Name, Yah [יה], and put it on him [*kehat*]: '*hakehati*'—a Heh at the beginning and a Yod at the end. . . . This was in order to guard [*mishmeret*] them until their days come" (NR 5:6).

If not for the families of Kehat, "Israel could not exist. . . . If Israel were soiled with something [a sin], and retribution came out of the *ohel moed* from the Shekhinah, immediately the Kehatites, who camped alongside the *ohel moed*, would rise and restrain it, so that it not come out upon them." Because they suffered such a role for Israel, the Kehatites needed special protection (NR 5:7).

TRANSFORMING VIOLENCE

That the Levites merited special status is particularly significant in light of the role that Levi played as the partner of Shimon—not only in the plundering of Shechem, but also in the plot against Joseph (see chapter 8).

Shimon and Levi's exceptionally cruel rage is compared to that of Esav, the archetype of male violence (GR 98:5). Jacob's "blessing" of them on his deathbed is in fact no blessing at all: He curses their anger and promises to "scatter them in Israel" (Gen. 49:5–7).

Both tribes were prevented from living in masses. The poor—the scribes and elementary teachers—were of the tribe of Shimon, in order that it should be dispersed (Rashi; GR 98:4). Levi, as we have seen, was landless altogether. The Shimonite scribes later served in synagogues, and the Levites, as Nachmanides noted, were the teachers and elders among Israel. Thus, although scattered throughout the Land, both tribes were given tasks that must have been intended to elevate them spiritually.

Levi apparently had a more passive role in the pair's violence than Shimon, who was the instigator. Perhaps the Levites' loyalty in Egypt and resistance to the golden calf did *teshuvah* for them, and so they were rewarded with a special relationship to God. The need to diminish the level of violence among them could even be the reason that God would make the tribe predominantly female: fewer males means less male violence.

Moses' blessing of Levi (Deut. 33:8–11) is vastly different from Jacob's, reflecting the tribe's special status after *teshuvah.* The Levites are called "Your pious ones" who merit wearing the *urim* and *tumim,* and are praised for their loyalty to God in a number of tests. "They shall teach Your Law to Jacob, and Your Torah to Israel. They shall place incense in Your nostrils and consume sacrifices on Your altar. May God bless his valor and the work of his hands."

Shimon, on the other hand, is completely omitted from Moses' blessing of the tribes, indicating the tribe's eventual fade into oblivion.

✳✳✳ 32 ✳✳✳

Sotah:
The Accused Wife

Naso (4:21–7:89)

S*otah*, the Hebrew term for the "accused wife," is a woman *suspected* by her hus-band of committing adultery. She must perform a ritual of drinking "bitter waters," the only instance in the Torah where an individual undergoes trial by ordeal.

The *actual* adultery of a married woman was a capital offense under Jewish law (Lev. 20:10; Deut. 22:22), just as it was throughout the ancient world. It may seem surprising that in pagan societies otherwise reputed for sexual licentiousness, the extramarital sexual activity of a woman would be punishable by death. This was due to changes in polygamy.

What about a married woman *accused* of adultery, with no actual evidence against her? Could social gossip serve as "testimony" to execute her? It is here that the Torah made a difference in women's lives by introducing due process of law. Pagan law, for an accused wife, was basically lynch law. The case of an accused wife illustrates how the Noachide law requiring gentiles to set up court systems helped civilize the pagan world.

In Babylonia, a married woman caught in the act of adultery was tied up with her lover and thrown in the river to drown (Code of Hammurabi 129). However, the husband could pardon his wife and the king could pardon the man (due to a legal parallel between husband–wife and king–subject relations). A woman who was only accused by her husband had to "make affirmation by god and return to her house" (Code of Hammurabi 131). This means her natal house—in other words, she was divorced, yet at least she lived. If "the finger was pointed at" her, however—in other words, there was social gossip against her concerning a particular man, although she had never been caught in the act with him—"she shall throw herself into the river for the sake of her husband" (Code of Hammurabi 132). This refers to a trial by ordeal in which the river acted as divine judge. The "water ordeal" was not unique to the Babylonians. It also appeared, for example, in medieval Europe. Although its exact methods varied, it was always stacked against the accused. In some cases, a woman was considered innocent if she sank and guilty if she floated.[1] In other cases, she was guilty if she sank and innocent if she floated, but a heavy stone was tied around her neck.[2]

Similarly, an accused Egyptian wife might be "killed by her husband and thrown to the dogs" or "burnt alive with her paramour and her ashes . . . thrown into the Nile."[3] Even as late as the days of early Rome, "there were no statutory penalties for adultery—probably because the husband took the matter into his own hands, or called on the family council to inflict the punishment."[4]

The Torah, on the other hand, prohibited the execution of an accused wife without a trial—that is, at least one witness had to testify that *intercourse* had taken place. This would be rare, since sexual activities, and especially illegal ones, do not generally have witnesses. The woman literally had to be caught in the act.

The accused wife with no evidence against her could not be executed, even if people were convinced of her guilt. Instead, she underwent the ritual of *sotah*, a water ordeal of drinking rather than dunking. *Sotah* was probably more common than court trials even in cases of actual adultery, since social gossip alone could not bring a woman to trial. Her innocence or guilt was to be established beyond a shadow of a doubt by God. Her fate was not left to a jealous husband, a court of men, an angry mob, or a pagan river god.

ADULTERY AND POLYGAMY

Only a married woman and a man (married or single) could be guilty of adultery under ancient legal codes, for in a polygynous society, the laws against adultery exist to maintain clear knowledge of paternity. Prohibiting what is frequently referred to in both Jewish and anthropological sources as men's "exchange of wives," ancient adultery laws were actually what initiated the breakdown of polygamy—by eliminating polyandry though allowing polygyny to continue.

---

1. See Margaret A. Murray, *The Witch-Cult in Western Europe* (London: Oxford University Press, 1921), p. 17; and Paul Carus, *The History of the Devil and the Idea of Evil* (New York: Bell, 1969), pp. 327–328.

2. Paul Veyne, *A History of Private Life from Pagan Rome to Byzantium* (Cambridge, MA: Harvard University Press, 1987), p. 471.

3. Mertz, p. 59; Montet, p. 54.

4. Otto Kiefer, *Sexual Life in Ancient Rome* (New York: Dorsett Press, 1993), p. 31.

The lesbian affair of a married woman was not adultery, nor was the sexual activity of an unmarried woman, whether she was single, widowed, or divorced. Extramarital sexual activity of a married man was only adultery if his affair was with a married woman. He might be fined or required to marry a single woman with whom he had intercourse, but he would not have committed adultery.

This one-sided definition of adultery is a clear sign of male sexual prerogative under polygyny. However, male sexual prerogative also flourished under full polygamy, for the addition of polyandry did not give women sexual "equality" with men. It simply extended men's license to pimp, "lend," and barter their wives in brotherhoods with each other (see chapter 9).

Under polyandry, adultery was defined by whether the woman's lover was part of her husband's clan, or by whether her affair was with her husband's knowledge and consent.

> In the former case there may be no penalty at all, while offenses on the part of strangers against marital claims are subject to vengeance, punishment or compensation. In numerous instances the temporary loan or exchange of wives takes place between members of the same marriage-group. . . . It is a serious offense only if the seducer belongs to a clan other than the husband's; if he be a "relative" (by which term we are presumably to understand a "clan-brother") there is no offense and no punishment.[5]

"Adultery" could, therefore, be charged by a jealous husband who "lends out" his wife to his buddies but gets upset when she initiates an affair herself with a stranger, without his consent, or when a man abducts her.[6] In other cases "the aggrieved husband has a right to kill the offender or to exact compensation" only if the act has occurred *outside* the home.[7]

By outlawing *all* extramarital sexual activity of women, ancient adultery laws eradicated the male ownership distinctions fostered by polyandry and were thus a first step in improving women's sexual status. It was a small step, to be sure, but it was a step nonetheless.

The eventual outlawing of polygyny as well takes the the spirit of the law to its logical conclusion, for polygyny is endemic to slavery. A man's wives and concubines live, under the watchful eyes of eunuch guards, in the harem, which is the most secluded and cloistered part of his house. In such a situation "it was quite simple to get rid of unwanted wives or [concubines] with perfect impunity; for no man, not even a police inspector, could enter another's harem."[8] Once a society has abolished slavery, polygyny too must go.

---

5. Briffault, 1:609, 642.
6. Ibid., 2:99–109.
7. Ibid., 3:257.
8. Alev Lytle Croutier, *Harem: The World behind the Veil* (New York: Abbeville Press, 1989), p. 161.

THE ACCUSED WIFE IN JEWISH LAW

Hashem spoke to Moses, saying, "Speak to the children of Israel and tell them [what to do] if any man suspects his wife of straying [*tisteh*] and deceiving [*maal*] him—if a man has lain with her and had a seminal emission, and it is concealed from the eyes of her husband, or she has secluded herself with him long enough to become *tamae*, and there is no witness against her, and she was not raped.

A spirit of jealousy [*ruach kinah*] has passed over him [the husband] and he has warned his wife and she has become *tamae*, or a spirit of jealousy has passed over him and he has warned his wife and she has not become *tamae*. The man must bring his wife to the priest. (Num. 5:11–15)

The Torah does not presume the *sotah*'s guilt. A woman has simply been *accused* by her husband, whom a "spirit of jealousy" has "passed over." Whether the woman herself has actually "become *tamae*" (i.e., had intercourse outside her marriage) would only be apparent once she drank the "bitter waters." She is therefore innocent until proven guilty.

Sotah (סוטה, Samekh, Vav, Tet, Heh) comes from the root *sut,* "to move about, be unsteady, to go astray" (Jastrow). Both of these words are spelled with a Samekh (ס), one of two Hebrew letters with an *s* sound. The other, Shin (ש), can also be pronounced as *sh*. *Tisteh* comes from a root spelled Shin, Tet, Heh, which means madness or folly. Adding a Vav to it thus spells *shotah* as well as *sotah* (שוטה).

A *shotah* is a madwoman or fool and a *shoteh* is a madman or fool—someone who operates out of a spirit of idiocy, folly, or even insanity. The classic definition of a *chasid shoteh* (a pious but foolish man) is one who does not save a drowning woman because he is forbidden by law to look at her or touch her (for sexual purposes). That he uses this law to stop himself from saving a dying human being shows what an idiot he is (Sot. 21b).

The Rabbis connected the concepts of straying and folly by noting that "a person does not go to a married woman unless he has gone out of his mind [*yetze midato*]," and "there is no prostituting a woman [*eino mezanah*] unless she has gone out of her mind" (NR 9:6). This latter statement is extremely meaningful in understanding the consequences of the sexual degradation of *znut*.

A woman's adultery is called *maal*—to deceive, defraud, to transgress, or "make inappropriate use of sacred property" (Jastrow). The "sacred property" is the woman's body and its reproductive organs. As a sacred vessel, the woman who commits adultery "causes degradation [*mezanah*] and renounces her husband, who has entrusted his body to her for safekeeping [*leshamro*]" (NR 9:2). As in *niddah*, the woman is a *shomeret,* keeping and guarding something sacred.

The concept that the woman's body is a sacred vessel for the man's seed is not a bad idea, in theory, as long as the man is held equally accountable for the consequences of where he puts his seed. That is, the "sacred vessel" view of sexuality must encourage male responsibility and not create a double standard in which women are the gatekeepers of morality while "boys will be boys."

Judaism, even in the midst of polygyny, has been very strict in treating men's (as well as women's) reproductive organs and capacities as "sacred vessels." Much of Jewish law concerning sexuality is based on telling men where they can put their penises and when (see, for example, *Zohar* II:3a–4a). The Torah's legislation against incest, adultery, marrying two sisters, homosexuality, intermarriage, physical contact during *niddah*, and "spilling seed" (which rules out masturbation as well as certain methods of birth control) all put more sexual restrictions on men than they had hitherto known. Circumcision added the "crowning touch." Now *sotah* would provide yet another limitation on male sexual prerogative.

A husband who *suspected* his wife of adultery had to publicly warn her twice not to speak to a particular man, whom he had to name. If she ignored these two warnings and continued to associate with the specified man in public, nothing further happened to her (Sot. 1:1–2).

Her husband could *accuse* her—that is, require her to undergo *sotah*—only if he could produce two witnesses of his warnings, and one witness that she had since been in a secluded place with the man long enough for the first stage of intercourse to occur. Although two witnesses are the standard requirement in Jewish law, only one witness was required to *make* an accused wife drink (by testifying to her *seclusion* with the man) or to *prevent* her from drinking (by testifying to her actual *intercourse* with the man) (Sot. 2a–3a).

An amusing discussion ensues among the Rabbis as to just how long it takes to get to the first stage of intercourse, based on their personal experiences. That Ben Azzai was not married made the others question how he could know (NR 9:10; Sot. 4a–b).

An accusation by a husband was no light thing, for he possibly "forbids her to himself for all time" (Sot. 2b). If the woman was a *kohenet*, she became prohibited from eating *trumah* as well. Some husbands were not allowed to bring accusations against their wives at all—for example, if either of them was blind, lame, armless, or mute (NR 9:42) or if the accused adulterer was a minor (Sot. 4:4). A wife could not be held accountable for sexual activity before marriage or after divorce, and her sexual activity after a divorce could not be brought up by a husband who had remarried her (Sot. 2:6). In other words, a woman's sexual past could not be used against her.

If an accused wife confessed, she was divorced by her husband without her *ketubah*, or monetary settlement. Nor was she allowed to marry her lover; hence, adultery could not be used as a means to force a divorce with that end in mind. If an accused wife maintained her innocence, her husband had to take her to the *kohen* to drink the bitter waters. In the wilderness, the performance of this rite meant walking across the camp to the Tabernacle, but in Temple times, it meant making a journey to Jerusalem from other parts of Israel. In the latter case, the husband took his wife to the local *bet din*, who supplied the couple with two *yeshivah bochers* to serve as chaperones on the trip. R. Judah's opinion that the husband could be trusted alone with his wife was rejected by the Sages (Sot. 1:3; NR 9:31).

THE JEALOUS HUSBAND

If I'm the least bit late getting home from work,
he screams at me, "Who were you f---ing?"

—a battered woman, describing
her husband's possessiveness

Obsessive, irrational jealousy is a major indicator
of lethality [potential for homicide] in a batterer.

Maureen Pasik, batterer intervention counselor
Cambridge, Massachusetts

The man must bring his wife to the priest. He must bring an offering for her of one-tenth an ephah of barley meal. He shall not pour oil on it, nor place frankincense on it, for it is a jealousy offering [*minchat kena'ot*], a memorial offering [*minchat zikaron*], a reminder of wrongdoing [*mazkeret avon*]. (Num. 5:15)

Who is being reminded of wrongdoing here? Clearly it is the husband, for the *minchah* is referred to as a *jealousy* offering, not a "straying" offering, even when the priest places it in *the woman's* hands (Num. 5:18). The jealous husband must bring an offering because of the gravity of the situation of making such an accusation against his wife. The burden of proof, and, hence, the sacrificial requirement are incumbent on him. Although he brings the offering "for her," that is, on her account, the behavior necessitating it is his.

This is also made clear by the last line of the entire section on *sotah*: "The man will be cleansed of his wrongdoing [*avon*], and the woman will carry [*tisa*] her wrongdoing" (Num. 5:31). If she is guilty, she has sinned and is punished. However, if she is innocent, *he* has sinned and must make atonement.

The law of *sotah* was not so much designed to punish unfaithful wives, although it did; it was primarily intended to protect innocent women from possessive, abusive husbands who were consumed by irrational fits of jealousy. It is wholly possible that most accused women were innocent. We have no way of knowing, but recall Rashi's statement that the copper washstand promoted domestic peace by giving the accused woman "an opportunity to prove her innocence."

Recall, too, Nachmanides' statement that women readily offered their copper mirrors for the laver because they "accepted the law [of *sotah*] upon themselves with joy." Women evidently saw the ritual as a mechanism for self-protection. The law of *sotah* could have served to protect women from the violence of jealous men by creating a format for channeling the man's rage and deflecting it from his wife.

Battering, domineering, or otherwise abusive husbands are extremely possessive and jealous. In 1992, in Massachusetts alone, a woman was killed by such a man every eight days, which was an increase from one every twenty-two days just two years earlier.[9] By 1994, the figure had risen to one woman every *six* days.[10]

---

9. Alison Bass, "Domestic Violence: Roots Go Deep," *The Boston Globe,* June 5, 1992, p. 1.
10. Personal telephone interview with Andrew Klein, Quincy Court probation officer, May 2, 1994.

If violent jealousy is so common in our society, where men and women are (theoretically) held up to the same expectations concerning monogamy, it is even *more* prevalent in polygynous societies, where a man can demand monogamy from his wife without having to practice it himself. Given strict seclusion and segregation practices, an innocent woman could easily be falsely accused simply because she exercised more freedom of movement than her society and her husband were willing to tolerate.

A hint of the jealous husband's possessive nature is indicated in the rabbinic assertion that the section on *sotah* follows a verse on *trumah* because "if one has *trumah* and tithes and does not give them to the priest, in the end he will require the priest's services to deal with his wife" (Br. 63a). That is, a man who is possessive of his crops, hoarding what is rightfully due to the priests, will most likely be possessive of his wife as well.

The commentators, unlike the Torah itself, presume the woman's guilt. *Ish ish,* "every man" (which might simply mean "any man"), is interpreted as referring to an offense against two "men"—her husband and God (Rashi; NR 9:2). This not only posits God as a man but as one who is automatically on the side of the jealous husband! A double male bias is thus set up.

Similarly, the offering is explained in terms of *her alleged behavior* as if it were certain, when it is not. Barley rather than wheat is said to have been used because "just as her actions were like the acts of a beast, so was her offering the food of a beast" (Sot. 2:1). Oil was omitted, the theory goes, "because oil is called light, and she acted in darkness," and frankincense was not added "because the matriarchs are called frankincense . . . while she departed from their paths" (Rashi; NR 9:13).

However, we do not yet know if the woman has done anything wrong! At this point her jealous husband has merely accused her. If she is innocent, then *his* behavior is what is bestial, dark, and deviating from the paths of the matriarchs. Indeed, he dare not arouse the spirit of the matriarchs with frankincense if he has wrongfully accused an innocent woman of adultery.

The following parallels are perhaps more enlightening. Only two grain offerings were barley rather than wheat; the other was the *omer,* the offering of the barley harvest. *Sotah,* too, was a "harvest" offering, for the woman would reap exactly what she had sown. If she was innocent, she would be cleared, while if she was guilty, she would be harmed.

Only two grain-offerings omitted oil and frankincense; the other was the *choteh,* the grain *chatat* of an individual who could not afford a mammal or a bird. This "variable" *chatat* was brought for an unintentional violation of the laws of *tumah* or for failure to fulfill an oath to testify as a witness. *Sotah,* too, was concerned with both *tumah* and the lack of a witness.

The sexist bias of ancient and medieval commentators makes it difficult to see the true nature of *sotah,* but even modern commentary does not necessarily help. Even if the accused wife were innocent of adultery, one contemporary rabbinic source declares her guilty of "any step leading to it." Having "brought suspicion upon herself" by "conduct[ing] herself in a manner which causes her husband to suspect her of infidelity," this "sinful woman" is accused of straying from the Torah and adopting non-Jewish habits of sexual immodesty.[11] She is blamed just for being accused, while her husband's motives are automatically assumed to be beyond question.

Such opinions only provide further illustration of why the rite of *sotah* was needed—because an accused wife was (and is) usually presumed by men to be guilty until proven innocent. Like a rape or an incest victim, she is believed to have "provoked" the situation, even a false accusation.

The Torah thus provided "a fairly simple, safe way for a woman to clear her name with divine approval, sanctioned by the priest and the Temple ritual." The pagan water ordeal was "transformed from a formidable test weighted toward guilt to an easy one, strongly biased in favor of demonstrating innocence . . . [and] changed from a measure threatening women to a mechanism for their protection."[12]

THE WATERS OF BITTERNESS AND CURSES

The priest shall take holy water in a clay vessel and put dust from the floor of the *mishkan* into the water. The priest shall have the woman stand before Hashem. . . . In the hand of the priest are the waters of bitterness and curses [*mei ha-marim ha-me'arrim*].

The priest administers an oath to the woman, saying, "If a man has not lain with you and you have not strayed in *tumah* from your husband, you will be unharmed by these waters of bitterness and curses. But if you have strayed and become *tamae* and had intercourse with a man other than your husband. . . . Hashem will make you into a curse and an oath among your people, causing your thigh to fall and your belly to swell. These curse-waters will come into your bowels, to make your belly swell and your thigh fall." And the woman says, "Amen, amen."

The priest writes these curses in a scroll [*sefer*] and dissolves it in the waters of bitterness. He then makes the woman drink the waters of bitterness and curses, and the curse-waters come into her for bitterness. . . . When he makes her drink the waters, if she had become *tamae* and deceived her husband, the curse-waters for bitterness come into her and her belly swells and her thigh falls, and the woman becomes a curse among her people. But if the woman had not become *tamae* but was *tahor*, she is cleared and will conceive. (Num. 5:17–28)

Bitter waters that bear a curse—a pun in Hebrew—were not used only in *sotah*. A "mass testing" occurred at Marah (see chapter 16), where the drinking water is said to have been made bitter by God on purpose. "The Egyptians claimed to be the parents of the children of Israel, and many [men] among Israel suspected their wives in the matter. So the Holy One brought them to that place . . . to put them to the test." Interestingly, both women *and* men were tested here to see if they had had sexual contact with an Egyptian. "And all, male and female, were proved to be *tahor*" (*Zohar* III:124b).

---

11. Weissman, 4:57–58, 60.
12. Biale, p. 187.

Moses administered a potion, made from water and the ground-up metal of the golden calf, that killed those who had "rejoiced in their hearts" but did not actively participate in the festivities (see chapter 20).

Thus, in all these cases, bitter waters were administered where unfaithfulness was alleged but could not be proven. A physically harmless (although perhaps foul-tasting) concoction had an effect far beyond its mere physical properties, differentiating the faithful from the unfaithful and saving the innocent from the indiscriminate violence of jealous anger (NR 9:45). In the golden calf waters, Aharon is even called the "paramour" who is punished along with the unfaithful (NR 9:47).

The golden-calf waters were a punishment for the obliteration of the writing caused when Moses broke the tablets and the letters flew off (NR 9:48). The waters of *sotah*, however, *consisted* of an obliteration—of God's Name! The four-letter Name was written on a scroll in soluble ink and then dissolved in the water just before the woman drank. There is no other situation where the Name of God is allowed to be erased in this way. This was truly a unique potion.

The Mishnah refers to the scroll as the woman's *megillah,* and it was indeed hers alone. Only one woman could be tested at a time (Sot. 8a). If she confessed or refused to drink after the Name had been written but *before* it was dissolved, her *megillah* could not be used to test another woman—it had to be buried with other sacred scriptures that could not be thrown away. If she confessed *after* the Name had been dissolved, the waters were poured out. If she refused to drink after the Name had been dissolved, however, she was forced to drink (Sot. 3:3).

If the *sotah* was innocent, not only was she completely unharmed by the waters, but she would soon conceive a child as a "reward." Hannah, the mother of the prophet Samuel, used this quite cleverly to get a child. Praying to overcome her barrenness, she told God that if she did not conceive, she would seclude herself with a man in order to be forced to undergo *sotah*. Because she would be innocent, God would *have to* give her a child (Br. 31b; 1 Sam. 1:11). Her boldness in trying to "trick" God in this way is quite remarkable.

If the *sotah* was guilty, the bitter waters affected her "measure for measure," *midah kneged midah.* The adulterer was harmed in the same way as the woman, even though he did not drink (Sot. 5:1; NR 9:21; 10:1). The main effect was on the "thigh" and "belly," the pelvic area, because the sin was sexual, yet "all the rest of the body did not escape" (Sot. 1:7).

Her (and his) face turned sickly pale, the eyes bulged, and the veins swelled up (NR 9:31; Sot. 3:4). The water is called "bitter" because it effected "divine retribution": "If she was white it made her black; if red, it made her green; her mouth would smell bad, her throat would swell, her flesh would decay; she would become a *zavah,* and she would feel bloated and languid" (NR 9:21).

The waters could even test women who tried to evade them. The story is told of a woman who drank on behalf of her lookalike sister because the latter, accused by her husband, was indeed guilty. When the innocent sister returned home after drinking, the guilty sister hugged and kissed her—and instantly died (NR 9:9).

It is asserted, however, that the punishment of a guilty woman could be held in abeyance for a year or two, or even three, if she had "merit." (No such statement is made about the guilty man.) It is immediately protested that that would simply make the whole rite ineffective, for most women have *some* merit to protect them. Innocent women would not be cleared, but merely presumed to be getting a delayed punishment. Nevertheless, it is concluded, a guilty woman may walk away from the ritual alive, but she "will not bear children nor will she continue in good health, but she will gradually waste away and die of it" (Sot. 3:4–5).

It is in this context that we find the famous remark of R. Eliezer allegedly opposing teaching women Torah. Ben Azzai maintained, "It is a person's obligation to teach his daughter Torah so that if she has to drink, she will know that her merit will suspend her punishment." R. Eliezer responded that "whoever teaches his daughter Torah, it is as if he teaches her *tiflut* [frivolity]."

While his response has been widely interpreted as a general proscription against teaching women Torah, it is highly possible that the statement is merely contextual—that is, it is a specific response to Ben Azzai's logic, for Ben Azzai's assertion is similar to saying that we should teach our children Torah so that they know their sins will be forgiven once a year if they go to shul on Yom Kippur. Teaching Torah *in that way* is indeed frivolous; perhaps that is all R. Eliezer meant to say.

THE *SOTAH*'S DEGRADATION AND FINAL VINDICATION

The priest stands the woman before Hashem and uncovers the woman's head [*rosh*]. (Num. 5:18)

The priest seizes her clothes—and if they rip, they rip; if they tear apart, they tear apart—so that her bosom [lit., "heart"] is exposed, and he loosens her hair. R. Judah says, "If her bosom is pretty he does not uncover it. If her hair is pretty he does not loosen it. (Sot. 1:5)

It would be hard to find a more glaring departure from the written Torah than this *mishnah*. As we noted in the Introduction, the Mishnah is not the *exact* words of God but reflects different rabbinic interpretations of the oral traditions acquired at Sinai. Does the degradation of the *sotah* described here represent the true will of God, or does it possibly reflect some sociological license taken by men? Although the woman is still innocent until proven guilty, she is treated by the priest and the Sanhedrin as if she were guilty until proven innocent. R. Judah's view, although it is rejected, shows just how far the level of exploitation might go.

The written Torah says that the priest uncovers her head. All this tells us, at most, is that married women *did* cover their hair, yet in a strange leap of logic, the Rabbis deduced from this verse that married women *must* cover their hair. The Torah also tells us that women wore nose-rings—Eliezer gave one to Rivkah (Gen. 24:47). Why do we not then have a law that women must still wear nose-rings? Why do we not require men to wear long, dresslike tunics instead of pants?

Ripping one's garment at the heart and "loosening" one's hair—that is, letting it grow and not cutting it—are both Jewish mourning practices. A *metzora* (Lev. 13:45) had to do these, too; yet the Mishnah says that only a male *metzora* does so, while a female does not. Similarly, a man who is stoned to death for a crime is stripped naked first, but a woman is not (Sot. 23a; San. 44b). Modesty and the preservation of women's dignity are a foremost consideration of the law, even for a criminal about to be executed.

Nonetheless, the *sotah*—who has not even been found guilty—supposedly had her "bosom" exposed. This probably means nothing more than what one would see by looking at Elizabeth Taylor in an evening gown, especially since the Mishnah then says a rope was tied around her to hold up her dress (Sot. 1:6).

The priests walked her around to make her tired (Sot. 8a). Great pressure was exerted to induce her to confess "so the great Name of God, written in sanctity, would not be erased by the waters." She was persuaded to admit if wine, laughter, or evil neighbors might have made her do it, and the Sanhedrin told her the stories of Judah and Tamar and Reuven and Bilhah, "things which neither she nor the family of her father's house is worthy to hear" (Sot. 1:4).

The community was encouraged to come and witness her ordeal, as a kind of moral deterrent. "All who want to see come to see, except her male and female slaves, because her heart is haughty toward them. All women are permitted to see her, as it is said, that all women may be taught not to do after your lewdness" (Sot. 1:6). "Permitted" is an understatement; Raba says that men are permitted but women are *obliged* (Sot. 8b).

The ordeal of *sotah* was eventually abolished because it ceased to be effective due to male behavior. The waters could only test a woman whose husband had never committed adultery or any other sexual violation himself (NR 9:44). That is, a woman could not be held accountable for something her accuser was guilty of doing. Thus, by around 70 C.E., "when adulterers increased in number, the rite of the bitter waters was stopped, and it was R. Jochanan ben Zakai who stopped it" (Sot. 9:9). In issuing this decree, he quoted Hosea 4:14: "I will not punish your daughters who sexually degrade themselves, nor your daughters-in-law who commit adultery, for they [the men] themselves go off with the common prostitutes [*zonot*], and sacrifice with the sacred prostitutes [*kedeshot*]. And the people that does not understand this will be miserable."

The God of Israel clearly rejects a double standard of sexual morality. The people that does not understand this will *indeed* be miserable!

SOTAH AND *NAZIRUT*

The topic of *sotah* is followed in the Torah by *nazirut*, the vow to abstain from wine (Num. 6). This indicates that "whoever witnesses a *sotah* in her disgrace should abstain from wine" (Sot. 2a).

> When they made the *sotah* drink they said to her, "Much is caused by wine," and all of
> Israel were standing by, men and women. . . . And Israel, the men and women who had
> seen it, came into their homes and said, "Oy to that man and that woman who drank

wine, got drunk, committed a transgression [crossed the line], and died! I swear I will never drink wine, so that something like his death does not happen to me!" And the women said the same. (NR 10:1)

The *nazir*—the person who took the Nazirite vow—abstained from all grape products and observed the mourning custom of not getting haircuts—while, like a priest, avoiding contact with the dead! At the end of the time period for which the vow was taken, the *nazir* brought several offerings—an *olah*, a *chatat*, a *shlamim*, and a *minchah*—and shaved off a lock of hair from the crown of the head, offering it on the fire with the *shlamim*. Hair is thus another link between *sotah* and *nazirut*.

The topic of *nazirut* is followed by *Birkat Kohanim*, the priestly blessing, indicating that the priests must not be drunk when they bless the people. The three-way proximity of *sotah*, *nazirut*, and *Birkat Kohanim* indicates that from the *sotah* who "was cleared and conceived seed, priests emanated from her who blessed Israel" (NR 10:25).

It is said to be "the way of a woman to separate from wine like a Nazirite." Any adult Jew, man or woman, could take the Nazirite vow. The law was meant "to make the women like men" (NR 10:7).

✱✱✱ 33 ✱✱✱

Remember Miriam

Behaalotkha (8:1–12:16)

Remember what Hashem your God did to Miriam as you went on the way out of Egypt.
(Deut. 24:9)

Miriam did a lot of wonderful things for the Jewish people for which she should be remembered. Her name, meaning "bitter sea," indicates her capacity to swim against the tide of society when necessary.

- As Puah, assistant to her mother, the midwife Yokheved/Shifrah, she secretly saved baby boys from Pharaoh's extermination plan.
- As a little girl, she had the *chutzpah* to challenge her father for divorcing her mother, saying he was worse than Pharaoh in that he was causing the "extermination" of baby girls as well as baby boys.
- She guarded Moses in the Nile until he was rescued by Pharaoh's daughter, Batyah, and then cleverly arranged for the baby's own mother to serve as his wet nurse for the next two years.
- She was a prophet who led the women as Moses led the men—for example, in celebration after crossing the Red Sea, and in preparation for the Revelation at Sinai. "All the righteous women of that generation come to Miriam. . . . The women on the eves of Sabbaths and festivals all come to Miriam to gain knowledge of the Sovereign of the Universe. Happy is that generation above all other generations" (*Zohar* III:163a).
- She suffered the death of her son, Chur, when he tried to stop other men from building and worshiping the golden calf.
- Because of her merit, her great-grandson, Betzalel, was appointed by God to supervise the construction of the Tabernacle.

• She was the source of water (in the form of a traveling well) for the people throughout their journeys in the wilderness.

These are just the things the Torah *tells* us, which means they are the most important. Who knows what other little daily acts of heroism were a significant part of her life? However, for none of these positive behaviors are we commanded to remember Miriam. Rather, we are told to remember what happened to her on the way out of Egypt—the only negative thing ever recorded about her.

Why should this be? Why, Nachmanides asks, should we remember only the punishment God inflicted upon this great prophet for questioning one action of a brother she loved and whose life she saved by guarding him at the Nile? Furthermore, "she spoke nothing wrong to his face, but only in privacy" with her other brother, Aharon. Nevertheless, all her great deeds could not negate the seriousness of this act and save her from its consequences.

MIRIAM'S DEFENSE OF ZIPPORAH

Miriam and Aharon spoke against Moses because of the Cushite woman woman he had married, for he had married a Cushite woman. "Has Hashem only spoken to Moses? Doesn't Hashem also speak to us?" And Hashem heard it. But the man Moses was very humble, more so than all the people on the face of the earth. (Num. 12:1–3)

Miriam is mentioned first because she initiated the conversation (Rashi). Earlier (Num. 11), the people had complained that there was no meat to eat and had even indulged in the slave mentality of wishing they were back in Egypt. "Meat" may just be a euphemism, however; tradition holds that they were upset because they could no longer commit incest (Yom. 75a). Moses, who was despairing over being in charge of such a people, was instructed by God to appoint seventy elders to help ease his burden.

To do this, Moses chose six men from each of the twelve tribes and then used a lottery system to eliminate two of them (San. 17a). These two, Eldad and Meidad, began prophesying. When Zipporah heard this, she exclaimed, "Oy to their wives if [the men] become involved in prophecy, for they will separate from their wives as my husband separated from me!" (Rashi).

Miriam thus made her statement sheerly out of sympathy for Zipporah, and not with any malicious intent toward Moses. She wanted to know why she could be a prophet and stay married to Calev and Aharon could be a prophet and stay married to Elisheva, but Moses had to leave Zipporah in order to prophesy. Although Moses had come to this conclusion on his own in order to be constantly ready to receive the Shekhinah, his decision was approved on high (Shab. 87a)—something that Miriam might not have known. Hence, we are taught, if an unintentionally disparaging remark deserves such punishment, how much more so does an intentionally disparaging one (Rashi)?

MOSES' PROPHECY

Hashem suddenly said to Moses and to Aharon and to Miriam, "All three of you go to the Tabernacle." Hashem descended in a pillar of cloud and stood at the tent's entrance, calling to Aharon and Miriam, and they both came out. [God] said, "Now hear My words. When there is a prophet among you, I make Myself known in a vision, I speak in a dream. But it is not so with My servant Moses—in all My house he is faithful. Mouth to mouth I speak to him, in a vision and not riddles, so that he sees a picture of Hashem. Why are you not afraid to speak against My servant Moses?" (Num. 12:4–8)

"For Moses gazed into the clear mirror of prophecy, whereas all the other prophets looked into a hazy mirror. Moses received the divine message standing and with all his senses unimpaired, and he comprehended it fully . . . whereas other prophets fell on their faces in a state of exhaustion and did not obtain a perfectly clear message" (*Zohar* I:170b–71a; Yev. 49b; LR 1:14). Remember the women and their copper mirrors! Moses alone, of all the Jewish men and women who were capable of prophecy, did not need the "vision of God" to be deflected.

While God frequently communicated with Moses and Aharon (and, we might presume, Miriam), there are thirteen instances where God spoke to Moses alone (NR 14:19; Rashi on Lev. 1:1). These include all communications made in Egypt, on Mount Sinai, and inside the Tabernacle. This is what is meant by saying that the Shekhinah spoke only to Moses.

Miriam and Aharon learned the significance of this when God called to them "suddenly, and they were *tamae* from sexual relations. They cried, 'Water, water!' [for immersion]. This was to show them that Moses had acted properly in separating from his wife, since the Shekhinah revealed Herself to him constantly, and there was no fixed time for communication" (Rashi).

THE CONSEQUENCES OF GOSSIP

Hashem got angry at them and went away. The cloud departed from the tent and Miriam had *tzaraat*, [a skin disease making her white] like snow. Aharon turned to Miriam and she was a *metzora*. And Aharon said to Moses, "Please, my lord, do not lay upon us the sin we have foolishly committed. Do not let her be like a dead person [i.e., a stillborn baby] who comes out of its mother's womb with its flesh half-consumed."

And Moses cried to Hashem, "Please, God, heal her, please!" Hashem said to Moses, "If her father had spit in her face, would she not be ashamed for seven days? Let her be shut outside the camp for seven days, and then she can be taken in." Miriam was quarantined outside the camp for seven days, and the people did not travel until she was brought in. Afterwards the people traveled from Chatzerot to the wilderness of Paran. (Num. 12:9–16)

The *tumah* of a *metzora*—a person inflicted with *tzaraat*, a skin disease usually mistranslated as "leprosy"—is described in gory detail in Leviticus 13–14. It could also appear on garments made of wool, linen, or leather, and on walls of houses—the latter only in Israel (Nachmanides).

The Midrash lists a number of sins as causing *tzaraat:* cursing God, sexual immorality, murder, falsely ascribing a negative trait to someone, arrogance, encroaching upon another's domain, lying, robbery, making a false oath, desecrating the Name of Heaven, idolatry (NR 7:5), and the "evil eye," which is described as selfishness in refusing to lend out one's possessions (DR 6:8).

Generally, however, *tzaraat* is believed to be caused by *lashon hara,* an "evil tongue." This includes (but is not limited to) slander, a false statement causing damage to someone's reputation. *Lashon hara* may be a true statement, however, so "gossip" is a more accurate translation.

The case of Miriam is cited as proof that *lashon hara* causes *tzaraat:* "The pious Miriam is a warning to all gossipers" (DR 6:9). The Rabbis add their own misogyny in asserting that women are gossipers by nature, and they even have the audacity to attribute such a sentiment to Moses himself (DR 6:11). The fact that the Torah uses the case of Miriam to illustrate the consequences of gossip does not imply anything about women in general (or even Miriam in general), yet once again the Torah is left to bear the blame for men's sexism.

Unlike those with other kinds of *tumah,* a *metzora* had to be isolated from people by being quarantined outside the camp. Because gossip sets people apart, the gossiper—the cause of the rift—had to be set apart as well (Rashi). A *metzora* had to tear his or her clothing and let his or her hair grow, like a mourner, cover the head and face, and call out, "*Tamae, tamae,*" so that people would know and keep their distance.

Miriam's seclusion took place on 22 *Sivan* (Ta. 29a) (see Table 20–1). While a *metzora* usually just traveled separately from the rest of the camp, in Miriam's case *the entire nation came to a standstill* and did not move on until she was ready to go. This was her reward for watching over Moses in the Nile (Rashi). It is also a clear indication of her status as leader of the people.

A person had to be examined by a priest to be declared a *metzora,* and again after seclusion to be declared *tahor,* yet Aharon could not perform this role with Miriam, since she was his relative. Nor could Moses, who was not a *kohen.* Therefore, it was God alone who examined her and decided whether she was *tamae* or *tahor* (Zev. 101b–2a).

According to R. Akiva, Aharon became a *metzora* as well. While his view is not clearly confirmed or disproved, he is chastised for even saying it, when the Torah does not: "Akiva! In either case you will be held accountable! If you are right, the Torah shielded him, while you disclose him; and if not, you cast a stigma upon a righteous man" (Shab. 97a).

From Moses' prayer, the Rabbis concluded that it is not necessary to mention the name of a person for whom one is praying (Br. 34a). The prayer was brief "so that Israel should not say, 'His sister is in trouble, and he stands and offers long prayers!' or 'On behalf of his sister he offers a long prayer, but on our behalf he does not offer a long prayer!'" (Rashi).

✻✻✻ 34 ✻✻✻

Women and the Land

Shlach Lekha (13:1–15:41)

The story of the ten spies who give a disparaging report about the Land of Israel—which God had promised would be a "land of milk and honey" (Ex. 3:17)—follows immediately upon the account of Miriam's *lashon hara* and punishment. This juxtaposition illustrates that "she was punished on account of the speech she uttered against her brother, yet these evil ones saw it and did not learn a lesson from it" (Rashi; NR 16:6).

Twelve men of rank, one from each tribe, were selected by Moses to scout out the territory the Jews were about to enter. These men were not the patrilineal heads listed as tribal princes in Numbers 1 but rather tribal princes of another kind. Calev, Miriam's husband, was the man chosen from Judah, while Joshua was chosen from the men of Efraim. The twelve spies left on 29 *Sivan* and returned forty days later, on 8 *Av*.

Showing Moses and the community some lush fruit that they had brought back with them, the men reported that the Land was indeed abundant, but the cities and the inhabitants were both large and strong. Only Calev, with Joshua's support, voiced the opinion that the Israelites could conquer the Land against such odds. The other ten spies stated that the Land ate up its inhabitants, who were the mighty descendants of the giants of old (see chapter 2).

"We were like grasshoppers in our own eyes, and so we must have been in their eyes," the ten men said (Num. 13:33). Herein lay their sin, for here were community leaders who, despite a high status in their own society, crumbled in the face of a challenge whose positive outcome had already been guaranteed by God. Their fear of fighting was normal, but they projected their lack of self-confidence onto the Canaanites. They let insecurity about their smaller stature create a self-fulfilling prophecy that could easily set them up for defeat, for how we see ourselves determines the kind of image we project, which in turn determines how others see and treat us.

"When the spies said, 'We were like grasshoppers in our own eyes,' the Holy One said, 'I will forgive them for that.' But when they said, 'And so we must have been in their eyes,' Hashem said, 'You know what I made you like in their eyes!? Who says you weren't like angels in their eyes? What have your brought upon yourselves?'" (NR 16:11).

THE FAILURE OF TEN MEN

Hashem told Moses, saying, "Send for yourselves men [*Shlach lekha anashim*] to explore the land of Canaan that I am giving to the children of Israel." (Num. 13:1–2)

The Hebrew word *anashim* can mean either "men" or "people," as with "mankind" in English. Here, it is used to denote importance: at the time of their appointment the twelve tribal leaders were worthy—that is, suitable, appropriate, and fit for the task. It was only later that they failed (Rashi).

"In every instance where it says *anashim,* it means righteous people [*bnei adam tzadikim*]. . . . Can you then call them fools? They were only called fools because of their report on the Land. . . . Nevertheless they were great people, yet they made fools of themselves." Moses presented each man's name and tribal affiliation to God for approval. That divine approval was given indicates that it was only "afterwards, at the end of 40 days they changed and made all the trouble. . . . When they were selected they were righteous and then they changed" (NR 16:5).

That is not the whole story, however. We are told, by another source, that God gave Moses some extremely interesting advice:

With My knowledge from seeing into the future, it would be better to send women, who cherish the Land because they don't count its faults. But for you [*lekha*], with your knowledge, if you think that they [masc.] are fit and the Land is dear to them, then send men. Therefore, send *for yourselves,* according to *your* level of knowledge, men. But according to My level of knowledge, it would be better to send women, as I said. (Kli Yakar)

If a psychic, claiming insight into the future, told a client that one plan is better than another, many people would follow that advice, and so would any *chasid* hearing it from his rebbe. That Moses could get such a warning from God and *not* heed it is astounding indeed. It illustrates how preposterous such a plan must have seemed to him and how preposterous he felt it would have sounded to the men in the wilderness if he had explained it to them. Many women in the wilderness would also, no doubt, have scoffed at the idea—having internalized a belief that *their* smaller stature made them weak and inferior for such a task! Indeed, many men (and some women) today would still think it preposterous to send twelve women out on a military expedition to explore the terrain.

However, physical height and muscular strength were not what was needed, not to scout out the Land nor to conquer it. Again, however,—as with slavery, polygyny, and child marriage—God did not push a higher level of consciousness on humans than they (or the majority) were able to tolerate at the time.

This meant, unfortunately, that male shortsightedness set the pace for community action. From here it was all downhill for the Jewish people, for even the *best* of men— which is who were chosen for this mission—could not match the suitability that the *average* woman would bring to the task. Calev and Joshua are the kind of men known in modern feminist parlance as "exceptional."

The ten spies had already decided during their travels to bring back a negative report (Rashi). Thus, upon their return they spoke in a deliberate attempt to discredit the Land. Their motive was power, pure and simple: "They were all righteous, but they were misled by false reasoning. They said, 'If Israel enters the Land, we will be superseded, since it is only in the wilderness that we are accounted worthy to be leaders.'" (*Zohar* III:158a).

They began their speech with a positive comment, but this was only a calculated tactic to gain credibility for the negativity to follow. "Such is the way of those who utter *lashon hara,* to begin with the good and conclude with the bad" (NR 16:17).

However, the positive comment was about the abundance of the Land—the facet that, God told Moses, women cherish more than men! Had Moses taken God's advice—and had the community allowed him to do so—the results would probably have been quite different. Women might not so readily have had their appreciation for the Land overcome by a lust to preserve their political power (assuming they had any). Male ego was thus the major cause of the spies' downfall.

The spies invoked men of very large stature to strike fear in the hearts of the Jewish people. First they mentioned the giants of old, then they cited Amalek, the prototypical attacker of the Jews, "to frighten and terrify them" (Nachmanides). The Midrash describes it as a strategy like child abuse, a way to create submission through intimidation: "What reason did they see to begin with Amalek? It is like a child who misbehaved and was beaten with a strap. Whenever people wanted to frighten him, they used to remind him of the strap with which he had been beaten. In the same way Amalek was Israel's evil strap" (NR 16:18).

It was not the first time that ten men had bonded together to commit a terrible act. Ten men sold their brother into slavery in Egypt, causing the whole Jewish people to descend into slavery in Egypt. Now, ten men were about to cause an entire generation of males to die in the wilderness. From this the Rabbis derived the norm of the *minyan* (the minimum number required for communal prayer) as ten men. The *minyan* may thus be seen as a kind of *teshuvah* for the negative consequences of male bonding. This illustrates a fundamental principle in Jewish law: when *only* men may fulfill a certain function, it is an indication that it is an atonement for a sin that *only* men committed. (This should not, however, be confused with positive time-bound activities from which women are exempt but not prohibited.)

THE DECREE UPON MEN IN THE WILDERNESS

As you have spoken in My ears, so I will do to you. In this wilderness your corpses will fall and all that were numbered in the counting from 20 years up, those who brought you to revolt against Me, you shall not come into the Land. (Num. 14:28–30)

For Hashem had told them that they would all die in the wilderness, and not a single man of them would survive, except Calev ben-Yefuneh and Joshua ben-Nun. (Num. 26:65)

After the ten spies finished talking, mass hysteria broke out. This occurred on the night of 9 *Av*, Tisha B'Av (see Table 20–1). It was the first of several major tragedies to befall the Jews on this date for the rest of history, from the destruction of both Temples to the expulsion of Spanish Jews in 1492 c.e.

"For Israel had wept on the night of Tisha B'Av, and the Holy One said to them: 'You have wept a causeless weeping before Me. I will therefore fix for you a weeping for all generations.' At that hour it was decreed that the Temple should be destroyed and that Israel should be exiled among the nations" (NR 16:20).

Plans were being made by men in the community to appoint a leader to take them back to Egypt. When Calev and Joshua pleaded with them not to give up faith in God, the men threatened to stone them to death. Imagine how it must have felt for Miriam, who witnessed her son Chur being stoned to death by the golden-calf mob, to now see her husband facing the same fate!

As a result, God decreed that all the twenty- to sixty-year-old men counted in the census (see chapter 31) would die in the wilderness. The 10 spies died immediately in a plague, but the other 603,540 men died only when they reached the age of sixty. "A man who was twenty years old died whether he was of the same mind as the spies or not. . . . Nevertheless, no one died under sixty years of age" (NR 16:23). "Not one of them died younger than sixty years old. Therefore forty years was decreed so that those who were twenty years old should reach the age of sixty" (Rashi). In other words, the decree not only meant that 603,550 men would die; it also was the reason that the Jews had to spend forty years in the wilderness—so that all these deaths could be spread out over time. If not for the sin of the spies, the Jews would have entered the Land immediately.

Fortunately for the women, the children, the elderly, and the Levites who survived, the elimination of the adult males was a gradual process, so the campsite did not turn into an immediate mass grave. Like the generation of the Flood and the men of Sodom, the spies and the men who died in the wilderness are said to have no portion in the world to come (San. 108a).

Calev and Joshua were the only exceptions to the decree. Boys under twenty and men over sixty in the eleven tribes also survived, as did 22,000 Levite males of all ages. This decree was, in fact, the very reason why God commanded the census of Levite males to be separate from the other adult males: "The Holy One foresaw that a decree would stand against all who had been counted from twenty years up, that they would die in the wilderness. God therefore said, 'Let these [the Levites] be the exception, because they are Mine, since they did not go astray with the calf" (Rashi on Num. 1:49; NR 1:12, 2:19, 3:7).

Women did not die at all. "But upon the women the decree of the spies was not decreed, because they cherished the Land" (Rashi). Thus, here, as with the Exodus and the golden calf, there is a "women and Levites" linkage in terms of faithfulness to God. Women and Levites did not worship idols in Egypt; therefore, the Jews merited the Exodus. Women and Levites did not participate in making or worshiping the golden calf. Women and Levites did not doubt God's promise about the Land; therefore, they did not die in the wilderness.

We should try to imagine as vividly as possible what this desert community must have looked like as men consistently died at or around their sixtieth birthday. Society was composed primarily of adult women and their children—mothers, girls, boys, teenagers, grandmothers, and grandfathers. The single-parent (i.e., mother only) family is an old institution, indeed.

Fathers were the "missing generation." They died at a very young age (sixty). Other than Calev and Joshua, the oldest non-Levitical male who entered the Land of Israel would have been fifty-nine years old (nineteen at the time of the decree). The decree was made in the second year in the wilderness after the Exodus—9 Av 2449 A.M. During the rest of the time the Jews lived in the wilderness, there was no direct communication between Moses and the Shekhinah until the last year (Ta. 30b).

Thus, when the Jewish people entered and settled in the Land of Israel, it was primarily the women who maintained any memory of life in the wilderness.

❊❊❊ 35 ❊❊❊

Korach's Rebellion

Korach (16:1–18:32)

Numbers 16–17 tells of the rebellion fomented against Moses and Aharon by Korach, Datan, Aviram, and 250 "men of rank." Pretending to be concerned with democracy and equality ("Everyone in the community is holy" [Num. 16:3]), Korach and his supporters were actually motivated by arrogance and a greed for more power than they already had—and the power they had was certainly substantial.

Korach in no way represented the underdog or the disenfranchised. Far from being a revolt of the powerless against the powerful, Korach's rebellion was a purely "upperclass" phenomenon. Not only was Korach a Levite, he was from the family of Kehat, the most special Levitical branch, responsible for carrying the ark and other vessels (see chapter 31). The Kehatites were praised for their humility, making Korach's arrogance even more immense by comparison. He was not satisfied with the vast amount of privilege he had; he wanted it all.

Korach was the first cousin of Moses, Aharon, and Miriam. Kehat, the second son of Levi, had four sons (Ex. 6:18, 6:21; Num. 3:19). Amram was the eldest, so his sons, Moses and Aharon, got the highest positions of authority. As the firstborn of Kehat's second son, Yitzhar, Korach felt that he should be next in line for any authority conferred. Hence, he was angry that Elitzafan, the son of Kehat's youngest son, Uziel, was made patrilineal head of the Kehatites instead of him. According to one opinion, that is when this rebellion occurred (Num. 3:30; NR 18:2). In addition to his Levitical status, Korach was an extremely wealthy man. "The keys of Korach's treasure house were a load for 300 white mules" (San. 110a; Pes. 119a). He had gained this wealth as an assimilated Jew in Egypt, for "he was controller in Pharaoh's palace and in charge of the keys of his treasury" (NR 18:15).

Korach was misled by a prophetic vision, which he misinterpreted. He foresaw that his descendants would include the prophet Samuel and twenty-four rotations of

Levitical singers in the Temple. As a result, he could not believe that all this dignity would come from him while he himself remained unrecognized. However, he perceived the vision wrong; his sons repented for their rebellious attitude and did not die. Hence, Samuel and the singers descended from them (Rashi; NR 18:8).

KORACH'S COHORTS

Korach's chief allies in the rebellion were Datan and Aviram, two Reuvenite brothers. Datan, we recall, was a Jewish officer in Egypt and Shlomit's husband. He was the man who was being beaten by the Egyptian taskmaster whom Moses then killed (see chapter 13). That he could challenge Moses' authority after Moses risked his own life to save Datan illustrates how arrogant and ungrateful he was. He refused to even come *speak* to Moses at the latter's request!

The tribe of Reuven was situated on the southern side of the camp, adjacent to the Kehatites, but it was not only physical proximity that made the Reuvenites vulnerable to persuasion by Korach. They were angry that Moses had taken away the status of firstborn from Reuven and had given it to Joseph (Nachmanides).

A second opinion of when the rebellion occurred places it at the time when the Levites were substituted for the firstborn sons (Ibn Ezra). However, Datan and Aviram were not firstborn sons, and would not have been motivated by that. Nevertheless, this view is supported by the fact that the *parshah* concludes with instructions about the duties of the Levites (Num. 18). A third opinion holds that the rebellion took place at Chatzerot, where Miriam was quarantined for a week (Rashi). This is interesting because it implies that without Miriam, the community fell apart, disintegrating into factionalism.

A fourth view, that the rebellion happened when it is mentioned—namely, after the spies returned—maintains that it was motivated by the decree on men in the wilderness (Nachmanides). However, Korach was a Levite and would not have been affected by that. This could apply to Datan and Aviram, and it may be implied in their assertion to Moses, "Isn't it enough that you brought us out of [Egypt] just to kill us in the wilderness?" (Num. 16:13). However, that might only have been a general complaint. A very strong argument against this opinion is that there was direct communication between God and Moses (16:20, 16:23), which did not happen after the incident of the spies until the fortieth year.

Korach also assembled 250 "men of rank" by persuading them that he had their interests at heart (Rashi). These were heads of the Sanhedrin and most of them were also Reuvenites, including that tribe's patrilineal prince, Elitzur (NR 18:3). Compare the descriptions in Numbers 1:16 and 16:2—"the elect of the congregation, princes of the tribes of their fathers, heads of the thousands of Israel" and "princes of the congregation, the elect of the assembly, men of name."

These were "outstanding men of the congregation . . . [who] knew how to intercalate the [leap] years and fix the months. . . They had a name among all" (NR 18:20). As Sanhedrin leaders—judges knowledgeable in the law—these men were expected to behave in a manner befitting their position as role models for the community. They were therefore held to a higher standard than "common" men, making their behavior that much worse.

The rebels tried to outsmart Moses and make him look foolish. Dressing in robes of pure *tekhelet* (indigo blue wool) they came before Moses to ask if such a garment was exempt from *tzitzit*—the fringes, each containing a blue thread, required on any four-cornered piece of clothing worn by adult males. Moses ruled that *tzitzit* were required. "A garment that is entirely blue does not exempt itself, yet four blue threads do exempt it?!" they mockingly replied. They then asked him if a house full of religious books required a *mezuzah* on the doorpost. When he said yes, they again mocked his legal authority: "The whole Torah . . . does not exempt the house, but one section [of it] in the *mezuzah* does exempt the house?!" (NR 18:3).

It is even said that Korach and his cohorts went so far as to erect a sanctuary in opposition to the Tabernacle (Kaplan). After the golden calf, the complaint about manna and the yearning for meat, and the report of the spies, this was now the fourth incident in which the Jews—primarily the men—descended into a slave mentality and clamored to return to Egypt (NR 18:6).

While Korach, Datan, and Aviram were swallowed up by the earth, the 250 princes were consumed by fire. Another 14,700 members of the congregation died in a plague because they blamed Moses for having killed the others.

MRS. KORACH AND MRS. ON

Datan and Aviram went out and stood at the entrance of their tents, along with their wives, their children, and their infants. . . . The earth opened its mouth and swallowed them and their houses, along with all the people that were with Korach and their property. (Num. 16:27, 16:32)

Why were Datan and Aviram's wives killed? (Is Datan's "wife" here only Shlomit, or did he have other wives as well?) We are not given a reason. We might presume that they encouraged their husbands to rebel against Moses—but such an assumption of guilt could be erroneous, since it certainly does not explain why the infants died.

"How difficult is dissent! The *bet din* above [the Heavenly Court] does not punish anyone unless they are at least 20 years old, and the *bet din* below [the earthly court] unless they are 13. Yet in Korach's strife, babies of a day old were burned and swallowed up in the underworld [*sheol tachtit*]" (NR 18:4).

The archetypal female earth is not the only active feminine presence in this story, however. The Talmud describes the influence of two "women behind the men"—the wives of Korach and On, a Reuvenite man who started out in the rebellion but did not stay with it and so did not die (Num. 16:1). Korach started his rebellion after a consultation with his wife (NR 18:4). Only then did he approach Moses and say, "You have laid upon us a burden greater than Egyptian slavery! It was better for us under the Egyptians than under your rule!" Was this his wife's opinion too, or did she just want her husband to have more power? Did she suggest the rebellion, or did she just support him in his own idea?

We are not given Mrs. Korach's name or the answers to any of these questions. We are only told that, in the end, her wickedness was so great it even quenched the flames of Gehenna: "The wife of Korach, when she descended into Gehenna, extinguished it [lit., 'her']" (NR 18:15).

We noted in chapter 1 the story of a pious couple who got divorced and each remarried. The man's remarriage was to a wicked woman; as a result he became bad. The woman 's remarriage was to a wicked man; as a result, he became good! Thus, in both cases the men were changed by the women, and not vice versa. Here we are told a somewhat similar story. Korach—whose character was not so great to begin with—definitely became worse after consulting with his wicked wife.

On the other hand, On started out as a rebel in Korach's party but *left* because of his wife's advice, for while On became caught up in the drive for power, Mrs. On was more realistic—she knew that her husband would not gain anything by rebelling. Her story is told in *Numbers Rabbah* 18:20 and *Sanhedrin* 109b–110a:

> On, the son of Pelet, was saved by his wife. She said to him: "What does this [rebellion] matter to you? If one [Moses] is the master, you're still [going to be] the disciple!"
> He replied, "What can I do? I have sworn to join them."
> She said, "I know that everyone in the congregation is holy. Stay here and I will save you." She got him drunk on wine and put him to bed. Then she sat down at the doorway with her daughter and and undid her hair, so that any man who came to see On would turn away.

Her scheme worked because of the law forbidding men to look at a married woman's hair. Korach and his rebels would have maintained such a strict level of halakhic observance because at that time and in that place it was normative for married women to cover their heads. A woman who refused to do so would be stigmatized as "loose" and perhaps even divorced by her husband. Today, in most communities, women would not be so easily able to manipulate men in this fashion.

Meanwhile, Korach's wife came and said [to On], "See what Moses has done! He has become king; he has appointed his brother high priest; and he has made his brother's sons assistant high priests. If *trumah* is brought he says, 'Let it be for the priest.' If *maaser* is brought he says, 'Give a tenth to the priest.'"

Mrs. Korach thus gained entry where the male rebels could not. As a woman, she did not have to turn away because she saw Mrs. On's hair. She did her best to rekindle On's resentment of Moses and provoke him to rebel. In the end, however, she failed, for On listened to his wife and stayed at home. Hence, his life was spared. Nevertheless, he spent the rest of his adult life as a mourner (*onen*) in atonement for his original willingness to join the rebellion.

✿✿✿ 36 ✿✿✿

The Waters of Life

Chukat (19:1–22:1)

This *parshah* is all about water. The term *mayim chayim,* meaning *living waters,* is a metaphor for the Torah itself, the lifespring sustaining the Jewish people. The theme of water is predominant in the following scenarios:

Mei niddah, the waters of the Red Heifer: This was a potion made from the ashes of a young red cow which had been burned with cedarwood, hyssop, and crimson wool. Sprinkling this concoction on a person or an object who was *tamae met*—in a state of *tumah* from contact with a corpse—rendered that person or object *tahor* (Num. 19). However, the men involved in the slaughter and burning of the cow, and the *ish tahor* (man or woman) who removed her ashes from the altar to outside the camp, were rendered *tamae* by the process, and had to immerse in a *mikvah* to become *tahor.* *Mei niddah* thus made the *tamae tahor* and the *tahor tamae.* It differed in this way from the *mikvah,* whose waters make the *tamae tahor,* but do not change the status of anything from *tahor* to *tamae.*

Miriam's Well: The death and burial of Miriam at Kadesh was followed by a lack of water for the community (Num. 20:1–2). Immediately, some irritable thirsty people began to blame Moses and Aharon for even bringing them out of slavery to begin with. A song is sung in honor of Miriam's Well, the water that had accompanied the Jews through the wilderness until her death.

Mei Merivah, Waters of Dispute: To get drinking water, Moses struck the rock instead of speaking to it as God had commanded; as a result he and Aharon were told they would not enter the Promised Land (Num. 20:7–13). Aharon then died on *Rosh Chodesh Av* of that year (Num. 20:24). This incident was the "misfortune through water" that Pharaoh's astrologers had foreseen in Moses' life but misinterpreted as him drowning in the Nile (see chapter 13).

Pledge of the Envoys: The Jews promised the Edomites (Num. 20:14–21) and the Amorites (Num. 21:21–22) not to drink their water as they passed through these king-

361

doms on their way to Canaan. Neither one allowed the Jews to pass through. The Amorites, however, went further than Edom and actually *attacked* the Jews, even after Israel had taken a circuitous route to avoid their territory. Israel defeated the Amorites and their king, Sichon, capturing and settling in all their cities.

The Copper Snake: Those who had jumped on the bandwagon of blaming Moses and Aharon for the lack of water after Miriam's death started squabbling about it a second time. They were punished with a snake plague (Num. 21:6) that was mitigated only when they begged Moses for mercy, who prayed on their behalf and built a copper snake image at God's command (Num. 21:9).

THE RED HEIFER: BLOOD WATERS

Mei niddah, the waters of the Red Heifer (Num. 19:9, 19:13, 19:20–21), literally means "the waters of *niddah*." *Niddah*, the term used for a menstruant and for a mother the week or two after childbirth, is defined by the separation of a woman at these times from sexual activity, entering the Tabernacle, and eating sacrificial food.

The waters of the Red Heifer, however, were used to make *tahor* a person who had become *tamae* through contact with the (human) dead. *Mei niddah* thus seems to have no apparent relationship to *niddah* in the "female-blood" sense. However, the waters affect—indeed, contain the mystery of—the distinct boundaries of *tumah* and *taharah*. Moreover, the quintessence of the Red Heifer is that she be red and female.

A heifer is, in fact, a nulliparous cow, a female that has not yet borne any young. To qualify as the Red Heifer, a young cow had to have been a vaginal birth herself, not a Caesarean section, and she could never have been yoked for any human benefit (Par. 2:3). She had to be completely red—as few as two hairs of any other color disqualified her.

She was then burned with cedar (red wood), crimson yarn (red wool), and hyssop. Thus, three of the four species had to be red by nature. The fourth species, hyssop, was red by association, for it was the herbal "paintbrush" used for putting ram's blood on the doorways of the Jewish households in Egypt. Painting this blood on the doorposts and lintel in the shape of a Heh prevented the bloodshed of the Jewish firstborn on the night of the Exodus. It also stood for Jewish resistance and heroism under Egyptian slavery, as symbolized by the blood of menstruation, childbirth, and circumcision (see chapter 15).

CLEANING UP AFTER "MAMA'S BOY"

Mei niddah had to be made from a red *cow* and not a bull, according to Jewish tradition, because the Red Heifer served as atonement for the golden calf in the way that a mother cleans up after her baby who makes a mess in the king's palace (NR 19:8). This is probably why a heifer, and not an adult cow, was required—the golden calf was her "only child."

The red and gold colors, the mother cow and her bull calf, are fundamentally Egyptian symbols. As red-haired men were sacrificed by Egyptian kings at the grave of Osiris as a precaution against famine (see chapter 15), "the oxen which were sacrificed had also to be red; a single black or white hair found on the beast would have disqualified it for the sacrifice."[1] Joseph, we have seen, eclipsed Osiris as the Egyptian "bull and corn" god by providing grain to the people in time of famine (see chapters 10 and 12).

The Jews, scared of being without Moses, built and worshiped the most common image known to them from living in Egypt—a golden bull, symbol of Pharaoh in relation to a mother-cow goddess. Cow and bull deities were the target of the fifth plague which God brought upon Egypt, pestilence (see chapter 14). That the Jews could revert to the worship of a golden bull indicates the depth of the slave mentality that possessed them.

The Torah took these images and utilized them in its attempt to wean human consciousness from the slave mentality of idolatry. Red and gold were major colors in the materials used to construct the Tabernacle: gold vessels in the Sanctuary, copper altar and laver in the courtyard, red ram's skins on the roof, and crimson wool and gold thread in the curtains and in the high priest's vestments.

Red, as the color of blood, continued to symbolize atonement; but the use of ritual bloodshed to effect atonement was greatly limited by the Torah, in contrast to the massive bloodbaths of pagan sacrifices (see chapters 22 and 23). The blood and smoke of sacrifices form the kabbalistic symbolism of turning red (God's anger, or Judgment) into white (God's forgiveness, or Mercy).

The Red Heifer's function as atonement for the golden calf is related to the use of its waters to make people *tahor* from "death *tumah*." The Jewish community, as a result of the golden calf, had a lot of "death *tumah*" in its midst. The three species burned with the heifer correspond to the three thousand firstborn sons killed by the Levites for sacrificing to the calf (Rashi). Because of the golden calf, the community had been in contact with numerous corpses—Chur, the firstborn males, the people who died in the plague, and the people who died from drinking the bitter waters. It affected the community as a whole, not just a few individuals and their families.

Crimson wool was also a prominent ingredient in the Yom Kippur rite of Azazel. The first Yom Kippur was the day of atonement for the golden calf, when Moses came down from Sinai with the second set of tablets, indicating God's forgiveness. The crimson wool, tied around the goat's neck, symbolized the sins of the community. When atonement was effected, the red yarn turned white. Red as the color of "sin" stems from the bloodshed of idol worship.

Azazel and the Red Heifer are two major examples of a category of Jewish law known as *chukim* (NR 19:5), legal statutes that have no rational explanation and that may cause the world to scoff at Jews for observing them. The nonrational nature of the waters of the Red Heifer led at least one pagan to suggest that it was *kishuf*, or sorcery. R. Jochanan ben Zakai responded by comparing it to the man's knowledge

---

1. Frazer, p. 441.

of how to expel a demon of madness from someone possessed (NR 19:8). The waters of the Red Heifer might thus be likened to a kind of spiritual herbal medicine.

The ritual was entrusted to Elazar even in Aharon's lifetime because of Aharon's role in building the golden calf (Rashi). The priest who was to burn the Red Heifer was separated from his household seven days beforehand, just like the high priest who performed the Yom Kippur service (Par. 3:1; Yom. 1:1).

GENDER, THE CALF, AND THE HEIFER

The most fascinating linkage of all between the Red Heifer and the golden calf is found in the mirroring of the gender distinctions of involvement with them. There were, we recall, three levels of involvement with, and accountability for, the calf:

• Only men made it, and only men sacrificed to it. Three thousand firstborn sons, the standard priesthood of the ancient world, were stabbed to death by the male Levites at God's command, and the Jewish priesthood was born.
• Both men and women participated in the merrymaking (*letzachek*) which accompanied the worship of the calf—feasting, drinking, and orgiastic sexual activity, including embracing and kissing the image. These people were killed in a plague by God.
• Both men and women who did not actively participate, but nevertheless "rejoiced in their hearts," died from drinking a potion of waters made from the ashes of the burnt calf.

In the case of the Red Heifer:

• Only men could make it, and only men could sprinkle the waters on a *tamae met* person. This was because only men had made the calf, and only men were responsible for the killing associated with it. A woman could hold the waters, but a man had to dip and sprinkle. Sprinkling was time-bound; it could only be done by daylight (Par. 12:10-11; Yom. 42b).
  The sprinkler could not even be a *tumtum* or a hermaphrodite. A hermaphrodite, in Jewish law, sometimes has the status of a man, sometimes of a woman, sometimes of both, and sometimes of neither (Bik. 4:1–5). Here, such a person holds the status of a woman. This indicates that complete maleness was required for the atonement of a sin committed completely by men.
• Both men and women could gather up the ashes and move them outside the camp. This task was not time-bound but rather could be done by day or by night. R. Judah, the second-century codifier of the Mishnah, whose word was final, agreed that women are permitted, but he disqualified minors (Yom. 43a). Since this task corresponds to the merrymaking that accompanied the worship of the calf, it appears that women were as culpable as men, but that children would not be held accountable for "playing."

• Both men and women could make the potion of waters from the ashes of the burnt heifer, according to the Mishnah, with minors, the insane, and the deaf being disqualified. However, R. Judah permitted (male) minors, as well as disqualifying women and hermaphrodites (Par. 5:4). Since this task corresponds to the waters made from the golden calf, it would seem to indicate that boys, more than adult women, died from the potion striking those who had "rejoiced in their hearts."

MIRIAM'S DEATH, MIRIAM'S WELL

All the congregation of the children of Israel came to the wilderness of Zin. In the first month the people settled in Kadesh and there Miriam died and was buried. The people did not have any water, so they began demonstrating against Moses and Aharon. (Num. 20:1–2)

The death of Miriam is said to follow immediately upon the preparation and use of the waters of the Red Heifer because "as the Red Heifer effects atonement, so does the death of the righteous effect atonement" (M.K. 28a; LR 20:12; Rashi). This may be true, but it is equally significant that the theme of water follows the death of Miriam as well as precedes it.

A link between Miriam and water was established immediately after the Exodus, when the Song at the Sea is followed by two accounts (at Marah and Rephidim) of a lack of water, before the Jews even reached Sinai. At Rephidim, Moses was told by God to strike a rock to get water. During the next thirty-nine years in the wilderness, the people got water through Miriam's merit from this rock, which was known as Miriam's Well (see chapter 16).

Created by God on the sixth day, Miriam's Well appears throughout the Torah with the matriarchs and the patriarchs: It is where Hagar had her vision and later found water for Ishmael. It is where Eliezer found Rivkah, where Jacob met Rachel, and where Moses met Zipporah. It was claimed by Avraham in a treaty with Avimelekh in Gerar (Gen. 21:25–30). After Avraham's death, the Philistines plugged up all the wells out of jealousy over Isaac's prosperity. In redigging them, Isaac found "a well of living waters" (Gen. 26:19). In Egypt, when Joseph died, "all the wells and springs were dried up, and the captivity began for all the tribes" (*Zohar* II:156a).

In the wilderness, Miriam's Well took the form of a rock shaped like a beehive which rolled along with the Jews wherever they went. When the people camped and the Tabernacle was set up, "that same rock would come and settle down in the court of the *ohel moed* and the princes would come and stand upon it and say, 'Rise up, O Well,' and it would rise" (NR 1:2). This is the song sung by the people in honor of the well after Miriam's death (Num. 21:17–18).

Miriam died on 10 *Nisan* 2487 at age 126 (see Table 20–1). The tenth of *Nisan* is also the day when the Pesach lamb was chosen and set aside. After her death, Miriam's Well "vanished and took a place among the other rocks" (Rashi). When God told Moses and Aharon to speak to a rock to get water at Merivah (Num. 20:7–11), it was assumed that the rock would be Miriam's Well, but it was not clear which rock God meant. When they spoke to one rock, as instructed, but nothing happened, Moses struck another rock. This one brought forth a few drops of water, so he struck it a second time (Rashi).

Later, when people again started complaining (Num. 21:5–9), God killed them with a snake plague that was stopped only by looking at the image of a copper snake. Here, again, we see the color red used to stay God's Judgment. This animal image of red metal built by Moses also seems to parallel the animal image of gold metal built by Aharon—for, like the golden calf, the copper snake (*nechash nechoshet*, which is a pun in Hebrew) became an object of Jewish communal idol worship. This got so out of hand that the copper snake was eventually destroyed, along with pagan images, in the time of the Prophets (2 Kings 18:4).

The location of Miriam's Well, since the Jews got out of the wilderness, is believed to be cited right in the Torah: "It is seen upon the face of Yeshimon" (Num. 21:20). "Anyone who ascends to the top of Mount Yeshimon will see something like a small sieve in the sea of Tiberias. This is Miriam's Well. R. Jochanan b. Nuri says: 'Our Rabbis have calculated its position, which is directly opposite the middle gate of the ancient synagogue of Tiberias'" (LR 22:4). Mount Yeshimon is elsewhere identified as Mount Carmel (Shab. 35a).

People's afflictions have been healed by the waters of Miriam's Well (NR 18:22), including "a certain man suffering from boils who went down to bathe in Tiberias. It so happened that he floated into Miriam's Well, and he bathed there, and was healed" (LR 22:4). This is quite interesting, as the biggest tourist attractions in Tiberias to this day are its hot springs on Lake Kinneret, the Sea of Galilee.

Like Moses and Aharon, Miriam died by the Divine Kiss (*al pi* Hashem, or "by the Mouth of God"). Those who die in this way do not convey "corpse *tumah*" (Nachmanides). However, why is this fact not stated about Miriam, as it is of Moses (Deut. 34:5) and Aharon (Num. 33:38)? This is because, the Rabbis suggest, it would be "disrespectful" of God to say such a thing about a woman (Rashi; M.K. 28a). The implication here is that it would have erotic connotations. Such an interpretation is borderline idolatrous, for it presumes that God really *is* a male!

The "Mouth of God" might, in fact, relate to divine communication about one's death, for Moses and Aharon were forewarned, while Miriam was not. God told both Moses and Aharon that Aharon was going to die so that the high priest's vestments could be transferred to Elazar (Num. 20:26). God also told Moses when he was about to die so that he could bless the tribes and name Joshua as his successor (Deut. 32:50). On the contrary, no one knew of Miriam's death ahead of time (NR 19:17), nor does the Torah indicate that God gave her any specific instructions which would have informed her it was about to happen.

Miriam was buried near the site of her death (M.K. 28a). The Torah's primary purpose in mentioning her death "was to show the unworthiness of Israel, for whom water was made to flow forth only through the virtue of Miriam. Hence Miriam's death was not recorded with such full details as that of Sarah," even though she was just as significant and righteous a figure (*Zohar* I:124b).

AHARON'S DEATH AND THE HOUSE OF ISRAEL

All the congregation saw that Aharon had expired, and all the House of Israel mourned Aharon for 30 days. (Num. 20:29)

The House of Israel means the women, as the structure and foundation ("home") of the Jewish people (see chapter 17). Aharon's death occurred on *Rosh Chodesh Av*, the first of the nine days leading up to Tisha B'Av. Tisha B'Av, which is rooted in the decree on men in the wilderness, marks the destruction of the First and Second Temples.

Hence there is a subtle pun involved in the linkage here: The House of Israel (women) mourned the death of Aharon in the month that would later become the mourning period for the House of Israel (the Temple). The reason for the predominance of the "house" theme is Aharon's role in fostering *shalom bayit*, "domestic peace."

Aharon's death was mourned by the women as much as the men, the Rabbis say, because he "pursued peace and promoted love between contending parties and between a man and his wife" (Rashi). We have learned that Aharon's pacifism was a double-edged sword, which earned him the priesthood as both a reward and an atonement (see chapter 23). The atonement, as usual, was for the golden calf. The reward was for the great contribution he made in stemming anger and violence, both between men and between husband and wife.

"When two men had quarreled with one another, Aharon would go and sit with one of them . . . until he had removed all enmity from his heart. Then Aharon would go and sit with the other . . . until he had removed all enmity from his heart. Later, when the two met, they embraced and kissed each other" (*Avot d'Rabbi Natan,* chap. 12).

In reconciling husbands and wives, *how* he did so is the key to understanding why women felt his loss so acutely. That women mourned his death enough for the Torah to make special note of it is highly significant. Aharon must have been very sensitive to women's needs and concerns. Surely he would not have been mourned so greatly by women had he told them to put up with a bad situation in the name of *shalom bayit.* The source quoted previously continues with an account indicating how his influence might have helped women with abusive, criminal, or even simply irresponsible husbands: "Whenever Aharon walked along the road and met a wicked man, he would offer him greetings. On the following day, when the man was about to commit a transgression, he would say, 'Oy! How can I lift up my eyes after doing that and look Aharon in the face?! I should be ashamed before him, since he greeted me.' Consequently the man withheld himself from transgression." As a result, "many thousands in Israel were given the name Aharon, since but for him they would not have come into the world" (*Avot d'Rabbi Natan*, chap. 12). That is, couples who reunited would name their next baby boy after the man who was responsible for saving their marriage.

❋❋❋ 37 ❋❋❋

Kazbi: Midianite Princess

Balak (22:2–25:9)

The name of the Midianite woman who was killed was Kazbi, the daughter of Zur, head of a patrilineal line in Midian. (Num. 25:15)

Kazbi, a Midianite princess, is a major character in the story of the Moabite women who "lured" thousands of Jewish men into the worship of the god Baal-Peor. This episode occurs after Balak, the king of Moav, tried unsuccessfully to have Israel cursed. Balak and Zur are actually the same person (NR 20:24).

MIDIAN AND MOAV

Midian, one of the six sons of Keturah, was the ancestor of five nations (Gen. 25:1, 25:4). It was the Midianites who pulled Joseph out of the pit and sold him to the Ishmaelites (Gen. 37:28). Zipporah, Moses' wife, was the eldest of seven daughters of the Midianite high priest, Yitro, who resigned because he saw the falsehood of idolatry. One of Zipporah's sisters, Bat-Putiel, married Aharon's son Elazar, and they had a son named Pinchas (see chapter 14). Now that Aharon was dead, Elazar had become the high priest and Pinchas was the *segan*, the assistant high priest.

Moav, the son of Lot's firstborn daughter, was the ancestor of Ruth, King David, and the Messiah. Because Moav bore the stigma of incest openly in his name, Israel provoked fear in the Moabites' hearts even though they did not attack them. On the other hand, Ben-Ami, the son of Lot's younger daughter, had a euphemism for a name and bore no open stigma; thus, the Ammonites did not fear Israel (see chapter 4).

Ammon, Moav, Edom, and Midian were located, from north to south, respectively, in what is now Jordan and the northwestern tip of Saudi Arabia. In the time of Esav, the Edomites defeated the Midianites in a battle in Moav (Gen. 36:35). Some of the territory of Moav was later captured and occupied by the Amorites; this land was, in turn, captured by Israel in its repulsion of the Amorites' attack (Num. 21:26). Israel's acquisition of Amorite-occupied Moav in this war of self-defense is said to have made the land *tahor* (Chul. 60b).

After hearing of Israel's victory over the Amorites, Moav's fear led it to form an alliance with its traditional enemy, Midian, against the Jews (Rashi; San. 105a; NR 20:4). Thus, there is a strong link in this chapter between the activities of the Midianites and the Moabites, which makes the two peoples appear almost interchangeable at times.

BALAK AND BILAM

When Balak, son of Zippor, saw all that Israel had done to the Amorites, the Moabites became deathly afraid because the people [of Israel] were so numerous. (Num. 22:2–3)

Balak, king of Moav, was the grandfather of Eglon (Judges 3:12–25), who was himself the father or grandfather of Ruth (Hor. 10b; Naz. 23b). Balak was also a Midianite prince (Rashi) and a descendant of Yitro (*Zohar* III:196b). Balak's father was called Zippor, the masculine form of Zipporah, because he practiced bird divination (Kaplan).

Balak was called "'son of a bird,' for he used birds for all his magic arts. He used to mark a bird plucking an herb or flying through the air, and on his performing certain rites and incantations that bird would come to him with grass in its mouth and he would put it in a cage. He would tie knots before it and it would tell him certain things." He also made a bird out of silver and gold that he set in the window, and when he pricked it with a needle it would talk (*Zohar* III:184b).

Balak sent the elders of Moav and Midian "with divination in their hands" (Num. 22:7) to Babylonia to fetch Bilam, a well-known sorcerer, to come and put a curse on Israel. Balak was more of an expert at divination and enchantment than Bilam (Rashi; NR 20:18), but Bilam was the master of sorcery. He and Yitro had both been advisors to Pharaoh during the latter's attempt to kill Jewish boys—Yitro was "minister of worship" of the stars and Bilam was "arch-sorcerer" (*Zohar* II:69a).

Bilam was the son of Beor, who was either Lavan or Lavan's son (see chapter 5). In either case, the name Beor alludes to his penchant for bestiality *(beir)*. Bilam learned sorcery "first from his father, but it was in the mountains of the East . . . that he obtained a mastery of all the arts of magic and divination" (*Zohar* I:126a).

BILAM'S PROPHECY

Bilam, like his father, engaged in bestiality for occult purposes (San. 105a). This is why the Torah specifically describes his donkey as a female, *aton,* rather than using *chamor,* the generic term for the species (Num. 22:21–32). A link between sorcery and bestiality is established by the proximity of the prohibitions on them (Ex. 22:17–18).

According to the *Zohar*, a sorcerer would practice bestiality in order to make himself *tamae*, for a person in a state of *tumah* has enhanced magical powers. A menstruating woman, for example, "is in close touch with the spirit of *tumah*, and therefore at such a period she will be more successful in the use of magical arts than at any other time" (*Zohar* I:126b).

The serpent is the *Zohar*'s symbol of the "spirit of *tumah*"; the snake's communication with Chavah, not Adam, in the Garden of Eden is the reason that "many kinds of magic and divination are found only in women" (*Zohar* I:126a).

> All species of witchcraft are linked up with, and proceed from, the primeval serpent who is the spirit of *tumah*. Hence all sorceries are called *nechashim* [serpents]. . . . For this reason, in order to draw toward himself the spirit of *tumah* from that supernal serpent, the wicked Bilam sullied himself every night by intercourse with his donkey, and he would then proceed to his divinations and sorceries.
>
> First he would take one of the familiar serpents, tie it up, break its head, and extract its tongue. Next he would take certain herbs and burn them as incense. Then he would take the head of the serpent, split it into four sections, and offer it up as a second offering. Finally, he traced a circle around himself, mumbled some words and made some gestures, until he became possessed by the spirits of *tumah*, who told him all that they knew from the side of the heavenly dragon; and he thus continued his magical practices until he became possessed by the spirit of the primeval serpent. (*Zohar* I:125b–26a)

God's presence with Bilam is thus somewhat puzzling. "Why did . . . the Shekhinah rest upon a wicked gentile? So that the nations should have no excuse to say, 'If we had prophets, we would have changed for the better,' [God] raised up prophets for them. Yet they broke down the fence of the world, because at first they guarded themselves from sexual immorality, but this one [Bilam] advised them to commit themselves to *znut*." God appeared to gentile prophets only at night, "like a person who goes to his concubine secretively" (Rashi; LR 1:13).

Bilam's level of prophecy is compared with that of Moses. While God appeared to Moses while he was standing, Bilam had to be lying down. God spoke to Moses mouth to mouth and face to face, but to Bilam only in parables. Moses did not always know when God would speak to him, or what the topic of conversation would be, but Bilam did (NR 14:20).

Bilam wanted to go with the elders because he hated the Jews even more than Balak did (Rashi; *Zohar* III:206b). God was angry with Bilam for his eagerness and sent an angel to block his way. Only Bilam's donkey saw the angel, however, so Bilam began to beat her when she stopped in the road. Not only did this animal have superior vision to her "bestial" owner, she was also given the power of human speech by God in order to defend herself!

Bilam was unable to curse Israel; every time he opened his mouth to do so, a blessing came out!

Bilam was possessed by an evil eye, and whatever he fixed his gaze on, he drew the destroying spirit. Knowing this, he sought to fix his gaze on Israel, in order that he might destroy everything upon which his look should fall. . . . Israel, however, was immune. . . . He saw the Shekhinah hovering over them and kept in position by the 12 tribes beneath, and his eye had no more power over them. (*Zohar* I:68b)

Israel was immune because "Rachel was there, and when she saw that his eye was sharpened to hurt them, she went forth and spread her wings over them and covered her children." Rachel protected Israel from Bilam's gaze, just as Joseph had protected her from Esav's gaze (*Zohar* III:202b).

Although (or because) he could not curse Israel, Bilam advised Balak that he could bring about the nation's downfall through sexual immorality, for "their God hates *zimah,* and they really like linen. Erect for them curtained booths, and place within them *zonot*—old women outside, and young girls inside, to sell linen garments" (San. 106a).

"Balak saw by his stargazing that Israel would fall by his hand. Therefore, he offered his daughter for prostitution, and through her 24,000 fell" (NR 20:7). This daughter was Kazbi.

THE MOABITE WOMEN

Israel was staying in Shitim when the people began to commit sexual degradation to [*liznot el-*] the daughters of Moav. They [the women] called the people to the sacrifices of their gods, and the people ate and bowed down to their gods. Israel became attached to Baal-Peor, and God got angry at Israel. (Num. 25:1–3)

"People" (*am*) in this passage is interpreted by all commentators to mean the men, same as with the golden calf (see Ex. 32:1, 32:3). No one asserts that Jewish women were being sexual with the Moabite men, and certainly no one tries to say that Jewish women engaged in lesbianism with the Moabite women!

English translations of this passage generally state that the men were committing sexual degradation "with" the Moabite women. However, the Hebrew preposition *el* always means "to." Hence, even though the Moabite women invited the men to their religious festival, responsibility for the *znut* is placed on the men.

The reason for this is that the women's behavior was a result of *chilul habat,* desecration of the daughter (see chapter 28). "Truly, the *znut* was not instigated as a plan of the women, but was done upon the advice of their men and their leaders" (Nachmanides). Moabite men, following the example of their king, Balak, readily pimped their daughters in an attempt to bring Israel down (and the men of Israel just as readily snapped at the "bait").

The underlying dynamic of *chilul habat,* we have noted, is *zimah*—which Bilam had told Balak the God of Israel hates—in which father–daughter incest sets a girl up for a life of prostitution. The willingness of Moabite men to prostitute their daughters, combined with their ancestral heritage of openly acknowledged father–daughter incest (embodied by Moav himself), strongly indicates that such incest was rampant in their society.

A further clue to the nature of Moabite men's treatment of women is found in the fact that a Moabite man may never convert and marry a Jewish woman, but a Moabite woman may convert and marry a Jewish man. The prohibition on entering the Jewish community applied only to Moabite men because they refused to bring bread and water to the Jews coming out of Egypt. The Rabbis did not hold Moabite women responsible for this, because it was not customary for the women to go out (Deut. 23:4–5; Yev. 76b).

In other words, the women of Moav were secluded, like Canaanite women in the time of Dinah (chapter 8), like Egyptian women in the time of Joseph (chapter 12), and like Saudi Arabian women today. The seclusion of women is found in any society where women are kept in harems. Although such seclusion is defended by men as a means of "protecting" women, it does not in any way prevent sexual and physical abuse. On the contrary, such abuse flourishes when women are hidden from public view. However, the abuse is successfully kept secret and the rapist or batterer is always a family member, not an acquaintance or a stranger on the street.

Nor does the seclusion of the women stop the men from using prostitutes and (in modern times) pornography. A huge double standard of sexual morality is thus intrinsic to the situation.[1]

In the ancient pagan world, the same men who secluded women and girls with such intense possessiveness and control might also choose to pimp them. This may seem contradictory at first, unless one understands that the primary purpose of seclusion is not so much to preserve a daughter's virginity (or even a wife's faithfulness), but to stifle women's freedom of movement. A father will fly into a rage if his daughter goes out with a man on her own, yet this same father might sell her to a temple or barter her to a friend or business colleague for his own benefit. The significant factor is that he, not she, decides what man (or men) will have her when.

This, then, is what the Moabite men were like. "Every man placed his daughter and wife at the door of his tent" so that a Jewish man would stop to talk, eat, and drink. Once he was drunk, "they placed before him a beautiful young woman and he did with her as he liked" (SY 284). This was the first time the Israelite men had indulged in *znut* since the days of Avraham (NR 20:22). As with modern prostitutes, it is not necessary (or realistic) to assert that all Moabite women were coerced. Many of them no doubt were, especially the young girls. Others, however (especially older women jaded by years and years of sexual abuse and exploitation), may have participated "willingly." The role of the older women actually resembles that of a "madam," a woman who has been "promoted" to the position of supervising other

---

1. For some eye-opening accounts of this phenomenon in modern Saudi Arabia, see Jean P. Sasson, *Princess* (New York: Avon Books, 1992); Sandra Mackey, *The Saudis* (Boston: Houghton Mifflin Co., 1987), pp. 122–168; and Soraya Altorki, *Women in Saudi Arabia* (New York: Columbia University Press, 1986). Although Saudi Arabia is a fundamentalist Moslem country, the most brutal practices described by these authors are in fact pre-Islamic, dating back to pagan Bedouin days.

prostitutes for the pimp. The "outing" from their seclusion might even have seemed like an interesting diversion from the women's normal, humdrum daily existence. In a society where free choice for women was minimal, this might have been the biggest "choice" of their lives.

Therefore, following Bilam's advice, the Moabites

made curtained booths for themselves and placed in them *zonot* in whose hands were all kinds of desirable objects. An old woman would sit outside and keep watch for the girl who was inside the shop. When Israel passed by to purchase an article in the bazaar, the old woman would say to him: "Do you want some linen clothing that comes from Bet Shean?" She would show it to him and say: "Go inside and you will see some lovely articles!" The old woman would ask him for more [money] and the girl for less. After this the girl would say to him: "You are now like a son of the house! Sit down and select something for yourself!"

A flask of wine was next to her, and the wine of gentiles had not yet been forbidden. A young woman would come out adorned and perfumed and would entice him, saying, 'Why is it that although we love you, you hate us? Take this article for nothing! Are we not all the children of one man, the children of Terach, the father of Avraham? If you do not want to eat of our sacrifices and our cooking, here, we have calves and cocks! Slaughter them according to your commandments and eat!' Then she would make him drink the wine and the *satan* would burn within him and he would be led astray after her. . . .

Once he propositioned her she would say to him, "I will not listen to you until you slaughter this [animal] to Peor and bow down to him." He would object, "I do not bow down to idols." She would answer him, "You will only appear as if you were uncovering yourself." He would be led astray after her and do so. . . . In the beginning they entered privately, but by the end they were coming in pairs, like a yoke of oxen. (NR 20:23; San. 106a)

The Jew did not realize at first that by uncovering himself, he *was* worshiping Peor. Once he realized it, however, it was too late.

THE WORSHIP OF BAAL-PEOR

A person who uncovers oneself before Baal-Peor [is guilty of idolatry], because this is his mode of worship. (San. 7:6)

The eating and orgiastic activity mentioned in the worship of Baal-Peor calls to mind the merrymaking (*letzachek*) associated with the worship of the golden calf. Such festivity accompanied all idol worship, but the actual worship itself was unique to each specific god.

Baal-Peor was so named because people "uncovered (*paar*) the anus in front of him and defecated—this was his mode of worship" (Rashi). "A gentile woman once was sick. She vowed, 'If I recover, I will go and serve every idol in the world.' She recovered, and proceeded to serve all idols. On reaching Peor, she asked its priests,

'How is this worshiped?' They replied, 'People eat beets, get drunk, and then defecate before it.' She replied, 'I would rather get sick again than serve a god in that
way'" (San. 64a).

Not only did Jewish men participate in a form of worship that was repugnant even
to a gentile woman used to serving idols; but when Jews reverted to idolatry, they
often *surpassed* the pagans in their fervor! The Talmud continues with the following
example:

> Savta ben-Alas once hired his donkey out to a gentile woman. When she came to Peor,
> she said to him, "Wait while I enter and come out again." On coming out, he said to
> her, "Now you wait for me while I go in and come out again." She said, "But aren't
> you a Jew?" He replied, "What's it to you?" He entered, uncovered himself before it,
> and wiped himself on its nose. Those attending the idol shouted out in praise of him,
> saying, "Never has anyone served this [god] like that!"

In ancient times, a Jew could nullify a pagan idol by abusing it in some way.
However, there were two notable exceptions to this rule: Baal-Peor and Merculis
(known as Mercury to the Romans and Hermes to the Greeks), who was worshiped
by throwing stones at it. For instance, a statue of the Greek goddess Aphrodite (known
as Venus to the Romans) could be nullified by urinating on it, while a statue of Baal-
Peor could not, for urination was not a mode of worship of Aphrodite, while it was
of Baal-Peor (A.Z. 44b). Thus, "a person who uncovers oneself to Baal-Peor has
worshiped him, even if one's intention was to show contempt for him. A person who
throws a stone at Merculis has worshiped him, even if one's intention was to attack
him" (San. 64a).

The story is then told of a Rabbi who saw an idol and threw a stone at it in disgust.
When he found out the statue was Merculis, in dismay he went to consult with his
fellow Rabbis, asking them if he should go and remove the stone he had thrown. They
told him not to, "because every stone removed makes room for another."

The Jewish men at Shitim (note the English pun in the name) were not defecating in
front of Baal-Peor out of contempt, however, but knowingly participating in his worship. This was even more serious than the golden calf (NR 20:23). Hence, while three
thousand men were killed for the worship of the calf, eight times as many—twenty-
four thousand men—were put to death for the worship of Baal-Peor. Once again, Jewish
men strayed and sinned while Jewish women remained faithful to Hashem.

ZIMRI AND PAGAN SEX RITES

> An Israelite man brought near to his brethren the Midianite woman, before the eyes of
> Moses and the eyes of the whole congregation of Israel, who were weeping at the en-
> trance of the Tabernacle. Pinchas, the son of Elazar the son of Aharon the *kohen*, saw
> this, and rose up from among the congregation and took a spear in his hand. He came
> after the Israelite man into the inner chamber [*kubah*] and stabbed both of them, the
> Israelite man and the woman in her womb [*kavatah*]. (Num. 25:6–8)

No sooner had Israel been told to kill the worshipers of Baal-Peor than Zimri, a tribal prince of Shimon (Num. 25:14) brought Kazbi, the Midianite princess and daughter of Balak, to the Tabernacle, where they had sex.

Kazbi's name was actually Shvilanai, but she was called Kazbi because she was false (*kazbah*) to her father, who had told her to only give herself to the greatest man in Israel, Moses. Another interpretation is that she said to her father, "Devour for me [*kos bi*] this people" (San. 82b). Zimri is here identified as a descendant of Shaul, the son of Shimon and Bunah, "the Canaanite woman" (see chapter 9).

When Moses told the judges of Israel to execute the men who had committed idolatry (Num. 25:5), the tribe of Shimon went to Zimri, their leader, and asked him to intervene. This was because the twenty-four thousand men executed were all Shimonites (*Zohar* III:237a).

Zimri then went to Kazbi and demanded that she submit to him sexually. She replied that she was a king's daughter and that her father had told her to surrender only to Moses. According to one view, she thought he was Moses because she saw fifty-nine thousand Shimonites rise before him (III:190a). According to another view, Zimri informed her that he was a prince and claimed that his tribe, because it was the secondborn of Jacob, was greater than Moses' tribe, which was only the thirdborn.

"He then seized her by her hair and brought her before Moses. 'Son of Amram,' he challenged, 'is this woman forbidden or permitted? Should you say that she is forbidden, who permitted Yitro's daughter to you?' At that moment Moses forgot the law and all the people burst into tears" (San. 82a; NR 20:24). Zimri had caught Moses off guard, for since Moses himself had married a Midianite woman, how could he say that a Midianite woman was forbidden to Zimri? Pinchas, himself the son of a Midianite woman (Bat-Putiel, Zipporah's sister), stabbed Zimri and Kazbi through their groins while they were in the midst of intercourse. However, was *znut*, or even the public (immodest) nature of the act, the motivation for Pinchas' zealotry?

It is highly likely that their sex act was more than passion; rather, it was the enactment of a pagan rite, and hence a form of idolatry. This is because Kazbi, as a pagan princess, would also have been a priestess. As the priestess of a god—Baal-Peor—her function would have been to have sex with kings playing the role of this god (see chapter 3). Zimri, as a prince, would fit the bill. Moreover, why else would having sex with Kazbi be Zimri's *response to a plea that he intervene to save lives*, if not to effect some kind of life-giving "fertility" magic on behalf of the worshipers of the god he was embodying?

Furthermore, the fact that they do the act in the Tabernacle is yet another indication of its ritual nature, for pagan sex rites usually took place in temples. There is a very significant pun in the Torah verse related to this. *Kubah*, the inner chamber of the Tabernacle, is of the same root as *kavah*, *womb*, meaning the "inner chamber" of a woman. *Kubah* also means "tent of prostitution" (Jastrow), which is what Zimri and Kazbi were reducing the Tabernacle to with their act.

An interesting note is that two stars in the constellation of Leo are named Zosma and Coxa. Perhaps it is a bit remote, but the names do sound strikingly similar to Zimri and Kazbi. Stars, as well as constellations and planets, usually bear names from

pagan mythology. In this case, Zosma means "girdle" and Coxa means "loincloth"![2]
Can this be mere coincidence? Zimri is also described as being proud and haughty
(NR 20:24), qualities traditionally ascribed to the astrological sign of Leo.

God performed a number of miracles for Pinchas: their mouths stayed shut so they
did not cry out; the spear pierced her belly with Zimri's penis inside, so that no one
could accuse Pinchas of having gone in to satisfy his own desire with her; the spear
was lengthened to pierce them both and its handle did not break when he lifted them
up; he was given extra strength to lift them up and the lintel was raised as he carried
them out above his head; their bodies stayed together and did not slide off the weapon;
they did not shed any blood and their souls stayed with their bodies, so Pinchas did
not become *tamae*; and finally, an angel struck the tribe of Shimon to prevent them
from attacking Pinchas when he came out (NR 20:25; San. 82b).

The murder of Zimri and Kazbi actually saved lives, for God's command to kill
the worshipers of Baal-Peor meant that more than 150,000 men should have died,
"but the act of Pinchas protected them" (Nachmanides).

Significantly, Pinchas's zealotry was rewarded by God with a "covenant of peace"
(Num. 25:12). While modern sensibilities about violence make it difficult to understand how stabbing someone can create "peace," it actually illustrates a very subtle
truth: violence is committed when wrongdoing is allowed to go unchecked simply
by being ignored.

Would it have been "violent" for the United States to bomb Auschwitz when it
was requested to do so?[3] Who is more "violent," the battered woman who kills her
husband in his sleep or the society that ignores her plight, blames her for his behavior, and reinforces male aggressiveness every day in myriad ways? Who is more cruel,
the jury that calls for the execution of a Nazi war criminal or one that gives him a
short prison sentence because, after all, it was "so long ago" and now he is just an
old man leading a quiet life? Misplaced compassion, as well as apathy in the face of
oppression, can potentially lead to the greatest violence of all.

---

2. Chet Raymo, *365 Starry Nights* (New York: Prentice Hall Press, 1982), p. 61.
3. See David S. Wyman, *The Abandonment of the Jews* (New York: Pantheon, 1984), pp. 288–
307.

❊❊❊ 38 ❊❊❊

The Daughters of Zelophechad

Pinchas (25:10–30:1)

It is the end of forty years in the wilderness. Miriam and Aharon have died, as have all the twenty- to sixty-year-old men who came out of Egypt. Another "mass elimination" of males has just occurred as a result of the worship of Baal-Peor. Moses, who has suffered many challenges from the people throughout these years, is about to undergo one more before God tells him to prepare for death. This time, however, the challenge is a positive one, coming not from a bunch of rebellious men but from some very smart women. The episode begins with a third and final census of adult males.

THE THIRD CENSUS

After twenty-four thousand men were killed for worshiping Baal-Peor, another census of twenty- to sixty-year-old males was commanded by God, for "on every occasion when they fell they were required to be counted" (NR 21:7) (see Table 20–1).

The men numbered in the current census had all been age nineteen or younger at the time of the last census, for none of the men numbered then were alive anymore. "Among these there was not a man counted by Moses and Aharon the priest when they counted the children of Israel in the wilderness of Sinai" (Num. 26:64). This time, Moses and Elazar did the counting.

This census was taken to number soldiers for a war of revenge against Midian, but since it was also for the purpose of land division in Israel, the Levites were again tallied separately. The patrilineal nature of the census was also meant to disprove the assertions of the gentiles that Jewish children were all products of rape under Egyptian slavery.

"The nations spoke disparagingly of them, saying, 'How can they trace their descent by their tribes? Do they think that the Egyptians did not overpower their mothers? If they [the Egyptians] ruled their [Jewish men's] bodies, how much more so [did they rule the bodies of] their wives!'" (Rashi). This alerts us to the reason why matrilineal descent was common among pagans—not because women were "honored" or had superior status, but because the prevalence of rape and other forms of sexual exploitation and abuse made a knowledge of paternity virtually impossible.

A number of families that had gone down to Egypt no longer existed by the time of the third census—five from Benjamin and one from Shimon (compare Numbers 26 with Genesis 46:9–24). This may have been a result of deaths under the decree, but it is also attributed to the deaths after Baal-Peor (Rashi; NR 21:8).

A comparison of this census with the second census (Num. 1) shows a vast decrease in the number of Shimonite males, due primarily to their execution for worshiping Baal-Peor (see Table 38–1). Benjamin, in spite of having only half as many families as it did originally, shows an increase in males. Judah, Zevulun, Yisakhar, Asher, Dan, and Menasheh also increased, indicating that their male birthrate exceeded the male rate of death under the decree. The male populations of Reuven, Gad, Naftali, and Efraim decreased. The number of Levite males, which are not cited in Table 38–1, increased from 22,000 to 23,000.

Thus, in spite of the decree against adult males and the punishment of Baal-Peor's worshipers, in the final year in the wilderness there were only about two thousand fewer adult male Israelites than there were in the year after the Exodus.

THE LAWS OF INHERITANCE

Zelophechad ben-Chefer did not have sons, but daughters. The names of the daughters of Zelophechad were Machlah, Noah, Chaglah, Milkah, and Tirtzah. (Num. 26:33)

Machlah, Tirtzah, Chaglah, Milkah, and Noah, the daughters of Zelophechad, married the sons of their [paternal] uncles. (Num. 36:11)

The five daughters of Zelophechad were the seventh generation of Joseph and descendants of his son Menasheh. Their lineage is emphasized because "as Joseph cherished the Land [wanting his bones brought up from Egypt], so his daughters cherished the Land" (Rashi). When the time came to allot portions of property to each tribe, the women registered a protest.

"Our father died in the wilderness," they stated. "He was not among the members of Korach's congregation who gathered against Hashem, but he died because of his own sin, and he did not have sons. Why should our father's name be diminished from among his families because he didn't have a son? Give us a portion of land among our father's brothers!" (Num. 27:3–4).

TABLE 38–1. The Second and Third Censuses

Tribe	Second Census	Third Census
Reuven	46,500	43,730
Shimon	59,300	22,200
Judah	74,600	76,500
Zevulun	57,400	60,500
Yisakhar	54,400	64,300
Gad	45,650	40,500
Asher	41,500	53,400
Dan	62,700	64,400
Naftali	53,400	45,400
Efraim	40,500	32,500
Menasheh	32,200	52,700
Benjamin	35,400	45,600
	603,550	601,730

Zelophechad may have been the man who was stoned to death for gathering sticks on the Sabbath (Num. 15:32). "Our Rabbis taught: The gatherer was Zelophechad: . . . this is R. Akiva's view. R. Judah b. Batyra said to him, 'Akiva! In either case you will be held accountable! If you are right, the Torah shielded him, while you disclose him; and if not, you cast a stigma upon a righteous man'" (Shab. 96b). (This is the same discussion that ensued when R. Akiva said that Aharon was struck with *tzaraat* along with Miriam.) R. Judah b. Batyra, on the other hand, believed that Zelophechad was one of the men who were killed trying to fight the Canaanites after the spies returned, at a time when God's Presence was not with them (Num. 14:44–45).

A third view reads *midbar* ("wilderness") as *medaber* ("speak"):

> Why did the daughters of Zelophechad so particularly state that their father had died in the wilderness, seeing that so many thousands of others had also died in the wilderness? . . . Zelophechad was one of the principal men of the sons of Joseph, but because he did not know the ways of the Torah sufficiently he did not become their prince.
>
> His fault was that he was not careful with his speech and his tongue in front of Moses. Hence, because he sinned in his speech against Moses, his daughters thought that Moses bore a grudge against him, and therefore they drew near before Moses and Elazar and all the princes, and spoke with Moses only in their presence, because they were afraid of his anger. From this we learn that one who is afraid of a judge should bring a large audience before him. (*Zohar* III:205b)

The petition of the five women is called *mishpatan* ("their case"), giving it the status of a legal inquiry (Num. 27:5). After coming before the Sanhedrin—the courts established by Yitro to relieve Moses of the responsibility of simple judicial questions—the daughters of Zelophechad finally stood before the tribal princes, the high priest Elazar, and Moses himself (Num. 27:2). In modern terms, their case had reached the Supreme Court.

However, not even Moses knew how to answer their challenge! It was a totally new idea to him that women should inherit land, so he consulted with God to find out what should be done. God told Moses point-blank: "The daughters of Zelophechad are right. Give them a hereditary portion of land alongside their fathers' brothers. Let their father's hereditary property pass over to them" (Num. 27:7).

God then established a general rule to provide for inheritance of any kind of property (land or movable) by daughters: If a man dies and has no son(s), his property shall pass over to his daughter(s). Only if he has no daughter(s) shall his property pass on to any other male relatives (Num. 27:8–11).

It would be easy to denigrate this decision from a modern viewpoint and ask, "So why didn't God say daughters should inherit even when there *are* sons?" However, as conservative as it appears to us, the new law was indeed a revolutionary change in the world at that time.

Furthermore, the term *inherit* is somewhat misleading, for in modern usage it refers to *any* receipt of money or property from the deceased. In Jewish law, however, while sons have priority in "inheritance," daughters (and widows) have priority in "maintenance." Maintenance is actually an open-ended inheritance. That is, before a fixed amount is left to each son, a man's widow and daughters must be given enough to support them, *in the style to which they are accustomed,* until their own deaths or (re)marriage. This means that if the estate is small, by the time the women are provided for, there may be nothing left for the sons! In effect, widows and daughters usually ended up with as much as, if not more than, sons did from the estate of a deceased man.[1]

That this system is meant to favor women is stated explicitly in the Mishnah. "When one dies and leaves sons and daughters, if the estate is large, the sons inherit and the daughters are maintained; if the estate is small, the daughters are maintained and the sons go begging. Admon [a judge of civil law in Jerusalem] stated, 'Must I be at a disadvantage because I am male?' R. Gamliel said, 'I see what Admon means'" (B.B. 9:1; Ket. 13:3). His sympathy for Admon's view, however, did not change the law.

A feminist is likely to think that equality would be better for women than favoritism. That sounds fine in theory, but in practice it would be devastating, because it presumes a basis of economic equality that simply did not exist—either then *or* now. "No-fault divorce" is a modern example of this. Treating men and women as equals under divorce law has only enriched the men and impoverished the women, for without alimony, a so-called "privilege," a divorced woman's income declines by 73 percent in the first year while that of a divorced man increases by 42 percent.[2]

Regarding the issue of land inheritance in the Torah, a system had to be devised so that the land apportioned to a tribe would stay within that tribe. Since tribal descent is patrilineal, land inheritance by sons only would keep each tribal allotment intact, regardless of whom they married. However, when a daughter inherited land,

---

1. For further elucidation of this concept, see Kaufman, pp. 202–204; and Moshe Meiselman, *Jewish Woman in Jewish Law* (New York: Ktav, 1978), pp. 84–95.

2. "Divorce American Style," *Newsweek,* Jan. 10, 1983, pp. 42–48.

if she married a man from a different tribe, she—and hence, her portion—would become part of *his* tribe. No one else could effect a transfer like that, since even land that was *sold* reverted back to its original owner in the Jubilee year. Inherited land did not.

This dilemma was brought to Moses by some men of Menasheh, who did not want to see their tribal portion diminished should the daughters of Zelophechad marry non-Menashites. These men were not misogynists complaining about women's right to inherit land. They, like the five women, were declared by God to have a just claim. Hence it was established that when a woman inherited land, she would have to choose a husband from within her natal tribe (Num. 36). While this did restrict a woman's marital choice, it still gave her thousands of men from whom to pick.

In the section discussing their marriages, the daughters of Zelophechad are listed by age because they were married in the order they were born. In the section discussing their petition to Moses, however, they are listed according to their wisdom (Rashi).

WOMEN OF WISDOM

Their eyes saw what Moses' eyes did not see. . . . Happy is the person with whose words the Holy One agrees! (Rashi)

The Holy One said [to Moses], "The law that you do not know is decided by the women!" (NR 21:12)

No one else in the entire Torah is ever credited with having a finer perception of the law than Moses! Here, the Rabbis unanimously praise the daughters of Zelophechad for their wisdom as well as their righteousness.

In this way, these five sisters are very important role models for modern Jewish women. In arguing that the law was being interpreted in a way that was unfair to them as women—which is today a common complaint about certain aspects of *halakhah*—the daughters of Zelophechad were extremely knowledgeable in the law and able to argue on *its* terms rather than from an appeal to common sense or from some outside philosophy.

Thus, when Moses first told them that daughters could not be heirs, they replied, "If we do not have the right to inherit, then shouldn't our mother have to perform the levirate marriage?" Indeed, if daughters were not heirs, then Mrs. Zelophechad, a widow with no sons, should have had to marry her dead husband's brother! However, she did not, for a child of *either* gender nullified that requirement. Hence, this was clearly a situation in which girls *are* considered to be their father's heirs. This indeed stumped Moses, and "it tells us that [the five sisters] were wise women" (Rashi).

Their timing was also perfect. They brought the subject up when Moses was teaching the Torah to Israel, probably in the review right before his death (Deut. 1:3): "They were wise and righteous women. What was their wisdom? They spoke at just the right moment, for Moses was engaged in [teaching] the section on inheritance. . . . They said to him,'If we have the status of a son, let us inherit like a son; if not, let our mother perform the levirate marriage.' . . . They were righteous, for they only married those who were worthy of them" (NR 21:11; B.B. 119b). None of the daughters of Zelophechad married until the age of forty—and nobody in the Jewish community was nagging them about it! On the contrary, they were praised for being so selective.

Finally, the five sisters knew how to be successfully persuasive. By couching their demand for equal rights in a concern that their "father's name not be diminished," they spoke in a language cleverly guaranteed to evoke male empathy rather than male defensiveness. Thus, they were able to set a precedent in Jewish law that would forever affect future generations of Jewish women—and they acted not out of egotistical motives, but out of love for the Land of Israel.

In this love they were typical of *all* the women in the wilderness. "In that generation the women built up fences while the men broke them down." Not only did women refuse to participate in the worship of the golden calf and Baal-Peor, they did not succumb to the spies' negative report. Thus, in contrast to the men, who clamored to return to Egypt rather than enter the Land, "the women drew near to ask for an inheritance in the Land." This is why the story of the daughters of Zelophechad follows a reference to the death decree on men in the wilderness, "for it was there that the men broke down the fences and the women built them up" (NR 21:10; Rashi).

If Jewish women today emulate the wisdom and the strategies of the daughters of Zelophechad, perhaps male rabbis will emulate the wisdom of Moses by taking women's protests seriously and "running to God" for some answers that are free of misogynist social prejudices.

✻✻✻ 39 ✻✻✻

A Woman's Vow

Matot (30:2–32:42)

The topic of this chapter, the power given by God to men to annul women's vows (Num. 30), is one of the most challenging sections of the Torah from a feminist point of view. For one thing, there is nothing in rabbinic sources overtly stating that these laws would not still be applicable today, if vows were made (which they are not).

However, it is difficult for a self-affirming, modern Jewish woman to accept that such male domination is indeed "God's will." If it were, marriage would not be an equal partnership; the best a woman could hope for in a husband would be a "benevolent master." The slave of a benevolent master is, of course, still a slave; and we have seen from our examination of marriage in Jewish law (chapter 18) that the Torah does not subordinate a wife to her husband like a slave to a master. On the contrary, she is raised out of the position of servitude so common in non-Jewish marriage arrangements.

Therefore, let us examine the annulment of vows closely to see what sense we can make of it.

THE NATURE OF VOWS

A "vow" (*neder*) and an "oath" (*shevuah*) are two different things in Jewish law. A vow involves the prohibition of an *object*—for example, "I vow to not eat broccoli on Tuesdays." An oath, on the other hand, involves the prohibition of an *action*—such as, "I swear to not eat on Tuesdays." In the first case, the object broccoli is forbidden, while in the second case, the act of eating is forbidden. For the sake of convenience, however, it is possible to use the term *vow* to include both.

A vow could only prohibit something permitted; it could not permit something forbidden, prohibit something already forbidden, or permit something already permitted. Thus, a Jew could vow to not eat broccoli, but could *not* vow to eat ham, to not eat ham, or to eat broccoli.

Taking a vow was no light matter. Nor was it just any kind of statement or promise of a certain behavior. There was a specific way in which it had to be phrased: the term *konam* was used to indicate that the prohibition was being consecrated as an offering to God, as if one were bringing a sacrifice to the Tabernacle. The Nazirite vow, which consisted primarily of an abstention from wine (see chapter 32), is a prime example.

"The making of vows would appear to have been a frequent practice in ancient life. People voluntarily denied themselves permitted pleasures, although the Rabbis frowned upon unnecessary asceticism, holding it a sin to abstain from legitimate enjoyment." Because vows were often made "to express anger or resentment . . . the Rabbis disapproved of the whole practice of vowing."[1] Therefore, it is said that "one who vows, even though [s]he fulfills the vow, is called a sinner" (Ned. 77b).

To make a vow and not fulfill it

> was considered rightly so great and heinous an enormity that the making of vows was deprecated and discouraged, and stress was laid on the need for the exercise of self-control and utmost urge to do right without the recourse to the incentive of vows, promises, and oaths. Rashness and lack of self-discipline, restraint and self-government often lead the individual to form vows which turn out to be impossible or immoral [to fulfill] with the result that relief has to be sought [through annulment,] and it may even be impossible in certain circumstances to disannul [*sic*] a vow however much it may be spiritually or physically or materially injurious or unpleasant to the vower or others concerned.[2]

Thus, we may conclude:

• A vow was not a positive thing, even when one fulfilled it, because asceticism is not valued in Judaism.
• Vows were often made on impulse; however, failing to follow through on a vow was a very grave offense. This was a deadly combination.
• The annulment of a vow was a desirable, though not always possible, way out of the situation.
• The annulment of a vow did not prevent the person from acting out the behavior of the vow; it simply made the behavior nonbinding. That is, if I vowed to not eat broccoli and my husband annulled my vow, I could still not eat broccoli, but my behavior would not have the status of a vow, so if I did give in and eat it occasionally, no sin would be committed.

---

1. Soncino, *Nedarim*, p. xi.
2. Blackman, *Nedarim*, p. 205.

Thus, all a vow did was to make inflexible a decision about a behavior. What good did that do that for anybody? It did no good at all, which is why the practice was discouraged and finally fell into oblivion.

Even today, however, the first thing we do on Yom Kippur is say a prayer called *Kol Nidre*: "All personal vows which we are likely to make, all personal oaths and pledges we are likely to take between this Yom Kippur and the next Yom Kippur, we publicly renounce. Let them all be relinquished and abandoned, null and void, neither firm nor established."[3] Note that we are not atoning for vows of the past, but annulling in advance any vows of the future. This is also why some religious Jews, whenever they make a promise, will quickly add, *bli neder*, "without a vow," meaning, "I have promised this, but it is not a vow."

A person in ancient times who made a vow and then regretted it could go to a Rabbi and (hopefully) be absolved from it—even on the Sabbath (Ned. 77a). If there was no legal expert available, then three "ordinary people"—that is, men—could do it (Rashi). In such a case, the vow was declared retroactively invalid, so no offense had been committed if the vow was violated before it was rescinded. When a man annulled his wife's or daughter's vow, however, it did not have a retroactive effect (Nachmanides).

THE LIMITS OF MALE CONTROL

Unlike some pagan cultures, a Jewish man did not have the power to *impose* a vow upon his wife or daughter.[4] His control was limited to annulling vows which she had made of her own free will. The following rules defined the free man's power to annul vows made by the members of his household.

A minor could not make a vow. Under Jewish law, a minor is defined as a girl under the age of twelve and a boy under the age of thirteen. In their twelfth and thirteenth years, however, minors might possibly make vows. From eleven years and a day to the twelfth birthday (for a girl), and from twelve years and a day to the thirteenth birthday (for a boy), the child's vow would be "investigated." If it were determined that the child understood "in Whose Name she [or he] has vowed," then the vow was binding (Rashi).

The day after his thirteenth birthday, a boy was legally considered an adult and could make a vow like any man. A girl, the day after her twelfth birthday, did not completely pass into adulthood, however. From the age of twelve years and a day to twelve years and six months, she was a *naarah*—this was the period of "adolescence" or puberty, in the ancient world, during which she would generally be betrothed. At the age of twelve years, six months, and one day, she became a *bogeret*—an "adult" woman.

---

3. Translation from Philip Birnbaum, *High Holyday Prayer Book* (New York: Hebrew Publishing Co., 1979), p. 490.
4. Soncino, p. xiii.

A *naarah* (unmarried "adolescent") could have her vow annulled by her father on the day that he heard of it. This applied to a daughter under her father's legal control, whether or not she actually lived with him (Rashi). If her father confirmed her vow, he could not then annul it; if he did, *he* would bear the guilt for any violation which might have occurred as a result of the confusion. If he remained silent when he heard of her vow, that was considered equivalent to confirmation.

"Day" was defined not as a twenty-four-hour period, but only as until sundown. Thus, if the daughter made a vow at night (and her father heard of it then), he had until the next evening to annul it. However, if she made a vow in the late afternoon (and he heard of it then), he only had until that evening to annul it.

A *bogeret* (unmarried "adult") was no longer under her father's legal authority. Thus, for example, a thirteen-year-old girl living with her parents was, halakhically speaking, an independent woman and could not have her vows annulled by her father.

Thus, a father's power to nullify his daughter's vows lasted no more than six months.

A *naarah-erusah* (betrothed "adolescent") had to have her vow annulled by both her father and her husband. (*Betrothal*, as it is used here, means *kiddushin* or *erusin*, the first stage of marriage in Jewish law; it does not refer to our modern usage of the term as *engagement*. A betrothed couple was legally married, and needed a *get* to be divorced, but they did not yet live together; hence, the *naarah-erusah* was still living in her father's house and was under his partial legal control.)

If one man annulled her vow but the other didn't, her vow was binding. If one man confirmed her vow, the other could not annul it. If one annulled it and the other confirmed it, and then the confirmer changed his mind, it was too late. The vow was confirmed and binding (Ned. 67a).

If the husband died on the same day he heard of her vow and he had not yet annulled it, then the father had sole power of annulment. However, if the father died on that day, the husband did not have sole power (Ned. 68a–b, 70a).

If the *naarah-erusah* was divorced on the day she made a vow, and then betrothed to someone else that same day, her father and the second husband (but not the first) could annul her vow (Ned. 71a).

A *bogeret-erusah* (betrothed "adult") could not have her vows annulled by either man. Her father had no control over her at all, and her husband could not annul her vows until they were fully married—that is, had gone through *nesuin*, the second stage of marriage effected under the *chuppah*, and were living together.

This was true even if *nesuin* had been delayed for some reason for more than a year. For if *kiddushin/erusin* lasted longer than twelve months, the husband was obliged to begin supporting her anyway. For this reason, R. Eliezer believed he could annul her vows, but his view was rejected (73b). This would appear to indicate that the husband's obligation to support his wife is *not* the reason he was given the power to annul her vows.

A *nesuah* (fully married woman) could have her vows annulled by her husband, regardless of her age (i.e., whether she was a *naarah* or a *bogeret*). Once her husband had confirmed her vow, he could not annul it; otherwise, a man who hated his wife would do this on purpose to make her guilty (Nachmanides).

Her husband could only annul vows of self-affliction (*le'anot nefesh*), according to the Torah (Num. 30:14). However, because the section concludes with the verse, "These are the statutes that Hashem commanded Moses between a man and his wife" (Num. 30:17), the Rabbis interpreted "between a man and his wife" to mean that the husband also had the power to annul *any* vow that affected their relationship (Ned. 79b). This creates a potential conflict in Jewish law, however, which we will examine shortly.

An *almanah* (widow) and a *gerushah* (divorcée) were, like the *bogeret*, independent adult women not under any man's control; hence their vows were binding. "This is the general principle: Once she has gone forth under her own authority for even one hour, he cannot annul her vow" (Ned. 89a).

A *yevamah* (woman awaiting levirate marriage) could not have her vows annulled by any of her dead husband's brothers, not even by the *yavam*, the one who agreed to marry her. R. Eliezer argued that the *yevamah* is betrothed like any *erusah*, but R. Akiva proved she is not, for if she had contracted a marriage with one brother-in-law and then slept with a second one, the sexual act merely invalidated the first one's claim and she would marry the second one. However, if an *erusah* slept with another man, that constituted adultery, a capital crime (and, if he was her brother-in-law, it was incest as well). Hence, "the *yevamah* is not so completely bound to the *yavam* as an *erusah* is to the *erus*" (Ned. 74a).

A slave could not make a binding vow under Jewish law because the Torah's commandment regarding vows "refers to one who is his own master"—that is, "whose life [*nefesh*] belongs to himself" (Naz. 61a). The Canaanite slave was not his own person. The male slave is certainly the subject under discussion here, for not even a freewoman in the ancient world was posited as being "her own master," much less a slavewoman!

However, as with sex, the Torah makes a definite distinction between a wife and a slave. A wife could at least *make* a vow, as long as her husband approved of it, while a slave could not make a vow at all. The one exception was *nazirut*: A slave could take the Nazirite vow. The master of the household could ignore it by forcing the slave to drink wine in *violation* of the vow, yet the master could not *annul* the slave's vow. On the other hand, he could *annul* his wife's vow but could not make her *violate* it (Naz. 9:1; NR 10:7).

This law really emphasizes the distinction, noted earlier, between a vow and its behavior. By forcing his slave to violate the vow, the master was making him drink wine. By annulling his wife's vow, however, all the husband was doing was releasing her from an obligation not to drink wine. He could not force her to actually drink any!

This law inadvertently serves as a model solution for the dilemma we referred to before: the husband's power to annul *any* vow his wife made that affected their relationship. What if her vow concerned sex?

THE VOW TO NOT HAVE SEX

Rav Kahana said: "If a wife vows, 'The pleasure of sex with me is prohibited to you,' *she is compelled to have sex with him*. But if she says, 'The pleasure of sex with you is prohibited to me,' he is forbidden and so he must annul it, since a person cannot be fed with something forbidden to him" [emphasis mine]. (Ned. 15b, 81b; Ket. 71b)

Rav Kahana makes a serious mistake: He assumes that a woman has a legal obligation to have sex with her husband, for in the first phrasing of the vow, he compels the woman to have sex against her will (in theory) because he sees it as her marital duty to give her husband pleasure; hence the vow is not valid to begin with, and he may make her violate it. (In actual practice, he could not rape her and instead had to divorce her.) In the second phrasing, however, since she is denying herself the pleasure, he sees the vow as valid; hence, it must be annulled for the husband to claim his alleged "right" to sex.

Although no one, man or woman, should be forced to stay in a sexless marriage, Rav Kahana's assertion goes too far. The basic foundation of sex in marriage under Jewish law is the asymmetrical notion that *sexual pleasure is the woman's right and the man's duty*. Hence, marital rape is automatically and always prohibited. Once the Rabbis start making any exceptions to this rule, they are embarking upon a very "slippery slope."

Unfortunately, however, a modern rabbi notes, "The majority of talmudic commentaries agree with the view of Rav Kahana that the wife is obligated to provide her husband with sexual relations."[5] Hence, a woman who refuses to have sex with her husband was included by the Rabbis in the definition of a *moredet*, the "rebellious wife" whose *ketubah* (monetary settlement upon divorce) is reduced by a certain amount each week until there is nothing left, after which she is divorced (Ket. 5:7).

A woman who is divorced takes with her any property she brought into the marriage; but if she came in with nothing, then theoretically (unless the *bet din* rules otherwise), she goes out with nothing. Hence, the threat of divorce without her *ketubah* can certainly be construed as a form of pressure bordering on coercion.

"*Moredet*" originally applied only to a wife who did not fulfill her end of the marriage contract—namely, to perform certain tasks in exchange for financial support (Ket. 5:5). Similarly, a man was a *mored*, a "rebellious husband," if he failed to support his wife in exchange for her work, or if he refused to have sex with her; he then had to add to her *ketubah*. The Rabbis thus created a more sexually symmetrical situation.

In all fairness to the Rabbis, it must be stated that their intention was not to make women sleep with husbands who were repulsive to them, for the law compels such a husband to divorce his wife (Ket. 7:9, 7:10). Rather, the situation referred to here is a case in which the wife's attitude is, "I like him but I wish to torment him" (Ket. 63b). That is, her "motivation is not to get a divorce but to withhold sexual relations

---

5. Shlomo Riskin, *Women and Jewish Divorce* (Hoboken, NJ: Ktav, 1989), p. 8.

in order to gain some desired end. . . . Since the Mishnah makes it clear that the woman does not want a divorce, but is instead employing sex as a bargaining tool, this *halakhah* emerges not as a penalty, but as a powerful deterrent to such action."[6]

The *halakhah* also refers to a situation in which a woman claimed that sex with her husband was unbearable to her but was lying in order to obtain a divorce and marry some other man. As a result the Rabbis ruled that she, too, was to be divorced without her *ketubah* (Ned. 11:12).

Such situations are indeed unfair to the husband, but is it "fair" that a woman had to lie to get a divorce in order to be with another man, when her husband might have more than one wife?

Is it "fair" that God made women and men differently, so that intercourse is impossible for him unless he is physically aroused, but possible and painful for her if she is not? Is it "fair" that orgasm is an inevitable result for the man, but not for the woman, in intercourse? Is it "fair" that the woman spends nine months being pregnant (with all the physical discomfort inherent in that), while the man has no biological role whatsoever after sex? There is indeed nothing "fair" or "symmetrical" about sex and its consequences!

By including sex in the definition of a *moredet*, the Rabbis set up a more mutual conjugal obligation, even though this had no basis in the Torah. For "although the Bible enjoins a husband to provide his wife with sexual gratification, there is no explicit biblical command for the wife to provide her husband with sexual satisfaction."[7]

The Torah's unabashed favoritism to the female in sexual legislation is definitely not "fair" to men at times, because it gives women a sexual power that it does not give to men. However, men already have a sexual power based in biology, so the Torah's asymmetry is just divine compensation for the greater sexual vulnerability inherent in being the "penetrated" rather than the "penetrator."

Thus, it may indeed be an unjustifiable male prerogative to attempt to reduce female privilege to a state of greater symmetry. It is surely understandable that men find it difficult to accept the sometimes blatant female chauvinism of the Torah. It is, after all, so diametrically opposed to the sense of entitlement to which men are accustomed, which derives from the sociological favoritism of the male. However, just as Admon's plea regarding inheritance law, "Must I be at a disadvantage because I am male?" is answered with a resounding "yes" (see chapter 38), so, too, is the case with the law of sex in marriage.

Hence, contrary to Rav Kahana, *the man does not have a "right" to sex from his wife*. Consequently, if a woman vows to not have sex with her husband, there is really nothing he can do about it. If he forces her to have sex with him (even if "only" through financial pressure), he is treating her as a slave and making her *violate* the vow. He may *annul* the vow but, as we have seen, that does not enable him to change her behavior—she can still refrain from sex with him. He should be able to divorce her

---

6. Ibid., p. 12.
7. Ibid., p. 7.

if she no longer wants a sexual relationship with him, but in no way should she be penalized financially because of it—regardless of the integrity of her motives.

To rule otherwise is to blur the distinction that the Torah has so carefully constructed between *wife* and *slave*.

WOMEN AND VOWS TODAY

This is the general principle: Once she has gone forth under her own authority for even one hour, he cannot annul her vow. (Ned. 89a)

[The law of vows] refers to one who is his own master ["whose life belongs to himself"]. (Naz. 61a)

If vows were made today, would men still have the right to annul women's vows as defined above? That is, is the Torah's command dependent on or independent of the sociological status of women?

Certain laws are true for all time, regardless of social change and the evolution of human consciousness. No matter how our understanding of women's roles may change, it will always be forbidden for a Jewish woman to (for example) eat cheeseburgers and porkchops, build a campfire on Saturday, commit adultery, have sex during menstruation, or engage in bestiality.

On the other hand, women accused of unfaithfulness by jealous husbands no longer drink a potion to prove their innocence, nor does a rapist pay fifty shekels and marry his victim. A bloody sheet is no longer brought forth to prove that a woman was a virgin on her wedding night. We do not sell our children into slavery or marry off our daughters when they become twelve years old. Therefore, anyone who says Torah law is "absolutely immutable" is not telling the whole truth. As social consciousness changes, so do the interpretations of certain biblical commands.

The question confronting us, then, is into which category does male authority over women's vows fall? Is it as immutable as porkchops and adultery or it is subject to reinterpretation as women become independent individuals in control of their own lives? I believe it falls into the latter category, and offer the following observations in defense of this position.

In many cases the Torah states that something is "a statute for all time" (*chukat olam*) or "for all generations" (*ledorotam*)—for example, the celebrations of Passover (Ex. 12:14), Shavuot (Lev. 23:21), and Sukkot (Lev. 23:41); Sabbath observance (Ex. 31:16); self-affliction on Yom Kippur (Lev. 16:31, 16:34, 23:31); the commandments not to sacrifice to pagan gods (Lev. 17:7) and not to eat new grain until the *omer* offering has been made (Lev. 23:14); priestly consumption of the showbread within the boundaries of the Tabernacle or Temple courtyard (Lev. 24:9); the wearing of *tzitzit* (Num. 15:37); the lack of land inheritance by the Levites (Num. 18:23); and the use of the waters of the Red Heifer to counteract death *tumah* (Num. 19:10, 19:21).

Many laws, it is true, are equally binding for all time even though they are stated with no qualifying phrase. The commandments regarding men's annulment of women's vows, however, conclude with a *partial* qualifying phrase, "These are the statutes [*chukim*]" (Num. 30:17). That is, the rest of the phrase, "for all time," is significantly absent.

The general principle that a man cannot annul a woman's vow "once she has gone forth under her own authority for even one hour" could be understood in light of women's modern status as independent persons. Men were given the power to annul women's vows in the past only because a woman was not "in her own control" (Sforno).

Women are no longer dependents who pass from a father's household to a husband's household. Hence, we have "gone forth under our own authority" for *more* than one hour! Because society has moved away from the practice of patrilocal marriage, a married woman today does not generally even move into her husband's household; rather, they set up a new household together or the man might even move into her house (which is not her father's).

On the other hand, a thirteen-year-old girl's vow might no longer be considered binding without her father's (and mother's) permission. For although a twelve-year-old girl is still an "adult" in terms of her obligation to observe the *mitzvot,* the modern concept of prolonged adolescence extends parental and social authority over her as a "child." Certainly no one would suggest lowering the drinking or driving ages to twelve, for example. Nor would statutory rape laws be possible if we were still marrying off twelve-year-old girls to twenty-one-year-old men.

Finally, the gap between *wife* and *slave* has significantly widened in modern consciousness. Slavery has, for the most part, been abolished, and the status of modern women is more akin to that of the "free man" in the ancient world. A woman is indeed "her own master" and "her life belongs to herself" more than ever before in history. She does not *need* to get married for economic reasons, but can *choose* to get married solely for love. She herself may even be the "head of the household."

Protective legislation (such as the annulment of vows) is fine as long as it really is protective; once it becomes restrictive to those it is meant to protect, however, it is no longer serving its purpose. Like vowing itself, it becomes obsolete.

❀❀ 40 ❀❀

Journey to the Land

Masei (33:1–36:13)

> *"When you cross the Jordan into the land of Canaan, you shall drive out all the inhabitants ahead of you and destroy all their stone places of worship. All their molten images you shall ruin, and all their altars you shall demolish. You shall inherit the Land and settle in it, for I have given you the Land to possess it. . . .*
>
> *If you do not drive out the inhabitants ahead of you, those who remain will become pricks in your eyes and thorns in your side and will oppress [tzarru] you upon the land which you settle. Furthermore, what I was going to do to them, I will do to you. (Num. 33:51–53, 33:55–56).*

Earlier, God had promised to send an angel (Ex. 23:23, 33:2), or possibly even a plague of hornets (Ex. 23:28), ahead of the Jews to drive the Canaanite nations out of the Land. Thus, it was not through any military might of their own but only through the power of God that this small band of runaway slaves would be able to displace seven mighty, well-established nations. (Remember the spies' "grasshopper"-like fear of the "giants" that was discussed in chapter 34.)

Then, as now, the Jews were warned not to make a treaty with the inhabitants or allow them to stay in the Land; for if they did, Israel would begin to "worship their gods, which would be a snare for you" (Ex. 23:33).

The root of the word used in the above verse for *oppress* (TZ-R-R, צרר) is also the root of *Mitzrayim* (*Egypt*)—meaning bondage, constriction, limitation, or confinement in a narrow place. It is a state akin to being tied up or strait-jacketed. Canaan and Mitzrayim were, in fact, closely related; their ancestral fathers were brothers, the children of Noach's son Cham (Gen. 10:6). That their customs were similar is indicated from their linkage in God's warning against them (Lev. 18:3).

Driving the Canaanites out of the land actually meant exterminating them. "You shall not allow a soul to remain alive. . . . You must wipe them out completely [*hacharem tacharim*], as Hashem your God has commanded you. This is so they will not teach you all the repugnant things [*toevah*] that they do for their gods, causing you to sin to Hashem your God" (Deut. 20:17).

The seven nations—the Canaanites, Jebusites, Hittites, Hivites, Amorites, Perizites, and Girgashites—were collectively known as Canaanites because they were all merchants (*kenani*). The Girgashites "arose and emigrated of their own accord" to Africa (LR 17:5, 17:6; Rashi on Ex. 33:2), so it was actually six nations that were to be annihilated.

What was so disgusting and revolting about these nations' practices that they had to be wiped off the face of the earth, down to the innocent babies? Does the command to exterminate these people differ in any fundamental way from a war of genocide against an indigenous population? We will attempt to answer these questions throughout part 5. For now, however, let us examine this concept of total annihilation, which is known as *cherem.*

CHEREM: CONSECRATION AND ANNIHILATION

The term *cherem,* when it first appears in the Torah, simply means "consecrated to God." For example, someone could dedicate a piece of property, such as a field or an animal, to the Temple. The consecrated property was then taboo for personal benefit and only a priest could use it. "All *cherem* is a holy of holies to God" (Lev. 27:21, 27:28; Num. 18:14).

Some human beings could even be *cherem.* A gentile slave, who was considered "property," could be dedicated to the Temple as a gift to the priests. A Jew who had been sentenced to death by the court for a capital crime could not be redeemed, but had to be put to death; such a person was also called *cherem* (Lev. 27:29; Rashi). In this latter case, we begin to see a shift in the term's meaning, from "consecration" to "annihilation."

The first time *cherem* refers to the annihilation of human beings in warfare is when the Canaanite king of Arad attacked the Jews in the Negev. "Israel made a vow to God, saying, 'If You will deliver this nation into my hand, I will make their cities *cherem.*' They made them and their cities *cherem.* Thus the place was named Charmah" (Num. 21:2–3). The meaning here is that they left no survivors. The implication of the "deal" made by Israel is that such total destruction would somehow be pleasing to God—an "offering," as it were, in exchange for the victory. Thus, we see the emergence of a definition of *cherem* that combines the two meanings—namely, consecration *through* annihilation.

Cherem was also practiced when Israel fought Og, king of Bashan: no captives were taken (Num. 21:35; Deut. 3:3, 3:6). The same was true in the battle against Sichon, king of the Amorites east of the Jordan River: "We conquered all his cities at that time, annihilating [*nacharem*] every city, the men, the women, and the children, leaving no survivors" (Deut. 2:34).

The Amorite men had assembled for war in one place, where they were all defeated; so when Israel arrived in the rest of the Amorite cities, "there was no one to stand up against them, for there were only women and children there" (Rashi on Num. 21:23). In addition to the Amorite women, the victims included Moabite women captured in the Amorite conquest (Num. 21:29). Israel then settled in Cheshbon, the Amorite capital, "and all its daughters"—meaning the adjacent towns (Num. 21:25, Num. 21:32).

These cases were exceptions to the general rule, however, for *cherem* was not the modus operandi in battles between Israel and the nations outside of Canaan. In these situations, Israel was instructed to first offer peace. If the peace offer was rejected, only then were they to fight. But they were to kill only the adult males. They had to spare the lives of the women and children, although they could take them as captives (Deut. 20:10–15; Rashi).

With the seven nations of Canaan, on the other hand, the Jews were told to practice *cherem*—to kill everybody. Thus, the distinguishing feature of *cherem* is actually the annihilation *of women and children.* What, if any, is the relationship here to consecration?

WOMEN AS WAR CAPTIVES

Modern wars are generally fought over territorial claims or political ideologies. Enemy soldiers may be captured, but this is generally just a side effect, and not a purpose, of the war. In the ancient world, however, taking war captives was not just a side effect on the way to conquering land. Rather, "the object of war [was] often the abduction of women. Wars [were] waged in order to secure women as wives, but also as workers and slaves."[1]

We have already noted that war captives provided a steady supply of slaves for the ancient world (see chapters 18 and 30). Generally, these captives became state, rather than private, slaves, and they might even be dedicated to temple service by the king in thanks to his god for the victory. Temple "service," for a pagan slave, could mean being sacrificed. We do not know if war captives used as slaves were mostly men or women, but it is safe to assume there were equal numbers of both. Given the female slave's additional "value" as concubine, it is possible that women even made up the majority of slave captives.

Female war captives also provided a steady supply of wives. Indeed, marriage-by-abduction is suggested by some to be

> the original and most primitive manner in which men obtained wives. . . . The forcible capture of women certainly occurs, and has occurred to a greater or less extent, in every part of the world and at all epochs. It is the natural accompaniment of primitive and barbaric warfare, and with several tribes has become the chief object of such warfare.

---

1. Franco Fornari, *The Psychoanalysis of War* (New York: Anchor, 1974), p. 44.

There is, nevertheless, remarkably little evidence in support of the view that in any primitive society the capture of women has ever been the usual mode of procuring a wife.[2]

Nevertheless, although the capture of women may not have been the *usual* mode, it was a common one:

Wholesale capture of women in warfare and tribal raids was prevalent among the more warlike tribes of northern and central Asia. The Germans and the Scandinavians captured women in the course of their wars; and so did the Slavs. The ancient Hebrews, in the course of their warfare among the tribes of Canaan, commonly captured women, as did all Semitic peoples. The archaic Greeks were constantly capturing women.[3]

When Shimon and Levi plundered Shechem in revenge for the rape of Dinah, they captured Hivite women and children and brought them home to be converted into slaves for Jacob's household. One of them, a girl named Bunah, became Shimon's wife (see chapter 8).

Thus, men clearly benefited, both economically and sexually, from war captives, and Jewish men were no exception. It is obvious that they would therefore *want* to capture women to bring home. *Cherem*, however, meant that the men were not allowed to do this. Killing the women rather than capturing them required a certain level of self-restraint and denial of gratification on men's part. Since the women were taboo for men's personal use, they were indeed (from the male point of view) "dedicated" or "consecrated" to God.

Moreover, considering the female victim's point of view, can anyone say for certain that slaughter is really a crueler fate than capture, enslavement, and marriage-by-abduction?

CAPTIVE MIDIANITE WOMEN

The Israelites took captive all the women of Midian and their children. . . . Moses said to them, "Why have you kept all the females alive? . . . Now kill every male child, and kill every woman who has slept with a man. But all the girls who have not slept with a man, you may keep alive for yourselves." (Num. 31:9, 31:15, 31:17)

Israel had been commanded by God to wage war against the Midianites as revenge for their role in Baal-Peor (Num. 25:16–18). The Midianites, but not the Moabites, were chosen as the object of war because the plan to use Moabite women had been devised by the elders of Midian (Nachmanides). Another reason why the Moabites were preserved was so that Ruth might descend from them. Furthermore, "the

2. Briffault, 2:230.
3. Ibid., 2:233.

Moabites acted out of fear, but the Midianites entered a quarrel that did not concern them" (Rashi).

Upon returning from battle, the soldiers immediately brought all the spoils of victory—captive women, children, animals, and property—to Moses and Elazar (Num. 31:12). "This informs you of their praiseworthiness, for they took nothing from the spoils without permission, but brought it before them [Moses and Elazar] first and only took from it later" (NR 22:4). Rashi calls the soldiers "kosher and righteous."

However, some of the men who had not fought were much less righteous and praiseworthy. Indeed, Moses and Elazar went out to meet the soldiers as they returned because they "saw the young men of Israel going out to snatch the spoils." These men recognized individual women as the ones with whom they (or their buddies) had slept at Shitim and were evidently ready to "claim" them again (Rashi on Num. 31:13, 31:16).

Thus, Moses was angry that these women had been kept alive and brought back, for it was evidently just going to re-create the situation that had already caused twenty-four thousand men to die! In ordering the deaths of the women and girls who had had sex with a man, a "virginity test" was devised to distinguish who should be spared. Each female was made to pass in front of the gold headband worn by the high priest, and if she was a virgin, her face would take on a pale, greenish tinge (Rashi; Yev. 60b).

Thus, along with sheep, cattle, and donkeys, 32,000 virgin girls were distributed among the men. Half the spoils went to the soldiers and the other half to the rest of the community. Of the soldiers' 16,000 girls, 1 out of every 500—that is, 32—were given to the priests as a "tithe." Of the community's 16,000 girls, 1 out of every 50—that is, 320—were given to the Levites as their "tithe" (Num. 31:27–30, 31:35, 31:40, 31:46–47).

What happened to the women afterwards is not described at this point. The laws instructing Jewish men how they must treat a captive woman are explained in Deuteronomy and will be the subject of chapter 46.

After killing the Midianites, the soldiers were *tamae*. To become *tahor*, they had to stay outside the camp for seven days, be sprinkled with the waters of the Red Heifer on the third and seventh days, and then immerse themselves in a *mikvah* at the end of the week. The Midianite girls also went through this process, not only because they, too, had been in contact with corpses, but also to make them Jewish (Num. 31:19, 31:24).

The laws of *tumah* and *taharah* usually only applied to Jews. That they also applied to gentiles in this case is a powerful statement about killing in warfare. Such killing was not to be glorified by Jews, even when it was commanded by God. An attitude of humility about it is apparent in the request of the army generals to make atonement (*lekhaper*), for the fact that no Jewish soldiers had been killed while killing (Num. 31:48–50).

Their atonement consisted of bringing gold items from the booty as an offering to God. This is reminiscent of the gold items that were brought to make the Tabernacle, in atonement for the golden calf. Now, as then, these items consisted of gold jewelry—including the *kumaz*, the primitive-type chastity belt worn by women (see chapter 21).

This was in order "to atone for the thoughts their hearts had entertained for the daughters of Midian" (Rashi). "Though we escaped from sin," the generals told Moses, "we did not escape from fantasizing about it" (Shab. 64a).

V

Entering the Land (Deuteronomy/ Devarim)

❀❀❀ 41 ❀❀❀

The Ashtarot

Devarim (1:1–3:22)

The word "nothing" describes the religion of the pagans, who do not bring the heavenly and the earthly into union, and adopt a faith of folly. (Zohar II:37a)

In this section we will examine the practices that led God to demand the complete annihilation of the seven nations of Canaan. While all pagan cultures worshiped idols, Canaan had the most repugnant behaviors, many of which were "religious rites" as well as social customs. This is why, for example, the matriarchs were chosen from Babylonia.

"The deeds of the Egyptians and the Canaanites were the most corrupt of all the nations, and the place where Israel lived [Goshen] was the most corrupt of all [of Egypt]. . . . The Canaanite peoples conquered by Israel were the most corrupt of all of them" (Rashi on Lev. 18:3). Egypt is linked here with Canaan, not only because Canaan was a vassal of Egypt for much of its history, but also because there was "a dense Canaanite population in Lower Egypt and a certain pervasion even of Egyptian life and religion by Canaanite elements."[1]

Another source states that "the Canaanite religion, in comparison with the religions of its neighbors, remained relatively primitive and aboriginal."[2] Since we have already seen that the Moabites, a non-Canaanite nation, worshiped Baal-Peor through defecation, we can only imagine what might be defined as more repugnant, corrupt, or primitive than that!

The answer may be found in Leviticus 18. God's prohibitions on all forms of incest, marriage to two sisters, sex during menstruation, wife-swapping, child sacri-

---

1. Gray, *The Canaanites*, p. 49.
2. Neumann, *Origins*, p. 73.

fice, sodomy, and bestiality were not merely theoretical but were an actual warning to Israel not to imitate the ways of the Canaanites upon entering the Land. "With all of these things the nations I am driving out from before you made themselves *tamae*. . . . All these abominations were done by the men of the Land before you, and they made the Land *tamae*" (Lev. 18:24, 18:27).

In this chapter, we will discuss the Ashtarot and its possible connection to bestiality and child sacrifice. Ashtarot, a term mentioned in both Torah and Prophets, has three meanings in Hebrew: it was the name of a city northeast of the Jordan River, it was the name of a goddess (or group of goddesses), and it also simply meant *lambs*. These three definitions are interrelated.

We have already explored the significance of various animals in the religions of the ancient Near East. Three major species—goats, cattle, and sheep—were worshiped as pagan deities; hence, these same animals were utilized by the Torah's sacrificial system to remove them from their pagan context and wean the Jews from their worship. We have so far looked at the symbolism of goats (satyrs and Azazel), cows (Isis and the Red Heifer), bulls (Osiris and the golden calf), and rams (sun gods and the Pesach sacrifice).

We will now examine evidence of a cult idolizing the ewe. Ewe worship was practiced in various parts of Egypt but was far more prevalent throughout Canaan. Perhaps this is because Canaan was a more nomadic society, while Egypt was primarily agricultural.

THE ABOMINATION OF EGYPT

Master of the Universe! From where have You brought them out? From Egypt, where everyone worships lambs! (ER 43:7)
            — Moses, responding to God's anger after the golden calf

We have noted the extensive worship of male sheep in ancient Egypt. As the symbol of the constellation Aries, the ram was sacred to sun gods, for when the sun enters Aries at the spring equinox, it is crossing the equator into the northern hemisphere after six months in the southern hemisphere (autumn and winter in the northern hemisphere). This return of the sun brings warmth and light; it was (and is) a cause for great celebration, especially among agricultural peoples. As a male, the ram (like the bull of Taurus) was also a symbol of Pharaoh, who was himself worshiped as a god.

The ewe (the female sheep) was also an object of worship. Like the cow, she was a goddess figure. Goddess idols were not sacrificed; only their sons were, so their blood could fertilize mother earth. Thus, while bulls and rams would occasionally be sacrificed, on the god's annual festival, ewes and cows were never killed for any reason. (In spite of its religious significance, this actually reflects practical agricultural concerns; for even today, when farming is completely secular, male animals are killed for meat, while females are kept alive for dairy products.)

When Jacob and his sons came down to Egypt, Joseph told Pharaoh that they were cattle herders *(anshei mikneh)* and shepherds *(roeh tzon)*. He then instructed his brothers to tell Pharaoh that they were cattle herders so they would be given land in Goshen, "for every shepherd is an abomination of Egypt" (Gen. 46:34). The brothers, however, told Pharaoh that they were shepherds (Gen. 47:3). Pharaoh then gave them the land they desired in Goshen.

The emphasis on shepherds is not accidental. One view holds that it was due to the worship of Aries (Kli Yakar), but why not emphasize cattle due to the worship of Taurus? The reason is that cattle were worshiped throughout Egypt as a whole, but "flocks" (which may include goats as well as sheep) were worshiped only in certain localities. Egypt was primarily an agricultural society; nomadic herdsmen were less numerous. Goshen was one of their more populous centers.

Herodotus reports that those "who live in the district of Thebes sacrifice goats but not sheep . . . Those who have a cult of the god of Mendes, or who live in the province of that city, sacrifice sheep but not goats."[3] In Mendes, a locale in Goshen, goats were "worshiped" through bestiality (see chapters 22 and 27).

If there were sexual "rites" conducted with sheep, it would be consistent with what we know of pagan ritual that the ewe was being "worshiped" by the shepherd in a type of fertility magic. Interestingly, both Moses and David are said to have been "tested by God through sheep" and "found trustworthy" (ER 2:2, 2:3). This means that they took gentle care of them and did not let them graze in other people's fields; but perhaps it also means more than that.

Bestiality would certainly explain why "every shepherd is an abomination of Egypt," for the phrase used by Joseph, *toavat Mitzrayim*, does indeed mean "an abomination *of* Egypt." It is usually translated as "an abomination *to* Egypt," but this is incorrect; *toavat* is the grammatical construct form of *toevah*, and the construct form always means "— of."

Thus, shepherds may not have been hated by the Egyptians, as modern commentators have asserted. Rather, Egyptian shepherds were an abomination *from the Torah's point of view* because their sheep "were goddesses [*elahot*] to them" (Rashi). Every shepherd was an idolator. Just as a farmer worshiped the cattle that pulled the plow to plant the crops, so, too, a shepherd worshiped the flocks that provided the wool.

Rashi's use of the feminine-gender form of *deities* tells us that this sheep worship was ewe worship, for even if it only *included* ewes, the masculine form, *elohim*, would be used as the generic. Another indication of ewe worship is the statement that those Egyptians who worshiped sheep not only refused to eat them but would not even drink their milk (Ibn Ezra).

EWE WORSHIP IN CANAAN

Og, king of Bashan, who lived in Ashtarot . . . (Deut. 1:4)

Blessed is the fruit of your belly, the fruit of your soil, the fruit of your beasts, the offspring of your cattle, and the lambs (*ashterot*) of your flocks." (Deut. 28:4)

They forsook Hashem and served the Baal and the Ashtarot. (Judges 2:13)

---

3. Carter, p. 109.

These three passages linguistically illustrate the connection between Ashtarot and ewe worship. Only one slight change in vowel-marks makes the difference between *lambs* and the goddess (or goddesses) referred to in the Book of Judges. Og's homeland (also known as Ashtarot-Karnayim) was one of Ashtarot's cult centers.

Commentary on the passage in Judges states that the Ashtarot were "images made in the form of female sheep" (Redak). Lambs are called *ashterot* in the blessing of Deuteronomy "because they enrich [*me'asherot*] their [fem.] owners" (Chul. 84b). Given the Talmud's exclusive use of the feminine gender here—as well as the blessing's context of human pregnancy, earth fertility, and animal birth—*ashterot* really means *female* lambs. (*Seh* and *taleh* are the Hebrew words for *male* lambs.)

Rashi asserts that Ashtarot, the place, means "rocks and hard things" (Deut. 1:4) and that *ashterot*, the lambs, is related to that by meaning "strength," that is, the "choicest of the flock" (Deut. 7:13).

Nachmanides combines all these interpretations. Ashtarot, he says, was "a place of high mountains upon which there were forms of rock. . . . There the flocks of sheep ascend." The rock forms were called Ashtarot because "the idol was made in the form of sheep in order to protect them, in accordance with [the people's] low mentality." The city of Ashtarot was well fortified and therefore difficult to capture—another way in which it was "strong" and "hard."

Ashtarot the place is also described as "pasture lands" (1 Chronicles 6:56), another obvious linkage with sheep. It was originally the home of the Rephaim, "a large and numerous people, as tall as the Anakim," the giants of old. After the Rephaim were defeated by the Canaanite kings, God promised their land to Avraham, and it was given to Lot's descendants. The Moabites referred to the Rephaim as Emim, while the Ammonites called them Zamzumim (Gen. 14:5, 15:20; Deut. 2:10–11, 2:20–21). The Perizites, one of the seven Canaanite nations, lived in the forests near the Rephaim (Joshua 17:15).

Og, who was defeated by Israel, was the last of the giants. "For only Og, king of Bashan, remained of the Rephaim. His bed was made of iron. It is in the Ammonite city of Rabbah, nine cubits [13½ feet] long and four cubits [6 feet] wide" (Deut. 3:11). This city, the former capital of Ammon, is now Amman, the capital of Jordan (Kaplan).

Ashtarot, east of the Jordan River, was not the only site where the Ashtarot were worshiped. West of the Jordan River, at Mt. Gilboa, there was a temple to this idol— Bet-Ashtarot, which means "House of Ashtarot" (1 Samuel 31:10). Ashtarot was clearly an indigenous Canaanite goddess, as indicated by Samuel's instructions to Israel to "remove the foreign gods *and* the Ashtarot from among you" (emphasis mine) (1 Samuel 7:3).

SYNCRETISM AND THE ASHTAROT

Syncretism refers to a fusion of deities or religious forms. For instance, when Christianity conquered the pagan lands of Europe, conversion was not always accomplished through force. It was much more effective for missionaries to convince the people that Mary and Jesus were just "other names" for the local mother goddess and her son, the god. (This is why, in many Catholic areas, the worship of the "blessed mother" still outshines that of the "son of God," even though *he,* according to Christian theology, is the divine one and she is only human.)

Syncretism is also defined by Webster as "the fusion into one of two or more differently inflected grammatical forms of a word." Both of these definitions indicate that the Ashtarot of Canaan may be linked with other goddesses of nearby areas.

Ashtarot can be the plural form of Ashtoret, the name of the goddess of Sidon, a city north of Canaan in Phoenicia (modern Lebanon). King Solomon, who married many foreign women who brought the worship of their deities with them to Jerusalem, himself "went after Ashtoret" (1 Kings 11:5, 11:33; 2 Kings 23:13).

Ashtoret is identified by secular writers (archaeologists, mythologists, historians, etc.) with Astarte, which is merely a different vocalization of the same consonants— עשתרת. (Ashtoret is never vocalized as Astarte in the Hebrew Bible, however.) Byblos, a city north of Sidon, was "one of the oldest and most important centers of Astarte worship."[4] Astarte was thus the name for Ashtoret north of Phoenicia (i.e., in Syria).

Astarte of Syria has also been likened to Ishtar of Babylonia, Isis of Egypt, and Aphrodite of Greece, all of whom were pagan personifications of the planet Venus (the planet simply bears the Roman name of this goddess). Astarte/Ashtoret has even been equated with the native Canaanite goddesses Anat and Asherah.

"It is often difficult to distinguish the like-named goddesses of the ancient Near East," writes a modern-day feminist goddess worshiper, "in part because the *persecuting Hebrews* blurred the distinctions between them. . . . What seems to have been shameful to the *patriarchal Hebrews* was the untrammeled sexuality of the goddess" [emphases mine].[5]

Actually, it is usually feminist goddess worshipers and male secular scholars who make strange bedfellows by blending together so many goddesses from different places and even different time periods. The Hebrew Bible discusses only Canaanite goddesses, and does so quite distinctly. The Ashtarot and the Asherah, for instance, do not seem to be the same deity at all, as we shall see in chapter 43.

Another name for Astarte, according to scholars, was Tanit, who was a goddess worshiped at Carthage in later times.[6] Since Astarte equals Ashtoret of Phoenicia and since Phoenicians lived in Carthage, the equation with Tanit is not farfetched, despite the difference in names. Tanit had a consort named Baal-Hammon. The word *baal* simply means "master" or "lord" and is always followed by the locale of the god (e.g., Baal-Peor was the "lord of Peor").

The name Baal-Hammon could indicate a linkage with Ammon. In Moav, an inscription has been found that refers to "Astarte-Chemosh," linking Astarte to the Moabite god Chemosh.[7] Ashtoret, Chemosh, and Milkom were all worshiped by Is-

---

4. Harden, p. 28
5. Patricia Monaghan, *The Book of Goddesses and Heroines* (New York: E. P. Dutton, 1981), p. 30.
6. Harden, pp. 87–88.
7. Ibid., pp. 104, 121.

rael, at altars built by King Solomon himself (1 Kings 11:5–7; 2 Kings 23:13). Milkom was the Ammonite version of Molekh, who was worshiped by burning children (see chapter 28).

Tanit and Baal-Hammon were also worshiped with the rites of a Molekh—i.e., "a bronze image . . . extending its hands, palms up and sloping toward the ground, so that each of the children when placed thereupon rolled down and fell into a sort of gaping pit filled with fire."[8]

Carthage is the site of "the largest cemetery of sacrificed humans ever discovered. Child sacrifice took place there almost continuously for a period of nearly 600 years."[9] In analyzing four hundred urns containing charred remains of children, lambs, and kids (baby goats), two archaeologists concluded, much to their own surprise, that "the demand for human infant sacrifice, as opposed to animal sacrifice, seems to increase rather than decrease with the passage of time."[10]

Given all these syncretistic connections, it is quite possible that child sacrifice was a rite of the Ashtarot of Canaan. It is surely significant that the same feminist sources that label the Jews as "patriarchal" and "persecuting" maintain complete silence about child sacrifice as a rite of pagan goddesses.

------

8. Lawrence E. Stager and Samuel R. Wolff, "Child Sacrifice at Carthage: Religious Rite or Population Control?" *Biblical Archaeology Review*, V 10:1 (Jan./Feb. 1984): 44.

9. Ibid., p. 32.

10. Ibid., p. 40.

❀❀❀ 42 ❀❀❀

The Prohibition of Imagery

Vaetchanan (3:23–7:11)

> *Guard yourselves very carefully—for you did not see any image on the day that God spoke to you on Chorev [Mount Sinai] from the midst of the fire—lest you ruin yourselves by making for yourselves a graven image, any form or shape, male or female.* (Deut. 4:15–16)

Any picture, statue, or image of God is strictly prohibited by the Torah. This passage goes on to forbid the visual representation of the Divine by any of God's creatures—not just humans—mammals, birds, reptiles, amphibians, and fish, as well as the sun, the moon, the stars, and the planets.

All these entities were common as deities throughout the pagan world. Even if Israel had evolved beyond worshiping them *as gods,* the people would still be tempted to venerate them as intermediaries *to* God or use them just to "represent" God. Hence they needed to "guard themselves very carefully."

However, even though all images are *equally* forbidden by the Torah and no weight is given to either male or female because both are *equally* idolatrous, one commentator maintains that a female image is worse! "How blasphemous and unnatural such a representation is to the Israelite mind can be gathered from the fact that the Hebrew language does not even possess a *word* for 'goddess'" (Hertz). This assertion is not true, as we saw in the last chapter from Rashi's use of *elahot*. However, even if it *were* true, the masculine license that is taken here with the Torah is astounding, for the Torah itself does not imply that a male image is any less "blasphemous" and "unnatural" than a female image.

Interesting, too, is the leap that Hertz makes from an actual physical and visual image of God to a mental and verbal one. Speaking of God in a particular gender is not idolatrous; that is, it is not a violation of the Torah's prohibition of "graven images." However, since Hertz has opened the door to such a connection, let us follow his logic through to its natural conclusion.

THE MASCULINE IMAGE OF GOD

If God is male, then the male is God.
                                        —Mary Daly
                                        Beyond God the Father[1]

Daly, a prominent feminist theologian, argues quite persuasively that an exclusively masculine image of God has had devastating consequences for women:

> The symbol of the Father God, spawned in the human imagination and sustained as plausible by patriarchy, has in turn rendered service to this type of society by making its mechanisms for the oppression of women appear right and fitting. If God in "his" heaven is a father ruling "his" people, then it is in the "nature" of things and according to divine plan and the order of the universe that society be male-dominated.[2]

Determining which came first, male supremacy or the masculine image of God, is an unresolvable chicken-or-the-egg dilemma. What is important is how exclusively male God-language "functions to legitimate the existing social, economic, and political status quo, in which women . . . are subordinate."[3] We are all made "in the image of God," yet this concept is greatly enhanced for men while it remains only theoretical for women when God is constantly called "He."

God, by definition, is all-powerful and all-knowing. How could the Creator of the Universe be anything *but* omnipotent and omniscient? It then becomes dangerous to posit such a Being as a father figure, for even in "enlightened" human societies, a father is still regarded as the "head" of his family. Women and children, as subordinate "wives and offspring" of men, are put in a position of servitude, humility, self-effacement, and obedience to the "master," the male head of household.

Submission, humility, and obedience are therefore loaded terms, yet they are the very qualities needed to live in relation to God's Will, the Divine Plan—which has absolutely nothing to do with any human head of household. However, it is easy to see why this metaphor became so common, for the entire universe is indeed God's "Household."

God's Will, or the Divine Plan (which includes, but is not limited to, the laws of nature), is contained in the Torah as the cosmic blueprint that preceded Creation. When adhered to, it "makes the world go round"; the universe runs in perfect harmony and justice. No human being can ever fully understand this Plan or claim to control it. It

---

1. Mary Daly, *Beyond God the Father* (Boston: Beacon Press, 1973), p. 19.
2. Ibid., p. 13.
3. Ibid., p. 19.

is the source of "divine providence" *(hashgachah pratit)* and karmic events, the subtle and cataclysmic lessons which form one's "destiny."

The difference between human submission to divine authority and human submission to human authority was once expressed beautifully by the late Rabbi Shlomo Carlebach: "When you bow down to another human being, you're a slave. When you bow down to God, you're standing as tall as you possibly can."[4]

CHRISTIANITY AND IDOLATRY

Unfortunately, many a clergyman has taken advantage of the "head of household" metaphor of God to demand that women be subordinate to men as humans are subordinate to God. Christianity has been much more guilty of this than Judaism, because the Catholic Church never accepted the prohibition on graven images. Protestantism did; the Reformation was, in large part, a reaction against image worship in the Church. However, that was a recent (16th-century) phenomenon in Christian history. The damage had already been done long before that.

For Christianity from its outset combined the first and second commandments into one: "I am Hashem ['the Lord'] your God; you shall have no strange gods before Me." By dropping the reference to Egypt from the first commandment, and using only the first sentence from the second commandment, the Church eliminated the essence of the second commandment, which is the prohibition of imagery.

This allowed the metaphor of "God the Father," which is a purely mental/verbal image in Judaism, to be crystallized into an actual physical image in Christianity— of an old (white) man with a white beard who has impregnated a "perfect" (but not divine) human mother, who gives birth to a "divine son." The divine son is nailed to a cross in order to "redeem humanity of its sins," and then he resurrects from the dead and bodily ascends to heaven, as does his mother.

One image of God spawned many more images, not only as statues and pictures in churches but as personal relics as well. Devout Catholics have carried "holy cards" (like bookmarks) and hung pictures in their homes depicting major theological scenes: the "blessed mother" being visited by an angel or going to heaven, the "divine son" at his birth, the last supper, and his torture, crucifixion, resurrection, and ascension.

Catholic churches have traditionally contained a pictorial meditation of fourteen images called "The Stations of the Cross."[5] The worshiper follows the divine son on his journey to crucifixion and death, stopping before each image to say a brief prayer, beseeching God for the ability to accept his or her own "crosses" in life. Jesus' suffering became the role model for people to endure their own suffering and oppression rather than challenge it. "God gives the heaviest crosses to bear to those He loves the most" used to be said as a source of comfort.

---

4. Stated during a Passover *seder*, April 1992.
5. See the *Saint Joseph Daily Missal* (New York: Catholic Book Publishing, 1959), pink pages at end.

A whole cult elevating suffering was thus created from the visual portrayal of the torture and death of a Jewish man from Nazareth at the hands of his Roman executioners in turn-of-the millennium Judea. This historical reality was combined with the pagan mythology of the god, who, as son of his mother, is sacrificed and reborn.

Thus, very early in its development, Christianity drastically departed from its "Jewish roots" and reverted back to pagan imagery. This imagery is such an essential element of Christianity that it is really quite false to speak of a singular "Judeo-Christian" tradition.

JUDAISM AND GOD-LANGUAGE

Judaism, since it never had statues, pictures, or relics, has never had a male physical image of God and, thus, no cult spawned by God's "wife" (or a "one-night stand" like Mary) and "son." Male God-language, however, predominated for two reasons: (1) the neuter gender in Hebrew is also the masculine gender; and (2) a male god served by male priests was the only model in pagan times of a religious service that was not sexual (see chapter 23).

However, exclusively male gender–language did not prevail throughout Jewish history. Jewish mysticism sought to redress the imbalance that had been created by referring to the Shekhinah, the immanent aspect of God, as She, the "bride" of the Holy One, the transcendent aspect of God referred to as He. (This resembles the concept of some Native American religions of Sky Father and Earth Mother. The more "remote" aspect of God is posited as male because the father is more biologically remote from a child than the mother, who carries the child in her body.)

In spite of this attempt at balance, the masculinity of God has nonetheless become an image "graven," so to speak, in the minds of most Jews. For sociological reasons (including the historical reality of an all-male rabbinate), an image of God the Father has predominated. God the Mother is barely recognized, if at all. The Talmud, for example, holds a discussion on the metaphor that "the Holy One puts on *tefillin*" (Br. 6a).

Nowhere do we find a corresponding rabbinic metaphor that the Shekhinah goes to the *mikvah* once a month! Why do they never describe Creation as God "giving birth" to the universe? Is not the Strong Hand that brought us out of Egypt the same security a small child feels in holding the hand of its mother? Is God, Who drowned the Egyptians in the Red Sea, a "man of war" or a "woman warrior"?

The Torah tells us to respect both our parents. In listing the Ten Commandments, it says, "Honor your father and your mother" (Ex. 20:12; Deut. 5:16), while in another passage it says to "fear one's mother and one's father" (Lev. 19:3). "Father" comes first in honoring because it is assumed that a child will more readily honor its mother; "mother" comes first in fearing because it is assumed that a child will more readily fear its father (Kid. 30b–31a).

The fact that each parent gets a turn at being mentioned first "teaches that both are equal. But the Sages have said: 'The father comes before the mother in every place, because both [a child] and its mother are obligated to honor the father'" (Kr. 6:9). Here we have a blatant discrepancy between divine law and sociology, for while the Torah teaches that the father and the mother are equals, the Rabbis decided that the father gets more honor than the mother! This contradicts their recommendation elsewhere that a man honor his wife more than himself (Yev. 62b). How can he do that when *her* duty to honor him is put on the same level as a child's? Should he also honor his children more than himself?

Since the Rabbis compare the respect and reverence due to the parents with the respect and reverence due to God (Kid. 30b), then God as Father does indeed validate second-class status for women. Even if the paternal metaphor of God were always of a *merciful* father, the exclusive masculine image would still be a problem.

However, God is even cast in the image of a *violent* father, who "struck his child with a mighty blow, and then put a plaster on his wound, saying to him, 'My child! As long as this plaster is on your wound you can eat and drink at will, and wash in hot or cold water, without fear. If you remove it, it will break out into sores.' So the Holy One spoke to Israel: 'My child! I created the *yetzer hara,* but I also created the Torah with which to temper it" (Kid. 30b).

In such imagery, the Shekhinah is reduced to a wife who tries to control her husband's violence. "And even when He threatens and raises the lash, the Mother comes and takes hold of His Right Arm so that the lash remains suspended, but does not descend" (*Zohar* II:190b).

The image of God as a battering father who hits his child so hard he needs bandaging is definitely *not* an effective way to teach Jewish women a love of God and Torah! At most, it will teach women to *fear* God and to keep the Torah out of an infantile dread for the consequences of disobedience. However, it is just as likely to impel women to rebel against Judaism altogether. This is especially true of women who have had authoritarian, abusive fathers. Any woman who has grown up with such a father is not likely to be eager to worship a God cast in the image of one.

THE FEMALE IMAGE OF MOSES

What flesh has heard the Voice of the Living God speak from the midst of the fire like we did and has survived? You [*Atah*] go near and hear what Hashem our God says [*yomar*]. You [*At*] tell [*tedaber*] us what Hashem our God tells [*yedaber*] you. We will hear it and we will do it. (Deut. 5:23–24)

—the people to Moses at Sinai

Moses said to Hashem, "Why are you treating Your servant so badly? Don't You like me anymore? Why did You put the burden of this people upon me? Was I pregnant with this people, did I give birth to them? You told me I must embrace them in my bosom like a nurse carries an infant . . . I am not able to bear this people alone, it is too heavy for me. If You [*At*] are going to do this to me, then kill me, please. (Num. 11:11–15)

—Moses to God during the craving for meat at Taverah

When the Ten Commandments were given at Mount Sinai, the people reportedly addressed Moses once in the masculine gender (Ex. 20:16). Here, in the first passage cited, Moses is recounting that incident to the Jewish people. He describes them as addressing him once as a male (*atah*, meaning *you*) and once as a female (*at*).

Moses was extremely disappointed that the people were afraid to hear God's Voice for themselves, wanting *him* to bear the full burden of transmitting the Torah to them. Imagine having the opportunity to hear the Torah directly from God, and turning it down! What Jewish woman today would not give her eyeteeth for an opportunity like that?

"You sapped [תַּשֵּׁשׁ] my strength like a female," Moses told them, "for I was vexed about you; you loosened my hands when I realized you were not anxious [*charedim*] to approach God out of love. Wouldn't it have been better for you to learn from the Mouth of the Almighty than from me?" (Rashi).

Rashi's (Moses') words refer to the dissipation of female strength through child-bearing and child rearing. Unfortunately, modern commentators have been completely sexist by translating the Hebrew as *weak*. They make it sound like women are weaker than men, when what is really being referred to here is the state of sheer exhaustion that women are in after labor. This labor is itself indicative of strength, an incredibly great strength, a uniquely female strength.

Moses' vexation (*tzaar*, צַעַר) was that of an overworked, stressed-out mother who needs help with the baby (or a good, affordable day care program). During one of several rebellions in the wilderness, he compares his burden of caring for this cranky people to the situation of a pregnant, birthing, and nursing mother. He would rather be dead than endure such agony! At this level of despair, Moses addresses God in the feminine gender (*At*).

Moses' role as a mother to the Jewish people was like Miriam's role with them (Nachmanides). Maternal imagery describes his burden because "it is the woman who bears the pain of children, in remembering what she endured for them from birth, pregnancy, and conception" (Nachmanides on Num. 11:12). Moses also addresses God as feminine for kabbalistic reasons—this is God as the attribute of justice, as alluded to in the fire at Sinai.

The *Zohar* calls Moses' words "an invocation to the Tree of Death," calling death "the realm associated with the female principle" (III:155b). This is indeed a strange association to make with the gender that gives birth!

Carrying the maternal imagery even further, we might also say that Moses needed God as El-Rachum (Ex. 34:6)—the God of Empathy, or *rachamim*, which is a specific form of compassion that comes from having a *rechem*, or womb. It goes beyond *Chesed,* sheer Mercy, because it enables one entity to identify *completely* with another, because the latter entity is or once was contained within the former.

In other words, what is good for a mother is good for her child. Unless a mother-to-be has been terribly damaged in some way, what she wants for herself will generally be consistent with what is best for the baby growing inside her. To know this is to acknowledge God as a Gracious Mother, El-Rachum veChanun.

The maternal imagery indicates that, contrary to "becoming weak like a woman,"

Moses *needed the strength of a woman* to deal with the Jewish people! This is the constitutional strength of endurance, not the muscle-bound strength, familiar to men, of domination through bigger size.

Feminine maternal imagery of both God and Moses relates also to their style of communication. God spoke to Moses as to the women at Sinai—with *le'emor*, a mild form of speech that communicates an overall structure to someone who is presumed to already have a certain level of knowledge. Moses, however, spoke to the people as God spoke to the men at Sinai—*lehagid*, with a stricter, more detailed set of instructions (see chapter 17).

Moses thus received the Torah *as a woman*, but he had to transmit it to the people *as men*—like children who needed limits set for them. Had all of Israel received all of the Torah directly from God, we might have all received it *le'emor*, "as a woman." However, we did not. By receiving it from Moses, we gave *him* the privilege of *le'emor* and put ourselves into the position of *lehagid*. Thus, by being afraid to hear the whole Torah directly from God, women lost even more at Sinai than men did!

Moses—a "female" in relation to the people as "male"—heard an "inner" Voice of God—of "a higher Heh and a lower Heh"; the "higher Heh is 'the great voice which did not cease,' the flow of which never ceases, and all those 'voices' were in it when the Torah was given to Israel" (*Zohar* III:261a).

The following two examples demonstrate how Moses taught the people on the level they required.

- "We will hear it and we will do it" in Moses' retelling reverses the pledge at Sinai itself, "We will do it and we will hear it." There a great faith was expressed, by promising to keep the Torah before they even knew what it said (Ex. 24:7). Moses' reversal of the word order is further evidence of his frustration with the people's faithlessness and concern for their future observance.
- In repeating the tenth commandment, Moses put "wife" separate from, and ahead of, the neighbor's possessions. He even used different words to describe "coveting" them. In Exodus, the commandment lists house, wife, slave, maid, ox, and donkey, in that order, and uses just one term for coveting them all. Forty years in the wilderness had apparently readied the Jews for hearing the radical social message that a wife is not a possession.

INTERMARRIAGE AND MATRILINEAL DESCENT

Do not intermarry with them. Do not give to his son, and do not take his daughter for your son, for he [it] will turn your son from Me and they will serve other gods. (Deut. 7:3–4)

Marriage is described here as the barter of daughters by their fathers, for that is what it was in the ancient world. Hence, God is addressing the Jewish father and telling him not to "trade" his daughter in marriage for the daughter of a gentile man. Besides instructing Jews not to marry anyone from the seven nations of Canaan, this Torah verse also sets up the law of matrilineal descent: a child is Jewish only if the mother is Jewish.

The question arises as to who is the "he" (or "it") in the above passage. Will "it"—intermarriage—"turn your son from Me?" Will "he"—meaning the gentile father—turn the Jewish son who marries his daughter away from Hashem? Alternately, will "he"—meaning the gentile son—turn the Jewish daughter's brother, the Jewish son, away from Hashem? The answer given is that the gentile son will turn his own son by the Jewish wife away from Hashem.

"The son of the gentile, when he marries your daughter, will turn away your grand-child from Me. This teaches you that your daughter's child by a gentile [man] is called your child, but your son's child by a gentile woman is not called your child, but her child" (Rashi; Kid. 68b).

The Torah is only concerned with the child of the Jewish daughter and her gentile husband, and not with the child of the Jewish son and his gentile wife, because only the former is Jewish according to Jewish law. A Jewish man cannot make Jewish children without a Jewish woman as mother. Hence, the Torah refers to the "turning away" of those it considers Jewish. Non-Jewish children are not spoken of as having been "turned away" from Judaism because they were not a part of it to begin with.

The use of matrilineal descent as the determining factor in Jewishness is as old as Avraham, for God insisted that the covenant pass to Sarah's son, and not *his* (first-born) son by Hagar. A Jewish father confers tribal affiliation to his children (e.g., *kohen* and *levi*), but not Jewishness itself. The Jewish soul comes only through a Jew-ish mother or a *mikvah*. This concept is no doubt related to the Torah's assertion re-garding animals, that the soul resides in the blood. It is the mother's, not the father's, blood that nourishes the baby *in utero*.

In a patriarchal world, where men have a strong sense of entitlement, it is difficult for them to stomach the notion that they have no independent control over the iden-tity of their children—especially when Jewishness is seen as just another "ethnicity." Hence, men have been arguing for patrilineal descent since rabbinic times.

When a man called Jacob of Nevorya ruled that the son of a Jewish father and a gentile mother should be circumcised on the Sabbath, R. Chagai ordered that he be flogged. Jacob of Nevorya defended his argument by citing the verse showing that tribal affiliation comes through the father (Num. 1:18). R. Chagai, in return, showed that matrilineal descent of Jewishness is *d'oraita* (from the Torah itself), by citing the verse from Deuteronomy (7:3–4) as the proof text (GR 7:2; NR 19:3).

Nevertheless, in 1983 c.e. the Reform branch of Judaism boldly passed a unilat-eral decision recognizing patrilineal descent within Judaism. Although nearly a third of Reform rabbis remain opposed to it, the resolution has held. Reform Judaism thus recognizes the child of a Jewish father and a gentile mother as a Jew as long as the child is being raised as a Jew. This has caused serious and unfortunate complica-tions, as the other branches of Judaism continue to adhere to the Jewish tradition of matrilineal descent.

Ironically, Jewish feminism has generally supported patrilineal descent in the spirit of "egalitarianism." However, there is nothing egalitarian about pregnancy and childbirth. By giving a Jewish man the power to make Jewish children without a Jewish woman, patrilineal descent reinforces the worst misogyny of patriarchy.

Patrilineal descent is racist as well, for it makes Jewishness something that is transmitted genetically, like being Italian or Cherokee. There is no such thing as being "part Jewish" or "half-Jewish." One either is or is not Jewish, depending solely on which parent is Jewish. Moreover, a non-Jew can *become* a Jew, something that is not possible with an ethnic or racial identity.

Jewishness as a purely ethnic, racial identity was the Nazi definition of a Jew. Patrilineal descent has often been defended with the argument, "If that person had been in Germany in the 1940s, he or she would have been killed as a Jew." That is indeed quite true. Nevertheless, it would be sadly ironic if the Jewish people were to give Nazism more authority to define "who is a Jew" than Jewish law itself.

✼✼✼ 43 ✼✼✼

The Asherah

Ekev (7:12–11:25)

Do not plant for yourselves an Asherah, or any tree, next to the altar of Hashem your God that you are making for yourselves. Do not erect a stone pillar [matzevah], something which Hashem your God hates. (Deut. 16:21–22)

Do not make for yourselves no-gods [elilim], a pedestal [pesel], or a stone pillar . . . for I am Hashem your God. (Lev. 26:1)

An altar, a stone pillar, and an Asherah tree were the three essential components of Canaanite worship. Israel was allowed to keep the altar, *mizbe'ach,* which was a pile of rocks from which to offer sacrifices, as long as the rocks were whole and not hewn (Ex. 20:22; Deut. 27:5–6). However, the stone pillar and the tree had to go. A tree could not be planted even for the sake of beautification (Rashi; Nachmanides).

Stone and wood were the essence of idolatry. Early Canaanite religion was an elementary, or "primitive," form of fertility worship and ancestor worship. A tree and a stone pillar were the simplest, crudest symbols of the forces of life and death. Carving the wood and hewing the stone into animal and human images was a later development, as was melting down metal.

The term for these stone and wood gods, *elilim,* is a play on אל—*al,* the negative in Hebrew, and *El,* the generic term for God. *Elilim* are "no-gods," nonentities that become gods only because people invest them with that status (Rashi on Lev. 19:4).

Asherah, the tree, was the Canaanite earth-mother goddess. The stone pillar was her son Baal, a vegetation god (like Osiris, Attis, Tamuz, and Adonis) who died and was reborn at the most significant turning points of the agricultural cycle. The stone pillar represented Baal in his dead aspect and also functioned as the totem of a dead ancestor.

The stone pillar, *matzevah,* is called *bimas* or *bimos* in the Mishnah (A.Z. 3:7). It is the same thing—one rock, unlike the altar, that was made from many rocks (Rashi). The different terms for the pillar may simply reflect the development from using a plain rock to one hewn into an image.

The stone pillar stood on a mound. Together the pillar and the mound formed a pedestal, which was set up on a hill. This was the *bamah,* the "high place" of worship. It is from the same root as *bimah,* the "high place" in the synagogue from which the Torah is read.

The *bamah* was located under an Asherah, "a tree that they worshiped" (Rashi). Any individual, family, or community could set up a *bamah* under a tree. A preexisting tree could be used or a tree could be planted for the purpose. Later in the evolution of pagan worship, a tree would be chopped down, carved into an image, and set up as a pole in a desired location. (This was the origin of the Christmas tree.)

A really elegant *bamah* would be located in a grove. The site would be a sacred shrine to the people of a town. A "shrine," as defined by Webster, is "a box of stone, metal, or wood used to hold sacred relics; a tomb, chapel, or other place held sacred because of the presence of such relics." The Asherah grove was a "box" of wood containing at least one sacred stone "relic."

THE TREE AS EARTH MOTHER

Whatever form the wood took—a preexisting tree, a tree planted for the sake of worship, or a wooden pole carved from a tree—this was called an Asherah. Asherah (אשרה) was the Canaanite mother goddess. In Canaanite epic poetry she is called "Lady Asherah of the Sea," Elat, and "creator of the gods."[1] The seaside resort of Eilat is her namesake. As "creator of the gods," Asherah was quite fecund. She had seventy children.

Primeval water, the generative force of the earth, is associated with the earth goddess's image as a tree, generated *from* the earth. The tree is commonly viewed in pagan mythology as a mother giving birth to a sun god.[2] The religious symbolism stemming from the relationship of the "mother" water-earth-tree to a sky-sun "son" has been prolific indeed, even appearing subtly in the Torah as well as more overtly in pagan and Christian mythologies.

The Garden of Eden, with its Tree of Life, Tree of Knowledge of Good and Evil, and four rivers, was the original "grove" in which humanity worshiped the Divine. A wooden ark, carrying one family within it on the waters of the Flood, rebirthed the entire human race. Moses' ark on the Nile was made of papyrus and clay, not wood, but the mother–child theme is still present—Yokheved did not have time to chop wood! To bury a body in a wooden coffin in the earth after death is to return it to its "mother." The wooden ark in the Tabernacle contained the *stone* tablets from Sinai.

1. Pritchard, pp. 98, 100, 105.
2. Neumann, *The Great Mother,* pp. 240–252.

The Christmas tree (which is put up at the winter solstice as the sun turns north-ward again from its southernmost point), the crib containing baby Jesus, and the cru-cifix (a wooden cross with the son god hanging on it) are all based on the tree–mother, sun–son symbolism. Vegetation gods were often sacrificed by being hanged on a tree; hanging from the gallows, as a means of execution, is related to this.

TREES AND THE DESTRUCTION OF AN ASHERAH

For their altars you must set afire; their stone pillars you shall break, and its Asherah you shall cut off. (Ex. 34:13)

What you must do to them is set their altars afire, break their stone pillars, chop their Asherim, and burn their pedestals in fire. (Deut. 7:5)

You must set their altars afire, break their stone pillars, burn their Asherim in fire, and chop the pedestals of their gods. Destroy them and their name from that place. (Deut. 12:3)

Do not destroy its trees. (Deut. 20:19)

The Jews were commanded to destroy an Asherah, but not to destroy trees as they fought the seven Canaanite nations. The destruction of the Asherah was not equiva-lent to the destruction of trees. The command to destroy an Asherah was phrased three different ways—cut off, chop, and burn—precisely to make this distinction. The term *cut off* is of the same root as *karet*, or spiritual excision. *Chop* is the term used for any tree or wood. *Burn* means to treat like kindling wood, whereas the term used for burning the altars means to set a fire that will spread.

The three types of destruction parallel three kinds of Asherah, as defined by the Mishnah (A.Z. 3:7):

- A tree that was planted for worship had to be burned.
- A tree from which a figure had been carved was chopped. The Asherah was in the figure, the "hands of a human" carving the wood into a statue. "What-ever has manual labor connected with it is forbidden" (A.Z. 3:5). If the carved part of the tree could be chopped off without destroying the roots of the tree, new shoots and sprouts could be started and the tree itself could be restored.
- A tree under which an idol was worshiped was permitted to remain if the idol was destroyed. "It once happened in Sidon at a tree they worshiped that they found a mound [gal] under it. R. Shimon told them to examine it. When they did so they found a form [tzurah]. He said, 'Since it is the form that they wor-ship, we permit the tree to you.'" This reflects a point in pagan religion where the worship of the son god preempted the worship of the mother goddess. Here, the Asherah was destroyed through spiritual excision, for the tree itself was no longer the primary object of worship and did not have to be physically destroyed. Only its pedestal did.

The question is raised about a preexisting tree—one that was not planted to *be* worshiped but subsequently *was* worshiped. The Rabbis agreed it was an Asherah that had to be destroyed, but they disagreed on how (A.Z. 45b). R. Jose, son of R. Judah, argued that it is like a tree that was planted for worship, and must be burned. The Rabbis, however, ruled that this tree came under the second category. Because of its preexisting state, it was more akin to a tree from which an Asherah was carved. Thus, it was chopped.

Their ruling is quite significant, for it meant that more trees could be chopped and regrown rather than being completely destroyed through burning. This prevented massive deforestation, such as that practiced by the Canaanites at the time of the Exodus: "When the Canaanites heard that the Israelites were about to enter the Land, they cut down all their trees. When they heard that they [the Jews] were being kept in the wilderness for forty years, they concluded that the wilderness would be their permanent home. So they planted trees again and tended to their growth. After that God had them [the Jews] enter the Land" (ER 20:16).

No benefit could be derived from an Asherah by a Jew. Vegetables could not be planted under an Asherah if its shade helped them grow or if its falling leaves had a fertilizing effect (A.Z. 3:8). The branch of a worshiped palm tree could not be made into a *lulav* for Sukkot (A.Z. 47a). Moreover, "for healing sickness anything may be used but the wood of an Asherah" (*Zohar* III:51b).

If the wood of an Asherah were used to heat a clay oven, the oven, if new, had to be broken; if old, it merely had to cool down before being used again. Bread baked in an oven heated with the wood of an *Asherah* could not be eaten; if only one loaf was baked in that oven but it got mixed up with other loaves from another oven, all the loaves were prohibited (A.Z. 3:9).

Sitting in the shade of an Asherah or walking or sitting under an Asherah were both forbidden. However, the former did not make a person *tamae*, while the latter did. This was because the remains of an idolatrous offering were presumed to be under the tree and because such remains in a covered area were akin to a corpse in a covered area. "Then they joined themselves to Baal-Peor, and ate the sacrifices of the dead" (Psalm 106:28). Thus, the shade was merely a forbidden benefit, but being *under* the Asherah was like being in a tent with a corpse because of the death worship connected with the stone pillar (A.Z. 48b).

THE STONE PILLAR AS TOTEM ANCESTOR

The stone pillars were "memorials of great ones among the ancestors of the community who had manifestly possessed the divine favor [*brakha*] and who . . . are the patron saints of the people."[3] Each pillar was a monument set up to a dead kinsman for an "intercessory function" on behalf of his relatives. The mound on which the pillar stood might even be the grave itself. (Here we see the origin of the headstone.)

---

3. Gray, *The Canaanites*, pp. 67–68.

The stone pillar was known to the patriarchs and used by them as a ritual object. "It was pleasing to [God] in the days of the patriarchs, but now [God] hates it because [the Canaanites] made it into a statute of idol worship" (Rashi).

When Jacob, on his way north fleeing from Esav, stopped to sleep at Bet-El, "he took stones [pl.] from the place and put them at his head" (Gen. 28:11). We might think he only meant to use them as a pillow. However, that night he dreamed of a stairway to heaven with angels running up and down it; God appeared to him in a vision, promising him descendants. Jacob woke up with a start, full of awe. He "took the stone [sing.] that he had put at his head and set it up as a pillar (*matzevah*), pouring oil on its head." He returned to this shrine later and poured wine and oil on it (Gen. 28:18; Gen. 35:14).

Years later, when Jacob was on his way back to Canaan with Rachel and Leah, and Lavan caught up with them, Jacob "took a stone and raised it as a pillar. 'Gather stones,' he told his family. They took stones and made a mound [*gal*]. They ate there on the mound. Lavan called it 'witness mound' [in Aramaic], but Jacob named it Galed [*gal ed*, 'witness mound' in Hebrew]. And Lavan said, 'This mound is a witness between us today. That is why it is called Galed'" (Gen. 31:45-48).

Lavan demanded a pledge from Jacob that he would not oppress his daughters, invoking God—first as Hashem and then as Elokim—as Witness if Jacob ever took any other wives. Lavan also called the *gal* and the *matzevah*, the mound and the pillar, as witnesses, and invoked the God of Avraham as Judge. Jacob swore by his father Isaac and slaughtered an animal, and a ritual feast was shared (Gen. 31:50–54).

When Moses prepared to ascend Sinai the first time (after the people told him they couldn't bear to hear God's Voice for themselves), he built an altar at the foot of Sinai along with twelve pillars, one for each tribe. He and the firstborn sons then sacrificed calves and sprinkled the blood on the altar (Ex. 24:4–6).

In all three scenarios we can hear echoes of the pillar as an ancestral totem connected to fertility worship: Jacob received a promise of descendants at one pillar, and swore by his father at another, when Lavan invoked the pedestal—a pillar and a mound—as "witnesses." Moses, the people's "mother," made a pillar for each tribe when he had to leave them, to somehow "hold them over" till he returned. However, their need for a visual image was so great that they made the calf anyway, for as soon as they thought he was late they panicked that he was never coming back.

The Torah itself was later engraved, at God's command, on twelve pillars, one for each tribe (Deut. 27:2–3; Kaplan). This visual image of the *mitzvot* no doubt helped to wean the Jews from the *matzevot*.

THE CANAANITE PANTHEON:
DIVINE DYSFUNCTIONAL FAMILY

Asherah had seventy children with her husband, El, the Canaanite father god. These made up the Canaanite pantheon. Information about these deities comes from epic poetry engraved on the Ras Shamra tablets discovered by archaeologists in the early part of the twentieth century. These epics are dated to fourteenth-century B.C.E. Ugarit, a site north of biblical Canaan.

Of Asherah and El's seventy children, Yam, the ruler of the sea, was the firstborn son.[4] Baal, the ruler of the sky, was the vegetation god and the ancestral spirit of the stone pillar. Mot, the ruler of the underworld, was death itself—the demon of plague and pestilence, drought and famine. He had "a constant urge to kill, to gather corpses in great number one upon the other, pile on pile, in vast multitudes. With both his hands he shovels them into his mouth, and he drinks their blood in a cup big as a pitcher."[5] There was also a daughter, Anat.

El was castrated by Baal. Yam, as the firstborn, went to take vengeance on Baal, but lost the battle and was killed. Mot then killed Baal to avenge the death of Yam, and Anat then killed Mot to avenge the death of Baal.[6]

Anat (ענת) is not mentioned in the Hebrew Bible, but various Canaanite cities bore her name: Bet-Anat, Bet-Anot, and Anatot (Joshua 15:59, 19:38; Judges 1:33; Jeremiah 1:1). Anah, the female Edomite tribal chief (chapter 6), could have been her namesake, for Anat's love of bloodshed was quite similar to that of Esav.

Anat was a virgin warrior goddess who was "distinguished for her heroic spirit and courage. She is a mighty fighter, who devastates her foes and loves to bathe her feet in the blood of those she has slain."[7] *Virgin* in this context refers only to abstinence from marriage, not from sex. Virgin goddesses remained independent of any one man but were usually quite promiscuous.

Warrior goddesses were also huntresses; shedding blood, human or animal, was their pleasure. Some say that Anat can be identified with Ashtoret, Astarte, and Ashtarot.[8] While these goddesses were not necessarily identical, they may be linked in that each was a "lady of the beasts,"[9] symbolized by animal rather than plant life. Anat, referred to as a cow several times in the epics,[10] has more in common with the Ashtarot, the ewe goddess, than either one does with Asherah, symbolized by plant life.

El (אל) was "the king paramount in the celestial court . . . who gives his sanction to all decisions among the gods affecting nature and society. He is the father of the divine family and president of the divine assembly."[11] He is often referred to in Canaanite epics as "Bull El." El was a remote, high, and transcendent god. Representing "the personification of the power believed to dwell in any object or phenomenon which excited a reaction of awe," El was like "a mild old gentleman delegating direct control to his children and himself acting merely as general supervisor and

4. Ulf Oldenburg, *The Conflict between El and Baal in Canaanite Religion* (Leiden, Netherlands: E. J. Brill, 1969), p. 32.

5. U. Cassuto, *The Goddess Anath* (Jerusalem: Magnes Press, 1971), p. 62.

6. Oldenburg, p. 132.

7. Cassuto, p. 64.

8. Raphael Patai, *The Hebrew Goddess* (New York: Avon, 1978), pp. 42–58.

9. Neumann, *The Great Mother*, pp. 268–280.

10. Pritchard, pp. 109, 112, 117.

11. John Gray, *Near Eastern Mythology* (London: Hamlyn, 1975), p. 70.

final arbiter between them."[12] His remoteness was "designed to conserve his dignity and the conception that the ultimate power of God is beyond disturbance."[13]

El's remoteness extended not only to the world at large but even to his family. Asherah "penetrates El's field and enters the pavilion of King Father Shunem. At El's feet she bows and falls down, prostrates herself and does him reverence."[14] This description calls to mind the trepidation with which Queen Esther approached King Achashverosh in the story of Purim. The queen may be the king's (primary) wife, but she is not "close" to him in any emotionally intimate sense.

Similarly, when Anat approached El, he "answered from seven chambers, from inside eight enclosures."[15]

EL, FERTILITY, AND THE PATRIARCHS

El is how God was known to the patriarchs. Both the singular and plural forms of this name are Names of God.[16] The plural form is used to denote the Divine as the indiscriminate forces of nature that evoke awe and fear.

Avraham first called upon God by name at an altar he built east of Bet-El, the "House of El" (Gen. 12:8, 13:4). Jacob set up a pillar at Bet-El after God appeared to him in a vision (Gen. 28:19), and he later set up an altar there to "El Who appeared to me" and "El Who answered me" (Gen. 35:1, 35:3, 35:7). At Bet-El Rivkah's nurse Devorah died and was buried under an oak tree (perhaps an Asherah) named the Weeping Oak.

Malkitzedek, the Canaanite king of Shalem (Jerusalem), was the priest of El-Elyon, "God Most High," and Avraham took an oath to "El-Elyon, Owner of heaven and earth" (Gen. 14:18–22). Avraham later planted a tree in Beersheva, calling upon El-Olam, "God of the Universe" (Gen. 21:33). Hagar made up the name El-Rai, "God of My Vision" (Gen. 16:13). God is also called El-Cana, "jealous God" (Ex. 34:14), a name that sounds suspiciously close to El-Canaan, El of Canaan.

El-Shaddai, "God Almighty," is the most significant name of all. God told Moses, "I am Hashem. I appeared to Avraham, Isaac, and Jacob as El-Shaddai, and did not let them know Me by my name Hashem" (Ex. 6:2–3). The tetragrammaton was known to the patriarchs but its inner significance was not. Only Moses received prophecy from a level associated with Hashem; the patriarchs received theirs from El-Shaddai (Kaplan).

The name El-Shaddai was used in God's fertility blessing to Avraham, "I will greatly multiply you" (Gen. 17:1–2), and to Jacob, "Be fruitful and multiply" (Gen.

---

12. Theodor H. Gaster, "The Religion of the Canaanites," in *Ancient Religions*, ed. Vergilius Ferm (N.Y.: Citadel, 1965), pp. 119, 121.

13. Gray, *Near Eastern Mythology*, p. 72.

14. Pritchard, p. 101.

15. Quoted in Cassuto, p. 103.

16. The reader should be aware that "El" and "Shaddai" are sacred Names of God that are usually not stated except in ritual. I have left them unchanged in this section, however, for the sake of clarity.

35:11, 48:3). It was used in Isaac's blessing of Jacob, "God Almighty will bless you, make you fruitful, and multiply you" (Gen. 28:3), and in Jacob's blessing of Joseph: "From your father's God, who will help you, Shaddai, who will bless you—blessings from the heavens above and the waters of the deep below, blessings of the breasts [*shaddaim*] and the womb" (Gen. 49:25).

In the latter instance, we see a clear linguistic connection between El-Shaddai and fertility. God Almighty is literally the God of Breasts.[17] El-Shaddai is a very maternal image—and is appropriate for blessing Avraham, Isaac, and Jacob with descendants, since they each had a barren wife! In revealing to them the truth of monotheism, the Sovereign of the Universe combined the qualities of the fecund mother Asherah with the transcendent father El, to become a new source of fertility.

BAAL: THE MASCULINE FRUCTIFIER

Baal (בעל), the son of Asherah and El, was a bull like his father. Unlike El, however, Baal was immanent and symbolized "the personification of that indwelling dynamic force which activated an object or phenomenon, gave it energy and determined its effectual and organic existence."[18]

Like other vegetation gods, Baal was worshiped through dead ancestors as well as through the forces responsible for crop growth. As the spirit of the dead ancestor, Baal was the "animating principle" of the pillar; as crop growth, he was the "animating principle" of vegetation.

Baal simply means "lord." The attachment of the name of a locale indicates the area's tribal ancestor—Baal-Peor was the totem of Peor, Baal-Hammon the totem of Hammon, Baal-Shalisha the totem of Shalisha (2 Kings 4:42), and so on. Baal-Zevuv of Ekron, who was consulted as an oracle by a man who fell through his roof in Samaria (2 Kings 1:2–6), literally means "lord of the fly" of Ekron.

There were many *Baalim*. Indeed, each man was a *baal*, meaning the "lord of his estate" and the "master of his household." *Baal* means "husband," who is the "lord" of a woman in the sexual sense, through *be'ilah* (בעילה), or intercourse. In the most primitive form of male supremacy, every wife was a "priestess" whose god was her husband or whose husband was her god.

However, a husband is called a *baal* in a strictly sexual sense. As a *baal,* an activating principle, he "brings his wife to sexual fulfillment and, so to speak, 'energizes' her womanhood; one who 'quickens' or cultivates soil is 'a *baal* of the earth' [and] . . . an eloquent man is 'a *baal* of the tongue.'"[19]

Baal, in Hebrew, means "fructifier." Bet-Baal, a House of Baal, means "a field sufficiently watered by rain and requiring no artificial irrigation" (Jastrow). Baal is

---

17. See David Biale, "The God with Breasts: El-Shaddai in the Bible," *History of Religions* 21: 3 (Feb. 1982): 240–256.
18. Gaster, p. 120.
19. Ibid.

called "rider of the clouds" in the epics because he ruled the sky forces responsible for crop growth—sun, rain, and clouds, hence thunder, lightning, and dew as well. His thunder aspect was called Baal-Hadad.[20] Lightning, dew, and "fatness of the earth"—Padriya, Taliya, and Artziya—were either his wives or his daughters (scholars disagree).[21]

Here we see how Baal's role as the vegetation god reflected Canaanite agriculture. Canaan, like Israel today, had two seasons, winter and summer. The soil depends upon winter rain for its fertility, unlike Egyptian soil, which depends upon natural irrigation from the Nile's annual inundation. Baal was therefore symbolized by sky forces, while Osiris was worshiped in more earth-related forms—such as the cornstalk, and the (earth's) moon—and whose regeneration was achieved by the "tears of Isis" welling up.

Baal, as rain god, lived in the winter and was dead in the summer—at which time Mot prevailed, according to those who say that Baal's death at the hands of Mot described an annual occurrence. Baal's consequent "resurrection" occurred with Anat recovering his corpse, as Isis did with Osiris. This event was celebrated as the recoronation of his kingship. It is not clear whether it occurred every fall, every seven years, or only when there was drought and famine.

A view disputing the annual celebration maintains that "the death of Baal and rule of Mot upon earth does not describe the normal change of seasons, but a special catastrophe of drought and infertility when the rain does not come in its season."[22] In a normal summer, following sufficient winter rains, Baal did not "die," but simply changed from a rain god to a sun god. In order to prevent drought, a ritual drama was enacted every seventh year.

As sun god, Baal was a *molekh*.[23] "In honor of Baal, who was both sun god and god of fire, the children were rolled down into a fiery pit in the shape of the image of the god; the image was itself known as a *molekh*."[24] Baal-the-Molekh was appeased by the roasted flesh of children. Adults may have been sacrificed as well, and perhaps even a person's own parents (Rashi on Deut. 12:31).

When 450 priests of Baal and 400 priests of Asherah had a confrontation with Elijah on Mount Carmel (1 Kings 18:17–26), they lost because the priests of Baal could not invoke their god *without using fire*. Hiel of Bet-El, who sacrificed his sons for the foundations of Jericho (1 Kings 16:34), "hid himself for the sake of Baal on Mt. Carmel in order to set fire to the wood" (ER 15:15), so the people would think Baal did it. He was punished by being bitten by a snake.[25]

20. Gray, *Near Eastern Mythology*, p. 66.

21. Pritchard, p. 98; Gray, *Near Eastern Mythology*, p. 81; Oldenburg, pp. 76–77; Gaster, p. 129; Cassuto, p. 113.

22. Oldenburg, p. 37.

23. For a discussion of whether Molekh was a specific god or just a generic term for any god worshiped with child sacrifice, see John Day, *Molech: A God of Sacrifice in the Old Testament* (London: Cambridge University Press, 1989), especially pp. 4–14, 34–36.

24. Davies, p. 51; see also Oldenburg, p. 82.

25. Soncino translation, ER, p. 180 n. 1.

Mount Carmel was not the first victory of Hashem over Baal. The "high places of Baal" (Num. 22:41) referred to the shrine to which Balak took Bilam to curse Israel, instructing him to build seven altars on which to sacrifice seven bulls and seven rams. There God also defeated Baal, for when Bilam opened his mouth to curse Israel, all he could do was utter a blessing.

BAAL-ZEPHON: THE "LAST IDOL" OF THE EXODUS

The highest "high place" of Baal was his northernmost summit. Zephon was the site of the temple built for Baal after he complained that he wanted one like all the other gods. He and Anat urged their mother to petition their father to build one for him. Asherah did so, and El agreed.[26]

Zephon was also the burial site of Baal after Mot killed him. When Anat found his corpse, she brought it to Zephon, where she "bewails him and buries him too, lays him in the hollows of the earth-ghosts." Afterward she is said to have sacrificed seventy buffalo, seventy cattle, seventy deer, seventy mountain goats, and seventy roebucks to him.[27]

Baal-Zephon is mentioned in the Torah (Ex. 14:2) as a location on the way out of Egypt—that is, north. It is contained in a set of directions God gave Israel in the wilderness in a ruse to make Pharaoh think they were trapped and come after them.

All the Egyptian deities had been struck dead by God's plagues except Baal-Zephon, who "remained of all the gods of Egypt in order to mislead them, that they should say he was difficult" (Rashi).

> What caused them to be struck by plague after plague? The fact that they trusted their idols. So what did God do? Struck their gods along with them. One of wood rotted, one of stone melted, those of silver, gold and copper were reduced to their original molten state. . . . All the idols of the world were destroyed then, except their Baal-Zephon. Why? In order to lead them astray. . . . When Israel came out of Egypt. . . . [God] summoned all the hosts and said to them, 'Do you not know that Baal-Zephon has assembled all the lions in the wilderness against Israel?' Then the prince of Egypt came down to destroy them. (ER 15:15)

Drowning the Egyptian army in the Red Sea was God's victory over Baal-Zephon.

RAIN AND THE EYES OF GOD

> The Land which you are about to possess is not like Egypt, which you left, where you could sow your seed and water it with your feet, like a vegetable garden. The Land

---

26. Pritchard, pp. 100–103.
27. Ibid., p. 111.

which you are crossing over to possess is a land of mountains and valleys which is watered by the rain of the heavens. It is a Land which Hashem your God examines carefully; the Eyes of Hashem your God are always on it, from the beginning of the year to the end of the year.

If you are careful to keep My commandments which I am commanding you today, to love and serve Hashem your God with all your hearts and all your souls, I will give the rain of your Land in its season, the early rains [in the fall, beginning at Sukkot] and the late rains [in the spring, ending at Passover] so that you may gather in your grain, your wine, and your oil. I will give the grass in your field for your animals, and you will eat and be satisfied.

Guard yourselves lest your hearts be misled and you turn aside and serve other gods and bow down to them. For Hashem will get angry with you and shut up the heavens, and there will be no rain and the ground will not give forth its crops. (Deut. 11:10–17)

This passage is a clear statement that the God of Israel rises above, replaces, and completely incorporates the fertility functions of the Canaanite rain god Baal as well as those of his mother, Asherah. Like the pagans, Israel learned that its God had to be appeased or placated in order for production (rain and crops) as well as reproduction (children and animal births) to occur.

Special fasts were decreed throughout Jewish history because of drought. An entire talmudic tractate, *Taanit*, is devoted to this subject. "Three Keys" are said to be in God's Hands alone, not entrusted to any emissary, angel or human: the Key of Rain, the Key of Life (Birth), and the Key of the Revival of the Dead. An additional one, the Key of Sustenance (*parnasah*), was added in one opinion but was said to be included in the Key of Rain (Ta. 2a–b).

The winter rains in Israel are so important that to this day, even Jews *outside* Israel pray for them fervently. As well as saying Deuteronomy 11:13–17 in the daily prayer known as the *Shma*, Jews recite a number of other "incantations," so to speak, to make the heavenly waters come at their appropriate times.

- *Tefillat Geshem*, the Prayer for Rain, is said on Shmini Atzeret, the eighth day festival marking the end of Sukkot, the autumn holiday which begins the rainy season in Israel.
- *Tefillat Tal*, the Prayer for Dew, is said on the first day of Passover, the spring holiday which ends the rainy season in Israel.
- The phrase, "Who causes the wind to blow and the rain to fall" is added to the daily prayers from the end of Shmini Atzeret to the beginning of Passover. It is inserted before the phrase, "You sustain the living with Mercy, and revive the dead with empathy [*rachamim*]." The link of rain with life-giving fertility as well as death is made very obvious.
- From the beginning of December (which corresponds to *Kislev*, the first winter month) until Passover, the phrase, "Bestow dew and rain for a blessing" is recited in the daily prayers instead of simply, "Bestow a blessing."

The behavior required to placate or appease the God of Israel, however, was of a very different nature than that required of the pagans by their gods. The God of Israel brings fertility and abundance only if Israel keeps the Torah. Lest Israel think that the rites of Asherah and Baal are essential for the fecundity of humans, animals, and the earth, Hashem makes it very clear that the worship of these idols will not only be ineffective, it will produce the very *opposite* effect.

However, the insecurity of the Jews in letting go of pagan rites must have been great indeed, for what else was known to people at that time? Hence, the God Who brought them out of Egypt reassured them that the Divine Eyes would be constantly watching. Israel was like a little child who needs to know that its mama will not let her baby crawl out of her sight. God repeatedly links "keeping My commandments" with the blessings of human and animal fertility and a bountiful harvest (Deut. 7:12–14, 8:11–13). It is here that *Birkat Hamazon*, the Grace After Meals, is commanded; the satisfaction that Jews experience after eating must be acknowledged as stemming from God's gift of the bounty of the Land (Deut. 8:10).

It is also here that Jews are instructed to remember that God gives us our *parnasah* (Deut. 8:17–18). Jewish tradition holds that health, wealth, and one's soulmate (the proper marriage partner) are predestined. This does not mean we can sit back lazily and not look for a job, and expect to get rich anyway. Nor does it mean that the wealthy can be selfish or the poor should be blamed for their poverty. It simply means that whatever provision, sustenance, or maintenance with which we are endowed in our lifetime—through job, salary, or professional success—comes from God, and not from any personal ego power apart from our relationship to God.

✵✵✵ 44 ✵✵✵

The Snare of Idolatry

Re'eh (11:26–16:17)

Do not make a covenant with them [the Canaanites] or their gods. Do not let them stay in the Land, lest they cause you to sin against Me. For if you worship their gods it will be a snare [mokesh] to you. (Ex. 23:32–33; see also Ex. 34:12 and Deut. 7:16)

Be careful not to be ensnared by going after them, after they have been exterminated from before you, lest you inquire about their gods, saying, "How did these nations serve their gods? I would also like to do so." (Deut. 12:30)

The Torah repeatedly emphasizes that the worship of Canaanite deities would be a "snare" to Israel. Because of this, there could be no coexistence with the people in whose image those gods were made. Even metal adornments on the statues could not be melted down to be used for other purposes but had to be utterly destroyed (Deut. 7:25).

Canaanite religion was apparently so enticing and seductive that Israel would not be able to resist it unless it was completely abolished, which included annihilating those addicted to its practices. It was not a question of simply changing people's theological belief system, for the intellect was not the level on which pagan religion had its appeal.

Canaanite worship did not differ in *essence* from the practices of the surrounding cultures, all of whom worshiped an earth-mother goddess and her son, a vegetation god. It was a difference in *degree* that seems to be why God chose to settle Israel in Canaan rather than in Egypt, Babylonia, Syria, or Asia Minor (let alone the rest of the world).

When crops were harvested (cut from the earth), the god "died"; when seeds were sown, he was "buried"; when the first sprouts popped out of the ground, he was "reborn." This yearly agricultural cycle of death, burial, and resurrection was observed with weeklong festivals at each season. First, the death and burial of the god would be mourned through ritual bloodshed—human and animal sacrifice, castration, and skin gashing. His rebirth would then be celebrated—indeed, brought about—through the sympathetic magic of orgiastic sex rites, accompanied by feasting and general merrymaking.

This is the origin of the linkage, in Jewish law, of idolatry, bloodshed, and forbidden sex. A Jew must die rather than worship an idol, murder someone, or commit *ervat gilah* (the sexual prohibitions listed in Leviticus 18). These are the only Torah violations requiring martyrdom, according to Maimonides (*Foundations of Torah*, chap. 5). In any other case, such as *Shabbat* or *kashrut*, one may violate the Torah in order to save one's life.

THE MOURNING RITES: SPILLING BLOOD

The prohibition against "murder" as it is linked with idolatry is called *shfikat damim*, which literally means "spilling of blood." The Hebrew term generally used for murder, such as in the Ten Commandments, is *ratzach*. Murder is the only form of bloodshed for which one must die to avoid committing, but it is actually just the most severe example of a range of activities which included castration, skin gashing, and eating the blood of sacrifices. The Canaanite worship of Asherah and Baal followed the pattern of other pagan cults in beginning its festivals with these rites.

We have already discussed priestly castration (see chapter 23). The priests of Asherah were eunuchs whose penises (perhaps gilded or mummified) were an "offering" to the goddess. These priests had a house attached to the Temple in Jerusalem when an Asherah was put there and women made weavings for her (2 Kings 23:7). Women who worshiped Asherah carried a *mifletzet*, a phallus used for sexual purposes (A.Z. 44a; 1 Kings 15:13). It is not clear whether these were artificial or actual "preserved" specimens.

Ritual Self-Mutilation

Ritual self-mutilation, or skin gashing, was also a Canaanite practice, but it was by no means unique to the Canaanite nations. Rashi calls it an Amorite custom (Deut. 14:1), yet we have already seen evidence to the contrary. Egyptian lamenters mourned the dismemberment and death of Osiris by shaving their heads, hitting themselves, slashing their shoulders, and ripping open their old wounds (see chapter 10).

In Asia Minor, the death of Attis was observed by a ritual in which the high priest drew blood from his arms and presented it as an offering to the goddess Cybele, while the other eunuch priests also slashed themselves with pieces of broken pottery or knives. In Syria and Phoenicia, Adonis was mourned in the same way (see chapter 23).

In Sumeria (early Babylonia), the description in epic poetry of what was done to Dumuzi ("they gashed him with axes") parallels the cutting of crops, and the mourning of the goddess, Inanna ("She tore at her eyes, she tore at her mouth, she tore at her thighs") parallels what the worshipers did to themselves.[1]

Baal's worshipers, like those of other vegetation gods, mourned him in a way that literally imitated the gods, for upon hearing of Baal's death at the hands of Mot, his father El "cuts a gash with a stone. . . . He gashes his cheeks and his chin, he harrows the roll of his arm. He plows his chest like a garden, harrows his back like a plain."[2] When Baal's sister, Anat, found his body, she did the same thing to herself.

When the priests of Baal were defeated at Mount Carmel, "they cried aloud and cut themselves according to their regulations [*mishpatim*] with knives and lances, till the blood gushed out upon them" (1 Kings 18:28). The term *mishpatim* indicates a set of laws carried out with rational precision, and not simply random acts of spontaneous, sporadic passion. It even implies a preset pattern of incisions that the worshiper would make on his or her body.

It was the cool, dispassionate precision with which people mutilated themselves that was so dangerous. A modern analogy might be the perversion of sensation found in sexual sadomasochists, many of whom engage in ritual cutting, which they call "blood sports." Sadomasochism (S&M) manuals give very matter-of-fact instructions on "how" to cut without inflicting fatal injuries.

Ritual cutting is still practiced in organized settings as well. In certain cults, it (along with sexual abuse) is inflicted on children of cult members. Animal and child sacrifice are also frequently practiced by these cults—which, although they are usually called "satanic," are by no means limited to worshipers of the Christian devil. In fact, some seemingly "mainstream" organizations are often involved.[3] These groups provide the closest modern parallel possible to the Canaanites. Reading about them gives one an idea of what Canaanite religion might have been like and why such a society would have to be destroyed (its evil was far beyond any possibility of rehabilitation).

Children who have survived ritual abuse often engage in compulsive self-mutilation as adults. In fact, self-mutilation has only recently come to be recognized as an aftereffect of "regular" (i.e., nonritualized) sexual abuse. It is resorted to by someone who is unable to express some very deep emotional pain and so converts it into physical pain, a format that is much more manageable by comparison.

> The incest survivor is a candidate for self-injury. She cannot allow herself to experience her emotional pain, but she has developed a huge tolerance for physical abuse. . . . Cutting distracts her, relieves the tension, and provides a kind of hypnotic state or high. The woman who injures herself may or may not feel pain from the act. For some

1. Quoted in Wolkstein and Kramer, pp. 71, 83.
2. Pritchard, p. 110.
3. Readers who are skeptical of the existence of modern ritual cult abuse are urged to examine the evidence—the testimony of survivors as well as the experiences of clinicians who have treated such children. See Valerie Sinason, ed., *Treating Survivors of Satanic Abuse* (New York: Routledge, 1994); Margaret Smith, *Ritual Abuse* (New York: HarperCollins, 1993); and Elizabeth S. Rose, "Surviving the Unbelievable," *Ms.*, 3:4 (Jan./Feb. 1993): 40–45.

women whose connection with the sensation of their bodies is nearly severed, to feel the pain of self-injury is a signal that their mind-body split is being repaired.[4]

Consider the following account of a teenage Jewish girl from a well-known autobiographical novel.[5]

> She had the top of a tin can, which she had found on one of her walks and picked up. . . . The edges were rippled and sharp. She dragged the metal down the inside of her upper arm, watching the blood start slowly from the six or seven tracks that followed the metal down below the elbow. There was no pain, only the unpleasant sensation of the resistance of her flesh. The tin top was drawn down again, carefully and fastidiously following the original tracks. She worked hard, scraping deeper, ten times or so up and back until the inside of the arm was a gory swath. Then she fell asleep.

The healing of this mental patient began to be effected when she could no longer cut or burn herself without feeling pain. Putting a lighted cigarette on her arm, "she felt the warmth of it, the heat, the burn. The first singe of hair brought a red-hot stab with it so that she jerked her arm away, astonished."

To facilitate the healing of *one* person in this condition is immensely difficult. Imagine an entire *culture* in a similar state of mind—only not as an unusual, freak compulsion but a normative, mainstream religious custom. The linkage between self-mutilation and incest is quite relevant to our discussion of the Canaanites, as we shall see later in this chapter.

The Jewish mourning custom of ripping one's clothing may be yet another "weaning device" of the Torah, a civilized alternative to ripping one's flesh. *Tefillin,* which are placed on the arm and on the head "between the eyes," the place where a bald patch was made by pagan mourners (Deut. 14:1), may be another.[6]

The Torah prohibits ritual self-mutilation "for the dead"; however, this could also be vocalized and read as "for Mot." Anat's revenge on Mot was not only severely mutilating, it was simultaneously a description of harvesting, threshing, and sowing grain: "She seizes the godly Mot. With sword she cleaves him. With fan she winnows him. With fire she burns him. With handmill she grinds him. In the field she sows him."[7]

While it was Asherah, the mother goddess, who "required" bloodshed, it was Anat, the daughter and sister goddess, who carried it out with such gusto. Her bloodthirstiness was not limited to Mot but was rather a regular activity from which she derived great pleasure:

> Anat gives battle, mightily she cuts in pieces the sons of the two cities. . . . She hangs heads on her back, she fastens hands on her girdle. She plunges her knees in the blood

---

4. Blume, p. 185.
5. Hannah Green, *I Never Promised You a Rose Garden* (New York: Signet, 1964), pp. 51, 239.
6. Theodor Reik, *Pagan Rites in Judaism* (New York: Noonday Press, 1964), pp. 122–123.
7. Pritchard, pp. 112–113.

of swift ones, her thighs in the gore of fast ones. . . . She smites exceedingly, and says: Anat hews in pieces and rejoices, her liver extends with laughter, her heart is filled with joy, for in Anat's hand is success. . . . She battles in the house until she is sated.[8]

Eating Blood

These pagan bloodbaths are the reason that this Torah portion links two major topics: the prohibition of idol worship and the consumption of animal flesh. The commands regarding animal flesh are as follows:

- Once the Jews entered the Land, they could only offer sacrifices in the location stipulated by God—namely, the Temple—and not at a *bamah* (Deut. 12:13–14).
- While meat could only be eaten in the wilderness after the animal was sacrificed as a *shlamim* (peace-offering) at the Tabernacle, once Jews were in the Land, meat eating could be a secular (i.e., nonsacrificial) activity as well (Deut. 12:15, 12:20).
- An animal could only be eaten if it was slaughtered according to the laws of *shechitah* (Deut. 12:21, 14:21).
- The species of animals that may not be eaten are reiterated (Deut. 14:3–20).
- The prohibition of cooking an animal in its mother's milk is emphasized for the third time (Deut. 14:21).
- The prohibition of eating blood is also emphasized for the third time (Deut. 12:16, 12:23–27).

The first time eating blood was prohibited (Lev. 7:26–27) was in relation to the *shlamim*. The second time (Lev. 17:10–14) was in the context of prohibiting sacrifices outside the Tabernacle as a way of weaning Jews from satyr worship; this is immediately followed by the sexual prohibitions, a juxtaposition that is highly significant. Now, in the third mention of the command to not eat blood, the Torah admonishes Israel to "be strong" in it, which implies that this will take some self-discipline. This is because the pagans "were addicted to eating blood" (Rashi).

Israel, too, had become

attached to blood in Egypt. . . . They always slaughtered their sacrifices to the satyrs. . . . The worship consisted of eating from the blood, because the blood would cause the demons to assemble. They would eat over it and from it, as if they were invited by the demons to eat at the table of those demons, and they became friendly with them. . . . They were addicted to it, and pursued it very much. They used to prophesy by means of it and tell of things to come. (Nachmanides)

If Israel allowed the Canaanites to stay in the Land, when "they lust [*zanu*] after their gods and sacrifice to their gods, they will invite you and you will eat from their sacrifices" (Ex. 34:15). This is exactly what happened with Baal-Peor.

---

8. Quoted in Cassuto, pp. 87–89.

THE FERTILITY RITES: *ERVAT GILAH*

After the bloodshed was over, an orgy took place. This was supposed to function as fertility magic for animals, crops, and humans. The midrashic statement that the men of the generation of the Flood "spilled their semen upon the trees and stones" (see chapter 2) takes on added meaning, now that we understand the ritual significance of trees and stones.

Four terms are used interchangeably in rabbinic literature to refer to idolatry. *Avodah zarah*, "strange worship," is the generic term as well as the name of the talmudic tractate on the subject. *Avodat kokhavim* means "star worship," which is the deification of the planets and constellations. *Avodat elilim* means "the worship of no-gods," or statues of stone, wood, and metal.

Avodat gilulim, the fourth term, comes from *gilul*, or "filth" (Jastrow). It relates to *gal*, "mound," as well as *galal*, to "roll or unfold." (The Galilee is so named because its terrain is made up of rolling hills.) *Avodat gilulim* may therefore refer specifically to the form of idol worship that took place on the mounds and hills of the Asherah groves. This is indicated by R. Akiva's statement, "Any place you find a high mount or a lofty hill and a green tree, you can be sure there is *avodat gilulim!*" (A.Z. 3:5). Oracles were obtained in these groves at a shrine called Bet-Galia, "house of revelation" (A.Z. 46a; Jastrow).

"Revelation" comes from *gilah*, to reveal or "uncover." This is the word that forms the term *ervat gilah*, which literally means "uncovering nakedness." Batyah, Pharaoh's daughter, immersed herself in the Nile to "cleanse herself of her father's *gilul*"; we have already surmised that this meant his incest as well as his worship of idols (see chapter 13).

Avodat gilulim thus appears to be a pun that refers to pagan fertility rites—that is, the sex (*gilah*) that took place on the mounds (*gal*) of the Asherah groves. The six sexual prohibitions defined as *ervat gilah*—incest, adultery, sodomy, bestiality, sex during menstruation, and sex with a living wife's sister—were probably the essence of ritual fertility acts and not just everyday customs.

This is suggested by comparing these behaviors to sexual prohibitions that are *not ervat gilah*. Rape, a husband's affair with a single woman, lesbianism, intermarriage (sex with a gentile), and premarital sex are all prohibited under Jewish law, yet *none of these are ervat gilah*. The penalty for them is not as severe, nor does one have to die rather than commit them. What is the distinguishing factor here?

Clearly, the factor is not logic, for if we were to categorize sexual behaviors by logic, then surely rape, incest, bestiality, and the adultery of *either* spouse would head the list of offenses. Male homosexuality and lesbianism would probably be in the same category. Sex with a gentile would be differentiated by gender, due to the different status of the children as Jews; that is, a Jewish man's intermarriage would be a more serious offense than that of a Jewish woman. Sex with one's wife during menstruation or with an ex-wife's sister once the divorce is final would be less serious offenses belonging to another category. Premarital sex—if it really was prior to a marriage and not promiscuous—would be in a class by itself and hardly an offense at all!

However, that is not how it works. *Ervat gilah* includes incest but not rape, a wife's adultery but not a husband's, male homosexuality but not lesbianism, and so on. The only way the Torah's distinctions make any sense is if the behaviors called *ervat gilah* were *avodat gilulim*, pagan fertility rites. This would also explain why the list of forbidden sex acts comes right after the topics of sacrifices, satyr worship, and eating blood. The Torah deals with them in the same sequence as they occurred in pagan rites—from blood to sex and from mourning to celebration.

Let us review the evidence we have gathered so far in support of this theory, starting with the weakest proof and working our way up to the strongest.

Wife's sister: We have not seen any evidence that would differentiate this as a ritual activity from a marriage custom. It would, however, be included in any orgiastic free-for-all.

Menstrual sex: We also have no evidence that this was anything more than men claiming constant sexual access to women. However, it could have been ritually important as the point at which blood and sex converged—even providing the original meaning of the term *bloodlust*.

Adultery: The men of Sodom had four annual festivals in which they swapped wives (see chapter 4). "Four annual festivals" immediately suggests seasonal, agricultural rites. That wife-swapping was an integral part of an orgiastic free-for-all is indicated by a description of a festival in the Canaanite epics—"the one hands over to another his wife, to a foreigner his beloved."[9] Adultery would also have been a ritual act if any of the *kedeshot*, the priestesses who functioned as embodiments of the goddess for ritual sex, were married women.

Sodomy: It is difficult to see how male homosexuality could function as imitative "fertility" magic, yet nevertheless, this seems to have been the case. A eunuch transvestite priest served as a *kadesh*, a "sacred prostitute" for men in pagan rites. The *kedeshim* were called "dog-priests"[10] (a reference, probably, to the physical position required for such activity), and their earnings are euphemistically referred to by the Torah as "the price of a dog" (see chapter 23).

Bestiality: *Nirbah* and *rovea*, the terms for a female and a male animal used for sex by a man and a woman, respectively, come from a Hebrew root that means "to fructify the ground" and "to inundate for the sake of improving the soil" (see chapter 22). The ritual nature of bestiality is thus made very clear. That its purpose was as fertility magic for the crops, and not for the animals, gives us a clue as to how ritual sodomy must have been perceived. The sex of the fertility rites did not have to be *actually* capable of impregnating.

Goats were employed in sex rites by both men and women in Goshen, Egypt (chapter 27). The Egyptian Apis bull was "worshiped" by women in an orgiastic manner (chapter 12). Ewes may have been "worshiped" in a similar way by male shepherds

---

9. Quoted in Ivan Engnell, *Studies in Divine Kingship in the Ancient Near East* (Oxford, England: Basil Blackwell, 1967), p. 159.

10. Graves and Patai, p. 169.

(chapter 41). Bilam abused his donkey in order to enhance his powers of sorcery (chapter 37). Bestiality was so prevalent in the ancient world that it was a criterion for choosing which animals to take on the ark (chapter 2), and a Jew could not even leave a domestic animal at the inn of an idolator because of the likelihood that it would be sexually abused (A.Z. 2:1).

Incest: Since patrilineal incest was not taboo prior to the giving of the Torah, father-daughter incest was normative in the pagan world and hence would be included in any orgy. In addition, the ritual defloration of girls was often done by their own fathers (chapter 5).

Incest, like bloodshed, was common in the Canaanite dysfunctional divine family—even between matrilineal relatives. For humans to engage in it would thus be nothing less than an imitation of the divine powers, and imitating the gods was the essence of religious ritual.

INCEST AND THE GODS

The entire Canaanite pantheon was the result of incestuous rape, for El's wives were his sisters. After usurping his own father's kingship by castration, he "takes the female household of his father." Resistance by the women is quelled, for El "catches his sisters, when they go against him to kill him by craft, and makes them his wives, and he has numerous progeny by them." He also impregnates his daughter, Anat.[11]

Baal, when he castrated El, did the same thing, for "the wife of the predecessor was identical with the right to the throne." Hence, Asherah became "the wife of Baal, and they probably were believed to provide fertility magically, by sexual intercourse." This mother–son incest was also rape, for as a result Asherah hated Baal, participated in plotting his overthrow, and even rejoiced at his death.[12]

We might surmise that the ritual castration of a priest who served the mother goddess was a symbolic revenge on her son for castrating his father and raping ("marrying") her. If this is all beginning to sound like the Greek myth of Oedipus, it is no coincidence, for in Phoenician documents, El is called El-Kronos. Kronos, in Greek mythology, also had three sons, who ruled the sky (Zeus, like Baal), the sea (Poseidon, like Yam), and the underworld (Hades, like Mot). It is thus quite probable that "the Greek myths . . . have their origin in Eastern countries."[13]

We can also see why scholars disagree as to whether the three women mentioned in the last chapter were Baal's wives or his daughters. Given the history of this family, they were probably both! All that is left to complete the incestuous circle is for Baal to have slept with Anat. This was indeed the case—complete with the cow and bull imagery we saw with Isis and Osiris in *their* incestuous relationship (as well as

11. Oldenburg, p. 109, 110, 115.
12. Ibid., pp. 20, 115–119.
13. Cassuto, p. 57.

a link with Ashtarot, the ewe goddess): "Like the heart of a cow for her calf, like the heart of a ewe for her lamb, so is the heart of Anat for Baal."[14]

Anat is called "fairest among Baal's sisters. Before her he rises, he stands, at her feet he kneels and falls down," and begs to be allowed to "anoint her horns." Then "he seizes and holds her womb; she seizes and holds his stones." The resulting offspring are "calves the cows drop. An ox for maiden Anat. . . . [A] wild ox is born to Baal, a buffalo to the rider of clouds."[15]

Unlike Asherah, who was angry at Baal for his incestuous rape of her, Anat appears to have nothing but love for her brother. "Nobody is as ready to serve Baal as Anat. . . . Anat adores her young heroic brother and is devoted to him."[16] Nor does she generally get angry with her father. She makes only one threat against El: "I shall trample him down like a lamb to the ground, I shall bring down his hoary head with blood to the grave, the gray hair of his old age with his gore."[17] This was a one-time occurrence, relating to her demand that he build a temple for Baal. However, the disproportionate level of her anger at this one offense is certainly significant.

We can now understand, from a modern psychological perspective on incest, why Anat was such a bloodthirsty woman. The anger the victim rightfully feels toward her perpetrator (then *or* now) has to be suppressed, for her own safety. As a result of its repression, it accumulates, becomes distorted, and explodes as rage toward the "entire gender or ethnic group of the perpetrator."[18] If this holds true in our own culture, where most men are *not* incest perpetrators, how much more so would it have been true in Canaan, where incest was normative!

Anat at least had enough remnants of self-esteem to be *outwardly* aggressive and destructive. She did not—like so many abused women and girls, in our time as well as hers—turn her anger inward and cut *herself* into bloody shreds! Herein lies her appeal to feminists (and the appeal of similar goddesses). The epithet *manhater* is frequently hurled against women whose passionate response to male supremacy comes from the depths of their hearts, souls, and childhood experiences. Manhating may be the *healthiest* response one can muster in such a situation. Those who are upset by manhating should work to eliminate the reason it occurs instead of condemning the women who feel it.

WOMEN AND THE ENTICEMENT TO IDOLATRY

If there is found among you . . . a man or a woman who does evil in the Eyes of Hashem your God by transgressing the covenant, going and serving other gods, . . . you shall

---

14. Pritchard, p. 112.
15. Ibid., pp. 116–118.
16. Oldenburg, pp. 71–72.
17. Quoted in Cassuto, p. 99.
18. Blume, pp. xviii–xix; see also pp. 131–144. The "ethnic" part of this dynamic should be explored as a significant reason for intermarriage by Jewish women.

bring that man or that woman who did this evil thing out to your gates. You shall stone the man or the woman to death with rocks. (Deut. 17:2–5)

Your sons will marry his [the Canaanite's] daughters. His daughters will lust after their gods and cause your sons to lust after their gods. (Ex. 34:16)

[If] men who have thrown off the yoke [of heaven] go out from among you and entice the residents of their city, saying, "Let's go worship other gods" . . . (Deut. 13:14)

Most passages in the Torah do not make a point of saying "a man or a woman," but use either *adam* ("human being") or *ish* (which can mean "person" as well as "man"). In the penalty for idol worship, however (Deut. 17:2–5 quoted previously), both sexes are specifically stated, as if to emphasize women. Why was this done? "Because of *kalut dat,* the woman can be enticed to *avodat gilulim* by signs and wonders done before her," Nachmanides asserts, offering three points as evidence: Exodus 22:17 refers to a sorceress, even though a sorcerer is equally liable; certain forms of divination were practiced primarily by women; and many women in the time of the prophet Jeremiah worshiped the goddess.

Given the attraction that witchcraft and goddess worship hold for many feminist women today, his explanation seems plausible. Even *kalut dat* may not have as offensive a meaning as sexist interpreters have given it. Although the phrase is usually translated as "light-mindedness," or even "frivolity"—as if women are flighty and incapable of serious mental activity—the word *kalut* means "swiftness" as well as "lightness" (Jastrow).

Kalut dat can therefore mean "quick-mindedness," implying that women have a greater mental flexibility and subtle perceptiveness than men. This sounds like *Binah*, the higher level of understanding in women that made the serpent talk to Chavah rather than Adam and is at the root of women's exemption from the positive time-bound commandments. It would certainly make women more adept at various kinds of occult practices.

However, even if we interpret *kalut dat* in a positive way, Nachmanides is still saying that women are more easily persuaded than men to worship idols. There is good reason to question this premise, especially since he uses the term *avodat gilulim.* Who wanted to make the golden calf? Who worshiped Baal-Peor? Not the women: it was the *men* who were enticed into idolatry. Nachmanides would have been more accurate if he had said that "the man can be enticed to *avodat gilulim* by sexual seduction," for sex, after all, was much more essential to that type of worship than "signs and wonders."

We see another reference to men's vulnerability to enticement through sex in the second passage (Ex. 34:16). Canaanite women, through marriage to Jewish men, would lead them to worship idols. However, there is no corollary statement that marriage to Canaanite men would lead Jewish women to worship idols. The precedent for this distinction is Baal-Peor: Jewish men were enticed through sex, but Jewish women were not enticed at all.

Therefore, the emphasis on women in the first passage cannot be because Jewish women were *more* prone to idolatry, for up to that point they had been *less* prone. It is as if the Torah were saying, "You must punish women *too,* if they do what you have so far only seen men do."

However, Nachmanides then offers another explanation that makes more sense. The punishment of an individual Jew who worships an idol had to be explicitly stated as applying to women as well as men because this was not the case when Jews *collectively* worshiped an idol. Then, men alone were held responsible (Deut. 13:14).

If an entire city of Jews was enticed into idolatry, it made a difference whether the instigators were men or women. If they were women, then the idol worshipers were punished as individuals, as in any other case. However, if the enticers were men, the whole city was condemned (*ir hanidachat*). It was placed under *cherem;* all the inhabitants were annihilated by the sword and the city could never be rebuilt (Deut. 13:13–19; San. 10:4). The issue was only theoretical, it seems, for it is asserted that "there never was a condemned city, and never will be" (San. 71a).

There are two possible ways of looking at this. If women were indeed more prone to idolatry, then requiring the instigators to be men was a way of making the criterion stricter, so that fewer cities would be condemned. If women were more easily enticed, they would also be more likely to act as enticers, and therefore cities might be condemned sooner and more often. Men, in this view, would succumb less readily, so by the time they were enticed and acting as enticers, the women would already be practicing idolatry.

On the other hand, we have seen that Jewish women had no precedent as either the enticed or the enticers. It was pagan women who acted as enticers and Jewish men who were enticed. However, a Jewish city was not condemned if it was enticed by pagans; the enticers had to be Jews. Thus, requiring the instigators to be Jewish men was a stricter criterion here, too, but for a different reason. A Jewish city would not be condemned for a Baal-Peor type of incident, in which men were seduced in large numbers by pagan women.

Once such seduced Jewish men became enticers, their success in recruiting other Jews would be limited, since they could not use sex as the pagan women did. The rest of the men would not be any more easily enticeable than the women—presumably, they could resist "signs and wonders" more easily than sexual temptation! Thus, Jewish women and children would not be condemned to death because of Jewish men's sexual weaknesses.

That this second view is the accurate one is supported by Nachmanides himself when he describes the destruction of the condemned city as "the men who have been enticed" and "the women who were dragged or pulled [*nigraru*] after the men." Similarly, Maimonides refers to "the children and wives of the worshipers," indicating that the transgressors were men (*Idolatry* 4:6).

✻✻✻ 45 ✻✻✻

The Pursuit of Justice

Shoftim (16:18–21:9)

Justice, justice you shall pursue. (Deut. 16:20)

In this Torah portion, God instructs Israel to set up courts of law. Each tribe had its own court with its own judges and police. If a dispute could not be settled within a local court, the parties went to the Jewish Supreme Court, the Sanhedrin, which convened at the Temple in Jerusalem (Deut. 17:8–9). With the destruction of the Second Temple, the Sanhedrin fell into oblivion, and local Jewish courts have very limited power in the world today, even in Israel.

Justice had to be meted out as fairly and impartially as possible. Bribes were not to be taken, but just as the rich were not to be favored over the poor, so, too, the poor were not to be favored over the rich (Lev. 19:15). The perversion of justice makes the Land *tamae*, desecrates God's Name, removes the Shekhinah, causes Israel to fall by the sword, and exiles Jews from the Land (Rashi on Lev. 19:35).

A Jewish court is not like an American court, where decisions are left to one judge or a jury of twelve laypeople. There are no lawyers in a Jewish court. Civil cases are tried by three judges, who question the witnesses. Capital cases are tried by twenty-three judges, and cases that affect a whole community, by seventy-one judges (San. 1:1–6).

The purpose of having an odd number of judges was to break a tie. In capital cases, if the vote differed by one in favor of acquittal, the verdict held, but if the vote differed by one in favor of conviction, more judges were added until a clearer verdict could be made. A conviction could be changed to an acquittal, but an acquittal could never be changed to a conviction. A convicted defendant was not executed until the following day, in order to give some additional time for evidence favoring acquittal to surface (San. 5:5).

Thus, a system that utilized the death penalty was balanced by rules that did everything possible to acquit a defendant. The arguments for and against capital punishment—whether it is a necessary deterrent or an unjustifiable evil—were debated in rabbinic times, just as today.

"A Sanhedrin that puts to death one person in seven years is called tyrannical," the Mishnah (Mak. 1:10) maintains. R. Elazar ben Azariah asserts, "One person in seventy years." R. Tarfon and R. Akiva go even further: "If we were on the Sanhedrin, no one would ever be put to death." R. Shimon ben Gamliel, arguing for deterrence, accuses the liberals on the court: "They would therefore increase the shedders of blood in Israel."

PAGAN IDOLATRY AND SOCIAL JUSTICE

The Jewish court was a radical system of justice in the ancient world. The Torah's requirement that non-Jews also set up court systems (one of the seven Noachide laws) encouraged gentiles to develop a more civilized and humane approach towards dealing with crime. Until then, blood vengeance and bodily mutilation (e.g., cutting off the hand of a thief) were common.

Sotah, we have noted (chapter 32), was an early antidote to the societal privilege that allowed a jealous man to kill his wife if he so much as *suspected* her of sexual infidelity. A court trial for a woman accused of adultery by her husband came relatively late in the ancient world. In Rome, which was founded in 753 B.C.E., the punishment of a woman's adultery was the husband's prerogative until 18 B.C.E., when the Lex Julia de Adulteriis "took jurisdiction over adultery away from the family and made it a public crime."[1]

Pagan courts were a first step in modifying lynch law and surely must have helped to decrease the number of murdered wives, as well as other barbarities. However, because they remained linked to idolatry, they did not achieve the same level of justice as the Jewish court system. The Babylonian Code of Hammurabi, which predated the Revelation of the Torah by about five hundred years, was a fairly advanced legal system for its time. Nonetheless, it contained many instances of bodily mutilation as the prescribed punishment for a crime, which was itself defined by whether the injured person was a nobleman, a commoner, or a slave.

The concept of justice in the pagan world was completely bound up with idol worship. Egyptian laws, for example, were believed to come from Maat, who was personified as the goddess of truth and justice:

> a quality not of men but of the world, built into it by the gods at the moment of Creation. As such, it represented the gods' will. . . . Thus it precluded any serious questioning of the structure of society or any possibility of reforming it. The world and

---

1. Julia O'Faolain and Lauro Martines, eds., *Not in God's Image* (New York: Harper & Row, 1973), p. 46.

everything in it had been created by the gods precisely in the form they wanted . . . The idea briefly emerged that Maat was not just a passive quality inherent in the world, but that the god-king's subjects had a right to expect its exercise. This was a step toward the development of a concept of social justice, but it did not long survive.[2]

Because the laws were believed to originate with the gods, the execution of justice was originally in the hands of the divine king and his priests. Independent judges were probably a later development. In early Babylonia, "every temple was a place of justice and every priest was entitled to pronounce judgments, but there were also regular judges appointed by the king, and certain of the higher officials such as the mayor of the city and . . . the governor of the province possessed judicial functions."[3]

There was no separation of religion and state, or of executive, legislative, and judicial branches. The legal system served to legitimize social hierarchy and class privilege. Egyptian judges were often in charge of the treasury and the granaries, and were usually governors of towns as well. As time went on, "the number of offices they then held grew to be enormous."[4]

"When anyone appealed to justice, those whose business it was to protect the tax-payer took bribes to acquit the guilty and to condemn the innocent victim who could not afford to purchase their favor." While the king sometimes punished "his own administrative officers in the interests of the privileged priestly class, . . . we may nevertheless question whether equally severe penalties were exacted for injustice to a free laborer or workman."[5]

When temple robbers were arrested, which was rare, they "purchased their freedom with a little gold and resumed their operations, having taken advantage of their removal from the prison of the mayors of the town to that of the high priest to make their escape."[6] While Egyptian temple robbers were thus protected by the prison or town of the high priest, in Judaism a similar concept was used to protect those who had committed manslaughter.

BLOOD VENGEANCE IN THE ANCIENT WORLD

Ancient pagan legal codes often make no mention of either murder or manslaughter:

The absence of a specific clause dealing with murder has been noticed . . . in both the Code of Hammurabi and in the Assyrian laws, [which] . . . is due to the fact that murder was still extra-judicial, a thing to be settled by private vengeance. That the blood-feud still survived in the Hittite Old Kingdom is clear. . . .

---

2. Casson, p. 75.
3. C. Leonard Wooley, *The Sumerians* (New York: W. W. Norton and Co., 1965), p. 93.
4. Erman, p. 89.
5. Montet, pp. 258–259.
6. Ibid., p. 267.

> In a primitive society punishment is synonymous with revenge, and it is impossible to distinguish "civil" from "criminal" offenses. The injured party will avenge himself as best he can upon the wrongdoer, or if he is dead, vengeance becomes the duty of his relatives, and there arises a blood-feud.[7]

Not only was the killer held accountable by the blood avenger, but "the guilt attaches to the whole family of the wrongdoer, and . . . its members may all be involved in [the] punishment."[8] Thus, we can see how one murder—even an accidental one—could set off an escalating, neverending cycle of bloodshed. The Torah put a plug on this in two major ways: providing cities of refuge for manslayers, and creating a ritual atonement for an unsolved murder, a ceremony we will call the River Heifer.

Cities of Refuge

If someone was killed intentionally, the murderer—*after* being tried and convicted—was handed over by the court to the blood avenger (Num. 35:19, 35:21; Deut. 19:11–12; Mak. 12a). The murderer would be executed, and the family of the victim got the emotional satisfaction of carrying out the court's sentence. If the victim had no blood avenger, the court appointed one (San. 45b), and the blood feud officially ended.

If someone was killed accidentally, the manslayer was sent to a city of refuge (*ir hamiklat*). Six cities of refuge were established within the Land of Israel—three in Canaan and three on the east side of the Jordan River (Num. 35:11–28; Deut. 19:1–9). The manslayer had to stay there until the high priest died—whether that was one day or ninety years.

If the high priest died during the trial, the manslayer's term was dependent on the lifespan of the next appointed high priest. If the high priest died right at the end of the trial, the manslayer did not have to go to a city of refuge at all. However, if the high priest himself was the victim *or* the manslayer or if a trial ended when no high priest was in office, the manslayer could never leave the city of refuge (Mak. 2:6, 2:7).

The mother of the high priest (with the help of mothers of other priests—probably those in line for the high priesthood) distributed food and clothing to the inhabitants of the cities of refuge. The manslayers would naturally want the high priest to die, in order to expedite their release. The high priest's mother, by providing goodies for them (e.g., baking cookies and knitting sweaters) was attempting to keep them comfortable so they would not pray for her son's death (Mak. 2:6).

At the time of the high priest's death, all the manslayers returned to their homes. If a manslayer left the city of refuge before the death of the high priest, was found outside its boundaries, and was killed by the blood avenger, the latter was not held culpable.

---

7. O. R. Gurney, *The Hittites* (London: Penguin, 1990), pp. 77–78, 80.
8. Ibid., p. 81.

The River Heifer

The Torah also curbed the bloodshed by creating a ritual atonement for an unsolved murder (Deut. 21:1–9). In the ancient world, the lack of knowledge of the murderer's identity did not stop blood vengeance.

Instead, "the nearest village is responsible for compensating the victim's family if the murderer has escaped. . . . There are parallels in the Code of Hammurabi. . . . The unique feature of the Hittite law is the three-mile limit, outside which responsibility ceases."[9]

Thus, the Torah has the elders of the city who are closest to the corpse perform this rite. Like the Red Heifer, the River Heifer had to be a young cow that had never given birth, been yoked, or done any work for human benefit. The elders of the nearby city brought her to a river. The spot of land chosen, like the heifer herself, must never have been worked or sown (i.e., fertilized). There, they decapitated her (actually, they broke her neck), washed their hands, and made a pledge that the murderer was unknown. The priests then asked God's forgiveness for the innocent blood that was shed.

Decapitation was the means used to slaughter the River Heifer because that was how a convicted murderer was executed (San. 52b; 9:1). If the murderer was found before the cow's neck was broken, she was set free; if not, she was buried at the place where she was slaughtered (Kr. 6:2).

DIVINATION AND JUDGMENT

There shall not be found among you . . . one who practices stick divination, who predicts auspicious times, who uses omens, sorcery, or incantations, who consults mediums and oracles, or who practices necromancy. (Deut. 18:10–11)

Before there were pagan courts and judges separate from the temples and priesthoods, how did pagan priests "judge" cases? In Egypt, temple idols were consulted as oracles, not just to prophesy the future, but to solve crimes and settle legal disputes (see chapter 19). Thus, decisions were sometimes rendered by "talking statues."

The practices listed in the previous quotation, which were methods of divination for predicting the future, could also be used to obtain legal judgments. This is why these activities are prohibited in the context of establishing a judicial system. They are called *toevah,* "repugnant abominations," and they made God wipe out the Canaanites. Although we may not learn to *do* them, we may learn *about* them in order to understand them and teach how corrupt they are (Rashi). Let us examine each one.

---

9. Ibid., pp. 80–81.

Stick Divination

A *kosem kesamim* is a person "who seizes one's stick and says, 'Shall I go, or shall I not go?'" (Rashi). People asked advice of their staff, or "divining rod," and believed that it answered them. Maimonides gives a more generic definition and some other examples.

> What is a *kosem*? This refers to a person who performs certain deeds to make oneself fall into a trance and have one's mind cleared of all thoughts until one can predict the future, saying, "This will happen," or "This will not happen," or saying, "It is proper to do such-and-such. Be careful to do so."
> There are some diviners who use sand or stones. Others prostrate themselves on the ground, make strange motions and scream. Others look at a metal or crystal mirror, meditate, and speak. Still others carry a staff and lean on it and tap with it until they fall into a trance and speak. (*Idolatry* 11:6, 11:7)

It is not only forbidden to divine in this way, but also to inquire of such a diviner. Moses and Aharon had a magical staff. It turned into a snake at the burning bush and a crocodile which swallowed up the staffs of Pharaoh's magicians, brought on the first three plagues in Egypt and water out of a rock in the wilderness, and sprouted almond blossoms to show God's choice for the priesthood after Korach's rebellion. In all these cases, the magical effect occurred specifically at God's command and clearly through God's power.

Auspicious Times

A *me'onen* literally means one who divines by cloud (*anan*) patterns. It is generally interpreted as one who predicts whether a certain time (*onah*) is good or bad for any given activity. Another interpretation links it to "eye" (*ayin*) and sees it as one who deceives through optical illusion. R. Shimon said, "It is one who applies seven kinds of semen to one's eye" (San. 65b; Rashi).

Maimonides says it is the use of astrological calculations to determine "good" days, "bad" days, the opportune time to begin a task or to set out on a journey, and so forth. He also mentions delusion through the performance of magical tricks (*Idolatry* 11:8, 11:9). The key factor in astrological divination of "auspicious times" is fatalism. One can determine auspicious times without using astrology, and one can know astrology without using it to determine auspicious times.

A person is not a *me'onen* for believing that planetary motion has some cosmic meaning, for Maimonides himself says that "all the stars and planets have a soul [*nefesh*], knowledge [*de'ah*], and intellect [*haskel*]," and that the knowledge of the stars and planets is greater than that of humans (*Foundations of Torah* 3:9). Both the Talmud and the *Zohar* acknowledge that planetary influences are real but that Israel, through the Torah, rises above them (Shab. 156a; *Zohar* III:216b). Samuel of Nehardea, a talmudic sage, studied astrology at times when he could not study Torah—"when I am in the bathroom" (DR 8:6).

To be a *me'onen*, one must use astrological knowledge in a limiting, fatalistic way—for example, not having a party on a certain night because the moon is in Capricorn, or saying "Our relationship will never work because you're a Gemini and I'm a Scorpio." Even positive planning of events (e.g., picking a wedding date) through the use of an ephemeris can be just as limiting and is forbidden.

The ancient Egyptian calendar labeled each day of the year "very favorable," "mostly favorable," "mostly adverse," or "very adverse," based on the alleged activities of the gods. On bad days, Egyptians were warned such things as, "Anyone born on this day will die of blindness," "Do not go in a boat on this day," "If you see a lion, he will kill you," "Do not leave your house at night," "Do not shout at anyone on this day," "Do not do anything on this day," or "Anyone born on this day will not live." The favorable days were much less varied and more benign, for example, "If you see anything on this day, it will be good."[10] Nothing illustrates better the spiritual enslavement of idolatry.

Many religious Jews believe the following:

> The Nine Days [leading up to Tisha B'Av] in Jewish history [are] replete with tragedy and misfortune, because the *mazal* [lit., "constellation"] of Israel is inauspicious [not favorable] during these days. Therefore, if a Jew has a lawsuit with a non-Jew scheduled for this period, he should try to postpone it until the month of Elul [considered "auspicious" for lawsuits] or at least until after Tisha B'Av.[11]

At what point does such a belief make one a *me'onen*?

Omens

A *menachesh* is a person who finds ominous meaning in the fact that the bread falls out of his mouth, her stick falls out of her hand, his son calls after him, a raven calls after her, a deer crosses his path, a serpent comes at her right hand, or a fox comes at his left. It also includes the use of weasels, birds, and fish to obtain omens (San. 65b–66a).

The Hittites used to ascertain divine will through "extispicy," or deformities in the entrails of sacrificed animals; "augury," the activity of birds; and "some form of lottery [that is] the specialty of certain female soothsayers called simply the 'Old Women.' . . . The Hittites, like the other ancient peoples, always consulted the omens before a military campaign or other important enterprise; but they also applied this traditional lore as a means of ascertaining the cause of a god's anger."[12]

The Babylonians had a very intricate system of examining animal entrails; this is why the Torah required these parts to immediately be burned when an animal was sacrificed. The diviner prayed to the gods to

---

10. Brier, pp. 228–251.
11. Rabbi Shimon D. Eider, *A Summary of the Halachos of the Three Weeks* (Lakewood, NJ: author, 1978), p. 5.
12. Gurney, p. 132.

"write" their message upon the entrails of the sacrificed animal. He then investigates, in traditional sequence, the animal's organs, such as the windpipe, the lungs, the liver, the gall bladder, and the coils in which the intestines are arranged, looking for deviations from normal state, shape, and coloring. Predictions are based on atrophy, hypertrophy, displacement, special markings, and other abnormal features of the organs.[13]

Liver omens were the most common.

The flight patterns or chirping of birds were also commonly "read" for meaning. Modern equivalents of the *menachesh* might be a person who reads tea-leaf patterns or believes it is a bad omen when a black cat crosses one's path.

Maimonides exempts from this prohibition a person who sees a *good* omen in something already completed, "since the person did not perform an act or hold oneself back from performing an act, but only considered something that had already happened as a sign" (*Idolatry* 11:5). Thus, calling a fortunate coincidence "a good omen" is not forbidden.

Sorcery

For a discussion of the *mekhashef*, see chapter 18. In short, it is a person who uses witchcraft or magic to gain influence and control over another.

Incantations

A *chover chaver* is "one who gathers snakes or scorpions or other creatures into one spot" (Rashi). Imprisoning such creatures through charms, spells, and incantations, even to prevent them from biting or stinging, is forbidden (San. 65a). However, a person who has been bitten or stung may recite an incantation over the wound, even on the Sabbath, says Maimonides, "in order to settle one's mind and strengthen one's heart" (*Idolatry* 11:11).

A *chover* uses charms and incantations and casts spells. Maimonides includes in the definition one "who whispers an incantation over a wound and then recites a verse from the Torah, who recites a verse over a baby so it will not become scared, or who places a Torah scroll or *tefillin* over a child so it will sleep" (*Idolatry* 11:12).

Throughout Jewish history, many Jewish people, from kabbalistic Rabbis to peasant women, have used incantations and amulets for protection. Various rationales have been given for these practices.[14]

13. A. Leo Oppenheim, *Ancient Mesopotamia* (Chicago: University of Chicago Press, 1977), p. 212.

14. See T. Schrire, *Hebrew Magic Amulets* (New York: Behrman House, 1982), esp. pp. 12–16, "The Halachic Attitude to Amulets." See also Joshua Trachtenberg, *Jewish Magic and Superstition* (New York: Atheneum, 1977).

Mediums and Oracles

The *ov* and *yidoni* are two forms of possession by spirits of the dead. The *ov* is a spirit named Pitom who speaks from a person's armpit after a corpse has been raised there, while the *yidoni* is the bone of an animal which speaks when put into a person's mouth (Rashi; San. 7:7). The *ov* speaks only from between a person's joints, but the *yidoni* speaks on its own (San. 65b). The Talmud also states that an *ov* is "one who raises [a corpse] with his penis and one who consults a skull."

Raising a corpse with one's penis seems to have included necrophilia, for Rashi's talmudic commentary is, "He raises and sets the corpse on his penis." The corpse conjured up like this is said to rise not "in the normal way" nor on the Sabbath, while a corpse that is raised to consult its skull does rise "in the normal way" and on the Sabbath (San. 65b).

"Why does this day [the Sabbath] differ from all other days?" a Roman governor of Judea once asked. R. Akiva responded by challenging him to raise his father from the dead:

> He went and made a test with his own father; every day he came up, but on the Sabbath he did not come up. After the Sabbath he brought him up. "Father," said [the Roman governor], "have you become a Jew after death? Why did you rise during the whole week but not on the Sabbath?" "One who does not keep the Sabbath among you by free will must keep it here in spite of himself." "But what toil do you have there?" he said. "The whole week we undergo judgment, but on the Sabbath we rest." (GR 11:5)

The ancient practice of consulting a skull was illustrated by Lavan's *terafim* (see chapter 7). The ephod, the apronlike garment worn by the Jewish high priest, atoned for the use of *terafim* (chapter 19). The ephod was the setting for the breastplate containing the *urim* and *tumim*, twelve tribal gemstones, and the Names of God. It, spelled out messages by lighting up. This was the only means by which Israel was ever to "divine" God's Will; it is called *mishpat,* "law" (Ex. 28:30; Num. 27:21).

While the Talmud puts phallic corpse raising and skull consultation under the definition of an *ov*, Rashi calls it necromancy.

Necromancy

A person who attempts to inquire of the dead (e.g., through a seance) is called a necromancer, or *doresh el-hametim*. The Talmud gives the following definition of necromancy: "This is a person who fasts [lit., 'starves himself'] and goes to sleep in a cemetery, so that a spirit of *tumah* will rest upon him" (San. 65b).

Maimonides says it is "a person who fasts and goes to sleep in a cemetery so that the deceased will come in a dream and reply to what is asked. There are others who wear special clothes, say certain words, burn special incense, and sleep alone so that the deceased will come and speak to them in a dream" (*Idolatry* 11:13).

THE JEWISH KING

Jews were different from pagans in not having a divine king. In the pagan world, the king was a god. Born of the goddess in the form of the queen, the king personified the vegetation son. In very ancient times this meant he would be sacrificed; in later times the king's son, another man, or a male animal was substituted (see chapters 6, 15).

After such sacrifices had ceased, the king simply underwent a symbolic suffering, death, and resurrection at the new year festival, when he would be coronated or reenthroned. In Babylonia this was in the spring, from 1 to 11 *Nisan*; this is why *Nisan* is called "the New Year for kings" in the Mishnah (R.H. 1:1). The king's temporary humiliation (e.g., being slapped and having his ears pulled) atoned for the sins of all the people, and the destiny of the entire country for the year, especially its fertility, was fixed at this time.[15]

The Canaanites "had an elaborate worship controlled by the local king. . . . At the larger temples of the Canaanite towns there was a dramatic cult comprising the fights, death, resurrection, and enthronement of the god," who had an "ox-nature," and in which "sexual rites played a great part."[16]

The sexual rites, involving the "sacred marriage" of the god and goddess, were "an important element in early Canaanite ritual." It was enacted by the king and queen—who were sometimes called *kohen*-Ashtarot (or Ashtoret/Astarte) and *kohenet*-Ashtarot—as well as by other priests and priestesses, and it was imitated by the participants in general.[17]

Thus we see why Jews were not supposed to have a king. No human being must ever be worshiped as an embodiment of the divine. Hashem was the only "King"; Rosh Hashanah and Yom Kippur, the Jewish New Year, carried on the themes of annual atonement and the fixing of destiny.

However, God foresaw that the Jews would eventually want to "be like everybody else" by having a king, so the instructions on setting up a judicial system conceded to that by providing one with limitations to remind him he was only human. For instance, even though every Jewish man had to have his own Torah scroll at home, a Jewish king had to write an extra one to keep with him wherever he went as a reminder that he was not superior to other Jews (Deut. 17:14–20).

As with the Jewish priesthood, the sexual element of worship was eliminated in the Jewish kingship by eliminating the female role, the queen. Hence, the Jews could appoint "a king, but not a queen" (Nachmanides). Without a queen, the king could not function as a divine son and consort. Unfortunately, the pagan reason for this prohibition was not kept in mind, and Maimonides ruled that *all* positions of authority in Israel must *always* be filled by men (*Kings and Their Wars* 1:5). This ruling is

---

15. See Engnell for a complete treatment of this subject.
16. Ibid., p. 76.
17. Ibid., pp. 77–78, 103, 130, 160.

still cited by Orthodox men who argue that women may not be political leaders or even synagogue presidents.

The Jewish king could have no more than eighteen wives and concubines (San. 2:4). By ancient standards, this was extremely strict. A pagan king could take any woman he wanted at any time, and he generally did. "It was the custom in Canaan that its kings took for themselves women, whomever they liked, from foreigners and made them their wives."[18]

A woman who was taken into the king's harem—that is, who slept with him once, whether as a wife or as a concubine—could never marry anyone else. This was as true of Jewish kings as pagan kings, according to Maimonides (*Kings and Their Wars* 2:2). Hence, pagan kings' harems consisted of thousands of women, some of whom had sex once in their lives and never again.

Remember, for instance, the story of Purim. Achashverosh, the Persian king, rounded up all the virgins in his empire—which stretched from Ethiopia to India—and, after spending a night with each one, picked Esther from among them to be his queen. Some of the other women who had been captured remained in the primary harem as (secondary) wives or concubines, if the king intended to sleep with them again. The rest of the women were shunted off to the secondary harem (Esther 2:14)—never being called back to sleep with the king again, nor allowed to marry any other man because they had once slept with the king.

The Jewish king was above the rest of Israel in one significant way: "The king can neither judge nor can they judge him; he may not give testimony, nor may testimony be brought against him" (San. 2:2). According to Maimonides, this applied only to the kings of Israel and not to the kings of Judah, because the former "are arrogant and the matter may cause a tragedy and loss to the faith" (*Kings and Their Wars* 3:7). Elsewhere, he says that it is "because they resort to violence and do not submit to the authority of judges" (*Evidence* 11:9). The king was above the court system because "no human being may judge the king, only God" (DR 5:8).

It is consistent and fair that a person who cannot be a judge or a witness in a court may also not be brought to trial by that court. This was the king's status. It is very different from the status of a Jewish woman, who cannot be a judge or a witness in court but *may* be brought to trial by that court. This difference needs to be emphasized, for many rabbis try to rationalize women's exclusion by equating her status with that of the king. This is a very disingenuous argument.

WOMEN AND THE JEWISH COURT

One witness [*ed echad*] shall not testify against a person [*ish*] on any wrongdoing or any sin. . . . A case must be established on the testimony of two witnesses [*edim*] or on the testimony of three witnesses. If a witness of violence testifies falsely against a person

18. Oldenburg, p. 123.

[*ish*], the two men [*anashim*] with strife between them shall stand before Hashem, before the priests and the judges that exist in those days. (Deut. 19:15-17)

We have seen in several instances that *ish* can mean "man" or "person," and its plural, *anashim,* can mean "men" or "people." Although this difference occurs between sentences or sections of the Torah, is it likely to have two different meanings in the same sentence?

The Rabbis apparently believed so, for this is the basis on which they prohibited women from giving testimony in a Jewish court. Although the *ish* is clearly a man or a woman—for it is undisputed that testimony may be brought *against* a woman by two or more witnesses—the *anashim* immediately following supposedly "teaches that there is no testimony by women" (Rashi).

Maimonides disqualifies women as witnesses not through *anashim,* but by *edim,* the masculine form of "witnesses" (*Evidence* 9:2). This is even more absurd, for most of the Torah's commands use the masculine gender as the generic. If Maimonides' logic were applied consistently, 99 percent of the Torah would no longer apply to women! Joseph Caro, author of the *Shulchan Arukh,* noted this.[19]

The exclusion of women from courts was normative in the ancient world. Courts were made by men for men. Babylonian, Egyptian, and Canaanite women did not go to court, nor did Greek women even in later times. Roman women could give testimony in court but could not be witness to a will.[20]

A "woman's testimony" is linguistically an oxymoron, for the etymology of *testimony* (and *testate*) is *testes,* the male reproductive organ. A man would "testify" by placing his hand on one of his testicles and swearing an oath. Precourt examples of this practice are found with Avraham and Eliezer (Gen. 24:2) and Jacob and Joseph (Gen. 47:29). The term "thigh" used in these passages is a euphemism (Kaplan). This practice was eventually replaced with swearing on a "testament," that is, a Torah scroll or *tefillin* (Shevu. 38b) or, for Christians, the Bible.

If women cannot be witnesses, they cannot be judges; since they cannot be judges, they cannot be rabbis. Thus, while the Jewish court system has limited power in the world today, the repercussions of this interpretation are still quite significant. It is the reason there are no female Orthodox rabbis. It is also why three *men* must witness a conversion (halakhically), and two *men* must witness a wedding—a "maid of honor" is not a Jewish tradition. It is why *Sheva Brakhot* (the seven wedding blessings) are recited only by men at an Orthodox wedding and why a *mezuman* (for the Grace After Meals) is made up of three women *only if* there are fewer than three men.

Men in general have used three rationales to exclude women from courts: competency, emotional sensitivity, and privacy. Let us examine each of these in regard to Jewish women.

19. Elon, p. 606.
20. O'Faolain and Martines, p. 62.

Competency

Competency refers to the reliability of a person's testimony. A competent witness must be mentally stable, mature enough to understand what is happening, unbiased, and of trustworthy character. Maimonides lists ten classes of ineligible witnesses: women, slaves, minors, the mentally deficient, the deaf, the blind, transgressors, the "self-abased," relatives of the defendant, and anyone with a vested interest in the case (*Evidence* 9:1).

Some of these people are ineligible because of incompetency while others are ineligible for other reasons. A *tumtum* and a hermaphrodite were included with women, but a eunuch was included with men (*Evidence* 9:3, 9:7). The deaf and the blind were disqualified because oral, not written, testimony was required, as was *hearing* the judge and *seeing* the evidence (*Evidence* 9:11–12).

Mental deficiency is clearly a competency issue. *Self-abased* is defined as those who eat while walking down the street, those who take charity publicly from a non-Jew when they could do so privately, "and those who walk about naked in the street while they are engaged in a repugnant occupation" (*Evidence* 11:5).

A "transgressor" is incompetent because he is untrustworthy. This is not only one who violates a negative commandment but also people who "have taken by force money that does not belong to them" (*Evidence* 10:4). Maimonides lists those who lend or borrow on interest, those who coerce a sale, herdsmen (for their cattle graze in others' fields), those who breed small cattle within Israel (but not those who breed large cattle or outside Israel), tax farmers (tax collectors who keep a profit), pigeon-flyers (who decoy other people's pigeons along with their own), those who sell *Shmitah* produce (which is supposed to be ownerless), and gamblers ("dice-players").

The Mishnah lists only four of these: gamblers, usurers, pigeon-flyers, and *Shmitah* produce-traders (San. 3:3). In discussing who is eligible to give testimony of sighting the New Moon (to set the calendar), the Mishnah again lists these four, plus slaves, and then states, "This is the general principle: All evidence that a woman is not eligible to give, these also are not eligible to give" (R.H. 1:8).

This linkage thus makes it appear as if women are incompetent witnesses. Maimonides fosters this view because he links women and children as *en datan shlemah*—they don't have "complete minds" or "full knowledge" (*Idolatry* 11:16). Elsewhere, he says that women have "poverty of mind" (*Talmud Torah* 1:13). Women's exemption from positive time-bound commandments has also been offered as a rationale for her disqualification as a witness (B.K. 88a).

A woman's credibility is not the real issue, however, for in any case where one witness is sufficient, a woman can be that witness. One witness cannot convict a person in a Jewish court, but "one witness" is the rule throughout the rest of Jewish life and law. Sometimes women did give court testimony. "Women are admitted as competent witnesses in matters within their particular knowledge, for example, on customs or events in places frequented only by women. . . . In post-talmudic times, the evidence of women was often admitted where there were no other witnesses available."[21]

One witness (man or woman) is sufficient to establish that a kitchen is kosher, that meat has been prepared according to the laws of *shechitah*, that one is or is not a *niddah*, or that a girl has or has not attained puberty (defined by two pubic hairs). A midwife's word is accepted on which twin is the firstborn, a woman who claims to be the mother of an abandoned baby is believed, and if several women sleep together in a bed and blood is found, as soon as one says she is menstruating, the others are presumed to be *tahor* (GR 85:13).

Only one witness was required to make an accused wife either undergo *sotah* or not undergo it. A woman was permitted to remarry on the testimony of one witness that her husband was dead. The River Heifer was not slaughtered if there was one witness to the murder, according to Maimonides (*Evidence* 5:2).

In spite of this, the issue of women's credibility is not completely absent from rabbinic dialogue. Regarding *niddah* and puberty, the Rabbis say, "A woman is trusted *(ne'emenet ishah)* " (Nid. 20b, 48b)—which implies, intentionally or not, that trust *is* the issue! Even in these cases, her testimony is only valid if it restricts rather than relaxes the law. Thus, a woman's testimony can be used to *deny* an eleven-year-old girl the right to perform *miun* or *chalitzah* but not to *permit* the girl to do either.

Emotional Sensitivity

A universal belief that women are too "emotionally sensitive" for court proceedings is as old as written history. As late as 1873 c.e., the U.S. Supreme Court upheld an Illinois decision denying Myra Bradwell admission to the bar by using this argument: "The natural and proper timidity and delicacy which belongs to the female sex evidently unfits it for many of the occupations of civil life."[22]

Although Bradwell had successfully proved that male-gender language frequently includes women, the Illinois Court had ruled against her on the grounds that "God designed the sexes to occupy different spheres of action," and that the courtroom atmosphere might "tend to destroy the deference and delicacy with which it is the pride of our ruder sex to treat her."[23]

More than a century later, Orthodox Jewish men are still asserting the same drivel. Citing "divine decree," one author writes:

> The essentially private role of women in Jewish life is not one that is consonant with the public role of the witness in court. . . . The feminine sensitivity does not lend itself to the stresses of public testimony and the associated rigorous examination, close questioning, and cross-examination. . . . Judaism considered it imperative that the woman not be placed

21. Elon, p. 606.
22. *In re Bradwell*, 55 Ill. Sup. Ct. Rep. 535, quoted in Karen Berger Morello, *The Invisible Bar* (New York: Random House, 1986), p. 20.
23. Ibid., pp. 16, 18.

in a position where she would be obligated to perform an act that would be in conflict with her nature. She is too sensitive to take personal part in an execution.[24]

Women who have killed their batterers or rapists might disagree with that last point. Female sensitivity is being *used against* women in this argument, perhaps because so many men mistakenly equate it with a lack of strength, endurance, or stamina.

Privacy

The privacy argument is very much related to the sensitivity argument. Because women are so sensitive (delicate, fragile, etc.), it follows that they must be "protected" from the harsh public realm. Thus "man's role is to confront the external sphere of existence, woman's is to direct the inner sphere, the one relating to the home."[25]

It is one thing to appreciate and value women's domestic tasks and nurturing abilities; it is quite another to use that as an excuse to *restrict* women to the home. We have already discussed the dangers and double standards inherent in the seclusion of women. "The glory of the king's daughter is within her" (Psalm 45:14)—rabbinically interpreted to mean that women should stay at home—is cited by the Talmud as the reason why a woman may not testify in court (Shevu. 30a).

Recall the Illinois court's statement that men (the "ruder sex") tend to drop all pretense of chivalry in the courtroom. Because making a woman wait in a crowd of men was deemed to cheapen and disgrace her *(zilutah)*, the Talmud teaches that a woman is always to be taken care of first in any public arena—for example, the distribution of tithes on the threshing floor or the hearing of lawsuits in a court. A woman's case was to be heard before a man's (Yev. 100a). Even where it is necessary for a woman to go to court to get financial support for her child from its father, her first husband, the Talmud maintains that she would be so ashamed to go to court that she would "kill" her child—that is, she would let it die rather than undergo the ordeal of a lawsuit (Yev. 42b).

All this says nothing about women; it says a great deal, however, about *men's behavior toward* women. If a woman is disgraced and cheapened by being in a crowd of men, it is because the men disgrace and cheapen her—by looking her up and down, calling her "sweetie," smacking their lips at her, or making obscene remarks and unwanted sexual advances. If the men treat her respectfully, there *is* no disgrace!

Thus, once again a restriction has been imposed on *women* as a means of controlling *men*, namely, by, minimizing their opportunities to be crude and obnoxious in front of "the ladies." This is like restricting Jews in order to "protect" them from anti-Semitism. Historically, Christian pogroms could be prevented by legislating that Jews must stay indoors the week before Easter; however, that actually *legitimizes and reinforces* the violence of the anti-Semites, for it puts the onus on the victim and leaves the perpetrator free to roam at will.

---

24. Kaufman, pp. 200–201.
25. Ibid., p. 26.

In 1876, a Wisconsin court ruled that Lavinia Goodell could not be a lawyer.[26] "The peculiar qualities of womanhood, its gentle graces, its quick sensibility, its tender susceptibility, its purity, its delicacy, its emotional impulses, its subordination of hard reason to sympathetic feelings, are surely not qualifications for forensic strife. . . . Woman is modeled for gentler and better things," the judge asserted. Since a court deals with "all that is selfish and extortionate, knavish and criminal, coarse and brutal, repulsive and obscene in human life," then "it would be revolting to all female sense of innocence and sanctity for their sex. . . . Reverence for all womanhood would suffer in the public spectacle of woman so interested and so engaged." For women to be present at discussions "unfit for female ears . . . would tend to relax the public sense of decency and propriety."

A Wisconsin newspaper wisely responded, "If her purity is in danger, it would be better to reconstruct the court and bar than to exclude the women."

The same may be said of the Jewish court. If it is too degrading for a woman to be there, that is no justification for keeping women out; rather, it is an argument for holding men accountable for their own behavior. If that fails, then perhaps men should be kept at home and women should run the court system! All the qualities cited to exclude the female sex would no doubt immensely enhance the execution of justice.

Justice, justice you shall pursue.

---

26. *In re Goodell*, 39 Wis. 232, quoted in Morello, p. 25.

✻✻✻ 46 ✻✻✻

The Captured Woman

Ki Tetze (21:10–25:19)

The "captured woman" is the theme of *Parshat Ki Tetze*. Thirteen situations of female captivity are addressed:

1. a war captive;
2. a hated wife whose firstborn is her husband's (patrilineal) firstborn;
3. a mother whose adolescent son is out of control;
4. a female transvestite;
5. a mother bird whose eggs are taken from her nest by a human;
6. a new bride who is supposed to be made happy by her husband, but instead he hates her and accuses her of not being a virgin in order to defame her;
7. an adulteress caught in the act;
8. a rape victim;
9. a father's wife (whose stepson has his eye on her);
10. a prostitute;
11. a woman divorced by her husband;
12. a widow; and
13. a woman who grabs a man's testicles in a fight.

In most of these cases, the nature of the entrapment is fairly evident.

Ki Tetze contains many laws whose fundamental principle is respect and concern for others. A corpse must be buried on the day of death, a lost article must be returned to its owner, a fallen animal must be helped, and a guardrail must be built on one's roof. Species may not be interbred, runaway slaves must be given refuge, and interest may not be charged between Jews. Farmworkers may eat as they harvest crops, wages must be paid on time, and harvesters must leave fallen sheaves and the corners of the field for the poor. Even the ox may not be muzzled while it threshes. Morever, all weights and measures must be fair and honest.

455

This is clearly not a law code that exploits the oppressed. Sympathetic laws for all other groups (slaves, workers, the poor, animals, and even a corpse) are not likely to be interspersed with sanctions to abuse women. The laws regarding women are indeed sympathetic to female oppression, but in ways which are difficult to see from a modern perspective, especially when rabbinic interpretations are misogynist. Thus, to understand each issue, we must (1) view it within its pagan context, and (2) distinguish rabbinic sexism, where it exists, from the Torah itself.

Levirate marriage is a good example of the importance of pagan context. Widows are an impoverished population vulnerable to exploitation. *Ki Tetze* forbids taking a widow's clothes as security for a loan (Deut. 24:17), yet it also requires her to marry her brother-in-law if she is childless (Deut. 25:5–10). This was a pagan practice; the Torah did not invent it and, in fact, limited it severely (see chapter 9). In the Torah's version of levirate marriage, a man could only marry his *brother's* widow, and not the widow of his father, son, or uncle.

His father's widows are specifically prohibited here (Deut. 23:1), for it was normative in the pagan world for a son to "inherit" his father's harem upon the latter's death. According to R. Judah, the prohibition on a father's "wives" extended to any women with whom he had sex, whether it was rape or premarital sex (Yev. 11:1). The uncle's widows are also included in the prohibition (Rashi).

The female war captive is a good example of the distinction to be made between Torah law and rabbinic sexism.

RAPE IN WARFARE

When you go out to war against your enemies and Hashem your God gives them into your hands, you will capture captives. If you see among the captives a woman of beautiful form [*yefat-toar*] and lust for [*chashak*] her and would take her for a wife, you shall bring her into the midst of your house.

She shall shave her head and do her nails, remove the clothing of captivity from herself, and stay in your house and weep for her father and her mother a month [lit., 'moon days']. After that you shall come to her and be her husband, and she shall be your wife.

If you no longer desire [*chafatz*] her, you must set her free [lit., 'send her away for herself']. You may not sell her for money or treat her harshly, for you have violated her [*initah*]. (Deut. 21:10–14)

This passage appears at first to be cruel. God seems to be sanctioning the abduction and rape of women conquered in warfare. Instead of telling men *not* to do it, the Torah is telling men *how* to do it. Why is this so?

The Torah's Strategy

The Torah says: "*When* you go out to war and capture captives . . ." It therefore assumes an already existing reality. It has been a universal practice, from ancient times down to the present, for soldiers victorious in warfare to take the "spoils" of the conquered people, and this includes raping the women.

"In the name of victory and in the power of the gun, war provides men with a tacit license to rape. In the act and in the excuse, rape in war reveals the male psyche in its boldest form, without the veneer of 'chivalry' or civilization."[1] The captive woman's total vulnerability as a member of the conquered people gives the victorious soldier the license to extend his conquest to sexual domination as well.

His urge for sexual domination is called *chashak,* meaning "to press, tie, surround, to be attached to" (Jastrow). The term clearly implies pressure, trapping, binding. The description of the woman as a "beautiful form" (*yefat-toar*) refers to her treatment as a sexual object. Any "beauty" is sheerly in the eyes of the beholder (Ibn Ezra). The law applies "even if she is ugly" (Nachmanides).

This is the closest the commentators come to understanding that domination, and not sexual attraction, is the motivating force behind rape. The woman's looks are irrelevant. Any woman, even a grandmother or a little girl, is vulnerable to becoming a *yefat toar*, a woman abducted in warfare.

Battlefield rapists are like gang rapists. Indeed, military rape is the ultimate gang rape, the biggest "fraternity bash" of all. Studies of gang-rapists have shown that they are not usually rapists in their individual lives, but the male bonding, bravado, and peer pressure of the situation creates a mob mentality. The soldier who rapes is not likely to be a rapist in his civilian life. Herein lies the key to the Torah's solution.

The Torah understands that simply *telling soldiers not to rape would be useless*, so instead, it set up a system that "postponed" the rape by allowing the soldier, in the lust of victory, to think he would get to do it later. After a month back in his civilian life, it was very likely that "in cool blood he would altogether recoil from his intentions."[2]

The Jewish soldier could do nothing to a woman on the battlefield. He had to take her home and he could only take one woman for himself: not more than one and not one for anybody else (his father, brother, son, etc.). He could also not capture any Canaanite women in the Land of Israel, for they were under *cherem* (Rashi).

Taking the *yefat toar* home, where the soldier probably already had a wife and children, gave his warfare mentality a chance to subside. It is stated that he must bring the captive woman "into the midst of" his house. She had to live in *his* part of the house—not in the harem, the women's quarters—so that he would come in contact with her every day (Rashi).

This was in order to humanize the *yefat toar* to the soldier. In warfare the enemy is dehumanized; in rape the victim is dehumanized; thus the *yefat toar* is doubly dehumanized. The soldier can only do what he does to her because she is "the enemy." After a month of being back in his normal peacetime environment and seeing the woman every day in *that* setting, the chances were quite good that he would lose the impulse to violate her humanity in this way.

---

1. Brownmiller, p. 32–33.
2. Soncino, *Kiddushin,* p. 104 n. 6.

The Torah's delaying tactics work precisely because rape involves domination and not attraction. However, many commentators miss the point, and misinterpret the Torah's rules as being connected to the woman's looks.

Rashi claims that pagan women "adorned" themselves to seduce enemy soldiers—but the Torah is talking about the rape of conquered women, *not* prostitution in warfare! These are two different phenomena (although they are related in terms of women being used to "service" men at war). Even the prettiest women of a people just conquered are not exactly at their most glamorous. They are generally distressed, disheveled, starving, and scared. Far from wanting to "lure" soldiers, female survivors are usually huddled in hiding, hoping fervently that enemy soldiers will *not* find them.

Rashi also asserts that the reason why the *yefat toar* must live in the man's part of the house is so "he sees her endless crying, he sees her disheveled appearance, so she becomes repulsive to him." He continues this line of thinking by playing on women's feelings of rivalry with each other under polygyny. The captured pagan woman is given time to mourn, he claims, only in order to contrast her to the soldier's wife: "The Jewish woman is happy while the other [the *yefat toar*] is sad; the Jewish woman adorns herself while the other neglects her appearance."

Maimonides (*Kings and Their Wars* 8:5) agrees. He and Rashi both interpret shaving her head and "doing" her nails according to the "attraction" theory, claiming she *grows* her nails in order to become "repulsive." Nachmanides shows the fallacy of this logic by pointing out that long nails are generally considered to be attractive to men, not repulsive.

Nachmanides (citing a discussion in Yev. 48a) says she *cuts* her nails—which, along with head-shaving and a thirty-day period, were mourning customs. A month of mourning is required, not to make her "repulsive," nor even out of compassion for her losing her family, he maintains, but "because she is leaving her religion and joining another people." It serves purely "to eliminate the names of idols from her mouth and from her heart." If she immediately renounces idolatry, there is no need to wait a month.

The *yefat toar* underwent a change in status similar to the Canaanite slave in a Jewish household. Any gentile war captive, in order to be set free and live in the Land of Israel, had to renounce idolatry and accept the Noachide laws. However, to stay and live in a Jewish household, he or she had to go to the *mikvah* and keep most of the commandments (see chapter 18).

Like the Hivite captives who entered Jacob's household, the *yefat toar* had to "change her clothes"—which means ritual immersion. Even in modern times, this is preceded by nail cutting. Shaving the head before immersion was part of the Levites' initiation rite (Num. 8:7), as well as the *metzora's* return to the camp after isolation (Lev. 14:8).

The *yefat toar* could not be kept as a concubine or a domestic servant, nor be sold in the slave market, which was the standard means of "disposal" of war captives in the ancient world. Like the Jewish maidservant, the *yefat toar* had to be given all the rights of a wife (after converting) or be set free (as a Noachide).

Her captor is told by the Torah, "you have violated her." That in itself was no doubt new to men's ears. "What do you mean I violated her? I just did what any red-blooded male would do," one can just hear these men protest. The root of "violated" is *anat*, ענה, which is the name of the vengeful Canaanite goddess raped by her father and her brother. It is the same verb used to describe the rape of Dinah (Gen. 34:2) and the Egyptian oppression of the Jews (Ex. 1:11–12, 3:7).

Rabbinic Concessions

The Torah's strategy of gaining freedom for the *yefat toar*—as a Noachide or a willing Jew—would have worked in theory, given the nature of male psychology. However, in practice there was one major hindrance—male interpretation.

All the Rabbis gave license for some form of coercion. Some allowed the soldier to rape the woman immediately, despite the Torah's instructions to the contrary, while even those who did not said she could be forcibly converted. Thus, one way or another, she was coerced, contrary to the Torah's intent.

Nachmanides believed that the *yefat toar* could be "converted against her will. No one asks her whether she desires to leave her religion and become Jewish, as is usually done with converts. Instead the *baal* [her captor] tells her that she must keep the Torah of Israel against her will."

Maimonides, on the other hand, said she could not be forced to convert (*Kings and Their Wars* 8:7). However, he only gives the woman this leniency because *he has already permitted the soldier to rape her*! His view follows an opinion expressed in the Babylonian Talmud (Kid. 21b–22a), allegedly by Rav.

The Rabbis considered the laws of the *yefat toar* to be a "concession" to men's *yetzer hara*, or evil inclination. They compared it to ritually slaughtering a dying animal in order to eat its meat. While a Jew is prohibited from eating *any* dying animal, ritually slaughtering one prior to its death is preferable to eating it as *nevelah*, after it has already died on its own. The notion that one prohibition is "preferable" to the other is based on the realistic assumption that the person is going to do the forbidden act regardless.

Maimonides (8:1) permits a Jewish soldier to eat *nevelah*, *trefah*, or even pork if that is all he can find to eat. Necessity is broadly defined, however; a person does not "need" wine, yet Maimonides permits a Jewish soldier to drink wine that has been dedicated to an idol! An analogy with male sexual gratification follows (8:2), in which the age-old excuse of the rapist is reiterated—his passion "overpowers" him and he just cannot "control" himself.

The Rabbis who give the soldier license to rape immediately operate on a technicality. They agree that he cannot do it *on the battlefield*, but once he gets her *back to his house* he can—this is their interpretation of bringing her into the "midst" of his house. What a loophole this provides! Only *after* this initial act of rape does the monthlong period begin, they claim. In this view, a *kohen* was permitted to rape a captive woman but forbidden to marry her later. (Here Samuel, a colleague of Rav, disagrees.)

Nachmanides, the proponent of forced conversion, insists that she cannot be raped immediately. He cites the Jerusalem Talmud (Mak. 2:6), where R. Jochanan accuses the Babylonian Rabbis of saying "things in the name of Rav which are not so," and emphasizes that no sex may take place until the man has complied with all the regulations, which means waiting a month.

We have here an incredible example of how a Torah policy that was meant to help women can be undermined by men. Allowing the soldier to rape the woman in the house *before* the thirty days begins sabotages the Torah's whole purpose of protecting women from battlefield rape! R. Jochanan's accusation shows quite clearly that the rabbinate has included men who, in the name of a "concession to the evil inclination," were merely conceding to their own.

However, even forced conversion is problematic. How many of our "Jewish foremothers" were originally captured pagan women? It is a discomforting thought, and highly ironic in light of the amount of rabbinic resistance to conversion in modern times.

The Rabbis did agree that setting the *yefat toar* free was preferable to marrying her. For a man who marries a woman he has abducted will come to hate her, says Rashi. (Does he not hate her already?) This is why the topic of the captive woman is followed by that of the hated wife (Deut. 21:15–17). If a man has two wives, one he loves and one he hates, and the hated wife is the mother of a patrilineal firstborn son (see chapter 15), the man cannot usurp that son's inheritance rights in favor of a firstborn son of the loved wife.

This topic is then followed by the rowdy son, who is so out of control that he may be put to death if *both* his mother and his father agree to it (Deut. 21:18–21). This juxtaposition shows that a man who has abducted his wife and hates her is likely to have such sons (Rashi). Children who are products of coerced sex will somehow bear the imprint of that violence.

King David is said to have had four hundred sons by *yefat toar*s. (He, like King Solomon, apparently did not obey the Torah rule limiting him to eighteen women in his harem. Nor could he have obeyed the Torah's one-woman rule of capture, unless he fought *many* battles!) These sons all wore their hair in pagan style, drove gold chariots, and were "the strong men" of David's army, who were sent out to terrorize enemy forces (San. 21a; Kid. 76b).

VIRGINITY AND THE DEFAMED BRIDE

If a man marries a woman and comes to her and hates her, bringing false charges against her and defaming her, saying, ". . . I have not found her to be a virgin." (Deut. 22:13–14)

A new bride is supposed to be "gladdened" by her groom. For that reason, a married man may not be called for army service in the first year after the wedding. A betrothed man cannot be put into combat but only supply food and water or repair the roads (Deut. 20:7, 24:5; Rashi). The war against the Canaanites was an exception; in that case "all [went] forth, even a bridegroom from his chamber and a bride from her canopy" (Sot. 8:7).

However, the Torah also addresses another possible reality for a new bride: Her husband hates her and falsely accuses her of not being a virgin on their wedding night. *The Torah's wording makes it very clear that the woman is innocent.* If he claims she lost her virginity *after* their betrothal, he is falsely accusing her of adultery. If he claims it happened *before* their betrothal, he is falsely accusing her of premarital sex.

A woman who *really did* commit adultery—whether after *erusin* or after *nesuin*—is discussed in other verses (Deut. 22:20–24). This includes three situations: an *erusah* who is caught with her lover, a *nesuah* who is caught with her lover, and a *nesuah* whose husband accuses her of not being a virgin and produces two witnesses who saw her have sex with another man *after erusin.*

We have noted, in discussing *sotah* (chapter 32), that witnesses to actual sexual activity were probably quite rare. Nevertheless, only if there were such witnesses, with no one to refute their testimony, were the adulteress and her lover executed. Once capital and corporal punishments were abolished in Judaism, an adulteress was simply forbidden to her husband and divorced without her *ketubah.*

A fourth situation—a *nesuah* whose husband accuses her of not being a virgin and produces two witnesses who saw her have sex *before erusin*—was treated differently, for this was premarital sex and not adultery. Reflecting the value that men have traditionally (and obsessively) placed on virginity, the Rabbis set the *ketubah* of a virgin at two hundred *zuzim* and the *ketubah* of a nonvirgin at one hundred *zuzim.* The definition of a *virgin* was marital and not sexual: a woman never married before was presumed to be a virgin, while a widow and a divorcee were presumed to not be virgins.

An accused bride who *really did* have premarital sex had her *ketubah* reduced from two hundred to one hundred *zuzim,* but the couple could still remain married (Ket. 11b). The premarital sexual activity of a woman was not a punishable offense; it simply reduced her marriage "market value."

Those are the four cases involving a woman who really did commit the sexual activity of which she was accused. Now let us return to the innocent bride who is defamed by her hateful husband. The Torah instructs her parents to take "the signs of virginity," *betulim,* to the elders, who make up a court of twenty-three judges (San. 1:1). The "signs" referred to the bedsheet *(sudar)* with hymeneal blood on it (Ket. 6b, 10a). One view unconvincingly claims that this was just a figurative expression for witnesses on her behalf, so that "the matter is made as clear as a new garment" (Ket. 46a).

The public display of the bedsheet after the wedding night has been a common custom throughout the world that originated in pagan times and still survives in parts of the world today. In one view, "the hymeneal blood [is] exhibited so that the demonic effects of this blood can be charmed away by magical defense measures."[3]

---

3. Nemecek, pp. 43–44.

Great importance is attached to the demonstration among Semitic peoples. Among the Bedawi [Bedouin] it used to be the rule to hang the bloodstained cloth bearing the proofs of the bride's virginity on a lance in the middle of the camp or village, and to leave it there for several days. Throughout Egypt and the Sudan, those "proofs" are obtained by digital defloration. . . . The proofs were in every case exhibited to the guests, hung out of the window, or carried in triumph to neighbors' houses. . . .

The public exhibition of the "proofs of virginity" was until lately customary among the peasantry in most countries of southern Europe. In Greece the bride's nightgown was left hanging for some days at the window, and the same custom obtained in Sicily.[4]

That the hymen can be broken without shedding blood or in ways other than through sex is completely denied by those who practice this degrading custom. In most of the modern Arab world, "if there was no blood, a girl would be disgraced and returned to her father. . . . Bloodied sheets are still proudly handed to the mother-in-law of the bride so that she can show friends and relatives that a woman of honor and purity has joined her family."[5]

The consequences for women of not having hymeneal blood to show have been so severe that many have resorted to extreme measures to fool their husbands—plastic surgery, setting the wedding date at menstruation, or even placing a small bag of chicken blood or a sheep's liver inside their vaginas![6] The women's cleverness and the men's gullibility would be quite amusing if the former's desperation were not so painfully sad.

The Torah limited the custom by requiring an exhibition only when a woman was accused. Both parents brought the "evidence" to court. The mother was "a partner in this affair because women occupy themselves with the subject of the sheet, for it is they who are knowledgeable and expert in blood, and it is proper for the mother to take hold and bring it to court" (Nachmanides).

However, because only the father is described as speaking to the elders, Rashi makes a grand leap that *as a general rule* a woman is not allowed to do the talking when she and her husband bring a case together! From this, the Rabbis also conclude that a father, but not a mother, can betroth a minor daughter without her consent (Sot. 23b).

The court flogged the defamer and fined him one hundred shekels. This fine applied only if the bride was a *naarah* and not a minor (Ket. 40b), and was the same regardless of her social status, whether she be "the greatest of the priesthood or the least of Israel" (Arak. 3:5).

Although it is perfectly clear that the Torah is discussing an innocent woman, the Rabbis do the same thing to her that they did in *sotah*: they presume her guilty until proven innocent. Rashi calls her "evil," and Silbermann reinforces this misogyny: "Although it has not yet been proved that she is guilty, the fact that the husband dares to suspect her of unchastity shows that her character cannot be faultless. 'There is no

4. Briffault, 3: 342–343.
5. Sasson, p. 180.
6. Ibid., pp. 180–181; Wikan, p. 224.

smoke without fire'!"[7] This blame-the-victim mentality completely ignores the Torah's statement that the husband is motivated by hatred—that *his* character is not faultless! Imagine if such logic were applied to anti-Semites' accusations against Jews!

The Gemara asserts that a man is believed when he says, "I have found an open opening" (Ket. 9a–10a)—that is, because penetration was not difficult, the woman must not be a virgin! This view is based on the phallic fallacy that "a man is able to state with certainty that a woman is not a virgin on the basis of his subjective experience during sexual intercourse."[8]

It is suggested that when a charge is brought by a man who has never been married before, he should be believed but also should be flogged because he must have gotten his knowledge from going to prostitutes (10a). A Judean man could not bring a charge at all because it was customary there for couples to be alone together during *erusin*—so if she was not a virgin, *he* was suspected (12a).

Four cases brought to R. Gamliel are discussed (10a–b). In one, he suggested to the man that he must have penetrated without breaking the hymen. In another, he washed the sheet and discovered that the man's semen had covered up the woman's blood. In a third case, he found that the woman came from a family where none of the women menstruated or had hymeneal blood. In a fourth case, he tested the woman by sitting her on a cask of wine. He had discovered, he claimed, by experimenting with two gentile slavewomen, that the smell of wine spreads through the body of a nonvirgin but not of a virgin. When asked why he first tried the procedure on non-Jewish women, R. Gamliel replied that until he was certain the test was valid, "it would not be proper to deal lightly with the daughters of Israel."

In general, however, the Rabbis believed men more than women. "The husband claims he is sure that his wife was not a virgin, and the wife claims with equal conviction that her virginity was intact. Thus, *there is no reason* to favor the wife's claim over that of the husband, and the husband is believed to make her forbidden to him [as an adulteress], for a person is believed when he declares that something is forbidden to himself [emphasis mine]."[9]

How can there be "no reason"? What about the hatred *the Torah says* he has for her? He wants to get rid of her without paying her *ketubah* (Nachmanides). Yet another view ignores—indeed, denies—the Torah's assertion by claiming that no man would go to the trouble of preparing a wedding feast only to waste the money he spent by making up a lie (10a). This shows a great deal of naivete about the nature of abusive husbands.

In a catch 22 dilemma, the woman was believed only if she admitted she was *not* a virgin. Then, if she said it was due to premarital sex or rape (rather than adultery), her word was taken. Many innocent women would have been backed into a corner this way—in other words, they would be better off lying than being honest! Unless

---

7. Silbermann, 5: 110 n. 2.

8. *The Talmud: The Steinsaltz Edition,* vol. 7, *Tractate Ketubot*, pt. 1 (New York: Random House, 1991), p. 106.

9. Ibid., p. 107.

a woman were married to a *kohen*, she would also be better off saying it was rape rather than premarital sex. The same men who set up a situation that encouraged a woman to lie about rape would no doubt be very quick to condemn her for doing so.

We have here an excellent illustration of the danger inherent in an all-male rabbinate. These Rabbis certainly *intended* to be fair. It would be absolutely wrong to accuse them of malicious cruelty toward women or of purposely twisting the Torah. It simply shows that even men with good intentions can be blinded by ignorance and unconscious male bias.

THE RAPE VICTIM

The Torah's next topic is the *anusah*, the rape victim. A distinction is made between whether the *anusah* is married or not. The Torah appears to be participating in the misogynist notion that rape is a crime against the man who "owns" the woman's sexuality, rather than against the woman herself. In fact, it simply reflects the depth of women's oppression in the ancient world.

First, a distinction is made between the seduction (i.e., adultery) and the rape of a betrothed girl. While the *erusah* is discussed, the same laws certainly applied to a *nesuah*. Because of the former's "in-between" status—she is technically married but still living in her father's house and not yet sleeping with her husband—perhaps her case needed special clarification.

If an *erusah* had consensual sex with a man other than her betrothed, that was adultery and both she and her lover were put to death. The Torah describes this situation as "a man finds her in the city and lies with her" (Deut. 22:23–24).

If an *erusah* was raped, the rapist was executed, for his crime was on the same level as murder. The Torah describes this situation as "a man finds [her] in the field, seizes her, and lies with her" (22:25–27). The word *seizes* (*hechezik*) indicates the woman's resistance, and is the key to distinguishing rape from consensual sex in these passages. Also significant are the phrases "in the city"—where the woman might be saved if she cried for help—and "in the field"—where there would be no one around to come to her aid even if she did scream. These phrases are meant to be symbolic.

A woman can certainly be raped in a city (or have consensual sex in a field). However, if the rapist is holding a knife to her throat, or has gagged her, she cannot cry out. Some women open their mouths to scream, but nothing comes out because their voices are paralyzed with terror. Thus, the Torah only mentions "crying out" as "the common case," and *not as a literal criterion* (Nachmanides).

Rashi seems to mistake the consensual sex for rape and then blames the victim. Because the man found a woman outdoors in the city, "therefore he lay with her. A breach invites the thief. If she had stayed at home ['as becomes a chaste Jewish girl,' Silbermann takes the liberty of adding[10]], this would not have happened to her."

---

10. Silbermann inserts these words in his translation of Rashi's commentary on Deut. 22:23 (Silbermann 5:112).

The Torah then deals with the rape of a girl who was not betrothed (Deut. 22:28–29). The seduction of an unmarried girl was discussed in Exodus (see chapter 18). The rape of an unmarried girl was not a capital crime; hence, this rapist was not executed. Instead, he paid four fines—the same three that the seducer paid, plus an additional one for the pain he inflicted. Unlike the seducer, the rapist could be forced to marry his victim—against *his* will, but not against *hers.*

> Either the girl or her father can withhold consent, for it is not proper that he should marry her against her will, and do two evils to her. Sometimes she may be of a more honorable family than he, and it is inconceivable that she should be further disgraced by his sinful act. The proper law is that the decision of marriage be left up to her and not up to him . . . so that violent men should not take liberties with the daughters of Israel. (Nachmanides)

As strange as it may sound to us today, the notion that the rape victim could choose *not* to marry her rapist was a radical one, for in ancient Canaan, rape was a typical means by which wives were acquired: "Marriage conventions [in Canaan] are particularly well attested. The Krt legend [from the Ras Shamra tablets], depicting the royal wooing as a military expedition to besiege the stronghold of the bride's father, preserves the tradition of marriage by force, which survives in the Arab idiom of 'snatching the bride.'"[11]

Another scholar gives a similar account:

> "The military expedition" is . . . the manifestation merely of the well-known rite of "marriage-by-capture." . . . The idea of the bride having to cut off every bond uniting her with her own family in order to be completely incorporated in that of her husband finds its legendary expression in a tale of the dynasty founder's robbing his wife from her father's house through martial violence.[12]

Remember Dinah's experience in Canaan. What Shechem did to her was typical, especially for a prince. "It is usually the sons of prominent families who rape the daughters of those less-known families who have no power against them" (Nachmanides). After raping her, Shechem *expected* to marry her, and he saw nothing wrong or unusual in this behavior. However, although marriage by rape was acceptable in Canaan, it was "an obscenity in Israel" (Gen. 34:7).

Remember, too, how Dinah did not want to leave Shechem's palace, and had to be kidnapped by her brothers. Women were so oppressed that marriage to one's rapist saved the victim from an even worse fate—unmarriageability. In a society where there is no place for women except as wives and mothers, to be unmarried is an even worse fate than being barren! Dinah never was married and lived with her brother the rest of her life. There was no other option for her in that era.

---

11. Gray, *The Canaanites,* p. 113.
12. Engnell, pp. 146–147.

Today, thankfully, women have come far enough that there are other options after being raped. No modern rabbi, even the most sexist, would ever recommend that an *anusah* marry her perpetrator! This is an indication of how the Torah is meant to be flexible enough to keep up with the evolution of human consciousness.

DIVORCE

The Torah states that if a man wishes to divorce his wife, he must "write her a bill of divorce and place it in her hand, and send her away from his house" (Deut. 24:1).

In the pagan world, a man divorced his wife by verbally dismissing her. This is still true in modern Islam. A Moslem man simply says, "I divorce you" three times in the presence of two male witnesses, and the woman is divorced. She cannot contest it, nor can she initiate any similar proceeding against him.

In Deuteronomy 24:1, the Torah is clearly describing divorce in a time when it was a unilateral right of men. Does this mean, however, that the Torah *wants* divorce to be a unilateral right of men? The Orthodox rabbinate appears to think so, for the absence of any reverse command—what a woman must do to divorce a man—is interpreted quite literally to indicate that there *is* no way.

This makes it very difficult for a woman to divorce an abusive husband who will not let her go even though he hates her. Indeed, women do not *divorce* men in Judaism; women *are divorced by* men. The rabbinic interpretation requires the man to initiate and the woman to receive, along the traditional sexist stereotypes of active male, passive female.

The *agunah*—the "chained wife," the woman who cannot get a divorce because her husband will not give her one—is probably the most pressing halakhic problem in modern Judaism. There are thousands of such women in the Jewish community today. Their plight is not just that they cannot remarry, for even if they do not want to, they are still subjected to blackmail by their husbands. Many women have gotten their *gets* (divorce documents) only by forfeiting their houses, furniture, bank accounts, and child support payments. The use of prenuptial agreements may help to prevent the problem in the future, but it does nothing for the women who are already *agunot*.

The Rabbis did empower a *bet din* to force a man to give a woman a *get*, but it had to be done in a roundabout way—"They press him until he says, 'I wish to do it'" (Rashi on Lev. 1:3). Beating him up, boycotting his business, refusing him synagogue honors, or (in Israel) revoking certain civil rights, such as holding a driver's license or being elected to public office, may indeed make him "want" to give the *get*. However, the validity of a *get* given under the slightest duress remains highly disputed.

Theoretically, a woman can also refuse to receive a *get* and thus can prevent her husband from obtaining the divorce he wants. However, the Rabbis were able to find a loophole. The man need only get the signatures of one hundred rabbis and he will have his divorce. Due to the polygynous definition of adultery as a married *woman's* unfaithfulness, even if he remarries without a Jewish divorce, his children are not *mamzers*, while the children of a woman who remarries without a Jewish divorce *are*. Thus, a man cannot be trapped by a marriage as a woman can. *Is this the Torah speaking?*

All the solutions that have been proposed to help the *agunah* are doomed to fail, for they keep her dependent on the goodwill of men—either her husband or the Rabbis. As long as the woman is kept in the position of passive recipient in divorce, marriage will be a potential prison for her—she can get in but she may never get out!

Only by empowering the woman to give a *get* can this change. The Rabbis will say this cannot be done, it is "against the Torah." However, making divorce mutual rather than unilateral is no more "against the Torah" than is eliminating the practices of bride-price and marrying one's rapist. The Rabbis allowed these innovations in spite of specific Torah verses, because they understood the legitimacy of social changes which upgraded women's status.

Once again, the pagan context provides a means by which to understand the Torah's intent. The Torah was given in a world where a man could divorce his wife on a whim. Requiring him to *write* a bill of divorce was a big step in protecting women, for a written document takes forethought and cannot be done in the impulsive heat of anger, as a verbal dismissal can. How ironic that a Torah law meant to *protect* women from male abuse has been turned into another *form* of male abuse! To say this is "God's Will" is indeed a *chilul Hashem*.

GENDER BOUNDARIES: A TORAH VIEW

No masculine vessel [*kli gever*] shall be on a woman, and a man shall not wear the dress of a woman, for all who do these are an abomination of Hashem your God. (Deut. 22:5)

We have explored the Torah's prohibitions of castration (Deut. 23:2), prostitution (23:18–19), and male transvestism in light of the pagan priesthoods. Transvestites have had a distinct role in a number of societies.

Among Native Americans, a person who adopts the dress and behavior of the opposite sex is known by the (European) term *berdache*. Documented in over 130 tribal cultures, *berdache*s "were known to belong to religious societies; to confer special, sacred names; to participate in sacred ceremonies; to become religious leaders or to maintain other spiritual roles." Kauxuma Nupika, an early nineteenth-century Kootenai female *berdache*, was a prophet and "a shaman with healing powers."[13]

Among the Arabs of Oman, a transvestite male is called a *xanith*.[14] *Xanith*s are "an integral part of the local social organization and very much in evidence." In Sohar,

---

13. Arlene Hirschfelder and Paulette Molin, *The Encyclopedia of Native American Religions* (New York: Facts on File, 1992), pp. 14–15, 144–145.

14. Here and following, see Wikan, pp. 168–186.

the third largest town, "well above one in every 50 males has a past or present history as a *xanith*." All male servants who are not slaves are *xanith*s, and all *xanith*s are homosexual prostitutes. They have their own mode of dress which is neither male nor female. They are socially categorized as women (for purposes of sexual segregation), but have the legal status of men (they do not require a male guardian as women do). A man may move back and forth, within his lifetime, between the *xanith* and male roles. There is no such thing as a female *xanith*, but the verb for female prostitution is *yitxanith*.

Androgyny, the artificial blurring of gender boundaries by anatomically distinct males and females, is not a Jewish ideal. However, Judaism *has* recognized people who are *not* anatomically one gender. The Talmud frequently discusses the hermaphrodite, a person *who is born* as both male and female, and the *tumtum,* a person of indeterminate gender. Such people may have been quite common before the advent of modern surgery. One opinion (Yev. 64a) even asserts that Avraham and Sarah were each originally a *tumtum*!

The Mishnah (Bik. 4:1–5) concludes that "a hermaphrodite is a creature unto itself" and defines the legal status of such a person. Sometimes the hermaphrodite was treated like a male, sometimes like a female, sometimes like both, and sometimes like neither. For instance, a hermaphrodite in *zivah* (having a genital emission) was not held liable for entering the Temple, as either a *zav* or *zavah* was! This material is fascinating, but it applies to a natural phenomenon, not a man-made one.

The transvestite is not a hermaphrodite but an anatomically distinct male or female. Male transvestites are said to be "effeminate" and to dress "like women," but what they call "feminine" dress and behavior (at least in the West) is actually a caricature or even a mockery of femaleness. Makeup, jewelry, high heels, bouffant hairdos, evening gowns, push-up bras, silk stockings, swinging hips, and removal of body hair are *not* the essence of womanhood! Indeed, many *women* would feel that they were dressed "in drag" if they had to look like that! The transvestite male does not take on femaleness; rather, he adopts the *accoutrements* of second-class female *status*, which reduces women to "dolls" and sex objects.

Although transvestism and homosexuality often overlap, the vast majority of transvestite men in America are heterosexuals who like to dress up in their wives' lingerie. "He's his first woman. It's like living with a man who has a mistress," one wife of a transvestite lamented on a television talk show.

Some transvestites have a male gender identity. Others are transsexuals: they believe that they are women "born in the wrong body" and so have surgery to create an "artificial vagina." This castrated, estrogenized male is then considered a woman by both the legal and the medical professions (and even by some feminists). Freud's notion that a woman is nothing more than a castrated man is evidently still accepted.

One may sympathize with the anguish felt by such a man without accepting medical mutilation as the solution. Social liberation from rigid sex roles would be a much more radical and effective antidote. Significantly, the first transsexual surgery was done in Germany, in 1931, and at least one concentration camp victim, a thirteen-year-old boy, was experimented on in this way.[15]

Female transvestites (and transsexuals) are much less common than males. Rashi mistakenly asserts that women dress like men "in order to consort with men, for this can only be for the purpose of adultery." On the contrary, women have passed as men in order to gain access to careers or other opportunities that were unfairly denied to them (remember the movie, *Yentl)* or to be the "butch" partner of a lesbian couple in the time before lesbian role-playing was liberated by feminism in the 1970s.

The Torah speaks of *gever* and not *zakhar,* and *vessel,* not *clothing.* It is not discussing stereotypical "masculine" traits, such as aggressiveness, or comfortable clothing such as pants. Rather, it is specifically prohibiting women from aping male "might" or macho bravado. The Gemara interprets it to mean that "a woman should not go out to war bearing weapons" (Naz. 59a). War is indeed man's game; the phallic symbolism of weapons—guns, swords, missiles—is no coincidence.

However, even here a distinction might be made between senseless wars of conquest and necessary wars of defense.

> For there is in the world causeless and purposeless slaughter and bloodshed, as well as slaughter and bloodshed in the course of war. The first proceeds from the male principle of the evil powers, the second from the female principle. The male aspect is concerned in mere bloodshed, whereas the female aspect is at the root of mutual wars of people against people; and all such wars proceed from the female principle. (*Zohar* II:243a)

Some rabbis have interpreted *kli gever* to include pants, yarmulkes, *tallis, tzitzit,* and *tefillin.* Others maintain there is no reason to prohibit such articles when they are either neutral or made specifically for women. However, even if a woman wears men's pants for practical reasons—because the sexist fashion industry makes them more durable and with more pockets—she is not trying to "pass" as a man.

We have noted that R. Judah obligated women to wear *tzitzit* (see chapter 17). One would be hard-pressed to assert that the codifier of the Mishnah wanted women to cross-dress! Similarly, were Rashi's daughters "transvestites" because they wore *tefillin?* On this issue, modern rabbis have been much stricter than their predecessors.

THE TESTICLE-GRABBER

> When men are fighting together, a man and his brother, and the wife of one approaches to rescue her husband from the hand that strikes him, and she puts out her hand and seizes his testicles, you shall cut off her hand, and not show any pity. (Deut. 25:11–12)

---

15. Janice Raymond, *The Transsexual Empire* (Boston: Beacon Press, 1979), p. 152; Joseph Wechsberg, ed., *The Murderers among Us* (New York: McGraw-Hill, 1967), p. 155.

This law immediately follows *chalitzah*, in which the *yevamah* is instructed to spit at the face of the brother-in-law who refuses to marry her. This is to illustrate that even though one woman has a *religious obligation* to disgrace and shame a man, the other does not (Sforno).

The law applies only where the woman could have saved her husband by some other means and, like other bodily mutilations mentioned in the Torah (such as "an eye for an eye"), the Rabbis interpreted the punishment as monetary compensation (B.K. 28a). Her hand was *not* cut off, and there was no fine at all if it was the only way she could rescue her husband.

There is, unfortunately, a dearth of commentary on this subject. Did women in the ancient world really go around grabbing men's testicles? The verse sounds similar to the one which describes a pregnant woman intervening in a fight (see chapter 18). What is the likelihood that *any* woman is going to intervene in a fight between two men? Is it possible that here, as there, the description is a euphemism for the woman *herself* being under attack?

A perpetrator who intends to kill or rape is called a *rodef* and must be killed, if necessary, to prevent him from carrying out his violent intent (San. 8:7). If two men are merely fighting without any murderous intent between them, a bystander may not kill one to stop them from fighting.

Grabbing a man's testicles is akin to castration and can even cause it if it is done long and hard enough. Castration is totally forbidden under Jewish law, even with a *rodef*. Thus, a woman may kill her rapist in self-defense but not castrate him! The case of Lorena Bobbitt, who castrated her batterer-rapist husband, illustrates this. She would have been more correct under Jewish law had she killed him, for a batterer (even one who does not rape) is certainly a *rodef*. (Battered women *know* that their husbands are capable of killing them, even if the rest of the world does not!)

Why the Torah prefers killing in self-defense to mutilating in self-defense is indeed an interesting question.

✻✻✻ 47 ✻✻✻

Festivals and Tithes

Ki Tavo (26:1–29:8)

There are three festivals in Judaism:

- Pesach, or Passover (early spring);
- Shavuot (late spring); and
- Sukkot (autumn).

At these three times of year, every adult Jewish male was obliged to be "seen before God" at the Temple in Jerusalem, bearing sacrifices from the firstfruits of his crops and the firstborn of his flocks (Ex. 23:17, 34:23; Deut. 16:16). Jewish women came, too, with or without sacrifices, but if for some reason they did not make it, no one could criticize them, for just as they were not *forbidden* to participate, neither were they *obliged.*

Jewish men were *required* to make these sacrifices because they were substitutes for the bloody orgiastic rites of Baal, the Canaanite male vegetation god who was "sacrificed" in spring by cutting the crops from the earth, "dead" throughout the summer dry season, and "resurrected" (restored to "kingship") in autumn with the onset of the rainy season.

"Canaan celebrated its agricultural festivals at the main seasonal crises of the beginning of the barley harvest, the end of the wheat harvest, conventionally 50 days or seven weeks later, and the Ingathering at the New Year season."[1] These holidays are first mentioned in the Torah (Ex. 23:15–16) as "the *matzah* festival" (*chag hamatzot*), "the reaping festival" (*chag hakatzir*), and "the gathering festival (*chag ha-asif*) at the end of the year."

---

1. Gray, *Near Eastern Mythology*, p. 77.

The transformation of these pagan harvest rites into festivals of the God of Israel is subtly evident in the Torah's juxtapositions. The first actual *description* of the festivals (Lev. 23:4–44) comes after the differentiation of the Jewish priesthood from pagan priesthoods through the prohibitions around death, sex, and physical mutilation, followed by a discussion of sacrifices, *trumah*, and the prohibition of using mutilated animals.

A second description of the festivals, with more detail about their sacrifices (Num. 28:16–29:39), appears after Jewish men had participated in sacrificing to Baal-Peor and were then counted in a final census for the war against Midian. The daughters of Zelophechad were described in the midst of this to illustrate the stark contrast between men and women in faithfulness to God. The third account of the three festivals (Deut. 16:1–17) occurs after a discussion of sacrifices, idolatry, dietary laws, tithes, *Shmitah*, and firstborn male animals.

Each of these accounts repeatedly emphasizes that the festivals are dedicated *to Hashem.*

THE SEASONAL RITES

Although the Jewish festivals were given national historical meaning—the Exodus (Pesach), the Revelation at Sinai (Shavuot), and living in the wilderness (Sukkot)— they are essentially nature festivals, which are rooted in the seasonal cycles of the Land itself. Because of this, their structure and symbols are found among the Canaanites. The Torah retained the basic *format* of the festivals but changed their *mode of worship*, in order to eliminate the bloodshed and the orgies.

Pesach

Pesach, the weeklong spring festival from 15 to 21 *Nisan* (the Canaanite month of *Aviv*), is actually two festivals in one: the sacrifice of a lamb from one's flock on the fourteenth of *Nisan*, and the *matzah* feast on the fifteenth. Lambs were born and barley began to be harvested at the full moon of the spring equinox. On the sixteenth, the firstfruits of the barley harvest were offered and the counting of the *omer* began.

"Pesach as a spring festival is very old. Jews observed a spring festival long before the deliverance from Egypt."[2] Lot baked *matzahs* for his three guests in Sodom because this event took place during Pesach (Gen. 19:3; Rashi). Moses told Pharaoh the Jews needed to leave Egypt to celebrate a festival; later, the festival became a celebration of their leaving. This was right after God had destroyed the Egyptian barley crop with the plague of hail.

Pesach was originally a time when firstborn sons were sacrificed[3]—in imitation of the male vegetation god himself. Thus, Pharaoh became willing to let the *males*

---

2. Hayyim Schauss, *The Jewish Festivals* (New York: Schocken, 1962), p. 39.
3. Reik, p. 121.

go. The sacrifice of the firstborn male lambs of men's flocks became a substitute for the sacrifice of their sons. The ram ritual "was not tied up with any sanctuary or priesthood; it was a family festival, conducted by the head of the family."[4]

The lamb sacrifice was a nomadic festival and the *matzah* feast was an agricultural one. "Both were spring festivals, but the Feast of Unleavened Bread was observed by the entire community gathered in a holy place, while Pesach was celebrated in the home as a family festival."[5] The two festivals became joined together by the historical event of the Exodus.

The word *Pesach* comes from a root meaning "to leap over" (Jastrow). In the holiday's historical meaning, this is explained as God passing or "leaping" over the houses with blood on the doorposts; hence the name Passover. However, it appears that part of the nature festival involved "the performance of a *leaping dance* such as characterizes harvest festivals in many parts of the world. The idea is that as high as the people leap, so high may the crops grow."[6]

Shavuot

Shavuot, the end of the wheat harvest, occurred fifty days (or seven weeks) later. It is called Yom Habikkurim, the Day of Firstfruits (Num. 28:26). In the context of this holiday, Israel was instructed in the harvest laws of *peah* and *leket* (Lev. 23:22).

Peah means leaving the corners of one's field (or orchard) unharvested, and *leket* means not picking up any stalks of grain (or pieces of fruit) that fall during harvesting. These unharvested and fallen crops have to be left for the poor to come and collect. The same is done with any stalks (or fruit) that one forgets—this is called *shikhchah* (Deut. 24:19). Similar practices apply to vineyards (Lev. 19:10): *peah*, the corners; *peret*, fallen grapes; *olelot*, undeveloped clusters; and *shikhchah*, forgotten clusters.

The seven weeks of the *Omer*, culminating in the fiftieth day, are echoed in the concepts of *Shmitah*, the seventh year, and *Yovel*, the fiftieth year, which follows seven cycles of seven years. All produce was ownerless in these years, so no crops were harvested. The poor could come and take whatever they needed, while the owner of the field was supposed to have stocked up extra provisions from the previous year's harvest.

Among the Canaanites, every seventh year the death god Mot prevailed over Baal. Hence, the land lay fallow, and "an artificial famine [was] observed in order that the powers of sterility might have free play and exhaust themselves so that the next period might be one of plenty."[7] Anat then killed Mot, which "secure[d] the unlimited rule of Baal for the next cycle of seven years."[8]

---

4. Schauss, p. 40.
5. Ibid., p. 43.
6. Gaster, p. 133.
7. Gray, *Near Eastern Mythology*, p. 88.
8. Oldenburg, p. 38.

The end of the Canaanite sabbatical year was marked by the "sacred marriage." This was a sex rite reenacting El's intercourse with his wife Asherah and his daughter Anat, "a ritual drama which was performed in the presence of the king and queen and other dignitaries of the community at a great religious feast in order that the gods might provide fertility for the coming cycle of seven years."[9]

From this act were born Shachar and Shalem, the gods of dawn and dusk. Their identification with the mythological twins of the constellation Gemini, Castor and Pollux, also indicates a link between *Shmitah* and Shavuot, for Shavuot occurs in *Sivan*, which corresponds to the solar month of Gemini (late May through mid-June). In fact, the birth of Shachar and Shalem "appears to have formed the cult-myth of a festival celebrated in June."[10]

The end of the wheat harvest in late spring was followed by the summer dry season. The Fast of 17 *Tamuz* at midsummer is related historically to the golden calf, as well as the siege of Jerusalem leading to the destruction of the Temple. In nature rites, however, it was a time to mourn the dead god. *Tamuz*, the name of the midsummer month, was also the name of the Babylonian vegetation god, the equivalent of Baal.

Fasting was a common pagan mourning practice, as was wailing by women. In Egypt, wailing at funerals was a female profession; women were considered to be the best mourners and were literally hired to weep.[11] (They must have had a lot to cry about!) In the time of the prophet Ezekiel, Jewish women were still weeping for Tamuz. They did not, however, mutilate themselves as did pagan women, who would "bare and lacerate their breasts and rend their disheveled hair."[12]

Sukkot

Sukkot, the weeklong autumn festival from 15–21 *Tishre*, celebrates the harvest of grapes and the gathering of crops from the threshing floor for winter storage. During this week, beginning at the full moon of the autumn equinox, observant Jews eat every meal in the *sukkah*, a temporary hut or tabernacle, unless it is raining (or, in the diaspora, snowing).

Sukkot begins five days after the completion of the Days of Awe—the ten days from Rosh Hashanah, the Jewish New Year, to Yom Kippur, the Day of Atonement. Rosh Hashanah is not referred to by this name in the Torah, leading one scholar to surmise that these three holidays were originally all one festival.[13] The Torah separated them but maintained the pagan cycle of self-affliction followed by revelry— the Days of Awe, a solemn introspective period culminating in a fast, followed by

9. Ibid., pp. 19, 122.

10. Ibid., p. 19; Gaster, pp. 123–124, 139.

11. Gay Robins, *Women in Ancient Egypt* (Cambridge, MA: Harvard University Press, 1993), p. 164; Murray, *Splendor*, p. 104; Casson (illustration), p. 83.

12. Gray, *Near Eastern Mythology*, p. 87.

13. Schauss, p. 113.

the rejoicing of Sukkot. The *nature* of the affliction and revelry, however, was completely transformed.

Unlike the Babylonians, whose new year (and king coronation) was in *Nisan*, the Canaanite new year was in their autumn month of *Etanim* (equivalent to *Tishre*). The kingship of Baal was declared and renewed as the autumn rains were about to begin. "It was probably the Canaanite liturgy that introduced the conception of the Kingship of God to Israel, who did not at first think of God as a king."[14]

The tabernacles "built in Israel at this seasonal festival were, in the Canaanite prototype of the New Year festival, symbolical in some way of the building of the 'house' of Baal."[15] "According to some scholars, the Feast of Booths originated in the worship of Adonis [the Syrian equivalent of Baal] or from the ritual drama of the Canaanites—whose autumn festival included a banquet of the gods and the erection of a pavilion for them."[16]

The booths were also originally "the walled cabins in which the harvesters lodged during the season. . . . Building a shack and living in it during the harvest time was an ordinary occurrence."[17]

The Krt legend speaks of a seven-day autumn harvest: "In the field is hewing of wood, on the threshing floors gathering in of grain, in the well drawing of water, at the spring filling up." These are "rites pertaining to the postulated Sukkot festival, viz., perhaps, the erecting of the 'reed hut,' and water-fetching rites connected therewith. . . . Gathering of wood is another of those rites bound up with the ancient Canaanite Sukkot festival."[18]

Water-drawing was pagan sympathetic magic used "to induce rainfall."[19] "Why did the Torah tell us to pour out water on Sukkot? The Holy One said, 'Pour out water before Me on Sukkot, so that the rains of the year will be a blessing for you. Also recite before Me on Rosh Hashanah *Malkiyot* ["Kingship," a part of the prayer service] . . . so that you may proclaim Me King over you" (R.H. 16a). The substitution of the God of Israel for Baal as king and rain-god is obvious. This water-drawing ceremony, *Simchat Bet Hashoevah*, is still part of Sukkot festivities in the modern Jewish world. It is described in detail in the Mishnah, which concludes, "One who has not seen *Simchat Bet Hashoevah* has never seen rejoicing in one's life" (Suk. 4:9–10, 5:1).

Along with the water-drawing there was also a fire ceremony. Men holding burning torches sang and danced while the Levites played their instruments. Two priests blasting trumpets walked to the east, faced west, and declared, "Our ancestors who were in this place had their backs to the Temple and their faces to the east, and bowed down eastward to the sun. But our eyes are towards God" (Suk. 5:2–4). This was clearly a renunciation of pagan sun worship (Baal's summertime role while his rain-god incarnation was "dead").

14. Gray, *Near Eastern Mythology*, p. 80.
15. Ibid., p. 81.
16. Reik, p. 5.
17. Ibid., pp. 9–10.
18. Engnell, p. 161.
19. Reik, p. 6.

People had so much fun at the Sukkot water and fire celebrations that their rejoicing seems to have approached the pagan style of merrymaking. "At no season of the year did they [Jews] drink and sing as much as they did during the autumn festival. . . . Those participating in the celebration often went beyond the limits in revelry and drink, and the festival often became a tumultuous, wild bacchanalia. The more serious-minded amongst the Jews protested against this character of the festival."[20]

Thus, the sexes were separated and a women's gallery was eventually constructed in the Temple. (This is the root of the practice of separate seating in Orthodox synagogues.) At first, both men and women were on the ground level of the outermost (eastern) courtyard. It is clear from the original style of separation that the purpose was not to exclude women, for the women were up front!

"Originally the women were on the inside while the men were on the outside, but as this led to frivolity [*kalut rosh*], it was instituted that the women should sit on the outside and the men on the inside. But there was still frivolity, so it was instituted that the women should sit above and the men below" (Suk. 51b).

Yet another practice of Sukkot is the waving of the Four Species. A palm branch, with myrtle and willow branches attached to it, is waved with a citron in the four directions, as well as up and down. This was, no doubt, originally a supplication rite for a bountiful harvest; invoking the "spirits" of the four directions for blessings and protection is a universal pagan rite even in modern times. On the seventh day, Hoshana Raba, the willow branches were beaten into the earth at the sides of the altar. This custom was originally "a talisman for making the earth fertile, because the willow grows only in moist places, and anything which grows in a damp place, and is very vigorous, is a symbol of growth and life" in the pagan view.[21]

After the seven days of Sukkot, the autumn rites conclude with Shmini Atzeret-Simchat Torah, the eighth (and diaspora ninth) day rain and Torah-dancing festival(s). This "Jewish rain dance" ushers in the rainy season in Israel. For some reason, Shmini Atzeret is mentioned only in the first (Lev. 23:36) and second (Num. 29:35–39) listings of the festivals; it is omitted in the third (Deut.).

THE PROHIBITION OF MIXING MEAT AND MILK

You shall bring the firstfruits of your soil to the House of Hashem your God; do not cook a kid in its mother's milk. (Ex. 23:19, 34:26)

Do not cook a kid in its mother's milk. Take a tithe from the harvest each year and eat it before Hashem your God in the place chosen for the Name to dwell. (Deut. 14:21)

The prohibition of "cooking a kid in its mother's milk" is the root of the Jewish practice of not mixing *any* meat with dairy products. The fact that it is said three

---

20. Schauss, pp. 171–173.
21. Ibid., p. 205.

times is interpreted to mean that a Jew may not cook such a mixture, eat it, or derive any benefit from it whatsoever.

Nachmanides says that the reason for this *mitzvah* is so "we not become a cruel and incompassionate people by milking the mother and cooking her offspring in it. Any meat in milk is included in this prohibition, because any nursing animal is called 'mother' and any suckling offspring is called 'kid,' and if they are cooked together it is always cruel."

Mystically, the "mother" is said to be the Shekhinah, and the "kid" is the "other side," the power of evil. Thus, "Israel hastened to bring the firstfruits" so that evil would not be nourished by Her strength, "the Sanctuary be not defiled, and Judgment be not aroused" (*Zohar* II:125a).

Nachmanides equates this prohibition with two others concerning mother animals and their young: not to slaughter (for meat) a cow, ewe, or female goat with its calf, lamb or kid on the same day (Lev. 22:28), and not to take a mother bird with her eggs (Deut. 22:6). "The reason for both of these is so we should not have a cruel heart and be incompassionate." Killing the mother and its young on the same day, or taking the mother bird with her eggs, is like destroying that whole species, he says.

While Nachmanides believes that God means to teach *humans* compassion through these commandments, Maimonides asserts that God is being compassionate to the mother *animal*. Her feelings of tenderness for her young and her distress at their death are no different from the feelings a human mother has for her child, for these are not a product of intellect or reason (*Guide of the Perplexed* III:48).

Neither of these commentators seems to have been intimidated by the statement of the Mishnah that anyone who claims compassion is God's reason should be silenced (Br. 5:3).

Nachmanides' equation of all three mother-offspring *mitzvot* is questionable, however. The prohibition of mixing meat with milk was rabbinically extended to include poultry—animals that do not have mammary glands! Nor is it forbidden to eat a chicken egg and a hen together (which would make sense if the prohibition was really about mothers and offspring).

Maimonides, in fact, only speaks of compassion in regards to the bird's nest and the slaughtering for meat; he does not associate the meat-and-milk prohibition with the mother animal at all. Rather, he says, "idolatry had something to do with it. Perhaps such food was eaten at one of the ceremonies of their cult or at one of their festivals."

Maimonides is indeed quite right. The practice of cooking a kid or a lamb in its mother's milk was a Canaanite custom and is mentioned in the Ras Shamra tablets. According to one interpretation, it was "a ritual ceremony designed to draw the blessing of fertility to the earth."[22] In another view its purpose was "to promote dairy produce."[23]

---

22. Cassuto, p. 50.
23. Engnell, p. 130.

Whether its alleged benefit was to crops or dairy products, cooking meat in milk was clearly a fertility rite. This explains why it is always mentioned next to tithing. Jews were being told to tithe their firstfruits *instead of* cooking an animal in milk.

TITHING THE CROPS

Tithing, or offering a portion of one's produce, was originally also a form of fertility magic. A pagan man sacrificed his firstborn son in the belief that this would gain him more sons, the firstborn of his animals as a way to make sure more animals would be born, and the firstfruits of his crops in order to have a bountiful harvest.

A Jewish man had to bring the firstfruits of seven species—wheat, barley, grapes, figs, pomegranates, olives, and dates—in a basket to the Temple in Jerusalem once a year, sometime between Shavuot and Sukkot (Bik. 1:6). There he would make a declaration in front of the priest relating how Jacob settled in Egypt, the Jews were enslaved, and God liberated them and gave them the Promised Land (Deut. 26:1–10). This passage, rather than the actual events in the Book of Exodus, is used to tell the story of Passover at the *seder* every year.

A woman, a hermaphrodite, and a *tumtum* could also bring firstfruits but did not make the declaration (Bik. 1:5). The Mishnah says this is because they cannot say the Land was given *to them* (for it was divided among males). However, this is a weak argument—what about the daughters of Zelophechad and other female land-owners? It is more likely that the declaration was made only by those who were obligated, and the obligation was on men for the reason we explained at the beginning of this chapter.

The tithe of firstfruits was called *bikkurim*. The Torah commanded several other tithes in addition to that. Tithing applies only in the Land of Israel and is required of women as well as men. To eat *tevel*, food from which tithes have not been taken, is akin to eating *nevelah* or *trefah*.

- *Trumah*—Priest's Portion: an average of one-fiftieth of one's crop was given to a *kohen*. This was in addition to firstborn animals and a portion of meat from the *shlamim* sacrifices (Num. 18:8–19; Deut. 18:3–4).
- *Maaser rishon*—First Tithe: after *trumah* was taken, one-tenth of the remainder of the crop was given to a Levite (Num. 18:24).
- *Trumah maaser*: the Levite then gave one-tenth of the First Tithe he received to a *kohen* (Num. 18:26–29).
- *Maaser sheni*—Second Tithe: after *trumah* and the First Tithe had been taken, one-tenth of the remainder of the crop was eaten by the owner in Jerusalem, along with a firstborn from the cattle or flock. If it was too difficult to transport all of this, the owner could sell it, add one-fifth to the sum, and use that money to buy produce and meat in Jerusalem. This was done every first, second, fourth, and fifth year of a *Shmitah* cycle (Lev. 27:30–31; Deut. 14:22–26).

- *Maaser ani*—Tithe of the Poor: every third and sixth year, instead of taking the Second Tithe, the owner distributed that portion to the poor, who could eat it anywhere (Deut. 14:28–29). In modern times, a Jew is required to give one-tenth of his or her income to the poor.

After one complete tithing cycle—that is, at the end of every third and sixth year—the owner made a declaration that all tithes had been properly performed (Deut. 26:12–15). Included in this was a statement that no part of the Second Tithe had been "given to the dead." This is interpreted as using the money to buy a shroud or a coffin (Rashi), but it is more likely a reference to the pagan practice of making and eating food offerings to the dead.

THE ESSENCE OF THE COVENANT

The tender woman among you, the woman of leisure whose foot never touches the ground out of delicacy and fragility, her eye will be evil towards her husband [lit., 'the man of her bosom'], her son, her daughter, the afterbirth that comes out from between her legs, and the children she shall bear. For she will eat them, out of total deprivation, in secret, because of the desperation when your enemies besiege your gates. (Deut. 28:56–57)

If Israel kept God's covenant, it would become "the highest of all the nations on earth." There would be abundant fertility of plants, animals, and children. No enemy could come near them, and the nations of the world would be in awe of this people who were a living manifestation of God's Name (Deut. 28:1–10).

Israel did *not* keep God's covenant after it entered the Land, however. Instead, the Jewish people reverted back to pagan practices, including the most repugnant ones, even though they had been warned this would bring the fate of the Canaanites upon them. For God had explicitly stated that if the Jews took on such practices, "What I was going to do to them, I will do to you" (Num. 33:56).

What is the definition here of "covenant"? It does not refer to just any violation of Jewish law. Rather, it refers specifically to the repudiation of *avodat gilulim*—the bloody, orgiastic rites that the Canaanites misguidedly believed were the source of fertility and abundance. These rites are summarized as the three big sins of Judaism: murder, idolatry, and incest.

In order to impress upon the Jewish people just how perverse and horrible these rites were, the God of Israel could not just render them *ineffective*—which would be too passive—but had to make them *actively destructive*. If Jews practiced skin gashing, castration, human sacrifice, incest, adultery, bestiality, or sodomy in the belief that this would aid fertility, the message had to be delivered loud and clear that these would not only *not cause* fertility but would *bring about* famine, barrenness, poverty, starvation, disease, and plague, to the point that normally sensitive people would become depraved enough to cannibalize their own children!

The fate of the "woman of leisure" described in the previous passage from Deuteronomy 28:56 is a nearly verbatim repetition of the fate of a "tender and delicate" *man* of leisure (Deut. 28:54–55). There was no sex discrimination in the consequences of breaking the covenant; these terms are not intended to imply any sexist notion of female "weakness."

This section is parallel to Leviticus 26, where God promises to keep increasing the punishments sevenfold every time Israel refuses to listen and adhere. The Leviticus account refers to the Babylonian conquest and the destruction of the First Temple; the Deuteronomy account refers to Roman rule and the destruction of the Second Temple (Sforno).

The Roman exile, according to Sforno (who cites *Sotah* 9:9–15), occurred because people stopped tithing. On the surface, this may appear to be a minor violation; however, if we recall that tithing was a substitute for certain pagan fertility rites, its importance becomes evident. Sexual immorality and murder had also become rampant, so much so that the rites of *sotah* and the River Heifer were rendered ineffective and had to be discontinued. The Sanhedrin ceased to function, justice was completely nullified, and "men of violence" became powerful.

The failure to tithe—that is, to share one's fertility and abundance with the less fortunate—is particularly relevant to references to the (man and) woman "of leisure." The Talmud illustrates the verse from Deuteronomy (28:56) with the example of Marta bat Boetus (Git. 56a). Marta was "one of the richest women in Jerusalem" during the siege leading to the destruction of the Second Temple. Her father, Boetus, had been high priest. Her first husband died; she had a son from that marriage who was so strong he could carry an entire sacrificial bull up the altar ramp by himself, a rite that was usually required to be performed by twenty-four priests (Suk. 52b).

Marta was then betrothed to Joshua b. Gamla, a *kohen*. She used her wealth to bribe Agrippa II to appoint Joshua as high priest around 64 C.E.[24] Once Joshua was appointed high priest, Marta, as a widow, would normally have been forbidden to marry him. However, because they had already undergone *erusin*, they were permitted to undergo *nesuin* and consummate the marriage (Yev. 6:4).

The Zealots, a group of Jews who refused to surrender to the Romans, had organized to fight a war of self-defense. The Rabbis opposed this, believing it could not succeed. The Zealots then burned down the storehouses of wheat and barley in order to cause a famine. It was in this context that Marta sent one of her servants to buy the finest wheat flour, which was sold out. The servant returned, telling her that there was only white flour. She sent him out again to get some of that, but by the time he arrived, it was also sold out. Again he returned, saying that all that was left was dark (whole wheat) flour. Therefore, she sent him out to get some of that, but again it was too late. By that time, only barley flour was left. For a fourth time, she sent him out to get some, but by the time he arrived, it too was all gone.

Marta (who obviously did not usually have to go shopping for herself) declared, "I will go out and see if I can find anything to eat." When she went out, "some dung

24. Soncino translation, *Sukkah,* p. 252 n. 4.

stuck to her foot and she died." R. Jochanan applied to her the verse, "the tender woman among you, the woman of leisure whose foot never touches the ground out of delicacy and fragility."

But others say she died from eating a fig left by R. Zadok, who "observed fasts for 40 years in order that Jerusalem might not be destroyed." He became so anorexic that "when he ate anything the food could be seen" as it passed down his throat. He would occasionally suck the juice out of a fig to restore himself and throw the rest away. It was one of these disposed figs that Marta allegedly ate.

"When Marta was about to die, she brought out all her gold and silver and threw it in the street, saying, 'What good is this to me?'" (Git. 56a). Her last act before dying was to "tithe," that is, to share her wealth.

✳✳✳ 48 ✳✳✳

Canaanites and the Covenant

Nitzavim (29:9–30:20)

The covenant that God made with Israel began with the matriarchs and patriarchs and was carried on by their descendants—the people who left Egypt, stood at Sinai, and lived in the wilderness.

All along, there were pagans who joined the Jews, either as full-fledged converts to Judaism or as slaves living in Jewish households. A slave had an "in-between" status; he or she had to renounce idolatry, become a Noachide (a monotheistic gentile), and take on most of the *mitzvot* while living in a Jewish household. If a pagan slave actually converted to Judaism, this was concurrent with manumission (Yev. 46a).

Quite a few Canaanites joined the Jews, even some who survived *cherem* (see chapter 40). "Surviving complete annihilation" sounds like a contradiction, but it happened. *Cherem* was not as complete in practice as it was in theory.

THE "STRANGER IN YOUR CAMP"

You are standing today, all of you, before Hashem your God: your tribal leaders, your elders, your law enforcers, every person [*ish*, meaning "freeman"] of Israel, your infants, your women, and your stranger [*ger*] inside your camp, from the woodcutters to the water-drawers. You are being brought into the covenant of Hashem your God. (Deut. 29:9–11)

All "your" Israelites—various categories of men, the children, and the women— are described in the plural with a plural possessive suffix *(-khem)*. "Your" stranger, however, is described in the singular with a singular possessive suffix *(-kha),* as if to emphasize that this person was an exceptional, individual case.

Who is this "stranger"? It refers to "Canaanites who came to convert in the days of Moses. . . . Moses made them woodcutters and water-drawers" (Rashi). Moses could not make a "covenant"—that is, a mutual treaty—with them, for God had specifically prohibited that (Ex. 23:32; Deut. 7:2). Instead he brought them into *the* covenant through the semistatus of slaves.

Canaanite slaves had been with the Jews since the time of the patriarchs—for example, Avraham's servant, Eliezer, and Shimon and Levi's Hivite captives. Canaanites were also captured in the wars prior to entering the Land (e.g., against the Midianites), for only Canaanites living *inside* the Land were subject to *cherem.* Canaanites who lived *outside* the Land were not, so they—that is, the women and children—could be spared (Rashi on Deut. 20:11; Sot. 35b).

The phenomenon that Rashi is describing "in the days of Moses," however, does not concern war captives. Rather, these were Canaanites who knew the Jews were about to enter the Land and did not want to be slaughtered. Therefore, they came to "convert" in the same way that the Givonites came later (Joshua 9:4)—with *armah,* "prudence, deliberation, subtlety" (Jastrow), to get Israel to accept them. *Armah* has the same Hebrew root as *arum,* the term used to describe the serpent's cunning with Chavah in the Garden of Eden (Gen. 3:1). It implies a very clever use of persuasion, or even deception.

Once Jews entered the Land, the six nations *within* the boundaries of the Land—the Canaanites, Hittites, Hivites, Amorites, Perizites, and Jebusites—were subject to *cherem.* (The Girgashites had fled to Africa.) While this makes it seem unlikely that any of these people would survive and live with the Jews, this could have happened according to Maimonides' view of *cherem,* which differs from Rashi's in a fundamental way.

Maimonides maintains that, just as in any other war, even the Canaanites *inside* Canaan had to first be offered peace. If they accepted the Noachide laws and agreed to second-class status—namely, serving as woodcutters and water-drawers—their lives could be spared *(Kings and Their Wars* 6:1). Nachmanides also shares this view (Deut. 20:10).

Only when the Canaanites did not accept these terms were they subject to *cherem.* While *cherem* was a positive commandment incumbent upon the Jewish people as a whole, the prohibition against allowing a Canaanite to live was a negative commandment incumbent upon the individual.[1] This may be why "your" stranger is in the singular possessive: responsibility for the Canaanite's existence fell on the individual Jew.

OBLIGATORY VERSUS OPTIONAL WARS

An "obligatory war" in Jewish law is called a *milchemet mitzvah.* Sometimes it is also called *milchemet chovah,* but the meaning is basically the same (Sot. 44b). The

---

1. Touger commentary on *Kings and Their Wars,* p. 83.

only obligatory wars were: (1) against the Canaanite nations; (2) against Amalek, who attacked the Jews from behind as they fled from Egypt (Ex. 17:8); and (3) against any enemy who attacks the Jews first—namely, a war of self-defense (Maimonides, *Kings and Their Wars* 5:1).

We are commanded, oxymoronically, to "erase the memory of Amalek and not forget" (Deut. 25:17–19). How does one "erase a memory" but "not forget"? Perhaps we are meant to eradicate his evil but still remember why he caused it. Amalek was the son of Timna, a Horite princess who was refused as a convert by the patriarchs and so entered the house of Esav as a concubine of his son (see chapter 8).

Any concubine was disadvantaged by not having the legal rights of a wife. For a woman who had been a princess, however, this type of subjugation must have been especially demeaning. Amalek probably learned a lot about anger and hostility from his mother, while also imitating the bullying, macho behavior of his father's side of the family. This was a deadly combination!

However, even though the war against Amalek was a *milchemet mitzvah*—which, by definition, requires *cherem*—Israel "cut off the heads of the strong men, leaving only the weak among them, and did not kill them all. From this we may learn that they acted according to the words of the Shekhinah" (Rashi on Ex. 17:13).

In a *milchemet mitzvah,* victory was not effected by the might of the soldiers but only by the power of God. Many statements in the Torah make this absolutely clear in reference to the war against the Canaanites.

The Jews were the smallest in number of any nation in the world, in contrast to those they were about to fight (Deut. 7:7).

If the Jews got scared thinking about this, and wondered how they would be able to drive out nations more numerous than themselves, they were to remember what God did for them in Egypt and realize that similar divine powers would be exerted with the Canaanites. Hashem would attack the nations with hornets, place their kings in Israel's power, and uproot the Canaanites little by little so that wild animals would not proliferate in the Land (Deut. 7:17–24).

The Jews would dispossess nations greater and mightier than themselves, even though the inhabitants were as tall as giants. God would go before Israel as a consuming fire, annihilating and expelling the nations. The Jews were not to think, mistakenly, that their own virtue or integrity led God to do this. Rather, the evil of the Canaanites was the only reason. They had to be eliminated so Israel would not learn their repugnant ways of worship (Deut. 9:1–6, 20:17–18).

The Jews, armed only with swords, knives, and other such weapons on foot, were not supposed to panic when they saw the horses, war chariots, and organized armies of their enemies. A special "war-priest" anointed for the purpose gave the Jewish soldiers a pep talk so that they would not be afraid and reminded them that God "is going with you to fight for you against your enemies, and will rescue you" (Deut. 20:1–4).

A war of aggression that a king wanted to fight in order to expand his territory or increase his wealth was called a *milchemet reshut*, an "optional war." To start such a war, says Maimonides (*Kings and Their Wars* 5:2), he first had to get the permission of the Great Sanhedrin, which consisted of seventy-one judges (San. 1:5, 2:4). This means that since the dissolution of the Sanhedrin, Jews are only allowed to fight wars of self-defense, namely, to stop a collective *rodef.*

Most non-Jewish wars throughout history would fall under the category of *milchemet reshut*—wars of aggression. However, Christianity, in claiming the "Old Testament" as its own, has appropriated the concept of *milchemet mitzvah* ("holy war") to rationalize its own atrocities—for example, the Crusades, the Inquisition, and the decimation of Native Americans. The list is endless.

Thus, one scholar asserts, "This ongoing identification between contemporary situations and the warring scenes of the Hebrew Bible is *a burden the tradition must guiltily bear.* The particular violence of the Hebrew Scriptures has inspired violence, has served as a model of and model for persecution, subjugation, and extermination for millennia beyond its own reality" (emphasis mine).[2]

However, this author then admits that the Christian "use of Hebrew Scriptures surely says more about their own forms of self-articulation than about ancient Israelite attitudes and traditions. . . . Paradoxically, the harsh ideology of the Puritans is somehow blamed on the Jews."[3]

The notion that the Torah legitimizes the conquest of indigenous peoples as modern idolators is a myth that must be exploded once and for all. Judaism maintains that the Canaanites are past history, that *there will never be another people like them again.* Christianity, however, does indeed bear a guilty burden in using Jewish Scriptures to rationalize its persecution of native peoples. This distortion—quite similar to its misuse of Chavah's story to rationalize the oppression of women—is a basic form of Christian anti-Semitism.

CHRISTIAN "COVENANT" AND NATIVE AMERICANS

This wilderness was the place which God decreed to make a Canaan to you.
—Urian Oakes, Protestant minister (and Harvard College president),
in a sermon given in Cambridge, Mass., 1673 C.E.[4]

The Anglo-Saxon pilgrims of colonial America believed they were "commissioned to uphold a sacred and exclusive covenant between themselves and God. . . . Within one generation, New England's own record of providential threatenings and deliverances was engrafted onto Israel's, with the same revelatory significance."[5]

Christian theology was grounded in the notion that God's covenant with Israel, the "Old Testament," had been broken and replaced by another covenant, the "New

---

2. Susan Niditch, *War in the Hebrew Bible* (New York: Oxford University Press, 1993), p. 4.
3. Ibid., pp. 4–5.
4. Quoted in Harry S. Stout, *The New England Soul* (New York: Oxford University Press, 1986), p. 73.
5. Ibid., pp. 7–8.

Testament." Events and objects in the Hebrew Bible were interpreted as merely "pre-figuring" Jesus Christ and the Church. This included, for the Puritans, "the promised land of Canaan prefiguring the promised land of New England."[6]

"Israel had always been New England's typological model . . . but after 1660 this theme became an obsession . . . God's New World people were in fact less a New *England* than a New *Israel* ; genealogy tied them to the Old World, but providence linked them to ancient Israel so thoroughly and explicitly that words in the Old Testament could be taken as if literally intended for New England."[7]

Thus, religious persecution in England was Egyptian bondage, the pilgrims were the "outcasts of Zion" and God's "chosen people," their journey across the Atlantic was the Exodus across the Red Sea, their leaders were Moses and Aharon (and later, the prophets and kings), their journey across land was the wandering in the wilderness, and New England was the promised land. "Israel's sins and judgments" were taken as "a solemn warning and mirror of New England's own endangered status."[8]

The next logical step of this mentality was a perception of the indigenous inhabitants as New Canaanites, whose extermination as "idolators" could then be easily rationalized. However, Native American religions are not at all equivalent to Canaanite modes of worship. Only a superficial knowledge of both could lead a person to such a conclusion.

There is not just one Native American "religion," but many religions. Some appear to be polytheistic while others are clearly monotheistic, and some contain an evolution from the former to the latter *within* them. While certain pagan elements are clearly present, such as sun worship or divination, the most heinous practices of the ancient Near East are noticeably rare, and for the most part totally absent. There are no sex orgies in fertility rites, religious dances are not at all eroticized, and there is strict adherence to incest, menstrual, and (in some cases) death taboos. The Native American reverence towards mother earth "is not the outstanding mother goddess who blossomed in the Old World. . . . North America had almost no sacrifice, even of animals. Mother Earth did not demand it."[9]

Apparently, some groups have practiced skin gashing as a mourning rite or to induce visions, but this "was incidental, used by some tribes and not at all by others." While this practice is certainly anathema from a Jewish point of view, it was not a universal rite in native North America as it was in the ancient Near East. It is certainly no excuse for *persecution by Christians*, for it was "no worse than the torture inflicted on themselves by medieval monks."[10]

The British settlers conveniently ignored that, unlike the Jews, they were not a smaller nation fighting a larger, more powerful one. They believed that their con-

6. Ibid., p. 45.

7. Ibid., p. 54.

8. Ibid., p. 174.

9. Ruth M. Underhill, *Red Man's Religion* (Chicago: University of Chicago Press, 1965), pp. 47–48.

10. Ibid., pp. 79, 97, 145, 150.

quest of Native Americans was, like the war against the Canaanites, not only *sanctioned* by God but *effected* by God; divine intervention, not military might, was responsible for victory in battle. Each victory was followed by a special weekday "thanksgiving sermon" delivered by the local minister. One such "thanksgiving day" was celebrated in 1637 after a massacre of Pequot Indians.[11]

In this massacre, seven hundred men, women, and children who were giving thanks to their Creator for the annual corn harvest—a four-day festival at the first new moon after the autumn equinox—were shot down or burned alive. The governor of the Massachusetts Bay Colony proclaimed the next day an official holiday, Thanksgiving Day. Governors of other states followed suit throughout the next century.[12]

Eventually the states' Thanksgiving Days were consolidated into one national holiday. The true origins of this American holiday belie the quaint little notion, taught in the white man's history books, that it commemorates the pilgrims and Indians "sharing a meal together." While the traditional foods and the spirit of thanks do indeed come from the Pequot harvest festival, the holiday, as it is observed today, commemorates a Christian crusade against the indigenous peoples of North America.

Ironically, even some religious Jews, who otherwise repudiate the observance of Christian holidays, celebrate Thanksgiving in the belief that it is a "secular" holiday. One rabbi has even asserted that "there is no American holiday more in keeping with the Jewish spirit than Thanksgiving. It is such a Jewish celebration."[13]

This rabbi, reiterating the "shared meal" myth of the holiday's origin, takes a naive delight in the fact that "Christopher Columbus envisioned himself to be King David fighting against Goliath, [that] our Pilgrim fathers saw themselves as the children of Israel, fleeing across the Red Sea as they sailed the ocean to the New World, which was their 'promised land.' . . . The Pilgrim fathers, in their love of the Old Testament, patterned their first Thanksgiving Day after the celebration of Sukkot."

This view is oblivious to Christian anti-Judaism, the physical and cultural attack on Native Americans, and—most important—*the linkage between the two*. It is no accident, for instance, that Queen Isabella and King Ferdinand sent Christopher Columbus off on his expedition the very same year they expelled the Jews from Spain.[14] Persecution of Jews at home and conquest of native peoples abroad go hand-in-hand.

The use of Jewish Scriptures by Christian covenant theology does not imply love of Jews; indeed, it is quite the contrary. The report of one anthropologist on missionary activities among the Amuesha Indians of Peru clearly illustrates this—Amuesha

---

11. Stout, p. 28.

12. "Thanksgiving Day Celebrates a Massacre," *Akwesasne Notes* (Summer 1980): 12. This newspaper is published by the Mohawk Nation of upstate New York.

13. Leonard Winograd, "Thanksgiving: A Unity Holiday," *The Jewish Advocate*, November 15, 1990, p. 8.

14. See, for example, Jane Frances Amler, *Christopher Columbus's Jewish Roots* (Northvale, NJ: Jason Aronson Inc., 1991); and Cecil Roth, *A History of the Marranos* (New York: Sepher-Hermon Press, 1992).

culture is denigrated by missionary teachings *as Jewish*: "The teacher was telling the gathering that they were 'Jews' because they don't believe in anything, and for that reason, they are killing the Christian god, just like the Jews persecuted and killed Jesus."[15]

The naivete of the rabbi quoted here about Thanksgiving Day is not unique. There are quite a few religious Jews today who believe that evangelical Christians are great allies because they appear to support the state of Israel. This short-sighted view ignores the long-range theology *behind* the support: The return of the Jews to Israel is to be followed by the "Second Coming" of Christ. Jews who do not accept the Christian messiah the second time around will perish in the Armageddon.

If there is indeed any "covenant" of a shared destiny, it is not between Jews and European Christians, Native Americans and Canaanites, Native Americans and Arabs, or Arabs and Canaanites.[16] It is between Jews and Native Americans. Many similarities can be seen between these two groups.[17] For both, the basis of religious beliefs and practices is an attachment to a specific piece of sacred land. The Jews regained their indigenous homeland after 1,878 years of exile. In the last twenty years or so, Native American nations have become more aggressive in reclaiming land, fishing, and hunting rights. In some cases, significant strides have been made.[18]

"Hashem your God will bring you to the Land that your ancestors possessed, and you will repossess it. [God] will be good to you and make you flourish even more than your ancestors" (Deut. 30:5).

---

15. Richard Chase Smith, "The Summer Institute of Linguistics: Ethnocide Disguised as a Blessing," in *Is God an American?*, ed. Soren Hvalkof and Peter Aaby (Copenhagen, Denmark: IWGIA and Survival International, 1981), p. 127.

16. An assertion that Palestinian Arabs are descendants of the Canaanites was made, for obvious political reasons, by Francis H. Russell, "The Palestinians: Who They Are," *The Christian Science Monitor*, Oct. 26, 1976, pp. 18–19.

17. For a brief summary of these, see Ed Sloan, "Jews and Native Americans—A Striking Resemblance," *The Jewish Advocate*, Nov. 8, 1991, p. 9.

18. See, for instance, Judith Gaines, "Tribe to Claim One-Third of New England," *The Boston Globe*, Aug. 10, 1990, p. 1; Yvonne Daley, "Vermont Judge Rules That Indians Hold Fishing and Hunting Rights," *The Boston Globe*, Aug. 15, 1989, p. 17; Nick King, "Native Americans May Finally Win One," *The Boston Globe*, Jul. 31, 1983, p. A13; and Frank Trippett, "Should We Give America Back to the Indians?" *Time*, Apr. 11, 1977, pp. 51–52.

✻✻✻ 49 ✻✻✻

Women and the Torah

Vayelekh (31:1–30)

At the end of seven years, at an appointed time of the Shmitah *year on the festival of* Sukkot, *when all of Israel comes to appear before Hashem your God in the place that [God] will choose, you must read this Torah before all of Israel within their hearing. Assemble the people—the men, the women, the children, and your stranger that is in your gates—so they may hear, so they may learn and will be in awe of Hashem your God, and carefully do all the words of this Torah.* (Deut. 31:10–12)

The Torah Assembly was actually held at the beginning of every eighth year, on the second day of Sukkot—the first intermediate day (*chol Hamoed*) of the festival in Israel. A wooden platform was built in the Temple courtyard where the king would sit and read specific sections of the Torah (Sot. 7:8).

These sections, all from Deuteronomy, were Moses' review of the journey through the wilderness, the cities of refuge, and Moses' review of the Ten Commandments (Deut. 1:1–6:3); the first two paragraphs of the *Shma* (6:4–9, 11:13–21); the Second Tithe (14:22–28); the tithing declaration (26:12–15); the laws of a king (17:14–20); and the blessings and the curses (27:15–26).

A deaf person was exempt from this *mitzvah,* since the Torah says, "so they may hear" (Chag. 3a). This Gemara then asserts that "the men came to learn, the women came to hear," and asks, "Why did the children come? In order to give a reward to those who bring them."

Thus, although the Torah itself clearly puts men and women on an equal footing—*both* are to "hear" *and* to "learn"—the Rabbis tried to minimize women's participation, rendering it more passive and superficial than men's. Men "learn"—that is, grapple with texts—while women "hear"—that is, are spoon-fed lectures.

Nachmanides says that "the women too heard and learned to be in awe of Hashem."

He acknowledges that women "learn," but makes the object of that verb "awe of God," not "Torah." Men presumably learn both.

Rabbinic debate over the centuries has focused not so much on whether women *should* study Torah, but on what, how much, where, how, and when. It is generally agreed that women *have to* be taught practical *halakhah*—for example, the laws of *Shabbat, kashrut*, and *niddah*—in order to be able to keep those laws. That is simply common sense, a bottom-line logic in which even the most sexist rabbi has an investment. If he expects his wife to cook all the meals, for instance, he needs to feel confident that she knows how to keep things kosher!

The Rabbis have also generally believed that women may be taught the written Torah. They could hardly deny women the right to study the written Torah when the written Torah itself required them to be present at its communal reading.

Thus, in a combination of these two views—written Torah plus the need to know practical laws for daily living—women have traditionally been taught Bible and *halakhah*, which are the beginning and end points of the Jewish legal process. The debatable issue in women's Torah study has been the oral tradition—the Talmud, or Mishnah and Gemara. (Mysticism, too, has historically been off-limits to women, but it was also off-limits to most men, all except for the most erudite.)

Mishnah and Gemara contain a wide variety of rabbinic discussions, debates, and interpretations illustrating the thought processes by which a Torah verse becomes a law or a set of laws. How, for example, do all the laws of *kashrut* regarding meat and milk derive from the verse saying not to "cook a kid in its mother's milk"? If this middle part of the process is omitted from a person's education, the student is not being taught to think, question, debate, and understand, but only to obey.

The arguments for and against teaching women the oral tradition are much too large in scope to be properly dealt with here in just one chapter. The topic is treated fully elsewhere.[1] Rabbinic arguments have historically ranged from the most incredibly misogynist—that women's minds are not "suited" for such study (the mode of which has been defined by and for men)—to the most liberal—that women can and should study.

The same range of opinions is still found among modern-day rabbis, although there are many more at the liberal end of the spectrum than there used to be. One of the most unqualified positive statements was made by the late Lubavitcher Rebbe, Menachem Schneerson:

> The present-day emphasis on the education of Jewish women . . . must be seen as one of the steps which both heralds and hastens the coming of the Redemption. In this connection, it must be emphasized that a woman's study of Torah should not be superficial. She should probe deeply into Torah study without reservations or qualms about the restrictions that applied to studying certain subjects in the past. Moreover, this study should also include the Torah's mystic truths.[2]

---

1. For a comprehensive treatment of this subject by an Orthodox woman, see Shoshana Pantel Zolty, *"And All Your Children Shall Be Learned"* (Northvale, NJ: Jason Aronson, 1993).

2. "Women, Redemption, and Happiness," *Ascent Quarterly* 10:2 (*Tamuz* 5754/Summer 1994): 8–9. This was a special commemorative issue published after the Rebbe's death on 3 *Tamuz*.

The misogynist mentality, however, is still prevalent in many right-wing circles. There is, for example, the statement by the founder of the Bet Yakov College for Girls in Bnei Brak: "If we succeed in instilling in our girl students that the purpose of their studies is to aspire to emulate our matriarchs, who did not study, then we have succeeded in educating our daughters."[3] Similar is the comment by the head of the Zikhron Meir religious court: "It is the nature of women that they cannot attain and understand the true point of the Torah, and as a result they trivialize the Torah's intentions."[4] (He would probably consider this book as proof!)

However, even the liberal view sometimes has an underlying, subtle misogyny. There is a paternalism inherent in assuming that the issue is even debatable. Who granted men the authority to give or withhold "permission" for women to study Torah? These men will say that God did, but this is the voice of male entitlement speaking, not God's Torah.

The Lubavitcher Rebbe's statement is exceptional even for the liberal view, which for the most part has gained ground *only* as secular education has become more open and available to women. Most of the liberal rabbis realized (sometimes too late) that Jewish women's intellects and values were in danger of being shaped more by secular education than by traditional Jewish learning. These rabbis began to encourage women's Torah study *in order to preserve Judaism*, and not out of any belief in the inherent legitimacy of women's own desires and aspirations.

Jews were given the mission to be "a light unto the nations," to set an example by leading the way. However, in women's education (and its legal consequences), traditional Judaism has dragged slowly *behind* the non-Jewish world. What kind of statement about Judaism does it make to a Jewish woman (and to the rest of the world) that she can be a judge in other people's court systems but not even so much as a witness in her own?

Should Jewish women's assimilation and/or intermarriage come as a surprise to us in such circumstances? Some older Jewish women who now function as neopagan priestesses admit that they might have become rabbis, had that opportunity existed, in the late 1960s, when they were becoming adults.[5] Another Jewish woman became an Episcopalian minister because Christianity was open to her in a way that Judaism was not; she received no Jewish education, while her brothers did.[6]

Mason's article cites a study that found that 66 percent of all Jewish apostates are women. The price to be paid for minimizing Jewish women's intellectual and spiritual aspirations continues to be high. Fortunately, however, there are now women who are taking it into their own hands to start women's yeshivas (and other educational formats), rather than waiting for male rabbis to do it "for" us.

3. Attributed to the late Rabbi Avraham Yosef Wolf. Quoted in El-Or, p. 65.
4. Rabbi Shmuel Halevy Vazner, "On the Prohibition Against Teaching Girls Commentators on the Torah in Depth," *Marveh Latsomeh* 45 (1986). Quoted in El-Or, p. 76.
5. Judith S. Antonelli, "Paganism's Allure Draws Women Alienated From Judaism," *The Jewish Advocate*, May 29–June 4, 1992, p. 11.
6. Ruth Mason, "Conversations with Jews Who Have Left Judaism," *The Jewish Advocate*, Aug. 16–22, 1991, p. 9.

SUSTAINING THE WORLD

One who concentrates one's mind on, and deeply penetrates into, the Torah sustains the world. For as the Holy One looked into the Torah and created the world, so humanity looks into the Torah and keeps the world alive. Hence the Torah is the cause of the world's creation, and also the power that maintains its existence. Therefore, blessed is one who is devoted to the Torah, for that person is the preserver of the world. (*Zohar* II:161b)

In December 1988, a group of women attending a Jewish feminist conference in Jerusalem decided to hold a halakhically observant prayer service and Torah reading at the Kotel (Western Wall). Upon doing so, they were verbally and physically attacked by a number of right-wing Orthodox men. Some right-wing Orthodox women also became upset when they saw the feminists praying as a group and holding a Torah scroll. According to various published reports, one of these women kept shouting, "The Torah is not for women!" and, "The Torah belongs to men!"[7]

"*The Torah belongs to men*": Although the woman who shouted this was living a Torah-observant life-style, she has been taught by men to believe that there is something wrong with women carrying and reading from a Torah scroll. "Those who carry babies don't carry Torahs," a college-age, modern Orthodox man once stated matter-of-factly to his female companion. What blatant womb envy!

By denying the petition of Women of the Wall (Jewish feminists who have the "audacity" to think the Torah belongs to them, too), the Israeli Supreme Court has in effect upheld the idea that "the Torah belongs to men." Supposedly "pious" Orthodox worshipers (men and women) are still shouting curses, throwing stones, and spitting at women who come to the Kotel in *yarmulkes* and prayer shawls.[8]

In America, the notion that "the Torah belongs to men" is nowhere more evident than in Orthodox synagogues on Simchat Torah. On this festive occasion, the joyful culmination of the autumn holidays that began with repentance, the Jewish people rejoice with the Torah by dancing in circles around a person holding a Torah scroll.

In most Orthodox synagogues, men dance while the women watch. In more progressive Orthodox synagogues, men and women each have their own circles, but women are not given a Torah. In only a few places do Orthodox women get a Torah scroll, too. In one case, the women of a particular synagogue had gotten a Torah and were dancing with it, and the rabbi came over and *took it away from them*!

Even when women do get a Torah, many women hesitate or even decline to take a turn holding it, mistakenly fearing that they are not physically strong enough and might drop it. This is very sad. For here we are, celebrating our *spiritual* acceptance of the Torah, but when it is *physically* held out to a woman to accept, she rejects it!

---

7. See, for instance, Pogrebin, p. 71; Ann F. Lewis, "The Jerusalem Agenda," *Ms.* (Mar. 1989): 23; and Roselyn Bell, "Wide-Awake Dreamers," *Hadassah* (Feb. 1989): 27.

8. "Israeli Supreme Court Rejects Women of the Wall," and "Hadassah Women Get Stoned," both in *Lilith* 19:1 (Spring 1994): 7.

Does she see the irony? Are women not "strong enough" to accept the Torah? One year a woman who hesitatingly took the scroll said joyfully, with tears in her eyes, "I've carried *out* the Torah all my life, but this is the first time I've ever *carried* one!"

The experience of dancing with a Torah in an all-women's circle is very powerful and far different from the dynamic in a mixed-gender circle. However, in some places, a religious woman is forced to choose between dancing with women without a Torah and dancing in a mixed group with a Torah. It is an unfortunate choice to have to make.

By denying Orthodox women the opportunity to dance among themselves with a Torah, men have appropriated the Torah for themselves and given this misogyny a divine stamp of approval. We should not be fooled by the assertions of men (or women, for that matter) who claim that women "don't want it." This is a common excuse. "When behavior is socially imposed, the people who have imposed it often claim that the behavior was freely chosen."[9]

This is not the way to "sustain the world."

---

9. Paula J. Caplan, *The Myth of Women's Masochism* (New York: E. P. Dutton, 1985), p. 70.

❈❈❈ 50 ❈❈❈

God's Daughters

Haazinu (32:1–52) and *VeZot HaBracha* (33:1–34:12)

You sapped the strength of the Rock that gave birth to you, and you forgot your Source. Hashem saw and was indignant from anger with [God's] sons and daughters. (Deut. 32:18–19)

Although God is called "Father" in an earlier verse (Deut. 32:6), here God is portrayed as a Mother, for the verb form used of the root Y-L-D means "to give birth," not "to beget." *Source* refers to "the One Who brought you forth from the womb" (Rashi). God is also described as an eagle hovering over its young in the nest, a clearly maternal image in spite of the grammatical neuter gender (Deut. 32:11).

Even though the Torah's custom is to use *banim* to mean "children," here it specifically uses *banim* ("sons") and *banot* ("daughters"). Nachmanides tries to explain this away with his theory that "women are more prone to idolatry," which, we have seen, is a false assumption (chapter 44). In fact, the masculine gender alone is used a few verses earlier to say that destruction is not caused by God but rather by defects in God's "children" (Deut. 32:5).

In this song before his death, Moses calls upon heaven (a masculine noun) and earth (a feminine noun) as witnesses, "for if Israel should say, 'We never accepted the covenant,' who can come and refute them?" Rain and crop fertility are the "testimony" given by these witnesses (Rashi on Deut. 32:1).

A male–female symmetry therefore persists throughout Moses' song. Followed only by the tribal blessings and Moses' death, the Torah thus ends as it began—with an equal balance between male and female.

WOMEN: THE DIVINE ESSENCE OF ISRAEL

All the women of Israel are blessed by the medium of the Community of Israel. (*Zohar* III:124a)

494

The Community of Israel, "which frequently occurs as the usual title of the Shekhinah, signifies the divine essence of the people Israel concentrated in the Shekhinah."[1] The Shekhinah, we are told, resides with *all* women but only with *married* men (*Zohar* I:228b).

The Community of Israel "is called the daughter of the king, the supreme King. . . . She is clothed and encompassed with supernal strength [*Gevurah*]. . . . On this account the earth is established, namely, when she takes hold of Judgment, and this we call 'the kingdom of heaven'" (*Zohar* I:237a). The Community of Israel as God's Daughter relates to the very nature of the soul itself (*Zohar* II:94b). The Community of Israel is also called Rachel, who weeps for her children and whose plea surpassed that of Avraham, Isaac, Jacob, and Moses in convincing God to return the Jews from exile (*Zohar* II:29b).

The caretaking of Israel by God is accomplished through righteous deeds. Here lies the role of the *tzaddik.* "When men repent and act virtuously then the mother returns and shelters the young, and this is called *teshuvah*" (*Zohar* I:219a). When the fifty gates of *Binah* are open, "there flows down drink and food for the Community of Israel through the intermediary of a righteous one. When this one moves towards her, many are those who stand and wait to be refreshed and to participate in the blessings from above" (*Zohar* I:208b).

"When the Community of Israel bestirs itself, there is a stirring among all the legions attached to it, both on high and below, Israel rising above them all. . . . 'The Community of Israel,' said R. Chiya, 'indeed brings her salvation from afar'" (*Zohar* II:50b).

Male supremacy, we noted in chapter 1, is a condition of exile. To restore women to their rightful place in the world is a task of incredible magnitude. Given women's central role in the blessings bestowed upon Israel, it is a task that the Jewish people cannot afford to ignore.

---

1. Tishby, 1:381.

Glossary

Adam The first human being; a sexually undifferentiated or hermaphroditic "earth creature."

Agunah The "chained wife," a woman who cannot get a divorce from her husband either because he is missing in action or because he refuses to give her the required divorce document.

Ailonit An anatomically abnormal woman who is incapable of conceiving.

Akarah An anatomically normal woman who is barren.

Akedah The binding of Isaac.

Aliyah Being called up to read from the Torah in the synagogue service; emigration to Israel. (Plural: *aliyot.*)

Almanah A widow.

Amah A Jewish maidservant. (Plural: *amahot.*)

Amora A Rabbi of the Gemara.

Androgynos A hermaphrodite: a person who is both male and female.

Andrololomosia Collective punishment, such as the Flood, that comes indiscriminately upon the world for sexual sins.

Aniut Oppression, violation, affliction, poverty; a term used to describe the rape of Dinah, enslavement in Egypt, and the abduction of a woman in warfare.

Anusah A rape victim.

Aravit The evening prayer; also called *Maariv.*

Arur Curse.

Asham Guilt-offering; a sacrifice that atoned for an uncertain violation of a prohibition punishable by *karet.*

Assiah The World of Action; the lowest of the Four Worlds of Jewish mysticism.

Atzilut The World of Emanation; the highest of the Four Worlds of Jewish mysticism.

Avodah zarah "Strange worship," the generic term for idolatry.

Avodat elilim The worship of "no-gods," statues of stone, wood, or metal.

Avodat gilulim Pagan fertility rites.

Avodat kokhavim "Star worship," meaning the deification of planets and constellations.

Baal teshuvah A secular Jew who becomes religious, that is, who "returns" to tradition.

Bamah The "high place" of pagan worship; a private altar used by Jews after entering Israel, before the Temple was built.

Baraita A collection of rabbinic statements contemporary with, but not included in, the Mishnah.

Bar mitzvah The coming of age of a Jewish boy at thirteen years old.

Bat-kohen The daughter of a priest.

Bat kol "Daughter voice," meaning a voice from heaven.

Bat mitzvah The coming of age of a Jewish girl at twelve years old.

Behemah A beast; specifically, a domestic animal.

Berdache The European term for a Native American transvestite, living in the tribal system, who has special religious functions.

Bet din A Jewish court of seventy-one, twenty-three, or three judges; in modern times, only those with three judges still exist.

Bet midrash House of study.

Betulah A virgin.

Bikkurim Tithe of the firstfruits of the seven species native to Israel: wheat, barley, grapes, figs, pomegranates, olives, and dates.

Bilineal descent Kinship through both the mother and the father.

Bilocal marriage A marriage in which the couple chooses which kin (husband's or wife's) with whom to live.

Bimah The raised platform in the synagogue from which the Torah is read.

Binah The quality of Understanding, which the Rabbis say God gave more of to women than men; the third *sefirah* of the Tree of Life, which is likened to Leah and characterized as a palace with fifty gates.

Birkat Hamazon The Grace After Meals.

Birkat Kohanim The priestly blessing, given in Numbers 6:24–26.

Boel niddah A man who has had sex with a menstruating woman and is considered a recipient of her blood.

Bogeret An adult female; a girl over twelve and a half years and one day old.

Boshet A fine paid by a seducer or a rapist for disgrace and indignity, the amount of which was determined by each party's social status.

Bride-price A monetary sum or goods presented by the groom's family to the bride's family; typical of patrilocal marriage.

Brideservice Work ("husbandry") done by a groom for a specified period of time for his bride's family (as Jacob did for Lavan); typical of matrilocal marriage.

Briyah The World of Creation; the second highest of the Four Worlds of Jewish mysticism.

Chalal A *kohen* who has lost his priestly status; also, the son of a forbidden priestly marriage who, although he is still technically a *kohen*, is disqualified from functioning as one.

Chalalah The daughter of a forbidden priestly marriage; she, too, is forbidden to marry a priest.

Chalitzah The repudiation of a brother-in-law (*levir*) by a childless widow.

Challah Braided bread used at Sabbath and holiday meals; in Temple times, the portion of dough that was pinched off the bread by its baker to be given as a tithe to the priest; today, the same pinch of dough is thrown into the fire of one's own oven.

Chalutzah A woman who has released her brother-in-law from the obligation of levirate marriage.

Chamas Violence, a cause of the Flood.

Chametz Leavened products, which may not be eaten during Passover.

ChaNaH The three *mitzvot* that are said to have special significance for women—*challah* (making bread), *niddah* (observing menstrual laws), and *hadlikat nerot* (lighting the Sabbath and festival lights).

Chanukah A postbiblical Jewish holiday, beginning on 25 *Kislev* and lasting eight days, that commemorates the rededication of the Second Temple in 165 B.C.E., during the long era of Jewish struggle against Roman oppression.

Chartumim Pharaoh's magicians.

Chasid A follower of Chasidism, a Jewish movement that is rooted in mysticism, emphasizes joy as a source of holiness, and is focused on a particular rabbi as the central figure.

Chatat Sin-offering; a sacrifice that atoned for an unintentional violation of a prohibition punishable by *karet*.

Chayot Four creatures on the Chariot in the prophet Ezekiel's vision.

Chelev The internal fat of an animal, which is forbidden to be eaten by a Jew under penalty of *karet*.

Cherem "Doomed thing"; killing women and children in warfare instead of taking them as "spoils" to be used by victorious soldiers as wives and slaves; also consecrated to God through annihilation.

Chesed The quality of Mercy, expansive loving-kindness; the fourth *sefirah* of the Tree of Life, which is likened to Avraham and Rivkah.

Chilel To desecrate, profane, or desacralize; to secularize something sacred and precious through common, everyday use.

Chilul habat Desecration of one's daughter.

Chilul Hashem Desecration of God's Name.

Chokhmah The quality of Wisdom; the second *sefirah* of the Tree of Life, which is characterized as the key that opens the palace (of *Binah*).

Chol Secular; common; for everyday use.

Chol hamoed The intermediate days of the festivals of Sukkot and Passover.

Choteh A grain *chatat* brought for an unintentional violation of the laws of *tumah*.

Chover chaver A person who uses charms, incantations, or spells.

Chukim Legal statutes of the Torah that have no rational explanation.

Chullin Common, secular, nonsacrificial food.

Chumash The written Torah; the Pentateuch; the Five Books of Moses: Genesis, Exodus, Leviticus, Numbers, and Deuteronomy.

Chuppah The wedding canopy.

Chutzpah Guts, nerve, gall, boldness.

Code of Hammurabi Babylonian legal code in use around 1700 B.C.E.

Couvade Male simulation of childbirth.

Cross cousin The child of one's mother's brother or father's sister.

Daven "Pray"; the anglicized "davening" is commonly used as a noun to refer to the Jewish prayer service.

Days of Awe The ten days from Rosh Hashanah to Yom Kippur, which are characterized by solemn introspection.

Derabbanan A rabbinic decree.

D'oraita A Torah law.

Doresh el-hametim A necromancer; one who inquires of the dead.

Dowry A monetary sum or goods presented by the bride's family to the groom's family; money or property brought to the marriage by the woman which, in Jewish law, must be returned to her upon divorce.

Du-partzufim Back-to-back; used in reference to the *adam*, which was created as a male and female joined together at the back.

Endogamy Marriage within one's (kinship) group; its main advantage is that it preserves wealth (or land) within the group, which is why the daughters of Zelophechad had to marry within their tribe.

Eretz Israel The Land of Israel.

Erev rav The "mixed multitude," Egyptians who left Egypt with the Jews; according to the *Zohar*, these were the sorcerers of Egypt.

Erev Shabbat Friday day, before sundown.

Erusah A betrothed woman; she is technically married but not yet living with her husband.

Erusin Betrothal, the first stage of marriage, which is effected by the groom giving the bride a ring; also called *kiddushin*; in ancient times, this was performed separately from the second stage of marriage, meaning that after *erusin*, the woman continued to live with her parents.

Ervat Nakedness.

Ervat gilah "Exiled nakedness," the perversion and violation of sexual boundaries; a sexual offense or prohibition; one of the six forbidden sexual relations enumerated in Leviticus 18: incest, female adultery, male homosexuality, bestiality, sex during menstruation, and sex with a living wife's sister.

Eshet-kohen The wife of a priest.

Etrog A citron, one of the Four Species waved at Sukkot; it corresponds to Sarah and the heart.

Exogamy Marriage outside one's (kinship) group; its main advantage is that it forges alliances.

Ezer knegdo "A help against him"; a description of woman in relation to man in Genesis 2:18.

Galli   The eunuch transvestite priests of Cybele and Attis.

Galut   Exile.

Gan Eden   The Garden of Eden, Paradise, "heaven," *olam haba*, the world to come.

Gehinom   A valley near Jerusalem, south of Mount Zion and west of Silwan, where pagan child sacrifice was conducted; the Jewish term for "hell."

Gemara   Rabbinic discussions of the Mishnah; together, Mishnah and Gemara form the Talmud.

Gematria   The numerical value of each Hebrew letter; adding these up in a Hebrew word gives the numerical value of that word; words with the same *gematria* —identical numerical value—are often interpreted to have some spiritual connection in meaning.

Ger   "Stranger"; *ger tzedek* is a convert to Judaism, while *ger toshav* is a gentile who lives among Jews and observes the Noachide laws.

Gerushah   A divorcée.

Get   A bill of divorce, a document that must be given by the husband to the wife.

Gevurah   The quality of Judgment, strength through limitation; the fifth *sefirah* of the Tree of Life, which is likened to Sarah and Isaac.

Gezel   Robbery, a cause of the Flood.

Halakhah   The corpus of Jewish law; the "way to go"; also one specific law. (Adjective: halakhic.)

Hallel   A song of praise recited on the festivals.

Hashem Elokim   Usually translated as "the Lord God"; Hashem is the name for the four-letter Name of God composed of the Hebrew letters Yod, Heh, Vav, and another Heh. Elokim is actually spelled with an *H* and not a *K*, but because we only pronounce Names of God in ritual acts, when we need to say these names in everyday conversation we change a letter.

Hashgachah pratit   Divine providence.

Hasmoneans   Leaders of the Chanukah rebellion.

Henotheism   The worship of one god while believing that others exist.

Hod   The quality of Glory; the eighth *sefirah* of the Tree of Life.

Hoshana Raba   The seventh day of Sukkot, which is observed by beating willow branches on the ground.

Imahot   Mothers; the matriarchs.

Ir hamiklat   A city of refuge to which manslayers fled for protection from blood avengers.

Ir hanidachat   A "condemned city," a Jewish town in which the majority of the population has been enticed, at the instigation of Jewish men, into practicing idolatry.

Ish   Man; a person with the status of a free man. (Plural: *anashim*, which can mean "men" or "people.")

Ish tahor   A man or woman who moved the ashes of the Red Heifer from the altar to outside the camp.

Ishah   Woman.

Isheh   The fire on the sacrificial altar.

Itzavon   "Toil"; used by God with Adam in relation to the earth and with Chavah in relation to child rearing. With the exile from the Garden of Eden, growing crops and raising children required hard work over a prolonged period of time.

Kabbalah   Jewish mysticism. (Adjective: kabbalistic.)

Kadashim   Sacred or sacrificial food of two types (*kodesh kadashim* and *trumah*), which had to be eaten within certain boundaries.

Kaddish   Sanctification of the dead; the prayer said by a mourner, usually for a deceased parent, for eleven months after the death.

Kadesh   A eunuch transvestite priest who served as a prostitute for men in pagan religions. (Plural: *kedeshim*.)

Kallah   A bride; a daughter-in-law.

Kalut dat   Quick-mindedness; mental flexibility.

Kalut rosh   Frivolity.

Kaporet   The gold cover of the ark in the Tabernacle.

Karet   The punishment of spiritual excision described by the biblical phrase, "that soul will be cut off from its people"; a consequence of thirty-six particular sins; according to various levels of interpretation, this means that one dies a premature death, loses one's place in the afterlife, or is not reincarnated as a Jew.

Kashrut   The Jewish dietary laws, whose basic principles concern what animals may be eaten, how such animals must be slaughtered, and the separation of meat from milk products.

Katlanit   A woman whose first and second husbands have died; she is believed to have "caused" this and is prohibited from remarrying.

Kedeshah   A pagan priestess who served a goddess through "sacred prostitution." (Plural: *kedeshot*.)

Kedushah   A state of holiness; sanctification through separation.

Kehatites   The most significant branch of the Levites, who carried the vessels of the Tabernacle through the wilderness between campsites.

Kehunah   The Jewish priesthood, which confers the right to eat *trumah*.

Kemitzah   A handful of flour scooped out of a grain-offering and burned on the altar.

Kesut   "Covering," lodging and clothing, the second of three obligations a husband has toward his wife, according to Jewish law.

Ketanah   A minor female; a girl from three years and one day to twelve years old.

Keter   Crown; the first *sefirah* of the Tree of Life.

Ketubah   The marriage contract; it guarantees the wife her food, lodging and clothing, and "conjugal rights" (i.e., sexual pleasure), as well as a monetary settlement in case of divorce.

Kiddush   Sanctification of wine; the blessing recited over a cup of wine on the Sabbath and holidays.

Kiddush Hashem   The sanctification of God's Name; martyrdom in the face of being commanded to commit murder, idolatry, or *ervat gilah*; the choice of a Jew to die rather than renounce Judaism.

Kiddushin   Sanctification of sex through betrothal, the first stage of marriage; also called *erusin*.

Kishuf Sorcery. (Plural: *keshufim.*)

Kli gever A "male vessel."

Knas A fifty-shekel fine paid by a seducer or a rapist.

Kodesh The sacred; sanctified through separation for rare and precious use; the Sanctuary, the front two-thirds of the Tabernacle, containing the showbread, menorah, and incense altar.

Kodesh kadashim Holy of Holies; the back third of the Tabernacle, containing the ark, which is entered only by the high priest on Yom Kippur; sacrificial food that had to be eaten within the boundaries of the Tabernacle or Temple courtyard.

Kohen A priest, a patrilineal descendant of Aaron. (Plural: *kohanim.*)

Kohenet A woman of the priestly class. (Plural: *kohanot.*)

Kol ishah The singing voice of a woman, which is considered sexually arousing to men by rabbinic tradition.

Kol Nidre A prayer said on Yom Kippur evening to renounce all vows.

Konam A term used in vowing to indicate that the prohibited object or activity was being consecrated to God.

Korban Sacrifice; "drawing near" to God.

Kosem kesamim A person who practices stick divination.

Kotel The Western Wall of the Temple, sometimes called the "Wailing Wall"; the holiest site in Judaism.

Kruvim The cherubim, angels with children's faces, who are depicted on top of the ark in the Tabernacle and the Temple.

Kubah Inner chamber of the Tabernacle; same root as *kavah*, or *womb*, the "inner chamber" of a woman.

Kumaz A women's body ornament in ancient times which was a primitive form of the chastity belt; given over by Jewish women to be melted down and used to build the Tabernacle.

Lashon hara An "evil tongue"; gossip, whether slanderous or true.

Lechem panim "Bread of faces," the showbread in the Tabernacle.

Leket Fallen stalks or fruit that must be left for the poor.

Letzachek "Playing" or "making sport"; sexual merrymaking, especially that of idol worship accompanied by feasting and drinking.

Leviah A woman of the tribe of Levi who is not a *kohenet.*

Levir The brother-in-law of a childless widow.

Levirate marriage The obligation of a man to marry the childless widow of his dead brother; done to preserve the patrilineal line of inheritance, but also as a means of security for a woman to remain in her patrilineal household even if her husband died; its correlate, sororate marriage, in which a woman married the childless widower of her dead sister, or the husband of her barren sister, was not practiced in biblical society.

Levite A patrilineal descendant of the families of Levi, especially of Yokheved and Amram; this includes Aharon and his descendants (the *kohanim*), Moses and his patrilineal descendants, and Miriam, but not her descendants, who were of their father's tribe (Judah).

Lulav A palm branch, one of the Four Species waved at Sukkot; corresponds to Rivkah and the spine; branches of willow (Rachel, mouth) and myrtle (Leah, eyes) are also attached to it.

Maariv The evening prayer; also called *Aravit*.

Maaseh Merkavah A form of Jewish mysticism, concerning Ezekiel's Chariot and its four creatures, symbolized in the women's weavings for the Tabernacle.

Maaser ani Tithe of the Poor; every third and sixth year, the Second Tithe was given to the poor instead of being eaten by its owner in Jerusalem.

Maaser rishon First Tithe; after *trumah*, a tithe of 10 percent of the remainder of one's crop was given to the Levites for their duty of caring for the Tabernacle.

Maaser sheni Second Tithe; after *trumah* and First Tithe, 10 percent of the remainder of one's crop was eaten by the owner in Jerusalem.

Makom kodesh The Tabernacle/Temple and its courtyard, where *kodesh kadashim* had to be eaten; also called the *mikdash*.

Makom tahor The camp in the wilderness and (later) the city of Jerusalem, the boundaries within which *trumah* could be eaten.

Malkhut Sovereignty, manifest energy; the tenth *sefirah* of the Tree of Life, which is likened to Rachel.

Mamzer The offspring of incest, adultery, or sex with a living wife's sister; from *mum zar*, meaning "strange blemish"; commonly translated as "bastard," it is not, however, equivalent to the gentile definition of a child born out of wedlock.

Manna The food from heaven that fell in the wilderness.

Mashal An example; a fable.

Mashkeh akarot A drink given to women to make them barren, which was used in the generation of the Flood and perhaps in the time of the matriarchs as well.

Matrilineal descent Kinship through the mother; mother-to-daughter lineage; inheritance passes from uncle to maternal nephew; the tradition that a child is Jewish only if its mother is Jewish, regardless of the father.

Matrilocal marriage A marriage in which the couple lives with the wife's kin after marriage.

Matzevah A stone pillar used in pagan worship as an ancestral totem.

Mayim chayim "Living waters," a metaphor for the Torah.

Mazal "Constellation"; fate or "luck" based on astrological timing.

Megillah "Scroll," such as *Megillat Esther*, the Scroll (or Book) of Esther, or the *megillah* of a *sotah*, the scroll written for an individual woman accused of adultery by a jealous husband.

Mei Merivah "Waters of dispute"; where Moses' experienced misfortune through water, striking the rock instead of speaking to it, and consequently was not permitted to enter the Promised Land.

Mei niddah "Waters of *niddah*"; a potion made from the ashes of a red heifer burnt with cedarwood, hyssop, and crimson wool, which, when sprinkled on a person who was *tamae* from contact with a corpse, made him or her *tahor*.

Mekhashefa A sorceress.

Mekor dameha   The "fountain of her blood"; the womb, the source of the blood of childbirth and menstruation.

Menachesh   One who bases one's actions on omens or "signs."

Mensch   A good person, one with integrity.

Me'onen   One who predicts "auspicious times" and acts according to them.

Messianic Era   A time of peace and perfection in the world, when all forms of exile will end, Jews will be regathered in Israel, and the Temple will be rebuilt.

Met   Death *tumah* conveyed by a corpse (human carcass).

Metzora   A person with the skin disease *tzaraat*.

Mezuman   Three people of the same gender who have shared a meal, and thus begin *Birkat Hamazon* with a specific formula.

Mezuzah   A scroll with Torah verses put upon the doorposts of a Jewish home.

Midah kneged midah   Measure for measure, "tit for tat"; the Jewish notion of "karma," that what you sow (do to others) you will reap (will come back to you).

Midrash   Rabbinic exposition and interpretation of the Torah, usually of a nonhalakhic nature.

Mifletzet   A phallus carried by women who worshiped Asherah.

Mikdash   Sanctified space, the Tabernacle/Temple and its courtyard; also called *makom kodesh*.

Mikseh   The roof of the Tabernacle.

Mikvah   Ritual bath used to change the status of a person or a vessel from *tamae* to *tahor*.

Milchemet mitzvah   Obligatory war; a war of self-defense.

Milchemet reshut   Optional war; a war of aggression.

Minchah   Grain-offering; the afternoon prayer.

Minchat kena'ot   "Jealousy offering"; the barley sacrifice required of a jealous husband who has accused his wife of adultery.

Minyan   A group of ten Jews for any required purpose; for example, ten adult Jewish males required for prayer or ten adult Jews of either gender before whom one must die rather than commit murder, idolatry, or *ervat gilah*.

Miriam's Well   The archetype of all the wells and "living waters" mentioned in the Torah; in the wilderness, a beehive-shaped rock that rolled along with the Jews wherever they went, and settled in the Tabernacle courtyard when they camped.

Mishkan   The Tabernacle structure; also called *ohel moed*.

Mishmeret   Vigilantly guarding something to preserve its sanctity; a sacred duty of watchfulness, observance, keeping, guarding, and preserving; for example, keeping the Sabbath, staying with a corpse until it is buried, and observing *niddah*; the *mishmarot* were the rounds of Levites assigned to guard the Tabernacle.

Mishnah   The oral Torah, compiled and written down by 200 c.e.

Mishpatim   Social ordinances of the Torah that can be rationally explained in ethical terms.

Mitzvah   One of 613 commandments incumbent upon the Jewish people; there are 248 positive and 365 negative. (Plural: *mitzvot*.)

Miun   The situation in which a minor daughter who has been married off by her mother or brother may repudiate the marriage when she reaches the age of twelve, whereupon the marriage is dissolved without a divorce; the girl is called a *mema'enet*.

Mohar   The Hebrew term for bride-price.

Mored   A "rebellious husband," one who fails to live up to his terms of the marriage contract (the three obligations listed under "*ketubah*").

Moredet   A "rebellious wife," one who fails to live up to her terms of the marriage contract (to perform certain household tasks if her husband is financially supporting her); the Rabbis added to this definition a woman who refuses to have sex with her husband.

Muktzah   An animal which has been dedicated as a sacrifice to a pagan idol (and may not be used for Jewish purposes); anything which may not be touched on Shabbat.

Mum   "Blemish"; an imperfection or bodily asymmetry (not necessarily a physical disability) which disqualifies a *kohen* from acting as a priest or an animal from being a sacrifice.

Naarah   A pubescent female; a girl from twelve years and one day to twelve and a half years old.

Naditu   A pagan priestess who served a god through the *hieros gamos* or "sacred marriage."

Nazirut   A vow to abstain from wine, all grape products, haircuts, and contact with the dead for at least thirty days.

Nechash nechashat   A copper snake built by Moses to stop a snake plague in the wilderness; it was destroyed in later times when it became an object of Jewish communal idol worship.

Neder   A vow; prohibiting an object to oneself.

Ne'evad   An animal that has been worshiped as a deity.

Nefesh   Life force; animal soul; the lowest level of the human soul.

Neolocal marriage   A marriage in which the couple lives in its own independent domestic unit.

Neshamah   The divine soul, what distinguishes humans from animals.

Nesuah   A (fully) married woman.

Nesuin   The second stage of marriage, effected by the *chuppah* ceremony, at which point the couple lives together; in modern times the two stages of marriage are performed simultaneously.

Netzach   The quality of Eternity; the seventh *sefirah* of the Tree of Life.

Nevelah   Death *tumah* conveyed by an animal carcass; either a nonkosher mammal or a kosher mammal that died through any means other than ritual slaughter.

Niddah   Procreative *tumah* conveyed by menstruation; a menstruating woman; the period of sexual separation between husband and wife at this time.

Nirbah An animal used for bestiality by a man.

Noachide laws Seven obligations incumbent upon gentiles from the Torah: to not commit murder, robbery, idolatry, blasphemy, *ervat gilah*, or tear the limb off a living animal, and to set up courts of law.

Ohel Tent; mystically, the manifestation of celestial light.

Ohel moed The Tabernacle structure; also called *mishkan*.

Olah Burnt-offering; a voluntary sacrifice that atoned for neglecting a positive commandment.

Olelot Undeveloped clusters of grapes that must be left for the poor.

Omer The seven weeks between Passover and Shavuot; also called *Sefirah*.

Onah "Conjugal rights," the third of three obligations that a husband has toward his wife, according to Jewish law.

Orlah "Foreskin"; "uncircumcised"; a sheath or covering; the fruit of a fruit tree for the first three years, which may not be eaten; the hair of a boy's head for the first three years, which may not be cut.

Ov A medium for a spirit named Pitom, who speaks out of an individual's armpit.

Parallel cousin The child of one's mother's sister or father's brother.

Pareve Neither meat nor milk; grains, nuts, vegetables, and fruits, as well as fish and eggs.

Parnasah The sustenance (wealth, income, job, career) endowed to us by God.

Parokhet The veil covering the Holy of Holies.

Parshah Torah portion of the week; each of fifty-four divisions of the Five Books of Moses, which are each called "*Parshat* [first word or two of the passage]."

Patrilineal descent Kinship through the father; father-to-son lineage and inheritance; the notion, adopted by the Reform movement, that a child can be Jewish even if only its father is Jewish and its mother is not.

Patrilocal marriage A marriage in which the couple lives with the husband's kin after marriage.

Peah "Corner"; the crops of the corner of one's field, vineyard, or grove which must be left unharvested for the poor; the hair of the corner of a man's head which may not shaved off, forming the earlocks known as *peyos*.

Peret Fallen grapes that must be left for the poor.

Pesach Passover, the spring harvest festival commemorating the Exodus from Egypt.

Pgam A fine paid by a seducer or a rapist for "blemish" or "deterioration," the amount of which was determined by the victim's value at the slave market.

Pidyon haben Redemption of the firstborn son; a compensation for pagan sacrifice of firstborn sons.

Polyandry One woman has several husbands; in fraternal polyandry, the most common form, the husbands are brothers; this practice is still found in parts of Tibet, Nepal, and India.

Polygamy Marriage to more than one person (simultaneously) by both men and women; the term means polyandry and polygyny *together*.

Polygyny One man has several wives; in sororal polgyny, the most common form, the wives are sisters; in nonindustrial societies, this increases a man's wealth.

Pru urvu The command given by God to procreate; an obligation incumbent upon men only.

Purim A postbiblical holiday, on 14–15 *Adar*, which commemorates how Esther, a Jewish woman of the fifth century B.C.E., became queen of Persia and saved the Jews from annihilation by Haman, the king's prime minister.

Rachamim Empathy; from *rechem*, meaning "womb"; complete identification with another entity, like a pregnant woman with her fetus.

Ras Shamra tablets A twentieth-century C.E. archaeological discovery containing epic poetry of fourteenth-century B.C.E. Ugarit, an area just north of biblical Canaan; from these tablets come most of our knowledge of Canaanite mythology and religion.

Red Heifer A ritual concoction whose ashes were used to make *tahor* a person who was *tamae met*.

Rephaim "Mighty ones," the giants of old.

Resurrection of the dead The Jewish belief that in the Messianic Era, the physical bodies of the dead will rise from their graves.

River Heifer A ritual in which a cow's neck was broken to atone for an unsolved murder.

Rodef A "pursuer"; such a person, who is coming to rape or kill someone, must be killed, if necessary, to stop him or her.

Rosh Chodesh The New Moon, which marks the beginning of each Jewish month.

Rosh Hashanah The New Moon of the seventh month; the Jewish New Year; commemorates the sixth day of Creation and the days on which both Sarah and Rachel conceived.

Rovea An animal used for bestiality with a woman.

Ruach hakodesh The spirit of prophecy; divine inspiration.

Ruach kinah A spirit of jealousy.

Saignade Male simulation of menstruation.

Sanhedrin The Jewish courts of seventy-one judges (Great Sanhedrin) and of twenty-three judges (Small Sanhedrin); these ceased to exist with the destruction of the Second Temple.

Saris A eunuch; also means "officer," referring to a man who was castrated in order to serve as a harem guard or other palace official.

Satan The "prosecuting angel" that argues against a person to God; combined with the pagan satyr to form the Christian devil.

Satyr A pagan god that was part man and part goat; a man with satyriasis, an abnormal "uncontrollable" sexual desire.

Sefirah One of ten spheres, or emanations, of the Tree of Life, representing aspects of God; another name for the *omer*.

Segan Assistant high priest.

Shabbat The Jewish Sabbath, from sundown on Friday to starlight on Saturday; treated as Queen, a Bride, or God's Daughter.

Shachrit The morning prayer.

Shalom bayit   Domestic peace.

Shalom zakhor   A ceremony welcoming the birth of a boy (separate from the circumcision ceremony); can mean "welcome male" as well as "remember peace," a linkage that acknowledges that violence in the world overwhelmingly comes from the male of the species.

Shavuot   The harvest festival, occurring fifty days after Passover, which commemorates the Revelation at Sinai.

Shechitah   The Jewish method of ritual slaughter of a permitted animal for meat, which renders it kosher.

She'er   "Sustenance" or "maintenance," the first of three obligations a husband has toward his wife, according to Jewish law.

Sheketz   Something to be shunned and avoided; a gentile man. (Feminine: *shiktzah*).

Shekhinah   The Divine Presence; divine immanence; the tangible manifestations of God; God as perceived through the physical senses; characterized as female by Jewish mystics.

Sheretz   Death *tumah* conveyed by the carcass of any one of eight kinds of reptiles or small mammals, whose common trait is that they burrow underground and live *in* the earth rather than on it.

Shevuah   An oath; prohibiting an action to oneself.

Shfikat damim   Spilling blood; refers to murder halakhically, but actually encompasses all pagan ritual bloodshed.

Shifchah   A female slave, usually Canaanite.

Shikhchah   Forgotten crops that must then be left for the poor.

Shikhvat zera   Procreative *tumah* conveyed by a seminal emission.

Shirah   The feminine form of *shir*, "song," which is used to refer to spiritual musical expressions of the Jews, such as the song of the Shekhinah (the song sung by the Jews after crossing the Red Sea).

Shlamim   Peace-offering; a voluntary offering of celebration or thanks; the only sacrifice in which the owner received a portion of the meat.

Shma   The Jewish prayer declaring that God is One.

Shmini Atzeret   The eighth-day festival marking the end of Sukkot, on which Jews pray for rain.

Shmitah   The Sabbatical Year; the "earth's Sabbath" every seventh year, in which the Land lies fallow, crops are not harvested, and all produce is ownerless; associated with *Malkhut*.

Shofar   A ram's horn, blown at Rosh Hashanah and Yom Kippur.

Shotah   A madwoman or fool; one who operates out of a spirit of idiocy, folly, or even insanity. (Masculine: *shoteh*.)

Shugetu   A low-ranking priestess in Babylonia.

Simchat bat   Celebration of the birth of a girl.

Simchat bet hashoevah   The water-drawing ceremony of Sukkot.

Simchat Torah   A festival of dancing with the Torah; the culmination of the autumn holidays that begin with Rosh Hashanah.

Smikhah   Laying one's hands on a sacrificial animal; rabbinic ordination.

Sotah The "accused wife"; a ritual undergone by a woman *suspected* of adultery by her jealous husband.

Subincision A male initiation rite in which the underside of the penis is slit to make it bleed; a form of saignade; as a result, the man must urinate sitting or squatting, like a woman.

Sudar The bedsheet from the wedding night which was supposed to prove the bride was a virgin by having hymeneal blood on it.

Sukkah The temporary hut that Jews build to eat their meals in during Sukkot.

Sukkot The autumn harvest festival commemorating the forty years in the wilderness.

Suttee The Hindu term for the sacrifice of a widow by immolation on her husband's funeral pyre.

Tabernacle The *mishkan* or *ohel moed*; the portable structure, predating the Temple, used in the wilderness.

Taharah A state in which a person may enter the Tabernacle/Temple, eat sacrificial food, and have sex; part of a cycle with *tumah*; body–spirit unity beginning at birth and ending at death.

Tahor In the state of *taharah*; complete.

Tamae In the state of *tumah*; separated.

Tamim (or tam) Pure, whole, perfect, unblemished, innocent, simple.

Tanakh The Hebrew Bible, comprising Torah, Prophets, and Writings; the "Old Testament."

Tanna A Rabbi of the Mishnah.

Tefillin Leather boxes containing Torah verses traditionally worn by Jewish men on their heads and left arms during prayer.

Tehorot Ritual objects used in the Tabernacle and the Temple.

Tekhelet Indigo blue wool.

Tekiah A single, long blast of the *shofar*.

Temple The House of God in Jerusalem. Built by Solomon, the First Temple was destroyed by the Babylonians; the Second Temple was destroyed by the Romans.

Terafim Statues of idols serving as household gods, often made from the shrunken heads of sacrificed firstborn sons and used for divination.

Teshucah "Yearning" or "longing"; used to describe women's sexual desire for men, the rain's need to fall upon the earth, God's longing for Israel, and the evil inclination's attraction to Cayin.

Teshuvah "Return"; repentance.

Tevel Food from which tithes have not been taken.

Tiferet The quality of Beauty, truth and harmony; the sixth *sefirah* of the Tree of Life, which is likened to Jacob.

Tikkun olam "Repair of the world"; a process, in which every Jew is required to participate, of making the world a better place in order to bring about the Messianic Era.

Tisha B'Av   The ninth day of the fifth month; the date of the decree on men in the wilderness; a fast day to mourn the destruction of the Temple(s) and other tragedies in Jewish history.

Tnufah   "Wave-offering"; the ritual of waving a sacrifice in the four directions to prevent "misfortune and bad winds."

Todah   A *shlamim* offered in thanks for rescue from grave peril.

Toevah   An "abomination" or repugnant practice.

Tree of Life   A kabbalistic diagram consisting of ten *sefirot*, or emanations, which represent aspects of God as well as the pattern of Creation.

Trefah   An animal that has a fatal organic flaw, being torn or blemished in such a way that it will die within a year, and is thus unfit to sacrifice and/or eat.

Trumah   "Elevated-offering"; the ritual of elevating a sacrifice up and down to keep away "evil dews"; the priestly portion of the *shlamim*, and the priestly tithe from crops; the voluntary gifts donated to make the Tabernacle.

Trumah maaser   A tithe of 10 percent from the Levites to the *kohanim*.

Tumah   A state in which a person may not enter the Tabernacle/Temple, eat sacrificial food, or have sex; part of a cycle with *taharah*; a condition that affects any form of life that is born and dies; three types: death *tumah*, procreative *tumah*, and sickness *tumah*.

Tumat erev   The state of being *tamae* for a day.

Tumat shivah   The state of being *tamae* for a week.

Tumtum   An individual of indeterminate gender.

Tzaar   A fine paid by a rapist for inflicting pain.

Tzaddik   A righteous person.

Tzaraat   Sickness *tumah* conveyed by a skin disease, usually mistranslated as "leprosy," which turned the body white and was caused by speaking *lashon hara*; it could also appear in fabric or on walls of houses.

Tzel   "Shadow"; the root of the name Zillah, the wife of Lemekh, who lived in his shadow.

Tzela   "Side"; often translated as "rib."

Tzitzit   Ritual fringes on any four-cornered garment traditionally worn by Jewish men.

Tzovot   The hosts of women who assembled at the entrance of the *ohel moed* to learn Torah, pray, and do some kind of service for the Tabernacle.

Urim and tumim   A parchment on which were written the Names of God and placed in the breastplate of stones (one gem per tribe) worn by the high priest; used for communication with God.

Xanith   An Arab male of Oman who is a transvestite, a slave, and a homosexual prostitute.

Yaldah   A girl up to three years old.

Yavam   A man who is obligated to marry his dead brother's childless widow.

Yefat toar   A woman abducted in warfare.

Yeshivah bocher   A young man whose major activity is the study of Talmud.

Yesod   Foundation; the ninth *sefirah* of the Tree of Life.

Yetzer hara   The "evil inclination"; a person's area of spiritual or moral weakness; often used to refer specifically to male sexual temptation.

Yetzirah   The World of Formation; the second lowest of the Four Worlds of Jewish mysticism.

Yevamah   A childless widow who must perform levirate marriage, that is, must marry her deceased husband's brother, unless she undergoes *chalitzah*.

Yibum   Levirate marriage.

Yidoni   A person who speaks an oracle derived from putting the bone of an animal (a *yidoa*) into one's mouth.

Yiud   The designation of a Jewish maidservant for marriage by her master; akin to the *kiddushin* of a free woman.

Yoledet   Procreative *tumah* conveyed by childbirth; a woman who has given birth to a boy in the last forty days or a girl in the last eighty days.

Yom Kippur   The Day of Atonement.

Yovel   The Jubilee Year; the fiftieth year in the Land's cycle, following seven *Shmitah* years (in which no crops are sown or harvested); associated with *Binah*.

Zakhar   Male.

Zakhor   Remember.

Zar   An Israelite man who marries a *kohenet*.

Zav   A man who has a nonseminal genital emission.

Zavah   A woman who has a nonmenstrual genital emission (of blood).

Zekenah   An old, postmenopausal woman.

Zekhukhah   A *yevamah* who has neither been married by her brother-in-law nor released through *chalitzah*; akin to an *agunah*.

Zimah   Lewdness; "*znut* that is thought of in secret"; in the Torah itself, the term is used only in reference to father–daughter incest and *chilul habat*; the underlying dynamic by which a victim of incest is set up for a life of prostitution.

Zivah   Sickness *tumah* conveyed by an abnormal genital emission; the state of being a *zav* or a *zavah*.

Znut   Sexual degradation; prostitution, promiscuity, licentiousness, lust; the seduction and degradation of idolatry.

Zonah   A "common" or "secular" prostitute; a woman who is ineligible to marry into the priesthood because a man has committed *ervat gilah* with her. (Plural: *zonot*.)

Bibliography

BOOKS

Abel, E. L. *Moon Madness.* Greenwich, CT: Fawcett, 1976.

Adler, Margot. *Drawing Down the Moon.* Boston: Beacon Press, 1979.

Aharoni, Yohanan, and Avi-Yonah, Michael. *The Macmillan Bible Atlas.* New York: Macmillan, 1968.

Aiken, Lisa. *To Be a Jewish Woman.* Northvale, NJ: Jason Aronson, 1992.

Altorki, Soraya. *Women in Saudi Arabia.* New York: Columbia University Press, 1986.

Amler, Jane Frances. *Christopher Columbus's Jewish Roots.* Northvale, NJ: Jason Aronson, 1991.

Aquinas, Thomas. *Summa Theologica of St. Thomas Aquinas.* Vol. 1. New York: Benziger Brothers, 1947.

Arditti, Rita, Klein, Renate Duelli, and Minden, Shelley, eds. *Test-Tube Women.* Boston: Pandora Press, 1984.

Barry, Kathleen. *Female Sexual Slavery.* New York: Avon Books, 1979.

Benedict, Helen. *Virgin or Vamp: How the Press Covers Sex Crimes.* New York: Oxford University Press, 1992.

Berkovits, Eliezer. *Jewish Women in Time and Torah.* Hoboken, NJ: Ktav, 1990.

Biale, Rachel. *Women and Jewish Law.* New York: Schocken, 1984.

Birnbaum, Philip. *Daily Prayer Book.* New York: Hebrew Publishing Co., 1977.

———. *High Holyday Prayer Book.* New York: Hebrew Publishing Co., 1979.

Blackman, Philip. *Mishnayoth.* 6 vols. Gateshead: Judaica Press, 1990.

Blume, E. Sue. *Secret Survivors: Uncovering Incest and Its Aftereffects in Women.* New York: John Wiley and Sons, 1990.

Blumstein, Philip, and Schwartz, Pepper. *American Couples.* New York: William Morrow and Co., 1983.

Bolton, Brett L. *The Secret Powers of Plants.* New York: Berkley Publishing, 1974.

Boston Women's Health Book Collective. *Our Bodies, Ourselves.* New York: Simon and Schuster, 1973.

Boswell, John. *Christianity, Social Tolerance, and Homosexuality.* Chicago: University of Chicago Press, 1980.

Brier, Bob. *Ancient Egyptian Magic.* New York: Quill, 1981.

Briffault, Robert. *The Mothers.* Vols. 1–3. New York: Macmillan, 1927.

Brownmiller, Susan. *Against Our Will.* New York: Simon and Schuster, 1975.

Buckley, Thomas, and Gottlieb, Alma. *Blood Magic: The Anthropology of Menstruation.* Berkeley: University of California Press, 1988.

Budapest, Zsuzsanna Emese. *The Holy Book of Women's Mysteries.* Part 2. Los Angeles: author, 1980.

Budge, E. A. Wallis. *Babylonian Life and History.* New York: Dorset Press, 1992.

Caplan, Paula J. *The Myth of Women's Masochism.* New York: E. P. Dutton, 1985.

Carter, Harry, trans. *The Histories of Herodotus.* Vol. 1. New York: Heritage Press, 1958.

Carus, Paul. *The History of the Devil and the Idea of Evil.* New York: Bell, 1969.

Casson, Lionel. *Ancient Egypt.* Alexandria, VA: Time-Life, 1965.

Cassuto, U. *The Goddess Anath.* Jerusalem: Magnes Press, 1971.

Cavendish, Richard. *The Black Arts.* New York: G. P. Putnam's Sons, 1967.

Chavel, Rabbi Dr. Charles B. *Ramban (Nachmanides) Commentary on the Torah.* 5 vols. New York: Shilo, date per volume.

Cleaver, Eldridge. *Soul on Ice.* New York: Dell-Delta/Ramparts, 1968.

Contenau, Georges. *Everyday Life in Babylon and Assyria.* New York: St. Martin's Press, 1954.

Corea, Gena. *The Mother Machine.* New York: Harper and Row, 1979.

Croutier, Alev Lytle. *Harem: The World Behind the Veil.* New York: Abbeville Press, 1989.

Daly, Mary. *Beyond God the Father.* Boston: Beacon Press, 1973.

————. *Gyn/Ecology.* Boston: Beacon Press, 1978.

Davidson, Basil. *The African Slave Trade.* Boston: Little, Brown and Co., 1980.

Davies, Nigel. *Human Sacrifice.* New York: William Morrow, 1981.

Davis, Elizabeth Gould. *The First Sex.* Baltimore, MD: Penguin, 1972.

Dawood, N. J., trans. *The Koran.* Harmondsworth, England: Penguin, 1974.

Day, John. *Molech: A God of Sacrifice in the Old Testament.* London: Cambridge University Press, 1989.

Delaney, Janice, Upton, Mary Jane, and Toth, Emily. *The Curse: A Cultural History of Menstruation.* New York: New American Library, 1977.

Dingwall, Eric John. *The Girdle of Chastity: A History of the Chastity Belt.* New York: Dorset Press, 1992.

Doane, Doris Chase. *Time Changes in the U.S.A.* San Francisco, CA: Quarto, 1973.

Dover, K. J. *Greek Homosexuality.* Cambridge, MA: Harvard University Press, 1978.

Edwards, I. E. S., Gadd, C. J., and Hammond, N. G. L., eds. *Cambridge Ancient History.* Vol. 1, part 1. New York: Cambridge University Press, 1970.

Eider, Rabbi Shimon D. *A Summary of the Halachos of the Three Weeks.* Lakewood, NJ: author, 1978.

Elon, Menachem. *The Principles of Jewish Law.* Jerusalem: Keter, n.d.

El-Or, Tamar. *Educated and Ignorant.* Boulder, CO: Lynne Rienner, 1994.

Engnell, Ivan. *Studies in Divine Kingship in the Ancient Near East.* Oxford, England: Basil Blackwell, 1967.

Epstein, Rabbi Dr. I. *The Babylonian Talmud.* 17 vols. London: Soncino Press, date per volume.

Erman, Adolf. *Life in Ancient Egypt.* New York: Dover, 1971.

Estrich, Susan. *Real Rape.* Cambridge, MA: Harvard University Press, 1987.

Feldman, David M. *Marital Relations, Birth Control, and Abortion in Jewish Law.* New York: Schocken, 1974.

Finkel, Avraham Yaakov. *The Great Torah Commentators.* Northvale, NJ: Jason Aronson, 1990.

————. *The Responsa Anthology.* Northvale, NJ: Jason Aronson, 1990.

Finkelhor, David. *Child Sexual Abuse: New Theory and Research.* New York: Free Press, 1984.

Fisch, Harold. *The Holy Scriptures.* Jerusalem: Koren, 1989.

Fornari, Franco. *The Psychoanalysis of War.* New York: Anchor, 1974.

Frazer, James. *The Golden Bough.* Abridged ed. New York: Macmillan, 1922.
Freedman, Rabbi Dr. H. *Midrash Rabbah.* 5 vols. New York: Soncino Press, 1983.
Gaster, Theodor H. "The Religion of the Canaanites." In *Ancient Religions,* ed. Vergilius Ferm, pp. 111–143. New York: Citadel, 1965.
Gimbutas, Marija. *The Goddesses and Gods of Old Europe.* Los Angeles: University of California Press, 1982.
Ginsburgh, Rabbi Yitzchak. *The Alef-Beit: Jewish Thought Revealed through the Hebrew Letters.* Northvale, NJ: Jason Aronson, 1991.
Glazerson, Matityahu. *Hebrew: Source of Languages.* Jerusalem: Raz Ot, 5748.
Goldenberg, Naomi R. *Changing of the Gods.* Boston: Beacon Press, 1979.
Goodrick-Clarke, Nicholas. *The Occult Roots of Nazism.* Wellingborough, England: Aquarian Press, 1985.
Gordon, Murray. *Slavery in the Arab World.* New York: New Amsterdam Books, 1989.
Gottlieb, Freema. *The Lamp of God.* Northvale, NJ: Jason Aronson, 1989.
Graves, Robert. *The Greek Myths.* Vol. 1. New York: Penguin, 1960.
Graves, Robert, and Patai, Raphael. *Hebrew Myths: The Book of Genesis.* New York: McGraw-Hill, 1966.
Gray, John. *The Canaanites.* London: Thames and Hudson, 1964.
———. *Near Eastern Mythology.* London: Hamlyn, 1975.
Green, Hannah. *I Never Promised You a Rose Garden.* New York: Signet, 1964.
Guillaume, Alfred. *Islam.* Harmondsworth, England: Penguin, 1956.
Gurney, O. R. *The Hittites.* London: Penguin, 1990.
Harden, Donald. *The Phoenicians.* New York: Praeger, 1962.
Hart, George. *A Dictionary of Egyptian Gods and Goddesses.* London: Routledge and Kegan Paul, 1986.
Hays, H. R. *The Dangerous Sex: The Myth of Feminine Evil.* New York: Pocket, 1966.
Henry, Sondra, and Taitz, Emily. *Written Out of History: Our Jewish Foremothers.* Fresh Meadows, NY: Biblio Press, 1983.
Herman, Judith Lewis. *Father–Daughter Incest.* Cambridge, MA: Harvard University Press, 1981.
Higgens, Elford. *Hebrew Idolatry and Superstition.* New York: Kennikat Press, 1983.
Hillel, Rabbi Yaakov. *Faith and Folly: The Occult in Torah Perspective.* Jerusalem: Feldheim, 1990.
Hirschfelder, Arlene, and Molin, Paulette. *The Encyclopedia of Native American Religions.* New York: Facts on File, 1992.
Hooks, Bell. *Ain't I a Woman: Black Women and Feminism.* Boston: South End Press, 1981.
Horney, Karen. *Feminine Psychology.* New York: W. W. Norton & Co., 1967.
Hosken, Fran P. *Female Sexual Mutilations.* Lexington, MA: Women's International Network News, 1980.
Hunter, Mic. *Abused Boys: The Neglected Victims of Sexual Abuse.* New York: Fawcett, 1990.
Jay, Karla, and Young, Allen. *The Gay Report.* New York: Summit Books, 1977.
Jeyes, Ulla. "The Naditu Women of Sippar." In *Images of Women in Antiquity,* ed. Averil Cameron and Amelia Kuhrt, pp. 260–272. Detroit, MI: Wayne State University Press, 1983.
Jones, Carl. *After the Baby Is Born.* New York: Dodd, Mead and Co., 1986.
Kantor, Mattis. *The Jewish Time Line Encyclopedia.* Northvale, NJ: Jason Aronson, 1992.
Kaplan, Aryeh. *Meditation and Kabbalah.* York Beach, ME: Samuel Weiser, 1982.
———. *Sefer Yetzirah.* York Beach, ME: Samuel Weiser, 1990.
Kaufman, Michael. *The Woman in Jewish Law and Tradition.* Northvale, NJ: Jason Aronson, 1993.
Keuls, Eva. *The Reign of the Phallus: Sexual Politics in Ancient Athens.* Berkeley: University of California Press, 1985.
Kevles, Bettyann. *Females of the Species.* Cambridge, MA: Harvard University Press, 1986.
Kiefer, Otto. *Sexual Life in Ancient Rome.* New York: Dorsett Press, 1993.

Kinsey, Alfred C., Pomeroy, Wardell B., Martin, Clyde E., and Gebhard, Paul H. *Sexual Behavior in the Human Female*. Philadelphia: W. B. Saunders, 1953.

Kitov, Eliyahu. *The Book of Our Heritage*. Vol. 1. New York: Feldheim, 1978.

Knight, Richard Payne, and Wright, Thomas. *A History of Phallic Worship*. New York: Dorset Press, 1992.

Krüll, Marianne. *Freud and His Father*. London: Hutchinson, 1986.

Lacey, Louise. *Lunaception*. New York: Warner, 1976.

Lederer, Wolfgang. *The Fear of Women*. New York: Harcourt Brace Jovanovich, 1968.

Lehmann, Johannes. *The Hittites: People of a Thousand Gods*. New York: Viking Press, 1977.

Levin, Moshe. *The Tabernacle*. Tel Aviv: Soncino, 1969.

Lew, Mike. *Victims No Longer*. New York: HarperCollins, 1988.

Lovelace, Linda. *Ordeal*. New York: Berkley Books, 1981.

Lust, John. *The Herb Book*. New York: Bantam, 1974.

Luzzatto, Moses. *General Principles of the Kabbalah*. New York: Samuel Weiser, 1970.

Lynch-Fraser, Diane. *The Complete Postpartum Guide*. New York: Harper and Row, 1983.

Mackey, Sandra. *The Saudis*. Boston: Houghton Mifflin Co., 1987.

Martin, Emily. *The Woman in the Body*. Boston: Beacon Press, 1989.

Masson, Jeffrey Moussaiff. *The Assault on Truth*. New York: Penguin, 1984.

———. *The Complete Letters of Sigmund Freud to Wilhelm Fliess 1887–1904*. Cambridge, MA: Harvard University Press, 1985.

McLean, Scilla, and Graham, Stella Efua, eds. *Female Circumcision, Excision and Infibulation*, report no. 47. London: Minority Rights Group, 1983.

Mead, Margaret. *Male and Female*. New York: William Morrow & Co., 1975.

Meiselman, Moshe. *Jewish Women in Jewish Law*. New York: Ktav, 1978.

Mendelsohn, Isaac. *Slavery in the Ancient Near East*. Westport, CT: Greenwood Press, 1949.

Mertz, Barbara. *Red Land, Black Land*. New York: Peter Bedrick, 1990.

Monaghan, Patricia. *The Book of Goddesses and Heroines*. New York: E. P. Dutton, 1981.

Montet, Pierre. *Everyday Life in Ancient Egypt*. Philadelphia: University of Pennsylvania, 1981.

Mopsik, Charles. "The Body of Engenderment in the Hebrew Bible, the Rabbinic Tradition, and the Kabbalah." In *Fragments for a History of the Human Body*, ed. Michel Feher, pp. 49–72. Cambridge, MA: MIT Press, 1989.

Morello, Karen Berger. *The Invisible Bar*. New York: Random House, 1986.

Murray, Margaret A. *The Witch-Cult in Western Europe*. London: Oxford University Press, 1921.

———. *The Splendor That Was Egypt*. New York: Hawthorn, 1963.

Nemecek, Ottokar. *Virginity: Prenuptial Rites and Rituals*. New York: Philosophical Library, 1958.

Neumann, Erich. *The Origins and History of Consciousness*. Princeton, NJ: Bollingen, 1954.

———. *The Great Mother*. Princeton, NJ: Bollingen, 1955.

Niditch, Susan. *War in the Hebrew Bible*. New York: Oxford University Press, 1993.

Oates, Joan. *Babylon*. London: Thames and Hudson, 1979.

O'Faolain, Julia, and Martines, Lauro, eds. *Not in God's Image*. New York: Harper and Row, 1973.

Oldenburg, Ulf. *The Conflict between El and Baal in Canaanite Religion*. Leiden, Netherlands: E. J. Brill, 1969.

Oppenheim, A. Leo. *Ancient Mesopotamia*. Chicago: University of Chicago Press, 1977.

Oratz, Ephraim. *The Pentateuch: Translation of the text and excerpts from the commentary of Samson Raphael Hirsch*. New York: Soncino Press, 1986.

Parise, Frank. *The Book of Calendars*. New York: Facts on File, 1982.

Patai, Raphael. *The Hebrew Goddess*. New York: Avon, 1978.

Pateman, Carole. *The Sexual Contract*. Stanford, CA: Stanford University Press, 1988.

Pelcovitz, Rabbi Raphael. *Sforno Commentary on the Torah*. 2 vols. New York: Mesorah Publications, 1989.

Pennick, Nigel. *Hitler's Secret Sciences*. Suffolk, England: Neville Spearman, 1981.

Pines, Shlomo. *Moses Maimonides Guide of the Perplexed*. 2 vols. Chicago: University of Chicago Press, 1963.

Plaskow, Judith. *Standing Again at Sinai*. San Francisco: Harper and Row, 1990.

Pogrebin, Letty Cottin. *Deborah, Golda, and Me*. New York: Crown, 1991.

Pritchard, James B. *The Ancient Near East*. Vol. 1. Princeton, NJ: Princeton University Press, 1958.

Qualls-Corbett, Nancy. *The Sacred Prostitute*. Toronto, Canada: Inner City Books, 1988.

Rackman, Emanuel. *One Man's Judaism*. New York: Philosophical Library, 1970.

The Random House College Dictionary. Rev. ed. New York: Random House, 1982.

Raymo, Chet. *365 Starry Nights*. New York: Prentice Hall Press, 1982.

Raymond, Janice. *The Transsexual Empire*. Boston: Beacon Press, 1979.

————. *A Passion for Friends*. Boston: Beacon Press, 1986.

Reed, Evelyn. *Woman's Evolution*. New York: Pathfinder Press, 1975.

Reik, Theodor. *Pagan Rites in Judaism*. New York: Noonday Press, 1964.

Riskin, Shlomo. *Women and Jewish Divorce*. Hoboken, NJ: Ktav, 1989.

Robins, Gay. *Women in Ancient Egypt*. Cambridge, MA: Harvard University Press, 1993.

Rosenberg, Rabbi A. J. *Judaica Books of the Prophets*. 14 vols. New York: Judaica Press, date per volume.

Roth, Cecil. *A History of the Marranos*. New York: Sepher-Hermon Press, 1992.

Rush, Florence. *The Best-Kept Secret: Sexual Abuse of Children*. Blue Ridge Summit, PA: Tab, 1980.

Russell, Diana E. H. "Pornography and Violence: What Does the New Research Say?" In *Take Back the Night: Women on Pornography*, ed. Laura Lederer, pp. 216–236. New York: Bantam, 1980.

————. *The Secret Trauma: Incest in the Lives of Girls and Women*. New York: Basic Books, 1986.

St. Joseph Daily Missal. New York: Catholic Book Publishing, 1959.

Sasson, Jean P. *Princess*. New York: Avon Books, 1992.

Sayce, A. H. *The Hittites: The Story of a Forgotten Empire*. London: Religious Tract Society, 1982.

Schauss, Hayyim. *The Jewish Festivals*. New York: Schocken, 1962.

Schrire, T. *Hebrew Magic Amulets*. New York: Behrman House, 1982.

Seligmann, Kurt. *Magic, Supernaturalism, and Religion*. New York: Pantheon Books, 1948.

Shaarawi, Huda. *Harem Years*. Trans. by Margot Badran. New York: Feminist Press, 1987.

Sheres, Ita. *Dinah's Rebellion*. New York: Crossroad, 1990.

Shulman, Eliezer. *The Sequence of Events in the Old Testament*. Israel: Bank Hapoalim and Israel Ministry of Defense, 1987.

Silverstein, Charles, and Picano, Felice. *The New Joy of Gay Sex*. New York: HarperCollins, 1992.

Sinason, Valerie. *Treating Survivors of Satanic Abuse*. New York: Routledge, 1994.

Sjöö, Monica, and Mor, Barbara. *The Great Cosmic Mother*. San Francisco, CA: Harper and Row, 1987.

Sklar, Dusty. *The Nazis and the Occult*. New York: Dorset Press, 1977.

Smith, Margaret. *Ritual Abuse*. New York: HarperCollins, 1993.

Smith, Richard Chase. "The Summer Institute of Linguistics: Ethnocide Disguised as a Blessing." In *Is God an American?* ed. Soren Hvalkof and Peter Aaby, pp. 121–132. Copenhagen, Denmark: IWGIA and Survival International, 1981.

Sperling, Harry, and Simon, Maurice. *The Zohar*. 5 vols. London: Soncino Press, 1984.

Stanton, Elizabeth Cady, and the Revising Committee. *The Woman's Bible*. New York: European Publishing Co., 1898. Reprint, Seattle, WA: Coalition Task Force on Women and Religion, 1974.

Starhawk. *The Spiral Dance*. New York: Harper and Row, 1979.

Starzecpyzel, Eileen. "The Persephone Complex: Incest Dynamics and the Lesbian Preference." In *Lesbian Psychologies*, ed. Boston Lesbian Psychologies Collective, pp. 261–282. Urbana: University of Illinois, 1987.

Stone, Merlin. *When God Was a Woman*. New York: Harcourt Brace Jovanovich, 1976.

Stout, Harry S. *The New England Soul*. New York: Oxford University Press, 1986.

The Talmud: The Steinsaltz Edition. Vol. 7, *Tractate Ketubot*, pt. 1. New York: Random House, 1991.

Tannen, Deborah. *You Just Don't Understand: Men and Women in Conversation*. New York: William Morrow, 1990.

Terrell, John Upton, and Donna M. Terrell. *Indian Women of the Western Morning*. New York: Anchor, 1976.

Tishby, Isaiah. *The Wisdom of the Zohar*. Vols. 1–3. New York: Oxford University Press, 1989.

The Torah. Philadelphia: Jewish Publication Society, 1962.

Touger, Rabbi Eliyahu. *Rambam Mishneh Torah*. 18 vols. to date. New York: Moznaim, date per volume.

Trachtenberg, Joshua. *Jewish Magic and Superstition*. New York: Atheneum, 1977.

Underhill, Ruth M. *Red Man's Religion*. Chicago: University of Chicago Press, 1965.

Veyne, Paul. *A History of Private Life from Pagan Rome to Byzantium*. Cambridge, MA: Harvard University Press, 1987.

Waite, Robert G. L. *The Psychopathic God: Adolf Hitler*. New York: Basic Books, 1977.

Walker, Lenore E. *The Battered Woman*. New York: HarperPerennial, 1979.

Warren, Mary Anne. *Gendercide: The Implications of Sex Selection*. Totowa, NJ: Rowman and Allanheld, 1985.

Weaver, Graham. *A to Z of the Occult*. London: Everest Books, 1975.

Webster's Dictionary. New Lexicon Encyclopedic Edition. New York: Lexicon, 1987.

Wechsberg, Joseph. *The Murderers Among Us*. New York: McGraw-Hill, 1967.

Weiss, Avraham. *Women at Prayer*. Hoboken, NJ: Ktav, 1990.

Weissman, Rabbi Moshe. *The Midrash Says*. Vols. 1–5. New York: Benei Yakov, 1980.

West, James King. *Introduction to the Old Testament*. New York: Macmillan, 1981.

Wikan, Unni. *Behind the Veil in Arabia: Women in Oman*. Chicago: University of Chicago Press, 1991.

Wolkstein, Diane, and Kramer, Samuel Noah. *Inanna: Queen of Heaven and Earth*. New York: Harper & Row, 1983.

Wooley, C. Leonard. *The Sumerians*. New York: W. W. Norton and Co., 1965.

———. *Ur 'of the Chaldees.'* Ithaca, NY: Cornell University Press, 1982.

Wulff, Wilhelm. *Zodiac and Swastika*. New York: Coward, McCann and Geoghegan, 1973.

Wyman, David S. *The Abandonment of the Jews*. New York: Pantheon, 1984.

Zolty, Shoshana Pantel. *"And All Your Children Shall Be Learned."* Northvale, NJ: Jason Aronson, 1993.

ARTICLES

Abramowitz, Yosef I. "Conservative Movement Begins to Struggle with Homosexuality." *The Jewish Advocate*, Dec. 13–19, 1991, p. 10.

Antonelli, Judith S. "Paganism's Allure Draws Women Alienated from Judaism." *The Jewish Advocate*, May 29–June 4, 1992, p. 11.

Bass, Alison. "Domestic Violence: Roots Go Deep." *The Boston Globe*, June 5, 1992, pp. 1, 11.

Bell, Roselyn. "Wide-Awake Dreamers." *Hadassah*, February 1989, pp. 24–27.

Biale, David. "The God with Breasts: El-Shaddai in the Bible." *History of Religions* 21: 3 (Feb. 1982): 240–256.

Crossette, Barbara. "As Thai Sex Trade Increases, So Do Abuses." *The New York Times*, Oct. 6, 1986, p. A10.

Daley, Yvonne. "Vermont Judge Rules That Indians Hold Fishing and Hunting Rights." *The Boston Globe*, Aug. 15, 1989, p. 17.

Daum, Annette. "Blaming Jesus for the Death of the Goddess." *Lilith*, 7 (1980/5741): 12–13.

Dell'Olio, Anselma. "The Sexual Revolution Wasn't Our War." *Ms.* (Spring 1972): 104–110.

"Divorce American Style." *Newsweek*, Jan. 10, 1983, pp. 42–48.

Edemikpong, Hannah. "Nigeria: A Direct Appeal." *Ms.* 1:3 (Nov./Dec. 1990): 10.

Edwards, Carolyn McVickar. "Shekhinah: The Door to the Soul." *Lilith* 17:4 (Fall 1992): 5.

Eilberg-Schwartz, Howard. "Why Not the Earlobe?" *Moment* 17:1 (Feb. 1992): 28–33.

Erlanger, Steven. "Thriving Sex Industry in Bangkok Is Raising Fears of an AIDS Epidemic." *The New York Times*, Mar. 30, 1989, p. A3.

Eytan, Edwin. "Barbie Ordered Back to Courtroom for Witnesses' Identification." *The Jewish Advocate*, May 28, 1987, p. 3.

Foderaro, Lisa W. "Parents and a Brother Slain by Self-Styled Rambo." *The New York Times*, Mar. 23, 1989, p. B3.

Gaines, Judith. "Tribe to Claim One-Third of New England." *The Boston Globe*, Aug. 10, 1990, pp. 1, 15.

"Gays Not Permitted Banner in Parade." *Weekly News Digest* (Jewish Telegraphic Agency), Apr. 1, 1993, p. 3.

"The Gender Gulf." *Ms.* 1:5 (Mar./Apr. 1991): 87.

Gendler, Mary. "Cornstalks, Conch Shells and My Jewish Problem." *Lilith* 16:4 (Fall 1991): 32.

Goleman, Daniel. "Violence against Women in Films." *Response* 8:1 (Winter 1985): 21–22.

Grossman, Jerome. "U.S. Shares in Barbie's Guilt." *The Jewish Advocate*, Aug. 6, 1987, p. 2.

"Hadassah Women Get Stoned." *Lilith* 19:1 (Spring 1994): 7.

Hornblower, Margot. "The Skin Trade." *Time*, June 21, 1993, pp. 45–51.

"If a Boy Is What You Want." *Parade*, Jan. 8, 1984, p. 8.

"Israeli Supreme Court Rejects Women of the Wall." *Lilith*, 19:1 (Spring 1994): 7.

King, Nick. "Native Americans May Finally Win One." *The Boston Globe*, Jul. 31, 1983, pp. A13–14.

"The Koran, Israeli Law, and Women's Rights." *The Jerusalem Post*, June 27, 1987, p. 17.

Lehman, Betsy A. "Upping the Odds That 'It's a Boy!'" *The Boston Globe*, Nov. 18, 1985, p. 42.

Lerman, Rhoda. "In Memoriam: Elizabeth Gould Davis." *Ms.* (Dec. 1974): 74–75, 95.

Leo, John. "Baby Boys, to Order." *U.S. News and World Report*, Jan. 9, 1989, p. 59.

Lewis, Ann F. "The Jerusalem Agenda." *Ms.* (Mar. 1989): 23–27.

Malamuth, Neil M., Haber, Scott, and Feshbach, Seymour. "Testing Hypotheses Regarding Rape: Exposure to Sexual Violence, Sex Differences, and the 'Normality' of Rapists." *Journal of Research in Personality* 14 (1980): 121–137.

Mason, Ruth. "Conversations with Jews Who Have Left Judaism." *The Jewish Advocate*, Aug. 16–22, 1991, p. 9.

Metzger, Deena. "What Dinah Thought." *Lilith* 15:2 (Spring 1990): 8–12.

Musleah, Rahel. "When the Goddess Calls, Jewish Women Answer." *Lilith* 18:4 (Fall 1993): 8–13.

Nealon, Patricia. "Killer Seeks Return of His Pornography." *The Boston Globe*, Apr. 29, 1992, p. 51.

———. "Inmate's Erotica Ordered Returned." *The Boston Globe*, June 24, 1992, p. 29.

"The People of 'Millennium.'" *Cultural Survival Quarterly* 16:2 (Spring 1992): 68.

Plaskow, Judith. "Blaming Jews for Inventing Patriarchy." *Lilith* 7 (1980/5741): 11–12.

"Researchers Study the Relation between Exercise and Menstrual Irregularities." *Harvard Gazette*, Jan. 25, 1980, p. 5.

Rose, Elizabeth S. "Surviving the Unbelievable." *Ms.* 3:4 (Jan./Feb. 1993): 40–45.

Russell, Francis H. "The Palestinians: Who They Are." *The Christian Science Monitor*, Oct. 26, 1976, pp. 18–19.

Sandison, A. T. "The Use of Natron in Mummification in Ancient Egypt." *Journal of Near Eastern Studies*, no. 22 (1963): 259.

Sloan, Ed. "Jews and Native Americans—A Striking Resemblance." *The Jewish Advocate*, Nov. 8, 1991, p. 9.

Stager, Lawrence E., and Wolff, Samuel R. "Child Sacrifice at Carthage: Religious Rite or Population Control?" *Biblical Archaeology Review* 10:1 (Jan./Feb. 1984): 31–51.

Steinem, Gloria. "Women in the Dark: Of Sex Goddesses, Abuse, and Dreams." *Ms.* 1:4 (Jan./Feb. 1991): 35–37.

"Thanksgiving Day Celebrates a Massacre." *Akwesasne Notes* (Summer 1980): 12.

"Tie Found between Risk of Adult Rape and Being Raped as a Child." *The New York Times*, Aug. 17, 1992, p. A17.

Trippett, Frank. "Should We Give America Back to the Indians?" *Time*, Apr. 11, 1977, pp. 51–52.

Wadley, Susan S. "Female Life Changes in Rural India." *Cultural Survival Quarterly* 13:2 (1989): 35–38.

Walker, Adrian. "Fighting Rape's Stigma." *The Boston Globe*, Apr. 17, 1991, pp. 1, 18.

Winograd, Leonard. "Thanksgiving: A Unity Holiday." *The Jewish Advocate*, Nov. 15, 1990, p. 8.

"Women, Redemption, and Happiness." *Ascent Quarterly* 10:2 (*Tamuz* 5754/Summer 1994): 8–9.

❋❋❋ ❋❋❋

Acknowledgments

Every effort has been made to ascertain the owner of copyrights for the selections used in this volume and to obtain permission to reprint copyrighted passages. For the use of the passages indicated, the author expresses her gratitude to those whose names appear below. The author will be pleased, in subsequent editions, to correct any inadvertent error or omission that may be pointed out.

From *Ancient Egyptian Magic* by Bob Brier. Copyright © 1980 by Bob Brier. Reprinted by permission of William Morrow & Company, Inc.

From *Blood Magic: The Anthropology of Menstruation* by Thomas Buckley and Alma Gottlieb (eds.). Copyright © 1988 by The Regents of the University of California. Reprinted with permission of the University of California Press and Thomas Buckley.

From *Human Sacrifice* by Nigel Davies. Copyright © 1981 by Nigel Davies. Reprinted by permission of William Morrow & Company, Inc.

From "Nigeria: A Direct Appeal" by Hannah Edemikpong. Copyright © 1990 by Lang Communications, Inc. Reprinted with permission of *Ms*. Magazine.

From *Life in Ancient Egypt* by Adolf Erman. Copyright © 1971 Dover Publications, Inc. Reprinted with permission of Dover Publications.

Reprinted with the permission of Simon & Schuster, Inc., from *The Golden Bough: A Study in Magic and Religion* by Sir James George Frazer. Copyright © 1922 by Macmillan Publishing Company, renewed 1950 by Barclays Bank, Ltd.

From *A Dictionary of Egyptian Gods and Goddesses* by George Hart. Copyright © 1986 George Hart. Reprinted with permission of Routledge & Kegan Paul Ltd., New York.

Neumann, Erich; *The Origins and History of Consciousness*. Copyright © 1954/1970 by Princeton University Press. Reprinted by permission of Princeton University Press.

From *Babylon* by Joan Oates. Copyright © 1979 Thames and Hudson Ltd., London. Reprinted with permission of Thames and Hudson.

From *The Woman's Bible* by Elizabeth Cady Stanton and the Revising Committee. Copyright © 1974 Coalition Task Force on Women and Religion, Seattle, WA. Reprinted with permission of Coalition Task Force on Women and Religion.

Index of Torah Verses

All biblical verses cited as references in this book are listed below. A boldface page number indicates that the verse is quoted at the beginning of a chapter section and usually forms the basis of discussion of that section.

General Index

Abortion, 25, 73, 196–197
Acha ben Jacob, Rabbi, 178
Achashverosh, King, 109, 422, 449
Adah (Esav's wife), 68–69
Adah (Lemekh's wife), 14–16, 21
Adam (human being), 4–6, 16, 178, 239, 242, 437
Adam, xxi, 15–17, 180, 233, 271
   creation of, 3–5, 91, 178–179
   sin and exile of, 10–13, 323, 370, 437
Adinah (Levi's wife), 113, 137
Adinah (Lavan's wife), 74–75, 82
Adiva, 112
Adler, Margot, xxvii
Admah. *See* Sodom
Admon, 380, 389
Adonis, 156, 234, 243, 253, 416, 429, 475
Adultery, 100, 290, 297, 337–340, 346, 390, 455; *see also* Polyandry;
   Sexuality, prohibited forms of
   accusation of. *See* Wife, accused
   as capital crime, 110, 132, 299, 336, 461
   as cause of Flood, 22–23
   committed by David, 91
   committed by Esav, 63
   committed by Ishmael, 36
   as fertility rite, 401, 433–434, 479
   and priestly marriages, 316–318, 340
   Tamar and, 108
Aflelet, 113
Africa, 107, 139, 188, 223, 282, 286; *see also* Ethiopia
   Girgashites in, 393, 483

Agriculture, 402
   cycles of. *See* Festivals, pagan
   laws of, 455–456, 473
   origins of, 12, 119
Ahalivamah, 68–69, 102
Aharon, xxxii, 292, 331, 333
   birth of, 137–138
   death of, 366–367, 377
   and golden calf, 213, 216–218, 245, 247–248, 344, 364, 366
   and Miriam, 142, 349–351
   and Moses, 145, 148, 249, 357, 361, 377, 444
   as peacemaker, 247, 367
   and priesthood, 146, 209, 212, 218, 245, 247–248, 254, 315, 321, 379
   sons of, 146, 147, 148, 218, 247; *see also* Elazar; Itamar; Nadav and Avihu
Akiva, Rabbi, 317, 351, 379, 387, 433, 440, 447
Aliyat (Bat-Shua), 112
Altar
   at foot of Sinai, 420
   incense, 297, 208, 237, 334
   private, on high place (*bamah*), 245, 416–418, 422, 425, 432
   sacrificial, 203, 205, 229–230, 233, 237, 241–242, 248–249, 255, 334–335
Amalek, 101–102, 217, 320, 354, 484
Amatlai, 27–28
Amazons, xxiv, 70
Amemar, 200
Amenophis I, 116

531

of kings of Israel, 449
of Korach and his followers, 357–358
lack of, 177, 334
of Nadav and Avihu, 256
and slaves, 31, 35, 346
of Sodom, 41
of Zimri, 376
Artemis, 251
Asher, 83
daughter of. *See* Serach
tribe of, 378
wives of, 113, 123
Asherah, xxvii, 234, 405, 416–427, 431,
433
and incest, 435, 436, 474
worshiped in Temple in Jerusalem, 429
Ashtarot (Ashtoret), xxvii, 402–406, 421,
435, 448
Asia Minor, 69, 428
deities of, 234, 429
Asnat, 114–115, 118, 121–122, 125, 130,
187
Astarte, 234, 251, 253–254, 312
and Ashtarot, 405, 421
as Tanit, 405–406
Astrology, 200; *see also* Zodiac
Balak's use of, 371
Benjamin's use of, 124
fatalistic use of, xxxix, 444–445
Nimrod's use of, 27
Pharaoh's use of, 126, 139, 141, 248,
249, 361
Yitro as minister of, 369
Rachel's pregnancy and, 85, 126
Zelikhah's use of, 109, 121
Atonement (*kaparah, teshuvah*), 224, 238,
319, 495
circumcision as, 270, 273
Day of. *See* Yom Kippur
death as, 256, 296, 365
for golden calf, 220, 222, 228, 247, 363,
367; *see also* Red Heifer
Levites and, 335
maleness and, 354, 364
name change as, 58
for Rivkah's deception, 64
Sabbatical Year and, 325
sacrifice as, 233, 235, 242, 244–245,
341, 363
for unsolved murder. *See* River Heifer
for warfare, 396
Attis, 234–235, 250–251, 416, 429

Avimelekh, 32, 34, 36, 38, 365
Avraham, 62, 64, 73, 81, 101, 292, 420,
468, 495
Aryan myth of, xxiv
Babylonian background of, 27–28, 161–
162, 292, 373
and binding of Isaac, 38, 79, 163–164,
167, 233
circumcision and, 270–271, 273–274
covenant with, 36–38, 233, 404, 414,
422–423
daughter of, 51–52, 75, 111, 316
and Eliezer, 41, 52–53, 74, 187, 450,
483
and Hagar, 30–31, 34–36, 80
hospitality of, 36, 55, 91, 105
and Keturah, 58–59, 80
and Lot, 40, 42–44
with Sarah in Egypt and Gerar, 32–34,
45, 91, 97, 109
tent of, 57, 168
Azariah, Rabbi, 21
Ay, 134
Azazel, 245, 296, 363, 402

Baal, 67, 234, 403, 416, 423–427, 471,
473–475
and incest, 435–436
as Molekh, 309–311, 424
as rain god, 153, 421, 424, 426, 475
and skin gashing, 243, 251, 429–430
Baal-Hammon, 405–406, 423
Baal-Peor, 382, 395, 401, 405, 423
Jews and, 368, 371, 373–378, 419, 432,
437–438, 472
Baal-Zephon, 425
Babel, Tower of, 27
Babylonia, 242, 369, 428, 445
deities of, 29–30, 71, 210, 429; *see also*
Dumuzi; Inanna; Ishtar; Tamuz
exile to. *See* Exile, Babylonian
historical periods of, 30
kings of. *See* King, Babylonian
matriarchs and, 401
Padan Aram, 52–54, 60, 69, 72–74, 98,
112
slavery in, 186–189, 326, 440
women of, 28–31, 199, 336–337, 450;
see also Priestesses, pagan
Bachrach, Rabbi Yair Chaim, xxix
Balak, 368–371, 375, 425
Bar Kappara, 20

ABOUT THE AUTHOR

Judith S. Antonelli is a writer and a freelance editor who lives in Boston, Massachusetts. She has been a feminist since the late 1960s and a religious Jew since the mid-1980s. Judith has degrees in psychology, women's studies, and journalism and has spent many years studying Judaism and other Western spiritual traditions. From 1986-1992, she was the associate editor of *The Jewish Advocate* newspaper, in which she published over 600 articles.